THROUGH
the YEAR
with
MARTIN
LUTHER

THROUGH
the YEAR
with
MARTIN
LUTHER

A SELECTION OF SERMONS
CELEBRATING THE FEASTS AND SEASONS
OF THE CHRISTIAN YEAR

HENDRICKSON PUBLISHERS

Through the Year with Luther

© 2007 Hendrickson Publishers, Inc.
P. O. Box 3473
Peabody, Massachusetts 01961-3473

ISBN 978-1-59856-123-4

Printed in the United States of America

First Printing — March 2007

Cover art: Cover Art: Cranach, Lucas the Elder (1472-1553). Portrait of Martin Luther. Located in the Germanisches Nationalmuseum, Nuremberg, Germany. Photo Credit: Scala / Art Resource, NY. Used with permission.

Contents

The First Sunday in Advent.............................9
Faith, Good Works, and the Spiritual Interpretation
of This Gospel
MATTHEW 21:1–9

The Second Sunday in Advent............................41
The Comfort Christians Have from the Signs of the Day of
Judgment; and the Spiritual Interpretation of These Gospel Signs
LUKE 21:25–36

The Third Sunday in Advent.............................62
Christ's Answer to the Question John Asked Him, His Praise
of John, and the Application of This Gospel
MATTHEW 11:2–10

The Fourth Sunday in Advent...........................82
The Witness and Confession of John the Baptist
JOHN 1:19–28

Christmas Day 97
Of the Birth of Jesus, and of the Angels' Song of Praise
at His Birth
LUKE 2:1–14

Christmas Day 118
Christ's Titles of Honor and Attribute; Christ's Coming;
His Becoming Man; and the Revelation of His Glory
JOHN 1:1–14

The Sunday After Christmas 158
Of Simeon; of Anna; of the Return of the Parents of Jesus
to Nazareth, and the Childhood of Christ
LUKE 2:33–40

New Year's Day 198
The Circumcision, and Choosing the Name,
as Was the Custom at Circumcision
LUKE 2:21

Epiphany. 207
  On the Visit of the Magi
  MATTHEW 2:1–12

The First Sunday in Lent 284
  The Fast and the Temptation of Christ
  MATTHEW 4:1–11

The Second Sunday in Lent 295
  The Faith of the Syrophenician Woman, and the Spiritual
  Interpretation of This Gospel
  MATTHEW 15:21–28

The Third Sunday in Lent. 300
  Christ's Defense Against Those Who Slandered Him
  LUKE 11:14–23

The Fourth Sunday in Lent. 308
  The Feeding of the Five Thousand
  JOHN 6:1–15

The Fifth Sunday in Lent 313
  Christ's Defense Against His Enemies
  JOHN 8:46–59

Palm Sunday 320
  Christ: An Example of Love
  PHILIPPIANS 2:5–11

Maundy Thursday 329
  Of Confession and the Lord's Supper

Good Friday. 345
  How to Contemplate Christ's Holy Sufferings

Easter Sunday 352
  Of Christ's Resurrection
  MARK 16:1–8

Easter Sunday 360
  The Manifestation of Christ After His Resurrection,
  and the Sermon He Preached to His Disciples
  LUKE 24:36–47

The Sunday After Easter...............................372
Of True Piety, the Law and Faith, and of Love
to Our Neighbor
JOHN 20:19–31

The Second Sunday After Easter.......................383
Christ's Office and Kingdom: A Sermon on
the Good Shepherd
JOHN 10:11–16

The Third Sunday After Easter 394
A Sermon of Comfort That Christ Preached
to His Disciples
JOHN 16:16–23

The Fourth Sunday After Easter 405
Of Sin, of Righteousness, and of the Cross
JOHN 16:5–15

The Fifth Sunday After Easter or Prayer Sunday 411
A Sermon by Christ on Prayer
JOHN 16:23–30

The Day Of Christ's Ascension into Heaven 419
Christ Upbraids and Commissions His Disciples
MARK 16:14–20

The Sunday After Christ's Ascension......................430
A Sermon of Comfort and of Admonition
JOHN 15:26–16:4

Pentecost 438
Or, the Festival of the Outpouring of the Holy Spirit
JOHN 14:23–31

Trinity Sunday 447
The Doctrine of the Trinity
ROMANS 11:33–36

Preface

Martin Luther, 1483–1546

A safe stronghold our God is still,
A trusty shield and weapon;
He'll help us clear from all the ill
That hath us now o'ertaken.
The ancient prince of hell
Hath risen with purpose fell;
Strong mail of craft and power
He weareth in this hour,
On earth is not his fellow.

God's word, for all their craft and force,
One moment will not linger,
But spite of hell, shall have its course;
'Tis written by his finger.
And, though they take our life,
Goods, honour, children, wife,
Yet is their profit small;
These things shall vanish all:
The city of God remaineth.

— *"A Safe Stronghold"* BY MARTIN LUTHER,
TRANSLATED BY THOMAS CARLYLE, 1795–1881

For the modern reader, the long version of Martin Luther's story relies on an unusual vocabulary. A bull? (An official, sealed document issued by the pope.) A diet? (An assembled court of law.) Worms? (A city in Germany.) The Diet of Worms? (Consider the possibilities.)

Martin Luther was born in eastern Germany in 1483. That's some forty years after the German Johann Gutenberg invented a printing press using movable metal type and nearly a decade before Columbus sailed the ocean blue. Having not inherited the family's farm, Luther's father turned to mining and founding metals. Being his father's hope for a son with a secure academic profession, Martin was educated in Latin and then attended the University of Erfurt, receiving a bachelor's and master's in law in 1505.

Martin was a particularly sensitive child, subject to mood swings—highs and lows. Influenced by his region's Germanic, peasantry brand of Christianity, he was haunted by fear—of demons and devils as well as of God the Judge, quick to condemn sinners to interminable punishment. Becoming a monk or priest was considered one sure way of gaining God's favor. For Martin, the decision to enter a monastery came in a July 1505 thunderstorm, when a bolt of lightning knocked him off his feet. On the brink of eternity, he cried out, imploring the aid of Saint Anne: "Help me," and promised, "I will become a monk."

Ordained in an Augustinian order in 1507, he continued educational pursuits, eventually being assigned to the University of Wittenberg to teach moral theology. Young Martin was not a happy man. How could he love God the Judge who was appeased at such a high price? He felt the burden of perfection, including stringent fasting and deprivations that he hoped would "compensate for his sins," to quote Roland Bainton in his acclaimed 1950 biography *Here I Stand*. There was the burden of confession, for scrupulous Martin several hours a day, wracking his brain to find offenses that would potentially separate him from God. There was the financial or physical cost of indulgences; papal bulls decreed that people could buy a proportioned amount of the righteousness of Jesus or a saint and thereby decrease a predeceased loved one's time in purgatory; some bulls went further, offering forgiveness of sin to a living person. Some indulgences were accessible only at churches or shrines containing relics, such as bones of saints. During a 1510 trip to Rome, Martin crawled up the purported (and displaced) steps of Pilate's palace, hopefully praying his grandfather out of purgatory.

After earning a theological doctorate, Martin taught biblical studies at Wittenberg, lecturing principally on the Psalms and then Romans and Galatians. In the writings of Paul, he rediscovered some classical theology of Augustine. Roland Bainton describes what Luther saw in Romans: "It is not that the Son by his sacrifice has placated the irate Father. ...It is that in some inexplicable way, in the utter desolation of the forsaken Christ, God was able to reconcile the world to himself."

Luther's long-time arguments with, even animosity toward, God withered. He later explained that he had previously taken the phrase "the righteousness of God" to mean "that righteousness whereby God is righteous and deals righteously in punishing the unrighteous." But after much grappling, "I grasped the truth that the righteousness of God is that righteousness whereby, through grace and sheer mercy, he justifies us by faith. Thereupon I felt myself to be reborn and to have gone through open doors into paradise. The whole of Scripture took on a new meaning, and whereas before 'the righteousness of God' had filled me with hate, now it became to me inexpressibly sweet in greater love."

At first Martin thought that his new insight would change the emphasis of his preaching and classroom teaching. But things got complicated. The small university town of Wittenberg was becoming a known center for acclaimed relics and the selling of indulgences. In surrounding areas, some Dominicans were selling even more indulgences, with geographical and cultural implications; German money was being whisked away to Rome to pay for the greatest reliquary of all: Saint Peter's Basilica. This political element helped to fuel the fire that resulted after Martin posted "Ninety-five Theses"—largely against the indulgences industry—in Latin on the door of the Castle Church in Wittenberg on October 31, 1517. If his intent was to engage academic debate, in actuality, he changed the course of the Western church and world.

Translated into German the document was reproduced by an enterprising printer and widely distributed, agitating local peasants. A copy went to Rome. Dominicans took sides against Augustinians. Luther dug in his heels, hitting at the authority of the pope by appealing to the higher authority of Scripture.

By the next summer, like the apostle Paul, Martin was subpoenaed, to appear in Rome, to answer charges of heresy and insubordination. But Luther's local political ruler, Frederick the Wise, had previously assured him that any trial would take place in Germany. A long, three-year tussle—including Luther's claim that the pope was the Antichrist and a papal bull decreeing Luther's excommunication in 1520—resulted in Luther's secular trial, at the Diet of Worms in early 1521.

The Holy Roman emperor himself, Charles V, presided over the trial. First-hand reports quote Martin as holding his ground, refusing to recant, saying, "Here I stand. I can do no other." Found guilty by a depleted number of jurors, Luther might well have been martyred, if not for one friend on the court, Saxony's elector, Frederick the Wise, who organized an abduction, in which Luther was spirited away to a fortress, Wartburg Castle. For about a year in hiding, Luther translated the New Testament from Greek into German, intent on getting the Scriptures into the hands of his people, even though his translation was outlawed by Charles V.

Martin Luther's message spoke freedom for and empowered German's "common man." His early writings (1520) include an *Appeal to the German Ruling Class,* in which he rallied local rulers to reform the church and protect their people from its extortion and oppression. Here he laid out his understanding of the "priesthood of all believers," in contrast to the prevailing view of the clergy as a caste set apart with special access to God. Here he also proposed that priests be allowed to marry.

The title and contents of another document fueled unrest: *Babylonian Captivity of the Church* (1520) in which he discounted five of seven church sacraments, claiming that only two, Eucharist and Baptism, were biblically instituted. In terms of Eucharist, he insisted that "the cup" to be offered to all believers, not reserved for the clergy only, and he argued against the literalness of transubstantiation—that in the Mass the bread and wine in substance became flesh and blood.

In a third early document (1520), *The Freedom of a Christian,* he explained the tenet of justification by grace through faith alone, not as a result of good works, which were the fruit rather than a contributing source of salvation.

The Diet of Worms decreed that these publications be burned. Many bonfires blazed, but the public had been churned up, and other academics, clerics, and some public officials caught Luther's vision, which opened roads to political as well as spiritual freedom. Priests were marrying. Congregants were sipping Communion wine. The Mass was being said in German. Though it was not part of Martin's "agenda," pictures and statues of the saints were being desecrated. The Wittenberg community was ideologically split, to the point of violence, and in 1522 the city council boldly asked Martin to return to town, in Bainton's view, "probably...to exert a moderating influence" in the fray. Cautiously, courageously Martin returned to Wittenberg and indeed he preached "patience, charity, and consideration for the weak. ...No one can be intimidated into belief." Returning to Wittenberg, Luther was in effect its mayor and priest, leading the town to real reform. Another diet, at Nürnberg, in 1523 revisited charges made at Worms, but a juridical impasse allowed Luther to continue his work, writing, teaching, preaching, leading in circles beyond Wittenberg.

Politics and religion. It's hard for us to understand how intricately intertwined the two were in central Europe in Luther's day. Two publications later that year reflect the scope of Luther's influence. *On Civil Government* was followed by *On the Order of Worship,* an initial attempt at a revised Eucharistic liturgy in which he introduced the idea of congregational singing.

In *Christian History* magazine Paul Grime notes, "Music in congregational worship remains one of Luther's most enduring legacies." To fill a gap he'd created, Martin accepted yet another task—that of writing hymns not in Latin but in German. With ramifications he didn't even understand, Luther was empowering his people. His appeal to all believers to take their stand as equal before God, even to rally in song, contributed to such unrest that by 1525 he was surrounded by a populist uprising known as the Peasants' War. Again he tried to serve as a mediator, writing an *Admonition to Peace,* exhorting the rulers to be less severe and the populace to honor and obedience of secular authority. But when the rebellion didn't subside, Luther sided with the princes (*Against the Robbing and Murdering Horde of Peasants*), advocating a controversially harsh repression.

Into this whirlwind life, and despite some Pauline reservations ("my mind is averse to marriage because I daily expect the death decreed to the heretic"), he brought a bride. Katherina von Bora was a former nun fifteen years younger than himself. Though he married feeling some obligation to provide a home for her, she became a steadying, still point in his life, prompting him eventually to say, "I would not give my Katie for France and Venice together." In red-haired, feisty, Katie, Martin had met his match. While Martin was changing the landscape of Europe, Katie was reining him in at home; he was known to call her "my Lord Kate." She had her hands full, managing him, eventually their growing family (six children in all), and their large home (the very Augustinian monastery that Martin had lived in as a young man), which served in effect as a hotel for people passing through or a hostel for the needy and a hospital for the sick, especially in a 1527 plague epidemic that devastated Wittenberg. Some of Luther's best known writings are known as his *Table Talk,* more than 6,500 short discourses he gave to visitors, including disciples, around his dinner table.

One statement about his marriage sheds light back on Martin's public, spiritual persona. "In domestic affairs I defer to Katie. Otherwise, I am led by the Holy Ghost." Luther was sure he spoke for God, though often in exaggerated tones. As he aged his rancor and anger at his enemies is disturbing. He wrote, for instance, "I cannot deny that I am more vehement than I should be. …But they assail me and God's Word so atrociously and criminally that… these monsters are carrying me beyond the bounds of moderation." The word *Protestant* even then seemed an apt description. That word was first used at the 1529 Diet of Speyer, at which Emperor Charles V again attempted to enforce the Diet of Worms. *Protestant* stuck as a descriptor of the anti-Catholic group(s). Any number of theologians supported Luther in his stand against papal power and extrabiblical traditions and abuses. But as Rome itself headed toward a Counter-Reformation and lost some power in central Europe, Protestant reformers took issue with—even turned on—each other. Points of doctrine and worship, such as the predestination versus free will, the baptism of infants, the role of music and art, the exact role and meaning of the Lord's Supper, caused rifts among groups of disciples, sometimes along regional lines, notably the Swiss and Dutch disagreeing with the Germans.

The most contentious issue became the "real presence" of Christ in the Eucharistic bread and wine. Though Luther disavowed the Catholic "hocus pocus" of the elements becoming flesh and blood, he appealed to Jesus' "This is my body...This is my blood" to counter Ulrich Zwingli's position that Christ's presence in the elements was not real but symbolic and dependent on the faith of the receiver. In 1529 a German prince, Philip of Hesse, persuaded Luther to meet with Ulrich Zwingli and others in Marburg to restore Protestant unity. But there was no compromise and to this day the Reformed and Lutheran traditions are set apart from each other.

Though Luther was making enemies of reformers, he still was in conflict with the Holy Roman Empire. Again under virtual house arrest at a castle fortress, he could not attend a 1530 Diet of Augsburg, at which the Lutheran apologetic, coauthored by Luther and his colleague Philipp Melanchthon, was presented. Professor Eugene Klug of Concordia Theological Seminary notes that for Lutherans, this *Augsburg Confession* became a "standard" for theology, "a document with the weight of a Declaration of Independence."

In midlife Luther was juggling not only matters of state, but also the education of the common man, writing a long and a short version of a *Catechism* that in question and answer format lay out the basics of the faith. The *Small Catechism*, which has been called "the gem of the Reformation," was taught in homes, generation after generation, instilling basic doctrines to the youngest children; it includes phrase-by-phrase explanations of the Ten Commandments, the Apostles' Creed, and the Lord's Prayer. In his spare time, he also continued translating the Old Testament from Hebrew, his complete German Bible being published in 1534.

And, lest we forget, Luther at heart was a teacher and preacher; he left a legacy of more than two thousand sermons, only a portion of those he delivered. The nineteen sermons selected for this volume reflect seasonal themes of the liturgical calendar, the very purpose for which they were written. In 1520, Luther's benefactor, Frederick the Wise, requested that Luther prepare a postil, or sermon, for every Sunday in the church year. His postils were expository studies of the lectionary readings assigned to the Sunday, and were intended to serve as expository guides for other priests, to help them prepare their own preaching. These writings were completed over a period of years and finally became known as the *Church Postils*.

As one would expect, Luther's sermons are grounded in a particular scriptural passage. But from that jumping off point, especially in his later years, Luther slipped in an agenda that not only supported his theological points, but also bitterly denounced groups that disagreed with him, particularly Catholics and also Jews. These tirades against Jews were theological, not racial. (Anthropological distinction between "Aryans" and "Semites" was a nineteenth-century categorization.) His complaint was not that the first-century Jews had killed Jesus, but rather that Jews subsequently did not accept and believe in him. Roland Bainton says, "The supreme sin for him was the persistent rejection of God's revelation of himself in Christ." Where Luther took that line of thought, and how, had drastic consequences in Europe for centuries.

Threads of his disrespect of his contrarians are evident in the sermons in this volume, which should be read for their positive and scriptural insights rather than for their accusative harangues. In his lifetime Luther wrote some 60,000 pages of prose. He welcomed listeners and readers, and yet his deeper desire was that "the Holy Scriptures alone be read." In a similar spirit, may these selected sermons prompt you to search the Scriptures themselves, looking for the basics of Luther's theology, which has been reduced to four points: *sola Scripture* (Scripture alone being the authority, rather than extraneous tradition), *sola fide* (faith alone, not works, being the channel of our righteousness), *sola gratia* (grace alone—a gift of God—being the cause of our salvation)—all anchored in *solo Christo* (Christ alone). Dr. Timothy George notes that "each *sola* affirmed the centrality of Jesus Christ."

Martin Luther died in 1546, at age sixty-two, after years of continued productivity despite declining health. A year after his death, the emperor declared war on Protestants, set in motion at the Diet of Augsburg. The emperor initially defeated the Protestants, but the tide turned. The 1555 Peace of Augsburg allowed local princes to determine the religion of their districts. This legally recognized Protestantism, though Germany suffered sectarian violence, including the Thirty Years' War, for another century.

Historians feel that early-sixteenth-century Europe was ready for sweeping reform, seeded by John Wycliffe, John Huss, and Desiderius Erasmus, among others. If not Luther it would have been another cleric or academic bridging medieval and Renaissance culture. But it was Martin Luther, a powerful personality, a charismatic motivator, and systematic teacher who shook not just the church but the political world with a basic premise—that we cannot buy or work our way into the kingdom of God.

The First Sunday in Advent

❦

Faith, Good Works, and the Spiritual Interpretation of This Gospel

And when they drew nigh unto Jerusalem, and came unto Bethphage, unto the Mount of Olives, then Jesus sent two of his disciples, saying unto them, "Go into the village that is over against you, and straightway ye shall find an ass tied, and a colt with her: loose them, and bring them unto me. And if any one say aught unto you, ye shall say, 'The Lord hath need of them;' and straightway he will send them." Now this is come to pass, that it might be fulfilled which was spoken through the prophet, saying, "Tell ye the daughter of Zion, 'Behold thy King cometh unto thee, meek, and riding upon an ass, and upon a colt the foal of an ass.'" And the disciples went, and did even as Jesus appointed them, and brought the ass, and the colt, and put on them their garments; and he sat thereon. And the most part of the multitude spread their garments in the way; and others cut branches from the trees, and spread them in the way. And the multitudes that went before him, and that followed, cried, saying, "Hosanna to the son of David: Blessed is he that cometh in the name of the Lord; Hosanna in the highest." — MATTHEW 21:1–9

1. In the preface, I said that there are two things to be noted and considered in the Gospel lessons: first, the works of Christ presented to us as a gift and blessing on which our faith is to cling and exercise itself; secondly, the same works offered as an example and model for us to imitate and follow. All the Gospel lessons thus throw light first on faith and then on good works. We will, therefore, consider this Gospel under three heads: speaking first of faith; secondly of good works, and thirdly of the lesson story and its hidden meaning.

I. CONCERNING FAITH

2. This Gospel encourages and demands faith, for it prefigures Christ's coming with grace, whom none may receive or accept save he who believes him

to be the man, and has the mind, as this Gospel portrays in Christ. Nothing but the mercy, tenderness, and kindness of Christ are here shown, and he who so receives and believes on him is saved. He sits not upon a proud steed, an animal of war, nor does he come in great pomp and power, but sitting upon an ass, an animal of peace fit only for burdens and labor and a help to man. He indicates by this that he comes not to frighten man, nor to drive or crush him, but to help him and to carry his burden for him. And although it was the custom of the country to ride on asses and to use horses for war, as the Scriptures often tell us, yet here the object is to show that the entrance of this king shall be meek and lowly.

Again, it also shows the pomp and conduct of the disciples toward Christ who bring the colt to Christ, set him thereon, and spread their garments in the way; also that of the multitude who also spread their garments in the way and cut branches from the trees. They manifested no fear nor terror, but only blessed confidence in him, as one for whom they dared to do such things and who would take it kindly and readily consent to it.

3. Again, he begins his journey and comes to the Mount of Olives to indicate that he comes out of pure mercy. For olive oil in the Scriptures signifies the grace of God that soothes and strengthens the soul as oil soothes and strengthens the body.

4. Thirdly, there is no armor present, no war cry, but songs and praise, rejoicing, and thanksgiving to the Lord.

5. Fourthly, Christ weeps, as Luke 19:41 writes, weeps over Jerusalem because she does not know nor receive such grace; yet he was so grieved at her loss that he did not deal harshly with her.

6. Fifthly, his goodness and mercy are best shown when he quotes the words of the prophets, in Isaiah 62:11 and in Zechariah 9:9, and tenderly invites men to believe and accept Christ, for the fulfilling of which prophecies the events of this Gospel took place and the story was written, as the evangelist himself testifies. We must, therefore, look upon this verse as the chief part of this Gospel, for in it Christ is pictured to us and we are told what we are to believe, and to expect of him, what we are to seek in him, and how we may be benefited by him.

7. First he says, "Tell ye" the daughter of Zion. This is said to the ministry and a new sermon is given them to preach, namely, nothing but what the words following indicate, a right knowledge of Christ. Whoever preaches anything else is a wolf and deceiver. This is one of the verses in which the Gospel is promised of which Paul writes in Romans 1:2; for the Gospel is a sermon from Christ, as he is here placed before us, calling for faith in him.

8. I have often said that there are two kinds of faith. First, a faith in which you indeed believe that Christ is such a man as he is described and proclaimed here and in all the Gospels, but do not believe that he is such a man for you, and are in doubt whether you have any part in him and think, Yes, he is such a man to others, to Peter, Paul, and the blessed saints, but who knows that he is such to me and that I may expect the same from him and may confide in it, as these saints did?

9. Behold, this faith is nothing; it does not receive Christ nor enjoy him, neither can it feel any love and affection for him or from him. It is a faith about Christ and not in or of Christ, a faith which the devils also have as well as evil men. For who is it that does not believe that Christ is a gracious king to the saints? This vain and wicked faith is now taught by the pernicious synagogues of Satan. The universities (Paris and her sister schools), together with the monasteries and all papists, say that this faith is sufficient to make Christians. In this way they virtually deny Christian faith, make heathen and Turks [Muslims] out of Christians, as Saint Peter in 2 Peter 2:1, had foretold: "There shall be false teachers, who shall privily bring in destructive heresies, denying even the Master that bought them."

10. In the second place, he particularly mentions "the daughter of Zion." In these words, he refers to the other, the true faith. For if he commands that the following words concerning Christ be proclaimed, there must be someone to hear, to receive, and to treasure them in firm faith. He does not say, "Tell of the daughter of Zion," as if someone were to believe that she has Christ; but to her you are to say that she is to believe it of herself, and not in any wise doubt that it will be fulfilled as the words declare. That alone can be called Christian faith, which believes without wavering that Christ is the Savior not only to Peter and to the saints but also to you. Your salvation does not depend on the fact that you believe Christ to be the Savior of the godly, but that he is a Savior to you and has become your own.

11. Such a faith will work in you love for Christ and joy in him, and good works will naturally follow. If they do not, faith is surely not present; for where faith is, there the Holy Ghost is and must work love and good works.

12. This faith is condemned by apostate and rebellious Christians, the pope, bishops, priests, monks, and the universities. They call it arrogance to desire to be like the saints. Thereby they fulfill the prophecy of Peter, in 2 Peter 2:2, where he says of these false teachers, "By reason of whom the way of the truth shall be evil spoken of." For this reason, when they hear faith praised, they think love and good works are prohibited. In their great blindness they do not know what faith, love, and good works are. If you would be a Christian

you must permit these words to be spoken to you and hold fast to them and believe without a doubt that you will experience what they say. You must not consider it arrogance that in this you are like the saints, but rather a necessary humility and despair not of God's grace but of your own worthiness. Under penalty of the loss of salvation does God ask for boldness toward his proffered grace. If you do not desire to become holy like the saints, where will you abide? That would be arrogance if you desired to be saved by your own merit and works, as the papists teach. They call that arrogance which is faith, and that faith which is arrogance; poor, miserable, deluded people!

13. If you believe in Christ and in his advent, it is the highest praise and thanks to God to be holy. If you recognize, love, and magnify his grace and work in you, and cast aside and condemn self and the works of self, then are you a Christian. We say, "I believe in the holy Christian Church, the communion of saints." Do you desire to be a part of the holy Christian Church and communion of saints, you must also be holy as she is, yet not of yourself but through Christ alone in whom all are holy.

14. Thirdly he says, "Behold." With this word he rouses us at once from sleep and unbelief as though he had something great, strange, or remarkable to offer, something we have long wished for and now would receive with joy. Such waking up is necessary for the reason that everything that concerns faith is against reason and nature; for example, how can nature and reason comprehend that such a one should be king of Jerusalem who enters in such poverty and humility as to ride upon a borrowed ass? How does such an advent become a great king? But faith is of the nature that it does not judge nor reason by what it sees or feels but by what it hears. It depends upon the Word alone and not on vision or sight. For this reason Christ was received as a king only by the followers of the word of the prophet, by the believers in Christ, by those who judged and received his kingdom not by sight but by the spirit—these are the true daughters of Zion. For it is not possible for those not to be offended in Christ who walk by sight and feeling and do not adhere firmly to the Word.

15. Let us receive first and hold fast this picture in which the nature of faith is placed before us. For as the appearance and object of faith as here presented is contrary to nature and reason, so the same ineffectual and unreasonable appearance is to be found in all articles and instances of faith. It would be no faith if it appeared and acted as faith acts and as the words indicate. It is faith because it does not appear and deport itself as faith and as the words declare.

If Christ had entered in splendor like a king of earth, the appearance and the words would have been according to nature and reason and would have seemed to the eye according to the words, but then there would have been no room for faith. He who believes in Christ must find riches in poverty, honor in dishonor, joy in sorrow, life in death, and hold fast to them in that faith which clings to the Word and expects such things.

16. Fourthly, "Thy king." Here he distinguishes this king from all other kings. It is thy king, he says, who was promised to you, whose own you are, who alone shall direct you, yet in the spirit and not in the body. It is he for whom you have yearned from the beginning, whom the fathers have desired to see, who will deliver you from all that has hitherto burdened, troubled, and held you captive.

Oh, this is a comforting word to a believing heart, for without Christ, man is subjected to many raging tyrants who are not kings but murderers, at whose hands he suffers great misery and fear. These are the devil, the flesh, the world, sin, also the law and eternal death, by all of which the troubled conscience is burdened, is under bondage, and lives in anguish. For where there is sin there is no clear conscience; where there is no clear conscience, there is a life of uncertainty and an unquenchable fear of death and hell in the presence of which no real joy can exist in the heart, as Leviticus 26:36 says, "The sound of a driven leaf shall chase them."

17. Where the heart receives the king with a firm faith, it is secure and does not fear sin, death, hell, nor any other evil; for he well knows and in no wise doubts that this king is the Lord of life and death, of sin and grace, of hell and heaven, and that all things are in his hand. For this reason, he became our king and came down to us that he might deliver us from these tyrants and rule over us himself alone. Therefore, he who is under this king cannot be harmed either by sin, death, hell, Satan, man, or any other creature. As his king lives without sin and is blessed, so must he be kept forever without sin and death in living blessedness.

18. See, such great things are contained in these seemingly unimportant words, "Behold, thy king." Such boundless gifts are brought by this poor and despised king. All this reason does not understand, nor nature comprehend, but faith alone does. Therefore, he is called your king; yours, who are vexed and harassed by sin, Satan, death and hell, the flesh, and the world, so that you may be governed and directed in the grace, in the spirit, in life, in heaven, in God.

With this word, therefore, he demands faith so you may be certain he is such a king to you, has such a kingdom, and has come and is proclaimed for this purpose. If you do not believe this of him, you will never acquire such faith by any work of yours. What you think of him you will have; what you expect of him you will find; and as you believe so shall it be to you. He will still remain what he is, the king of life, of grace, and of salvation, whether he is believed on or not.

19. Fifthly, he "cometh." Without doubt, you do not come to him and bring him to you; he is too high and too far from you. With all your effort, work, and labor you cannot come to him, lest you boast as though you had received him by your own merit and worthiness. No, dear friend, all merit and worthiness is out of the question, and there is nothing but demerit and unworthiness on your side, nothing but grace and mercy on his. The poor and the rich here come together, as Proverbs 22:2 says.

20. By this are condemned all those infamous doctrines of free will, which come from the pope, universities, and monasteries. For all their teaching consists in that we are to begin and lay the first stone. We should by the power of free will first seek God, come to him, run after him, and acquire his grace. Beware, beware of this poison! It is nothing but the doctrine of devils, by which all the world is betrayed. Before you can cry to God and seek him, God must come to you and must have found you, as Paul says, in Romans 10:14–15, "How then shall they call on him in whom they have not believed? and how shall they believe in him whom they have not heard? and how shall they hear without a preacher, and how shall they preach except they be sent?" God must lay the first stone and begin with you, if you are to seek him and pray to him. He is present when you begin to seek. If he were not, you could not accomplish anything but mere sin, and the greater the sin, the greater and holier the work you will attempt, and you will become a hardened hypocrite.

21. You ask, How shall we begin to be godly and what shall we do that God may begin his work in us? Answer: Do you not understand, it is not for you to work or to begin to be godly, as little as it is to further and complete it. Everything that you begin is in and remains sin, though it shines ever so brightly; you cannot do anything but sin, do what you will. Hence the teaching of all the schools and monasteries is misleading, when they teach man to begin to pray and do good works, to found something, to give, to sing, to become spiritual and thereby to seek God's grace.

22. You say, however, Then I must sin from necessity, if by my free will I work and live without God? and, I could not avoid sin, no matter what I would do? Answer: Truly, it is so, that you must remain in sin, do what you will, and that everything is sin you do alone out of your own free will. For if out of your own free will you might avoid sin and do that which pleases God, what need

would you have of Christ? He would be a fool to shed his blood for your sin, if you yourself were so free and able to do aught that is not sin. From this, you learn how the universities and monasteries with their teachings of free will and good works, do nothing else but darken the truth of God so that we know not what Christ is, what we are and what our condition is. They lead the whole world with them into the abyss of hell, and it is indeed time that we eradicate from the earth all chapters and monasteries.

23. Learn then from this Gospel what takes place when God begins to make us godly, and what the first step is in becoming godly. There is no other beginning than that your king comes to you and begins to work in you. It is done in this way: The Gospel must be the first, this must be preached and heard. In it you hear and learn how all your works count for nothing before God and that everything is sinful that you work and do. Your king must first be in you and rule you. Behold, here is the beginning of your salvation; you relinquish your works and despair of yourself, because you hear and see that all you do is sin and amounts to nothing, as the Gospel tells you, and you receive your king in faith, cling to him, implore his grace, and find consolation in his mercy alone.

But when you hear and accept this it is not your power, but God's grace, that renders the Gospel fruitful in you, so that you believe that you and your works are nothing. For you see how few there are who accept it, so that Christ weeps over Jerusalem and, as now the papists are doing, not only refuse it, but condemn such doctrine, for they will not have all their works to be sin, they desire to lay the first stone and rage and fume against the Gospel.

24. Again, it is not by virtue of your power or your merit that the Gospel is preached and your king comes. God must send him out of pure grace. Hence not greater wrath of God exists than where he does not send the Gospel; there is only sin, error, and darkness, there man may do what he will. Again, there is no greater grace than where he sends his Gospel, for there must be grace and mercy in its train, even if not all, perhaps only a few, receive it. Thus the pope's government is the most terrible wrath of God, so that Peter calls them the children of execration, for they teach no Gospel, but mere human doctrine of their own works as we, alas, see in all the chapters, monasteries, and schools.

25. This is what is meant by "Thy king cometh." You do not seek him, but he seeks you. You do not find him, he finds you. For the preachers come from him, not from you; their sermons come from him, not from you; your faith comes from him, not from you; everything that faith works in you comes from him, not from you; and where he does not come, you remain outside;

and where there is no Gospel there is no God, but only sin and damnation, free will may do, suffer, work, and live as it may and can. Therefore you should not ask, where to begin to be godly; there is no beginning, except where the king enters and is proclaimed.

26. Sixthly, he cometh "unto thee." Thee, thee, what does this mean? Is it not enough that he is your king? If he is yours how can he say, he comes to you? All this is stated by the prophet to present Christ in an endearing way and invite to faith. It is not enough that Christ saves us from the rule and tyranny of sin, death, and hell, and becomes our king, but he offers himself to us for our possession, that whatever he is and has may be ours, as Saint Paul writes, in Romans 8:32, "He that spared not his own Son, but delivered him up for us all, how shall he not also with him freely give us all things?"

27. Hence the daughter of Zion has twofold gifts from Christ. The first is faith and the Holy Spirit in the heart, by which she becomes pure and free from sin. The other is Christ himself, that she may glory in the blessings given by Christ, as though everything Christ is and has were her own, and that she may rely upon Christ as upon her own heritage. Of this Saint Paul speaks, in Romans 8:34, "Christ maketh intercession for us." If he makes intercession for us he will receive us and we will receive him as our Lord. And 1 Corinthians 1:30 says, "Christ was made unto us wisdom from God, and righteousness and sanctification, and redemption." Of the twofold gifts Isaiah speaks in 40:1–2, "Comfort ye, comfort ye my people, saith your God. Speak ye comfortably to Jerusalem; and cry unto her, that her warfare is accomplished, that her iniquity is pardoned, for she hath received of Jehovah's hand double for all her sins."

Behold, this means that he comes to you, for your welfare, as your own; in that he is your king, you receive grace from him into your heart, so that he delivers you from sin and death, and thus becomes your king and you his subject. In coming to you he becomes your own, so that you partake of his treasures, as a bride, by the jewelry the bridegroom puts on her, becomes partner of his possessions. Oh, this is a joyful, comforting form of speech! Who would despair and be afraid of death and hell if he believes in these words and wins Christ as his own?

28. Seventhly, "Meek." This word is to be especially noticed, and it comforts the sin-burdened conscience. Sin naturally makes a timid conscience, which fears God and flees, as Adam did in paradise, and cannot endure the coming of God, the knowing and feeling that God is an enemy of sin and severely punishes it. Hence it flees and is afraid, when God is only mentioned, and is concerned lest he go at it tooth and nail. In order that such delusion and timidity may not pursue us he gives us the comforting promise that this king comes meekly.

As if he would say, Do not flee and despair for he does not come now as he came to Adam, to Cain, at the flood, at Babel, to Sodom and Gomorrah, nor as he came to the people of Israel at Mount Sinai; he comes not in wrath, does not wish to reckon with you and demand his debt. All wrath is laid aside, nothing but tenderness and kindness remain. He will now deal with you so that your heart will have pleasure, love, and confidence in him, that henceforth you will much more abide with him and find refuge in him than you feared him and fled from him before. Behold, he is nothing but meekness to you, he is a different man, he acts as if he were sorry ever to have made you afraid and caused you to flee from his punishment and wrath. He desires to reassure and comfort you and bring you to himself by love and kindness.

This means to speak consolingly to a sin-burdened conscience, this means to preach Christ rightly and to proclaim his Gospel. How is it possible that such a form of speech should not make a heart glad and drive away all fear of sin, death, and hell, and establish a free, secure, and good conscience that will henceforth gladly do all and more than is commanded.

29. The evangelist, however, altered the words of the prophet slightly. The prophet says in Zechariah 9:9, "Rejoice greatly, O daughter of Zion; shout, O daughter of Jerusalem: behold, thy king cometh unto thee; he is just, and having salvation; lowly, and riding upon an ass, even upon a colt, the foal of an ass." The evangelist expresses the invitation to joy and exultation briefly in these words, "Tell the daughter of Zion." Further on he leaves out the words, "just and having salvation." Again the prophet says, "he is lowly," the evangelist, "he is meek." The prophet says, "upon the colt, the foal of an ass," he mentions the last word in the plural number; the evangelist says, "upon the colt, the foal of an ass that is used for daily and burden-bearing labor." How shall we harmonize these accounts?

30. First, we must keep in mind that the evangelists do not quote the prophets word by word; it is enough for them to have the same meaning and to show the fulfillment, directing us to the Scriptures so that we ourselves may read, what they omit, and see for ourselves that nothing was written which is not richly fulfilled. It is natural, also, that he who has the substance and the fulfillment, does not care so much for the words. Thus we often find that the evangelists quote the prophets somewhat changed, yet it is done without detriment to the understanding and intent of the original.

31. To invite the daughter of Zion and the daughter of Jerusalem to joy and gladness the prophet abundantly gives us to understand that the coming of this king is most comforting to every sin-burdened conscience, since he

removes all fear and trembling, so that men do not flee from him and look upon him as a severe judge, who will press them with the law, as Moses did, so that they could not have a joyful confidence in God, as the knowledge and realization of sin naturally come from the law. But he would arouse them with this first word to expect from him all grace and goodness. For what other reason should he invite them to rejoice and command them even to shout and be exceeding glad! He tells this command of God to all who are in sorrow and fear of God. He also shows that it is God's will and full intent, and demands that they entertain joyful confidence in him against the natural fear and alarm. And this is the natural voice of the Gospel which the prophet here begins to preach, as Christ speaks likewise in the Gospel and the apostles always admonish to rejoice in Christ, as we shall hear further on.

It is also full of meaning that he comes from the Mount of Olives. We shall notice that this grace on account of its greatness might be called a mountain of grace, a grace that is not only a drop or handful, but grace abundant and heaped up like a mountain.

32. He mentions the people twice while the evangelist says only once, daughter of Zion. For it is one people, daughter of Zion and daughter of Jerusalem, namely, the people of the same city, who believe in Christ and receive him. As I said before, the evangelist quotes the Scriptures only briefly and invites us to read them ourselves and find out more there for ourselves. That the evangelist does not invite to joy like the prophet, but simply says, "Tell it to the daughter of Zion," he does it to show how the joy and exultation shall be carried on. None should expect bodily but spiritual joy, a joy that can be gathered alone from the Word by the faith of the heart. From a worldly aspect there was nothing joyful in Christ's entrance. His spiritual advent must be preached and believed, that is, his meekness; this makes man joyful and glad.

33. That the prophet gives Christ three titles—lowly, just, and having salvation—while the evangelist has only one—meek—is again done for brevity's sake, he suggests more than he explains. It seems to me that the Holy Ghost led the apostles and evangelists to abbreviate passages of the Scriptures for the purpose that we might be kept close to the holy Scriptures, and not set a bad example to future exegetes, who make many words outside the Scriptures and thereby draw us secretly from the Scriptures to human doctrines. As to say, If I spread the Scriptures verbatim everyone will follow the example and it will come to pass that we would read more in other books than in the holy writings of the principal book, and there would be no end to the writing of books and we would be carried from one book to another until, finally, we would get

away from the holy Scriptures altogether, as has happened in fact. Hence with such incomplete quotations he directs us to the original book where they can be found complete, so that there is no need for everyone to make a separate book and leave the first one.

34. We notice, therefore, that it is the intention of all the apostles and evangelists in the New Testament to direct and drive us to the Old Testament, which they call the holy Scriptures proper. For the New Testament was to be only the incarnate living Word and not Scripture. Hence Christ did not write anything himself, but gave the command to preach and extend the Gospel, which lay hidden in the Scriptures, as we shall hear on Epiphany Sunday.

35. In the Hebrew language the two words "meek" and "lowly" do not sound unlike, and mean not a poor man who is wanting in money and property, but who in his heart is humble and wretched, in whom truly no anger nor haughtiness is to be found, but meekness and sympathy. And if we wish to obtain the full meaning of this word, we must take it as Luke uses it, who describes how Christ at his entrance wept and wailed over Jerusalem.

We interpret therefore the words lowly and meek in the light of Christ's conduct. How does he appear? His heart is full of sorrow and compassion toward Jerusalem. There is no anger or revenge, but he weeps out of tenderness at their impending doom. None was so bad that he did or wished him harm. His sympathy makes him so kind and full of pity that he thinks not of anger, of haughtiness, of threatening or revenge, but offers boundless compassion and good will. This is what the prophet calls lowly and the evangelist meek. Blessed he who thus knows Christ in him and believes in him. He cannot be afraid of him, but has a true and comforting confidence in him and entrance to him. He does not try to find fault either, for as he believes, he finds it; these words do not lie nor deceive.

36. The word "just" does not mean here the justice with which God judges, which is called the severe justice of God. For if Christ came to us with this who could stand before him? Who could receive him, since even the saints cannot endure it? The joy and grace of this entrance would thereby be changed into the greatest fear and terror. But that grace is meant, by which he makes us just or righteous. I wish the word *justus, justitia,* were not used for the severe judicial justice; for originally it means godly, godliness. When we say, He is a pious man, the Scriptures express it, He is *justus,* justified or just. But the severe justice of God is called in the Scriptures, severity, judgment, tribunal.

The prophet's meaning, therefore, is this, Thy king cometh to thee pious or just, i.e., he comes to make you godly through himself and his grace; he knows well that you are not godly. Your piety should consist not in your deeds, but in his grace and gift, so that you are just and godly through him. In this sense Saint Paul speaks, in Romans 3:26, "That he might himself be just, and the justifier of him that hath faith in Jesus." That is, Christ alone is pious before God and he alone makes us pious. Also, in Romans 1:17, "For therein is revealed a righteousness of God from faith unto faith," that is the godliness of God, namely, his grace and mercy, by which he makes us godly before him, is preached in the Gospel. You see in this verse from the prophet that Christ is preached for us unto righteousness, that he comes godly and just, and we become godly and just by faith.

37. Note this fact carefully, that when you find in the Scriptures the word God's justice, it is not to be understood of the self-existing, imminent justice of God, as the papists and many of the fathers held, lest you be frightened; but, according to the usage of Holy Writ, it means the revealed grace and mercy of God through Jesus Christ in us by means of which we are considered godly and righteous before him. Hence it is called God's justice or righteousness effected not by us, but by God through grace, just as God's work, God's wisdom, God's strength, God's Word, God's mouth, signifies what he works and speaks in us. All this is demonstrated clearly by Saint Paul, in Romans 1:16, "I am not ashamed of the Gospel of Christ; for it is the power of God (which works in us and strengthens us) unto salvation to everyone that believeth. For therein is revealed a righteousness of God," as it is written in Habakkuk 2:4, "The righteous shall live by his faith." Here you see that he speaks of the righteousness of faith and calls the same the righteousness of God, preached in the Gospel, since the Gospel teaches nothing else but that he who believes has grace and is righteous before God and is saved.

In the same manner you should understand Psalm 31:1, "Deliver me in thy righteousness," i.e., by your grace, which makes me godly and righteous. The word Savior or Redeemer compels us to accept this as the meaning of the little word "just." For if Christ came with his severe justice he would not save anyone, but condemn all, as they are all sinners and unjust. But now he comes to make not only just and righteous, but also blessed, all who receive him, that he alone as the just one and the Savior be offered graciously to all sinners out of unmerited kindness and righteousness.

38. When the evangelist calls his steed a burden-bearing and working foal of an ass he describes the animal the prophets mean. He wants to say, The prophecy is fulfilled in this burden-bearing animal. It was not a special animal trained for this purpose, as according to the country's custom riding animals are trained, and when the prophet speaks of the foal of the ass it is his meaning that it was a colt, but not a colt of a horse.

II. CONCERNING GOOD WORKS

39. We have said enough of faith. We now come to consider good works. We receive Christ not only as a gift by faith, but also as an example of love toward our neighbor, whom we are to serve as Christ serves us. Faith brings and gives Christ to you with all his possessions. Love gives you to your neighbor with all your possessions. These two things constitute a true and complete Christian life; then follow suffering and persecution for such faith and love, and out of these grows hope in patience.

40. You ask, perhaps, What are the good works you are to do to your neighbor? Answer: They have no name. As the good works Christ does to you have no name, so your good works are to have no name.

41. Whereby do you know them? Answer: They have no name, so that there may be no distinction made and they be not divided, that you might do some and leave others undone. You shall give yourself up to him altogether, with all you have, the same as Christ did not simply pray or fast for you. Prayer and fasting are not the works he did for you, but he gave himself up wholly to you, with praying, fasting, all works, and suffering, so that there is nothing in him that is not yours and was not done for you. Thus it is not your good work that you give alms or that you pray, but that you offer yourself to your neighbor and serve him, wherever he needs you and every way you can, be it with alms, prayer, work, fasting, counsel, comfort, instruction, admonition, punishment, apologizing, clothing, food, and, lastly, with suffering and dying for him. Pray, where are now such works to be found in Christendom?

42. I wish to God I had a voice like a thunderbolt, that I might preach to all the world, and tear the word "good works" out of people's hearts, mouths, ears, books, or at least give them the right understanding of it. All the world sings, speaks, writes, and thinks of good works, everyone wishes to exercise themselves in good works, and, yet, good works are done nowhere, no one has the right understanding of good works. Oh, that all such pulpits in all the world were cast into the fire and burned to ashes! How they mislead people with their good works! They call good works what God has not commanded, as pilgrimages, fasting, building and decorating their churches in honor of the saints, saying Mass, paying for vigils, praying with rosaries, much prattling and bawling in churches, turning nun, monk, priest, using special food, raiment or dwelling—who can enumerate all the horrible abominations and deceptions? This is the pope's government and holiness.

43. If you have ears to hear and a mind to observe, pray, listen and learn for God's sake what good works are and mean. A good work is good for the reason that it is useful and benefits and helps the one for whom it is done; why

else should it be called good! For there is a difference between good works and great, long, numerous, beautiful works. When you throw a big stone a great distance it is a great work, but whom does it benefit? If you can jump, run, fence well, it is a fine work, but whom does it benefit? Whom does it help, if you wear a costly coat or build a fine house?

44. And to come to our papists' work, what does it avail if they put silver or gold on the walls, wood, and stone in the churches? Who would be made better if each village had ten bells, as big as those at Erfurt? Whom would it help if all the houses were convents and monasteries as splendid as the temple of Solomon? Who is benefited if you fast for Saint Catherine, Saint Martin, or any other saint? Whom does it benefit if you are shaved half or wholly, if you wear a gray or a black cap? Of what use were it if all people held Mass every hour? What benefit is it if in one church, as at Meissen, they sing day and night without interruption? Who is better for it if every church had more silver, pictures, and jewelry than the churches of Halle and Wittenberg? It is folly and deception; men's lies invented these things and called them good works. They all pretend they serve God thus and pray for the people and their sins, just as if they helped God with their property or as if his saints were in need of our work. Sticks and stones are not as rude and mad as we are. A tree bears fruit, not for itself, but for the good of man and beast, and these fruits are its good works.

45. Hear then how Christ explains good works in Matthew 7:12, "Whatsoever ye would that men should do unto you, even so do ye unto them; for this is the law and the prophets." Do you hear now what are the contents of the whole law and of all the prophets? You are not to do good to God and to his dead saints, they are not in need of it; still less to wood and stone, to which it is of no use, nor is it needed, but to men, to men, to men. Do you not hear? To men you should do everything that you would they should do to you.

46. I would not have you build me a church or tower or cast bells for me. I would not have you construct for me an organ with fourteen stops and ten rows of flute work. Of this I can neither eat nor drink, support neither wife nor child, keep neither house nor land. You may feast my eyes on these and tickle my ears, but what shall I give to my children? Where are the necessaries of life? O madness, madness! The bishops and lords, who should check it, are the first in such folly, and one blind leader leads the other. Such people remind me of young girls playing with dolls and of boys riding on sticks. Indeed, they are nothing but children and players with dolls, and riders of hobbyhorses.

47. Keep in mind that you need not do any work for God nor for the departed saints, but you ask and receive good from him in faith. Christ has

done and accomplished everything for you, atoned for your sins, secured grace and life and salvation. Be content with this, only think how he can become more and more your own and strengthen your faith. Hence direct all the good you can do and your whole life to the end that it be good; but it is good only when it is useful to other people and not to yourself. You need it not, since Christ has done and given for you all that you might seek and desire for yourself, here and hereafter, be it forgiveness of sins, merit of salvation, or whatever it may be called. If you find a work in you by which you benefit God or his saints or yourself and not your neighbor, know that such a work is not good.

48. A man is to live, speak, act, hear, suffer, and die for the good of his wife and child, the wife for the husband, the children for the parents, the servants for their masters, the masters for their servants, the government for its subjects, the subjects for the government, each one for his fellowman, even for his enemies, so that one is the other's hand, mouth, eye, foot, even heart and mind. This is a truly Christian and good work, which can and shall be done at all times, in all places, toward all people. You notice the papists' works in organs, pilgrimages, fasting, etc., are really beautiful, great, numerous, long, wide, and heavy works, but there is no good, useful, and helpful work among them and the proverb may be applied to them, It is already bad.

49. But beware of their acute subtleties, when they say, If these works are not good to our neighbor in his body, they do spiritual good to his soul, since they serve God and propitiate him and secure his grace. Here it is time to say, You lie as wide as your mouth. God is to be worshiped not with works, but by faith; faith must do everything that is to be done between God and us. There may be more faith in a miller-boy than in all the papists, and it may gain more than all priests and monks do with their organs and jugglery, even if they had more organs than these now have pipes. He who has faith can pray for his fellowman, he who has no faith can pray for nothing.

It is a satanic lie to call such outward pomp spiritually good and useful works. A miller's maid, if she believes, does more good, accomplishes more, and I would trust her more, if she takes the sack from the horse, than all the priests and monks, if they kill themselves singing day and night and torment themselves to the quick. You great, coarse fools, would you expect to help the people with your faithless life and distribute spiritual goods, when there is on earth no more miserable, needy, godless people than you are? You should be called, not spiritual, but spiritless.

50. Behold, such good works Christ teaches here by his example. Tell me what does he do to serve himself and to do good to himself? The prophet

directs all to the daughter of Zion and says, "He cometh to thee," and that he comes as a Savior, just and meek, is all for you, to make you just and blessed. None had asked nor bidden him to come; but he came, he comes of his own free will, out of pure love, to do good and to be useful and helpful.

Now his work is manifold, it embraces all that is necessary to make us just and blessed. But justification and salvation imply that he delivers us from sin, death, hell, and does it not only for his friends, but also for his enemies, yea, for none but his enemies, yet he does it so tenderly, that he weeps over those who oppose such work and will not receive him. Hence he leaves nothing undone to blot out their sin, conquer death and hell, and make them just and blessed. He retains nothing for himself, and is content that he already has God and is blessed—thus he serves only us according to the will of his Father, who wishes him to do so.

51. See then how he keeps the law, "Whatsoever ye would that men should do unto you, even so do ye unto them." Is it not true, everyone heartily wishes that another might step between man and his sin, take it upon himself and blot it out, so that it would no more sting his conscience, and deliver him from death and hell? What does everyone desire more deeply than to be free from death and hell? Who would not be free from sin and have a good, joyful conscience before God? Do we not see how all men have striven for this, with prayer, fastings, pilgrimages, donations, monasteries, and priestdom? Who urges them? It is sin, death, hell from which they would be saved. And if there were a physician at the end of the world, who could help here, all lands would become deserted and everyone would hasten to this physician and risk property, body, and life to make the journey.

And if Christ himself, like we, were surrounded by death, sin, and hell, he would wish that someone would help him out of it, take his sin away, and give him a good conscience. Since he would have others do this for him, he proceeds and does it for others, as the law says; he takes upon himself our sins, goes into death, and overcomes for us sin, death, and hell, so that henceforth all who believe in him, and call upon his name, shall be justified and saved, be above sin and death, have a good, joyful, secure, and intrepid conscience forever, as he says in John 8:51, "If a man keep my word, he shall never see death," and John 11:25–26, "I am the resurrection, and the life; he that believeth on me, though he die, yet shall he live, and whosoever liveth and believeth on me, shall never die."

52. Behold, this is the great joy, to which the prophet invites, when he says, "Rejoice greatly, O daughter of Zion; shout, O daughter of Jerusalem!" This is the righteousness and the salvation for which the Savior and king

comes. These are the good works done for us by which he fulfills the law. Hence the death of the believer in Christ is not death but a sleep, for he neither sees nor tastes death, as is said in Psalm 4:8, "In peace will I both lay me down and sleep, for thou, Jehovah, alone makest me dwell in safety." Therefore death is also called a sleep in the Scriptures.

53. But the papists and their disciples, who would get rid of death, sin, and hell by their own works and satisfaction, must remain in them eternally for they undertake to do for themselves what Christ alone did and could do, of whom they should expect it by faith. Therefore they are foolish, deluded people who do works for Christ and his saints, which they should do for their neighbor. Again, what they should expect of Christ by faith they would find in themselves and have gone so far as to spend on stone and wood, on bells, and incense what they should spend on their neighbors. They go on and do good to God and his saints, fast for them, and dedicate to them prayers, and at the same time leave their neighbor as he is, thinking only, let us first help ourselves! Then comes the pope and sells them his letter of indulgence and leads them into heaven, not into God's heaven, but into the pope's heaven, which is the abyss of hell. Behold, this is the fruit of unbelief and ignorance of Christ, this is our reward for having left the Gospel in obscurity and setting up human doctrine in its place. I repeat it, I wish all pulpits in the world lay in ashes, and the monasteries, convents, churches, hermitages and chapels, and everything were ashes and powder because of this shameful misleading of souls.

54. Now you know what good works are. Think of it and act accordingly. As to sin, death, and hell, take care that you augment them not, for you cannot do anything here, your good works will avail nothing, you must have someone else to work for you. To Christ himself such works properly belong; you must consent to it that he who comes is the king of Zion, that he alone is the just Savior. In him and through him you will blot out sin and death through faith. Therefore, if anyone teaches you to blot out your own sin by works, beware of him.

55. When in opposition to this they quote verses of the Bible like Daniel 4:27, "Break off thine iniquities by showing mercy to the poor," and 1 Peter 4:8, "Love covereth a multitude of sins," and the like, be not deceived; such passages do not mean that the works could blot out or remove sin, for this would rob Christ of his word and advent, and do away with his whole work. But these works are a sure work of faith, which in Christ receives remission of sins and the victory over death. For it is impossible for him who believes in Christ, as a just Savior, not to love and to do good. If, however, he does not

do good nor love, it is sure that faith is not present. Therefore man knows by the fruits what kind of a tree it is, and it is proved by love and deed whether Christ is in him and he believes in Christ. As Saint Peter says in 2 Peter 1:10, "Wherefore, brethren, give the more diligence to make your calling and election sure; for if ye do these things, ye shall never stumble," that is, if you bravely practice good works you will be sure and cannot doubt that God has called and chosen you.

56. Thus faith blots out sin in a different manner than love. Faith blots it out of itself, while love or good works prove and demonstrate that faith has done so and is present, as Saint Paul says, in 1 Corinthians 13:2, "And if I have all faith, so as to remove mountains, but have not love, I am nothing." Why? Without doubt, because faith is not present where there is no love, they are not separate the one from the other. See to it then that you do not err and be misled from faith to works.

57. Good works should be done, but we should not confide in them, instead of in Christ's work. We should not touch sin, death, and hell with our works, but direct them from us to the Savior, to the king of Zion, who rides upon an ass. He who knows how to treat sin, death, and hell will blot out sin, overcome death, and subdue hell. Do you permit him to perform these works while you serve your neighbor—you will then have a sure testimony of faith in the Savior who overcame death. So love and good works will blot out your sin for you that you may realize it; as faith blots it out before God where you do not realize it. But more of this later.

The Lesson Story and the False Notions the Jews Held Concerning the Messiah

58. In the story of this Gospel we will first direct our attention to the reason why the evangelist quotes the words of the prophet, in which was described long ago and in clear, beautiful, and wonderful words, the bodily, public entrance and advent of our Lord Jesus Christ to the people of Zion or Jerusalem, as the text says. In this the prophet wanted to show and explain to his people and to all the world, who the Messiah is and how and in what manner he would come and manifest himself, and offers a plain and visible sign in this that he says, "Behold, thy king cometh unto thee, meek, and riding upon an ass," etc., so that we would be certain of it, and not dispute about the promised Messiah or Christ, nor wait for another.

He therewith anticipates the mistaken idea of the Jews, who thought, because there were such glorious things said and written of Christ and his kingdom, he would manifest himself in great worldly pomp and glory, as a king against their enemies, especially the Roman empire, to the power of which they were subject, and would overthrow its power and might, and in their place set up the Jews as lords and princes. They thus expected nothing in the promised Christ but a worldly kingdom and deliverance from bodily captivity. Even today they cling to such dreams and therefore they do not believe in Christ, because they have not seen such bodily relief and worldly power. They were led to this notion, and strengthened in it by their false priests, preachers, and doctors, who perverted the Scriptures concerning Christ and interpreted them according to their own worldly understanding as referring to bodily, worldly things, because they would fain be great earthly lords.

59. But the dear prophets plainly foretold and faithfully gave warning that we should not think of such an earthly kingdom nor of bodily salvation, but look back and pay attention to the promises of a spiritual kingdom and of a redemption from the pernicious fall of mankind in paradise; of which it is said in Genesis 2:17, "In the day that thou eatest thereof thou shalt surely die." The first prophecy of Christ is also against it, in Genesis 3:15, "The seed of woman shall bruise the serpent's head." This means he shall deliver all mankind from the power of the devil and the captivity of sin and eternal death and, instead, bring justification before God and eternal life. Hence this prophet calls him "just and having salvation." This truly is a different salvation from that of bodily freedom, bodily power and glory, the end of which is death, and under which everything must abide eternally.

They ought to have considered this and rejoiced in it, since the prophets had heartily yearned and prayed for it, and this prophet admonishes to such great joy and gladness. But they and their shameless preachers made a temporal affair out of this misery and unhappiness, as if it were a joke about sin and death or the power of the devil, and considered it the greatest misfortune that they lost their temporal freedom and were made subject to the emperor and required to pay taxes to him.

60. The evangelist therefore quotes this saying of the prophet, to punish the blindness and false notions of those who seek bodily and temporal blessings in Christ and his Gospel, and to convince them by the testimony of the prophet, who shows clearly what kind of a king Christ was and what they should seek in him, in that he calls him just and having salvation and yet adds this sign of his coming by which they are to know him, "He cometh to thee meek, and riding upon a colt, the foal of an ass." As if to say, A poor, miserable, almost beggarly horseman upon a borrowed ass who is kept by the side of its mother not for ostentation but for service. With this he desires to lead them away from gazing and waiting for a glorious entrance of a worldly king.

And he offers such signs that they might not doubt the Christ, nor take offense at his beggarly appearance. All pomp and splendor are to be left out of sight, and the heart and the eyes directed to the poor rider, who became poor and miserable and made himself of no kingly reputation that they might not seek the things of this world in him but the eternal, as is indicated by the words, "just and having salvation."

61. This verse first clearly and effectively does away with the Jewish dream and delusion of a worldly reign of the Messiah and of their temporal freedom. It takes away all cause and support for excuse, if they do not receive Christ, and cuts off all hope and expectation for another, because it clearly and distinctly announces and admonishes that he would come on this wise and that he has fulfilled everything. We Christians thus have against the Jews a firm ground and certain title and conviction from their own Scripture that this Messiah, who thus came to them, is the Christ predicted by the prophets and that no other shall come, and that in the vain hope of another's coming they forfeit their temporal and eternal salvation.

III. THE SPIRITUAL INTERPRETATION OF THIS GOSPEL

62. This has been said about the history of this Gospel. Let us now treat of its hidden or spiritual meaning. Here we are to remember that Christ's earthly walk and conversation signify his spiritual walk; his bodily walk therefore signifies the Gospel and the faith. As with his bodily feet he walked from one town to another, so by preaching he came into the world. Hence this lesson shows distinctly what the Gospel is and how it is to be preached, what it does and effects in the world, and its history is a fine, pleasing picture and image of how the kingdom of Christ is carried on by the office of preaching. We will consider this point by point.

And when they drew nigh unto Jerusalem,
and came unto Bethphage, unto the Mount of Olives.

63. All the apostles declare that Christ would become man at the end of the world, and that the Gospel would be the last preaching, as is written in 1 John 2:18, "Little children, it is the last hour, and as ye have heard that Antichrist cometh, even now hath there arisen many Antichrists; whereby we know that it is the last hour," etc. He mentions here the Antichrist. Antichrist in Greek means he who teaches and acts against the true Christ. Again, 1 Corinthians 10:11, "All these things were written for our admonition, upon whom the ends of the ages are come." As the prophets came to man before the first advent of Christ, so the apostles are the last messengers of

God, sent before the last advent of Christ at the last day to preach it faithfully. Christ indicates this by not sending out his apostles to fetch the ass, until he drew nigh unto Jerusalem, where he was now to enter. Thus the Gospel is brought into this world by the apostles shortly before the last day, when Christ will enter with his flock into the eternal Jerusalem.

64. This agrees with the word "Bethphage," which means, as some say, mouth-house, for Saint Paul says in Romans 1:2, that the Gospel was promised afore in the holy Scriptures, but it was not preached orally and publicly until Christ came and sent out his apostles. Therefore the church is a mouth-house, not a pen-house, for since Christ's advent that Gospel is preached orally which before was hidden in written books.

It is the way of the Gospel and of the New Testament that it is to be preached and discussed orally with a living voice. Christ himself wrote nothing, nor did he give command to write, but to preach orally. Thus the apostles were not sent out until Christ came to his mouth-house, that is, until the time had come to preach orally and to bring the Gospel from dead writing and pen-work to the living voice and mouth. From this time, the church is rightly called Bethphage, since she has and hears the living voice of the Gospel.

65. The sending shows that the kingdom of Christ is contained in the public oral office of preaching, which shall not stand still nor remain in one place, as before it was hidden with the Jewish nation alone in the Scriptures and foretold by the prophets for the future, but should go openly, free, and untrammeled into all the world.

66. The Mount of Olives signifies the great mercy and grace of God, that sent forth the apostles and brought the Gospel to us. Olive oil in Holy Writ signifies the grace and mercy of God, by which the soul and the conscience are comforted and healed, as the oil soothes and softens and heals the wounds and defects of the body. And from what was said above, we learn what unspeakable grace it is that we know and have Christ, the justified Savior and king. Therefore he does not send into the level plain, nor upon a deserted, rocky mountain, but unto the Mount of Olives, to show to all the world the mercy which prompted him to such grace. There is not simply a drop or handful of it, as formerly, but because of its great abundance it might be called a mountain. The prophet also calls in Psalm 36:6, such grace God's mountain and says, "Thy righteousness is like the mountains of God," that is, great and abundant, rich and overflowing. This he can understand who considers what it means that Christ bears our sin, and conquers death and hell, and does everything for us that is necessary to our salvation. He does not expect us to do anything for it, but to exercise it toward our neighbor, to

know thereby whether we have such faith in Christ or not. Hence the Mount of Olives signifies that the Gospel was not preached nor sent until the time of grace came; from this time on, the great grace goes out into the world through the apostles.

> *Then Jesus sent two disciples, saying unto them,*
> *"Go into the village that is over against you."*

67. These two disciples represent all the apostles and preachers sent into the world. The evangelical sermon is to consist of two witnesses, as Saint Paul says in Romans 3:21, "A righteousness of God has been manifested, being witnessed by the law and the prophets." Thus we see how the apostles introduce the law and the prophets, who prophesied of Christ, so that it might be fulfilled that Moses spoke in Deuteronomy 17:6 and Christ in Matthew 18:16, "At the mouth of two witnesses or three, every word may be established."

68. When he says, "Go into the village over against you," not mentioning the name, it signifies that the apostles are not sent to one nation alone, as the Jews were separated from the gentiles and alone bore the name "People of God" and God's Word and promise of the future Messiah were with them alone. But now when Christ comes, he sends his preachers into all the world and commands them to go straight forward and preach everywhere to all the heathen, and to teach, reprove, without distinction, whomsoever they meet, however great and wise and learned and holy they may be.

When he calls the great city of Jerusalem a village and does not give her name, he does it for the reason that the name Jerusalem has a holy significance. The kingdom of heaven and salvation are the spiritual Jerusalem that Christ enters. But the apostles were sent into the world among their enemies who have no name.

69. The Lord here comforts and strengthens the apostles and all ministers when he calls the great city a village and adds, she is over against you. As if he would say, like Matthew 10:16, "Behold, I send you forth as sheep in the midst of the wolves," I send you into the world, which is against you, and seems to be something great, for there are kings, princes, the learned, the rich, and everything that is great in the world and amounts to anything, this is against you. And as he says in Matthew 10:22, "Ye shall be hated of all men for my name's sake." But never fear, go on, it is hardly a village, do not be moved by great appearances, preach bravely against it, and fear no one. For it is not possible that he should preach the Gospel truth, who fears the multitude and does not despise all that the world esteems highly. It is here decreed that this village is against the apostles; therefore they should not be surprised if the great,

high, rich, wise, and holy orders do not accept their word. It must be so, the village must be against them; again, the apostles must despise them and appear before them, for the Lord will have no flatterer as a preacher. He does not say, Go around the village, or to the one side of it. Go in bravely and tell them what they do not like to hear.

70. How very few there are now who enter the village that is against them. We gladly go into the towns that are on our side. The Lord might have said: Go ye into the village before you. That would have been a pleasing and customary form of speech. But he would indicate this mystery of the ministry, hence he speaks in an unusual way: Go into the village that is over against you. That is: Preach to them that are disposed to prosecute and kill you. You shall merit such thanks and not try to please them, for such is the way of hypocrites and not that of the evangelists.

"And straightway ye shall find an ass tied, and a colt with her;
loose them and bring them unto me."

71. This is also offered as consolation to ministers that they should not worry as to who would believe or receive them. For it is decreed in Isaiah 55:11, "My word shall not return unto me void." And Saint Paul says, in Colossians 1:6, "The Gospel is in all the world bearing fruit." It cannot be otherwise than that where the Gospel is preached there will be some who accept it and believe. This is the meaning of the mystery that the apostles shall find the ass forthwith and the colt, if they only go. As if he would say, Only go and preach, care not who they are that hear you. I will care for that. The world will be against you, but be not afraid, you will find such as will hear and follow you. You do not know them yet, but I know them; you preach, and leave the rest to me.

72. Behold, in this way he consoles them that they should not cease to preach against the world, though it withstands and contradicts them ever so hard, it shall not be in vain. You find people now who believe we should be silent and cause no stir, because it is impossible to convert the world. It is all in vain, they say; pope, priests, bishops, and monks reject it and they will not change their lives; what is the use to preach and storm against them? This is the same as if the apostles had said to Christ, You tell us to go into the village that is over against us; if it is against us, what use is it that we enter there; let us rather stay outside.

But the Lord refutes this and says, Go there and preach, what does it matter if it is against you? You will find there what I say. We should now do likewise. Although the masses storm against the Gospel and there is no hope that they will be better, yet we must preach. There will yet be found those who listen and become converted.

73. Why does he have them bring two asses or not both young or old ones, since one was enough for him to ride upon? Answer: As the two disciples represent the preachers, so the colt and its mother represent their disciples and hearers. The preachers shall be Christ's disciples and be sent by him, that is, they should preach nothing but Christ's doctrine. Nor should they go to preach except they be called, as was the case with the apostles. But the hearers are old and young.

74. Here we should remember that man in Holy Writ is divided into two parts, in an inner and an outer man. The outer man is called according to his outward, visible, bodily life and conversation; the inner man, according to his heart and conscience. The outer man can be forced to do the good and quit the bad, by law, pain, punishment, and shame, or attracted by favor, money, honor, and reward. But the inner man cannot be forced to do out of his own free will, what he should do, except the grace of God change the heart and make it willing.

Hence the Scriptures say all men are liars, no man does good of his own free will, but everyone seeks his own and does nothing out of love for virtue. For if there were no heaven nor hell, no honor nor disgrace, none would do good. If it were as great an honor and prize to commit adultery as to honor matrimony, you would see adultery committed with much greater pleasure than matrimony is now held sacred. In like manner all other sins would be done with greater zeal than virtues are now practiced. Hence all good conduct without grace is mere glitter and semblance; it touches only the exterior man, without the mind and free will of the inner man's being reached.

75. These are the two asses: The old one is the exterior man; he is bound like this one, with laws and fear of death, of hell, of shame, or with allurements of heaven, of life, of honor. He goes forward with the external appearance of good works and is a pious rogue, but he does it unwillingly and with a heavy heart and a heavy conscience.

Therefore the apostle calls her "*subjugalem*," the yoked animal, who works under a burden and labors hard. It is a miserable, pitiable life that is under compulsion by fear of hell, of death, and of shame. Hell, death, and shame are his yoke and burden, heavy beyond measure, from which he has a burdened conscience and is secretly an enemy to law and to God. Such people were the Jews, who waited for Christ, and such are all who rely upon their own power to fulfill God's commands, and merit heaven. They are tied by their consciences to the law; they must, but would rather not, do it. They are carriers of sacks, lazy beasts of burden, and yoked rogues.

76. The colt, the young ass, of which Mark and Luke write, on which never man rode, is the inner man, the heart, the mind, the will, which can never be subject to law, even if he be tied by conscience and feels the law. But he has no desire nor love for it until Christ comes and rides on him. As this colt was never ridden by anyone, so man's heart has never been subject to the good; but, as Moses says in Genesis 6:5 and 8:21, is evil continually from his youth.

77. Christ tells them to loose them, that is, he tells them to preach the Gospel in his name, in which is proclaimed grace and remission of sins, and how he fulfilled the law for us. The heart is here freed from the fetters of conscience and things. Thus man is loose not from the law, that he should and joyful, willing, and anxious to do and to leave undone all things. Thus man is loose not from the law, that he should do nothing, but from a joyless, heavy conscience he has from the law, and with which he was the enemy of the law, that threatens him with death and hell. Now he has a clear conscience under Christ, is a friend of the law, neither fears death nor hell, does freely and willingly, what before he did reluctantly. See, in this way the Gospel delivers the heart from all evil, from sin and death, from hell, and a bad conscience through faith in Christ.

78. When he commands them to bring them to him, he speaks against the pope and all sects and deceivers, who lead the souls from Christ to themselves; but the apostles bring them to Christ; they preach and teach nothing but Christ, and not their own doctrine nor human laws. The Gospel alone teaches us to come to Christ and to know Christ rightly. In this the stupid prelates receive a heavy rebuke at their system of bringing souls to themselves, as Paul says, in Acts 20:29–30, "I know that after my departing grievous wolves shall enter in among you, not sparing the flock; and from among your own selves shall men arise, speaking perverse things, to draw away the disciples after them." But the Gospel converts men to Christ and to none else. Therefore he sends out the Gospel and ordains preachers, that he may draw us all to himself, that we may know him as he says, in John 12:32, "And I, if I be lifted up from the earth, will draw all men unto myself."

> "And if any man say aught unto you, ye shall say,
> The Lord hath need of them; and straightway he will send them."

79. Saint Paul, in Galatians 4:2, compares the law to guardians and stewards, under whom the young heir is educated in fear and discipline. The law forces with threats that we externally abstain from evil works, from fear of death and hell, although the heart does not become good thereby. Here are,

as Luke writes, the masters of the ass and its colt, speaking to the apostles, What, do ye loose the colt? Where the Gospel begins to loose the conscience of its own works, it seems to forbid good works and the keeping of the law. It is the common speech of all the teachers of the law, and of the scribes and doctors, to say, If all our works amount to nothing and if the works done under the law are evil, we will never do good. You forbid good works and throw away God's law; you heretic, you loose the colt and wish to make bad people free. Then they go to work and forbid to loose the colt and the conscience and to bring it to Christ and say, You must do good works, and keep people tied in bondage to the law.

80. Our text shows how the apostles should act toward such persons. They should say, "The Lord hath need of them." They should instruct them in the works of the law and the works of grace, and should say, We forbid not good works, but we loose the conscience from false good works, not to make them free to do evil deeds, but to come under Christ, their true Master and, under him, do truly good works; to this end he needs them and will have them. Of this Paul treats so well in Romans 6, where he teaches that through grace we are free from the law and its works; not so as to do evil, but to do truly good works.

81. It all amounts to this, that the scribes and masters of the law do not know what good works are; they therefore will not loose the colt, but drive it with unmerciful human works. However, where wholesome instruction is given concerning good works, they let it pass, if they are at all sensible and honest teachers of the law, as they are here represented. The mad tyrants, who are frantic with human laws, are not mentioned in this Gospel. It treats only of the law of God and of the very best teachers of the law. For without grace, even God's law is a chain and makes burdened consciences and hypocrites whom none can help, until other works are taught, which are not ours, but Christ's, and are worked in us by grace. Then all constraint and coercion of the law is ended and the colt is loose.

Now this is come to pass, that it might be fulfilled, which was spoken through the prophet, saying, "Tell ye the daughter of Zion."

82. This verse has already been sufficiently explained. The evangelist introduces it that we may see how Christ has come not for the sake of our merits, but for the sake of God's truth. For he was prophesied long ago before we, to whom he comes, had a being. God out of pure grace has fulfilled the promises of the Gospel to demonstrate the truth that he keeps his promises in order to stir us confidently to trust in his promise, for he will fulfill it.

And this is one of the passages, where the Gospel is promised, of which Paul speaks in Romans 1:2, "Which he promised afore through his prophets in the holy Scriptures, concerning his Son Jesus Christ," etc. We have heard how in this verse the Gospel, Christ, and faith are preached most distinctly and consolingly.

And the disciples went, and did even as Jesus appointed them, and brought the ass, and the colt, and put on them their garments, and he sat thereon, (and they set him thereon).

83. These are the ministers who by the Gospel have freed the consciences from the law and its works and led them to the works of grace, who made real saints out of hypocrites, so that Christ henceforth rides upon them.

84. The question arises here, whether Christ rode upon both animals. Matthew speaks as if the disciples put him on both, while Mark, Luke, and John mention only the colt. Some think he sat first on the colt and, because it was too wanton and untamed, he then sat on its mother. These are fables and dreams. We take it that he rode only on the colt. He had them both brought to him on account of the spiritual significance above mentioned. When Matthew says he sat on them as though he rode on both, it is said after the manner of the Scriptures and the common way of speaking by synecdoche, where a thing is ascribed to the community, the whole people, which applies only to a few of them; for example, Matthew writes, The thieves on the cross reviled him, while only one did it, as Luke tells us. Christ says in Matthew 23:37 that the city of Jerusalem stoned the prophets, while only a few of the city did it. You say, the Turks [Muslims] killed the Christians, although they killed only a few. Thus Christ rode on the asses, though he rode only on the colt, because the two are compared to a community. What happened to one is expressed as if it happened to all.

85. Now consider the spiritual riding. Christ rides on the colt, its mother follows, that is, when Christ lives through faith in the inner man we are under him and are ruled by him. But the outer man, the ass, goes free, Christ does not ride on her, though she follows in the rear. The outer man, as Paul says, is not willing; he strives against the inner man; nor does he carry Christ, as Galatians 5:17 says, "The flesh lusteth against the Spirit, and the Spirit against the flesh; for these are contrary, the one to the other; that ye may not do the things that ye would." Because the colt carries Christ, that is, the Spirit is willing by grace, the ass, that is, the flesh, must be led by the halter, for the Spirit chastises and crucifies the flesh, so that it becomes subject.

86. This is the reason Christ rides upon the colt and not upon its mother, and yet uses both for his entrance into Jerusalem, for both body and soul must be saved. If, here upon earth, the body is unwilling, not capable of grace and Christ's leading, it must bear the Spirit, upon which Christ rides, who trains it and leads it along by the power of grace, received through Christ. The colt, ridden by Christ, upon which no one ever rode, is the willing spirit, whom no one before could make willing, tame, or ready, save Christ by his grace. However, the sack-carrier, the burden-bearer, the old Adam, is the flesh, which goes riderless without Christ; it must for this reason bear the cross and remain a beast of burden.

87. What does it signify that the apostles, without command, put their garments on the colt? No doubt again not all the disciples laid on their garments, nor were all their garments put on, perhaps only a coat of one disciple. But it is written for the spiritual meaning, as if all the garments of all the disciples were used. It was a poor saddle and ornaments, but rich in meaning. I think it was the good example of the apostles, by which the Christian Church is covered, and adorned, and Christ is praised and honored, namely, their preaching and confession, suffering and death for Christ's sake, as Christ says of Peter, that he would glorify God by a like death, in John 21:19. Paul says in one of his Epistles, we shall put on Christ, by which he doubtless wishes to show that good works are the garments of the Christians, by which Christ is honored and glorified before all people. In the Epistle, Paul says, in Romans 13:12, "Let us put on the armor of light." By this he means to show that good works are garments in which we walk before the people, honorably and well adorned. The examples of the apostles are the best and noblest above all the saints; they instruct us best and teach Christ most clearly. Therefore they should not, like the rest, lie on the road, but on the colt, so that Christ may ride on them and the colt go under them. We should follow these examples, praise Christ with our confession and our life, and adorn and honor the doctrine of the Gospel as Titus 2:10 says.

88. Hear how Paul lays his garments on the colt in 1 Corinthians 11:1, "Be ye imitators of me, even as I also am of Christ," and in Hebrews 13:7, "Remember them that had the rule over you, men that spake unto you the Word of God; and considering the issue of their life, imitate their faith." No saint's example is as pure in faith as that of the apostles. All the other saints after the apostles have an addition of human doctrine and works. Hence Christ sits upon their garments to show that they are true Christian and more faithful examples than others.

89. That they set him thereon must also signify something. Could he not mount for himself? Why does he act so formal? As I said above, the apostles would not preach themselves, nor ride on the colt themselves. Paul says, in 2 Corinthians 1:24, "Not that we have lordship over your faith." And in 2 Corinthians 4:5, "We preach not ourselves, but Christ Jesus as Lord, and ourselves as your servants for Jesus' sake." Again, in 1 Peter 5:3, "Neither as lording it over the charge allotted to you." They preached to us the pure faith and offered their examples, that Christ might rule in us, and our faith remain undefiled, that we might not receive their word and work as if it were their own, but that we might learn Christ in their words and works. But how is it today? One follows Saint Francis, another Saint Dominic, the third this, and the fourth that saint; and in none is Christ alone and pure faith sought; for they belong only to the apostles.

And the most part of the multitude spread their garments in the way;
and others cut branches from the trees, and spread them in the way.

90. The garments are the examples of the patriarchs and prophets, and the histories of the Old Testament. For, as we shall learn, the multitude that went before, signifies the saints before the birth of Christ, by whom the sermon in the New Testament and the way of faith are beautifully adorned and honored. Paul does likewise when he cites Abraham, Isaac, Jacob, and Peter cites Sarah and, in Hebrews 11, many patriarchs are named as examples, and by these are confirmed faith and the works of faith in a masterly way. The branches mean the sayings of the prophets, one of which is mentioned in this Gospel, which are not stories nor examples but the prophecy of God. The trees are the books of the prophets. Those who preach from these cut down branches and spread them in the way of Christian faith.

91. All this teaches the character of an evangelical sermon, a sermon on the pure faith and the way of life. It must first have the word Christ commands the apostles, saying, Go, loose and bring hither. Then the story and example of the apostles must be added that agree with Christ's word and work—these are the garments of the apostles. Then must be cited passages from the Old Testament—these are the garments and branches of the multitude. In this way the passages and examples of both Testaments are brought home to the people. Of this Christ speaks in Matthew 13:52, "Every scribe who hath been made a disciple to the kingdom of heaven, is like unto a man that is a householder, who bringeth forth out of his treasure things new and old." This signifies the two lips of the mouth, the two points of a bishop's hat, the two

ribbons on it, and some other like figures. But now none of these is kept before the eyes, the devil through the papists throws sulphur and pitch in the way, himself rides on the colt and banishes Christ.

92. To spread garments in the way means that, following the example of the apostles, we should with our confession and our whole life, honor, adorn, and grace Christ by giving up all glory, wisdom, and holiness of our own and bowing to Christ in simple faith; also that we turn everything we have—honor, goods, life, power, and body—to the glory and advancement of the Gospel, and relinquish everything for the one thing needful. Kings and lords and the great, powerful, and rich should serve Christ with their goods, honor, and power; further the Gospel and for its sake abandon everything. The holy patriarchs, prophets, and pious kings in the Old Testament did so by their examples. But now everything is turned around, especially among the papal multitudes, who usurp all honor and power against Christ and thus suppress the Gospel.

93. To cut branches from the trees and spread them in the way means also the office of preaching and the testimony of the Scriptures and the prophets concerning Christ. With this the sermon of Christ is to be confirmed and all the preaching directed to the end that Christ may be known and confessed by it. John writes in John 12:13, that they took branches of palm trees and went forth to meet him. Some add, there must have been olive branches also, because it happened on the Mount of Olives. This is not incredible, although the Gospels do not report it.

94. There is reason why palm branches and olive branches are mentioned. They signify what is to be confessed, preached, and believed concerning Christ. It is the nature of the palm tree that when used as a beam, it yields to no weight but rises against the weight. These branches are the words of divine wisdom; the more they are suppressed, the higher they rise. This is true if you firmly believe in those words. There is an invincible power in them, so that they may well be called palm branches, as Saint Paul says in Romans 1:16, "The Gospel is the power of God unto salvation to everyone that believeth," and, as Christ says, "The gates of hell shall not prevail against it," in Matthew 16:18. Death, sin, hell, and all evil must bend before the divine Word, or only rise, when it sets itself against them.

95. Olive branches are named, because they are words of grace in which God has promised us mercy. They make the soul meek, gentle, joyful, as the oil does the body. The gracious Word and sweet Gospel is typified in Genesis 8:11, where the dove in the evening brought in her mouth an olive branch

with green leaves into the ark, which means the Holy Spirit brings the Gospel into the church at the end of the world by the mouth of the apostles.

And the multitudes that went before him, and that followed,
cried, saying, "Hosanna to the son of David: Blessed is he that cometh
in the name of the Lord; Hosanna in the highest."

96. For this reason they carried palm trees before kings and lords, when they had gained a victory and celebrated their triumph. Again, the carrying of palm branches was a sign of submission, especially of such as asked for mercy and peace, as was commonly done among ancient people.

By their pomp before Christ they indicated that they would receive him as their Lord and king, sent by God as a victorious and invincible Savior, showing themselves submissive to him and seeking grace from him. Christ should be preached and made known in all the world, as the victorious and invincible king against sin, death, and the power of the devil and all the world for those who are oppressed and tormented, and as a Lord with whom they shall find abundant grace and mercy, as their faithful priest and mediator before God.

The word of the Gospel concerning this king is a word of mercy and grace, which brings us peace and redemption from God, besides invincible power and strength, as Saint Paul in Romans 1:16, calls the Gospel "a power of God unto salvation" and "the gates of hell shall not prevail against it," as Christ says in Matthew 16:18.

97. Paul says, in Hebrews 13:8, "Jesus Christ is the same yesterday and today, yea, forever." All who will be saved from the beginning to the end of the world, are and must be Christians and must be saved by faith. Therefore Paul says, in 1 Corinthians 10:3–4, "Our fathers did all eat the same spiritual food; and did all drink the same spiritual drink." And Christ says in John 8:56, "Your father Abraham rejoiced to see my day; and he saw it and was glad."

98. Hence the multitudes going before signify all Christians and saints before Christ's birth; those who follow signify all the saints after the birth of Christ. They all believed in and adhered to the one Christ. The former expected him in the future, the latter received him as the one who had come. Hence they all sing the same song and praise and thank God in Christ. Nor may we give anything else but praise and thanks to God, since we receive all from him, be it grace, word, work, Gospel, faith, and everything else. The only true Christian service is to praise and give thanks, as Psalm 50:15 says, "Call upon me in the day of trouble, I will deliver thee, and thou shalt glorify me."

99. What does "Hosanna to the son of David" signify? Hosanna in Psalm 118:25–26, means, "Save now, we beseech thee, O Jehovah; O Jehovah, we beseech thee, send now prosperity. Blessed be he that cometh in the name of Jehovah." This verse was applied to Christ and is a well-wishing as we wish happiness and safety to a new ruler. Thus the people thought Christ should be their worldly king, and they wish him joy and happiness to that end. For "hosanna" means, O, give prosperity or Beloved, help or Beloved, save or whatever else you might desire to express in such a wish. They add, "to the son of David," and say, God give prosperity to the son of David! O God, give prosperity, blessed be, etc. We would say, O, dear Lord, give happiness and prosperity to this son of David, for his new kingdom! Let him enter in God's name that he may be blessed and his kingdom prosper.

100. Mark proves clearly that they meant his kingdom when he writes expressly in Mark 11:10 that they said, "Blessed is the kingdom that cometh, the kingdom of our father David: Hosanna in the highest." When some in the churches read it "Osanna," it is not correct; it should be "Hosanna." They made a woman's name out of it, and her whom they should call Susanna they call Osanna. Susanna is a woman's name and means a rose. Finally, after making a farce out of baptism, the bishops baptize bells and altars, which is a great nonsense, and call the bells Osanna. But away with the blind leaders! We should learn here also to sing Hosanna and Hazelihana to the son of David together with those multitudes, that is, joyfully wish happiness and prosperity to the kingdom of Christ, to holy Christendom, that God may put away all human doctrine and let Christ alone be our king, who governs by his Gospel, and permits us to be his colts! God grant it, Amen.

The Second Sunday in Advent

❧

*The Comfort Christians Have from the Signs of the Day of Judgment;
and the Spiritual Interpretation of These Signs*

A nd there shall be signs in the sun and moon and stars; and upon
the earth distress of nations, in perplexity for the roaring of the
*sea and the billows; men fainting for fear, and for expectation of the
things which are coming on the world: for the powers of the heavens
shall be shaken. And then shall they see the Son of man coming in a
cloud with power and great glory. But when these things begin to come
to pass, look up, and lift up your heads; because your redemption
draweth nigh."*

*And he spake to them a parable: "Behold the fig tree, and all the trees:
when they now shoot forth, ye see it and know of your own selves
that the summer is now nigh. Even so ye also, when ye see these things
coming to pass, know ye that the kingdom of God is nigh. Verily I
say unto you, This generation shall not pass away, till all things be
accomplished. Heaven and earth shall pass away: but my words shall
not pass away."* — Luke 21:25–36

I. THE SIGNS OF THE DAY OF JUDGMENT

1. The first thing for us to understand is that although the signs preceding
the judgment day are many and great, they will all be fulfilled, even though
none or very few men take note of or esteem them as such. For two things
must take place according to the Word and prophecy of Christ and the apostles: first, that many and great signs will be made manifest; and secondly, that
the last day will come unawares, the world's not expecting it, even though
that day be at the door. Though men see these signs, yea, be told that they are
signs of the last day, still they will not believe, but in their security mockingly
say, "Thou fool, hast thou fear that the heavens will fall and that we shall live
to see that day?"

2. Some, indeed, must see it, and it will be those who least expect it. That there will be such security and indifference among men, let us prove by the words of Christ and the apostles. Christ says in the 34th and 35th verses of Luke 21, "Take heed to yourselves, lest haply your hearts be overcharged with surfeiting, and drunkenness, and cares of this life, and that day come on you suddenly as a snare: for so shall it come upon all them that dwell on the face of all the earth." From these words it is clear that men in great measure will give themselves over to surfeiting and drunkenness and the cares of this life, and that, drowned as it were in these things, they will rest secure and continue to dwell on the earth as if the dreadful day were far away. For, were there no such security and heedlessness, that day would not break in unawares. But he says, it will come as a snare by which birds and beasts are caught at a time when most concerned about their food and least expecting to be entrapped. In this figure he gives us clearly to understand that the world will continue its carousing, eating and drinking, building and planting, and diligently seeking after earthly things, and will look upon the day of judgment as yet a thousand and more years off, when, in the twinkling of an eye, they may stand before the terrible judgment bar of God.

3. The words of Christ in Luke 17:24, say the same: "For as the lightning, when it lighteneth out of the one part under the heaven, shineth unto the other part under heaven; so shall the Son of man be in his day." See here again that the day will break upon the world with the utmost suddenness. The same further appears in what follows in verses 26–29: "As it was in the days of Noah, even so shall it be also in the days of the Son of man. They ate, they drank, they married, they were given in marriage, until the day that Noah entered into the ark, and the flood came, and destroyed them all. Likewise even as it came to pass in the days of Lot; they ate, they drank, they bought, they sold, they planted, they builded; but in the day that Lot went out from Sodom it rained fire and brimstone from heaven, and destroyed them all. After the same manner it shall be in the day that the Son of man is revealed." These words abundantly show that people will rest so secure and will be so deeply buried beneath the cares of this life, that they will not believe the day is at hand.

4. There is now no doubt that Christ did not foretell these signs in the expectation that no one would note nor recognize them when they should appear; although few indeed will do so, just as in the days of Noah and Lot but few knew the punishment in store for them. Were this not true, the admonition of Christ would have been in vain: "When ye see these things come to pass, know ye that the kingdom of God is nigh." Then, "Lift up your heads, because your redemption draweth nigh." There must then be some, at least, who do

recognize the signs, and lift up their heads and wait for their redemption, although they do not really know on what day that will come. We should be careful, therefore, to note whether the signs are being fulfilled now, or have been or will be in the future.

5. I do not wish to force anyone to believe as I do; neither will I permit anyone to deny me the right to believe that the last day is near at hand. These words and signs of Christ compel me to believe that such is the case. For the history of the centuries that have passed since the birth of Christ nowhere reveals conditions like those of the present. There has never been such building and planting in the world.

There has never been such gluttonous and varied eating and drinking as now. Wearing apparel has reached its limit in costliness. Who has ever heard of such commerce as now encircles the earth? There have arisen all kinds of art and sculpture, embroidery and engraving, the like of which has not been seen during the whole Christian era.

6. In addition men are so delving into the mysteries of things that today a boy of twenty knows more than twenty doctors formerly knew. There is such a knowledge of languages and all manner of wisdom that it must be confessed, the world has reached such great heights in the things that pertain to the body, or as Christ calls them, "cares of life"—eating, drinking, building, planting, buying, selling, marrying, and giving in marriage—that everyone must see and say either ruin or a change must come. It is hard to see how a change can come. Day after day dawns and the same conditions remain. There was never such keenness, understanding, and judgment among Christians in bodily and temporal things as now—I forbear to speak of the new inventions, printing, firearms, and other implements of war.

7. But not only have such great strides been made in the world of commerce, but also in the spiritual field have there been great changes. Error, sin, and falsehood have never held sway in the world as in these last centuries. The Gospel has been openly condemned at Constance, and the false teachings of the pope have been adopted as law though he practiced the greatest extortion. Daily Mass is celebrated many hundred thousand times in the world, and thereby the greatest sin committed. By confession, sacrament, indulgence, rules, and laws, so many souls are driven to condemnation that it seems God has given the whole world over to the devil. In short, it is not possible that there should be greater falsehood, more heinous error, more dreadful blindness, and more obdurate blasphemy than have ruled in the church through the bishops, cloisters, and universities. As a result, Aristotle, a blind heathen, teaches and rules Christians more than does Christ.

8. Moreover the pope has attempted to abolish Christ and to become his vicar. He occupies the throne of Christ on earth, would to God he occupied the devil's throne instead.

I forbear to speak of the grosser forms of sin, unchastity, murder, infidelity, covetousness, and the like, which are all practiced without shame or fear. Unchastity has taken forms against nature, and has affected no station or condition more than the spiritual character of the clergy—shall I call it spiritual, since it is so fleshly and void of all simplicity?

9. Whatever other signs may appear before Christ's coming, I know that, according to the words of Christ, these will be present: surfeiting and drunkenness, building and planting, buying and selling, marrying and giving in marriage, and other cares of this life. Just as certain to me is also the saying of Christ in Matthew 2:15, where he speaks of the abomination of desolation, the Antichrist, under whose rule gross error, blindness, and sin shall flourish, just as they now flourish under the pope in the most tyrannical and shameless form. This above all else compels me to believe that Christ will soon come to judgment; for such sins cry to heaven, and so provoke and defy the last day that it must soon break in upon them.

If it were only the unchastity of the antediluvian world, or the worldliness of Sodom, I would not believe the last day is so near at hand. But to destroy, root out, condemn, and blaspheme divine service, God's Word and the sacraments, the children of God, and everything that belongs to God; and to worship and honor the devil instead and to proclaim his lies for the Word of God—such sins, I am firmly convinced, will put an end to the world before we are aware of it. Amen.

10. But the apostles have also prophesied concerning this self-security of men as the judgment day approaches. Paul says in 1 Thessalonians 5:2–3, "The day of the Lord so cometh as a thief in the night. When they are saying, Peace and safety, then sudden destruction cometh upon them." Now we know that a thief never comes but when one feels most secure and least expects him. And, in 2 Peter 3:3–10, we read, "In the last days mockers shall come with mockery, walking after their own lusts, and saying, Where is the promise of his coming? From the day the fathers fell asleep, all things continue as they were from the beginning of the creation....But the day of the Lord will come as a thief in the night; in the which the heavens shall pass away with a great noise, etc." Who are they that walk after their own lusts but the papal clergy? They wish to be subject neither to God nor to man, but expect the world to recognize it as their right to live as they please and to do what they like. It is these that say, Where is the promise of his coming? Do you

think the last day will break in upon us so soon? Things will continue as they have in the past.

11. We also read in the history of the destruction of Jerusalem that many signs were fulfilled, yet they would not believe them to be tokens of the coming destruction until judgment was executed. Finally, from the beginning of the world, it has ever been so, that the unbelieving could not believe the day of calamity to be near—they always experienced it before they believed it. This is in fulfillment of Psalm 55:23, "Bloodthirsty and deceitful men shall not live out half their days," for they presume upon the continuance of their days and have no fear, and so the hour must come unawares. So here people are putting off the judgment for yet a thousand years when it may break in upon them in a night. This is the first class of signs that presage the nearness of the day of God. Let us now consider the second class.

"And there shall be signs in the sun."

12. This sign to be given in the sun is that it will lose its brightness, after the manner in which it has often occurred, as Matthew 24:29 says, "The sun shall be darkened." I will not trespass here again but express my opinion. Some think that the sun is to be darkened as never to shine again; but this cannot be the meaning, for day and night must continue to the end, as God foretells, in Genesis 8:22, "While the earth remaineth, seedtime and harvest, and cold and heat, and summer and winter, and day and night shall not cease." This sign must, therefore, not interfere with day and night and still be fulfilled before the judgment day, for it is a token of its coming. It cannot, therefore, be more than a darkening of the sun in its accustomed course.

13. Now at all times such a sign in the sun has been looked upon as foreboding misfortune or disaster, which also often followed, as history abundantly shows. Thus we have had, it seems to me, the last few years more and more frequent eclipses of the sun than in any other like period of time. God has spared us and no great evil has come upon us. For this reason these signs are not noticed. In addition, astronomers have told us, and rightly so, that these eclipses are but natural phenomena. As a result the tokens are still more despised and carnal security increased. Nevertheless God, in carrying on his work in silence, gives us security and moves forward in his plans. Whatever the natural course of the heavens may be, these signs are always tokens of his wrath and predict sure disaster for the future. If these are not seen, shall God make other suns and moons and stars and show other signs in them?

14. The course of the heavens has been so arranged from eternity that be-fore the last day these signs must appear. The heathen say that the comet

is a natural product; but God has created none that is not a token of future evil. Thus also the blind leader, Aristotle, writing a book about the phenomena of the heavens, attributes all to nature and declares these are no signs. Our learned men follow him and thus one fool fills the world with fools. Let us know that though the heavenly bodies wander in their courses according to law, God has still made these to be signs or tokens of his wrath.

"And in the moon."

15. This sign is given in Matthew 24:29, to the effect that "the moon shall not give her light"; that is, it will lose its brightness. The same is to be said of this as of the signs in the sun, no matter how natural it may be. Is it not true that scarcely a year has passed of late in which sun or moon or both have been eclipsed, sometimes one of them twice a year? If these are not signs, then, what are signs? It may be that at other times more were seen than now, but surely not in more rapid succession. When Jerusalem was to be destroyed, some signs preceded that had occurred before, but they were still new tokens.

"And in the stars."

16. According to Matthew 24:29, "the stars shall fall from heaven." This is seen almost daily. Whether it was seen as frequently in former days as now, I cannot say. Aristotle again talks about the nature of the thing; but the Gospel, which is the Word and wisdom of God, pronounces the falling of the stars a sign and there let the matter rest. Wherefore if the stars fall or the sun and moon fail to give their light, be assured that these are signs of the last day; for the Gospel cannot utter falsehood. While in these years there have been so many showers of stars, they are all harbingers of the last day, just as Christ says; for they must appear often in order that the great day may be abundantly pointed out and proclaimed. These signs appear and pass but no one considers them; so it shall be that they will wait for other signs just as the Jews are waiting for another Christ.

"And upon the earth distress of nations, in perplexity."

17. This is not to be understood that all nations and all people among these nations will so suffer; for you must note that these are to be signs. Stars do not fall from the heavens at all times; the sun does not lose its brightness for a whole year or a month, but for an hour or two; the moon does not refuse to give its light for a whole week or a whole night, but, like the sun, for an hour or two—that all these may be tokens without changing or perverting the order of things. Hence not many will suffer distress and anxiety, but only a

few; and even with these it will be only at times that they be signs to those
who despise the idea, and attribute all to the complexion or to the melancholy
or to the influence of the planets or to any other natural cause. Meanwhile
such clear harbingers of the day pass by unobserved, and there happens what
Christ said of the Jews in Matthew 13:14, that though hearing and seeing they
do not understand.

18. "Distress of nations in perplexity" does not refer to the body. For, as we
have already heard, there will be peace and joy in abundance. People will eat
and drink, build and plant, buy and sell, marry and be given in marriage, dance
and play, and wrap themselves up in this present life as if they expected to
abide here forever. I take it that it is the condition of agonized conscience. For
since the Gospel, by which alone the troubled conscience can be comforted, is
condemned, and in its stead there are set up doctrines of men, which teach us
to lay aside sin and earn heaven by works, there must come a burdened and
distressed conscience, a conscience that can find no rest, that would be pious,
do good and be saved, that torments itself and yet does not know how to find
satisfaction. Sin and conscience oppress, and however much is done no rest is
found. By these the sinner becomes so distressed that he knows not what to
do nor whither to flee. Hence arise so many vows and pilgrimages and worship of the saints and chapters for Mass and vigils. Some castigate and torture
themselves, some become monks, or that they may do more they become
Carthusian monks.

These are all works of distressed and perplexed consciences, and are in
reality the distress and perplexity of which Luke here speaks. He uses two
words which suggest this meaning, a man gets into close quarters as though
he were cast into a narrow snare or prison; he becomes anxious and does not
know how he may extricate himself; he becomes bewildered and attempts this
and that and yet finds no way of escape. Under such conditions he would be
distressed and perplexed. In such a condition are these consciences; sin has
taken them captive, they are in straits and are distressed. They want to escape
but another grief overtakes them, they are perplexed for they know not where
to begin—they try every expedient but find no help.

19. It is indeed true that the masses do not become so afflicted, but only
the few and generally the most sensible, scrupulous, and good-hearted individuals who have no desire to harm anyone and would live honorable lives. It
may be they foster some secret sin, as for example unchastity. This burdens
them day and night so that they never are truly happy. But this is game for the
monks and priests, for here they can practice extortion, especially with
women; here people confess, are taught, absolved, and go whithersoever the

confessor directs. Meanwhile the people are the Lord's token of the last day. To such the Gospel is light and comfort while it condemns the others.

20. Neither can anyone deny this sign, for it has been so common these hundreds of years that many have become insane over it, as Gerson informs us. Although at all times there have been people so distressed and perplexed, it was formerly not so common as now. From the beginning of the world no human doctrine exercised the tenth part or even the hundredth part of the influence, or tortured and seared so many consciences as the doctrines of the pope and his disciples, the monks and priests. Such perplexed hearts will necessarily grow out of the papal doctrine of confession, which has never been so earnestly promulgated as now. Therefore this has never been a token of the judgment until now. There must be many and great signs, therefore, and they be despised by most men.

"For the roaring of the sea and the billows."

21. This will take place through the winds, for all roaring of the waters comes by means of the storm. Therefore the Lord would say by these words that many and great storms will arise. By sea, however, is not to be understood simply the ocean but all gathered waters, according to the language of Scripture, in Genesis 1:10, "And the gathering together of the waters called he seas," be they oceans, seas, or lakes. Rivers, on the other hand, are changeable flowing waters.

22. It is not to be supposed that all waters, streams, lakes, seas, and oceans, will, at the same time and in the same way, become stormy and boisterous. Some seas are thus to be moved and this is to be the sign unto us. For as not all stars fall and not all nations are distressed in perplexity, so shall not all waters roar nor all places be visited by the storm.

23. Here heathen art will sit in the schools and with wide-open mouth will say, "Did you see the storm or hear the sea and the waves roaring? Aristotle clearly teaches that these are but natural phenomena." Let us pass these by and know that God's Word and tokens are despised by the wisdom of the gods. Do you hold fast to the Gospel—this teaches you to believe that storms and detonations in the sea are signs and tokens. And however many times such signals have been given in other days, they shall nevertheless become more numerous and terrible as the day of doom approaches.

24. It seems to me that within the space of ten or twelve years, there have been such storms and tempests and waters roaring as have never before been seen or heard. We are to consider, therefore, that although in former times these signs came singly and at less frequent intervals, now they appear many

and frequent. In our time both sun and moon are darkened, stars fall, distress of nations is present, winds and waves are roaring, and many other signs are being fulfilled. They are all coming in a heap.

25. We have lately also seen so many comets and so many calamities have fallen from the skies and there has arisen the hitherto unknown disease, syphilis. Also how many signs and wonders have been seen in the heavens, as suns, moons, stars, rainbows, and many other strange sights. Dear hearer, let them be signs, great signs, tokens that mean much; so that neither the astronomers nor heathen astrologers can say they simply follow the ordinary course of nature, for they knew nothing of them before nor did they prophesy of them.

26. No astronomer will say that the course of the heavens foretold the coming of the terrible beast that the Tiber threw up a few years ago; a beast with the head of an ass, the breast and body of a woman, the foot of an elephant for its right hand, with the scales of a fish on its legs, and the head of a dragon in its hinder parts, etc. This beast typifies the papacy and the great wrath and punishment of God. Such a mass of signs presages greater results than the mind of man can conceive.

Before proceeding further it might be well to consider the testimony concerning the last day which the celebrated teacher, Latantius Firmianus, gave about AD 320, in his work entitled *"Divinarum Institutionum,"* in the seventh book and fifteenth chapter: When the end of the world draws near, the condition of human affairs must materially change and take on a more wicked form. Then will malice and wickedness prevail to such a degree that our age, in which malice and wickedness have almost reached their highest pitch, will be looked upon as happy and treasured as golden in comparison with that time when no one will be able to help or give advice. Then will righteousness become practically unknown, and blasphemy, covetousness, impure desires, and unchastity become common. Then will the godly become a prey to the most wicked and be vexed and grieved by them. At the same time only the wicked will be rich and well to do, while the godly will be driven hither and thither in shame and poverty. Justice will be perverted, law will be overthrown, and no one will have aught else but that which he can secure by his own strength. Daring and strength will possess all. There will be neither faith nor confidence left in man, neither peace, nor loveliness, nor shame, nor truth, and as a result, no safety, no government, no rest of any kind from the reprobate. For all lands will become rebellious, everywhere men will rage and war with one another, the whole world will be in arms, and bring destruction to itself.

"Men fainting for fear, and for expectation of the things
which are coming on the world."

27. Here, again, it is not the profligate mass who disregard God's tokens and refer all to natural causes that shall realize these, but rather the better class, and the most distinguished, who take these things to heart and are given to reflection. By "men fainting for fear" is to be understood that they shall be frightened to death, or the next thing to death; and that their fear shall consume them and rob them of their strength. What do they fear and wait for? Christ says, "The things which are coming on the world"; that is, the last day, the terrible judgment, hellfire, and eternal death. Why do they fear and look for these things, and not the world upon whom they will come rather than upon them? Because these are the tokens of God that are to be despised and rejected by the world.

28. I am not yet able to say who these people are, unless it be those who are exposed to and have to do with the temptations of death and hell, concerning whom Tauler writes. For such temptations consume flesh and blood, yea, bone and marrow, and are death itself. No one can endure them except he be miraculously sustained. A number of patriarchs have tasted them—Abraham, Isaac, Jacob, Moses, David; but near the end of the world they will be more common. This token will then greatly increase, although it is present now more than is generally known. There are individuals who are in the perils of death and are wrestling with him; they feel that which will come over the whole world and fear that it will come upon and abide with them. It is to be hoped, however, that such people are in a state of grace. For Christ speaks as if he would separate the fear and the thing which they fear; and so divides these that he gives to them the fear and to the world that which they fear. It is to be presumed that by this fear and anxiety, they are to have their hell and death here, while the world, which fears nothing, will have death and hell hereafter.

"For the powers of the heavens shall be shaken."

29. By the powers of heaven some understand the angels of heaven. But since Christ speaks of signs, and says we shall see them and in them recognize the coming of the last day, they must surely be visible tokens and be perceived with the bodily senses. For those people whose consciences are in distress and whose hearts are failing from fear, though this be an affection of the soul, yet manifest it by word and countenance. Therefore these powers of heaven must be such as can be really shaken and so perceived.

30. But the Scriptures speak in a twofold way concerning the powers of

heaven. At one time they are spoken of as the powerful heavens or the heavens which are among all creatures the most powerful, as is written, in Genesis 1:8, "And God called the firmament"—that is, expanse or fortress—"heaven"; for every creature under heaven is ruled and strengthened by the light, heat, and movements of the heavens. What would the earth be without the heavens but a dark and desert waste? Like princes and nobles in the world, the Scriptures call the heavens powerful because they rule over the bodies beneath them.

31. At another time, the powers of heaven signify the hosts of heaven, as Psalm 33:6 says, "By the word of Jehovah were the heavens made, and all the host of them by the breath of his mouth." And in Genesis 2:1, "And the heavens and the earth were finished, and all the host of them." It is the common custom of the Scriptures to speak in this way of the powers of heaven. And it is clear from these passages that the hosts or powers of heaven include all that is in them; in the heavens, the sun, moon, stars, and other heavenly bodies; on earth, man and beast, birds and fish, trees, herbs, and whatever else lives upon it.

32. The passage before us may therefore mean the powers of heaven in both senses, probably chiefly the hosts of heaven. Christ would say that all creatures shall be shaken and shall serve as tokens of that day; sun and moon with darkening, the stars with falling, the nations with wars, men with hearts failing from fear, the earth with earthquakes, the waters with winds and roaring, the air with infection and pestilence, and the heavens with their hosts.

33. I do not know just what is meant by the moving of the hosts of heaven unless it be manifestations like those of the great constellation of the planets in 1524. For the planets are certainly among the most important of the powers and hosts of heaven, and their remarkable gathering together into one constellation is surely a token for the world. Christ does not say that all the hosts of heaven will be moved, but some of them only; for not all stars shall fall from their places, nor all men be overcome with fear, nor all waters at the same time be in noisy commotion, nor sun and moon be every day darkened; for these are to be but signs, which can occur only at particular times and in a few places, that they may be something special, and singled out as tokens from the great mass that are not such. It is quite probable, therefore, that these movements of the powers of heaven are such movements of the constellations of the planets. Astrologers interpret them to signify the coming of another flood; God grant that they may rather presage the coming of the last day.

34. Let us not be mistaken, however, and think that these constellations are the product of the natural course of the heavenly bodies. As such Christ calls them signs and desires us to take special note of them, appearing, as they do, not alone but with a multitude of other tokens. Let the unbeliever doubt

and despise God's tokens and speak of them as simply natural; but let us hold fast to the Gospel.

35. There are many other signs elsewhere described in the Scriptures, such as earthquakes, famine, pestilence, and wars as in Luke 17:20 and Matthew 24:7. We have seen much of these for they have been common at all times. Still they are tokens appearing by the side of others. It is a known fact also that wars at the present time are of such a character as to make former wars appear as mere child's play. But since our Gospel of today does not speak of these, let us not consider them further. Only let us consider them as signs, great signs, signifying great things; alas, they are already despised and forgotten!

> *"And then shall they see the Son of man*
> *coming in a cloud with power and great glory."*

36. Here power may again signify the hosts of angels, saints, and all creatures that will come with Christ to judgment (I believe this is the correct interpretation); or it may mean the special power and might that will characterize this coming of Christ in contradistinction to his first coming. He says not only that he will come, but that they shall see him come. At his birth he came also, but men did not recognize him. He comes now through the Gospel in a spiritual manner, into the hearts of believers. This also is not by observation. But his last coming will be such that all must see him as Revelation 1:7 says, "And every eye shall see him." And they shall see that he is none other than the man Christ Jesus, in bodily form, as he was born of the Virgin Mary and walked upon this earth.

He might have said they shall see me, but that would not have clearly indicated his bodily form. But when he says, "They shall see the Son of man," he clearly indicates that it will be a bodily coming, a bodily seeing in bodily form; a coming in great power and glory, accompanied by the hosts of heaven. He shall sit upon the clouds and be accompanied by all the saints. The Scriptures speak much of that day and everywhere point to the same. This, then, is said concerning the signs. The Savior adds words of comfort for Christians in the presence of these signs.

II. THE COMFORT CHRISTIANS HAVE WHEN THESE SIGNS APPEAR

> *"And when these things begin to come to pass, look up,*
> *and lift up your heads; because your redemption draweth nigh."*

37. Here you may say, who can lift up his head in the face of such terrible wrath and judgment? If the whole world is filled with fear at that day, and lets fall its head and countenance out of terror and anxiety, how shall we look up and lift up our heads, which evidently means, how shall we manifest any joy in and longing for these signs? In answer I would say that all this is spoken only to those who are really Christians and not to heathen and Jews. True Christians are so afflicted with all manner of temptations and persecutions that in this life they are miserable. Therefore they wait and long and pray for redemption from sin and all evil; as we also pray in the Lord's Prayer, "Thy kingdom come," and "Deliver us from evil." If we are true Christians, we will earnestly and heartily join in this prayer. If we do not so pray, we are not yet true Christians.

38. If we pray aright, our condition must truly be such that, however terrible these signs may be, we will look up to them with joy and earnest desire, as Christ admonishes, "When these things begin to come to pass, look up." He does not say, Be filled with fear or drop your heads; for there is coming that for which we have been so earnestly praying. If we really wish to be freed from sin and death and hell, we must look forward to this coming of the Lord with joy and pleasure.

Saint Paul also says, in 2 Timothy 4:8, "Henceforth there is laid up for me the crown of righteousness, which the Lord, the righteous judge, shall give to me at that day: and not only to me, but also to all them that have loved his appearing." If he gives the crown to those who love his appearing, what will he give to those who hate and dread it? Without doubt, to enemies, eternal condemnation. Titus 2:13 says, "Looking for the blessed hope and appearing of the glory of the Great God and our Savior Jesus Christ." And in Luke 12:6, "And be ye yourselves like unto men looking for their lord, when he shall return from the marriage feast."

39. But what do those do who are filled with fear and do not desire to have him come, when they pray, "Thy kingdom come, thy will be done," and "Deliver us from the evil one"? Do they not stand in the presence of God and lie to their own hurt? Do they not strive against the will of God who will have this day for the redemption of .the saints? It is necessary, therefore, that we exercise great care lest we be found to hate and to dread that day. Such dread is a bad omen and belongs to the damned, whose cold minds and hard hearts must be terrified and broken, if perchance they might reform.

40. But to believers that day will be comforting and sweet. That day will be the highest joy and safety to the believer, and the deepest terror and anguish to the unbeliever; just as also in this life the truths of the Gospel are

exceedingly sweet to the godly and exceedingly hateful to the wicked. Why should the believer fear and not rather exceedingly rejoice, since he trusts in Christ who comes as judge to redeem him and to be his everlasting portion.

41. But you say I would indeed await his coming with joy, if I were holy and without sin. I should answer, what relief do you find in fear and flight? It would not redeem you from sin if you were to be filled with terror for a thousand years. The damned are eternally filled with fear of that day, but this does not take away their sin; yea, this fear rather increases sin and renders man unfit to appear without sin on that day when it comes. Fear must pass out of the soul and there must enter in a desire for righteousness and for that day. But if you really desire to be free from sin and to be holy, then give thanks to God and continue to desire to be more free from sin. Would to God that such desire were so sincere and powerful in you as to bring you to your death.

42. There is no one so well prepared for the judgment day as he who longs to be without sin. If you have such desire, what do you fear? You are then in perfect accord with the purpose of that day. It comes to set free from sin all who desire it, and you belong to that number. Return thanks to God and abide in that desire. Christ says his coming is for our redemption. But do not deceive yourself and be satisfied, perhaps, with the simple desire to be free from sin and to await the coming of the day without fear. Perhaps your heart is false and you are filled with fear, not because you would be free from sin, but because in the face of that day you cannot sin free and untrammeled. See to it that the light within you be not darkness. For a heart that would be truly free from sin will certainly rejoice in the day that fulfills its desire. If the heart does not so rejoice there is no true desire to be loosed from its sin.

43. Therefore we must above all things lay aside all hatred and abhorrence of this day, and exercise diligence that we may really desire to have our sins taken away. When this is done, we may not only calmly await the day, but with heartfelt desire and joy pray for it and say, "Thy kingdom come, thy will be done." In this you must cast aside all feelings and conceit, hold fast to the comforting words of Christ, and rest in them alone.

44. Could he admonish, comfort, and strengthen you in a more delicate and loving manner? In the first place he says, You will hear of wars, but you should have no fears. And when he tells you to have no fears, what else does he mean than that he commands you to be of good cheer and to discern the signs with joy? Secondly, he tells you to look up; thirdly, to lift up your heads; and fourthly, he speaks of your redemption. What can comfort and strengthen you if such a word does not? Do you think he would deceive you and try to lead you into a false confidence? My dear hearer, let such a word not have been

said in vain: thank God and trust in it—there is no other comfort or advice if you cast this to the winds. It is not your condemnation but your redemption of which Christ speaks. Will you turn his words around and say, It is not your redemption but your condemnation? Will you flee from your own salvation? Will you not greet and thank your God who comes out to meet and to greet you?

45. He has no doubt also spoken this word for the fainthearted who, although they are devout and prepared for the last day, are yet filled with great anxiety and are hindered in taking part in his coming with that desire that should be found at the end of the world; therefore he calls attention to their redemption. For when at the end of the world sin will hold such sway, and by the side of sin the punishment for sin with pestilence, war, and famine, it will be necessary to give to believers strength and comfort against both evils, sin and its punishment. Therefore he uses the sweet and comforting word redemption which is so dear to the heart of man. What is redemption? Who would not be redeemed? Who would have a desire to abide in the desert of sin and punishment? Who would not wish an end to such misery and woe, such perils for souls, such ruin for man? Especially should this be the case when the Savior allures, invites, and comforts us in such an endearing way.

46. The godless fanatical preachers are to be censured who in their sermons deprive people of these words of Christ and faith in them, who desire to make people devout by terrifying them and who teach them to prepare for the last day by relying upon their good works as satisfaction for their sins. Here despair, fear, and terror must remain and grow and with it hatred, aversion, and abhorrence for the coming of the Lord, and enmity against God be established in the heart; for they picture Christ as nothing but a stern judge whose wrath must be appeased by works, and they never present him as the Redeemer, as he calls and offers himself, of whom we are to expect that out of pure grace he will redeem us from sin and evil.

47. Such is always the result where the Gospel is not rightly proclaimed. When hearts are only driven by commands and threats, they will only be estranged from God and be led to abhor him. We ought to terrify, but only the obstinate and hardened; and when these have become terrified and dejected also, we ought to strengthen and comfort.

48. From all this we learn how few there are who pray the Lord's Prayer acceptably even though it is prayed unceasingly in all the world. There are few who would not rather that the day would never come. This is nothing else than to desire that the kingdom of God may not come. Therefore the heart prays contrary to the lips, and while God judges according to the heart, they

judge according to the lips. For this reason they institute so many prayers, fill all the churches with their bawling, and think they pray aright when in reality their prayer is, "May thy kingdom not come, or not just yet." Tell me, is not such a prayer blasphemy? Is it not of such a prayer that the psalmist speaks in Psalm 109:7, "Let his prayer be turned into sin." How men are applying all the wealth of the world to fill every nook and corner of it with such blasphemy, and then are calling it a divine service!

49. Yet he who feels such fear must not despair, but rather use it wisely. He uses it wisely who permits such fear to urge and admonish him to pray for grace that this fear might be taken away and he be given joy and delight in that day. Christ has promised, in Matthew 7:8, "Everyone that asketh receiveth." Therefore those who are fearful are nearer their salvation than the hard-hearted and reprobate, who neither fear nor find comfort in that day. For though they do not have a desire for it, they have a something within which admonishes them to pray for such a desire.

50. On the other hand, he uses fear unwisely who allows it to increase and abides in the same, as though he could thereby be cleansed from sin. This leads to nothing good. Not fear, which, as John says, in 1 John 4:18, must be cast out, will remain in that day, but love which, Saint Paul says in 1 Corinthians 13:8, must abide. Fear is to be a power to drive us to seek such love and pray for it. Where fear is not cast out, it opposes the will of God and antagonizes your own salvation; it thus becomes a sin against the Holy Spirit. It is, however, not necessary to say that the individual must be altogether without fear, for we still have human nature abiding in us. This is weak and cannot exist altogether without the fear of death and the judgment; but the spirit must be uppermost in the mind, as Christ says, in Matthew 26:41, "The spirit indeed is willing, but the flesh is weak."

And he spake to them a parable: "Behold the fig tree, and all the trees:
when they now shoot forth, ye see it and know of your own selves
that the summer is now nigh. Even so ye also, when ye see these things
coming to pass, know ye that the kingdom of God is nigh."

51. Pure words of comfort are these. He does not put forth a parable from the fall or winter season when all the trees are bare and the dreary days begin; but a parable from the spring and summer season, when everything is joyous, when all creation buds forth and rejoices. By this he clearly teaches that we are to look forward to the last day with as much joy and delight as all creation shows in spring and summer. What is the meaning of this parable if in it he does not teach us this? He could have found others that were not so joyous.

52. In applying it, he does not say your hell or condemnation is at hand, but the kingdom of God. What else does it signify that the kingdom of God is at hand than that our redemption is near? The kingdom of God is but ourselves, as Christ says, in Luke 17:21, "For lo, the kingdom of God is within you"; therefore, it draws nigh when we are nearing our redemption from sin and evil. In this life it begins in the spirit; but since we must still battle with sin and suffer much evil, and since death is still before us, the kingdom of God is not yet perfect in us. But when once sin and death and all evil are taken away, then will it be perfect. This the last day will bring and not this life.

53. Therefore, my dear hearer, examine your life, probe your heart to ascertain how it is disposed toward this day. Do not put your trust in your own good life, for that would soon be put to shame; but think of and strengthen your faith so that the day may not be a terror to you as to the damned, but be your joy as the day of your salvation and of the kingdom of God in you. Then when you think or hear of the same, your heart will leap for joy and earnestly long for its coming. If you do not wish to pronounce judgment upon yourself, then do not think that you would be able to stand in that day even with the meritorious deeds of all the saints.

"Verily I say unto you, This generation shall not pass away,
till all things be accomplished. Heaven and earth shall pass away:
but my words shall not pass away."

54. Why does the Lord so fortify his Word and confirm it beyond measure by parables, oaths, and tokens of the generation that shall remain though heaven and earth pass away? This all happens because, as was said above, all the world is so secure and with open eyes despises the signs to such a degree that perhaps no word of God has been so despised as this that foretells and characterizes the judgment day. It will appear to the world that there are no signs; and even though people should see them, they will still not believe. Even the very elect of God may doubt such words and tokens, in order that the day may come when the world is never so secure and thus be suddenly overwhelmed in its security, as Saint Paul said above.

55. Therefore, Christ would assure us and wake us up to look for the day when the signs appear. We are to realize that though the signs be uncertain, those are not in danger who look upon them as tokens, while those who despise them are in the greatest danger. Hence let us play with certainties and consider the above-named signs as truly such lest we run with the unspiritual. If we are mistaken, we have after all hit the mark; if they are mistaken, it is a mistake for eternity with them.

56. Jesus calls the Jews "this generation." This passage, therefore, clearly indicates that the common saying is not true which holds that all the Jews will become Christians; and that the passage, John 10:16, "And they shall become one flock and one shepherd," is not fulfilled when the Jews go over to the heathen, but when the heathen came to the Jews and became Christians at the time of the apostles, as Saint Augustine often explains. Christ's words in John 10:16, indicate the same, "And other sheep I have, which are not of this fold; them also I must bring, and they shall hear my voice, and they shall become one flock and one shepherd." Note that he speaks clearly of the heathen who have come to the Jewish fold; therefore, the passage has been long since fulfilled. But here he says, "This generation shall not pass away" until the end come; that is, the Jews who crucified Christ must remain as a token. And although many will be converted, the generation and Jewish character must remain.

57. Some have also been concerned about how heaven and earth will pass away, and they again call Aristotle to their aid. He must interpret the words of Christ for them, and he says that heaven and earth will not pass away as to their essence but only as to their form. How much they think they are saying! If they so understood it that heaven and earth will continue to be something, they would indeed be right. But let us suffer the blind to go, and know that just as our bodies will be changed as to their essence, and yet be remade according to their essence, so heaven and earth at the last day with all the elements will be melted with fervent heat and turned to dust, together with the bodies of men, so that there will be nothing but fire everywhere. Then will everything be new-created in greatest beauty; our bodies will shine in brilliancy, and the sun be much more glorious than now. Peter speaks of this day, in 2 Peter 3:10–13, "But the day of the Lord will come as a thief; in the which the heavens shall pass away with a great noise, and the elements shall be dissolved with fervent heat, and the earth and the works that are therein shall be burned up. But, according to his promise, we look for new heavens and a new earth, wherein dwelleth righteousness."

Paul also testifies to the same in 1 Corinthians 3:13, that "the last day shall be revealed in fire." And in Isaiah 30:26, "The light of the moon shall be as the light of the sun, and the light of the sun shall be sevenfold as the light of seven days, in the day that Jehovah bindeth up the hurt of his people, and healeth the stroke of their wound." Likewise in Isaiah 65:17, "For, behold I create new heavens and a new earth; and the former things shall not be remembered, nor come into mind. But be ye glad and rejoice forever in that which I create." Therefore, this passing away is not only according to form but also as to essence; unless it be that you do not want to call it a passing away, if things turn to dust until no trace of them can be found, as the burned body turns to ashes and passes away.

58. But where do our souls dwell when the abode of every creature is afire and there is no earthly dwelling place? Answer: My dear hearer, where is the soul now? Or where is it when we sleep and are not conscious of what is taking place in our bodies and in the world around us? Do you think that God cannot so preserve or hold the souls of men in his hand that they will never know how heaven and earth passed away? Or do you think that he must have a bodily home for the soul, just as a shepherd has a stable for his sheep? It is enough for you to know that they are in God's hands and not in the care of any creature. Though you do not understand how it happens, do not be led astray. Since you have not yet learned what happens to you when you fall asleep or awaken, and can never know how near you are to waking or sleeping, though you daily do both, how do you expect to understand all about this question? The Scripture says, "Father, into thy hands I commend my spirit," and so let it be. Meanwhile there will arise a new heaven and a new earth, and our bodies will be revived again to eternal salvation. Amen. If we knew just how the soul would be kept, faith would be at an end. But now we journey and know not just whither; yet we put our confidence in God, and rest in his keeping, and our faith abides in all its dignity.

III. THE SPIRITUAL INTERPRETATION OF THESE GOSPEL SIGNS

59. Finally, we must find also a hidden or spiritual meaning in this Gospel. The sun is Christ, the moon is the church, the stars are Christians, the powers of heaven are the prelates or planets of the church. Now these earthly signs surely signify what has long since taken place and is now taking place among Christians; for they follow the service of sin and threaten and manifest the punishment resting upon them.

60. That the sun is darkened no doubt signifies that Christ does not shine in the Christian Church; that is, that the Gospel is not preached and that faith is expiring from the lack of divine service. This has come about through the teaching and works of men. The pope sits in the churches in the place of Christ and shines like dirt in a lantern—he with his bishops, priests, and monks. It is these that have darkened the sun for us, and instead of the true worship of God have set up idolatry and image worship with their tonsure and hoods and vestments and pipes and lutes and singing and playing, etc. Oh, what darkness! What darkness!

61. From this, it necessarily follows that neither the moon gives any light; that is, when faith died out, love had to die out, also, so that no real Christian deeds are any more seen, no example is found in which one Christian serves another; but all the people have been led into idolatry, and image worship, and there have been instituted Mass, vigils, altars, chapels, purifications, bells, and impostures. Again, what darkness!

62. I interpret the falling of the stars to mean the falling of man who has been baptized and become a Christian and then became a priest or monk. Whoever wants to believe me, may; whoever does not want to, need not do so, but I know what I am talking about. I do not say that they will all be lost; God can save even from the fire whom he will. But this I say, whoever becomes a priest or monk in the belief that he is taking up a holy estate falls from Christian faith into unbelief; for the falling of the stars does not signify the gross forms of sin, murder, adultery, theft, but a falling from faith. Priests and monks (unless God does wonders) are by virtue of their position renegade and apostate Christians, worse than whom no people dwell on the earth.

63. The Turks [Muslims] also are no Christians; but in two senses they are better than the papists: first, they have never been Christians or stars, therefore have not fallen from the faith; secondly, they do not sin against the sacrament of the Lord's body and blood. But the papists make a sacrifice out of the Mass and a meritorious work and do it daily and continually. This is certainly the most sacrilegious perversion upon which the sun has yet shined. In short, he who desires to become holy and be saved by works and holy orders, falls from the faith, falls from heaven; for the blood of Jesus Christ alone is able to save us. Therefore, whenever you see a star fall, then know that it signifies someone has become a priest, a monk, or a nun.

64. That men's hearts failed them for fear signifies the torments that the pope's saints and fallen stars suffer, for while they do great things their consciences are never at rest. The Scriptures say they are weary and heavy laden.

65. The roaring winds and seas are the worldly estates, both high and low. There is no ruler or land at peace with the other, no faith or trust in one another, everyone is looking only to his own interests. Neither is there reproof or discipline or fear upon the earth; and the whole world is so engaged in eating, drinking, unchastity, and the lusts of the flesh that it moans and roars.

66. The powers of heaven are our planets, our spiritual squires and tyrants, popes, bishops, and their companions, the universities, which are all so deeply sunk in worldly affairs, property, honor, and pleasures, that they think they are not planets, that is, errorists, for *planeta* in Greek means an errorist, one who does not travel on the right way, but travels backward and

to both sides as the planets also do in the heavens. This the Germans express in a proverb—the more learned, the more perverse; in other words, the spiritual government is only planets. But now when the Gospel shines forth and shows them their virtue and colors it with its own hue, and shows that they are unlearned idolaters and soul-deceivers, they get angry, begin to move, and form a constellation. They gather together, try to shelter themselves behind bulls and edicts, and threateningly predict a great flood. But it will do them no good; the day will come and its light cannot be placed under a bushel like a candle.

67. The parable of the fig tree seems to me to signify that the fig tree is the holy Scriptures that have so long been hidden in obscurity. They are now budding forth and taking leaves, their word is breaking forth into fruitage. For twelve centuries it has not been so well known, nor have its languages been so well known. There is no doubt in my mind, however, that the Scriptures are a fig tree that is easily preserved. It was fig leaves with which Adam and Eve covered their nakedness; for the old Adam always uses the Scriptures to adorn himself. Therefore the book must come forth, its leaves must become green, in spite of all the movements of the planets. The summer is not far distant— would to God that the fruit would also follow the leaves. I fear that there will be nothing but leaves, for we talk much about true faith but bring forth no fruit.

68. Enough has now been said concerning these signs; if anyone desires to consider the matter further, to him has been given here the impulse and a start. But the planets with their factious spirit will not believe in them, in order that the Scriptures may still be true in this, that they give these people great security and contempt for the Word, works, and signs of God.

The Third Sunday in Advent

Christ's Answer to the Question John Asked Him,
His Praise of John, and the Application of This Gospel

N
ow when John heard in the prison the works of the Christ, he
sent by his disciples and said unto him, "Art thou he that cometh,
or look we for another?" And Jesus answered and said unto them, "Go
and tell John the things which ye hear and see: the blind receive their
sight, and the lame walk, the lepers are cleansed and the deaf hear, and
the dead are raised up, and the poor have good tidings preached to them.
And blessed is he, whosoever shall find no occasion of stumbling in me."

And as these went their way, Jesus began to say unto the multitudes
concerning John, "What went ye out into the wilderness to behold? a
reed shaken with the wind? But what went ye out to see? a man clothed
in soft raiment? Behold, they that wear soft raiment are in kings'
houses. But wherefore went ye out? to see a prophet? Yea, I say unto
you, and much more than a prophet. This is he, of whom it is written,
Behold, I send my messenger before thy face, who shall prepare thy way
before thee." — MATTHEW 11:2–10

I. THE QUESTION JOHN PUTS TO CHRIST

1. The most I find on this Gospel treats of whether John the Baptist knew
that Jesus was the true Christ, although this question is unnecessary and of little import. Saint Ambrose thinks John asked this question neither in ignorance
nor in doubt, but in a Christian spirit. Jerome and Gregory write that John
asked whether he should be Christ's forerunner also into hell, an opinion that
has not the least foundation, for the text plainly says, "Art thou he that cometh
or look we for another?" This looking or waiting for Christ, according to the
words, relates to his coming on earth and pertains to the Jewish people, otherwise John ought to have asked, or do those in hell look for thee? And since
Christ with his works answered that he had come, it is certain that John

inquired about Christ's bodily coming, as Christ himself thus understood it and answered accordingly, although I do not deny that Christ also descended into hell, as we confess in our creed.

2. Hence it is evident John knew very well that Jesus was he that should come, for he had baptized him and testified that Christ was the Lamb of God that takes away the sin of the world, and he had also seen the Holy Spirit descending upon him as a dove, and heard the voice from heaven, "This is my beloved Son, in whom I am well pleased." All is fully related by all four evangelists. Why, then, did John ask this question? Answer: It was not done without good reasons. In the first place, it is certain that John asked it for the sake of his disciples, as they did not yet hold Christ to be the one he really was. And John did not come in order to make disciples and draw the people to himself, but to prepare the way for Christ, to lead everybody to Christ, and to make all the people subject to him.

3. Now the disciples of John had heard from him many excellent testimonies concerning Christ, namely, that he was the Lamb of God and the Son of God, and that Christ must increase while he must decrease. All this his disciples and the people did not yet believe, nor could they understand it, as they themselves and all the people thought more of John than of Christ. For this reason they clung so strongly to John, even to the extent that they for his sake became jealous and dissatisfied with Christ when they saw that he also baptized, made disciples, and drew the people to himself. They complained to John about this because they feared that their master would grow less in esteem, as we read, in John 3:26, "And they came unto John and said to him, Rabbi, he that was with thee beyond the Jordan, to whom thou hast borne witness, behold, the same baptizeth, and all men come to him."

4. To this error they were led by two reasons—first, because Christ was not yet known to the people, but only to John; neither had he as yet performed any miracle, and no one was held in high esteem but John. Hence it appeared so strange to them that he should point them and everybody else away from himself and to someone else, inasmuch as there was no one living besides John who had gained a great name and enjoyed great fame. The other reason was because Christ appeared so very humble and common, being the son of a poor carpenter and of a poor widow. Neither did he belong to the priesthood, nor to the learned, but was only a layman and a common apprentice. He had never studied, was brought up as a carpenter apprentice just like other laymen; hence it seemed as though the excellent testimony of John concerning Christ and the common layman and apprentice, Jesus of Nazareth, did not

at all harmonize with each other. Therefore, though they believed that John told the truth, they still reasoned, Perhaps it will be someone else than this Jesus, and they looked for one who might appear among them in an imposing way, like a highly learned leader among the priests, or a mighty king. From such delusion John could not deliver them with his words. They clung to him, and regarded Christ as being much inferior, meanwhile looking for the glorious appearing of the great person of whom John spoke. And should he really be Jesus, then he had to assume a different attitude; he must saddle a steed, put on bright spurs, and dash forward like a lord and king of Israel, just as the kings aforetime had done. Until he should do this, they would cling to John.

5. But when Jesus began to perform miracles and became famous, then John thought he would point his disciples away from himself and lead them to Christ, so they might not think of establishing a new sect and becoming Johnites; but that all might cling to Christ and become Christians, John sends them to Christ so that from now on they might learn not only from the witness he bore of Christ but also from the words and deeds of Christ himself that he was the one of whom John had spoken. It should not be expected that the works and coming of Christ would be attended by drums and bugles and like worldly pomp, but by spiritual power and grace, so there would be no riding and walking on streets paved and carpeted; but by virtue of such power and grace the dead would be raised up, the blind receive their sight, the deaf hear, and all kinds of bodily and spiritual evil be removed. That should be the glory and coming of this king, the least of whose works could not be performed by all the kings, all the learned, and all the rich in the world. This is the meaning of the text.

Now when John heard in the prison the works of the Christ,
he sent by his disciples and said unto him, "art thou he that cometh,
or look we for another?"

6. As though John would say to his disciples, There you hear of his works, such as I never accomplished, nor anyone else before him. Now go to him and ask him whether he is the one that cometh. Put away the gross worldly deception that he would ride on steeds in armor. He is increasing, but I must now decrease; my work must cease, but his must continue. You must leave me and cling to him.

7. How necessary it was for John to point his disciples away from himself to Christ is very clear. For what benefit would it have been to them if they had depended a thousand times on John's piety and had not embraced Christ? Without Christ there is no help or remedy, no matter how pious men may be. So at the present day what benefit is it to the monks and nuns to observe the

rules of Saint Benedict, Saint Bernard, Saint Francis, Saint Dominic, and Saint Augustine if they do not embrace Christ and him only, and depart also from their John? All Benedictines, Carthusians, Barefoot-Friars, Ecclesiastes, Augustinians, Carmelites, all monks and nuns are surely lost, as only Christians are saved. Whoever is not a Christian even John the Baptist cannot help, who, indeed, according to Christ, was the greatest of all saints.

8. However, John deals kindly with his disciples and has patience with their weak faith until they shall have grown strong. He does not condemn them because they do not firmly believe him. Thus we should deal with the consciences of men ensnared by the examples and regulations of pious men until they are freed from them.

II. CHRIST'S ANSWER, GIVEN IN WORDS AND DEEDS

And Jesus answered and said unto them, "Go and tell John the things which you hear and see; the blind receive their sight, and the lame walk, the lepers are cleansed, and the deaf hear, and the dead are raised up, and the poor have good tidings preached to them. And blessed is he whosoever shall find no occasion of stumbling in me."

9. Christ answered John also for the sake of his disciples. He answers in a twofold way: first, by his works; secondly, by his words. He did the same thing when the Jews surrounded him in the temple and asked him, "If thou art the Christ, tell us plainly," in John 10:24. But he points them to his works, saying, "I told you, and ye believe not, the works that I do in my Father's name, these bear witness of me," in John 10:25. Again, "Though ye believe not me, believe the works," in John 10:38. Here Christ first points them to the works, and then also to the words, saying, "And blessed is he, whosoever shall find no occasion of stumbling in me." With these words, he does not only confess that he is the Christ, but also warns them against finding occasion of stumbling in him. If he were not the Christ, then he who finds no occasion of stumbling in him could not be blessed. For one can dispense with all the saints, but Christ is the only one that no man can dispense with. No saint can help us, none but Christ.

10. The answer of his works is more convincing, first, because such works were never before accomplished either by John or by anyone else; and secondly, because these works were predicted by the prophets. Therefore, when they saw that it came to pass just as the prophets had foretold, they could and should have been assured. For thus Isaiah had said of these works, "The Spirit of the Lord Jehovah is upon me, because Jehovah hath anointed me to preach

good tidings unto the weak; he hath sent me to bind up the broken-hearted, to proclaim liberty to the captives, and the opening of the prison to them that are bound," in Isaiah 61:1. When Isaiah says, "He hath anointed me," he thereby means that Jesus is the Christ and that Christ should do all these works, and he who is doing them must be the Christ. For the Greek word Christ is Messiah in Hebrew, Unctus in Latin, and Gesalbter (anointed) in German. But the kings and priests were usually anointed for the kingdom and priesthood. But this anointed king and priest, Isaiah says, shall be anointed by God himself, not with real oil, but with the Holy Spirit that should come upon him, saying, "The Spirit of the Lord Jehovah is upon me." That is my anointment with which the Spirit anointed me. Thus he indeed preaches good tidings to the weak, gives sight to the blind, heals all kinds of sickness, and proclaims the acceptable year, the time of grace, etc.

Again Isaiah says, "Behold, your God will come with vengeance, with the recompense of God; he will come and save you. Then the eyes of the blind shall be opened, and the ears of the deaf shall be unstopped. Then shall the lame man leap as a hart, and the tongue of the dumb shall sing," etc., in Isaiah 35:4–5. Now, if they would compare the Scriptures with these works, and these works with the Scriptures, they would recognize John's witness by Christ's works, that he was the true Messiah. Luke says, in Luke 7:21, that Christ at that time, when John's disciples asked him, healed many of their diseases and plagues and evil spirits, and bestowed sight on many that were blind.

11. But here we must take to heart the good example of Christ in that he appeals to his works, even as the tree is known by its fruits, thus rebuking all false teachers, the pope, bishops, priests, and monks to appear in the future and shield themselves by his name, saying, "We are Christians"; just as the pope is boasting that he is the vicar of Christ. Here we have it stated that where the works are absent, there is also no Christ. Christ is a living, active, and fruit-bearing character who does not rest, but works unceasingly wherever he is. Therefore, those bishops and teachers that are not doing the works of Christ, we should avoid and consider as wolves.

12. But they say, Why, it is not necessary for everyone to do these works of Christ. How can all the pious give sight to the blind, make the lame walk, and do other miracles like those of Christ? Answer: Christ did also other works; he exercised himself in patience, love, peace, meekness, etc. This, everybody should do. Do these works, and then we also shall know Christ by his works.

13. Here they reply, Christ says, "The scribes and the Pharisees sit on Moses' seat; all things therefore whatsoever they bid you, these do and observe; but do not ye after their works; for they say, and do not," in Matthew 23:2–3.

Here Christ commanded to judge the doctrine but not the life. Answer: What do I hear? Have you now become Pharisees and hypocrites, and confess it yourselves? If we would say this about you then you would indeed become angry. Be it so, if you are such hypocrites and apply these words of Christ to yourselves, then you must also apply to yourselves all the other words Christ speaks against the Pharisees. However, as they wish to shield themselves by these words of Christ and put to silence the ignorant, we will further consider the same, inasmuch as the murderers of Christians at the Council of Constance also attacked John Huss with this passage, claiming that it granted them liberty for their tyranny, so that no one dared to oppose their doctrine.

14. It must, therefore, be observed that teaching is also a work, yea, even the chief work of Christ, because here among his works he mentions that to the poor the Gospel is preached. Therefore, just as the tyrants are known by their works, so are they known by their teachings. Where Christ is, there surely the Gospel will be preached; but where the Gospel is not preached, there Christ is not present.

15. Now in order to grant our Pharisees that not the life but the doctrine should be judged, be it so, let them teach, and we will gladly spare their lives; but then they are a great deal worse than the Pharisees who taught Moses' doctrine, though they did not practice it. But our blockheads are idols; there is neither letting nor doing, neither life nor doctrine. They sit on Christ's seat and teach their own lies and silence the Gospel. Hence this passage of Christ will not shield them; they must be wolves and murderers as Christ calls them, in John 10:1.

16. Thus Christ here wants them to hear the Pharisees but only on Moses' seat, that is, if they taught the law of Moses, the commandments of God.

In the same place Christ forbids to do according to their works, he mentions their teachings among their works, saying, "Yea, they bind heavy burdens and grievous to be borne, and lay them on men's shoulders; but they themselves will not move them with their finger," in Matthew 23:4. Observe here that Christ first of all forbids among their works their teachings grievous to be borne, as being of chief import, so that finally the meaning of the passage is, All that they teach according to Moses, you should keep and do, but whatever they teach and do besides, you should not observe. Even so should we listen to our Pharisees on Christ's seat only when they preach the Gospel to the poor, and not hear them nor do what they otherwise teach or do.

17. Thus you perceive how skillfully the rude papists made this passage the foundation of their doctrine, lies, and tyranny, though no other passage is more strongly against them and more severely condemns their teachings than

this one. Christ's words stand firm and are clear; do not follow their works. But their doctrine is their own work, and not God's. They are a people exalted only to lie and to pervert the Scriptures. Moreover, if one's life is bad, it would be strange indeed if he should preach right; he would always have to preach against himself, which he will hardly do without additions and foreign doctrines. In short, he who does not preach the Gospel identifies himself as one who is sitting neither on Moses' nor on Christ's seat. For this reason you should do neither according to his words nor according to his works, but flee from him as Christ's sheep do, in John 10:4–5, "And the sheep follow him, for they know his voice. And a stranger will they not follow, but flee from him." But if you wish to know what their seat is called, then listen to David, "Blessed is the man that walketh not in the counsel of the wicked, nor standeth in the way of the sinner, nor sitteth in the seat of scoffers, in Psalm 1:1. Again, in Psalm 94:20, "Shall the throne of wickedness have fellowship with thee, which frameth mischief by statute?"

18. But what does it mean when Christ says, "The poor have good tidings preached to them"? Is it not preached also to the rich and to the whole world? Again, why is the Gospel so great a thing, so great a blessing as Christ teaches, seeing that so many people despise and oppose it? Here we must know what Gospel really is, otherwise we cannot understand this passage. We must, therefore, diligently observe that from the beginning God has sent into the world a twofold Word, or message: the Law and the Gospel. These two messages must be rightly distinguished, one from the other, and properly understood for, besides the Scriptures, there never has been a book written to this day, not even by a saint, in which these two messages, the Law and the Gospel, have been properly explained and distinguished, and yet so very much depends on such an explanation.

The Difference Between the Law and the Gospel

19. The law is that Word by which God teaches what we shall do as, for instance, the Ten Commandments. Now, if human nature is not aided by God's grace, it is impossible to keep the law, for the reason that man, since the fall of Adam in paradise, is depraved and full of sinful desires, so that he cannot from his heart's desire find pleasure in the law, which fact we all experience in ourselves. For no one lives who does not prefer that there were no law, and everyone feels and knows in himself that it is difficult to lead a pious life and do good and, on the other hand, that it is easy to lead a wicked life and to do evil. But this difficulty or unwillingness to do the good is the reason we do not keep the law of God. For whatever is done with aversion and unwillingness is considered by God

as not done at all. Thus the law of God convicts us, even by our own experience, that by nature we are evil, disobedient, lovers of sin, and hostile to God's laws.

20. From all this, either self-confidence or despair must follow. Self-confidence follows when a man strives to fulfill the law by his own good works, by trying hard to do as the words of the law command. He serves God, he swears not, he honors father and mother, he kills not, he does not commit adultery, etc. But meanwhile he does not look into his heart, does not realize with what motives he leads a good life, and conceals the old Adam in his heart. For if he would truly examine his heart, he would realize that he is doing all unwillingly and with compulsion, that he fears hell or seeks heaven, if he be not prompted by things of less importance, as honor, goods, health, and fear of being humiliated, of being punished or of being visited by a plague. In short, he would have to confess that he would rather lead a wicked life if it were not that he fears the consequences, for the law only restrains him. But because he does not realize his bad motives, he lives securely, looks only at his outward works and not into his heart, prides himself on keeping the law of God perfectly, and thus the countenance of Moses remains covered to him, that is, he does not understand the meaning of the law, namely, that it must be kept with a happy, free, and willing mind.

21. Just as an immoral person, if you should ask him why he commits adultery, can answer only that he is doing it for the sake of the carnal pleasure he finds in it. For he does not do it for reward or punishment, he expects no gain from it, nor does he hope to escape from the evil of it. Such willingness the law requires in us, so that if you should ask a virtuous man why he leads a chaste life, he would answer, Not for the sake of heaven or hell, honor or disgrace, but for the sole reason that he considers it honorable, and that it pleases him exceedingly, even if it were not commanded. Behold, such a heart delights in God's law and keeps it with pleasure. Such people love God and righteousness, they hate and fear naught but unrighteousness. However, no one is thus by nature. The unrighteous love reward and profit, fear and hate punishment and pain; therefore, they also hate God and righteousness, love themselves and unrighteousness. They are hypocrites, disguisers, deceivers, liars, and self-conceited. So are all men without grace, but above all, the saints who rely on their good works. For this reason, the Scriptures conclude, "All men are liars," in Psalm 116:11; "Every man at his best estate is altogether vanity," in Psalm 39:5; and "There is none that doeth good, no, not one," in Psalm 14:3.

22. Despair follows when man becomes conscious of his evil motives, and realizes that it is impossible for him to love the law of God, finding nothing good in himself; but only hatred of the good and delight in doing evil. Now

he realizes that the law cannot be kept only by works, hence he despairs of his works and does not rely upon them. He should have love but he finds none, nor can have any through his own efforts or out of his own heart. Now he must be a poor, miserable, and humiliated spirit whose conscience is burdened and in anguish because of the law, commanding and demanding payment in full when he does not possess even a farthing with which to pay. Only to such persons is the law beneficial, because it has been given for the purpose of working such knowledge and humiliation; that is its real mission. These persons well know how to judge the works of hypocrites and fraudulent saints, namely, as nothing but lies and deception. David referred to this when he said, "I said in my haste, all men are liars," in Psalm 116:11.

23. For this reason, Paul calls the law a law unto death, saying, "And the commandment, which was unto life, this I found to be unto death," in Romans 7:10; and a power of sin. In 1 Corinthians 15:56, "And the power of sin is the law," and in 2 Corinthians 3:6, he says, "For the letter killeth, but the spirit giveth life." All this means, if the law and human nature be brought into a right relation, the one to the other, then will sin and a troubled conscience first become manifest. Man, then, sees how desperately wicked his heart is, how great his sins are, even as to things he formerly considered good works and no sin. He now is compelled to confess that by and of himself he is a child of perdition, a child of God's wrath and of hell. Then there is only fear and trembling, all self-conceit vanishes, while fear and despair fill his heart. Thus man is crushed and put to naught, and truly humbled.

Inasmuch as all this is caused only by the law, Saint Paul truly says, that it is a law unto death and a letter that killeth, and that through the commandment sin becomes exceedingly sinful, in Romans 7:13, provoking God's wrath. For the law gives and helps us in no way whatever; it only demands and drives and shows us our misery and depravity.

Concerning the Gospel

24. The other Word of God is neither law nor commandments, and demands nothing of us. But when that has been done by the first word, namely, the law, and has worked deep despair and wretchedness in our hearts, then God comes and offers us his blessed and life-giving word and promises; he pledges and obligates himself to grant grace and help in order to deliver us from misery, not only to pardon all our sins, but even to blot them out, and in addition to this to create in us love and delight in keeping his law.

25. Behold, this divine promise of grace and forgiveness of sin is rightly called the Gospel. And I say here, again, that by the Gospel you must by no

means understand anything else than the divine promise of God's grace and his forgiveness of sin. For thus it was that Paul's Epistles were never understood, nor can they be understood by the papists, because they do not know what the law and the Gospel really mean. They hold Christ to be a lawmaker, and the Gospel a mere doctrine of a new law. That is nothing else than locking up the Gospel and entirely concealing it.

26. Now, the word Gospel is of Greek origin and signifies in German *Frohliche Botschaft*, that is, glad tidings, because it proclaims the blessed doctrine of life eternal by divine promise, and offers grace and forgiveness of sin. Therefore, works do not belong to the Gospel, as it is not a law; only faith belongs to it, as it is altogether a promise and an offer of divine grace. Whosoever now believes the Gospel will receive grace and the Holy Spirit. This will cause the heart to rejoice and find delight in God, and will enable the believer to keep the law cheerfully, without expecting reward, without fear of punishment, without seeking compensation, as the heart is perfectly satisfied with God's grace, by which the law has been fulfilled.

27. But all these promises from the beginning are founded on Christ, so that God promises no one this grace except through Christ, who is the messenger of the divine promise to the whole world. For this reason he came and through the Gospel brought these promises into all the world, which before this time had been proclaimed by the prophets. It is, therefore, in vain if anyone, like the Jews, expects the fulfillment of the divine promises without Christ. All is centered and decreed in Christ. Whosoever will not hear him shall have no promises of God. For just as God acknowledges no law besides the law of Moses and the writings of the prophets, so he makes no promises except through Christ alone.

28. But, you may reply, is there not also much law in the Gospel and in the Epistles of Paul? and, again, many promises in the writings of Moses and the prophets? Answer: There is no book in the Bible in which both are not found. God has always placed side by side both law and promise. For he teaches by the law what we are to do and, by the promises, whence we shall receive power to do it.

29. But the New Testament especially is called the Gospel above the other books of the Bible because it was written after the coming of Christ, who fulfilled the divine promises, brought them unto us, and publicly proclaimed them by oral preaching, which promises were before concealed in the Old Testament Scriptures. Therefore, hold to this distinction, and no matter what books you have before you, be they of the Old or of the New Testament, read them with a discrimination so as to observe that when promises are made in

a book, it is a Gospel book; when commandments are given, it is a law book. But because in the New Testament the promises are found so abundantly, and in the Old Testament so many laws, the former is called the Gospel, and the latter the Book of the Law. We now come back to our text.

"And the poor have good tidings preached unto them."

30. From what has just been said, it is easily understood that among the works of Christ none is greater than preaching the Gospel to the poor. This means nothing else than that to the poor the divine promise of grace and consolation in and through Christ is preached, offered, and presented, so that to him who believes all his sins are forgiven, the law is fulfilled, conscience is appeased, and, at last, life eternal is bestowed upon him. What more joyful tidings could a poor sorrowful heart and a troubled conscience hear than this? How could the heart become more bold and courageous than by such consoling, blissful words of promise? Sin, death, hell, the world and the devil, and every evil are scorned when a poor heart receives and believes this consolation of the divine promise. To give sight to the blind and to raise up the dead are but insignificant deeds compared with preaching the Gospel to the poor. Therefore, Christ mentions it as the greatest and best among these works.

31. But it must be observed that Christ says the Gospel is preached to none but to the poor only, thus without doubt intending it to be a message for the poor only. For it has always been preached unto the whole world, as Christ says, "Go ye into all the world, and preach the Gospel to the whole creation," in Mark 16:15. Surely these poor are not the beggars and the bodily poor, but the spiritually poor, namely, those who do not covet and love earthly goods; yes, rather those poor, broken-hearted ones who in the agony of their conscience seek and desire help and consolation so ardently that they covet neither riches nor honor. Nothing will be of help to them, unless they have a merciful God. Here is true spiritual weakness. They are those for whom such a message is intended, and in their hearts they are delighted with it. They feel they have been delivered from hell and death.

32. Therefore, though the Gospel is heard by all the world, yet it is not accepted but by the poor only. Moreover, it is to be preached and proclaimed to all the world, that it is a message only for the poor, and that the rich men cannot receive it. Whosoever would receive it must first become poor, as Christ says, in Matthew 9:13, that he came not to call the righteous but only sinners, although he called all the world. But his calling was such that he desired to be accepted only by sinners, and all he called should become sinners. This they resented. In like manner, all should become poor who heard the

Gospel, that they might be worthy of the Gospel; but this they also resented. Therefore, the Gospel remained only for the poor. Thus God's grace was also preached before all the world to the humble, in order that all might become humble, but they would not be humble.

33. Hence you see who are the greatest enemies of the Gospel, namely, the work-righteous saints, who are self-conceited, as has been said before. For the Gospel has not the least in common with them. They want to be rich in works, but the Gospel wills that they are to become poor. They will not yield, neither can the Gospel yield, as it is the unchangeable Word of God. Thus they and the Gospel clash, one with another, as Christ says, "And he that falleth on this stone shall be broken to pieces; but on whomsoever it shall fall, it will scatter him as dust," in Matthew 21:44.

Again, they condemn the Gospel as being error and heresy; and we observe it comes to pass daily, as it has from the beginning of the world, that between the Gospel and the work-righteous saints there is no peace, no good will, and no reconciliation. But meanwhile Christ must suffer himself to be crucified anew, for he and those that are his must place themselves, as it were, into this vise, namely, between the Gospel and the work-righteous saints, and thus be pressed and crushed like the wheat between the upper and nether millstones. But the lower stone is the quiet, peaceable, and immovable Gospel, while the upper stone is the works and their masters, who are ranting and raging.

34. With all this John contradicts strongly the fleshly and worldly opinion his disciples entertained concerning Christ's coming. They thought that the great king, whom John extolled so highly, namely, that the latchet of whose shoe he was not worthy to unloose, in John 1:27, would enter in such splendor that everything would be gold and costly ornaments, and immediately the streets would be spread with pearls and silks. As they lifted up their eyes so high and looked for such splendor, Christ turns their look downward and holds before them the blind, lame, deaf, dumb, poor, and everything that conflicts with such splendor, and contrariwise he presents himself in the state of a common servant rather than that of a great king, whose shoe's latchet John considered himself unworthy to unloose, as though Christ would say to them, "Banish your high expectations, look not to my person and state, but to the works I do. Worldly lords, because they rule by force, must be accompanied by rich, high, healthy, strong, wise, and able men. With them they have to associate, and they need them, or their kingdom could not exist; hence they can never attend to the blind, lame, deaf, dumb, dead, lepers, and the poor.

But my kingdom, because it seeks not its own advantage, but rather bestows benefits upon others, is sufficient of itself and needs no one's help;

therefore, I cannot bear to be surrounded by such as are already sufficient of themselves, such as are healthy, rich, strong, pure, active, pious, and able in every respect. To such, I am of no benefit; they obtain nothing from me. Yea, they would be a disgrace to me, because it would seem that I needed them and were benefited by them, as worldly rulers are by their subjects. Therefore, I must do otherwise and keep to those who can become partakers of me, and I must associate with the blind, the lame, the dumb, and all kinds of afflicted ones. This the character and nature of my kingdom demand. For this reason, I must appear in a way that such people can feel at home in my company.

35. And now very aptly follow the words, "And blessed is he, whosoever shall find no occasion of stumbling in me." Why? Because Christ's humble appearance and John's excellent testimony of Christ seemed to disagree with each other. Human reason could not make them rhyme. Now all the Scriptures pointed to Christ, and there was danger of misinterpreting them. Reason spoke thus, Can this be the Christ, of whom all the Scriptures speak? Should he be the one, whose shoe's latchet John thought himself unworthy to unloose, though I scarcely consider him worthy to clean my shoes? Therefore, it is surely true that it is a great blessing not to find occasion of stumbling in Christ, and there is here no other help or remedy than to look at his works and compare them with the Scriptures. Otherwise, it is impossible to keep from being offended at Christ.

Two Kinds of Offenses

36. Here you observe that there are two kinds of offenses, one of doctrine and the other of life. These two offenses must be carefully considered. The offense of doctrine comes when one believes, teaches, or thinks of Christ in a different way than he should, as the Jews here thought of and taught Christ to be different than he really was, expecting him to be a temporal king. Of this offense the Scriptures treat mostly. Christ and Paul always dwell upon it, scarcely mentioning any other. Note well, that Christ and Paul speak of this offense.

37. It is not without reason that men are admonished faithfully to remember this. For under the reign of the pope this offense has been hushed entirely, so that neither monk nor priest knows of any other offense than that caused by open sin and wicked living, which the Scripture does not call an offense; yet they thus construe and twist this word.

On the contrary, all their doings and all their teachings by which they think to benefit the world, they do not consider to be an offense, but a great help; and yet these are dangerous offenses, the like of which never before existed. For they teach the people to believe that the Mass is an offering and a good work, that by works men may become pious, may atone for sin and be saved, all of which is nothing else than rejecting Christ and destroying faith.

38. Thus the world today is filled with offenses up to the very heavens, so that it is terrible to think of it. For no one now seeks Christ among the poor, the blind, the dead, etc.; but all expect to enter heaven in a different way, which expectation must surely fail.

39. The offense of life is, when one sees an openly wicked work done by another and teaches it. But it is impossible to avoid this offense, inasmuch as we have to live among the wicked, nor is it so dangerous, since everybody knows that such offense is sinful, and no one is deceived by it, but intentionally follows the known evil. There is neither disguise nor deception. But the offense of doctrine is that there should be the most beautiful religious ceremonies, the noblest works, the most honorable life, and that it is impossible for common reason to censure or discern it; only faith knows through the spirit that it is all wrong. Against this offense Christ warns us, saying, "But whoso shall cause one of these little ones that believe on me to stumble, it is profitable for him that a great millstone should be hanged about his neck, and that he should be sunk in the depth of the sea," in Matthew 18:6.

40. Whosoever does not preach Christ, or who preaches him otherwise than as one caring for the blind, the lame, the dead, and the poor, like the Gospel teaches, let us flee from him as from the devil himself, because he teaches us how to become unhappy and to stumble in Christ; as it is now done by the pope, the monks, and the teachers in their high schools. All their doings are an offense from head to foot, from the skin to the marrow, so that the snow is scarcely anything but water; nor can these things exist without causing great offense, inasmuch as offense is the nature and essence of their doings. Therefore, to undertake to reform the pope, the convents, and the high schools and still maintain them in their essence and character, would be like squeezing water out of snow and still preserving the snow. But what it means to preach Christ among the poor, we shall see at the end of our text.

III. HOW AND WHY CHRIST PRAISES JOHN

And as these went their way, Jesus began to say unto the multitudes concerning John, "What went ye out into the wilderness to behold? a reed shaken by the wind? But what went ye out to see? a man clothed in soft raiments? Behold, they that wear soft raiment are in kings' houses. But wherefore went ye out? to see a prophet? Yea, I say unto you, and much more than a prophet."

41. Inasmuch as Christ thus lauds John the Baptist, because he is not a reed, nor clothed in soft raiment, and because he is more than a prophet, he gives us to understand by these figurative words, that the people were inclined to look upon John as a reed, as clad in soft raiment, and as a prophet. Therefore we must see what he means by them, and why he censures and rejects these opinions of theirs. Enough has been said, that John bore witness of Christ in order that the people might not take offense at Christ's humble appearance and manner.

42. Now, as it was of great importance for them to believe John's witness and acknowledge Christ, he praised John first for his steadfastness, thus rebuking their wavering on account of which they would not believe John's witness. It is as though he would say, You have heard John's witness concerning me, but now you do not adhere to it, you take offense at me and your hearts are wavering; you are looking for another, but know not who, nor when and where, and thus your hearts are like a reed shaken by the wind to and fro; you are sure of nothing, and would rather hear something else than the truth about me. Now do you think that John should also turn his witness from me and, as is the case with your thoughts, turn it to the winds and speak of another whom you would be pleased to hear? Not so. John does not waver, nor does his witness fluctuate; he does not follow your swaying delusion; but you must stay your wavering by his witness and thus adhere to me and expect none other.

43. Again, Christ lauds John because of his coarse raiment, as though to say, Perhaps you might believe him when he says that I am he that should come as to my person; but you expect him to speak differently about me, saying something smooth and agreeable, that would be pleasant to hear. It is indeed hard and severe that I come so poor and despised. You desire me to rush forth with pomp and flourish of trumpets. Had John thus spoken of me, then he would not appear so coarse and severe himself. But do not think thus. Whoever desires to preach about me must not preach different than John is doing. It's to no purpose; I will assume no other state and manner. Those who teach different than John are not in the wilderness but in kings' houses. They are rich and honored by the people. They are teachers of man-made doctrines, teaching themselves and not me.

44. Christ lauds John, thirdly, because of the dignity of his office, namely, that he is not only a prophet, but even more than a prophet, as though to say, In your high-soaring, fluctuating opinion, you take John for a prophet who speaks of the coming of Christ, just as the other prophets have done, and thus again your thoughts go beyond me to a different time when you expect Christ to come, according to John's witness, so that you will in no case accept me. But I say to you, your thoughts are wrong. For just as John warns you not to

be like a shaken reed, and not to look for any other than myself, nor to expect me in a different state and manner from that in which you see me, he also forbids you to look for another time, because his witness points to this person of mine, to this state and manner, and to this time, and it opposes your fickle ideas in every way and binds you firmly to my person.

45. Now, if you want to do John justice, then you must simply accept his witness and believe that this is the person, the state and manner, and the time that you should accept, and abandon your presumption and your waiting for another person, state, and time. For it is decreed that John should be no shaken reed, not a man of soft raiment and, above all, not a prophet pointing to future times, but a messenger of present events. He will not write as did the prophets, but will point out and orally announce him who has been predicted by the prophets, saying,

"This is he, of whom it is written, 'Behold, I send my messenger before thy face, who shall prepare the way before thee.'"

46. What else can this mean than that you dare not wait for another, neither for another manner of mine, neither for another time. Here I am present, the one of whom John speaks. For John is not a prophet but a messenger. And not a messenger that is sent by the master who stays at home, but a messenger that goes before the face of his master and brings the master along with him, so that there is but one time for the messenger and for the master. Now if you do not accept John as such a messenger but take him for a prophet who only proclaims the coming of the Lord, as the other prophets have done, then you will fail to understand me, the Scriptures, and everything else.

47. Thus we see Christ pleads, mainly for them to take John as a messenger and not as a prophet. To this end, Christ quotes the Scriptures referring to the passage in Malachi 3:1, "Behold, I send my messenger, and he shall prepare the way before me," which he does not do in reference to the other points, namely, his person and manner. For to this day, it is the delusion of the Jews that they look for another time; and if they then had believed that the time was at hand and had considered John a messenger and not a prophet, then everything could easily have been adjusted as to the person and manner of Christ, inasmuch as they at last had to accept his person and manner, at least after the expired time. For there should be no other time than the days of John, the messenger and preparer of the way for his Master. But as they do not heed the time, and look for another time, it is scarcely possible to convince them by his person and manner. They remain shaken reeds and soft-raiment seekers as long as they take John for his prophet and not for his messenger.

48. We must accustom ourselves to the Scriptures, in which angel (angelus) really means a messenger, not a bearer of messages or one who carries letters, but one who is sent to solicit orally for the message. Hence in the Scriptures this name is common to all messengers of God in heaven and on earth, be they holy angels in heaven or the prophets and apostles on earth. For thus Malachi speaks of the office of the priest, "For the priest's lips should keep knowledge, and they should seek the law at his mouth; for he is the messenger (angel) of Jehovah of hosts," in Malachi 2:7. Again, "Then spake Haggai, Jehovah's messenger (angel) in Jehovah's message unto the people," in Haggai 1:13. And again, "And it came to pass, when the days were well nigh come that he should be received up, he steadfastly set his face to go to Jerusalem, and sent messengers (angels) before his face," in Luke 9:51.

Thus they are called God's angels or messengers and solicitors, who proclaim his Word. From this is also derived the word Gospel, which means good tidings. But the heavenly spirits are called angels chiefly because they are the highest and most exalted messengers of God.

49. Thus John is also an angel or Word-messenger, and not only such a messenger, but one who also prepares the way before the face of the Master in a manner that the Master himself follows him immediately, which no prophet ever did. For this reason, John is more than a prophet, namely, an angel or messenger, and a forerunner, so that in his day the Lord of all the prophets himself comes with this messenger.

50. The preparing here means to make ready the way, to put out of the way all that interferes with the course of the Lord, just as the servant clears the way before the face of his master by removing wood, stones, people, and all that is in the way. But what was it that blocked the way of Christ and John was to remove? Sin, without doubt, especially the good works of the haughty saints; that is, he should make known to everybody that the works and deeds of all men are sin and iniquity, and that all need the grace of Christ. He who knows and acknowledges this thoroughly is himself humble and has well prepared the way for Christ. Of this we shall speak in the following Gospel. Now is the opportunity for us to receive a blessing from this Gospel lesson.

IV. THE APPLICATION OF THIS GOSPEL

The Doctrine of Faith and Good Works

51. As we have said touching the other Gospels, that we should learn from them the two doctrines of faith and love, or accepting and bestowing good

works, so we should do here, extol faith and exercise love. Faith receives the good works of Christ; love bestows good works on our neighbor.

52. In the first place, our faith is strengthened and increased when Christ is held forth to us in his own natural works, namely, that he associates only with the blind, the deaf, the lame, the lepers, the dead, and the poor; that is, in pure love and kindness toward all who are in need and in misery, so that finally Christ is nothing else than consolation and a refuge for all the distressed and troubled in conscience. Here is necessary faith that trusts in the Gospel and relies upon it, never doubting that Christ is just as he is presented to us in this Gospel, and does not think of him otherwise, nor let anyone persuade us to believe otherwise. Then surely we learn Christ as we believe and as this Gospel speaks of him. For as you believe, so you will have it And blessed is he who finds here no occasion of stumbling in Christ.

53. Here you must with all diligence beware of taking offense. Who stumble at Christ? All that teach you to do works instead of teaching you to believe. Those who hold forth Christ to you as a lawmaker and a judge, and refuse to let Christ be a helper and a comforter, torment you by putting works before and in the way of God in order to atone for your sins and to merit grace. Such are the teachings of the pope, priests, monks, and their high schools, who with their masses and religious ceremonies cause you to open your eyes and mouth in astonishment, leading you to another Christ and withholding from you the real Christ. For if you desire to believe rightly and to possess Christ truly, then you must reject all works that you intend to place before and in the way of God. They are only stumbling blocks, leading you away from Christ and from God. Before God no works are acceptable but Christ's own works. Let these plead for you before God, and do no other work before him than to believe that Christ is doing his works for you and is placing them before God in your behalf.

In order to keep your faith pure, do nothing else than stand still, enjoy its blessings, accept Christ's works, and let him bestow his love upon you. You must be blind, lame, deaf, dead, leprous, and poor; otherwise, you will stumble at Christ. That Gospel which suffers Christ to be seen and to be doing good only among the needy will not belie you.

54. This means to acknowledge Christ aright and to embrace him. This is true and Christian believing. But those who intend to atone for sins and to become pious by their own works will miss the present Christ and look for another, or at least they will believe that he should do otherwise, that first of all he should come and accept their works and consider them pious. These are, like the Jews, lost forever. There is no help for them.

55. In the second place, Christ teaches us rightly to apply the works and shows us what good works are. All other work, except faith, we should apply to our neighbor. For God demands of us no other work that we should do for him than to exercise faith in Christ. With that he is satisfied, and with that we give honor to him, as to one who is merciful, long-suffering, wise, kind, truthful, and the like. After this, think of nothing else than to do to your neighbor as Christ has done to you, and let all your works together with all your life be applied to your neighbor. Look for the poor, sick, and all kinds of needy, help them and let your life's energy here appear, so that they may enjoy your kindness, helping whoever needs you, as much as you possibly can with your life, property, and honor. Whoever points you to other good works than these, avoid him as a wolf and as Satan, because he wants to put a stumbling block in your way, as David says, "In the way wherein I walk have they hidden a snare for me," in Psalm 142:3.

56. But this is done by the perverted, misguided people of the papists, who, with their religious ceremonies, set aside such Christian works, and teach the people to serve God only and not also mankind. They establish convents, masses, vigils, become religious, do this and that. And these poor, blind people call that serving God, which they have chosen themselves. But know that to serve God is nothing else than to serve your neighbor and do good to him in love, be it a child, wife, servant, enemy, friend; without making any difference, whoever needs your help in body or soul, and wherever you can help in temporal or spiritual matters. This is serving God and doing good works. O Lord God, how do we fools live in this world, neglecting to do such works, though in all parts of the world we find the needy, on whom we could bestow our good works; but no one looks after them nor cares for them. But look to your own life. If you do not find yourself among the needy and the poor, where the Gospel shows us Christ, then you may know that your faith is not right and that you have not yet tasted of Christ's benevolence and work for you.

57. Therefore, behold what an important saying it is, "Blessed is he, whosoever shall find no occasion of stumbling in me." We stumble in two respects. In faith, because we expect to become pious Christians in a different way than through Christ, and go our way blindly, not acknowledging Christ. In love we stumble, because we are not mindful of the poor and needy, do not look after them, and yet we think we satisfy the demands of faith with other works than these. Thus we come under the judgment of Christ, who says, "For I was hungry, and ye did not give me to eat, I was thirsty, and yet ye gave me no drink,"

in Matthew 25:42. Again, "Inasmuch as ye did it not unto one of these least, ye did it not unto me," in Matthew 25:45.

Why is this judgment right, if not for the reason that we do not unto our neighbor as Christ has done to us? He has bestowed on us needy ones his great, rich, eternal blessings, but we will not bestow our meager service on our neighbors, thus showing that we do not truly believe, and that we have neither accepted nor tasted his blessings. Many will say, "Did we not do wonders in thy name, did we not speak and cast out devils?" But he will answer them, "Depart from me, ye that work iniquity," in Matthew 7:23, and why? Because they did not retain their true Christian faith and love.

58. Thus we see in this Gospel how difficult it is to acknowledge Christ. There is a stumbling block in the way, and one takes offense at this, another at that. There is no headway, not even with the disciples of John, though they plainly see Christ's works and hear his words.

59. This we also do. Though we see, hear, understand, and must confess that Christian life is faith in God and love to our needy neighbor, yet there is no progress. This one clings to his religious ceremonies and his own works, that one is scraping all to himself and helps no one. Even those who gladly hear and understand the doctrine of pure faith do not proceed to serve their neighbor, as though they expected to be saved by faith without works; they see not that their faith is not faith, but a shadow of faith, just as the picture in the mirror is not the face itself, but only a reflection of the same, as Saint James so beautifully writes, saying, "But be ye doers of the Word, and not hearers only, deluding your own selves. For if anyone is a hearer of the Word and not a doer, he is like unto a man beholding his natural face in a mirror: for he beholdeth himself, and goeth away, and straightway forgetteth what manner of man he was," in James 1:22–25. So also there within themselves many behold a reflection of true faith when they hear and speak of the Word, but as soon as the hearing and speaking are done, they are concerned about other affairs and are not doing according to it, and thus they always forget about the fruit of faith, namely, Christian love, of which Paul also says, "For the kingdom of God is not in word, but in power," in 1 Corinthians 4:20.

The Fourth Sunday in Advent

⚜

The Witness and Confession of John the Baptist

And this is the witness of John, when the Jews sent unto him from Jerusalem priests and Levites to ask him, "Who art thou?" And he confessed, and denied not; and he confessed, "I am not the Christ." And they asked him, "What then? Art thou Elijah?" And he saith, "I am not." "Art thou the prophet?" And he answered, "No." They said therefore unto him, "Who art thou? that we may give an answer to them that sent us. What sayest thou of thyself?" He said, "I am the voice of one crying in the wilderness, 'Make straight the way of the Lord,' as said Isaiah the prophet." And they had been sent from the Pharisees. And they asked him, and said unto him, "Why then baptizest thou, if thou art not the Christ, neither Elijah, neither the prophet?" John answered them, saying, "I baptize with water: in the midst of you standeth one whom ye know not, even he that cometh after me, the latchet of whose shoe I am not worthy to unloose." These things were done in Bethany beyond the Jordan, where John was baptizing. — JOHN 1:19–28

I. THE WITNESS AND CONFESSION OF JOHN THE BAPTIST

1. With many words the evangelist describes and magnifies the testimony of John. Although it would have been sufficient if he had written of him, "He confessed," he repeats it and says, "He confessed and denied not." This was surely done in order to extol the beautiful constancy of John in a sore trial, when he was tempted to a flagrant denial of the truth. And now consider the particular circumstances.

2. First, there are sent to him not servants or ordinary citizens, but priests and Levites from the highest and noblest class, who were Pharisees, that is to say, the leaders of the people. Surely a distinguished embassy for a common man, who might justly have felt proud of such an honor, for the favor of lords and princes is highly esteemed in this world.

3. Secondly, they sent to him not common people, but citizens of Jerusalem, to wit, the capital, the Sanhedrin, and the leaders of the Jewish nation. So it was as if the entire people came and did honor to him. What a wind that was! and how he might have been inflated had he possessed a vain and worldly heart!

4. Thirdly, they do not offer him a present, nor ordinary glory, but the highest glory of all, the kingdom and all authority, being ready to accept him as the Christ. Surely a mighty and sweet temptation! For, had he not perceived that they wished to regard him as the Christ, he would not have said, "I am not the Christ." And Luke, in Luke 3:15–16, also writes that, when everybody thought he was the Christ, John spoke, "I am not he who you think I am, but I am being sent before him."

5. Fourthly, when he would not accept this honor, they tried him with another and were ready to take him for Elijah. For they had a prophecy in the last chapter of the prophet Malachi, where God says, "Behold, I will send you Elijah the prophet, before the coming of the great and dreadful day of the Lord; and he shall turn the heart of the fathers to the children, and the heart of the children to the fathers, lest I come and smite the earth with a curse."

6. Fifthly, seeing that he would not be Elijah, they go on tempting him and offer him the homage due to an ordinary prophet, for since Malachi they had not had a prophet. John, however, remains firm and unshaken, although tried by the offer of so much honor.

7. Sixthly and lastly, not knowing of any more honors, they left him to choose as to who or what he wished to be regarded, for they greatly desired to do him homage. But John will have none of this honor and gives only this for an answer, that he is a voice calling to them and to everybody. This they do not heed. What all this means, we shall hear later on. Let us now examine the text.

And this is the witness of John, when the Jews sent unto him from Jerusalem priests and Levites to ask him, "Who art thou?"

8. They sent to him, why did they not come themselves? John had come to preach repentance to the entire Jewish people. This preaching of John they did not heed; it is clear, therefore, that they did not send to him with good and pure intentions, offering him such honor. Neither did they truly believe him to be the Christ, or Elijah, or a prophet; otherwise, they would have come themselves to be baptized, as did the others. What then did they seek of him? Christ explains this, in John 5:33–35, "Ye have sent unto John, and he hath borne witness unto the truth. He was the lamp that burneth and shineth, and ye were willing to rejoice for a season in his light." From these words it is clear

they looked for their own honor in John, desiring to make use of his light, his illustrious and famous name, in order to adorn themselves before the people. For if John had joined them and accepted their proffered honor, they also would have become great and glorious before all the people, as being worthy of the friendship and reverence of so holy and great a man. But would not hereby all their avarice, tyranny, and rascality have been confirmed and declared holy and worthy? Thus John, with all his holiness, would have become a sponsor for vice; and the coming of Christ would justly have been regarded with suspicion, as being opposed to the doings of the priests and tyrants, with whom John, this great and holy man, would have taken sides.

9. Thus we see what rascality they practice and how they tempt John to betray Christ and become a Judas Iscariot, in order that he might confirm their injustice and they might share his honor and popularity. What cunning fellows they are, thus to fish for John's honor! They offer him an apple for a kingdom, and would exchange counters for dollars. But he remained firm as a rock, as is shown by the statement:

And he confessed, and denied not; and he confessed, "I am not the Christ."

10. John's confession comprises two things: first, his confessing, and secondly, his not denying. His confessing is his declaration about Christ, when he says, "I am not the Christ." To this belongs also that he confesses to be neither Elijah nor a prophet. His not denying is declaration of what he really is, when he calls himself a voice in the wilderness, preparing the way of the Lord. Thus his confession is free and open, declaring not only what he is but also what he is not. For if someone declares what he is not, such a confession is still obscure and incomplete, since one cannot know what is really to be thought of him. But here John openly says what is to be thought of him, and what not, this giving the people a certain assurance in confessing that he is not the Christ, and not denying that he is the voice preparing his advent.

11. Yet someone might say, the evangelist contradicts himself in calling it a confession when John declares himself not to be Christ, whereas this is rather a denial, for he denies that he is Christ. To say, "Nay" is to deny, and the Jews wish him to confess that he is Christ, which he denies; yet the evangelist says that he confessed. And again, it is rather a confession when he says, "I am the voice in the wilderness." But the evangelist considers this matter and describes it as it is before God and not as the words sound and appear to men. For the Jews desired him to deny Christ and not to confess what he really was. But since he confesses what he is and firmly insists upon what he is not, his act is before God a precious confession and not a denial.

And they asked him, "What then? Art thou Elijah?"
and he saith, "I am not."

12. The Jews, as said above, had the prophecy concerning Elijah, that he was to come before the day of the Lord, in Malachi 4:5. It is therefore also among Christians a current belief that Elijah is to come before the last day. Some add Enoch, others Saint John the Evangelist. Of this we shall have something to say.

13. In the first place, all depends upon whether the prophet Malachi speaks of the second coming of the Lord on the last day, or of his first coming into flesh and through the Gospel. If he speaks of the last day, then we have certainly yet to expect Elijah; for God cannot lie. The coming of Enoch and Saint John, however, has no foundation in Scripture, and is therefore to be considered as a fable. If, on the other hand, the prophet speaks of Christ's coming in the flesh and through the Word, then assuredly Elijah is no more to be expected, but John is that same Elijah announced by Malachi.

14. I am of the opinion that Malachi spoke of no other Elijah than John, and that Elijah the Tishbite, who went up to heaven with the chariot of fire, is no more to be expected. To this opinion I am forced first and foremost by the words of the angel Gabriel, in Luke 1:17, who says to John's father, Zacharias, "And he shall go before his face in the spirit and power of Elijah, to turn the hearts of the fathers to the children, and the disobedient to walk in the wisdom of the just." With these words the angel manifestly refers to the prophecy of Malachi, adducing even the words of the prophet, who also says that Elijah is to turn the hearts of fathers to children, as cited above. Now then, if Malachi had meant another Elijah, the angel doubtless would not have applied these words to John.

15. In the second place, the Jews themselves of old understood Malachi to speak of Christ's coming into the flesh. Therefore, they here ask John whether he is Elijah, who is to come before the Christ. But they erred in thinking of the original and bodily Elijah. For the purport of the text is indeed that Elijah is to come beforehand, but not that same Elijah. We do not read, Elijah the Tishbite is to come, as the Bible calls him in 1 Kings 17:1 and 2 Kings 1:3–8, but merely Elijah, a prophet. This Gabriel, in Luke 1:17, explains as meaning, "In the spirit and power of Elijah," saying, as it were, He will be a real Elijah. Just as we now say of one who has another's manner and carriage, He is a true X.; as I may say, e.g., the pope is a real Caiaphas; John was a real Saint Paul. In the same manner does God through Malachi promise one who is to be a true Elijah, i.e., John the Baptist.

16. Yet would I not trust the interpretation of the Jews alone, were it not confirmed by Christ, in Matthew 10:10ff. When, on Mount Tabor, the disciples saw Elijah and Moses, they said to the Lord, "Why then say the scribes that Elijah must first come?" They meant to say, "You have already come; yet Elijah has not come first, but only now, after you: and was it not said that he was to come before you?" This interpretation was not rejected but confirmed by Christ, who said, "Elijah truly shall first come, and restore all things. But I say unto you that Elijah is come already; and they knew him not, but have done unto him whatsoever they listed." Then the disciples understood, says Saint Matthew, that he spoke of John the Baptist. Saint Mark likewise says, in Mark 9:13, "But I say unto you that Elijah is come, and they have done unto him whatsoever they would, even as it is written of him."

17. Now there is no other prophecy concerning Elijah's coming but this one of Malachi, and Christ himself applies it to John. Thus it has no force if someone were to object. Christ says that Elijah is to come first and restore all things, for Christ interprets his own words by saying, "But I tell you that Elijah is come," etc. He means to say, It is right and true what you have heard about Elijah, that he is to come first and restore all things; thus it is written and thus it must come to pass. But they do not know of which Elijah this is said, for he is come already. With these words, therefore, Christ confirms the Scriptures and the interpretation concerning the coming Elijah, but he rejects the false interpretation concerning an Elijah other than John.

18. Most strongly, however, does Christ assert, in Matthew 11:13ff., that no other Elijah is coming. He says, "All the prophets and the law prophesied until John. And if you will receive it, this is Elijah that is to come. He that hath ears to hear, let him hear." Here it is made clear that but one Elijah was to come. Had there been another, he would not have said, "John is Elijah who was to come," but he would have had to say, "John is one of the Elijahs," or simply, "He is Elijah." But by calling John that Elijah whom everybody expects, who, doubtless, was announced to come, he makes it sufficiently clear that the prophecy of Malachi is fulfilled in John, and that after this no other Elijah is to be expected.

19. We insist, therefore, that the Gospel, through which Christ has come into all the world, is the last message before the day of judgment; before this message and advent of Christ John came and prepared the way. And although all the prophets and the law prophesy until John, it is not allowed to apply them, neglecting John, to another Elijah who is yet to come. Thus also the prophecy of Malachi must fit the times of John. He carries the line of the prophets down to John's times and permits no one to pass by. And so

we conclude with certainty that no other Elijah is to come, and that the Gospel will endure unto the end of the world.

"Art thou the prophet?" And he answered, "No."

20. Some think the Jews here asked concerning that prophet of whom Moses writes in Deuteronomy 18:15, "The Lord thy God will raise up unto thee a prophet from the midst of thee, of thy brethren, like unto me, etc." But this passage Saint Peter in Acts 3:22, and Saint Stephen in Acts 7:37, apply to Christ himself, which is the correct interpretation. The Jews also certainly held this prophet in equal esteem with Moses, above Elijah and, therefore, understood him to be Christ. They asked John whether he was an ordinary prophet, like the others, since he was neither Christ nor Elijah. For they had had no prophet since the days of Malachi, who was the last and concluded the Old Testament with the above-mentioned prophecy concerning the coming of Elijah. John, therefore, is the nearest to and first after Malachi, who, in finishing his book, points to him. The Jews then asked whether he was one of the prophets. Christ likewise says of him, in Matthew 11:9, "Wherefore went ye out? to see a prophet? Yea, I say unto you, and much more than a prophet." And Matthew says, in Matthew 21:26, "All hold John as a prophet."

21. Now the question arises, Did John really confess the truth when he denied that he was Elijah or a prophet, whereas Christ himself called him Elijah and more than a prophet? He himself knew that he had come in the spirit and power of Elijah, and that the Scriptures called him Elijah. To say, therefore, that he did not consider himself a prophet because he was more than a prophet, is disgraceful and makes him an empty boaster. The truth of the matter is, that he simply and in a straightforward manner confessed the truth, namely, that he was not that Elijah about whom they asked, nor a prophet. For the prophets commonly led and taught the people, who sought advice and help from them. Such a one John was not and would not be, for the Lord was present, whom they were to follow and adhere to. He did not desire to draw the people to himself, but to lead them to Christ, which was needful before Christ himself came. A prophet foretells the coming of Christ. John, however, shows him present, which is not a prophet's task. Just so a priest in the bishop's presence would direct the people away from himself to the bishop, saying, "I am not priest; yonder is your priest"; but in the bishop's absence, he would rule the people in the place of the bishop.

22. John likewise directs the people away from himself to Christ. And although this is a higher and greater office than that of a prophet, yet it is not so on account of his merit but on account of the presence of his Master. And in

praising John for being more than a prophet, not his worthiness but that of his Master, who is present, is extolled. For it is customary for a servant to receive greater honor and reverence in the absence of his master than in his presence.

23. Even so the rank of a prophet is higher than that of John, although his office is greater and more immediate. For a prophet rules and leads the people, and they adhere to him; but John does no more than direct them away from himself to Christ, the present Master. Therefore, in the simplest and most straightforward manner, he denied being a prophet, although abounding in all the qualities of a prophet. This he did for the sake of the people, in order that they might not accept his testimony as the foretelling of a prophet and expect Christ in other, future times, but that they might recognize him as a forerunner and guide, and follow his guidance to the Lord, who was present. Witness the following words of the text:

> They said therefore unto him, "Who art thou? that we may give
> an answer to them that sent us. What sayest thou of thyself?" He said,
> "I am the voice of one crying in the wilderness, Make straight
> the way of the Lord, as said Isaiah the prophet."

24. This is the second part of his confession, in which he declares what he is, after having denied that he was Christ, or Elijah, or a prophet. As though he were to say, Your salvation is much too near for a prophet to be required. Do not strain your eyes so far out into the future, for the Lord of all the prophets is himself here, so that no prophet is needed. The Lord is coming this way, whose forerunner I am; he is treading on my heels. I am not prophesying of him as a seer, but crying as a courier, to make room for him as he walks along. I do not say, as the prophets, "Behold, he is to come"; but I say, "Behold, he is coming, he is here. I am not bringing word about him, but pointing to him with my finger. Did not Isaiah long ago foretell that such a crying to make room for the Lord should go before him? Such I am, and not a prophet. Therefore, step aside and make room, permit the Lord himself to walk among you bodily, and do not look for any more prophecies about him."

25. Now this is the answer which no learned, wise, and holy men can bear; therefore, John must surely be a heretic and be possessed of the devil. Only sinners and fools think him a holy, pious man, listen to his crying, and make room for the Lord, removing whatsoever obstructs his way. The others, however, throw logs, stones, and dirt in his way, aye, they even kill both the Lord and his forerunner for presuming to say such things to him. And why? John tells them to prepare the way of the Lord. That is to say, they have not the Lord nor his way in them. What have they then? Where the Lord is not, nor

his way, there must be man's own way, the devil, and all that is evil. Judge then, whether those holy wise people are not justly incensed at John, condemn his word, and finally slay both him and his Master! Shall he presume to hand such holy people over to the devil, and denounce all their doings as false, wicked, and damnable, claiming that their ways are not the Lord's ways, that they must first of all prepare the Lord's ways, and that they have lived all their holy lives in vain?

26. Yet, if he quietly wrote it on a tablet, they might still hear it in patience. But he gives utterance to it, yea, he cries it aloud, and that not in a corner, but openly under the sky, in the wilderness, before all the world, utterly disgracing before everybody those saints with all their doings and discrediting them with all the people. Thus they lose all honor and profit which their holy life formerly brought them. This certainly such pious men cannot bear, but for God's and justice's sake they cannot damn that false doctrine, in order that the poor people may not be misled and the service of God be not corrupted; aye, finally, they will have to kill John and his Master, to serve and obey God the Father.

27. This, then, is the preparation of Christ's way and John's proper office. He is to humble all the world, and proclaim that they are all sinners—lost, damned, poor, miserable, pitiable people; that there is no life, work, or rank, however holy, beautiful, and good it may appear, but is damnable unless Christ our God dwell therein, unless he work, walk, live, be, and do everything through faith in him; in short, that they all need Christ and should anxiously strive to share his grace.

Behold, where this is practiced, namely, that all man's work and life is as nothing, there you have the true crying of John in the wilderness and the pure and clear truth of Christianity, as Saint Paul shows, in Romans 3:23, "All have sinned, and fall short of the glory of God." This is truly to humiliate man, to cut out and annihilate his presumption. Aye, this is indeed to prepare the way of the Lord, to give room and to make way.

28. Now here are found two kinds of people: some believe the crying of John and confess it to be what he says. These are the people to whom the Lord comes, in them his way is prepared and made even, as Saint Peter says, in 1 Peter 5:5, "God giveth grace to the humble"; and the Lord himself says, in Luke 18:14, "He that humbleth himself shall be exalted." You must here diligently learn, and understand spiritually, what the way of the Lord is, how it is prepared, and what prevents him from finding room in us. The way of the Lord, as you have heard, is that he does all things within you, so that all our works are not ours but his, which comes by faith.

29. This, however, is not possible if you desire worthily to prepare yourself by praying, fasting, self-mortification, and your own works, as is now generally and foolishly taught during the time of Advent. A spiritual preparation is meant, consisting in a thoroughgoing knowledge and confession of your being unfit, a sinner, poor, damned, and miserable, with all the works you may perform. The more a heart is thus minded, the better it prepares the way of the Lord, although meanwhile possibly drinking fine wines, walking on roses, and not praying a word.

30. The hindrance, however, which obstructs the Lord's way, is formed not only in the coarse and palpable sin of adultery, wrath, haughtiness, avarice, etc., but rather in spiritual conceit and Pharisaical pride, which thinks highly of its own life and good works, feels secure, does not condemn itself, and would remain uncondemned by another.

Such, then, is the other class of men, namely, those that do not believe the crying of John, but call it the devil's, since it forbids good works and condemns the service of God, as they say. These are the people to whom most of all and most urgently it is said, "Prepare the way of the Lord," and who least of all accept it.

31. Therefore John speaks to them with cutting words in Luke 3:7–8, "Ye offspring of vipers, who warned you to flee from the wrath to come? Bring forth therefore fruits worthy of repentance." But, as said above, the more just people are urged to prepare the Lord's way, the more they obstruct it and the more unreasonable they become. They will not be told that their doings are not the Lord's, and finally, to the glory and honor of God, they annihilate the truth and the word of John, himself and his Master to boot.

32. Judge, then, whether it was not a mighty confession on the part of John, when he dared to open his mouth and proclaim that he was not Christ, but a voice to which they did not like to listen, chiding the great teachers and leaders of the people for not doing that which was right and the Lord's pleasure. And as it went with John, so it still goes, from the beginning of the world unto the end. For such conceited piety will not be told that it must first and foremost prepare the way of the Lord, imagining itself to sit in God's lap and desiring to be petted and flattered by having long ago finished the way, before God even thought of finding a way for them—those precious saints! The pope and his followers likewise have condemned the crying of John to prepare the Lord's way. Aye, it is an intolerable crying—except to poor, penitent sinners with aggrieved consciences, for whom it is the best of cordials.

33. But isn't it a perverse and strange manner of speaking to say, "I am the voice of one crying"? How can a man be a voice? He ought to have said, I am

one crying with a voice! But that it speaking according to the manner of the Scriptures. In Exodus 4:16, God spoke to Moses, "Aaron shall be to thee a mouth." And in Job 29:15, we read, "I was eyes to the blind, and feet was I to the lame." Similarly, we say of a man that gold is his heart and money his life.

So here, "I am the voice of one crying" means, I am one who cries, and have received my name from my office; even as Aaron is called a mouth because of his speaking, I am a voice because of my crying. And that which in Hebrew reads *vox clamantis*, the voice of one crying, would be translated into Latin *vox clamans*, a crying voice. Thus Saint Paul in Romans 15:26, says *pauperes sanctorum*, the poor of the saints, instead of *pauperes sancti*, the poor saints; and in 1 Timothy 3:16, *mysterium pietatis* (the mystery of godliness) instead of *mysterium pium* (the godly mystery). Instead of saying, The language of the Germans, I had better say, the German language. Thus "a voice of one crying" means "a crying voice." In Hebrew, there are many similar phrases.

> *And they had been sent from the Pharisees. And they asked him,*
> *and said unto him: "Why then baptizest thou if thou be not the Christ,*
> *nor Elijah, neither the prophet?" John answered them, saying, "I baptize*
> *with water; in the midst of you standeth one whom ye know not,*
> *even he that cometh after me is preferred before me,*
> *the latchet of whose shoes I am not worthy to unloose."*

34. It seems as though the evangelist had omitted something in these words, and as if John's complete answer ought to be, "I baptize with water; but he has come among you who baptizes with fire." Thus Luke, in Luke 3:16, says, "I baptize you with water: but he shall baptize you with fire." And, in Acts 1:5, we read, "John baptized with water, but ye shall be baptized with the Holy Ghost." But although he here says nothing of this other baptism, he sufficiently indicates that there is to be another baptism, since he speaks of another who is coming after him and who, undoubtedly, will not baptize with water.

35. Now begins the second onset, whereby John was tried on the other side. For not being able to move him by allurements, they attack him with threats. And here is uncovered their false humility, manifesting itself as pride and haughtiness. The same they would have done had John followed them, after they had had enough of him. Learn, therefore, here to be on your guard against men, particularly when they feign to be gentle and kind; as Christ says, in Matthew 10:16–17, "Beware of men, be wise as serpents, and harmless as doves." That is to say, Do not trust those that are smooth, and do no evil to your enemies.

36. Behold, these Pharisees, who professed their willingness to accept John as the Christ, veer around when things turn out as they desired, and censure John's baptism. They say, as it were, "Since you are not Christ, nor Elijah, nor a prophet, you are to know that we are your superiors according to the law of Moses, and you are, therefore, to conduct yourself as our subordinate. You are not to act independently, without our command, our knowledge, and without our permission. Who has given you power to introduce something new among our people with your baptizing? You are bringing yourself into trouble with your criminal disobedience."

37. John, however, as he had despised their hypocrisy, likewise scorns their threats, remains firm, and confesses Christ as before. Moreover, he boldly attacks them and charges them with ignorance, saying, as it were, "I have no authority from you to baptize with water. But what of that? There is another from whom I have power; him you do not know, but he is amply sufficient for me. If you knew him, or wished to know him, you would not ask whence I have power to baptize, but you would come to be baptized yourselves. For he is so much greater than I, that I am not worthy to unloose his shoes' latchet.

38. John's words, "He it is who, coming after me, is preferred before me," three times quoted by the evangelist in this chapter, have been misinterpreted and obscured by some who referred them to Christ's divine and eternal birth, as though John meant to say that Christ had been born before him in eternity. But what is remarkable is the fact that he was born before John in eternity, seeing that he was born before the world and all other things. Thus he was also to come not only after him, but after all things, since he is the first and the last, in Revelation 1:11. Therefore, his past and his future agree. John's words are clear and simple, referring to Christ when he already was a man. The words "He will come after me" cannot be taken to mean that he would be born after him; John, like Christ, was at that time about thirty years old.

39. These words then evidently apply to his preaching. He means to say, "I have come, that is, I have begun to preach, but I shall soon stop and another will come and preach after me." Thus Saint Luke says, in Acts 1:22, that Christ began from the baptism of John; and, in Luke 3:23, that Jesus was thirty years old when he began. And it says in Matthew 11:3, "Art thou he that should come," that is, he who should begin to preach; for Christ's office does not begin until after his baptism, at which his Father had acknowledged and glorified him. Then also began the New Testament and the time of grace, not at the birth of Christ, as he himself says, in Mark 1:15, "The time is fulfilled, and the kingdom of God is at hand." Had he not begun to preach, his birth would have been of no use; but when he did begin to act and to teach, then

were fulfilled all prophecies, all Scriptures; then came a new light and a new world.

40. So we see what he means by saying, "He will come after me." But the meaning of the words "He is preferred before me; he was before me" is not yet clear, some referring them to Christ's eternal birth. We maintain in all simplicity that those words also were spoken concerning their preaching. Thus the meaning is, "Although he is not yet preaching, but is coming after me, and I am preaching before him, nevertheless he is already at hand and so close by that, before I began to preach, he has already been there and has been appointed to preach. The words "before me," therefore, point to John's office and not to his person. Thus, "he has been before my preaching and baptism for about thirty years; but he has not yet come, and has not yet begun." John thereby indicates his office, namely, that he is not a prophet foretelling the coming of Christ, but one who precedes him who is already present, who is so near that he has already been in existence so many years before his beginning and coming.

41. Therefore, he also says, "In the midst of you standeth one whom ye know not." He means to say, "Do not permit your eyes to wander off into future ages. He of whom the prophets speak has been among you in the Jewish nation for well nigh thirty years. Take care and do not miss him. You do not know him, therefore, I have come to point him out to you." The words "In the midst of you standeth one" are spoken after the manner of the Scriptures, which say, A prophet will arise or stand up. Thus in Matthew 24:24, "There shall arise false prophets." In Deuteronomy 18:15, God says, "The Lord thy God will raise up unto thee a prophet." John now wishes to show that this "raising up, arising, standing," etc., was fulfilled in Christ, who was already standing among them, as God had prophesied; the people, however, knew him not.

42. This then is the other office of John and of every preacher of the Gospel, not alone to make all the world sinners, as we have heard above (§24ff.); but also to give comfort and show how we may get rid of our sins; this he does in pointing to him who is to come. Hereby he directs us to Christ, who is to redeem us from our sins, if we accept him in true faith. The first office says, "You are all sinners, and are wanting in the way of the Lord." When we believe this, the other office follows and says, "Listen, and accept Christ, believe in him; he will free you of your sins." If we believe this, we have it. Of this we shall say more anon.

*These things were done in Bethany beyond the Jordan,
where John was baptizing.*

43. So diligently does the evangelist record the testimony of John, that he also mentions the places where it happened. The confession of Christ is greatly dependent on testimony, and there are many difficulties in the way. Undoubtedly, however, he wished to allude to some spiritual mystery of which we shall now speak.

II. THE SPIRITUAL MEANING OF THIS GOSPEL STORY

44. This is the sum and substance of it: In this Gospel is pictured the preacher's office of the New Testament—what it is, what it does, and what happens to it.

45. First, it is the voice of one calling, not a piece of writing. The law and the Old Testament are dead writings, put into books, and the Gospel is to be a living voice. Therefore, John is an image, and a type, and also a pioneer, the first of all preachers of the Gospel. He writes nothing but calls out everything with his living voice.

46. Secondly, the Old Testament or the law was preached among the tents at Mount Sinai to the Jews alone. But John's voice is heard in the wilderness, freely and openly, under the heavens, before all the world.

47. Thirdly, it is a calling, clear and loud voice, that is to say, one that speaks boldly and undauntedly and fears no one, neither death, hell, life, nor the world, neither devil, man, honor, disgrace, nor any creature. Thus Isaiah says, in Isaiah 40:6ff., "The voice of one saying, cry. And one said, What shall I cry? All flesh is grass, and all the goodliness thereof is as the flower of the field. The grass withereth, the flower fadeth, but the Word of our God shall stand forever." And further, "O thou that tellest good tidings to Zion, get thee up on a high mountain; lift up thy voice with strength; lift it up, be not afraid." The world cannot bear the Gospel, and hence there must be a strength, which scorns it and can call against it without fear.

48. Fourthly, John's raiment is of camel's hair and has a leather girdle, in Matthew 3:4. This means the strict and chaste life of preachers, but above all it points to the manner of the preachers of the Gospel. It is a voice not given to soft phrases, neither does it deal in hypocrisy and flattery. It is a sermon of the cross, a hard, rough, sharp speech for the natural man, and girds the loins for spiritual and bodily chastity. This is taken from the life and words of the patriarchs of old, who like camels have borne the burden of the law and of the cross. "He eats locusts and wild honey." This means those that accept the Gospel, namely, the humble sinners, who take the Gospel unto and into themselves.

49. Fifthly, John is on the other side of the Jordan. "Jordan" really means the holy Scriptures, which have two sides. One, the left side, is the external

meaning which the Jews sought in Holy Writ; here John is not. For this interpretation does not produce sinners, but saints proud of their works. The right
side is the true spiritual understanding, which discards and kills all works, in
order that faith alone may remain, in all humility. This meaning is brought out
in the Gospels, as Saint Paul does, in Romans 3:23, saying, "All have sinned."

50. Sixthly, here begins the dispute between true and false preachers. The
Pharisees cannot bear to hear John's voice; they despise his teaching and baptism, and remain obdurate in their doings and teachings. On account of the
people, however, they pretend to think highly of him. But because he opposes
their will, he must be possessed of the devil, they say, and finally he must be
beheaded by Herod. So it is now and so it has always been. No false teacher
wishes it to be said of him that he preaches without or against the Gospel, but
on the contrary that he thinks highly of it and believes in it. Nevertheless he
does violence to it, making it conform to his meaning. This the Gospel cannot
permit, for it stands firm and never lies. Then it is reviled as heresy and error,
aye as a devilish doctrine, and finally they apply violence prohibiting it and
striking off its head so that it may nowhere be preached or heard. This was
done by the pope in the case of John Huss.

51. Thus he is a truly Christian preacher who preaches nothing but that
which John proclaimed, and firmly insists upon it.

First, he must preach the law so that the people may learn what great
things God demands of us; of these we cannot perform any because of the
impotence of our nature which has been corrupted by Adam's fall. Then
comes the baptism in Jordan. The cold water means the teaching of the law,
which does not kindle love but rather extinguishes it. For through the law man
learns how difficult and how impossible of fulfillment the law is. Then he
becomes hostile to it, and his love for it cools; he feels that he heartily hates it.
This of course is a grievous sin, to be hostile to God's commands. Therefore
man must humble himself, and confess that he is lost and that all his works are
sins, aye, that his whole life is sinful. Herewith then John's baptism has been
accomplished, and he has been not only besprinkled but properly baptized.
Then he sees why John says, "Repent ye." He understands that John is right,
and that everyone must needs become a better man and repent. But Pharisees
and those holy in their works do not arrive at this knowledge, nor do they permit themselves to be baptized. They imagine that they do not need repentance and, therefore, John's words and baptism are foolishness in their eyes.

52. Furthermore, when the first teaching, that of the law, and baptism are
over and man, humiliated by the knowledge of himself, is forced to despair of
himself and his powers, then begins the second part of John's teaching, in

which he directs the people from himself to Christ and says, "Behold the Lamb of God that takes upon itself the sin of the world." By this he means to say, "First I have, by my teaching, made you all sinners, have condemned your works and told you to despair of yourselves. But in order that you may not also despair of God, behold, I will show you how to get rid of your sins and obtain salvation. Not that you can strip off your sins or make yourselves pious through your works; another man is needed for this; nor can I do it, I can point him out, however. It is Jesus Christ, the Lamb of God. He, he, and no one else either in heaven or on earth takes our sins upon himself. You yourself could not pay for the very smallest of sins. He alone must take upon himself not alone your sins, but the sins of the world, and not some sins, but all the sins of the world, be they great or small, many or few." This then is preaching and hearing the pure Gospel, and recognizing the finger of John, who points out to you Christ, the Lamb of God.

53. Now, if you are able to believe that this voice of John speaks the truth, and if you are able to follow his finger and recognize the Lamb of God carrying your sin, then you have gained the victory, then you are a Christian, a master of sin, death, hell, and all things. Then your conscience will rejoice and become heartily fond of this gentle Lamb of God. Then will you love, praise, and give thanks to our heavenly Father for this infinite wealth of his mercy, preached by John and given in Christ. And finally you will become cheerful and willing to do his divine will, as best you can, with all your strength. For what lovelier and more comforting message can be heard than that our sins are not ours any more, that they no more lie on us, but on the Lamb of God. How can sin condemn such an innocent Lamb? Lying on him, it must be vanquished and made to nothing, and likewise death and hell, being the reward of sin, must be vanquished also. Behold what God our Father has given us in Christ!

54. Take heed, therefore, take heed, I say, lest you presume to get rid of the smallest of your sins through your own merit before God, and lest you rob Christ, the Lamb of God, of his credit. John indeed demands that we grow better and repent; but that he does not mean us to grow better of ourselves and to strip off our sins by our own strength, this he declares powerfully by adding, "Behold the Lamb of God that taketh away the sin of the world." As we have said above (§29), he means that each one is to know himself and his need of becoming a better man; yet he is not to look for this in himself, but in Jesus Christ alone. Now may God our Father according to his infinite mercy bestow upon us this knowledge of Christ, and may he send into the world the voice of John, with great numbers of evangelists! Amen.

Christmas Day

～ॐ～

Of the Birth of Jesus, and of the Angels' Song of Praise at His Birth

Now it came to pass in those days, there went out a decree from Cæsar Augustus, that all the world should be enrolled. This was the first enrollment made when Quirinius was governor of Syria. And all went to enroll themselves, every one to his own city. And Joseph also went up from Galilee, out of the city of Nazareth, into Judea, to the city of David, which is called Bethlehem, because he was of the house and family of David; to enroll himself with Mary, who was betrothed to him, being great with child. And it came to pass, while they were there, the days were fulfilled that she should be delivered. And she brought forth her firstborn son; and she wrapped him in swaddling clothes, and laid him in a manger, because there was no room for them in the inn.

And there were shepherds in the same country abiding in the field, and keeping watch by night over their flock. And an angel of the Lord stood by them, and the glory of the Lord shone round about them; and they were sore afraid. And the angel said unto them, "Be not afraid; for behold, I bring you good tidings of great joy which shall be to all the people: for there is born to you this day in the city of David a Savior, who is Christ the Lord. And this is the sign unto you: Ye shall find a babe wrapped in swaddling clothes, and lying in a manger." And suddenly there was with the angel a multitude of the heavenly host praising God, and saying, "Glory to God in the highest, and on earth peace among men in whom he is well pleased." — LUKE 2:1–14

I. THE BIRTH OF JESUS

The Story of Jesus' Birth

1. It is written in Haggai 2:6–7, that God says, "I will shake the heavens; and the precious things of all nations shall come." This is fulfilled today, for

the heavens were shaken, that is, the angels in the heavens sang praises to God. And the earth was shaken, that is, the people on the earth were agitated; one journeying to this city, another to that throughout the whole land, as the Gospel tells us. It was not a violent, bloody uprising, but rather a peaceable one awakened by God, who is the God of peace.

It is not to be understood that all countries upon earth were so agitated, but only those under Roman rule, which did not comprise half of the whole earth. However, no land was agitated as was the land of Judea, which had been divided among the tribes of Israel, although at this time the land was inhabited mostly by the race of Judah, as the ten tribes led captive into Assyria never returned.

2. This taxing, enrollment, or census, says Luke, was the first; but in the Gospel according to Matthew, in Matthew 17:24, and at other places, we read that it was continued from time to time, that they even demanded tribute of Christ, and tempted him with the tribute money, in Matthew 22:17. On the day of his suffering, they also testified against him, that he forbade to give tribute to Cæsar. The Jews did not like to pay tribute and unwillingly submitted to the taxing, maintaining that they were God's people and free from Cæsar. They had great disputes as to whether they were obliged to pay the tribute, but they could not help themselves and were compelled to submit. For this reason, they would have been pleased to draw Jesus into the discussion and bring him under the Roman jurisdiction. This taxing was, therefore, nothing else but a common decree throughout the whole empire that every individual should annually pay a penny, and the officers who collected the tribute were called publicans, who in German are improperly interpreted notorious sinners.

3. Observe how exact the evangelist is in his statement that the birth of Christ occurred in the time of Cæsar Augustus, and when Quirinius was governor of Syria, of which the land of Judea was a part, just as Austria is a part of the German land. This being the very first taxing, it appears that this tribute was never before paid until just at the time when Christ was to be born. By this, Jesus shows that his kingdom was not to be of an earthly character nor to exercise worldly power and lordship, but that he, together with his parents, is subject to the powers that be. Since he comes at the time of the very first enrollment, he leaves no doubt with respect to this, for had he desired to leave it in doubt, he might have willed to be born under another enrollment, so that it might have been said it just happened so, without any divine intent.

4. And had he not willed to be submissive, he might have been born before there was any enrollment decreed. Since now all the works of Jesus are precious teachings, this circumstance cannot be interpreted otherwise than

that he by divine counsel and purpose will not exercise any worldly authority, but will be subject to it. This then is the first rebuke to the pope's government, and everything of that character, that harmonizes with the kingdom of Christ as night does with day.

5. This Gospel is so clear that it requires very little explanation, but it should be well considered and taken deeply to heart; and no one will receive more benefit from it than those who, with a calm, quiet heart, banish everything else from their mind and diligently look into it. It is just as the sun which is reflected in calm water and gives out vigorous warmth but which cannot be so readily seen nor can it give out such warmth in water that is in roaring and rapid motion.

Therefore, if you would be enlightened and warmed, if you would see the wonders of divine grace and have your heart aglow and enlightened, devout and joyful, go where you can silently meditate and lay hold of this picture deep in your heart, and you will see miracle upon miracle. But to give the common person a start and a motive to contemplate it, we will illustrate it in part and afterward enter into it more deeply.

6. First, behold how very ordinary and common things are to us that transpire on earth, and yet how high they are regarded in heaven. On earth it occurs in this wise: Here is a poor young woman, Mary of Nazareth, not highly esteemed, but of the humblest citizens of the village. No one is conscious of the great wonder she bears; she is silent, keeps her own counsel, and regards herself as the lowliest in the town. She starts out with her husband, Joseph; very likely, they had no servant, and he had to do the work of master and servant, and she that of mistress and maid. They were, therefore, obliged to leave their home unoccupied, or commend it to the care of others.

7. Now they evidently owned an ass, upon which Mary rode, although the Gospel does not mention it, and it is possible that she went on foot with Joseph. Imagine how she was despised at the inns and stopping places on the way, although worthy to ride in state in a chariot of gold.

There were, no doubt, many wives and daughters of prominent men at that time, who lived in fine apartments and great splendor, while the mother of God takes a journey in mid-winter under most trying circumstances. What distinctions there are in the world! It was more than a day's journey from Nazareth in Galilee to Bethlehem in the land of Judea. They had to journey either by or through Jerusalem, for Bethlehem is south of Jerusalem, while Nazareth is north.

8. The evangelist shows how, when they arrived at Bethlehem, they were the most insignificant and despised, so that they had to make way for others

until they were obliged to take refuge in a stable, to share with the cattle, lodging, table, bedchamber and bed, while many a wicked man sat at the head in the hotels and was honored as lord. No one noticed or was conscious of what God was doing in that stable. He lets the large houses and costly apartments remain empty, lets their inhabitants eat, drink, and be merry; but this comfort and treasure are hidden from them. O what a dark night this was for Bethlehem, that was not conscious of that glorious light! See how God shows that he utterly disregards what the world is, has, or desires; and furthermore, that the world shows how little it knows or notices what God is, has, and does.

9. See, this is the first picture with which Christ puts the world to shame and exposes all it does and knows. It shows that the world's greatest wisdom is foolishness, her best actions are wrong, and her greatest treasures are misfortunes. What had Bethlehem when it did not have Christ? What have they now who at that time had enough? What do Joseph and Mary lack now, although at that time they had no room to sleep comfortably?

10. Some have commented on the word *"diversorium,"* as if it meant an open archway, through which everybody could pass, where some asses stood, and that Mary could not get to a lodging place. This is not right. The evangelist desires to show that Joseph and Mary had to occupy a stable because there was no room for her in the inn, in the place where the pilgrim guests generally lodged. All the guests were cared for in the inn or caravansary, with room, food, and bed, except these poor people who had to creep into a stable where it was customary to house cattle.

This word *diversorium*, which by Luke is called *"katalyma,"* means nothing else than a place for guests, which is proved by the words of Christ, in Luke 22:11, where he sent the disciples to prepare the supper, "Go and say unto the master of the house, the Teacher saith unto thee, Where is the guest chamber, where I shall eat the Passover with my disciples?" So also here Joseph and Mary had no room in the *katalyma*, the inn, but only in the stable belonging to the innkeeper, who would not have been worthy to give shelter to such a guest. They had neither money nor influence to secure a room in the inn, hence they were obliged to lodge in a stable. O world, how stupid! O man, how blind thou art!

11. But the birth itself is still more pitiful. There was no one to take pity on this young wife who was for the first time to give birth to a child; no one to take to heart her condition that she, a stranger, did not have the least thing a mother needs in a birth night. There she is without any preparation, without either light or fire, alone in the darkness, without anyone's offering her service

as is customary for women to do at such times. Everything is in commotion in the inn, there is a swarming of guests from all parts of the country, no one thinks of this poor woman. It is also possible that she did not expect the event so soon, else she would probably have remained at Nazareth.

12. Just imagine what kind of swaddling clothes they were in which she wrapped the child. Possibly her veil or some article of her clothing she could spare. But that she should have wrapped him in Joseph's trousers, which are exhibited at Aix-la-Chapelle, appears entirely too false and frivolous. It is a fable, the like of which there are more in the world. Is it not strange that the birth of Christ occurs in cold winter, in a strange land, and in such a poor and despicable manner?

13. Some argue as to how this birth took place, as if Jesus was born while Mary was praying and rejoicing, without any pain, and before she was conscious of it. While I do not altogether discard that pious supposition, it was evidently invented for the sake of simple-minded people. But we must abide by the Gospel, that he was born of the Virgin Mary. There is no deception here, for the Word clearly states that it was an actual birth.

14. It is well known what is meant by giving birth. Mary's experience was not different from that of other women, so that the birth of Christ was a real natural birth, Mary being his natural mother and he being her natural son. Therefore, her body performed its functions of giving birth, which naturally belonged to it, except that she brought forth without sin, without shame, without pain, and without injury, just as she had conceived without sin. The curse of Eve did not come on her, where God said, "In pain thou shalt bring forth children," in Genesis 3:16; otherwise, it was with her in every particular as with every woman who gives birth to a child.

15. Grace does not interfere with nature and her work, but rather improves and promotes it. Likewise Mary, without doubt, also nourished the child with milk from her breast and not with strange milk, or in a manner different from that which nature provided, as we sing: *ubere de coelo pleno*, from her breast being filled by heaven, without injury or impurity. I mention this that we may be grounded in the faith and know that Jesus was a natural man in every respect just as we, the only difference being in his relation to sin and grace, he being without a sinful nature. In him and in his mother nature was pure in all the members and in all the operations of those members. No body or member of woman ever performed its natural function without sin, except that of this virgin; here for once God bestowed special honor upon nature and its operations. It is a great comfort to us that Jesus took upon himself our nature and flesh. Therefore, we are not to take away from him or his mother

anything that is not in conflict with grace, for the text clearly says that she brought him forth, and the angels said, unto you he is born.

16. How could God have shown his goodness in a more sublime manner than by humbling himself to partake of flesh and blood, that he did not even disdain the natural privacy but honors nature most highly in that part where in Adam and Eve it was most miserably brought to shame? so that henceforth even that can be regarded godly, honest, and pure, which in all men is the most ungodly, shameful, and impure. These are real miracles of God, for in no way could he have given us stronger, more forcible, and purer pictures of chastity than in this birth. When we look at this birth, and reflect upon how the sublime Majesty moves with great earnestness and inexpressible love and goodness upon the flesh and blood of this virgin, we see how here all evil lust and every evil thought is banished.

17. No woman can inspire such pure thoughts in a man as this virgin; nor can any man inspire such pure thought in a woman as this child. If in reflecting on this birth we recognize the work of God that is embodied in it, only chastity and purity spring from it.

18. But what happens in heaven concerning this birth? As much as it is despised on earth, so much and a thousand times more is it honored in heaven. If an angel from heaven came and praised you and your work, would you not regard it of greater value than all the praise and honor the world could give you, and for which you would be willing to bear the greatest humility and reproach? What exalted honor is that when all the angels in heaven cannot restrain themselves from breaking out in rejoicing, so that even poor shepherds in the fields hear them preach, praise God, sing, and pour out their joy without measure? Were not all joy and honor realized at Bethlehem, yes, all joy and honor experienced by all the kings and nobles on earth, to be regarded as only dross and abomination, of which no one likes to think, when compared with the joy and glory here displayed?

19. Behold how very richly God honors those who are despised of men, and that very gladly. Here you see that his eyes look into the depths of humility, as is written, "He sitteth above the cherubim" and looketh into the depths. Nor could the angels find princes or valiant men to whom to communicate the good news; but only unlearned laymen, the most humble people upon earth. Could they not have addressed the high priests, who it was supposed knew so much concerning God and the angels? No, God chose poor shepherds, who, though they were of low esteem in the sight of men, were in heaven regarded as worthy of such great grace and honor.

20. See how utterly God overthrows that which is lofty! And yet we rage and rant for nothing but this empty honor, as we had no honor to seek in heaven; we continually step out of God's sight so that he may not see us in the depths into which he alone looks.

21. This has been considered sufficiently for plain people. Everyone should ponder it further for himself. If every word is properly grasped, it is as fire that sets the heart aglow, as God says in Jeremiah 23:29, "Is not my Word like fire?" And as we see, it is the purpose of the divine Word to teach us to know God and his work, and to see that this life is nothing. For as he does not live according to this life and does not have possessions nor temporal honor and power, he does not regard these and says nothing concerning them, but teaches only the contrary. He works in opposition to these temporal things, looks with favor upon that from which the world turns, teaches that from which it flees, and takes up that which it discards.

22. And although we are not willing to tolerate such acts of God and do not want to receive blessing, honor, and life in this way, yet it must remain so. God does not change his purpose, nor does he teach or act differently than he purposed. We must adapt ourselves to him; he will not adapt himself to us. Moreover, he who will not regard his word, nor the manner in which he works to bring comfort to men, has assuredly no good evidence of being saved. In what more lovely manner could he have shown his grace to the humble and despised of earth than through this birth in poverty, over which the angels rejoice, and make it known to no one but to the poor shepherds?

23. Let us now look at the mysteries set before us in this history. In all the mysteries here, two things are especially set forth, the Gospel and faith, that is, what is to be preached and what is to be believed, who are to be the preachers and who are to be the believers. This we will now consider.

II. THE BIRTH OF JESUS CONSIDERED IN ITS SPIRITUAL MEANING

A. The Teaching Concerning Faith

24. Faith is first, and it is right that we recognize it as the most important in every word of God. It is of no value only to believe that this history is true as it is written; for all sinners, even those condemned believe that. The Scripture, God's Word, does not teach concerning faith that it is a natural work, without grace. The right and gracious faith which God demands is that you firmly believe that Christ is born for you, and that this birth took place for

your welfare. The Gospel teaches that Christ was born, and that he did and suffered everything in our behalf, as is here declared by the angel, "Behold, I bring you good tidings of great joy which shall be to all the people; for there is born to you this day a Savior, who is Christ the Lord." In these words, you clearly see that he is born for us.

25. He does not simply say, Christ is born, but to you he is born; neither does he say, I bring glad tidings, but to you I bring glad tidings of great joy. Furthermore, this joy was not to remain in Christ, but it shall be to all the people. This faith no condemned or wicked man has, nor can he have it; for the right ground of salvation which unites Christ and the believing heart is that they have all things in common. But what have they?

26. Christ has a pure, innocent, and holy birth. Man has an unclean, sinful, condemned birth; as David says, in Psalm 51:5, "Behold I was brought forth in iniquity; and in sin did my mother conceive me." Nothing can help this unholy birth except the pure birth of Christ. But Christ's birth cannot be distributed in a material sense neither would that avail anything; it is, therefore, imparted spiritually, through the Word; as the angel says, it is given to all who firmly believe so that no harm will come to them because of their impure birth. This it the way and manner in which we are to be cleansed from the miserable birth we have from Adam. For this purpose, Christ willed to be born, that through him we might be born again, as he says, in John 3:3, that it takes place through faith; as also Saint James says in James 1:18: "Of his own will he brought us forth by the word of truth, that we should be a kind of first-fruits of his creatures."

27. We see here how Christ, as it were, takes our birth from us and absorbs it in his birth, and grants us his, that in it we might become pure and holy, as if it were our own, so that every Christian may rejoice and glory in Christ's birth as much as if he had himself been born of Mary as was Christ. Whoever does not believe this, or doubts, is no Christian.

28. O, this is the great joy of which the angel speaks. This is the comfort and exceeding goodness of God that, if a man believes this, he can boast of the treasure that Mary is his rightful mother, Christ his brother, and God his father. For these things actually occurred and are true, but we must believe. This is the principal thing and the principal treasure in every Gospel, before any doctrine of good works can be taken out of it. Christ must above all things become our own and we become his, before we can do good works.

But this cannot occur except through the faith that teaches us rightly to understand the Gospel and properly to lay hold of it. This is the only way in which Christ can be rightly known so that the conscience is satisfied and made to rejoice. Out of this grow love and praise to God, who in Christ has bestowed upon us such unspeakable gifts. This gives courage to do or leave undone, and living or dying, to suffer everything that is well pleasing to God. This is what is meant by Isaiah 9:6, "Unto us a child is born, unto us a son is given," to us, to us, to us is born, and to us is given this child.

29. Therefore, see to it that you do not find pleasure in the Gospel only as a history, for that is only transcient; neither regard it only as an example, for it is of no value without faith; but see to it that you make this birth your own and that Christ be born in you. This will be the case if you believe, then you will repose in the lap of the Virgin Mary and be her dear child. But you must exercise this faith and pray while you live; you cannot establish it too firmly. This is our foundation and inheritance, upon which good works must be built.

30. If Christ has now thus become your own, and you have by such faith been cleansed through him and have received your inheritance without any personal merit, but alone through the love of God who gives to you as your own the treasure and work of his Son, it follows that you will do good works by doing to your neighbor as Christ has done to you. Here good works are their own teacher. What are the good works of Christ? Is it not true that they are good because they have been done for your benefit, for God's sake, who commanded him to do the works in your behalf? In this then Christ was obedient to the Father, in that he loved and served us.

31. Therefore since you have received enough and become rich, you have no other commandment to serve Christ and render obedience to him, than so to direct your works that they may be of benefit to your neighbor, just as the works of Christ are of benefit and use to you. For the reason Jesus said at the Last Supper, "This is my commandment that ye love one another; even as I have loved you," in John 13:34. Here it is seen that he loved us and did everything for our benefit, in order that we may do the same, not to him, for he needs it not, but to our neighbor; this is his commandment, and this is our obedience. Therefore, it is through faith that Christ becomes our own, and his love is the cause that we are his. He loves, we believe, thus both are united into one. Again, our neighbor believes and expects our love; we are, therefore, to love him also in return and not let him long for it in vain. One is the same as the other; as Christ helps us so we in return help our neighbor, and all have enough.

32. Observe now from this how far those have gone out of the way who have united good works with stone, wood, clothing, eating, and drinking. Of what benefit is it to your neighbor if you build a church entirely out of gold? Of what benefit to him is the frequent ringing of great church bells? Of what benefit to him is the glitter and the ceremonies in the churches, the priests'

gowns, the sanctuary, the silver pictures and vessels? Of what benefit to him are the many candles and much incense? Of what benefit to him is the much chanting and mumbling, the singing of vigils and masses? Do you think that God will permit himself to be paid with the sound of bells, the smoke of candles, the glitter of gold, and such fancies? He has commanded none of these. But if you see your neighbor going astray, sinning, or suffering in body or soul, you are to leave everything else and at once help him in every way in your power and, if you can do no more, help him with words of comfort and prayer. Thus has Christ done to you and given you an example for you to follow.

33. These are the two things in which a Christian is to exercise himself, the one that he draws Christ into himself, and that by faith he makes him his own, appropriates to himself the treasures of Christ, and confidently builds upon them; the other that he condescends to his neighbor and lets him share in that which he has received, even as he shares in the treasures of Christ. He who does not exercise himself in these two things will receive no benefit even if he should fast unto death, suffer torture, or even give his body to be burned, and were able to do all miracles, as Saint Paul teaches, in 1 Corinthians 13ff.

B. The Spiritual Meaning of the Doctrine of This Gospel

34. The other mystery, or spiritual teaching, is, that in the churches the Gospel only should be preached and nothing more. Now it is evident that the Gospel teaches nothing but the foregoing two things, Christ and his example and two kinds of good works, the one belonging to Christ by which we are saved through faith, the other belonging to us by which our neighbor receives help. Whosoever therefore teaches anything different from the Gospel leads people astray; and whosoever does not teach the Gospel in these two parts leads people all the more astray and is worse than the former, who teaches without the Gospel, because he abuses and corrupts God's Word, as Saint Paul complains concerning some, in 2 Corinthians 2:17.

35. Now it is clear that nature could not have discovered such a doctrine, nor could all the ingenuity, reason, and wisdom of the world have thought it out. Who would be able to discover by means of his own efforts, that faith in Christ makes us one with Christ and gives us for our own all that is Christ's? Who would be able to discover that no works are of any value except those intended to benefit our neighbor? Nature teaches no more than that which is wrought by the law. Therefore it falls back upon its own work, so that this one thinks he fulfills the commandment by founding some institution or order, that one by fasting, this one by the kind of clothes he wears, that one by going on pilgrimages; this one in this manner, that one in that manner; and yet all

their works are worthless, for no one is helped by them. Such is the case at the present time in which the whole world is blinded and is going astray through the doctrines and works of men, so that faith and love along with the Gospel have perished.

36. Therefore, the Gospel properly apprehended is a supernatural sermon and light that makes known Christ only. This is pointed out first of all by the fact that it was not a man that made it known to others, but that an angel came down from heaven and made known to the shepherds the birth of Jesus, while no human being knew anything about it.

37. In the second place, it is pointed out by the fact that Christ was born at midnight, by which he indicates that all the world is in darkness as to its future and that Christ cannot be known by mere reason, but that knowledge concerning him must be revealed from heaven.

38. In the third place, it is shown by the light that shined around the shepherds, which teaches that here there must be an entirely different light than that of human reason. Moreover, when Saint Luke says, *Gloria Dei*, the glory of God, shone around them, he calls that light a brightness, or the glory of God. Why does he say that? In order to call attention to the mystery and reveal the character of the Gospel. For while the Gospel is a heavenly light that teaches nothing more than Christ, in whom God's grace is given to us and all human merit is entirely cast aside, it exalts only the glory of God, so that henceforth no one may be able to boast of his own power, but must give God the glory, that it is of his love and goodness alone that we are saved through Christ.

See, the divine honor, the divine glory, is the light in the Gospel, which shines around us from heaven through the apostles and their followers who preach the Gospel. The angel here was in the place of all the preachers of the Gospel, and the shepherds in the place of all the hearers, as we shall see. For this reason, the Gospel can tolerate no other teaching besides its own; for the teaching of men is earthly light and human glory; it exalts the honor and praise of men, and makes souls to glory in their own works, while the Gospel glories in Christ, in God's grace and goodness, and teaches us to boast of and confide in Christ.

39. In the fourth place, this is represented by the name Judea and Bethlehem, where Christ chose to be born. Judea is interpreted, confession or thanksgiving; as when we confess, praise, and thank God, acknowledging that all we possess are his gifts. One who so confesses and praises is called *Judaeus*. Such a king of the Jews is Christ, as the expression is, *"Jesus Nazarenus Rex Judaeorum,"* Jesus the Nazarene, the king of the Jews, of those confessing God.

By this is shown that no teaching whatever can make such a confession except the Gospel, which teaches Christ.

40. Beth means house; *lehem* means bread—Bethlehem, a house of bread. The city had that name because it was situated in a good, fruitful country, rich in grain, so that it was the granary for the neighboring towns or, as we would call it, a fertile country. In olden times, the name of the city was Ephrata, which means fruitful. Both names imply that the city was in a fruitful and rich land. By this is represented that without the Gospel this earth is a wilderness and there is no confession of God nor thanksgiving.

41. Moreover, where Christ and the Gospel are, there is the fruitful Bethlehem and the thankful Judea. There everyone has enough in Christ and overflows with thanksgiving for the divine grace. But while men are thankful for human teachings, they cannot satisfy, but leave a barren land and deadly hunger. No heart can ever be satisfied unless it hears Christ rightly proclaimed in the Gospel. In this, a man comes to Bethlehem and finds him; he also comes to and remains in Judea and thanks his God eternally. Here he is satisfied; here God receives his praise and confession, while outside of the Gospel there is nothing but thanklessness and starvation.

42. But the angel shows most clearly that nothing is to be preached in Christendom except the Gospel; he takes upon himself the office of a preacher of the Gospel. He does not say, I preach to you, but "glad tidings I bring to you." I am an evangelist and my word is an evangel, good news. The meaning of the word Gospel is, a good, joyful message, that is preached in the New Testament. Of what does the Gospel testify? Listen! the angel says, "I bring you glad tidings of great joy," my Gospel speaks of great joy. Where is it? Hear again, "For there is born to you this day in the city of David a Savior, who is Christ the Lord."

43. Behold here what the Gospel is, namely, a joyful sermon concerning Christ, our Savior. Whoever preaches him rightly, preaches the Gospel of pure joy. How is it possible for man to hear of greater joy than that Christ has given to him as his own? He does not only say Christ is born, but he makes his birth our own by saying, to you a Savior.

44. Therefore the Gospel does not only teach the history concerning Christ, but it enables all who believe it to receive it as their own, which is the way the Gospel operates, as has just been set forth. Of what benefit would it be to me if Christ had been born a thousand times, and it would daily be sung into my ears in a most lovely manner, if I were never to hear that he was born for me and was to be my very own? If the voice gives forth this pleasant sound, even if it be in homely phrase, my heart listens with joy for it is a lovely sound which penetrates

the soul. If now there were anything else to be preached, the evangelical angel and the angelic evangelist would certainly have touched upon it.

C. The Spiritual Meaning of the Signs, the Angel, and the Shepherds

45. The angel says further, "And this is the sign unto you; Ye shall find the babe wrapped in swaddling clothes, and lying in a manger." The clothes are nothing else than the holy Scriptures, in which the Christian truth lies wrapped, in which the faith is described. For the Old Testament contains nothing else than Christ as he is preached in the Gospel. Therefore, we see how the apostles appeal to the testimony of the Scriptures and with them prove everything that is to be preached and believed concerning Christ. Thus Saint Paul says, in Romans 3:21, that the faith of Christ through which we become righteous is witnessed by the law and the prophets. And Christ himself, after his resurrection, opened to them the Scriptures, which speak of him, in Luke 24:27.

When he was transfigured on the mount, in Matthew 17:3, Moses and Elijah stood by him; that means, the law and the prophets as his two witnesses, which are signs pointing to him. Therefore, the angel says, the sign by which he is recognized is the swaddling clothes, for there is no other testimony on earth concerning Christian truth than the holy Scriptures.

46. According to this, Christ's seamless coat which was not divided and which during his sufferings was gambled off and given away, in John 19:23–24, represents the New Testament. It indicates that the pope, the Antichrist, would not deny the Gospel, but would shut it up violently and play with it by means of false interpretation until Christ is no longer to be found in it. Then the four soldiers who crucified the Lord are figures of all the bishops and teachers in the four quarters of the earth, who violently suppress the Gospel and destroy Christ and his faith by means of their human teachings, as the pope with his papists has long since done.

47. From this, we see that the law and the prophets cannot be rightly preached and known unless we see Christ wrapped up in them. It is true that Christ does not seem to be in them, nor do the Jews find him there. They appear to be insignificant and unimportant clothes, simple words, which seem to speak of unimportant external matters, the import of which is not recognized; but the New Testament, the Gospel, must open it, throw its light upon it, and reveal it, as has been said.

48. First of all, then, the Gospel must be heard, and the appearance and the voice of the angel must be believed. Had the shepherds not heard from

the angel that Christ lay there, they might have seen him ten thousand times without ever knowing that the child was Christ. Accordingly, Saint Paul says, in 2 Corinthians 3:16, that the law remains dark and covered up for the Jews until they are converted to Christ.

Christ must first be heard in the Gospel, then it will be seen how beautiful and lovely the whole Old Testament is in harmony with him, so that a man cannot help giving himself in submission to faith and be enabled to recognize the truth of what Christ says in John 5:46, "For if ye believed Moses, ye would believe me, for he wrote of me."

49. Therefore, let us beware of all teaching that does not set forth Christ. What more would you know? What more do you need if indeed you know Christ, as above set forth, if you walk by faith in God, and by love to your neighbor, doing to your fellow man as Christ has done to you. This is indeed the whole Scripture in its briefest form, that no more words or books are necessary, but only life and action.

50. He lies in the manger. Notice here that nothing but Christ is to be preached throughout the whole world. What is the manger but the congregations of Christians in the churches to hear the preaching? We are the beasts before this manger; and Christ is laid before us upon whom we are to feed our souls. Whosoever goes to hear the preaching, goes to this manger; but it must be the preaching of Christ. Not all mangers have Christ, neither do all sermons teach the true faith. There was but one manger in Bethlehem in which this treasure lay and, besides, it was an empty and despised manger in which there was no fodder.

Therefore, the preaching of the Gospel is divorced from all other things; it has and teaches nothing besides Christ. Should anything else be taught, then it is no more the manger of Christ, but the manger of warhorses full of temporal things and of fodder for the body.

51. But in order to show that Christ in swaddling clothes represents the faith in the Old Testament, we will here give several examples. We read, in Matthew 8:4, when Christ cleansed the leper, that he said to him, "Go, show thyself to the priest, and offer the gift that Moses commanded, for a testimony unto them." Here you perceive that the law of Moses was given to the Jews for a testimony, or sign, as the angel also here says, namely, that such law represents something different from itself. What? Christ is the priest, all men are spiritual lepers because of unbelief; but when we come to faith in him, he touches us with his hand, gives and lays upon us his merit, and we become clean and whole without any merit on our part whatever. We are, therefore, to show our gratitude to him and acknowledge that we have not become

pious by our own works but through his grace; then our course will be right before God. In addition, we are to offer our gifts, that is, give of our own to help our fellow man, to do good to him as Christ has done to us. Thus Christ is served and an offering is brought to the rightful priest, for it is done for his sake, in order to love and praise him.

Do you here see how, figuratively speaking, Christ and the faith are wrapped up in the plain Scriptures? It is here made evident how Moses in the law gave only testimony and an interpretation of Christ. The whole Old Testament should be understood in this manner, and should be taken to be the swaddling clothes as a sign pointing out and making Christ known.

52. Again, it was commanded that the Sabbath should be strictly observed and no work should be done, which shows that not our works but Christ's works should dwell in us; for it is written that we are not saved by our works but by the works of Christ. Now these works of Christ are twofold, as shown before—on the one hand, those that Christ has done personally without us, which are the most important and in which we believe; the others, those he performs in us, in our love to our neighbor. The first may be called the evening works and the second the morning works, so that evening and morning make one day, as it is written in Genesis 1:5, for the Scriptures begin the day in the evening and end in the morning, that is, the evening with the night is the first half, the morning with the day is the second half of the whole natural day. Now as the first half is dark and the second half is light, so the first works of Christ are concealed in our faith, but the others, the works of love, are to appear, to be openly shown toward our fellow man. Here then you see how the whole Sabbath is observed and hallowed.

53. Do you see how beautifully Christ lies in these swaddling clothes? How beautifully the Old Testament reveals the faith and love of Christ and of his Christians? Now, swaddling clothes are as a rule of two kinds, the outside of coarse woolen cloth, the inner of linen. The outer or coarse woolen cloth represents the testimony of the law, but the linen are the words of the prophets. As Isaiah says, in Isaiah 7:14, "Behold, a virgin shall conceive, and bear a son, and shall call his name Immanuel," and similar passages that would not be understood of Christ, had the Gospel not revealed it and shown that Christ is in them.

54. Here then we have these two, the faith and the Gospel, that these and nothing else are to be preached throughout Christendom. Let us now see who are to be the preachers and who the learners. The preachers are to be angels, that is, God's messengers, who are to lead a heavenly life, are to be constantly engaged with God's Word that they, under no circumstances,

preach the doctrine of men. It is a most incongruous thing to be God's messenger and not to further God's message. Angelus means a messenger, and Luke calls him God's messenger (*Angelus Domini*). The message also is of more importance than the messenger's life. If he leads a wicked life, he injures only himself, but if he brings a false message in the place of God's message, he leads astray and injures everyone that hears him, and causes idolatry among the people in that they accept lies for the truth, honor men instead of God, and pray to the devil instead of to God.

55. There is no more terrible plague, misfortune, or cause for distress upon earth than a preacher who does not preach God's Word, of whom, alas, the world today is full; and yet they think they are pious and do good when indeed their whole work is nothing but murdering souls, blaspheming God, and setting up idolatry, so that it would be much better for them if they were robbers, murderers, and the worst scoundrels, for then they would know that they are doing wickedly. But now they go along under spiritual names and show, as priest, bishop, pope, and are at the same time ravening wolves in sheep's clothing, and it would be well if no one ever heard their preaching.

56. The learners are shepherds, poor people out in the fields. Here Jesus does what he says, in Matthew 11:5, "And the poor have good tidings preached to them," and, in Matthew 5:3, "Blessed are the poor in spirit; for theirs is the kingdom of heaven." Here are no learned, no rich, no mighty ones, for such people do not as a rule accept the Gospel. The Gospel is a heavenly treasure, which will not tolerate any other treasure, and will not agree with any earthly guest in the heart. Therefore, whoever loves the one must let go the other, as Christ says, in Matthew 6:24, "You cannot serve God and mammon."

This is shown by the shepherds in that they were in the field, under the canopy of heaven, and not in houses, showing that they do not hold fast and cling to temporal things; and, besides, they are in the fields by night, despised by and unknown to the world, which sleeps in the night, and by day delights so to walk that it may be noticed; but the poor shepherds go about their work at night. They represent all the lowly who live on earth, often despised and unnoticed but dwell only under the protection of heaven. They eagerly desire the Gospel.

57. That there were shepherds, means that no one is to hear the Gospel for himself alone, but everyone is to tell it to others who are not acquainted with it. For he who believes for himself has enough and should endeavor to bring others to such faith and knowledge, so that one may be a shepherd of the other, to wait upon and lead him into the pasture of the Gospel in this world, during the nighttime of this earthly life.

At first, the shepherds were sore afraid because of the angel; for human nature is shocked when it first hears in the Gospel that all our works are nothing and are condemned before God, for it does not easily give up its prejudices and presumptions.

58. Now let everyone examine himself in the light of the Gospel and see how far he is from Christ, what is the character of his faith and love. There are many who are enkindled with dreamy devotion and, when they hear of such poverty of Christ, are almost angry with the citizens of Bethlehem, denounce their blindness and ingratitude, and think, if they had been there, they would have shown the Lord and his mother a more becoming service, and would not have permitted them to be treated so miserably. But they do not look by their side to see how many of their fellow men need their help, and which they let go on in their misery unaided. Who is there upon earth that has no poor, miserable, sick, erring ones, or sinful people around him? Why does he not exercise his love to those? Why does he not do to them as Christ has done to him?

59. It is altogether false to think that you have done much for Christ if you do nothing for those needy ones. Had you been at Bethlehem, you would have paid as little attention to Christ as they did; but since it is now made known who Christ is, you profess to serve him. Should he come now and lay himself in a manger, and would send you word that it was he, of whom you now know so much, you might do something for him, but you would not have done it before. Had it been positively made known to the rich man in the Gospel, to what high position Lazarus would be exalted, and he would have been convinced of the fact, he would not have left him lie and perish as he did.

60. Therefore, if your neighbor were now what he shall be in the future, and lay before you, you would surely give him attention. But now, since it is not so, you beat the air and do not recognize the Lord in your neighbor; you do not do to him as he has done to you. Therefore, God permits you to be blinded, and deceived by the pope and false preachers, so that you squander on wood, stone, paper, and wax that with which you might help your fellow man.

III. EXPLANATION OF THE ANGELS' SONG OF PRAISE

61. Finally, we must also treat of the angels' song, which we use daily in our service: *Gloria in Excelsis Deo*. There are three things to be considered in this song, the glory to God, the peace to the earth, and the good will to mankind. The good will might be understood as the divine good will God has toward men through Christ. But we will admit it to mean the good will that is granted unto men through this birth, as it is set forth in the words thus, *"en anthropis eudokia, hominibus beneplacitum."*

62. The first is the glory to God. Thus we should also begin, so that in all things the praise and glory be given to God as the one who does, gives, and possesses all things, that no one ascribe anything to himself or claim any merit for himself. For the glory belongs to no one but to God alone; it does not permit of being made common by being shared by any person.

63. Adam stole the glory through the evil spirit and appropriated it to himself, so that all men with him have come into disgrace, which evil is so deeply rooted in all mankind that there is no vice in them as great as vanity. Everyone is well pleased with himself, and no one wants to be nothing, and they desire nothing, which spirit of vanity is the cause of all distress, strife, and war upon earth.

64. Christ has again brought back the glory to God, in that he has taught us how all we have or can do is nothing but wrath and displeasure before God, so that we may not be boastful and self-satisfied, but rather be filled with fear and shame, so that in this manner our glory and self-satisfaction may be crushed, and we be glad to be rid of it, in order that we may be found and preserved in Christ.

65. The second is the peace on earth. For just as strife must exist where God's glory is not found, as Solomon says, in Proverbs 13:10, "By pride cometh only contention"; so also, where God's glory is, there must be peace. Why should they quarrel when they know that nothing is their own, but that all they are, have, and can desire is from God; they leave everything in his hands and are content that they have such a gracious God. He knows that all he may have is nothing before God; he does not seek his own honor, but thinks of him who is something before God, namely, Christ.

66. From this, it follows that where there are true Christians, there is no strife, contention, or discord; as Isaiah says, in Isaiah 2:4, "And they shall beat their swords into plowshares, and their spears into pruning hooks; nation shall not lift up sword against nation, neither shall they learn war any more!"

67. Therefore, our Lord Christ is called a king of peace and is represented by King Solomon, whose name implies rich in peace, that inwardly he may give us peace in our conscience toward God through faith and, outwardly, that we may exercise love to our fellow men, so that through him there may be everywhere peace on earth.

68. The third is good will toward men. By good will is not meant the will that does good works, but the good will and peace of heart, which is equally submissive in everything that may betide, be it good or evil. The angels knew very well that the peace, of which they sang, does not extend farther than to the Christians who truly believe; such have certainly peace among themselves.

But the world and the devil have no reproof; they do not permit them to have peace but persecute them to death, as Christ says, in John 16:33, "In me ye may have peace. In the world ye have tribulation."

69. Hence it was not enough for the angels to sing peace on earth; they added to it the good will toward men, that they take pleasure in all that God does, regard all God's dealing with them as wise and good, and praise and thank him for it. They do not murmur but willingly submit to God's will. Moreover, since they know that God, whom they have received by faith in Christ as a gracious Father, can do all things, they exult and rejoice even under persecution, as Saint Paul says in Romans 5:3, "We also rejoice in our tribulations." They regard all that happens to them as for the best, out of the abundant satisfaction they have in Christ.

70. Behold, it is such a good will, pleasure, good opinion in all things, whether good or evil, that the angels wish to express in their song; for where there is no good will, peace will not long exist. The unbelieving put the worst construction on everything, always magnify the evil, and double every mishap. Therefore, God's dealings with them does not please them; they would have it different, and that which is written in Psalm 18:25–26, is fulfilled: "With the merciful thou wilt show thyself merciful, with the perfect man thou wilt show thyself perfect; with the pure thou wilt show thyself pure," that is, whoever has such pleasure in all things that you do in him, you, and all yours, will also have pleasure, and, "with the perverse thou wilt show thyself forward," that is, as you and all you do, does not please him, so he is not well pleasing to you and all that are yours.

71. Concerning the good will, Saint Paul says, in 1 Corinthians 10:33, "Even as I also please all men in all things." How does he do that? If you are content and satisfied with everything, you will in turn please everybody. It is a short rule: if you will please no one, be pleased with no one; if you will please everyone, be pleased with everyone—insofar, however, that you do not violate God's Word for, in that case, all pleasing and displeasing ceases. But what may be omitted without doing violence to God's Word, may be omitted, that you may please everyone and at the same time be faithful to God, then you have this good will of which the angels sing.

72. From this song, we may learn what kind of creatures the angels are. Don't consider what the great masters of art dream about them; here they are all painted in such a manner that their heart and their own thoughts may be recognized. In the first place, in that they joyfully sing, ascribing the glory to God, they show how full of his light and fire they are, not praising themselves, but recognizing that all things belong to God alone, so that with great

earnestness they ascribe the glory to him to whom it belongs. Therefore, if you would think of a humble, pure, obedient, and joyful heart, praising God, think of the angels. This is their first step, that by which they serve God.

73. The second is their love to us as has been shown. Here you see what great and gracious friends we have in them, that they favor us no less than themselves; rejoice in our welfare quite as much as they do in their own, so much so that in this song they give us a most comforting inducement to regard them as the best of friends. In this way, you rightly understand the angels, not according to their being, which the masters of art attempt fearlessly to portray, but according to their inner heart, spirit, and sense, that though I know not what they are, I know what their chief desire and constant work is; by this you look into their heart. This is enough concerning this Gospel. What is meant by Mary, Joseph, Nazareth will be explained in Luke 1.

The Armor of This Gospel

74. In this Gospel is the foundation of the article of our faith when we say, "I believe in Jesus Christ, born of the Virgin Mary." Although the same article is founded on different passages of Scripture, yet on none so clearly as on this one. Saint Mark says no more than that Christ has a mother; the same is also the case with Saint John, neither saying anything of his birth. Saint Matthew says he is born of Mary in Bethlehem, but lets it remain at that without gloriously proclaiming the virginity of Mary, as we will hear in due time. But Luke describes it clearly and diligently.

75. In olden times, it was also proclaimed by patriarchs and prophets; as when God says to Abraham, in Genesis 22:17, "And in thy seed shall all the nations of the earth be blessed." Again he says to David, in Psalm 89:4 and Psalm 132:11, "Jehovah hath sworn unto David in truth; he will not return from it; of the fruit of thy body will I set upon thy throne." But those are obscure words compared with the Gospel.

76. Again, it is also represented in many figures, as in the rod of Aaron which budded in a supernatural manner, although a dry piece of wood, in Numbers 7:5. So also Mary, exempt from all natural generation, brought forth, in a supernatural manner, really and truly a natural son, just as the rod bore natural almonds, and still remained a natural rod. Again by Gideon's fleece, in Judges 6:37, which was wet by the dew of heaven, while the land around it remained dry, and many like figures which it is not necessary to enumerate. Nor do these figures conflict with faith, they rather adorn it; for it must at first be firmly believed before I can believe that the figure serves to illustrate it.

77. There is a great deal in this article, of which, in time of temptation, we would not be deprived, for the evil spirit attacks nothing so severely as our faith. Therefore, it is of the greatest importance for us to know where in God's Word this faith is set forth and, in time of temptation, point to that, for the evil spirit cannot stand against God's Word.

78. There are also many ethical teachings in the Gospel, as for example, meekness, patience, poverty, and the like; but these are touched upon enough and are not points of controversy, for they are fruits of faith and good works.

Christmas Day

~❧~

Christ's Titles of Honor and Attribute; Christ's Coming;
His Becoming Man; and the Revelation of His Glory

I n the beginning was the Word, and the Word was with God, and the
Word was God. The same was in the beginning with God. All things
were made through him; and without him was not anything made that
hath been made. In him was life; and the life was the light of men. And
the light shineth in the darkness; and the darkness apprehended it not.
There came a man, sent from God, whose name was John. The same
came for witness, that he might bear witness of the light, that all might
believe through him. He was not the light, but came that he might bear
witness of the light. There was the true light, even the light which
lighteth every man, coming into the world. He was in the world, and
the world was made through him, and the world knew him not. He
came unto his own, and they that were his own received him not. But
as many as received him, to them gave he the right to become children
of God, even to them that believe on his name: who were born, not of
blood, nor of the will of the flesh, nor of the will of man, but of God.
And the Word became flesh, and dwelt among us (and) we beheld his
glory, glory as of the only begotten from the Father, full of grace
and truth. — JOHN 1:1–14

CHRIST'S TITLES OF HONOR AND ATTRIBUTE

1. This is the most important of all the Gospels of the church year, and
yet it is not, as some think, obscure or difficult. For upon it is clearly founded
the important article of faith concerning the divinity of Christ, with which all
Christians ought to be acquainted, and which they are able to understand.
Nothing is too great for faith. Therefore, let us consider this Gospel lesson in
the simplest manner possible, and not as the Scholastics did with their fabricated subtleties, conceal its doctrine from the common people and frighten

them away from it. There is no need of many fine and sharp distinctions, but only of a plain, simple explanation of the words of the text.

2. In the first place, we should know that all that the apostles taught and wrote, they took out of the Old Testament; for in it all things are proclaimed that were to be fulfilled later in Christ, and were to be preached, as Paul says in Romans 1:2, "God promised afore the Gospel of his son Jesus Christ through his prophets in the holy Scriptures." Therefore, all their preaching is based upon the Old Testament, and there is not a word in the New Testament that does not look back into the Old, where it had been foretold.

Thus we have seen in the Epistle how the divinity of Christ is confirmed by the apostle from passages in the Old Testament. For the New Testament is nothing more than a revelation of the Old. Just as one receives a sealed letter which is not to be opened until after the writer's death, so the Old Testament is the will and testament of Christ, which he has had opened after his death and read and everywhere proclaimed through the Gospel, as it is declared, in Revelation 5:5, where the Lamb of God alone is able to open the book with the seven seals, which no one else could open, neither in heaven, nor on earth, nor under the earth.

I. CHRIST'S FIRST TITLE OF HONOR AND ATTRIBUTE: HE IS THE WORD

3. That this Gospel may be clearer and more easily understood, we must go back to the passages in the Old Testament upon which it is founded, namely, the beginning of the first chapter of Genesis. There we read, in Genesis 1:1–3, "In the beginning God created the heavens and the earth, and the earth was waste and void; and darkness was upon the face of the deep; and the Spirit of God moved upon the face of the waters. And God said, Let there be light, and there was light," etc. Moses continues how all things were created in like manner as the light, namely, by speaking, or the Word of God. Thus, "And God said, Let there be a firmament." And again, "God said, Let there be sun, moon, stars," etc.

4. From these words of Moses, it is clearly proved that God has a Word, through which or by means of which he spoke, before anything was created; and this Word does not and cannot be anything that was created, since all things were created through this divine utterance, as the text of Moses clearly and forcibly expresses it, when it says, "God said, Let there be light, and there was light." The Word must, therefore, have preceded the light, since light came by the Word; consequently, it was also before all other creatures, which also came by the Word, as Moses writes.

5. But let us go further. If the Word preceded all creatures, and all creatures came by the Word and were created through it, the Word must be a different being than a creature, and was not made or created like a creature. It must, therefore, be eternal and without beginning. For when all things began, it was already there, and cannot be confined in time nor in creation, but is above time and creation; yea, time and creation are made and have their beginning through it. Thus it follows that whatever is not temporal must be eternal; and that which has no beginning cannot be temporal; and that which is not a creature must be God. For besides God and his creatures, there is nothing. Hence we learn from this text of Moses, that the Word of God, which was in the beginning and through which all things were made and spoken, must be God eternal and not a creature.

6. Again, the Word and he that speaks it, are not one person; for it is not possible that the speaker is himself the Word. What sort of speaker would he be who is himself the Word? He must needs be a mute, or the word must needs sound of itself without the speaker. But Scripture here speaks in strong and lucid words, "God said." And thus God and his Word must be two distinct things.

If Moses had written, "There was an utterance," it would not be so evident that there were two, the Word and the Speaker. But when he says, "God said," and names the speaker and his word, he forcibly states that there are two; that the speaker is not the word, and the word is not the speaker, but that the word comes from the speaker, and has its existence not of itself but from the speaker. But the speaker does not come from the word, nor does he have his existence from it, but from himself. Thus the words of Moses point conclusively to the fact that there are two persons in the Godhead from eternity, before all creatures, that the one has its existence from the other, and the first has its existence from nothing but itself.

7. Again, the Scriptures firmly and everlastingly maintain that there is only one God, as Moses begins, saying, "In the beginning God created the heavens and the earth." And, in Deuteronomy 6:4, "Hear, O Israel; Jehovah our God is one God." Thus the Scriptures proceed in simple, comprehensible words, and teach such exalted things so plainly that everyone may well understand them, and so forcibly that no one can gainsay them. Who is there that cannot here understand from these words of Moses, that there must be two persons in the Godhead, and yet but one God, unless he wishes to deny the plain Scriptures?

8. Again, who is there so subtle as to be able to contradict this doctrine? He must distinguish or keep apart the Word from God, the speaker; and he must confess that it was before all creatures, and that the creatures were made

by it. Consequently, he must surely admit it to be God for, besides the creatures, there is nothing but God; he must also admit that there is only one God. Thus the Scriptures forcibly conclude that these two persons are one perfect God, and that each one is the only true, real, and perfect God, who has created all things; that the Speaker has his being not from the Word, but that the Word has its being from the Speaker, yet he has his being eternally and from eternity, and outside of all creation.

9. The Arian heretics intended to draw a mist over this clear passage and to bore a hole into heaven, since they could not surmount it, and said that this Word of God was indeed God, not by nature, however, but by creation. They said that all things were created by it, but it had also been created previously, and after that all things were created by it. This they said from their own imagination without any authority from the Scriptures, because they left the simple words of the Scriptures and followed their own fancies.

10. Therefore, I have said that he who desires to proceed safely on firm ground, must have no regard for the many subtle and hair-splitting words and fancies, but must cling to the simple, powerful, and explicit words of Scripture, and he will be secure. We shall also see how Saint John anticipated these same heretics and refuted them in their subterfuges and fabrications.

11. Therefore, we have here in the books of Moses the real gold mine, from which everything that is written in the New Testament concerning the divinity of Christ has been taken. Here you may see from what source the Gospel of Saint John is taken, and upon what it is founded; and, therefore, it is easy to understand.

This is the source of the passage, in Psalm 33:6, "By the Word of Jehovah the heavens were made." Solomon in beautiful words describes the wisdom of God, in Proverbs 3:22, saying that this wisdom had been in God before all things; and he takes his thoughts from this chapter of Moses. So almost all the prophets have worked in this mine and have dug their treasures from it.

12. But there are other passages by this same Moses concerning the Holy Ghost as, for example, in Genesis 1:22, "And the Spirit of God moved upon the face of the waters." Thus the Spirit of God must also be something different from him who breathes him into existence, sends him forth, and yet he must be before all creatures.

Again, Moses says in Genesis 1:28–31, "God blessed the creatures, beheld them, and was pleased with them." This benediction and favorable contemplation of the creatures point to the Holy Ghost, since the Scriptures attribute to him life and mercy. But these passages are not so well developed as those which refer to the Son; consequently, they are not so prominent. The ore is still halfway in the mines, so that these passages can easily be believed, if reason is so far in subjection as to believe that there are two persons. If anyone will take the time and trouble to compare the passages of the New Testament referring to the Holy Ghost with this text of Moses, he will find much light, as well as pleasure.

13. Now we must open wide our hearts and understanding, so as to look upon these words not as the insignificant, perishable words of man, but think of them as being as great as he is who speaks them. It is a Word which he speaks of himself, which remains in him, and is never separated from him.

Therefore, according to the thought of the apostle, we must consider how God speaks with himself and to himself, and how the Word proceeds from within himself. However, this Word is not an empty sound, but brings with it the whole essence of the divine nature. Reference has been made in the Epistle to the brightness of his glory and the image of his person, which constitute the divine nature, so that it accompanies the image in its entirety and thus becomes the very image itself. In the same manner, God of himself also utters his Word, so that the whole Godhead accompanies the Word and in its nature remains in, and essentially is, the Word.

14. Behold, here we see whence the apostle has taken his language, when he calls Christ an image of the divine essence, and the brightness of divine glory. He takes it from this text of Moses, when he says that God spoke the Word of himself; this can be nothing else than an image that represents him, since every word is a sign which means something. But here the thing signified is by its very nature in the sign or in the Word, which is not in any other sign. Therefore, he very properly calls it a real image or sign of his nature.

15. The word of man may also in this connection be used in a measure as an illustration; for by it the human heart is known. Thus we commonly say, I understand his heart or intentions, when we have only heard his words; as out of the fullness of the heart the mouth speaks, and from the word the heart is known, as though it were in the word. In consequence of this experience, the heathen had a saying, *Qualis quisque est talia loquitur* (As a man speaks, so is he.). Again, *Oratio est character animi* (Speech is an image of the heart.). When the heart is pure, it utters pure words; when it is impure, it utters impure words. With this also corresponds the Gospel of Matthew 12:34, where Christ says, "Out of the abundance of the heart the mouth speaketh." And again, "How can ye, being evil, speak good things?" Also John the Baptist says, in John 3:31, "He that is of the earth is of the earth, and of the earth he speaketh." The Germans also have a proverb: "Of what the heart is full, overfloweth out of the mouth." The bird is known by its song, for it sings according to its

nature. Therefore, all the world knows that nothing represents the condition of the heart so perfectly and so positively as the words of the mouth, just as though the heart were in the word.

16. Thus it is also with God. His Word is so much like himself, that the Godhead is wholly in it, and he who has the Word has the whole Godhead. But this comparison has its limits. For the human word does not carry with it the essence or the nature of the heart, but simply its meaning, or is a sign of the heart, just as a woodcut or a bronze tablet does not carry with it the human being, but simply represents it. But here in God, the Word does not only carry with it the sign and picture, but the whole being, and is as full of God as he whose word or picture it is. If the human word were pure heart, or the intention of the heart, the comparison would be perfect. But this cannot be; consequently, the Word of God is above every word, and without comparison among all creatures.

17. There have indeed been sharp discussions about the inner word in the heart of man, which remains within, since man has been created in the image of God. But it is all so deep and mysterious, and will ever remain so, that it is not possible to understand it. Therefore, we shall pass on, and we come now to our Gospel, which is in itself clear and manifest.

In the beginning was the Word.

18. What beginning does the evangelist mean except the one of which Moses says, "In the beginning God created the heavens and the earth"? That was the beginning and origin of creation. Other than this, there was no beginning, for God had no beginning, but is eternal. It follows, therefore, that the Word is also eternal, because it did not have its origin in the beginning, but it was already in the beginning, John says. It did not begin, but when other things began it was already in existence; and its existence did not begin when all things began, but it was then already present.

19. How prudently the evangelist speaks, for he does not say, "In the beginning the Word was made," but it was there, and was not made. The origin of its existence is different from the beginning of creation. Furthermore, he says, "In the beginning." Had he been made before the world, as the Arians maintain, he would not have been in the beginning, but he would have himself been the beginning. But John firmly and clearly maintains, "In the beginning was the Word," and he was not the beginning. Whence has Saint John these words? From Moses, in Genesis 1:3, "God said, Let there be light." From this text, evidently, come the words, "In the beginning was the Word." For if God spoke, there had to be a Word. And if he spoke it in the beginning,

when the creation began, it was already in the beginning, and did not begin with the creation.

20. But why does he not say, Before the beginning was the Word? This would have made the matter clearer, as it would seem; thus Saint Paul often says, Before the creation of the world, etc. The answer is, because, to be in the beginning, and to be before the beginning, are the same, and one is the consequence of the other. Saint John, as an evangelist, wished to agree with the writings of Moses, wished to open them up, and to disclose the source of his own words, which would not have been the case had he said, "Before" the beginning. Moses says nothing of that which was before the beginning, but describes the Word in the beginning, in order that he can the better describe the creation, which was made by the Word. For the same reason, he also calls him a word, when he might as well have called him a light, life, or something else, as is done later; for Moses speaks of a word. Now, not to begin and to be in the beginning are the same as to be before the beginning.

But if the Word had been in the beginning and not before the beginning, it must have begun to be before the beginning, and so the beginning would have been before the beginning, which would be a contradiction, and would be the same as though the beginning were not the beginning. Therefore, it is put in a masterly way, In the beginning was the Word, so as to show that it has not begun and, consequently, must necessarily have been eternal, before the beginning.

And the Word was with God.

21. Where else should it have been? There never was anything outside of God. Moses says the same thing when he writes, "God said, Let there be light." Whenever God speaks, the Word must be with him. But here he clearly distinguishes the persons, so that the Word is a different person than God with whom it was. This passage of John does not allow the interpretation that God had been alone, because it says that something had been with God, namely, the Word. If he had been alone, why would he need to say, The Word was with God? To have something with him, is not to be alone or by himself.

It should not be forgotten that the evangelist strongly emphasizes the little word "with," for he repeats it, and clearly expresses the difference in persons to gainsay natural reason and future heretics. For while natural reason can understand that there is but one God, and many passages of Scripture substantiate it, and this is also true, yet the Scriptures also strongly oppose the idea that this same God is only one person.

22. Thus arose the heresy of Sabellius, who said, The Father, Son, and Holy Ghost are only one person. And again, Arius, although he admitted that

the Word was with God, would not admit that he was true God. The former confesses and teaches too great a simplicity of God; the latter too great a multiplicity. The former mingles the persons; the latter separates the natures. But the true Christian faith takes the mean, teaches and confesses separate persons and an undivided nature. The Father is a different person from the Son, but he is not another God. Natural reason cannot comprehend this; it must be apprehended by faith alone. Natural reason produces error and heresy; faith teaches and maintains the truth, for it clings to the Scriptures, which do not deceive nor lie.

And God was the Word.

23. Since there is but one God, it must be true that God himself is the Word, which was in the beginning before all creation. Some change the order of the words and read, And the Word was God, in order to explain that this Word not only is with God and is a different person, but that it is also in its essence the one true God with the Father. But we shall leave the words in the order in which they now stand: And God was the Word; and this is also what it means; there is no other God than the one only God, and this same God must also essentially be the Word, of which the evangelist speaks; so there is nothing in the divine nature which is not in the Word. It is clearly stated that this Word is truly God, so that it is not only true that the Word is God, but also that God is the Word.

24. Decidedly, as this passage opposes Arius, who teaches that the Word is not God, so strongly it appears to favor Sabellius, for it speaks as though it mingled the persons, and thereby revokes or explains away the former passage, which separates the persons and says, The Word was with God.

But the evangelist intentionally arranged his words so as to refute all heretics. Here, therefore, he overthrows Arius and attributes to the Word the true essential of the Godhead by saying, And God was the Word; as though he would say, I do not simply say, the Word is God, which might be understood as though the Godhead was only asserted of him, and were not essentially his, as you, Arius, claim; but I say, And God was the Word, which can be understood in no other way than that this same being which everyone calls God and regards as such, is the Word.

Again, that Sabellius and reason may not think that I side with them, and mingle the persons, and revoke what I have said on this point, I repeat it and say again,

The same was in the beginning with God.

25. The Word was with God, with God, and yet God was the Word. Thus the evangelist contends that both assertions are true: God is the Word, and the Word is with God; one nature of divine essence, and yet not one person only. Each person is God complete and entire, in the beginning and eternally. These are the passages upon which our faith is founded and to which we must hold fast. For it is entirely above reason that there should be three persons and each one perfect and true God, and yet not three Gods but one God.

26. The Scholastics have argued much pro and con with their numerous subtleties to make this doctrine comprehensible. But if you do not wish to become entangled in the meshes of the enemy, ignore their cunning, arrogance, and subtleties, and hold to these divine words. Press into them and remain in them, like a hare in a rocky crevice. If you come out and deign to listen to human talk, the enemy will lead you on and overcome you, so that you will at last not know where reason, faith, God, or even yourself are.

27. Believe me, as one who has experienced and tried it, and who does not talk into an empty barrel, the Scriptures are not given us for naught. If reason could have kept on the right road, the Scriptures would not have been given us. Take an example in the case of Arius and Sabellius. Had they clung to the Scriptures and disregarded reason, they would not have originated so much trouble in the church. And our Scholastics might have been Christians, had they ceased fooling with their subtleties and had clung to the Scriptures.

All things were made through him.

28. Has this not been put clearly enough? Who would be surprised, if stubborn men reject every effort to convince them of their error, however plainly and earnestly the truth may be told them, when the Arians could evade this clear and explicit passage and say, All things are made by the Word, but the Word was itself first made, and afterward all things were made by it? And this in opposition to the direct words, "All things were made through him." And there is no doubt that he was not made and cannot be counted among the things that were made. For he who mentions all things excludes nothing, as Saint Paul also explains Psalm 8:6, when he says, in Hebrews 2:8, "Thou didst put all things in subjection under his feet. For in that he subjected all things unto him, he left nothing that is not subjected to him." Again, in 1 Corinthians 15:27, "For he put all things in subjection under his feet. It is evident that he is expected who did subject all things unto him."

So also the words, "All things were made through him," must certainly be understood to except him by whom all things were made, and without whom is nothing that is made. This passage is also based upon the first chapter of Genesis, where all created things are mentioned which God had made, and in each case it is said, "And God said, and it was so," in order to show that they were all made by the Word. But Saint John continues and explains himself still more fully when he says,

And without him was not anything made that hath been made.

29. If nothing was made without him, much less is he himself made without whom nothing was made; accordingly, the error of Arius should never have attracted any attention, and yet it did. There is no need of comment to explain that the Word is God and the real Creator of all created things, since without him nothing was made that ever was made.

30. Some have been in doubt about the order of the words in this text; the words "that was made" they take with the following words, in this way, "That which was made, was in him life." Of this opinion was Saint Augustine. But the words properly belong to the preceding words as I have given them, thus, "And without him was not anything made that hath been made." He means to say that none of the things that are made, are made without him; so that he may the more clearly express that all things were made through him, and that he himself was not made. In short, the evangelist firmly maintains that the Word is true God, yet not of himself, but of the Father. Therefore, we say, Made through him, and begotten of the Father.

II. CHRIST'S SECOND TITLE OF HONOR AND ATTRIBUTE: IN HIM WAS LIFE

31. On this passage there is generally much speculation, and it is often taken to mean something hard to understand in reference to the twofold existence of creation; in this, the Platonic philosophers are famous. They maintain that all creation has its being first in its own nature and kind, as it was created. Secondly, all creation has its being in divine Providence from eternity, in that he has resolved in himself to create all things. Therefore, as he lives so all things are living in him; and this creative existence in God, they say, is nobler than the existence in its own kind and nature. For in God things do live which in themselves have no life, as stones, earth, water, and the like.

And therefore Saint Augustine says that this Word is an image of all creation, and like a bedchamber is hung with images which are called Ideas (Greek for images), according to which the created things were made, each one according to its own image. Concerning these, John is to have said, "In him was life." Then they connect these words with the preceding ones, thus, That which was made was life in him, that is, all that was ever created, before it was created, had had its life in him.

32. But this is going too far and is a forced interpretation of this passage. For John speaks very simply and plainly, and does not mean to lead us into such hair-splitting, subtle contemplations. I do not know that the Scriptures anywhere speak of created beings in this way. They do say that all things were known, elected, and even ready and living in the sight of God, as though creation had already taken place, as Christ says of Abraham, Isaac, and Jacob in Luke 20:38, "He (God) is not the God of the dead, but of the living; for all live unto him." But we do not find it written in this sense that all things live in him.

33. This passage also implies something more than the life of the creature, which was in him before the world. It signifies in the simplest manner that he is the fountain and cause of life, that all things which live, live by him and through him and in him, and besides him there is no life, as he himself says, in John 14:6, "I am the way, the truth, and the life." Again, in John 11:25, "I am the resurrection and the life." Consequently, John calls him in 1 John 1:1, "The Word of Life"; and he speaks especially of the life which man receives by him, that is, eternal life; and it was for this very life that John set out to write his Gospel.

34. This is also apparent from the context. For he himself explains the life of which he speaks, when he says, "And the life was the light of men." By these words, he undoubtedly shows that he speaks of the life and the light Christ gives to man through himself. For this reason also, he refers to John the Baptist as a witness of that light. It is, therefore, evident how John the Baptist preached Christ, not in lofty terms of speculation, as some fable; but he taught in a plain, simple way how Christ is the light and the life of all men for their salvation.

35. Therefore, it is well to remember that John wrote his Gospel, as the historians tell us, because Cerinthus, the heretic, arose in his day and taught that Christ did not exist before his mother Mary, thus making a simple human being or creature of him. In opposition to this heretic, he begins his Gospel in an exalted tone and continues thus to the end, so that in almost every letter he preaches the divinity of Christ, which is done by none of the other evangelists. And so he also purposely introduces Christ as acting strangely toward his mother and, "Woman, what have I to do with thee?" he said to her, in John 2:4. Was not this a strange, harsh expression for a son to use in addressing his mother? So also on the cross he said, "Woman, behold thy son," in John 19:26. All this he does in order to set forth Christ as true God over against Cerinthus; and this he does in language so as not only to meet Cerinthus, but also Arius, Sabellius, and all other heretics.

36. We read also that this same pious John saw Cerinthus in a bathing house and said to his followers, "Let us flee quickly hence that we be not destroyed with this man." And after John had come out, the bathing house is said to have collapsed and destroyed this enemy of the truth. He thus points and directs all his words against the error of Cerinthus, and says, Christ was not only before his mother, nay, he was in the beginning the Word of which Moses writes in the very beginning, and all things were made by him, and he was with God and the Word was God, and was in the beginning with God; and thus he strikes Cerinthus as with thunderbolts.

37. Thus we take the meaning of the evangelist in this passage to be simply and plainly this: He who does not recognize and believe Christ to be true God, as I have so far described him, that he was the Word in the beginning with God, and that all things were made by him, but wishes to make him only a creature of time, coming after his mother, as Cerinthus teaches, is eternally lost, and cannot attain to eternal life; for there is no life without this Word and Son of God; in him alone is life. The man Christ, separate from, and without, God, would be useless, as he says himself in John 6:55, 63, "The flesh profiteth nothing. My flesh is meat indeed, and my blood is drink indeed."

Why does the flesh profit nothing, and yet my flesh is the only true meat? The plain reason is, because I am not mere flesh and simply man, but I am God's son. My flesh is meat not because it is flesh, but because it is my flesh. This is as much as to say, He who believes that I, who am man, and have flesh and blood like other men, am the Son of God, and God, finds in me true nourishment, and will live. But he who believes me to be only man, is not profited by the flesh, for to him it is not my flesh or God's flesh.

He also says, "Ye shall die in your sins, except ye believe that I am he," in John 8:24. Again, "If the son shall therefore make you free, ye shall be free indeed." This is also the meaning of the following passage, "In him was life." The Word of God in the beginning, who is himself God, must be our life, meat, light, and salvation. Therefore, we cannot attribute to Christ's human nature the power of making us alive, but the life is in the Word, which dwells in the flesh and makes us alive by the flesh.

38. This interpretation is simple and helpful. Thus Saint Paul is wont to call the doctrine of the Gospel "*doctrina pietatis*," a doctrine of piety—a doctrine that makes men rich in grace. However, the other interpretation which the heathen also have, namely, that all creatures live in God, does indeed make subtle disputants and is obscure and difficult; but it teaches nothing about grace, nor does it make men rich in grace. Wherefore, the Scriptures speak of it as "idle."

Just as we interpret the words of Christ, when he says, "I am the life," so also should we interpret these words, and say nothing philosophically of the life of the creatures in God; but on the contrary, we should consider how God lives in us, and makes us partakers of his life, so that we live through him, of him, and in him. For it cannot be denied that through him natural life also exists, which even unbelievers have from him, as Saint Paul says, "In him we live, and move, and have our being; for we are also his offspring," in Acts 17:28.

39. Yes, natural life is a part of eternal life, its beginning, but on account of death it has an end, because it does not acknowledge and honor him from whom it comes; sin cuts it off so that it must die forever. On the other hand, those who believe in him, and acknowledge him from whom they have their being, shall never die; but this natural life of theirs will be extended into eternal life, so that they will never taste death, as John says, in John 8:51, "Verily, verily, I say unto you, if a man keep my word, he shall never see death." And again, in John 11:25, "He that believeth on me, though he die, yet shall he live." These and similar passages are well understood when we rightly learn to know Christ, how he has slain death and has brought us life.

40. But when the evangelist says, "In him was life," and not, "In him is life," as though he spoke of things past, the words must not be taken to mean the time before creation, or the time of the beginning; for he does not say, "In the beginning life was in him," as he has just before said of the Word, which was in the beginning with God; but these words must be referred to the time of Christ's life or sojourn upon earth, when the Word of God appeared to men and among men; for the evangelist proposes to write about Christ and that life in which he accomplished all things necessary for our life. Just as he says of John the Baptist, "There came a man, sent from God"; and again, "He was not the Light, etc."; even so, he afterward speaks of the Word, "And the Word became flesh, and dwelt among us"; "He was in the world"; "He came unto his own, and they that were his own received him not"; etc. In the same manner does Christ also speak of John the Baptist, "He was the lamp that burneth and shineth," in John 5:35.

41. So he says also here, "In him was life"; and Christ says of himself, "When I am in the world, I am the light of the world," in John 9:5. The words of the evangelist, therefore, simply refer to the sojourn of Christ on earth. For as I said at first, this Gospel is not as difficult as some think; it has been made difficult by their looking for great, mysterious, and mighty things in it. The evangelist has written it for ordinary Christians, and has made his words

perfectly intelligible. For whoever will disregard the life and sojourn of Christ upon earth, and will wish to find him in some other way, as he now sits in heaven, will always fail. He must look for him as he was and as he sojourned while upon earth, and he will then find life. Here Christ was made our life, light, and salvation; here all things occurred that we are to believe concerning him. It has really been said in a most befitting manner, "In him was life," not, that he is not our life now, but that he does not now do that which he then did.

42. That this is the meaning can be seen from the words of the text when it says, "John the Baptist came for witness, that he might bear witness of the light, that all might believe through him." It is sufficiently clear that John came solely to bear witness of Christ, and yet he has said nothing at all of the life of the creatures in God supporting the above philosophical interpretation; but all his teaching and preaching were concerning the life of Christ upon earth, whereby he became the Life and Light of men. Now follows:

III. CHRIST'S THIRD TITLE OF HONOR AND ATTRIBUTE: HE WAS THE LIGHT

A. Christ Was the Light of Men

And the Life was the Light of men.

43. Just as the word "life" was interpreted differently from the meaning intended by the evangelist, so was also the word "light." There has been much foolish speculation as to how the Word of God in its divinity could be a light, which naturally shines and has always given light to the minds of men even among the heathen. Therefore, the light of reason has been emphasized and based upon this passage of Scripture.

44. These are all human, Platonic, and philosophical thoughts, which lead us away from Christ into ourselves; but the evangelist wishes to lead us away from ourselves into Christ. For he would not deal with the divine, almighty, and eternal Word of God, nor speak of it, otherwise than as flesh and blood, that sojourned upon earth. He would not have us diffuse our thoughts among the creatures which he has created, so as to pursue him, search for him, and speculate about him as the Platonic philosophers do; but he wishes to lead us away from those vague and high-flown thoughts and bring us together in Christ.

The evangelist means to say, Why do you make such extensive excursions and search for him so far away? Behold, in the man Christ are all things. He has made all things; in him is life, and he is the Word by whom all things were made. Remain in him and you will find all; he is the life and the light of all men. Whoever directs you elsewhere, deceives you. For he has offered himself in this flesh and blood, and he must be sought and will be found there. Follow the testimony of John the Baptist; he will show you no other life or light than this man, who is God himself. Therefore, this light must mean the true light of grace in Christ, and not the natural light, which also sinners, Jews, heathen, and devils have, who are the greatest enemies of the light.

45. But let no one accuse me of teaching differently from Saint Augustine, who interpreted this text to mean the natural light. I do not reject that interpretation, and am well aware that all the light of reason is ignited by the divine light; and as I have said of the natural life, that it has its origin in, and is a part of, the true life, when it has come to the right knowledge, so also the light of reason has its origin in, and is part of, the true light, when it recognizes and honors him by whom it has been ignited.

It, however, does not do this of itself, but remains separate and by itself, becomes perverted, and likewise perverts all things; therefore, it must become extinguished and die out. But the light of grace does not destroy the natural light. To the light of nature, it is quite clear that two and three make five. That the good is to be encouraged and the evil avoided is also clear to it; and thus the light of grace does not extinguish the light of nature, but the latter never gets so far as to be able to distinguish the good from the evil. It is with him as one who wishes to go to Rome with Rome behind his back; for he himself well knew that whoever would go to Rome must travel the right way, but he knew not which was the right road. So it is also with the natural light; it does not take the right road to God, nor does it know or recognize the right way, although it knows well that one must get on the right road. Thus reason always prefers the evil to the good; it would never do this if it fully realized with a clear vision that the good only should be chosen.

46. But this interpretation is out of place in this connection, because only the light of grace is preached here. Saint Augustine was only a man, and we are not compelled to follow his interpretation, since the text here clearly indicates that the evangelist speaks of the light of which John the Baptist bore witness, which is ever the light of grace, even Christ himself.

47. And since this is an opportunity, we shall further describe this deceptive natural light, which causes so much trouble and misfortune. This natural light is like all the other members and powers of man. Who doubts that man with all his powers has been created by the eternal Word of God like all other

things, and is a creature of God? But yet there is no good in him, as Moses says, in Genesis 6:5, "Every imagination of the thoughts of man's heart was only evil continually."

48. Although the flesh was created by God, yet it is not inclined to chastity, but to unchastity. Although the heart was created by God, it is not inclined to humility, nor to the love of one's neighbor, but to pride and selfishness, and it acts according to this inclination, where it is not forcibly restrained. So it is with the natural light; although it is naturally so bright as to know that only good is to be done, it is so perverted that it is never sure as to what is good; it calls good whatever is pleasing to itself, is taken up with it, and only concludes to do what it has selected as good. Thus it continues to pursue the evil instead of the good.

49. We shall prove this by examples. Reason knows very well that we ought to be pious and serve God; of this it knows how to talk, and thinks it can easily beat all the world. Very well, this is true and well said; but when it is to be done, and reason is to show how and in what way we are to be pious and serve God, it knows nothing, is purblind, and says one must fast, pray, sing, and do the works of the law; it continues to act the fool with works, until it has gone so far astray as to imagine that people are serving God in building churches, ringing bells, burning frankincense, whining, singing, wearing hoods, shaving their heads, burning candles, and other innumerable tomfoolery, of which all the world is now full and more than full. In this monstrously blind error, reason continues, even while the bright light shines on, that enjoins piety and service to God.

50. When now Christ, the light of grace, comes and also teaches that we are to be pious and serve God, he does not extinguish this natural light, but opposes the way and manner of becoming pious and serving God as taught by reason. He says, To become pious is not to do works; no works are good without faith.

51. Then begins the fight. Reason rises up against grace, and cries out against its light, accuses it of forbidding good works, protests against not having its own way and standard of becoming pious, being thus set aside; but continually rages about being pious and serving God, and so makes the light of grace foolishness, nay, error and heresy, and persists in persecuting and banishing it. See, this is the virtue of the light of nature, that it raves against the true light, is constantly boasting of piety, piety, and is always crying, "Good works!" "Good works!" but it cannot and will not stand to be taught what piety is and what good works are; it insists that which it thinks and proposes must be right and good.

52. Behold, here then you have the cause and origin of all idolatry, of all heresy, of all hypocrisy, of all error, of which all the prophets have spoken, on account of which they were killed, and against which all the Scriptures protest.

All this comes from the stubborn, self-willed arrogance and delusion of natural reason, which is self-confident and puffed up because it knows that we ought to be pious, and serve God; it will neither listen to, nor suffer, a teacher to teach them, thinks it knows enough, and would find out for itself what it is to be pious and serve God, and how it may do so. Therefore, divine truth cannot and must not submit to reason; for this would be the greatest mistake and be contrary to God's honor and glory. In this way, contentions and tribulations arise.

53. Therefore, it is clear, I think, that John does not speak here of the false light, nor of that bright natural light, which rightly claims that we must be pious, for it is already here, and Christ did not come to bring it, but to dim and blind this false, self-willed arrogance, and to set in its place the light of grace, to wit, faith. And this also the words themselves indicate, when they say, "The life was the light of men." If it is the light of men, it must be a different light from the one that is in men, since man already has the light of nature in him, and whatever enlightens man, enlightens the light of nature in man, and brings another light, which surpasses the light that is in man.

He does not say that it is the light of irrational animals, but of man, who is a rational being. For there is not a man found in whom there is not the natural light of reason, from which cause alone he is called man and is worthy to be a man. If the evangelist would have us understand by this light the natural light of reason, he would have said, The life was a light of darkness; as Moses writes in Genesis 1:2, "And darkness was upon the face of the deep." Therefore, this light must be that which was revealed in Christ on earth.

54. Notice also the order of the words. John puts the Life before the Light. He does not say, "The light was the life of men" but, on the contrary, "The life was the light of men," for the reason that in Christ there is reality and truth, and not simply appearance as in men. Saint Luke speaks of Christ's external life thus, in Luke 24:19, "He was a prophet mighty in deed and word" and in Acts 1:1, "Jesus began both to do and teach," where "doing" precedes the "teaching"; for where there is only teaching without doing, there is hypocrisy. Thus John says of John the Baptist, "He was the lamp that burneth and shineth," in John 5:35; for to be simply shining and not burning is deceptive. In order, therefore, that Christ may here also be recognized as the true, unerring light, John says that all things were life in him, and this same life afterward was the light of men.

55. It follows then that man has no other light than Christ, God's son in the flesh. And whosoever believes that Christ is true God, and that in him is life, will be illumined and quickened by this life. The light supports him, so that he may remain where Christ is. As the Godhead is an eternal life, this same light is an eternal light; and as this same life can never die, so also this light can never be extinguished; and faith in it cannot perish.

56. We may also especially notice that the evangelist assigns life to Christ, as the eternal Word, and not to Christ the man; for he says, "In him," eminently in the Word, "was the life." Although Christ died as man, yet he ever remained alive; for life could not and cannot die; and consequently, death was overcome and was swallowed up in life, so much so that his humanity soon again became alive.

This same Life is the light of men; for he who recognizes and believes in such a life in Christ, indeed passes through death, yet never dies, as has been stated above. For this Light of life protects him, so that death cannot harm him. Although the body must die and decay, the soul will not feel this death, because it is in that light, and through that light, that it is entirely comprehended in the life of Christ. But he who does not believe this, remains in darkness and death; and although his body is united to him, even as it will be forever at the day of judgment, yet the soul will nevertheless taste and feel death, and will die eternally.

57. From this, we may realize how great was the harm which Cerinthus threatened, and which all do who believe and teach that Christ is only man and not true God. For his humanity would profit us nothing if the divinity were not in it. Yet, on the other hand, God will not and cannot be found, save through and in his humanity, which he has set up as an ensign for the nations, gathering together the dispersed of Judah from the four corners of the earth, in Isaiah 11:12.

58. See now, if you will believe that in Christ there is such life that remains even in death, and has overcome death, this light will lighten you aright, and will remain a light and life within you even at the time of your death. It follows then that such Life and Light cannot be mere creatures, for no creature can overcome death, either in itself or in another. Behold, how easy and becoming this interpretation of the light is, and how much better it is for our salvation; but how very far they are from it who wish to make of this light only the natural light of reason. For this latter light does not improve anyone, nay, it leads only farther away from Christ into creation and to false reason. We must enter into Christ, and not look at the lights which come from him,

but gaze at his light, which is the origin of all lights. We must follow the streams which lead to the source and not away from it.

B. Christ Was the Light That Shineth in the Darkness

And the light shineth in the darkness
and the darkness apprehended it not.

59. This passage has also been interpreted with such lofty ideas, and made to mean that reason has a natural light, as I have just mentioned, and that the same is kindled by God; and yet reason does not recognize, understand, nor feel him, the real Light, by whom it is kindled; therefore, it is in darkness, and does not behold the Light from which nevertheless it receives all its vision.

60. Oh, that this interpretation, that reason has a natural light, were rooted out of my heart! How deeply it is seated there. Not that it is false or wrong in itself, but because it is out of place and untimely in this Gospel connection, and it will not allow these blessed and comforting words of the Gospel to remain simple and pure in their true meaning. Why do they not thus speak also of the natural life? For even the natural life is surely quickened by the divine life, just as much as the light of reason is kindled by the divine light.

They might just as well say that life quickens the dead and the dead apprehend it not, as to say that the light illumines dark reason and reason apprehends it not. I might also say that the eternal will makes the unwilling willing, and the unwilling do not apprehend it; and in like manner we might speak of all our other natural gifts and powers. But how does reason and its light fall on such speculations? The Platonic philosophers with their useless and senseless prating first led Augustine to his interpretation. The glitter was so fascinating that they were even called the divine philosophers. Augustine then carried us all with him.

61. What more can their talk teach than this, that reason is illumined by God, who is inconceivable and incomprehensible light? Just so, life is given by God, who is inconceivable life, and all our powers are made powerful by God, who is inconceivable power. And as he is near to the light of reason with his inconceivable life, and to the powers with his inconceivable power, as Saint Paul says, "In him we live, and move, and have our being," in Acts 17:28. Again, "Am I a God at hand, saith Jehovah, and not a God afar off? Do not I fill heaven and earth?" in Jeremiah 23:23, 24.

Thus we have just heard in the Epistle that "He upholds all things by the word of his power," in Hebrews 1:3. Therefore, he is not only near to the light of reason and illumines it, but he is near also to all creatures, and flows and pours into them, shines and works in them, and fills all things. Accordingly, we are not to think that Saint John speaks here of the light of reason; he simply sets mankind before him, and tells what kind of light they have in Christ, aside from and above the light of nature.

62. It is also a blind and awkward expression to say of the natural light that the darkness apprehended it not. What else would this be than to say that reason is illumined and kindled by the divine light, and yet, remains in darkness and receives no light? Whence comes this natural light? There can never be darkness where a light is kindled; although there is darkness from the want of the light of grace. But here they are not speaking of the light of grace, and so they cannot refer to like or spiritual darkness. Therefore, it is a contradiction of terms to say that the light illumined the darkness, and the darkness apprehended it not, or the darkness remained. One might as well say that life is given to a dead person, and the dead person does not apprehend it nor receive it, but remains dead.

63. But if someone should say that we are not able to apprehend him who gives light and life, then I really hear, what angel does apprehend him? What saint apprehends the one who offers him grace? Verily he remains concealed and unapprehended: but this does not mean, as the evangelist here says, that the Light is not apprehended in darkness; but as the words read, it means, the Light shines into the darkness, but the darkness remains darkness and is not illuminated; the Light shines upon the darkness, and yet the darkness remains; just as the sun shines upon the blind, and yet they do not perceive it. Behold how many words I must waste in order to remove this foreign and false interpretation of our text!

64. Therefore, let us cling to the simple meaning the words convey when we do no violence to them. All who are illumined by natural reason apprehend the light, each one being illumined according to his talent and capacity. But this Light of grace, which is given to men aside from and above the natural light, shines in darkness, that is, among men of the world, who are blind and without grace; but they do not accept it, yea, they even persecute it. This is what Christ means when he says, in John 3:19, "And as this is the judgment, that the light is come into the world, and men loved the darkness rather than the light." Behold, Christ was upon earth and among men before he was publicly preached by John the Baptist; but no one took notice of him. He was the Life and Light of men. He lived and did shine; yet there was nothing but darkness, and the darkness did not perceive him. Everybody was worldly blind and benighted. Had they apprehended who he was, they would have given him due honor, as Saint Paul says, "Had the rulers of this world known the wisdom of God, they would not have crucified the Lord of glory," in 1 Corinthians 2:8.

65. Thus Christ has always been the Life and Light, even before his birth, from the beginning, and will ever remain so to the end. He shines at all times in all creatures, in the holy Scriptures, through his saints, prophets, and ministers, in his word and works; and he has never ceased to shine. But in whatever place he has shone, there was great darkness, and the darkness apprehended him not.

66. Saint John may have indeed directed these words thus against the followers of Cerinthus, so that they saw the plain Scriptures and the truth that enlightened them, yet they did not apprehend their darkness. So it is at all times, and even now. Although the Scriptures are explained to blind teachers so that they may apprehend the truth, yet they do not apprehend it, and the fact remains that the light shines in the darkness and the darkness apprehends it not.

67. It is especially to be observed that the evangelist here says the light shines, *phaenei*, that is, it is manifest and present to the eyes in the darkness. But he who receives nothing more from it remains in darkness; just as the sun shines for the blind man, but he does not on that account see any better. So it is the nature of this light that it shines in darkness, but the darkness does not on that account become brighter. In believers, however, it not only shines, but it makes them transparent and seeing, it lives in them, so that it can properly be said that "The life is the light of men." On the other hand, light without life is a shining of darkness; therefore, no light is of any use to unbelievers, for however clear the truth is presented and shown to them, they still remain in darkness.

68. Let us, then, understand all these sayings of the evangelist as common attributes and titles of Christ, which he wishes to have preached in the church as a preface and introduction of that which he proposes to write of Christ in his whole Gospel, namely, that he is true God and true man, who has created all things, and has been given to man as Life and Light, although but a few of all those to whom he is revealed receive him.

This is what our Gospel lesson contains and nothing more. In the same manner, Saint Paul also composes a preface and introduction to his Epistle to the Romans, in Romans 1:1. Now follows the actual beginning of this Gospel:

C. Christ Was the Light of Which John Bore Witness

There came a man, sent from God, whose name was John.

69. Saint Mark and Saint Luke begin their Gospels with John the Baptist, and they should begin with him; as Christ himself says, "From the days of John the Baptist until now the kingdom of heaven suffereth violence," in Matthew 11:12. And Saint Peter says that Jesus began from the baptism of John, by whom he was also called and ordained to be a minister, in Acts 1:22. And Saint

John the Baptist himself testifies, "I have beheld the Spirit descending as a dove out of heaven," in John 1:32, and he heard the Father's voice saying, "This is my beloved Son, in whom I am well pleased," in Matthew 3:17. Then Christ was made a teacher, and his public ministry began; then only began the Gospel of Christ. For no one except Christ himself was allowed to begin the exalted, blessed, comforting mission of the Word. And for his sake, John must first come and prepare the people for his preaching, that they might receive the Life and the Light.

70. For, as we have heard, Christ is everywhere the Light which shines in the darkness and is not apprehended; so he was especially and bodily in his humanity present among the Jews, appeared to them; but he was not recognized by them. Therefore, his forerunner, John, came for the sole purpose of preaching him, in order that he might be recognized and received. This passage, therefore, fittingly follows the former one. Since Christ, the shining Light, was not recognized, John came to open the eyes of men and to bear witness of the ever-present, shining light, which afterward was to be received, heard, and recognized itself without the witness of John.

71. It is my opinion that we have now passed through the most difficult and most glorious part of this Gospel; for what is said henceforth is easy, and is the same as that which the other evangelists write of John and of Christ. Although, as I have said, this part is in itself not difficult, yet it has been purposely made so by natural and human interpretations. A passage naturally becomes difficult when a word is taken from its ordinary meaning and given a strange one. Who would not wish to know what a man is, and would not imagine all manner of wonderful things, if he were told that a man is something different from what all the world thinks? This is what happened here to the clear, simple words of the evangelist.

72. Still, John uses a peculiar style, since he always, because of Cerinthus, directs the testimony of John the Baptist to the divinity of Christ, which is not done by the other evangelists, who only refer to Christ, without especially emphasizing his divinity. But here he says, John came to bear witness of the Light, and to preach Christ as the Life, the Light, and as God, as we shall hear.

73. What, therefore, was said about John the Baptist in Advent, is also to be understood here, namely, that, like as he came before Christ and directed the people to him, so the spoken word of the Gospel is simply to preach and point out Christ. It was ordained by God for this purpose alone, just as John was sent by God. We have also heard that John was a voice in the wilderness, signifying by his office the oral preaching of the Gospel. Since the darkness was of itself unable to apprehend this Light, although it was present, John

must needs reveal it and bear witness of it. And even now the natural reason is not able of itself to apprehend it, although it is present in all the world: the oral word of the Gospel must reveal it and proclaim it.

74. We see now that through the Gospel this light is brought to us, not from a distance, nor do we need to go far to obtain it; it is very near us and shines in our hearts; nothing more is needed than that it be pointed out and preached. And he who now hears it preached, and believes, finds it in his heart; for as faith is only in the heart, so also this light is alone in faith. Therefore, I say it is near at hand and within us, but of ourselves we cannot apprehend it; it must be preached and believed. This is also what Saint Paul means when he says, referring to Deuteronomy 30:11–14, "Say not in thine heart, Who shall ascend into heaven? (that is, to bring Christ down), or, Who shall descend into the deep? (that is, to bring Christ up from the dead). But what saith it? The word is nigh thee, in thy mouth, and in thy heart; that is, the word of faith, which we preach," in Romans 10:6–8. Behold this is the light which shines in darkness and is not recognized until John and the Gospel come and reveal it. Then man is enlightened by it, and apprehends it; and yet it changes neither time, nor place, nor person, nor age, but only the heart.

75. Again, as John did not come of himself, but was sent by God, so neither the Gospel nor any sermon on this Light can come of itself or from human reason; but they must be sent by God. Therefore, the evangelist here sets aside all the doctrines of men; for what men teach will never show Christ, the Light, but will only obstruct it. But whatsoever points out Christ is surely sent by God, and has not been invented by man. For this reason, the evangelist mentions the name and says, His name was John. In Hebrew, John means grace or favor, to signify that this preaching and message was not sent on account of any merit of ours; but was sent purely out of God's grace and mercy, and brings to us also God's grace and mercy. Thus Saint Paul says, "How shall they preach, except they be sent?" in Romans 10:15.

76. From all this, we learn that the evangelist speaks of Christ in a manner that he may be recognized as God. For if he is the light which is everywhere present and shines in darkness, and it needs nothing more than that it be revealed through the Word, and recognized in the heart through faith, it must surely be God. No creature can to such a degree be so near in all places, and shine in all hearts. And yet the Light is God in a way as to be still man, and be preached in and by man. The words follow:

The same came for witness, that he might bear witness of the Light,
that all might believe through him.

77. From what has now been said, it is clear that the Gospel proclaims only this Light, the man Christ, and causes the darkness to apprehend it, yet not by reason or feeling, but by faith. For he says, "That all might believe through him." Again, "He came for a witness, that he might bear witness." The nature of bearing witness is that it speaks of that which others do not see, know, or feel; but they must believe him that bears testimony. So also the Gospel does not demand a decision and assent according to reason, but a faith which is above reason, for in no other way can this light be recognized.

78. It was said plainly enough above, in what way the light of reason is in conflict with and rages against this Light, to say nothing of its being adhered to or apprehended by it. For it is positively written, "The darkness apprehendeth the light not"; therefore, reason with its light must be taken captive and blinded; as is said in Isaiah 60:19, "The sun," that is, thy reason, "shall be no more thy light by day; neither for brightness shall the moon give light unto thee; but Jehovah will be unto thee an everlasting light and thy God thy glory," that is, through the Gospel or Word of God, or through the witness of John, which demands faith, and makes a fool of reason. Consequently, witness is borne of this Light through the Word, that reason may keep silent and follow this testimony; then it will apprehend the Light in faith, and its darkness will be illumined. For if reason were able to apprehend this Light of itself, or adhere to it, there would be no need of John or his testimony.

79. Therefore, the aim of the Gospel is to be a witness for reason's sake, which is self-willed, blind, and stubborn. The Gospel resists reason and leads it away from its own light and fancy to faith, through which it can apprehend this living and eternal Light.

He was not the Light, but came that he might bear witness of the Light.

80. Dearly beloved, why does he say this, and repeat the words that John was only a witness of the Light? Oh, what necessary repetition! First of all to show that this Light is not simply a man, but God himself; for, as I have said, the evangelist greatly desires to preach the divinity of Christ in all his words. If John, the great saint, be not that Light, but only a witness of it, then this Light must be something far different from everything that is holy, whether it be man or angel. For if holiness could make such a light, it would have made one of John. But it is above holiness, and must, therefore, be above the angels, who are not more than holy.

81. In the second place, to resist wicked preachers of man, who do not bear witness of Christ, the Light, but of themselves. For it is true indeed, that all who preach the doctrines of men make man the light, lead men away from

God to themselves, and set themselves up in the place of the true Light, as the pope and his followers have done. Therefore, he is the Antichrist, that is, he is against Christ, the true Light.

82. This Gospel text allows of no other doctrine beside it; it desires only to testify of Christ and lead men to him, who is the Light. Therefore, O Lord God, these words, "He was not the Light," are truly worthy to be capitalized and to be well remembered against the men who set themselves up as the light and give to men doctrines and laws of their own fabrication. They pretend to enlighten men, but lead them with themselves into the depths of hell; for they do not teach faith, and are not willing to teach it; and no one teaches it except John, who is sent of God, and the holy Gospel. Truly much could be said on this point.

83. In short, he who does not preach the Gospel to you, reject and refuse to hear him. He, however, preaches the Gospel who teaches you to believe and trust in Christ, the eternal Light, and not to build on any of your own works. Therefore, beware of everything told you that does not agree with the Gospel; do not put your trust in it, nor accept it as something external, as you regard eating and drinking, which are necessary for your body, and which you may use at your pleasure or at the pleasure of another; but by no means as something necessary to your salvation. For this purpose nothing is necessary or of use to you except this Light.

84. Oh, these abominable doctrines of men, which are now so prevalent and which have almost banished this Light! They all wish to be this light themselves, but not to be witnesses of it. They advocate themselves and teach their own fancies, but are silent about this Light, or teach it in a way as to preach themselves along with it. This is worse than to be entirely silent; for by such teaching they make Samaritans who partly worship God and partly worship idols, in 2 Kings 17:33.

D. He Was the Light That Lighteth Everyone

There was the true Light, which lighteth every man,
coming into the world.

85. Neither John nor any saint is the Light; but John and all evangelical preachers testify of the true Light. For the present, enough has been said of this Light—what it is, how it is recognized by faith, and how it supports us eternally in life and death, so that no darkness can ever harm us. But what is remarkable is, that he says, "It lighteth every man, coming into the world." If this be affirmed of the natural light, it would be contradicted when he says

that it is "the true Light." He had said before, "The darkness apprehends it not"; and all his words are directed toward the Light of grace. Then follow the words, "He was in the world, and the world knew him not," and "His own received him not." But he whom the true Light lights, is illumined by grace, and recognizes the Light.

86. Again, that he does not speak of the light of grace is evident when he says, "It lighteth every man, coming into the world." This manifestly includes all men who are born into the world. Saint Augustine says it means that no man is illumined except by this Light; it is the same as though we were to say of a teacher in a place where there is no other teacher, This teacher instructs all the city, that is, there is no other teacher in that city; he instructs all the pupils. By it is not said that he teaches all the people in the city, but simply that he is the only teacher in the city, and none are taught but by him.

So here the evangelist would have us know that John is not the Light, nor any man, nor any creature; but that there is only one Light that lights all men, and that no man comes into the world who can possibly be illumined by any other light.

87. And I cannot reject this interpretation; for Saint Paul also speaks in like manner in Romans 5:18, "As through one trespass the judgment came unto all men to condemnation; even so through one act of righteousness the free gift came unto all men unto justification of life." Although all men are not justified through Christ, he is, nevertheless, the only man through whom justification comes.

So it is also here. Although all men are not illumined, nevertheless this is the only light through which all illumination comes. The evangelist has used this manner of speech freely, and had no fear that some might take offense because he says "all men." He thought he would anticipate all such offense, and explains himself before and afterward, and says, "The darkness apprehended him not, and his own received him not." These words are sufficient proof to prevent anyone from saying that the evangelist meant to say that all men are illumined; but he did wish to say that Christ is the only Light that lights all men, and without him no man is lighted.

88. If this were said of the natural light of reason, it would have little significance, since it not only enlightens all men who come into the world, but also those who go out of the world, and even devils. For this light of reason remains in the dead, in devils, and in the condemned, yea, it becomes brighter, that they may be all the more tormented by it. But since only human beings who come into this world are mentioned, the evangelist indicates that he is speaking of the Light of faith, which lightens and helps only in this life; for

after death, no one will be illumined by it. The illuminating must take place in this life through faith in the man Christ, yet by his divinity. After this life, we shall clearly see his divinity without the humanity and without faith.

89. Therefore, the evangelist is careful to form his words so as not by any means to reject the man Christ, and yet so as to declare his divinity. For this reason, it was necessary for him to say "all men," so as to preach only one light for all, and to warn us not to accept in this life the lights of men or any other lights.

One man is not to lighten another, but this light alone is to lighten all men; and ministers are to be only forerunners and witnesses of this Light to men, that all may believe in this Light.

Therefore, when he had said, "Which lighteth every man," he realized that he had said too much, and so he added, "coming into the world," so that he might make Christ the Light of this world. For in the world to come this light will cease and will be changed into eternal glory, as Saint Paul says, "When he shall deliver up the kingdom to God," in 1 Corinthians 15:24; but now he rules through his humanity. When he delivers up the kingdom, he will also deliver up the Light; not as though there were two kinds of light, or as though we were to see something different from what we now see; but we shall see the same Light and the same God we now see in faith, but in a different manner. Now we see him in faith darkly, then we shall see him face to face. Just as though I beheld a gilded picture through a colored glass or veil, and afterward looked at it without these. So also Saint Paul says, "Now we see in a mirror, darkly; but then face to face," in 1 Corinthians 13:12.

90. Behold, you now know of what the evangelist speaks, when he says that Christ is the Light of men through his humanity, that is, in faith, by means of which his divinity is reflected as by a mirror, or is seen as in a glass or as the sun shines through bright clouds. But let us remember that the Light is attributed to his divinity, not to his humanity; and yet his humanity, which is the cloud or curtain before the Light, must not be thought lightly of.

91. This language is sufficiently plain and he who has faith understands very well what is the nature and character of this Light. It matters not if he who does not believe does not understand it. He is not to understand it, for it is better that he knew nothing of the Bible and did not study it, than that he deceive himself and others with his erroneous light; for he imagines it to be the light of Scripture, which, however, cannot be apprehended without true faith. For this Light shines in the darkness, but is not apprehended by it.

92. This passage may also mean that the evangelist has in mind the preaching of the Gospel and of faith in all the world, and so that this Light shines upon

all men throughout the world, just as the sun shines upon all men. Saint Paul says, "Be not moved away from the hope of the Gospel which ye heard, which was preached in all creation under heaven," in 1 Colossians 1:23. Christ himself says, "Go ye into all the world, and preach the Gospel to the whole creation," in Mark 16:15. The psalmist also says, "His going forth is from the end of the heavens, and his circuit unto the ends of it; and there is nothing hid from the heat thereof," in Psalm 19:6. How this is to be understood has been explained in the sermon on the Epistle for Christmas, in Isaiah 9:2.

93. By this easy and simple interpretation, we can readily understand how this Light lights every man, coming into the world, so that neither Jews nor anyone else should dare to set up their own light anywhere. And this interpretation is well suited to the preceding passages. For even before John or the Gospel bore witness of the Light, it had shone in darkness and the darkness apprehended it not; but after it has been proclaimed and publicly witnessed to, it shines as far as the world extends, unto all men, although all men will not receive it, as follows:

II. THE COMING OF CHRIST

He was in the world, and the world was made through him,
and the world knew him not.

94. All this is said of Christ as man and refers especially to the time after his baptism, when he began to give light according to John's testimony. He was ever in the world. But what place of the world knew it? Who received him? He was not even received by those with whom he was personally associated, as the following shows:

He came unto his own, and they that were his own received him not.

95. This also is said of his coming as a preacher, and not of his being born into the world. For his coming is his preaching and illumining. The Baptist says, "He it is who coming after me is preferred before me, the latchet of whose shoe I am not worthy to unloose," in Matthew 3:11, Luke 3:16, Mark 1:7, John 1:27. On account of this coming, John is also called his forerunner, as Gabriel said to his father, Zacharias, "He shall go before his face in the spirit and power of Elijah; to make ready for the Lord a people prepared for him," in Luke 1:17. For, as has been said, the Gospels begin with the baptism of Christ. Then he began to be the Light and to do that for which he came. Therefore, it is said that he came into the world to his own people and his own received him not.

If this were not said of his coming to give light by preaching, the evangelist would not thus reprove them for not having received him.

96. Who could know that it was he, if he had not been revealed? Therefore, it is their fault that they did not receive him; for he came and was revealed by John and by himself. Therefore, John says, "That he should be made manifest to Israel, for this cause came I baptizing with water," in John 1:31. And he says himself, "I am come in my Father's name, and ye receive me not; if another shall come in his own name, him ye will receive," in John 5:43. This is also evidently said of the coming of his preaching and of his revelation.

97. He calls the Jews his own people because they were chosen out of all the world to be his people, and he had been promised to them through Abraham, Isaac, Jacob, and David. For to us heathens or gentiles there was no promise of Christ. Therefore, we are strangers and are not called "his own"; but through pure grace we have been adopted, and have thus become his people; though, alas, we also allow him to come daily through the Gospel and do not esteem him. Therefore, we must also suffer that another, the pope, comes in his place and is received by us. We must serve the bitter foe because we will not serve our God.

98. But we must not forget in this connection that the evangelist refers twice to the divinity of Christ. First, when he says, "The world was made through him." Secondly, when he says, "He came unto his own." For it is the nature only of the true God to have his own people. The Jews were always God's own people, as the Scriptures frequently declare. If, then, they are Christ's own people, he must certainly be that God to whom the Scriptures assign that people.

99. But the evangelist commends to every thoughtful person for consideration, what a shame and disgrace it is that the world does not recognize its Creator, and that the Jewish people do not receive their God. In what stronger terms can you reprove the world than by saying that it does not know its Creator? What base wickedness and evil report follow from this fact alone! What good can there be where there is nothing but ignorance, darkness, and blindness? What wickedness where there is no knowledge of God! O woe! What a wicked and frightful thing the world is! The one who knew the world and duly pondered this would fall the deeper into perdition. He could not be happy in this life, of which such evil things are written.

But as many as received him, to them gave he the right to become children of God, even to them that believed on his name.

100. We see now what kind of a Light that is of which the evangelist has hitherto been speaking. It is Christ, the comforting light of grace, and not the light of nature or reason. For John is an evangelist and not a Platonist. All who receive the light of nature and reason receive him according to that light; how could they receive him otherwise? Just as they receive the natural life from the divine life. However, that light and that life do not give them any power to become the children of God. Yea, they remain the enemies of this Light, do not know it, nor acknowledge it. Therefore, there can be no reference in this Gospel to the light of nature, but only to Christ, that he may be acknowledged as true God.

101. From now on, this Gospel is familiar to all, for it speaks of faith in Christ's name, that it makes us God's children. These are excellent words and powerfully refute the teachers of the law, who preach only good works. Good works never bring about a change of heart. Therefore, although the work righteous are ever changing and think they are improving their deeds, in their hearts they remain the same, and their works only become a mantle for their shame and hypocrisy.

102. But, as has often been said, faith changes the person and makes out of an enemy a child, so mysteriously that the external works, walk, and conversation remain the same as before, when they are not by nature wicked deeds. Therefore, faith brings with it the entire inheritance and highest good of righteousness and salvation, so that these need not be sought in works, as the false teachers of good works would have us believe. For he who is a child of God has already God's inheritance through his sonship. If, then, faith gives this sonship, it is manifest that good works should be done freely, to the honor of God, since they already possess salvation and the inheritance from God through faith. This has been amply explained heretofore in the sermon on the second Epistle for this day.

Who were born, not of blood, nor of the will of the flesh,
nor of the will of man, but of God.

103. To explain himself, the evangelist here tells us what faith does, and that everything is useless without it. Here he not only does not praise nature, light, reason, and whatever is not of faith, but forcibly overthrows each. This sonship is too great and noble to originate from nature or to be required by it.

104. John mentions four different kinds of sonship: one of blood, another of the will of the flesh, a third of the will of man, the fourth of this will of God. It is evident that the sonship of blood is the natural sonship. With this, he refutes the Jews who boasted that they were of the blood of Abraham and

the patriarchs, relying on the passages of Scripture in which God promises the blessing and the inheritance of eternal salvation to the seed of Abraham. Therefore, they claim to be the only true people and children of God. But here he says, there must be more than mere blood, else there is no sonship of God. For Abraham and the patriarchs received the inheritance, not for blood's sake but for faith's sake, as Paul teaches in Hebrews 11:8. If mere blood relationship were sufficient for this sonship, then Judas the betrayer, Caiaphas, Ananias, and all the wicked Jews who in times past were condemned in the wilderness, would have a proper right to this inheritance. For they were all of the blood of the patriarchs. Therefore, it is said, they were born "not of blood, but of God."

105. The other two relationships, or sonships, to wit, "of the will of the flesh" and "of the will of man," I do not yet sufficiently understand myself. But I see very well that the evangelist thereby wishes to reject everything which is of nature and which nature can accomplish, and that he would retain the birth by God alone. Therefore, there is no danger in whatever manner we explain these two parts and variously attribute them to nature outside of grace. It is all the same. Some understand the sonship of the will of the flesh to come not of blood, but through the law of Moses. He commanded that the nearest kin to the wife of a deceased husband marry the widow, and raise a name and heir to the deceased one, that the name of his friend be not put out of Israel. To this interpretation belongs also the "step" relationship, which comes of the will of the flesh, and not of blood relationship.

106. But the evangelist here calls by the name of flesh man, as he lives in the flesh, which is the common scriptural designation. Therefore, the meaning is, not as men have children outside of their own line of descent, which is carnal and human, and takes place in accordance with man's free will, but what is born in the line of ancestral blood, takes place without the free will, according to nature, whether a man wills it or not.

107. The third kind of sonship mentioned is "of the will of man." This is taken to mean the sonship of strangers, commonly called "adoption," as when a man chooses and adopts a strange child as his own. Though you were Abraham's or David's real child, or stepchild, or you had been adopted, or you were a stranger, it would all be of no benefit to you unless you were born of God. Even Christ's own friends and relatives did not believe in him, as we are told, in John 7:5.

108. But those who wish may explain this relationship as follows: "Those born of blood" may mean all those who belong to the blood relationship, whether it be a full or a step relationship; "those born of the will of the flesh" may include all those who are not born of blood, or those who have been

adopted into the relationship. But "those who are born of the will of man" are spiritual children of those who are the disciples or followers of a teacher. Thus the evangelist rejects everything that might be accomplished by blood, flesh, nature, reason, art, doctrine, law, free will, with all their powers, so that no one may presume to help another by means of his own doctrine, work, art, or free will, or be allowed to help any man upon earth to the kingdom of God; he is to reject everything, except the striving after the divine birth.

I am also inclined to think that "man" in the Scriptures usually means a superior, who rules, leads, and teaches others. These are properly and before all others rejected, since no relationship is more stubborn, more insolently presumptuous, and confides more in itself than this, and does most strenuously oppose grace at all times, and persecutes the Lord of grace. In this respect, let everyone have his opinion, as long as he bears in mind that nothing avails which is not born of God. For if something else would have availed anything, the evangelist would without doubt have put it side by side with the divine birth, especially as he looks for it so carefully, and would not have exalted only this divine birth.

109. The divine birth is, therefore, nothing else than faith. How can this be? It has been explained above how the light of grace opposes and blinds the light of reason. If now the Gospel comes and bears witness to the light of grace, that man must not live and do according to his fancy, but must reject, put away, and destroy the light of nature, if this man accepts and follows such testimony, gives up his own light and fancy, is willing to become a fool, allows himself to be led, taught, and enlightened, he will be entirely changed, that is, in his natural light. His old light is extinguished and a new light, to wit, faith, is kindled. He follows this new light in life and in death, clings solely to the witness of John or the Gospel, even should he be compelled to abandon all he had and could do before.

Behold, he is now born again of God through the Gospel, in which he remains, and lets go his own light and fancy, as Saint Paul says, "For in Christ Jesus I begat you through the Gospel," in 1 Corinthians 4:15; again, "Of his own will he brought us forth by the word of truth, that we should be a kind of first fruits of his creatures," in James 1:18. Therefore, Saint Peter calls us "new born babes," in 1 Peter 2:2. It is for this reason also that the Gospel is called the womb of God, in which we are conceived, carried, and born as a woman conceives, carries, and bears a child in her womb. Isaiah says, "Hearken unto me, O house of Jacob, and all the remnant of the house of Israel, that have been borne by me from their birth, that have been carried from the womb," in Isaiah 46:3.

110. But this birth properly shows its power in times of temptation and death. There it becomes evident who is born again, and who is not. Then the old light, reason, struggles and wrestles and is loath to leave its fancies and desires, is unwilling to consider and resort to the Gospel, and let go its own light. But those who are born again, or are then being born again, spend their lives in peace and obedience to the Gospel, confide in and cling to the witness of John, and let go their light, life, property, honor, and all they have. Therefore, they come to the eternal inheritance as real children.

111. But when this light, reason, and man's old conceit are dead, dark, and changed into a new light, then the life and all powers of man must be changed and be obedient to the new Light. For where the will goes, reason follows, and love and pleasures follow the will. And so the whole man must be hid in the Gospel, become a new creature, and put off the old Adam, as the serpent puts off its old skin. When the skin becomes old, the serpent seeks a narrow crevice in the rock, crawls through it, sheds its old skin, and leaves it on the outside.

Thus man must resort to the Gospel and to God's Word, confidently trusting their promises, which never fail. In this way, he puts off the old Adam, sets aside his own light and conceit, his will, love, desire, speech, and his deeds, and becomes an entirely new man, who sees everything in a different manner than before, judges differently, thinks differently, wills differently, speaks and loves and desires differently, acts and conducts himself differently than he did before. He now understands whether all the conditions and works of men are right or wrong, as Saint Paul says, "He that is spiritual judgeth all things, and he himself is judged of no man," in 1 Corinthians 2:15.

112. He now sees clearly what great fools they are who pretend to become pious through their good works. He would not give one farthing for all the preachers, monks, popes, bishops, tonsures, cowls, incense, illuminations, burning of candles, singing, organs, prayers, with all their external performances; for he sees how all this is simple idolatry, and foolish dissimulation, just as the Jews prayed to Baal, Ashtaroth, and the calf in the wilderness, which they looked upon as precious things in the old light of stubborn, self-conceited reason.

113. From this, it is evident that no blood, nor relationship, nor command, nor doctrine, nor reason, nor free will, nor good works, nor exemplary living, nor Carthusian orders, nor any religious orders, though they were angelic, are of any use or help to this sonship of God; but they are only a hindrance. For where reason is not first renewed and in agreement with the new birth, it takes offense, becomes hardened and blinded, so that it will scarcely, if ever, be able to be righted; but thinks its doings and ways are right and

proper, storming and raving against all who disregard and reject its doings. Therefore, the old man remains the enemy of God and of grace, of Christ and of his light, beheads John and destroys his testimony, the Gospel, and sets up his own human doctrines. Thus the game goes on even now, in full splendor and power, in the doings of the pope and his clergy, who together know nothing of this divine birth. They prattle and speak nonsense in their doctrines and commandments of certain good works, with which they hope to attain grace, though still clad in the old Adam.

114. But what is here said remains unchangeable: Not of blood, not of the will of the flesh nor of man, but of God, is this new birth. We must despair of our own will, works, and life, which have been poisoned by the false, stubborn, selfish light of reason; in all things, listen to the voice and testimony of the Baptist; believe and obey it. Then the true Light, Christ, will enlighten us, renew us, and give us power to become the sons of God. For this reason, he came and was made man, as follows:

III. CHRIST'S INCARNATION

And the Word became flesh, and dwelt among us, (and we beheld his glory, glory as of the only begotten from the Father,) full of grace and truth.

115. By "flesh" we understand the whole man, body and soul, according to the Scriptures, which call man "flesh," as above, when it is said, "Not of the will of the flesh"; and in the creed we say, "I believe in the resurrection of the body" (German: flesh), that is, of all men. Again Christ says, "Except those days had been shortened, there would be no flesh saved," that is, no man, in Matthew 24:22. Again, "He remembered that they were but flesh, a wind that passeth away, and cometh not again," in Psalm 78:39. Again, "Thou gavest him authority over all flesh, that to all whom thou hast given him, he should give eternal life," in John 17:2.

116. I speak of this the more fully because this passage has occasioned so much offense on the part of heretics at the time when there were learned and great bishops. Some, as Photinus and Appollinaris, taught that Christ was a man without a soul, and that the divine nature took the place of the soul in him. Manichaeus taught that Christ did not have true, natural flesh, but was only an apparition, passing through his mother, Mary, without assuming her flesh and blood, just as the sun shines through a glass, but does not assume its nature. In opposition to all these, the evangelist uses a comprehensive word and says, "He became flesh," that is, a man like every other man, who has flesh and blood, body and soul.

117. Thus the Scriptures, one part after another, had to be tried and confirmed, until the time of the Antichrist, who suppressed them not in parts, but in their entirety. For it has been prophesied that at the time of Antichrist all heresy should be united into one parasitic whole and devour the world. This could not have happened at a better time than when the pope set aside the whole Scriptures, and in their place set up his own law. Therefore, bishops are now no more heretics, nor can they become heretics; for they have no part of the book by which heretics are made, to wit, the Gospel. They have piled up all heresy within and among themselves.

118. In times past, heretics, however bad they were, still remained in the Scriptures, and left some parts intact. But what is left since this divine birth and faith are no more acknowledged and preached, and in their stead only human law and works? What matters it, whether Christ is God or not God, whether he was flesh or a mere apparition, whether he had a soul or not, whether he had come before or after his mother, or whether all error and heresy which have ever been, would prevail? We would have no more of him than all those heretics and do not need him. He seems to have become man in vain, and all things written about him seem to be to no purpose, because we have ourselves found a way by which we may by our own works come to the grace of God!

119. Therefore, there is no difference between our bishops and all heretics that have ever lived, except this that we name Christ with our mouth and pen, for the sake of appearance. But among ourselves we speak of him, and are as little benefited by him, as though he were one with whom all heretics might play the fool. Thus Saint Peter has prophesied and said, "These shall be false teachers among you, who shall privily bring in destructive heresies, denying even the Master that bought them," in 2 Peter 2:1.

120. What does it profit, though Christ be not what the heretics make him, if he is no more to us than to them, and does no more for us? What does it profit to condemn the heretics, and know Christ aright, if we have no different faith in him than they had? I see no reason for the need of Christ, if I am able to attain grace by my works. It is not necessary for him to be God and man. In short, all that is written about him is unnecessary; it would be sufficient to preach God alone, as the Jews believe, and then obtain his grace by means of my works. What more would I want? What more would I need?

121. Christ and the Scriptures are not necessary, as long as the doctrine of the pope and his schools exist. Therefore, I have said that pope, bishops, and schools are not good enough to be heretics; but they surpass all heretics, and are the dregs of all heresies, errors, and idolatry from the beginning,

because they entirely suppress Christ and the Word of God, and only retain their names for appearance's sake. This no idolater, no heretic, no Jew has ever done, not even the Turk [Muslim] with all his violent acts. And although the heathen were without the Scriptures and without Christ before his birth, yet they did not oppose him and the Scriptures, as these do. Therefore, they were far better than the papists.

122. Let us be wise in these times in which Antichrist is powerful, and let us cling to the Gospel, which does not teach us that reason is our light, as men teach us, but which presents Christ as indispensable to our salvation, and says, The Word, by which all things were made, is life, and the life is the light of men. Firmly believe that Christ is the Light of men, that without him all is darkness in man, so that he is unable to know what to do or how to act, to say nothing about being able to attain the grace of God by his own works, as the foolish schools with their idol, the pope, teach and deceive all the world.

123. He came that he might become the Light of men, that is, that he might become known; he showed himself bodily and personally among men and was made man. He is the light on the candlestick. The lost piece of money did not of itself and with light in hand go after and seek the lighted candle, but the candle with its light sought the piece of money and found it; it has swept the house of this whole world in every nook and corner with its broom; and it continues to seek, sweep, and find even until the last day.

124. But that the Word and not the Father was made flesh, and that both are one complete, true God, is a great mystery. Yet faith apprehends it all, and it is proper that reason should not apprehend it; it happened and is written that reason should not apprehend it, but become altogether blind, dazzled, and stupefied, changing from its old false light into the new light.

125. Yet this article is not opposed to the light of reason, which says that we must serve God, believe, and be pious, which accords with this article. But if reason is called on to say exactly who this God is, it is startled and says, "This is not God," and so makes a God according to its fancy. Therefore, when it is informed that this Word is God and that the Father is the same God, it doubts, hesitates, and imagines the article to be wrong and untrue, continues in its conceit and fancy, and thinks it knows better what God is and who he is than anyone else.

126. Thus the Jews continue in their opinion, and do not doubt at all that God is to be believed and honored; but who this God is, they explain according to their own fancy, claim to be masters themselves, and even make God a liar. See then, thus reason does to all of God's works and words, continues to cry that God's work and Word are to be honored, but claims that it is its privilege

and judgment to say what is God's work and Word. It would judge God in all his works and words, but is unwilling to be judged by him. What God is or is not, must be according to its caprice.

127. Consider whether God does not justly express his anger in the Scriptures against such immeasurable wickedness, whether he does not rightly prefer open sinners to such saints. What would you think more vexatious than such wicked presumptuousness? I say this that we may recognize the delicious fruit to which the pope and his schools attribute so much, and which of itself and by its own exertions, without Christ, provides the grace of God. They are God's greatest enemies, and would annihilate him, in order that they might be God themselves, and succeed in making men believe that the grace of God is obtained as they prescribe. This surely is real darkness.

128. See, in this way reason must make idols, and cannot do otherwise; it knows very well how to talk of God's honor, but goes and bestows the same honor on him whom it fancies to be God. Such a one is certainly not God, but is reason's fancy and error, of which the prophets in various ways complained. Nor does it improve the matter, if anyone were to say, as the Jews do, "Yes, I mean the God who has created the heavens and the earth; here I cannot be mistaken, and must be right." In Isaiah 48:1, God himself answers, "Hear ye this, who swear by the name of Jehovah, and make mention of the God of Israel, but not in truth, nor in righteousness." And Jeremiah 5:2 says, "And though they say, as Jehovah liveth; surely they swear falsely."

129. How is this to be accounted for? It happens thus that he who does not accept God in the particular manner in which God has revealed himself, will profit nothing, if he afterward accepts God in the manner which he has selected for himself. If Abraham had said that it was neither God nor God's work that commanded him to sacrifice his son Isaac, but would have followed his reason and have said he would not sacrifice his son, but would serve the God who made heaven and earth in some other way, what would it have profited him? He would have lied; for he would in that very thing have rejected the God who created the heavens and the earth, and would have devised another God, under the name of the God who had created the heavens and the earth, and would have despised the true God, who had given him the command.

130. Behold, thus they all lie who say, they mean the true God who created the heavens and the earth, and yet do not accept his work and Word, but exalt their own opinion above God and his Word. If we truly believed in the God who had created heaven and earth, they would also know that the same God is a creator of their imagination, makes, breaks, and judges it as he pleases. But

as they do not allow him to be a creator of themselves and their fancies even in a small degree, it cannot be true that they believe him to be the creator of all creation.

131. Perhaps you will say, What if I were deceived, and he were not God? Answer: Do not worry, dear soul; a heart that does not trust in its own fancy God will not allow to be deceived; for it is not possible that he should not enter such a heart and dwell there. Mary says, "He hath filled the hungry with good things," in Luke 1:53. The psalmist says, "He satisfieth the longing soul," in Psalm 107:9. But if any is deceived, it is certain that he trusted in his own fancy, either secretly or openly. Therefore a hungry soul always stands in fear in those things that are uncertain, whether they be of God. But self-conceited persons are immediately taken with them, thinking it sufficient if the things glitter and take their fancy. Again, what is certain to be of God, the simple accept at once, but the arrogant persecute it.

132. Now there is no surer sign of a thing of God than that it is against or beyond our fancy. Likewise the arrogant think, there is no surer sign that a thing is not of God than that it is against their fancy. For they are makers and masters of God, and so make those things God and of God which accord with their fancy. Therefore, all those who depend upon themselves must be deceived, and all those who are simple-minded, and not preoccupied with themselves, are safe; they are they who keep the true Sabbath. Where this fancy goes so far as to employ the Word of God in defense of its arrogance and to apply the Scriptures according to its own light, there is neither hope nor help. Such people think the Word of God on their side, and they must safeguard it. This is the last fall, and is the real mischief of Lucifer, of whom Solomon speaks, "A righteous man falleth seven times, and riseth up again; but the wicked are overthrown by calamity," in Proverbs 24:16.

133. Of this, there is now enough; let us come back again to the Gospel. John says, "And the Word became flesh, and dwelt among us"; that is, he lived among men upon earth, as other men do. Even though he was God, he became a citizen of Nazareth and Capernaum, and conducted himself as other men did. Thus Saint Paul says, "Who, existing in the form of God, counted not the being man equality with a thing to be grasped, but emptied himself, taking the form of a servant, being made in the likeness of men; and being found in fashion as a man, he humbled himself, becoming obedient even unto death, yea, the death of the cross," in Philippians. 2:6–8.

134. Now this "likeness" and "dwelling" of Christ must not be understood of his human nature, in which he has been made like unto men. But these words must be understood as referring to his external being and mode

of living such as eating, drinking, sleeping, walking, working, resting, hearth and home, and standing, and all human conduct and deportment, by which no one could recognize him as God, had he not been so proclaimed by John in the Gospel.

IV. THE REVELATION OF CHRIST'S GLORY

135. He says further, "We behold his glory," that is, his divinity through his miracles and teachings. The word "glory" we have heard before in the Epistle, where it was said of Christ, that Christ is the "brightness of the Father's glory," which means his divinity. Our word "glory" comes from the Latin *"gloria."* The corresponding word in Hebrew is *"kabod"* and the Greek word is *"doxa."* Thus we speak of a ruler or a great man having achieved an accomplishment with great glory, and that everything passed off gloriously, when it has passed off well, successfully, and bravely.

Glory does not only mean a great repute, or far-famed honor, but it means also the things which give occasion for the fame, such as costly houses, vessels, clothes, servants, and the like, as Christ says of Solomon, "Consider the lilies of the field, how they grow; they toil not, neither do they spin; yet I say unto you, that even Solomon in all his glory was not arrayed like one of these," in Matthew 6:28–29. In the book of Esther, we read, "King Ahasuerus made a great feast…when he showed the riches of his glorious kingdom," in Esther 1:3–4. Thus we say, This is a glorious thing, a glorious manner, a glorious deed, *"gloriosa res."* This is also what the evangelist means when he says, "We have seen his glory," to wit, his glorious being and deeds, which are not an insignificant, common glory, but the glory as of the only begotten of the Father.

136. Here he expresses who the Word is, of whom he and Moses have been speaking, namely, the only begotten Son of God, who has all the glory of the Father. He calls him the only begotten, so as to distinguish him from all the children of God, who are not natural children as this one is. With these words is shown his true divinity; for if he were not God, he could not in preference to others be called the only begotten Son, which is to say that he and no other is the Son of God. This cannot be said of angels and pious men. For not one of them is the Son of God, but are all brethren and creatures of a like creation, children elected by grace, and not children born out of God's nature.

137. But the expression, "We beheld his glory," does not refer only to bodily sight; for the Jews also saw his glory, but did not regard it as the glory of the only begotten Son of God: it refers to the sight of the faithful, who

believe it in their hearts. Unbelievers, who beheld only the worldly glory, did not notice this divine glory. Nor can these two tolerate each other. He that would be glorious before the world for God's sake, will be glorious before God.

Full of grace and truth.

138. These two words are commonly used together in the Scriptures. "Grace" means that whatsoever Christ does is ever pleasing and right. Furthermore, in man there is only disfavor and guile; all that he does is displeasing to God. In fact, he is fundamentally untrue and puts on a vain show, as the psalmist says, "All men are liars," in Psalm 116:11. And again, "Surely every man at his best estate is altogether vanity," in Psalm 39:5.

139. This passage is opposed to the presumptuous papists and Pelagians, who find something outside of Christ, which they claim is good and true; and yet in Christ alone is grace and truth. It is indeed true, as has been said above, that there are some things outside of Christ which are true and pleasing, as the natural light, which teaches that three and two are five, that God should be honored, and the like.

But this light never accomplishes its end; for as soon as reason is to act, and make use of its light, and exercise it, it confuses everything, calls that which is good bad, and that which is bad good; calls that the honor of God which is his dishonor, and vice versa. Therefore, man is only a liar and vain, and unable to make use of this natural light except against God, as we have already said.

140. It is unnecessary to look for the armor in this Gospel; it is all armor and the chief part, upon which is founded the article of faith that Christ is true God and true man, and that without grace, nature, free will, and works are nothing but deception, sin, error, and heresy in spite of papists and Pelagians.

The Sunday After Christmas

❧

Of Simeon; of Anna; of the Return of the Parents of Jesus to Nazareth, and the Childhood of Christ

*A*nd his father and his mother were marveling at the things which were spoken concerning him; and Simeon blessed them, and said unto Mary his mother, "Behold, this child is set for the falling and the rising of many in Israel; and for a sign which is spoken against; yea and a sword shall pierce through thine own soul; that thoughts out of many hearts may be revealed." And there was one Anna, a prophetess, the daughter of Phanuel, of the tribe of Asher (she was of a great age, having lived with a husband seven years from her virginity, and she had been a widow even unto fourscore and four years), who departed not from the temple, worshiping with fastings and supplications night and day. And coming up at that very hour she gave thanks unto God, and spake of him to all them that were looking for the redemption of Jerusalem. And when they had accomplished all things that were according to the law of the Lord, they returned into Galilee, to their own city Nazareth.

And the child grew, and waxed strong, filled with wisdom, and the grace of God was upon him. — LUKE 2:33–40

1. It is very probable that today's Epistle has been selected by a pure misunderstanding, the one who appointed it for this Sunday probably thinking that it refers to the infant Christ, because it speaks of a young heir who is lord of all. Many other Epistles and Gospels have been selected for inappropriate days from similar misunderstandings. Nothing, however, depends upon the order of selection; it amounts to the same thing what is preached at the different seasons, if only the right meaning is preserved. Thus the events of this Gospel happened on the day of Candlemas, when Mary brought the child into the temple, and yet it is read on this Sunday. I mention all this, that nobody may be confused by the chronological order, or prevented from correctly

understanding the Gospel. We will divide it into two parts, the one treating of Simeon, and the other of Anna. It is indeed a rich Gospel and well arranged: first, the man Simeon; second, the woman Anna, both aged and holy.

I. OF SIMEON

And his father and his mother were marveling at
the things which were spoken concerning him.

2. What are those wonderful things spoken concerning him? They are the things concerning which Saint Simeon had spoken immediately before, when in the temple he took the child Jesus upon his arms, saying, "Now lettest thou thy servant depart, Lord according to thy word, in peace; for mine eyes have seen thy salvation, which thou hast prepared before the face of all peoples; a light for revelation to the gentiles, and the glory of thy people Israel." At these things, Saint Luke says, they marveled, namely, that this aged and holy man stood there before them in the temple, took the child in his arms and spoke of him so exultingly, calling him the light of the world, a Savior of all nations, a glory of all the people of Israel; Simeon himself thinking so highly of him that he would now fain depart this life after he had seen the child.

3. Now it must indeed excite wonder that such things were proclaimed openly by Simeon in that public and sacred place with reference to that poor and insignificant child, whose mother was so humble and lowly and whose father Joseph was not wealthy. How could such a child be considered the Savior of all men, the light of the gentiles, and the glory and honor of all Israel? At present, after we have had so many proofs of Christ's greatness, these words do no longer seem so wonderful; but then, when nothing as yet was known of Jesus, they were indeed marvelous, and this lowly child was very unlike the great and mighty being portrayed by Simeon. But Joseph and Mary believed it nevertheless, and just, therefore, they marveled. If they had not believed it, the words of Simeon would have appeared to them insignificant, untrue, and worthless, and not at all wonderful. Therefore, the fact that they were marveling, shows that Joseph and Mary possessed a strong and sublime faith.

4. But someone might say, Why, then, do they marvel at this? Had not the angels told them before that this child was Christ and the Savior, and had not the shepherds also spoken glorious things concerning him? It was also very wonderful that the kings or wise men had come from distant lands to worship him with their offerings. Mary knew well that she had conceived him of the Holy Spirit, and that wonderful events had attended his birth. Moreover,

the angel Gabriel had said that he should be great and be called the Son of the Most High. In short, all the preceding events had been marvelous, up to this time; now nothing wonderful occurs, but only those things are announced and proclaimed concerning him which have not happened and are not yet seen.

5. It seems to me that in this case we need not look very far for an explanation. The evangelist does not deny that they had also marveled before this. He simply desires to relate here what they did when Saint Simeon spoke such glorious things concerning the child. He means to say, When Saint Simeon spake thus, the child's parents did not despise his words, but believed them firmly. Therefore, they remained and listened to him and marveled at his utterances; what could they have done in addition to this? Thus it is not denied here that previously they marveled just as much, if not more.

6. We shall inquire later into the spiritual significance of this wonderment; now we are concerned about the literal sense, serving as an example of our faith and teaching us how wonderful are the works of God concerning us; for the end is very unlike the beginning. The beginning is nothing, the end is everything; just as the infant Christ here appears to be very insignificant, and yet he finally became the Savior and light of all nations.

7. If Joseph and Mary had judged according to outward appearances, they would have considered Christ more than a poor child. But they disregard the outward appearance and cling to the words of Simeon with a firm faith; therefore, they marvel at his speech. Thus we must also disregard all the senses when contemplating the works of God, and only cling to his words, so that our eyes and our senses may not offend us.

8. The fact that they were marveling at the words of Simeon is also mentioned to teach us that the Word of God is never preached in vain, as we read in Isaiah 55:11, "So shall my word be that goeth forth out of my mouth" (i.e., out of the mouth of God's messengers), "it shall not return unto me void, but it shall accomplish that which I please, and it shall prosper in the thing whereto I sent it." Thus the evangelist would say that Simeon delivered a warmhearted, beautiful sermon, preaching the pure Gospel and the Word of God. For the Gospel is nothing but a sermon whose theme is Christ, declaring him to be the Savior, light, and glory of all the world. Such preaching fills the heart with joy and wonder at this great grace and comfort, if it is received in faith.

9. But although this sermon was very beautiful and comforting, there were only a few who believed; nay, people despised it as being foolish, going hither and thither in the temple. Some prayed, others did something else, but they did not give heed to the words of Simeon. Yet, as the Word of God must produce results, there were indeed some who received it with joy and wonder,

namely, Joseph and Mary. The evangelist here also rebukes the unbelief of the Jews, for as this occurred publicly in the temple, there were many present, and yet they would not believe, the fact that the Savior was only a child causing them all to stumble. Thus we learn here that we should hear the Word of God gladly, for it will invariably produce good fruits.

The Spiritual Meaning of This Gospel Concerning Simeon

10. This leads us to the spiritual significance of this astonishment of Joseph and Mary. The temple is an abode of God, therefore, signifying every place where God is present. Among others, it also signifies the holy Scriptures, where God may be found as in his proper place. To bring Christ into the temple, means nothing else than to follow the example of the people mentioned in Acts 17:11. After they had received the Word with all readiness of mind, they went into the Scriptures, daily examining them whether these things were so.

11. Now we find in this same temple Simeon, who in his person represents all the prophets filled with the Holy Spirit, just as Saint Luke says of Simeon. They have spoken and written as they were moved by the Holy Spirit, and have waited for the coming of Christ, just like Simeon. They have never ceased to do this until Christ came, as Saint Peter says in Acts 3:24, that all the prophets have spoken of the days of Christ. And Christ himself says, in Matthew 11:13, that all the prophets and the law prophesied until John, i.e., until the baptism of Christ, when he began to show himself as the Savior and light of all the world.

12. All this is signified by Simeon, who was not to die until he had seen Christ. For this reason, he is called Simeon, which means "one who hears," for the prophets had only heard of Christ as of him who was as yet unborn and would come after them. Therefore, having him in their wake, as it were, they heard him. Now if we thus come into the temple with Christ and the Gospels and contemplate the Scriptures, all the sayings of the prophets are so kind to him, take him in their arms, so to speak, and declare all with great joy, This is indeed the Man of whom we have spoken, and now our utterances concerning him have come to their goal in peace and joy. And now they begin to give the most beautiful testimonies concerning him, as being Christ, the Savior, the light, the comfort, and the glory of Israel; and all this Simeon here declares and announces regarding him. Saint Paul speaks of this in Romans 1:2, where he says that God promised the Gospel afore through his prophets in the holy Scriptures, which shows us what is meant by Simeon and by the temple. We also refer to Romans 3:21, "But now apart from the law a righteousness of

God has been manifested, being witnessed by the law and the prophets," also to the words of Christ in John 5:39, "Ye search the Scriptures, because ye think that in them ye have eternal life; and these are they which bear witness of me," and, in verse 46, "For if ye believed Moses, ye would believe me; for he wrote of me." This might be proved by examples, but we have no time here. From the Epistle and Gospel for Christmas, we have seen what beautiful and very appropriate testimonies the apostles gathered from holy Scriptures. We have also discussed this in explaining the Christmas Gospel, when we spoke of the swaddling clothes in which the child was wrapped.

13. For the present, the prophecy of Moses may suffice, which we find in Deuteronomy 18:15, and which is quoted by the apostles in Acts 3:22 and in Acts 7:37, and in many other places, and reads as follows, "Jehovah thy God will raise up unto thee a prophet from the midst of thee, of thy brethren, like unto me; unto him ye shall hearken." Here Moses declares that the people will no longer hearken to him, and that his teaching will end when this prophet Christ appears, to whom they should hearken thenceforth. This also demonstrates that Christ was to be a light and Savior after Moses, and no doubt better than Moses; for otherwise, Moses would not have declared that his teaching and guiding would terminate, but that it would continue along with that of Christ. Isaiah also says, in Isaiah 28:16, "Behold, I lay in Zion for a foundation a stone, a tried stone, a precious cornerstone of sure foundation: he that believeth shall not be in haste." Behold, how beautifully these and other passages of Holy Writ agree with the Gospel, declaring of Christ what the apostles preached concerning him and what is proclaimed continually by all the holy Scriptures.

14. Therefore, Simeon had to be an aged man, so that he might completely and suitably represent the prophets of old. He does not take the child in his hands nor in his lap, but in his arms. There is a deeper meaning in this, but suffice it to say now that the prophecies and passages of Scriptures do not keep Christ to themselves, but exhibit and offer him to everybody, just as we do with those things we carry in our arms. Saint Paul refers to this in Romans 4:23 and in Romans 15:4, when he says that all was written not for their sake, but for our learning. And in 1 Peter 1:12, we read that the prophets have not ministered these things unto themselves, but unto us, to whom they have been announced.

15. For this reason, Saint Luke does not say that Joseph and Mary were marveling at the words of Simeon, but "at the things which were spoken concerning him." He passes over the name of Simeon in silence, deliberately

diverting our attention from Simeon to this spiritual significance, so that thereby we might understand the sayings of Scripture.

16. Only his father and his mother were marveling at these things. It is remarkable that the evangelist here does not mention the names of Joseph and Mary, but calls them father and mother, thereby giving no cause to point out the spiritual significance. Who is meant by the spiritual father and mother of Christ? He himself mentions his spiritual mother in Mark 3:34–35 and in Luke 8:21, "For whosoever shall do the will of God, the same is my brother, and sister, and mother." Saint Paul calls himself a father in 1 Corinthians 4:15, "For though ye have ten thousand tutors in Christ, yet have ye not many fathers; for in Christ Jesus I begat you through the Gospel." It is, therefore, clear that the Christian Church, that is to say, all those who believe, the spiritual mother of Christ, and all the apostles and teachers of the people who preach the Gospel, are his spiritual father. As often as faith is created in a man, Christ is born anew in him. These are the people who are marveling at the sayings of the prophets; for how beautifully and precisely do these apply to Christ and how gloriously do they speak of him, demonstrating in a masterly manner the truth of the whole Gospel. There is no greater delight in this life than to perceive and experience this in reading the Scriptures.

17. But the great multitude of unbelievers despise this Simeon, scoff at him, and pervert his words as those of a fool, carrying on their apish tricks and buffoonery in the temple and even rearing idols and the altar of Damascus there, as did King Ahab, in 1 Kings 16:32–33. These are the people who wantonly pervert the Scriptures and bring them into discredit; they judge them according to their human understanding and elevate their favorite idol, reason, thereby making of the Scriptures a doctrine of works and human laws. Finally, they desecrate and destroy this temple of the Scriptures altogether and carry on in it their sin and shame, as the pope with his decrees and the great seats of learning with their devotion to Aristotle have done and are still doing. At the same time, they are very devout and consecrate many churches, chapels, and altars of wood and stone, show their indignation against the Turks [Muslims] who desecrate and destroy these churches, and believe that God ought to reward them for desecrating and devastating ten thousand times more badly his most precious temple, which is immeasurably better and eternal. They are a blind, mad, clumsy people; let them go in their blindness to eternal destruction.

18. Some simple-minded people might be surprised that Luke calls Joseph the father of Christ, in spite of the fact that Mary was a virgin. But he speaks

thus according to the custom which prevailed among the people, and in keeping with the tradition of the law, according to which stepfathers were also called fathers, which indeed is the general custom everywhere and always. Moreover, Joseph is properly called his father because he was the affianced husband of his mother. The evangelist had sufficient reason to speak thus, for he had previously written very plainly about the virginity of Mary, so that he probably thought nobody would get the impression that Joseph was the real father of Christ. As there was consequently no danger, because of the precautions he had taken, he could write in this manner without any reserve. For the preceding narrative abundantly convinces us that Mary was his real mother and Joseph was his real father only in the conventional sense of the word; and thus it is true that he had both a father and a mother.

And Simeon Blessed Them

19. This blessing means nothing else but that he wished them happiness and joy, honor, and all prosperity. Luke relates that he did not bless only the child but every one of them, the child, his father, and his mother.

20. This blessing seems to be a useless and trivial matter, for people generally do this and wish each other all that is good. But to bless Christ and his parents is a great and exceptional deed, for the reason that Christ and our nature are entirely opposed to each other. Christ condemns all that the world elects, gives us the cross to bear and to suffer all evil, deprives this world of all its pleasures, possessions, and honors, and teaches that men deal in those things which are altogether foolish and sinful. And behold, nobody will nor can take this from him. Then they begin to execrate, blaspheme, and persecute Christ and all his disciples, and there are only a few Simeons who bless him; but the whole world is full of those who curse him and wish him all evil, disgrace, and misfortune. For he who is not disposed willingly to despise all things and to suffer everything, will not bless and praise Christ very long, but will speedily stumble.

21. There are indeed some who praise him, because he does what they desire and leaves them as they are. But then he is not Christ and does not do the works of Christ with them, but he is what they are and desire. When, however, he begins to be Christ to them and they are required to forsake their works and to let him alone dwell within them, there is nothing but flight, blasphemy, and execration.

22. There are also some who believe that, if they were to see the infant Christ before them with his mother, as did Simeon, they would also joyously bless him. But they lie; for his childhood and poverty and his contemptible

appearance would certainly cause them to stumble. They prove it by disregarding, hating, and persecuting such poverty and humble appearance in the members of Christ, and yet they might still find daily among them Christ their head. If they then shun the cross now and hate its contemptible appearance, they would certainly do the same thing if they were still to see him with their eyes. Why are they not showing such honor to the poor? Why will they not honor the truth? But Simeon was of a different mind. Outward appearances did not cause him to stumble but, on the contrary, he confessed that the Savior was to be a sign which is spoken against, and is pleased that Christ rejects the appearance of worldly greatness and exhibits the cross. Therefore, he does not bless Christ alone, but also his members, father and mother.

23. Thus Simeon, as a preacher and lover of the cross and an enemy of the world, in blessing the child, gave a remarkable example of exalting and honoring Christ, who was then despised, cursed, and rejected in his own person, and is now treated in the same manner in his members, who for his sake endure poverty, disgrace, death, and all ignominy. Yet nobody will come to their relief, receive and bless them, but people want to be pious Christians by praying and fasting, and by bequests and good works.

The Significance of the Blessing upon Christ's Mother and Father

24. Explaining this figuratively, we find that the spiritual Christ, or his spiritual father and mother, that is to say, the Christian Church, with its apostles and followers, is subjected on earth to all ignominy, being made as the filth of the world, the offscouring of all things, as Saint Paul says in 1 Corinthians 4:13. Therefore, it is indeed necessary that they receive blessing and consolation from some other source, from Simeon in the temple, which means from the prophets in the holy Scriptures, as Saint Paul says in Romans 15:4, "For whatsoever things were written aforetime were written for our learning, that through patience and through comfort of the Scriptures we might have hope."

25. A Christian must, therefore, not imagine, nor endeavor to bring it about, that he may be praised and blessed by the people of this world. No, it has already been decided that he must expect reproach and contempt and willingly submit to it. A blessing he can only expect from Simeon in the temple. The Scriptures are our comfort, praising and blessing all who are reproached by the world for Christ's sake. This is the whole teaching of Psalm 37, also of Psalm 9 and many others, which tell us that God will rescue all those who suffer in this world. Thus Moses writes, in Genesis 4:9 that God takes such great care of pious Abel after his death as to be moved to vengeance solely by his

blood, without having been petitioned for it, doing more for him after his death than while he was still living. This shows that he cannot forsake even the dead, nay, he will remember his believers more when they are dead than while they are living. Again, after Cain had been slain, he was silent, showing no interest in him.

26. These and similar passages of Scripture are our comfort and blessing, if we are Christians; to them we must cling and with them we must be satisfied. Here we see how blessed are those who suffer reproach, and how wretched are those who persecute us. The former, God will never forget nor forsake, and the latter, he will not acknowledge nor remember. Could we desire a more abundant, a greater comfort and blessing? What is the blessing and comfort of this world compared with this consolation and blessing of Simeon in the temple?

And he said unto Mary his mother, "Behold, this child is set for the falling and rising of many in Israel; and for a sign which is spoken against; yea and a sword shall pierce through thine own soul; that thoughts out of many hearts may be revealed."

27. Why does he not say this to the father also, and why does he call the mother by name? He desires here to address himself to the real mother, and not to the father. As Jesus was her own child, all that happened to him naturally also happened to her and caused her genuine and real pain. Simeon perhaps also addressed Mary alone for the reason that Joseph was not to live until the time of the sufferings of Christ, which the mother would experience alone; and in addition to all this sorrow, she was to be a poor and lonely widow, and Christ was to suffer as a poor orphan. This is a situation unspeakably pitiable, and God himself, according to the Scriptures, takes great interest in widows and orphans, calling himself a father of the fatherless, and a judge of the widows.

28. For Mary lived in all three estates—in the state of virginity, in that of matrimony, and in that of widowhood, the latter being the most pitiable, without any protection or aid. A virgin has her parents, a wife her husband, but the widow is alone. And in this pitiful condition, Simeon announces to her such great sorrow, thereby showing and explaining to her that his blessing is a blessing of God and not of the world. For in the sight of the world, all was to be reversed and she was not only to be not blessed, but her child also should become the target and aim of everybody's curses, just as bows and arrows are aimed at the target. Behold, this, in my opinion, means to be

blessed in the temple. It was indeed necessary that she should be strengthened and comforted by a spiritual and divine benediction against the arrows of future curses, for her soul alone was to bear and endure this great tempest of the execration of her child.

29. Simeon declares in the first place that Christ is set for the falling and the rising of many in Israel. This, then, is the first consolation which his mother was to experience in him and for which she was to educate him, namely, that many were to be offended in him, even in Israel, the chosen people. This is a poor comfort in the judgment of men, that she is the mother of a son who is to cause many to stumble and fall, even in Israel. Some have explained this text thus, that many have been stirred up by Christ and their pride has fallen, so that they might rise again in humility; just as Saint Paul fell and rose again, and all the self-righteous must fall, despair of their own strength, and rise again in Christ, if they would be saved. This is a good interpretation, but not exhaustive here. Simeon says of Christ that many Jews would take offense at him and stumble, thereby falling into unbelief, just as it has happened in the past and as it still occurs. It was indeed a dark picture and a terrible announcement to which this holy mother had to listen.

30. Not Christ, however, is the cause of this fall, but the presumption of the Jews. It happened in this wise. Christ came to be a light and Savior of all the world, as Simeon said, so that all might be justified and saved by faith in him. If this is to be brought about, all other righteousness in ourselves, sought for outside of Christ with works, must be rejected. The Jews would not hear of this, as Saint Paul says in Romans 10:3, "For being ignorant of God's righteousness, and seeking to establish their own, they did not subject themselves to the righteousness of God." Thus they take offense at faith, fall deeper and deeper into unbelief, and become hardened in their own righteousness, so that they have even persecuted with all their might all who believed.

31. All those who would be saved by their own righteousness must do the same thing. They depend upon their works, and when faith in Christ is demanded, they stumble and fall, burning, condemning, and persecuting all who reject their works or consider them useless. Such people are the pope, the bishops, the Scholastics, and all the papists. And this they do under the impression that they are earnestly serving God, defending the truth, and preserving Christianity, just as the Jews also pretended to preserve the true service of God and the law of Moses when they killed the apostles and other Christians, and persecuted them.

32. Therefore, as Simeon here tells the mother of Christ that not all the people of Israel will receive him as their light and Savior, and that not only a

few, but many, will take offense at him and fall, so also the spiritual mother of Christ, that is to say, the Christian Church, must not be surprised when many false Christians, even among the clergy, will not believe. For such are the people who depend upon works and seek their own righteousness, who stumble and fall because Christ demands faith, and who persecute and kill those that oppose them. This has been prophesied long ago by the spiritual Simeon, namely, the prophets, who almost with one accord have spoken of this fall. In Isaiah 8:11–15, we read as follows, "For Jehovah spoke thus to me with a strong hand, and instructed me not to walk in the way of this people, saying, Say ye not, A conspiracy, concerning all whereof this people shall say, A conspiracy; neither fear ye their fear, nor be in dread thereof. Jehovah of hosts, him shall ye sanctify; and let him be your fear, and let him be your dread. And he shall be for a sanctuary; but for a stone of stumbling and for a rock of offense to both the houses of Israel, for a gin and for a square to the inhabitants of Jerusalem. And many shall stumble thereon, and fall, and be broken, and be snared, and be taken." There are many more passages from which it can be shown that Christ must be a rock against which the best and greatest will stumble, as we read in Psalm 78:31, "And he slew of the fattest of them, and smote down the young men of Israel," for Christ is set as a Savior and cannot yield nor change. But these arrogant people are headstrong and obstinate, will not give up their vanity, and run their head against Christ, so that one of the two must break and fall. Christ, however, must remain and cannot fall; consequently, they fall.

33. Again, as firmly as he stands over against the legalists and will not yield before them, so immovably he stands also for all who would found their faith on him, as we read in Isaiah 28:16, "Behold, I lay in Zion for a foundation a stone, a tried stone, a precious cornerstone of sure foundation: he that believeth shall not be in haste." And in Matthew 16:18, he says himself, "Upon this rock I will build my church; and the gates of hell shall not prevail against it." Now, as by the falling and breaking spoken of in this connection, nothing else is meant but unbelief and dependence upon works, so rising and being built upon this rock means nothing but to believe and disregard his works. This is done by the believers, for the rising of whom alone Christ is set. And, as in the times of Christ, many among the people of Israel rose in him, so it will be until the end of the world, for nobody can rise through his works, or through the doctrines of men, but only through Christ. This is brought about by faith, as has often been said, without any merit or works; the works will only follow, after we have risen.

34. You will perceive, therefore, how the whole Scriptures speak only of faith, and reject works as useless, nay, as standing in the way of justification and preventing us from rising. For Christ will alone be set for the rising of many, and those who will not rise must fall. Nothing can be set beside him by which we might rise. Is not the life of the papists and priests abominable? For they run their heads against this rock, and their conduct is so directly opposed to Christianity that it may indeed be called the sway and government of the Antichrist. The spiritual Simeon also speaks of this rising to the spiritual mother of Christ. For all the prophets teach the Christian Church that only in Christ can all men rise, and Saint Paul, in Romans 1:17 and in Hebrews 10:38, quotes the passage from Habakkuk 2:4, "But the righteous shall live by his faith."

35. We see, therefore, this falling and rising by Christ must be understood spiritually, and that the falling and rising apply to different classes of people. The falling applies only to those who are great, learned, mighty and holy, and who trust too much in themselves. Thus the Gospel tells us that Christ never had a disagreement nor a conflict with sinners, but he treated them with the utmost kindness. But with the select people, the scribes and high priests, he cannot get along, neither is he gracious to them. If, then, only those can fall who are standing up, only those can rise who have fallen and are lying prostrate. These are the people who know their poverty and long for grace, who realize that they are nothing and Christ is everything.

36. It is noticeable that Simeon adds the word "Israel." For Christ had been promised by all the prophets only to the people of Israel. At the same time it was announced that many among that people would fall away only on account of their self-righteousness. This is indeed a terrible example to us gentiles, to whom nothing has been promised; but out of pure grace we have unexpectedly been brought into the kingdom and have risen through Christ, as Saint Paul tells us in Romans 15:9, and as we have said in explaining the Epistle for the second Sunday in Advent. For this reason, the example of Israel's fall should touch our hearts, as the apostle exhorts us in Romans 11:20, that we may not also fall, or perhaps fall more grievously than the Jews and Turks [Muslims], being seduced by Antichrist and bearing the name of Christ to the dishonor of God and our own harm.

37. In the second place, Simeon says that Christ is set for a sign which is spoken against. Is it not a great pity that the Savior and light of the world must be spoken against, condemned, and rejected, he whom the whole world ought to desire and seek? This shows us the character of the world, and how our human nature uses the freedom of the will. This world is the kingdom of

Satan and the enemy of God, and does not only transgress the commandments of God, but with senseless rage also persecutes and kills the Savior,
who would help them to keep God's commandments. But one sin leads to
another; those who take offense at him must also speak against him, and cannot do otherwise. On the other hand, those who rise through him must confess him, testify, and preach of him, and they also cannot do otherwise. But a
sword shall pierce through their souls, as we shall now see.

38. Now give heed to the text. Simeon does not say that Christ shall be spoken against, but that he is set for a sign which is spoken against; just as a butt
or target is set for the marksman, so that all bows and guns, arrows, and stones
may be aimed at it. Such a target is set up that the shots may be directed only
at it and nowhere else. Thus Christ is the mark which is noticed by everybody,
and all opposition is directed toward him. And although the opponents are at
variance with each other, yet they become united when they oppose Christ.
This is proved by Luke 23:12, where we read that Pilate and Herod became
friends in their opposition against Christ, while before they were at enmity
between themselves. The Pharisees and Sadducees could never agree, but in
their opposition to Christ, they were united. David speaks of this and
expresses his astonishment in Psalm 2:12, "Why do the nations rage, and the
people meditate a vain thing? The kings of the earth set themselves and the
rulers take counsel together, against Jehovah, and against his anointed."

39. In the same manner, the heretics, however strongly they differed with
each other and opposed each other, were nevertheless united in their opposition against the one Christian Church. Even now, when all the bishops, religious establishments, orders, and monasteries are at variance with each other,
so that there are nearly as many sects and different opinions as heads, yet they
are unanimous in their opposition against the Gospel. Asaph also writes, in
Psalm 83:6–8, that many nations conspired against the people of Israel, namely, Edom and the Ishmaelites, Moab and the Hagarenes, Gebal, and Ammon,
and Amalek, Philistia with the inhabitants of Tyre, and Assyria, yet they were
at enmity among one another. Wickedness and falsehood are at variance with
themselves, but they are united against truth and righteousness, every attack
and opposition being directed toward this mark. They believe to have good
reason for this. For every faction fights against its own adversary, Pilate against
Herod, the Pharisees against the Sadducees, Arius against Sabellius, the
monks against the priests. But every faction has its adherents and friends, and
their discord or harmony is only partial.

40. But Christ is very impolite and unreasonable, rebuking them all, Pilate
being as much to him as Herod, and the Pharisees as much as the Sadducees,

so that he does not take the part of any of them. Therefore, as he is against all of them, so they are all against him. Thus truth is opposed to all lies and falsehoods and, therefore, all lies are united against the truth and make of it a sign which is spoken against. It must needs be so. For Christ and the truth find not a single man pious and pleasing to God, as we read in Psalm 116:11, "All men are liars." Therefore, Christ must rebuke them indiscriminately and reject their works, so that they all may feel the need of his grace and long for it. But only a few will believe and accept this.

41. Thus we have here two Simeons. The literal Simeon tells Mary that Christ in his own person is set for a sign which is spoken against. In these words, he indicates what the spiritual Simeon, that is to say, the prophets, would teach the church concerning our Christian faith, namely, that this faith and Gospel, the living word of truth, is a rock at which many will stumble and by the help of which many will rise, and that it finally is a sign which is spoken against. Thus Isaiah expresses his surprise when he says, in Isaiah 53:1, "Who hath believed our message?" just as if he would declare that not many believe it. In Isaiah 8:15 and in Isaiah 28:13, we also read that many will stumble at this word, so that hardly the dregs of the people will be saved. The prophets have written copiously of this falling, rising, and speaking against.

42. Simeon has declared before that Christ is the light and Savior of all the world, which has also been declared by the prophets. This shows us the character of Christ and his attitude toward the world. But when Simeon speaks of falling, rising, and speaking against, he shows what Christ will achieve, what is the character of the world, and what attitude it takes toward Christ. Thus it appears that Christ is indeed willing and qualified to be the light and Savior of all the world, and abundantly demonstrates himself as such. But the world will not receive him and becomes only worse, opposing and persecuting him with all its strength.

43. This shows us that this world is the kingdom of Satan, not only full of wickedness and blindness, but also loving these things, as Christ says in John 3:19, "The light is come into the world, and men loved the darkness rather than the light." Behold, how we sojourn on earth among devils and the enemies of God, so that indeed this life ought to be a horror for us.

44. From this, we learn to be assured that we may comfort ourselves and cheerfully bear up when many people stumble at our Word and speak against our faith, especially the great, the learned, and the priests. This is a sign that our message and faith is right, for it receives the treatment foretold by Simeon and all the prophets. They must take offense at it, stumble over it, rise by it, and speak against it; it cannot be otherwise. He who would have it otherwise

must look for another Christ. Christ is set for the falling and rising of many in Israel, and for a sign which is spoken against; consequently, his members, or every Christian, must be like him on account of his faith and his message. He is called *"antilegumenous,"* he who is spoken against. His doctrine must be rejected, condemned, and execrated as the worst heresy, error, and foolishness. It is treated rightly when this is done; but when this does not take place, then we have neither Christ, nor his mother, nor Simeon, nor the prophets, nor faith, nor the Gospel, nor any Christians. For what does speaking against mean but to deny, blaspheme, curse, condemn, reject, prohibit, and persecute with all disgrace and ignominy as the worst heresy?

45. But we find still another consolation in our text. Simeon says that Christ is a sign which is spoken against, which, however, will not be overthrown or exterminated. The whole world may condemn my faith and my Word, call it heresy, and misrepresent and pervert it in the most shameful manner, but they must let it remain and cannot take it from me. With all their rage and fury they will accomplish nothing, but can only speak against me, and I must be their mark and target. Yet they will fall, and I shall stand. Let them speak against me as much as they desire; God will also oppose them and, with his deeds, contend against their words. We shall see who will win the victory. Here are the deeds of God, which establish this sign firmly and solidly upon a good foundation. A goal is set up by God; who will upset it? But the others have no more than fleeting words and an impotent breath of the mouth. The flies make a great fluttering with their wings and sharpen their bills, but they only defile the wall and must let it stand.

46. From this, it follows that the doctrine and faith of the pope, the bishops, the religious establishments, the monasteries, and the universities is of the world and of the devil, for no one takes offense at them or speaks against them, neither do they suffer any harm. They reap nothing but honor, power, riches, peace, and pleasure, and fatten themselves at the crib, with the exception of a few that may sometimes be found who are tormented by the devil with spiritual temptations concerning their faith and hope. For where Christ is and his faith, there is also opposition; otherwise, it is not Christ. If men do not oppose openly, devils do it secretly. These are sore temptations to unbelief, despair, and blasphemy. Such people may be preserved and saved. The great multitude, however, lives without Christ, without Mary, without Simeon, without the least truth but, meanwhile, they read many masses, sing high and low, wear tonsures and ecclesiastical vestments, and are the apes of Solomon and like Indian cats. As they will not suffer to be spoken against and are not

worthy of it, have nothing, and do nothing that would call forth opposition, they become opponents themselves. What else could they do? It is their work to condemn, forbid, curse, and persecute the truth.

47. I mention all this because I want to do my duty and point out to every Christian his danger, so that all may beware of the pope, the Scholastics, and the priests, and shun them as they shun the kingdom of Satan, for the Word of God does not prevail among them. Cling to the Gospel and find out where there is opposition and where there is praise. Where you find no opposition, there Christ is not present; and here we do not mean opposition from the Turks [Muslims], but from our nearest neighbors. Christ is not a sign set for the falling of many in Babylon or Assyria, but in Israel, that is to say, among the people in the midst of whom he dwells and who boast to be his own.

48. In the third place, Simeon says to Mary, "A sword shall pierce through thine own soul." This does not mean an actual sword, but must be understood figuratively, just like Psalm 107:10, "Such as sat in darkness and in the shadow of death, being bound in affliction and iron," and like Deuteronomy 4:20, "Jehovah hath taken you, and brought you forth out of the iron furnaces." It means that her heart was to be filled with great sorrow and grief, although her body would not be tortured. Everybody knows how this happened. Thus we must take these words as a Hebrew figure of speech, expressing great sorrow and grief, just as we speak of a "heart-rending sorrow," or use expressions like "my heart is breaking" or "my heart will burst."

49. We shall speak more about this during the Passion season, when we consider the sufferings of Christ. At present, we can only notice how Simeon interprets his blessing by predicting such sorrow, in order that it might not be understood as a worldly blessing. But what does it signify that Simeon here speaks only to Mary, the mother, and not to Joseph? It signifies that the Christian Church, the spiritual Virgin Mary, will remain on earth and will not be exterminated although the preacher and their faith and the Gospel, the spiritual Christ, are persecuted. Thus Joseph died before Christ suffered, and Mary in her widowhood was deprived of her child, yet she lived, and all this grief overwhelmed her soul. Thus the Christian Church will always be a widow, feeling great sorrow because the holy fathers, represented by Joseph, die, and the Gospel is persecuted. The church must feel the sword, and will yet remain until the last day.

50. What can be more painful for a Christian than to see and experience how furiously the tyrants and unbelievers persecute and exterminate the Gospel of Christ? This is done more at the present time under the pope than ever before With this agrees the name of Mary, which means a "sea of bitterness." This

declares that there is in her not only a drop, nor a river, but a whole sea of bitterness, for all the waves of sorrow go over her, so that she may indeed be called Mary, a bitter sea.

51. Finally, Simeon says that all this will happen that thoughts out of many hearts may be revealed. What a blessed and necessary fruit of this falling and speaking against! But in order to understand this, we must notice that there are two different kinds of temptation among men. There is the temptation to gross sins, as for instance to be disobedient to parents, to kill, to be unchaste, to steal, to lie and blaspheme, etc., which are sins against the second table of the law. The people who do these things need not take offense at a sign which is spoken against; their thoughts are sufficiently revealed by their evil life. The Scriptures speak little of this temptation.

52. But the most dangerous temptation is prefigured by Cozbi the daughter of Zur, a prince of Midian, because of whom twenty-four thousand were slain in Israel, as Moses writes in Numbers 25:15. This is the temptation through the bright and shining sins of good works and the service of God, which bring misfortune upon the whole world and against which nobody can guard sufficiently. These are the sins against the first table of the law, against faith, the honor of God, and his works.

53. For a life of good works, blameless conduct, and outward respectability is the greatest, most dangerous, and destructive stumbling block. The people leading such lives are so upright, reasonable, honorable, and pious that scarcely a single soul could have been preserved or saved, if God had not set up a sign against which they might stumble and by which the thought of their hearts might be revealed. Thus we see their hearts behind their beautiful words and good works, and find that these great saints and wise men are pagans and fools; for they persecute the faith for the sake of their works and will not suffer their ways to be rebuked. Thus their thoughts are laid bare and they become manifested as trusting in their own works and themselves, sinning not only continually against the first commandments, but endeavoring also in their enmity against God to exterminate and destroy all that belongs to God, claiming to do this for the sake of God and to preserve the truth. Behold, such are the pope, the bishops, and almost all the priests, who have filled the world with innumerable snares and stumbling blocks by making an external glitter of the spiritual life. Among them there is no faith, but only works; the Gospel does not prevail, but only human laws.

54. The whole Scriptures speak of this stumbling block, and God with all his prophets and saints contends against it. This is the true gate of hell and the

broad highway to eternal damnation, wherefore this harlot is well called Cozbi, *"mendacium meum,"* my lie. Everything that glitters lies and deceives, but her beautiful ornaments and embellishments deceive even the princes of Israel, and so she is not merely called *"mendacium,"* but *"meum mendacium,"* my lie, because with her deception she attracts and tempts almost everybody.

55. But in order to protect us, God has set up his Christ as a sign, at which they might stumble and fall and which they oppose, so that we may not be seduced by their works and words, nor consider them good and imitate them. We should rather know that before God no moral life without faith is acceptable; where there is no faith, there is only Cozbi, nothing but lies and deception. This becomes manifest as soon as we preach against them and consider their works worthless in comparison with faith. Behold, then, you must be a heretic with your faith; they reveal themselves and disclose their heart before you unwillingly and unknowingly. Then you perceive the shocking abominations of unbelief hidden behind that beautiful life, the wolves in sheep's clothing, the harlot adorned with the wreath, impudently demanding that you consider her disgrace and vice, her honor and virtue, or threatening to kill you. Therefore, God says to her, in Jeremiah 3:3, "Thou hadst a harlot's forehead, thou refusedst to be ashamed," and, in Isaiah 3:9, "The show of their countenance doth witness against them; and they declare their sin as Sodom, they hide it not." Would she not be considered a mad and impudent harlot who would have her adultery extolled even before her husband? But this is being done by all the preachers of works and faithless teachers, who shamelessly preach righteousness by works, but condemn faith, or conjugal chastity, who call their lewdness chastity, but true chastity they call lewdness. Now all this might remain hidden, and human nature and reason might never discover such vices, for their works are too attractive and their manners too polished. Indeed, human nature devises all this and delights in it, believing it to be well and right, persisting and becoming hardened in it. Therefore, God sets up a sign that our nature may stumble and everybody may learn how much higher is the Christian life than nature and reason. The virtues of nature are sins, its light is darkness, its ways are errors. We need an entirely new heart and nature; the natural heart reveals itself as an enemy of God.

56. This is prefigured by the Philistines, in 1 Samuel 5:6, whom God smote with tumors when the ark of God was with them. The tumors are the thoughts of unbelieving hearts, breaking out when the ark of God comes to them, that is to say, when the Gospel and Christ are preached, which they will not tolerate. Thus it happens, that the hearts of these saints, which otherwise

could not be known, become revealed when Christ is held up before them. Saint Paul says in 1 Corinthians 2:15, "But he that is spiritual judgeth all things, and he himself is judged of no man," for he knows their disposition and the attitude of their hearts when he perceives that they do not accept the Word of God and faith.

II. OF ANNA

The Second Part of This Gospel

> And there was one Anna, a prophetess, the daughter of Phanuel of the tribe of Asher (she was of a great age, having lived with a husband seven years from her virginity, and she had been a widow even unto fourscore and four years), who departed not from the temple, worshiping with fastings and supplications night and day.

57. Here some might say, From the example of Anna, you see that good works are exalted as, for instance, fasting and praying and going to church; therefore, they must not be condemned. But who has ever condemned good works? We only reject hypocritical and spurious good works. Fasting, praying, going to church are good works, if they are done in the right spirit. But the trouble is that these blockheads explain the Scriptures so awkwardly, noticing only the works and examples of the saints and thinking that now they are able to learn from them and imitate them. Thus they become nothing but apes and hypocrites, for they do not perceive that the Scriptures speak more of the heart than of the deeds of men. The sacrifice and works of Abel are praised in Scripture, but he himself a great deal more. They, however, disregard the person and observe only the example, take notice of the works and pay no heed to faith, eat the bran and throw away the flour, as we read in Hosea 3:1, "They turn unto other gods, and love cakes of raisins." If you desire to fast and pray like Anna, well and good. But take good care that first of all you imitate her character, and then her works. Be first of all like Anna. But let us see what Luke says of her works and her character, so that her example may be correctly understood.

58. In the first place, he says that she was a prophetess, and undoubtedly a devout, godly prophetess. Most assuredly, the Holy Spirit dwelled in her and, consequently, she was good and righteous regardless of all her works. Therefore, the works which she produced must also have been good and righteous. So you see that Luke does not want to say that through her works she became holy and a prophetess, but she was a holy prophetess before and, for this reason, her

works were also good. Why would you mutilate this example and pervert the Gospel, paying most attention to the works, while Luke describes first of all the whole person, and not only the works?

59. In the second place, he praises her as a widow, who did works becoming her widowhood and her station in life. But he would not represent them as being unusual and the only good works whereby we can serve God, rejecting all others. Saint Paul writes of the life of widows in 1 Timothy 5:3–6, as follows, "Honor widows that are widows indeed. But if any widow hath children or grandchildren, let them learn first to show piety toward their own family, and to requite their parents: for this is acceptable in the sight of God. Now she that is a widow indeed, and desolate, hath her hope set on God, and continueth in supplications and prayers night and day. But she that giveth herself to pleasure is dead while she liveth."

60. From this, you see that Anna must have been a widow, alone in the world, without any children or parents to take care of, otherwise, she would not have served God but the devil by not departing from the temple and neglecting her duty of managing her household according to the will of God. Luke indicates this when he writes that she had been a widow even for fourscore and four years. Everybody may then easily calculate that her parents must have been dead and her children provided for, so that as an aged mother she was cared for by them and she did not have anything to do but to pray and fast and forego all worldly pleasures. Luke does not say that all the eighty-four years of her life were spent in this manner; but at the time when Christ was born and brought into the temple, she began to lead such a life, when all things, as well as her children and parents, were provided for and she was entirely alone.

61. It is, therefore, a dangerous thing to take notice only of the works, and fail to consider the whole character of a person, as well as his station and calling. God cannot bear to see anyone neglect the duties of his calling or station in life in order to imitate the works of the saints. If, therefore, a married woman were to follow Anna in this respect, leave her husband and children, her home and parents, in order to go on a pilgrimage, to pray, fast, and go to church, she would do nothing else but tempt God, confound the matrimonial estate with the state of widowhood, desert her own calling, and do works belonging to others. This would be as much as walking on one's ears, putting a veil over one's feet, and a boot on one's head, and turning all things upside down. Good works should be done, and you ought to pray and fast, but you must not thereby be kept from or neglect the duties of your calling and station. The service of God does not consist in the performance of one or two special deeds, nor is it bound to any particular calling, but God may be served in every

calling. The duty of Anna and all widows who like her are alone, is praying and fasting, and here Saint Luke agrees with Saint Paul. The duty of married women is not only praying and fasting, but they should govern their children and household according to the will of God and care for their parents, as Saint Paul says in 1 Timothy 5:4. For this reason, the evangelist, in describing the life of Anna, takes such great care to mention her station and age, so that he may discourage those who would take notice only of her deeds and draw poison from roses. He first of all draws attention to her calling.

62. In the third place, the same reason prompts him to write that she lived with a husband seven years from her virginity. Here he exalts the state of matrimony and the duties of that estate, so that nobody may think that he considers only praying and fasting as good works. For she did not devote herself entirely to praying and fasting while she lived with her husband, or during the time of her maidenhood, but only after she had become an aged and lonely widow. Yet her virginity and her wedded life with its duties are also praised and help us as an example of truly good works. Why would you disregard them and only cleave to the deeds of the widow?

63. And with good purpose does the evangelist first praise her wedded life and then her widowhood, for he wanted to cut the ground entirely from under the feet of the blind legalists. She was a godly maiden, a godly wife, and a godly widow and, in all these three estates, she performed her respective duties.

64. May you then do likewise. Reflect on your condition, and you will find enough good works to do if you would lead a godly life. Every calling has its own duties, so that we need not inquire for others outside of our station. Behold, then we will truly serve God, just as Luke says that Anna worshiped with fastings and supplications night and day. But the legalists do not serve God, but themselves, nay, the devil, for they do not perform their duties and forsake their own calling. Thus it depends entirely upon the character of the person and his calling whether his works are good, as we have said above, in explaining the Gospel for the Day of Saint John the Evangelist. This may suffice for the present. Let us now see what Anna means spiritually.

The Spiritual Meaning of Anna the Prophetess

65. We said in §11 and 12 that by Simeon are signified the holy prophets, who have spoken of Christ in the holy Scriptures. Therefore, Anna must signify those who stand by and hear this message, assenting to it and applying it to themselves, as did Anna, who stood by when Simeon spoke of Christ. Thus Anna means nothing but the holy synagogue, the people of Israel, whose life

and history are recorded in the Bible. For Anna is found in the temple, that is to say, in the Scripture. And as Mary signifies the Christian Church, the people of God after the birth of Christ, so Anna signifies the people of God before Christ's birth. Therefore, Anna is well-nigh a hundred years old and near her death, while Mary is young and in the prime of life. Thus the synagogue was on the wane at the time of Christ, while the church was in its beginning.

66. It is then indicated here that the saints before the birth of Christ have understood and believed the message of the prophets, and all have been saved in Christ and by faith in him, as Christ says of Abraham, "Your father Abraham rejoiced to see my day; and he saw it, and was glad"; also, in Luke 10:24, "For I say unto you, that many prophets and kings desired to see the things which ye see, and saw them not; and to hear the things which ye hear, and heard them not." Paul says in Hebrews 13:8, "Jesus Christ is the same yesterday and today, yea and for ever," and more plainly, in 1 Corinthians 10:1–4, "For I would not, brethren, have you ignorant, that our fathers were all under the cloud, and all passed through the sea; and were all baptized unto Moses in the cloud and in the sea; and did all eat the same spiritual food; and did all drink the same spiritual drink: for they drank of a spiritual rock that followed them: and the rock was Christ." Such and similar passages prove that all the saints before the birth of Christ have like us been saved in Christ. Therefore, we read in Hebrews 11 of examples of faith, of Abel, Enoch, Noah, Abraham, Moses, and others, who spent their lives in Christ and for Christ, who heard him and, through the prophet's words, knew him, believed in him, and waited for his coming.

67. For this reason, all the narratives of the Old Testament so beautifully answer Christ and testify of him with one accord, standing around him just as Anna here literally stood near him. It is a great delight to read and perceive how they all look and point at Christ. Let us notice only one example. Isaac was sacrificed by his father and yet his life was spared, a ram being substituted for him, which Abraham saw behind him caught in the thicket by his horns. Here Christ, the Son of God, is prefigured, who like a mortal man died on the cross. Yet the divine nature did not die, the human nature being sacrificed in its place, which is designated in the ram that, by his horns (this is to say the preaching of the Gospel, rebuking and punishing the perversity and obstinacy of the scribes and priests), was caught in this thicket, being behind Abraham, that is to say, coming after him. Many more important lessons might be learned from this narrative.

68. So Joseph was sold into Egypt and, after having been in prison, became the ruler of the whole land, in Genesis 37 and Genesis 41. This

occurred and was recorded that Christ might be prefigured, who through his sufferings became the Lord of all the world. But who has time enough to explain all these narratives and to show how Samson, David, Solomon, Aaron, and others are appropriate and perfect types of Christ?

69. Luke, therefore, here uses the word *"epistasa"* with reference to Anna, which means that she stood over, or beside, or near that which happened to Christ in the temple. In the Latin text, we read *"superveniens,"* meaning that she came near at that time. This is also true, but the other expression, that she "stood over" what happened, is better. It means that she pressed forward with great earnestness to see him. Thus we say, How the people press forward to see this or that. Thus do the narratives of Holy Writ act toward Christ, in order that they may typify him.

70. Yet the saints would not have been saved by this, and probably they did not know at the time that by their deeds they became types of Christ. For our faith cannot be based upon figures and interpretations, but it must first of all be established upon clear passages of Scripture, which must be explained according to the natural meaning of the words. Then, after the foundation for faith has been laid by the words of Scripture, such interpretations of history must be based upon faith, which is thereby nourished and strengthened. Therefore, as I have said, they were types of Christ only in their outward conduct and works, through which nobody could have been sanctified, but they heartily believed in the Christ who was to come, whom they literally knew from clear passages of Holy Writ.

71. Thus Christ was promised to Adam and Eve after the fall, when God said to the serpent, in Genesis 3:15, "I will put enmity between thee and the woman, and between thy seed and her seed: he shall bruise thy head, and thou shalt bruise his heel." This promise holds good for Adam and Eve, and they believed in the seed of the woman, who was to bruise the head of the serpent. So it was until the time of Noah, to whom another promise was given when God said, in Genesis 6:18, "But I will establish my covenant with thee." When, therefore, Eve bore Cain, her first son, in Genesis 4:1, she rejoiced and believed him to be the seed of whom God had spoken, saying, "I have gotten a man with the help of Jehovah," as if she were to say, This will be the man, the seed, who is to fight against the serpent. She desired to see Christ, but the time was not yet come. Afterward, she realized that Cain was not the Savior and that her faith must look forward to another woman.

72. Then came the clear promise to Abraham, in Genesis 12:3 and in Genesis 22:18, to whom God said, "In thy seed shall all the nations of the earth be blessed," of which we have spoken in explaining the Epistle. The faith of all

the saints before the birth of Christ until the time of his coming was based upon this promise, so that this passage may also be referred to by the "bosom of Abraham," of which Christ speaks in Luke 16:22. Such a promise was indeed also made to David, but only by the virtue of the promise to Abraham. This child of Mary, then, is the seed of the woman, waging war against the serpent in order to destroy sin and death. Therefore, we read in the text that the seed is to bruise the head of the serpent, by which, undoubtedly, the serpent is meant that seduced Eve, namely, Satan in the serpent, and Adam and Eve certainly understood it thus. Who will show us another son or seed bruising the head? If it had been said of a mere man, it might as well be understood of Adam as of any of his children. Yet not Adam, nor a child of Adam, was to do it, but a woman's, a virgin's child.

73. It is well said, in distinction, that this seed is to bruise Satan's head, the seat of life; Satan, however, will not bruise the head of the seed, but his heel, or the sole of his foot. This means that Satan indeed injures, destroys, and kills the external, bodily life and activity of Christ; but the head, that is to say, the divine nature, remains alive and even raises from death the heel, or the human nature, which was bruised by Satan. So in all Christians, he injures and destroys their life and work, thus bruising their heels; but he cannot touch the head, or faith and, therefore, their life and work will also be restored. On the other hand, Satan's feet remain, his strength and fury are great; but his head, that is to say, sin and the inmost essence of his life, are bruised. Therefore, his feet must die eternally with sin and death. Behold, in this manner did God save the saints of old by his Word and their faith, and has kept them from sin and the power of the devil until the coming of Christ, signified by this saintly Anna.

74. For this reason, she does not take the infant Christ into her arms like Simeon, neither does she speak concerning him like Simeon, but she stands by and speaks about him to others. For the dear fathers of old and the saints have not uttered prophecies concerning Christ like the prophets, neither have they spoken of him, but they have taken the greatest interest in the announcement of the prophets, have believed them firmly, and transmitted them to other people and generations, just as Luke here says of Anna.

75. Everything agrees with this that Luke here relates of her. In the first place, she is a prophetess, that is to say, she has the insight of the prophets. Thus all the saints of old have apprehended Christ in the passages of Scripture by faith and, consequently, they were all prophets.

76. In the second place, she is called Anna, which in Latin is "gratia," meaning favor or grace. The two names, Anna and John (Johannes), are almost one in Hebrew. Anna means gracious, or one who is favored. This signifies that the

fathers and saints of old have not received such faith and the promise of God by their own merit, but by the favor and grace of God, according to whose mercy they were pleasing in his sight. In the same manner, all men are not acceptable and pleasing to God on account of their worthiness, but only by the grace of God. This is also the way of human nature, which often shows a predilection for something that is unattractive, and it is a common saying among us that love and favor may as likely fall upon a frog as upon purple, or that nobody can make us dislike what we love. Thus God loves us who are sinful and unworthy, and we are all favored by him. We are all Johns and Annas in his sight.

77. In the third place, she is a daughter of Phanuel. After Jacob had wrestled with the angel, in Genesis 32:30, he called the name of the place Peniel, or Phanuel, and said, "I have seen God face to face, and my life is preserved." *Peniel*, or *Phanuel*, means "face of God." Now, the face of God is nothing but the knowledge of God, and God can only be known by faith in his Word. The Word and promises of God declare nothing but comfort and grace in Christ, and whoever believes them beholds the grace and goodness of God. This is the knowledge of God, which cheers and blesses the heart, as David says in Psalm 4:6–7, "Jehovah, lift thou up the light of thy countenance upon us. Thou hast put gladness in my heart," and in Psalm 80:3, "And cause thy face to shine, and we shall be saved." We read much in Scripture concerning the hiding and showing of the countenance of God.

78. Behold, in this way, the fathers and saints of old were spiritual children of Phanuel, of divine knowledge and wisdom, which filled them with joy. To this, they attained by faith in the divine promise and thus they became prophets. But faith and the promises of God they obtained only because they were favored by him, out of God's pure grace and mercy.

79. This brings us to the fourth point, namely, that she was of the tribe of Asher. Asher means happiness, in Genesis 30:13. Faith makes us children of divine wisdom and blessedness. For faith destroys sin and redeems from death, as Christ says in Mark 16:16, "He that believeth and is baptized shall be saved." To be saved means nothing but redemption from sin and death.

80. Anna, then, is a daughter of Phanuel and Asher, full of wisdom and having a good conscience in the face of all sins and the terrors of death. All this is bestowed by faith in the divine promise of mercy; and thus, one follows the other: Anna, the prophetess, a daughter of Phanuel, of the tribe of Asher. This means that we obtain the promise of God and believe in it only by divine grace, whereby we learn to know God and his goodness thoroughly, which

fills the heart with joy, security, and blessedness, and delivers us completely from sin and death.

81. We come now in the fifth place to the more profound and spiritual interpretations. She lived with a husband seven years and, after that, was a widow for eighty-four years, without a husband. Had one sufficient time and skill, he might find the whole Bible contained in this number. But in order that we may see how, as Christians, we do not need Aristotle or human lore, but have in the Scriptures enough to study for all eternity, if we should so desire, let us also consider this number in connection with the wonders of Scripture mentioned before. The number seven is commonly taken to signify our temporal life, the life of this body, because all time is measured by the seven days of the week in Genesis 1, which is the first and best standard for the measurement of time, established by the Scriptures. For in Genesis 1, Moses writes that God first created days and appointed seven of them as a definite period of time. Of weeks were then made months and, of months, years, into which our whole life is divided. These seven years therefore signify the whole course of the temporal life and conduct of the saints of old.

82. But who was the husband? Saint Paul explains in Romans 7:2, that a husband signifies the law. For as a woman is bound to her husband while he lives, so all are bound to the law, who live under it. Now the law has been given to no people on earth except to this Anna, the Jewish people, as Paul says in Romans 3:2, that they were entrusted with the oracles of God. In Psalm 147:19–20, we read, "He showeth his word unto Jacob, his statutes and his ordinances unto Israel. He hath not dealt so with any nation; and as for his ordinances, they have not known them"; also in Psalm 103:7, "He made known his ways unto Moses, his doings unto the children of Israel." The Gospel, however, he did not reveal only to one nation, but to all the world, as we read in Psalm 19:4, "Their line is gone out through all the earth, and their words to the end of the world," which means the words of the apostles. Therefore, Anna, who lived seven years with her husband, signifies the people of Israel under the law, in their outward conduct and temporal life.

83. Now, we have heard in the Epistle for today that those who live under the law do not live aright, for they do the works of the law unwillingly and without delight, and are bond servants, not children. For the law will hold no one righteous who does not keep it willingly. Such willingness, however, is only bestowed by faith, as has often been said. Faith will produce righteous works and fulfill the law. It is all the same to the believer, whether he is under the law or free from it, seeing that Christ also was under the law.

84. But Saint Luke, or rather the Holy Spirit, desires to show that this saintly Anna, the holy people of old, was not only under the law and a bond servant. He points out that besides her life under the law she also walked in the freedom of faith and the Spirit, fulfilling the law not only with outward works like a bond servant, but rather in faith. This is signified by the eighty-four years of her widowhood, meaning the spiritual life of faith led by the saints of old. For the widowhood, the life without a husband, signifies freedom from the law. Thus the life under the law and the life of faith existed, side by side. The believers of old, as to their souls were justified without the works of the law, alone by faith, and in this respect they were truly widows; but in their external conduct and as to their bodies, they were subject to the law. They did not, however, believe that they were justified by works but, having been justified by faith, they kept the law voluntarily, cheerfully, and to the glory of God. He who lives in this manner may also do the works of the law, which will not harm him nor make a bond servant of him, for Christ and the apostles also have kept the law. Behold, these are the people who at the same time live seven years with a husband and eighty-four years without a husband, who at the same time are free from the law and yet under the law, as Saint Paul says of himself in 1 Corinthians 9:20, "I am to them that are under the law, as under the law, not being myself under the law."

85. How can he be at the same time under the law and free from the law? In order to gain others he gladly performed the external works of the law, but in his heart he clung to faith, by which he was justified, without the works of the law. For he fulfilled the law, and yet would not be justified by it, which indeed is impossible. In this manner, Anna, the holy people, has kept the law. For whoever believes and has been justified by faith, may keep not only the law of God, but the laws of the whole world, and they will not hinder him; for he keeps them voluntarily, not in the opinion that thereby he acquires righteousness. But those people who only follow Anna in this that they live seven years with a husband, and do not live eighty-four years without a husband, are without the Spirit and faith and are bond servants. They believe that by doing the works of the law, they become righteous. But in this manner, they can never become righteous and pious, as today's Epistle sufficiently explains. It is well arranged that first the seven years of wedded life and then the eighty-four years of widowhood are mentioned, for Saint Paul also says in 1 Corinthians 15:46, "Howbeit that is not first which is spiritual, but that which is natural."

86. If man is to become spiritual and a believer, he must necessarily first be under the law; for no one can know his faults without the law, and he who does not know his sin will not long for grace. But the law demands so much

that man must realize and confess that he is unable to satisfy those demands. Then he must despair of himself and in all humility sigh for the grace of God. Behold, therefore, the seven years come first, the law precedes grace as John the Baptist was the forerunner of Christ. The law kills and condemns the natural, sensual man, so that grace may lift up the spiritual, inner man.

87. There is, however, nothing said of the years of Anna's virginity, which signifies the unfruitful life before either the law or grace has been in operation, and which is worthless before God. Therefore, virginity as a barren state was altogether despised and disapproved in the Old Testament.

88. But how is it that faith or the spiritual life of the inner man, which without the law is widowed, without a husband, is signified by the number 84? Let us here follow the example of Saint Augustine and try to find out the allegorical significance. Everyone knows that the numbers seven and twelve are the most glorious in the holy Scriptures. For these two numbers are mentioned frequently, undoubtedly because there were twelve apostles who founded and established the faith in all the world, and who exalted only faith by their doctrine and life. Whereas the one Moses received the law from the angels, thereby uniting Anna to a husband and demanding outward works from men.

Thus the apostles, who were twelve times more in number than Moses, received the Gospel, not from angels, but from the Lord himself, and made us widows, free by faith and justified without works. Now the saints of old, as we have said before, possessed this apostolic faith along with the law. Therefore, they have not only acquired the number seven, but also the number twelve, have not only possessed the one Moses, but also the apostles who were twelve times more, have lived as well under the law as free from the law, as we have heard before. Thus the number seven signifies the one Moses, and the number twelve times as many as Moses. It is, therefore, unquestionable that the number twelve signifies the apostles, the apostolic doctrine, the apostolic faith, the true widowhood, the spiritual life without the law. So also the number seven signifies Moses, the teaching of Moses, the works of the law, the real matrimonial state of bondage.

89. The twelve apostles are typified by the twelve patriarchs, the twelve precious stones on the holy garment of Aaron, the twelve princes of the people of Israel, the twelve stones taken out of the Jordan, the twelve foundations and gates of the new Jerusalem, etc. For the whole Scriptures emphasize faith and the Gospel, preached and established by the apostles. Thus this faith is also signified by these eighty-four years, which contains the number twelve in a wonderful manner.

90. In the first place, eighty-four is equal to twelve times seven. This signifies that the teacher of the law is only one, Moses, being only one time seven, that is to say, the law and the life under the law. But the apostles are twelve, twelve times as many as Moses. Eighty-four bears the same relation to seven as twelve does to one. Now, as the law was given through one and the Gospel through twelve, it is evident that seven signifies Moses and eighty-four the apostles. So the disciples of Moses are represented by Anna in the state of matrimony, while the widow Anna signifies the followers of the apostles, the former emphasizing external conduct, the latter a life in the Spirit and in faith. This also signifies that faith exceeds the works as much as twelve exceeds the number one, or eighty-four the number seven. It comprises the whole sum and inheritance, as also the apostle calls it *"holokleros,"* the whole inheritance, in 1 Thessalonians 5:23; for the number twelve comprises all the people of Israel, divided into twelve tribes. He who believes, possesses all things, is an heir of heaven and a blessed child of God. Notice also the divine arrangement here. As Anna was not a widow for twelve years nor a married woman for one year, God ordained it so that the years of her wedded life were seven and those of her widowhood eighty-four in number, the former number bearing the same relation to the latter that one does to twelve. Besides this, there is thus also found, as we have seen, a greater spiritual significance in the number seven, in her wedded life and in the state of her widowhood.

91. In the second place, the arithmeticians divide numbers into so-called aliquot parts, that is to say, they examine how often a given number may be divided into equal parts. Thus the number twelve may be divided five times into equal parts. For twelve, in the first place, is twelve times one, all aliquot parts; secondly, six times two; thirdly, four times three; fourthly, three times four; fifthly, two times six. In this case, there can be no further division into aliquot parts. Seven and five are also twelve; likewise, three and nine, one and eleven, but those numbers are not aliquot parts of twelve. Now, they add together these aliquot parts to find their sum. Thus the aliquot parts of twelve are 1, 2, 3, 4, 6, which, added together, make 16, exceeding the number itself by four. This is called the abundant number, because the sum of the aliquot parts exceeds the number itself. Again, sometimes the aliquot parts of a number added together make less than the number itself. For instance, eight is eight times one, four times two, two times four. But 1, 2, and 4 make only seven, one less than eight. This is called the deficient number. Between these two is the perfect number, which is equal to the sum of its aliquot parts. Thus six is six times one, three times two, and two times three; now one, two, and three added together make six.

92. Notice here also that Moses, represented by the number seven, cannot thus be divided, as all odd numbers cannot. For this division is only possible with even numbers. But eighty-four, which signifies the apostles, is an abundant number and can be divided eleven times into aliquot parts. Judas, the traitor, does not belong to the abundant number, although he is one of the number. He is omitted here, so that there may not be twelve. He belongs to the number of the apostles in name, but not in reality. In the first place, eighty-four is 84 times one; then 42 times 2, 28 times 3, 21 times 4, 14 times 6, 12 times 7, 7 times 12, 6 times 14, 4 times 21, 3 times 28, 2 times 42. If you add together the aliquot parts 1, 2, 3, 4, 6, 7, 12, 14, 21, 28, 42, the result is 140, 56 more than the number itself.

93. All this signifies that Moses undivided, or the law, like the number seven, remained by itself, having not passed beyond the Jewish people nor exercised an influence upon other nations. But the spiritual life and the Gospel preached by the apostles has spread abundantly over all the world. And as the number one compared with twelve is very small and trifling, so that it could hardly look more unimportant, so also the number seven compared with eighty-four is very insignificant. For the law with its works confers nothing upon its servants but temporal possessions and worldly honor, a poor and wretched possession, which will not increase, but surely decrease. On the other hand, one is great and will multiply instead of decreasing; for faith has the blessing of God and abounds forever with possessions and honor. We have now rambled about sufficiently and have seen that no tittle of the Scriptures was written in vain. The dear fathers of old have shown us great examples of faith, and with their works have always pointed to that in which we should believe, namely, Christ and his Gospel. Therefore, we read nothing concerning them in vain, but their whole conduct strengthens and improves our faith. Let us now continue with Anna.

94. Luke says that she departed not from the temple. What a salutary and necessary exhortation! We have heard that by the temple is signified the holy Scriptures. It was a special sin of the people that they liked to listen to false prophets and human doctrines; this they proved by erecting altars outside of the temple, in high places and valleys. Moses spoke against this in Deuteronomy 5:32 and in Deuteronomy 12:32, when he said, "What thing soever I command you, that shall ye observe to do: thou shalt not add thereto, nor diminish from it." He desires, as it were, the people to be like Anna, who did not depart from the temple. They were however not all like Anna, but turned from the temple to their altars, from the law of God to their own devices and to false prophets.

95. But this was nothing compared with the state of affairs at the present time. We have not only been seduced by the pope and human doctrines to depart from the temple, but we have also arbitrarily destroyed and desecrated it with all kinds of profanations and abominations, more than we can express. But we ought to heed what Saint Anthony so diligently taught his disciples, namely, that nobody should do anything that has not been commanded or advised by God in the Scriptures, so that we might by all means remain in the temple. Psalm 1:1–2 speaks of this: "Blessed is the man that walketh not in the counsel of the wicked, nor standeth in the way of sinners, nor sitteth in the seat of scoffers: but his delight is in the law of Jehovah; and on his law does he meditate day and night." In 1 Peter 4:18, we read, "And if the righteous is scarcely saved, who is in the temple" (Luther's translation). This means that Satan also tempts those who trust only in the Word of God; they are scarcely saved. How then will those secure and reckless people be saved who base their faith upon the doctrines of men?

96. A holy life cannot endure human doctrines; they are a stumbling block and a dangerous snare. We must remain in the temple and never depart from it. This was done by the saints of old, of whom Saint Paul speaks in Romans 11:4, where he quotes the answer of God to Elijah, "I have left for myself seven thousand men, who have not bowed the knee to Baal." David complains of these persecutors and ensnarers in Psalm 140:45, "Keep me, O Jehovah, from the hands of the wicked; preserve me from the violent man: who have purposed to thrust aside my steps. The proud have hid a snare for me, and cords; they have spread a net by the wayside; they have set gins for me." All this is directed against human doctrines which take us away from the temple. For the Word of God and the doctrines of men cannot agree at all with each other in the same heart. Yet these senseless enemies of souls, the papists with their Antichrist, the pope, declare that we must teach and observe more than is found in the Bible. With their ecclesiastical ranks and orders, they lead the whole world to hell.

97. Finally, Luke says of Anna that she worshiped with fastings and supplications night and day. Here we see how good works follow faith. She must first be Anna, a prophetess, the daughter of Phanuel, of the tribe of Asher, a widow even unto fourscore and four years, not departing from the temple; then her fasting and praying is right, then the sacrifice of Abel is acceptable, then God may be served with fastings and supplications night and day. But whoever starts with works reverses all things and obtains nothing. Thus, after Saint Paul has taught the Romans faith, he begins in Romans 12:1, to teach them many good works, exhorting them to present their bodies a living sacrifice, holy,

acceptable to God, which would be their spiritual service. This is rendered to God in that the body is mortified by fasting, watching, and labors, which is done by Anna.

98. All the saints of old have done this, for fasting means all chastisement and discipline of the body. Although the soul is just and holy by faith, the body is not yet entirely free from sin and carnal appetites, wherefore it must be subdued and disciplined and made subject to the soul, as Saint Paul says of himself in 1 Corinthians 9:27, "But I buffet my body, and bring it into bondage: lest by any means, after that I have preached to others, I myself should be rejected." We also read in 1 Peter 2:5, that we should offer up spiritual sacrifices, that is to say, not sheep nor calves, as under the law of Moses, but our own body and ourselves, by the mortification of sin in our flesh and the discipline of the body. No one can do this who does not first believe.

99. Therefore, I have often said that the works which follow faith should not be done with the intention of meriting righteousness; for this must exist before good works can be done. They must be done with a view to discipline the body and to serve our neighbor. Good works are a true service of God if they are done freely and voluntarily, to the honor of God. Why should he desire us to fast if thereby we did not suppress our sin and flesh, which according to his will should be subdued? But many feast only to please the saints or at special seasons, not in order to discipline the body. Such fasting, however, is entirely worthless.

100. But Anna does not fast only on special days, on Saturdays and Fridays, on apostles' or ember days, nor does she know anything about a diversity of meats. But Luke says that she worshiped night and day and thereby served God, which means that she continually disciplined her body, not because she desired to do a meritorious work, but in order to serve God and to subdue sin.

101. Saint Paul also speaks of this fasting in 2 Corinthians 6:4–5, when he says among other things, that we should commend ourselves as ministers of God in fastings. But our foolish fasting contrived by men only consists in not partaking of meat, eggs, butter, or milk for a few days, not as a service of God and with the intention to discipline the body and subdue the flesh; but thereby we only serve the pope, the papists, and the fishmongers.

102. Anna worshiped night and day; therefore, she must certainly also have watched. But we must not believe that she prayed and fasted night and day without intermission, for she was obliged also to eat, drink, sleep, and rest. Fasting and praying were the mode of life she pursued night and day. Doing something during the day or at night does not mean that we do it all day and all night.

103. This is the second part of the service of God, by which the soul is offered up to him, as the body is by fasting. And by prayer we do not merely understand oral prayer, but also the hearing, proclaiming, contemplating, and meditating on the Word of God. Many psalms are prayers, although they hardly contain a petition; others teach some lesson or rebuke sin and, by meditating upon them, we converse with God, with ourselves, and with men. Behold, such was the service rendered to God by the dear fathers and saints of old, who sought nothing but the honor of God and the salvation of men. Thus we read of a great longing on the part of the ancient fathers in Scripture and their longing for Christ and the salvation of the world. This can especially be noticed by anyone in the Psalms.

104. But at the present time people only pray at stated times, count beads, and rattle off their prayers. Nobody thinks seriously of asking and obtaining something from God, but they only perform it as a duty obligatory upon them, and then are satisfied. As a thrasher who wields his flail, they move their tongue, and only earn bread for the body. Much less do they trouble themselves by serving God with their prayers and petitioning him to relieve the general need of Christendom, but even the best among them believe they have done enough when they are pious for themselves and pray only for themselves. Therefore, hypocrites as they are, they deserve nothing but hell with their prayers, for they serve neither God nor men, but only their own body and advantage. If they wished to serve God and their neighbor as they ought, they would not think of the number of prayers and psalms they repeat, but with all their hearts would seek the honor of God and the salvation of men, which would be a true service of God. Then for one thing they earnestly desire they would often pray a whole day. This would indeed be praying and worshiping like Anna. When Luke writes that she worshiped God with supplications, he condemns the multitude of our foolish prayers, whereby we only increase and multiply our sins, because we do not serve and seek God. Now let us return again to our text.

And coming up at that very hour she gave thanks unto God, and spoke of him to all them that were looking for the redemption of Jerusalem.

105. Our Latin texts read, "for the redemption of Israel," but the Greek has, "that were looking for the redemption of Jerusalem." Anna spoke to those who were in Jerusalem and were waiting for the redemption. For, as she did not depart from the temple, she could only speak to those who were in Jerusalem, either to the inhabitants or to visitors. In the spiritual interpretation, we have spoken sufficiently of the meaning of her standing near. For

when we come with Christ into the temple of the Scriptures to present him to God with thanksgiving, there is found at that very hour also this holy Anna, with all the saints of the whole synagogue, who unanimously look and point at him with their faith and their whole life.

106. We also notice here the great distinction conferred upon this holy woman, who was favored more than many great people when she recognized this poor child as the true Savior. There were undoubtedly priests present who received the offerings of Joseph and Mary, but did not know the child and perhaps considered the words of Simeon and Anna as mere old wives' talk. She must have been specially illumined by the Holy Spirit, and a saintly woman in the sight of God, who enlightened her more than others.

107. Behold, five persons are here brought together: the infant Christ, his mother Mary, Joseph, Simeon, and Anna. By this small number of people, every station in life is represented—husband and wife, young and old, virgin and widow, the married and the unmarried. Here Christ begins to gather around him people of every honorable station, and will not be alone. Whoever, then, is not found in one of these states, is not on the way to salvation.

108. "She gave thanks unto God." In the Hebrew tongue different meanings are attached to the word "confess", for which we need various expressions, as for instance: to confess (sins), to acknowledge, to give thanks. Thus to give thanks is in Hebrew expressed by the word "confess," and very appropriately so. For to give thanks is nothing but to acknowledge the kindness of the benefactor and that the gift is not deserved confess that we have received benefits. He who will acknowledge and confess this will also sincerely give thanks. To "confess" means also to admit something. Thus Christ says in Matthew 10:32-33: "Every one therefore who shall confess me before men, him will I also confess before my Father who is in heaven. But whosoever shall deny me before men, him will I also deny before my Father who is in heaven."

109. Now, as it has been said above in explaining the blessing of Simeon that it is a great and extraordinary virtue to bless Christ whom all the world rejects, so it is also a remarkable deed to give thanks to God for Christ. It is done by those who know him, but there are only a few of them. The others blaspheme God, condemn, persecute, and oppose Christ and his doctrine. They treat him and God his Father as they treat his doctrine, according to his words, in Luke 10:16, "He that rejecteth you rejecteth me; and he that rejecteth me rejecteth him that sent me." It is a terrible thing that the world is full of blasphemers and persecutors, and that we must live among them. Saint Paul predicts in 2 Timothy 3:1–2, that in the last days there will be many railers. This prophecy is now being fulfilled by the pope and the great schools, the

convents, and monasteries that do nothing else but reject, persecute, and condemn the Gospel of Christ.

110. May you, therefore, consider it a manifestation of the grace of God in you when you learn to know Christ and give thanks to God for him, when you do not regard him an accursed heretic and seducer, and do not blaspheme, despise, and forsake God and his teaching, as is done by the great multitude. For Christ does not first of all want his person and name exalted, which is done by all his enemies, but he requires that his doctrine be honored, which is the greatest art. He himself says in Luke 6:46, "And why call ye me, Lord, Lord, and do not the things which I say?" and in Mark 8:88, "For whosoever shall be ashamed of me and of my words in this adulterous and sinful generation, the Son of man also shall be ashamed of him." You perceive here that he cares most for his doctrine. The pope and the papists also call him Lord, indeed, in his name, to his honor and, in his service, they reject his doctrine, slay his Anna, and persecute her throughout the world. It is dreadful and unbearable to see how great multitudes of people blaspheme God and his Christ, and in their fanaticism go down to hell.

111. He is a sign which is spoken against, and more stumble and fall against him at the present time than ever before. *Deo gratias* (Thanks be to God!) is a common saying, but there is scarcely one among a thousand who says it in truth. At the time of Elijah, which was still a gracious time, there were left only seven thousand among the Jewish people, who without doubt numbered more than a million; but how many may be left in these last times which Daniel calls the times of the indignation, in Daniel 11:36? We might indeed ask God with the words of Psalm 89:49, "Lord, where are thy former lovingkindnesses, which thou swarest unto David in thy faithfulness?"

112. Anna did not only give thanks unto God but she also spoke of him to all them that were looking for the redemption of Jerusalem. Luke has a special reason for adding that Anna spoke of Christ only to those who were looking for the redemption. There were certainly not many of them, and none at all among the highly educated priests. What could these great, holy, and cultured people learn of such an old, foolish woman! They considered themselves the real leaders of the people. Thus the words of Anna were undoubtedly despised by these great gentlemen. For the Word of God concerning Christ must necessarily be contemptible, foolish, heretical, sacrilegious, and presumptuous to the ears of these great, learned, and spiritual men. Therefore, it is only received by the hungering, longing souls that look for the redemption, as Luke says here, who feel their sin and desire grace, light, and consolation, who know nothing of any wisdom and righteousness of their own.

113. Now faith and the knowledge of Christ cannot be silent. They break forth and testify, so that others may be helped and receive the light, as we read in Psalm 116:10, "I believe, for I will speak." Faith is too kind and bountiful to keep all such treasures to itself. But when it speaks, it is persecuted by all the unbelieving saints; yet it does not care and goes right ahead. And who knows how Anna was treated! But perhaps they spared her on account of her age and sex, and simply despised her as a silly fool. Otherwise, her life would hardly have been preserved, because she proclaimed such error and heresy, declaring of Christ such marvelous things, in opposition to all the doctrines and systems of the learned priests and teachers of the law, who are filled with wisdom and righteousness to such a degree that they do not need any redemption, but deserve only a crown and reward for their good works and great merits. For if we speak of the redemption of Christ, we declare that they are bound in sin and blindness. This, however, is too much for these great saints, to be called blind sinners! Therefore, they cannot endure hearing anything of Christ and his redemption and, consequently, they condemn it as a dangerous error and a diabolical heresy.

114. We now easily understand how it was that the spiritual Anna gives thanks to God and speaks of Christ to all that are looking for the redemption of Jerusalem. For the dear saints of the Old Testament knew Christ well. Therefore, by their whole life they praise God and give thanks to him, exemplifying the Bible and proclaiming only this redemption, how Christ came solely for those who need him and hunger after him. This is proved by all the narratives of the Old Testament. For God never assisted those who consider themselves strong and not forsaken. On the other hand, he never forsook those who were needy and desired his help. This might here be corroborated by all the stories of the Bible, but it is sufficiently clear and manifest to all who will read them.

115. The evangelist, in writing of these things, mentions especially Jerusalem, for the reason that Jerusalem means a vision of peace and signifies the hearts that are peaceable, not quarrelsome. Saint Paul writes in Romans 2:8, that the people who are factious will not obey the truth. Divine truth demands tranquil hearts that listen attentively and are desirous to learn. But those who brawl and bluster, who are pigheaded and demand signs and reasons before accepting the truth, will never find it. They are in the turmoil of Babylon and do not know the peace of Jerusalem. Therefore, they neither look for the redemption, nor listen to the words of Anna. But we may also read "Israel" instead of "Jerusalem"; it does not matter much which one of these two words is here used.

III. THE RETURN OF THE PARENTS OF JESUS TO NAZARETH, AND THE CHILDHOOD OF CHRIST

And when they had accomplished all things that were according to the law of the Lord, they returned into Galilee, to their own city Nazareth.

116. The Gospel for the day of Candlemas will explain what the things are which they accomplished according to the law of the Lord. The significance of Galilee and Nazareth will be explained in the Gospel for the festival of the Annunciation. But we must refer here to the words of Saint Matthew in Matthew 2:13ff., who writes that after the wise men had departed, who found Christ in Bethlehem and offered unto him gifts, gold and frankincense and myrrh, an angel appeared to Joseph in a dream and bade him flee into Egypt with the child and his mother, and that Joseph did so. How does this agree with the narrative of Luke, according to whom they returned to Nazareth after six weeks had passed, and they had accomplished all things that were according to the law of the Lord? We must here either assume that they went into Egypt immediately after the expiration of the six weeks of purification, and then returned to Nazareth from Egypt in due time, or we must believe, which is also my opinion, that they returned home, immediately after the six weeks had elapsed, as Luke relates here. Then the appearance of the angel who commanded them to flee into Egypt, whereof Matthew speaks, occurred not in Bethlehem, but at Nazareth; and indeed it took place after the departure of the wise men, as Matthew says, but not directly afterward. But Matthew writes thus because immediately after the departure of the wise men, he records the flight into Egypt, and omits what Luke relates here of the presentation in the temple. Thus it is clear that the two evangelists do not disagree.

117. It is also pointed out here how they were obliged to take up their cross. After the poor mother had been away from home for seven or eight weeks on account of the sudden birth of her child, and after having now returned and settled down to rest from their travels, they must again leave everything behind and, without delay, start on a much longer journey. Thus the Lord Christ begins his journeys in his earliest childhood, always wandering on this earth and having no definite place or abode where he might stay. How differently from other children is this royal child reared and treated; how did he, especially in this case, taste the sorrows and troubles of life! The poor mother must flee with the poor child into Egypt from the wrath of Herod. We shall speak more of this when this Gospel is explained.

And the child grew, and waxed strong, filled with wisdom:
and the grace of God was upon him.

118. Some inquisitive people who were not satisfied with the information given in the Scriptures have desired to know what Christ did in his childhood, and have received their reward for their curiosity. Some fool or knave has fabricated a legendary book on the childhood of Christ, and has not been afraid nor slow to write down his lies and frauds, relating how Christ went to school and a great deal more of absurd and blasphemous tomfoolery. Thus he jests with his lies at the expense of the Lord, whom all the angels adore and fear, and before whom all creatures tremble, so that this rascal would have deserved that a great millstone had been hanged about his neck and he had been sunk in the depth of the sea, because he did not esteem the Lord of all more than to make him an object of his absurd buffoonery. Yet people may still be found who print this book, read and believe it, which, in fact, was the object of this miscreant. Therefore, I say that such books ought to be burned by the pope, the bishops, and the universities, if they would follow Christ. But they produce books that are a great deal worse, are blind leaders, and remain such.

119. Christ never went to school, for no schools like ours existed at that time. He did not even have an elementary education, as we read in the Gospel of Saint John 7:15, the Jews were marveling, saying, "How knoweth this man letters, having never learned?" We also read in Mark 6:2–3, that they were astonished at his wisdom and said, "What is the wisdom that is given unto this man, and what mean such mighty works wrought by his hands? Is not this the carpenter, the son of Mary?" They thought it strange that a layman and the son of a carpenter should have such great knowledge, having never studied. Therefore, they were offended in him, as the evangelist relates, and thought that he must be possessed of an evil spirit.

120. Let us, therefore, be satisfied with the narrative of the Gospel, which tells us enough of his childhood. Luke writes that "the child grew, and waxed strong, filled with wisdom," etc. Later on, he writes that he was subject to his parents. What else should he have related? The time was not yet come when he performed miracles. He was brought up like other children, with the exception, that as some children excel others in ability, Christ also was an extraordinarily clever child. Thus no more could be written concerning him than is recorded by Luke. If he had related how he ate, drank, and what he did every day, how he walked, stood, slept, and watched, what kind of a narrative would it have been?

121. It is not necessary to believe, neither do I think it is true, that his coat which was woven from the top throughout, grew with him in size from his youth. Probably his mother made it, and in that country it was the common garment of the poor. We should have a pure faith that accepts nothing which is not found in the Scriptures. Enough is contained in the Scriptures that we may believe, especially since Christ did not begin to perform his miracles and mighty deeds until after his baptism, as it is written in John 2:11 and in Acts 10:37.

122. Some hairsplitters are perplexed by the words of Luke according to which Christ, although he was God, waxed strong, filled with wisdom. That he grew, they admit, which is indeed surprising, as they are very swift in inventing miracles where there are none and despise those in which they should believe. The reason for their perplexity and their anxious questions is this, that they have invented an article of faith according to which Christ from the first moment of conception was filled with wisdom and the spirit to the highest possible degree, just as if the soul were a wineskin which may be completely filled. They themselves do not understand what they say, nor whereof they confidently affirm, as Saint Paul writes in 1 Timothy 1:7.

123. Even if I could not understand what Luke means when he says that Christ waxed strong, filled with wisdom, I should yet believe his word because it is the Word of God, and should honor it as the truth, although I might never find out how it could be true; and I should abandon my imaginary article of faith as human foolishness, which is far too worthless to be a standard of divine truth. We all must acknowledge that Christ was not always cheerful, notwithstanding the fact that he who is filled with the Spirit is also full of joy, since joy is the fruit of the Spirit, according to Galatians 5:22. Neither was Christ always gentle and calm, but sometimes he was indignant and vexed, as for instance when he cast the Jews out of the temple, in John 2:15–17, and when he was angry and grieved at the hardening of their hearts, in Mark 3:5.

124. Therefore, we must understand the words of Luke simply as applying to the human nature of Christ, which was an instrument and temple of the Godhead. And although he was always filled with the Spirit and with grace, yet the Spirit did not always move him, but prompted him now to do this, now something else, just as necessity required. Although the Spirit was in him from the first moment of the conception, yet as his body grew and his reason naturally developed as in other men, so also was he filled and moved by the Spirit more and more. It is no delusion when Luke says that he waxed strong and advanced in wisdom, but the words tell us plainly in age and in stature and, as he grew in stature, his reason developed and, with the development of his

reason, he became stronger in the Spirit and filled with wisdom before God, in himself, and before men, which needs no further explanation. This is a Christian explanation which can be accepted without any danger, and it does not matter whether it overthrows any imaginary articles of faith.

125. Saint Paul agrees with this when he says in Philippians 2:7, that Christ, who existed in the form of God, emptied himself, taking the form of a servant, being made in the likeness of men, and being found in fashion as a man. Saint Paul does not speak here of the likeness of Christ's human nature to our own, but he says, Christ, the man, after he had taken upon himself human nature, was made in the likeness of men, and found in fashion as a man. Now, as all men grow naturally in body, reason, mind, and wisdom, which is a universal experience, Luke agrees with Paul when he says that Christ grew in the same manner, yet being an extraordinary child that developed more rapidly than others. For his bodily constitution was nobler, and the gifts and graces of God were bestowed upon him more abundantly than upon others. Thus the sense of Luke's words is easily understood, perspicuous, and simple, if only these wiseacres would leave out their subtleties. So much on this Gospel.

New Year's Day

❦

The Circumcision, and Choosing the Name, as Was the Custom at Circumcision

A*nd when eight days were fulfilled for circumcising him, his name was called Jesus, which was so called by the angel before he was conceived in the womb.* — LUKE 2: 21

1. It is the custom "to distribute the New Year" from the pulpit on this day, as if there were not enough other useful and salutary matter to preach, and it were necessary to present such useless fables in place of the Word of God, and to make a sport and disgrace of so serious an office. The Gospel requires us to preach on the circumcision and the name of Jesus; and this we will do!

I. OF THE CIRCUMCISION OF JESUS

2. First, let us ask the wise woman, Dame Jezebel, natural reason: Is it not a foolish, ridiculous, useless command, when God demands circumcision? Could he find no member of the body but this? If Abraham had here followed reason, he would not have believed that it was God who demanded this of him. For in our eyes, it is such a foolish thing that there can scarcely be anything more absurd. The Jews had to endure great infamy and disgrace on account of it, were despised by everybody, and treated as an abomination. Moreover, there is no use in it. What benefit is it, if the body is mutilated? Man is made no better by it, for everything depends upon the soul.

3. But such are all of God's commandments and works, and such they are to be. In our eyes, they appear most foolish, most contemptible, and most useless, in order that haughty reason, who deems herself clever and wise, may be put to shame and blinded, and may surrender her self-conceit and submit to God, give him honor, and believe that whatever he appoints, is most useful, most honorable, and most wise, although she does not see it and thinks quite differently. If God had given a sign which would have been suitable to her and useful, wise, and honorable in her estimation, she would have

remained in her old skin, would not have surrendered her haughtiness, would have continued in her custom of seeking and loving only honor, gain, and wisdom on earth, and so would have become ever more deeply rooted in worldly, temporal things. But now that he presents to her foolish, useless, and contemptible things, he tears her away from the seeking after gain, honor, and wisdom, and teaches her to regard only the invisible, divine wisdom, honor, and gain and, for its sake, willingly to suffer the lack of temporal honor, gain, and wisdom, and to be a fool—poor, unprofitable, and despised for God's sake. Therefore, God was not concerned about the circumcision, but about the humiliation of proud nature and reason.

4. So we also have baptism in the New Testament, in order that we should be buried in the water, and believe that we are thereby cleansed from sins and saved; also, that Christ's body is in the bread of the altar; also, that we worship the crucified man as Lord and God. All this is immeasurably far above, and contrary to, reason. So the works and words of God are all contrary to reason and this, in turn, is also contrary to God and recoils at the sign that is spoken against. Before men, it was a very foolish speech, when Noah built the ark and said the world would be flooded. So Lot must needs have been a fool when he said Sodom and Gomorrah would perish. Moses and Aaron were fools before King Pharaoh. In short, God's Word and his preachers must be fools, as Saint Paul says, in 1 Corinthians 1:21. In all this, God seeks nothing but this humility, that man bring his reason into captivity and be subject to divine truth. Abraham and his seed received the foolish rite of circumcision, in order that by it they should give glory to God and suffer him alone to be wise.

5. Now circumcision was an external mark, by which God's people were known in distinction from other nations; just as we see that every prince gives his people and army his standard and watchword, by which they are known among themselves and by which foreigners can tell, to what lord they belong. Thus God has never left his people without such a sign or watchword, by which it can outwardly be known in the world where his people are to be found. Jews are known by circumcision; that was their divine mark. Our mark is baptism and the body of Christ. Therefore, the ancient fathers called these signs, characters, symbols, *tesseras*, that is, watchwords or standards, what we now call sacraments, that is, sacred signs. For where there is baptism, there certainly are Christians, be they where they will in the world. It matters not if they are not under the pope, as he claims; for he would like to make of himself a sacrament and a Christian watchword.

6. Let this be enough concerning the temporal reason for circumcision. We will now also look at the spiritual reason and its significance. First, why did

he not command to circumcise a finger, hand, foot, ear, or eye, or some other member? Why did he select just that which in human life serves for no work or employment and which was created by God for natural birth and multiplication? If evil was to be cut off, then certainly the hand or the tongue, of all members, ought to have been circumcised; for by the tongue and hands all wickedness is perpetrated among men.

7. It is said that it was done for the reason, that evil lust manifests itself most in this member of the body; wherefore also Adam and Eve felt the disobedience of their flesh there, and sought a covering for their nakedness. That is all true; but in addition to that, it also signifies, as we are wont to say, that God does not condemn or save the person on account of his works, but his works on account of the person. Accordingly, our fault lies not in our works, but in our nature. The person, nature, and entire existence are corrupt in us because of Adam's fall. Therefore, no work can be good in us, until our nature and personal life are changed and renewed. The tree is not good; therefore, its fruits are bad.

8. Thus God has here taught everyone, that nobody can become righteous by works or laws, and that all works and labors to become righteous and be saved are in vain, as long as the nature and person are not renewed. You see now that, had he commanded to circumcise the hand or the tongue, this would have been a sign that the fault to be changed lay in the words or works; that he was favorable to the nature and person, and hated only the words and works. But now, in selecting that member which has no work except that the nature and personal existence arise thereby, he gives clearly to understand that the fault lies in the entire state of the nature, that its birth and its origin are corrupt and sin. This is original sin, or the sin of the nature, or the sin of the person, the truly chief sin. If this did not exist, there would neither be any actual sin. This sin is not done, like all other sins; but it exists, lives, and does all sins, and is the essential sin, that sins not for an hour or a season; but wherever and as long as the person exists.

9. God looks at this sin of the nature alone. This can be eradicated by no law, by no punishment, even if there were a thousand hells: but the grace of God alone, which makes the nature pure and new, must purge it away. The law only manifests it and teaches how to recognize it, but does not save from it; the law restrains only the hand or member, it cannot restrain the person and nature from being sinful; for in birth, the nature has already anticipated the law, and has become sin before the law could forbid it. Just as little as it lies in one's human power to be born and to receive natural existence, so little does it lie in his power to be without sin or to escape from it. He who has created us, he

alone must take it away. Therefore, he first gives the law, by which man recognizes this sin and thirsts for grace; then he also gives the Gospel and saves him.

10. In the second place, why does he command to circumcise males only, when nature and birth involve the woman also? The prophet also complains more of the mother than of the father, when he says, in Psalm 51:5, "Behold, I was brought forth in iniquity; and in sin did my mother conceive me." It was surely done on account of Christ and his mother, because he was to come, and because it was possible that a natural man and person could be born of a woman without sin and natural intercourse. But in all conception from a man, the man sins as well as the woman, and sin on either side cannot be avoided. Therefore, Christ willed not to be conceived of a man, in order that his mother also might not be under the necessity of sinning and of conceiving him in sin. Therefore, he made use of her womanly flesh and body for natural birth, but not for natural conception, and was conceived and born a true man without sin. Since, therefore, it is possible that a pure, innocent birth, nature, and person may be derived from a woman, but from a man, only a sinful birth, nature, and person, therefore, circumcision was imposed upon males only, in order to signify that all birth from man is sinful and condemned, requiring circumcision and change; but that a birth derived only from a woman without a man, is innocent and uncondemned, requiring no circumcision or change. And here one may apply what John writes, in John 1:12–13, "To them gave he the right to become children of God, even to them that believe on his name: who were born not of blood, nor of the will of the flesh, nor of the will of man, but of God," with the understanding that "the will of man" refers to birth from man. If it were possible now that more women could bear without men, these births would be altogether pure and holy; but this has been reserved for this one mother alone.

11. In the third place, why was it necessary to perform it on the eighth day? Here again, the sin of nature is indicated. For the poor babe has no actual sin of its own; nevertheless, it must be circumcised and assume the sign of purification from sin. If he had commanded to circumcise after eight years, one might say it was done for sins committed and for the avoidance of future sins. But by commanding to circumcise on the eighth day, he excludes both ideas, that it is done for sins committed and for the sake of future sins; without doubt, because a greater than any actual sin is born and ingrained in human nature.

12. But here it might be objected that Abraham and his servants and household were circumcised when they were grown and old, in Genesis 17:23; therefore, circumcision might signify actual committed sins. The answer is,

Scripture anticipates and abolishes the idea that Abraham was justified by circumcision, for he was already justified of his sins when he received circumcision; for it is written, in Genesis 15:6, that he was made righteous by his faith before his circumcision, when he was eighty years old or a little more, and circumcision he received when he was ninety-nine years old; so that circumcision was instituted almost twenty years after his justification. From this, Saint Paul, in Romans 4:11, concludes, against the Jews, that not circumcision, but faith without circumcision, justifies, as Abraham's example cogently shows. Therefore, circumcision is not a putting off of sin, but a sign of such putting off, which is accomplished by faith alone, as was the case with Abraham. Therefore, it demands, as in Abraham so in all men, faith, which removes the sin of nature and makes the person righteous and accepted.

13. If now Abraham's faith had not been described before his circumcision, it would have been a certain sign of original sin in him, as it is in the case of children, whose faith is not described beforehand. The Scriptures have ordered it so, that Abraham first believed and afterward was circumcised, and others were first circumcised and afterward believed, in order that both truths might stand: first, that circumcision is only a sign of justification and nobody is justified by it; secondly, that faith justifies alone without the cooperation of circumcision and, therefore, faith and its sign are clearly distinguished, to the discomfiture of the righteousness that trusts in works.

14. Perhaps the eighth day was also appointed for bodily reasons, in order that the babe might first grow stronger, lest it might appear that it had died from the circumcision, if it were circumcised directly after birth and had died from weakness.

15. But the spiritual significance is of greater importance. Seven days signify the time of this world until the last day, because this present time is measured by the week, or seven days, described in Genesis 1. The eighth day is the last day after the present time, when weeks, months, and years will cease, and there will be only an eternal day. On that day, circumcision shall be fulfilled, when not only the soul, but also the body, shall be redeemed from sin, death, and all impurity, and shall shine as the sun. Meanwhile, the soul is circumcised from sin and an evil conscience by faith.

16. So we see that the Scriptures in all places urge to faith, but only to faith in Christ. Therefore, circumcision was not given by the law of Moses, nor to the fathers before Abraham, but to Abraham, to whom Christ, his seed, was promised for a blessing, so that the bodily circumcision might everywhere be in accord with the spiritual circumcision.

17. Why then has it ceased, if that same faith in Christ, to which it points, still remains? The answer is, God has always, from the beginning of the world to the end, maintained one faith in Christ, but he has not given only one sign of it. If all the signs which refer to faith remained, who could keep them? But since faith is inward and invisible, God has foreshadowed it to men by many external signs, in order that they might be incited to believe as by many examples, and has permitted each to continue for its time. How many signs did Moses alone do in Egypt and in the wilderness, which have all passed away and lasted during their time, and still were all signs of faith? So when God promised to Abraham the blessings in his seed and gave to him a sign of it, namely, circumcision, it could not exist by virtue of that promise longer than the fulfillment of the promise. But when Christ, the blessed seed, came, the promise was finished and fulfilled; it was no longer to be expected. Therefore, the sign also necessarily was finished and fulfilled; why should it continue any longer, when the promise on which it depended was finished? But that which it signified, faith, remains always, whether the promise with its sign passes away or remains.

18. Yet circumcision has not been abolished in such a way that it is sin to be circumcised, as Saint Jerome and many others contend; but it has become free. If anybody wishes, he may circumcise himself, or not circumcise himself, as long as he does not act from the opinion that it is necessary and commanded, or that the promise of God to Abraham is unfulfilled and still to be expected. For faith can endure none of these opinions. Therefore, it does not depend upon the work, but upon the imagination and opinion of the one doing the work. If anybody circumcise himself with the same opinion with which he cuts his hair, beard, or skin, in love and service to another, he would not commit sin; for he would do it bound not by the law and by necessity of justification, nor against the fulfilled promise of God, but from free volition and his own choice, because the promise is fulfilled and the sign attached to it is finished.

19. Moreover, God never has had the custom of establishing a sign again, when once it has come to an end, but he has always instituted other new signs. So after the fulfillment of his promise, after the coming of Christ, he instituted for Abraham's seed another new sign, namely, baptism. This indeed is the last sign to be instituted before the last day, because he instituted it in person. Nevertheless, the same faith in Christ, which was in Abraham, abides always; for it knows neither day nor night, nor any outward transformation. This baptism has the same significance as circumcision, as is to be shown at the proper time.

II. THE NAMING OF JESUS, AS WAS THE CUSTOM AT CIRCUMCISION

20. Finally, it was the custom to give the child its name in circumcision, as we see here and in the instance of John the Baptist, to whom his name was also given in his circumcision. However, just as Christ was not obliged to be circumcised and this sign was empty in this case, so also his name had been given to him before by the angel, so that he did not obtain it by circumcision. This was done and is written, to the end that he should be altogether free from the law and from sin above all other men, and only serve us by submitting to the law and becoming like unto us in order to redeem us from it, as Saint Paul said in the last Epistle, "He was born under the law, that he might redeem them that were under the law," in Galatians 4:4–5.

21. For when death fell upon him and slew him, and yet had no right or cause against him, and he willingly and innocently submitted and suffered himself to be slain, death became liable to him, did him wrong, and sinned against him, and completely exposed itself, so that Christ has an honest claim upon it. Now, the wrong which death became guilty of toward him, is so great that death can never pay nor atone for it. Therefore, it must be subject to Christ and in his power forever, and so death is overcome and killed in Christ. Now, Christ did not do this for himself, but for us, and has bestowed upon us this victory over death in baptism. Therefore, all who believe in Christ must also be lords over death, and death must be their subject, nay, their criminal, whom they are to judge and execute, even as they do when they die and at the last day. For by the gift of Christ, death has also become guilty to all those who have received this gift from Christ. Behold, this is the sweet and joyous redemption from death through Christ; these are the spiritual victories of Joshua over the heathen of Canaan, notably the five kings, upon whose necks the princes of Israel put their feet by his command, in Joshua 10.

22. So also circumcision did Christ wrong, for he was not subject to it. Therefore, it is justly subject to him and he has power over it, has conquered it, and has granted to us, that it must cease and has lost its right over those who believe in Christ. He has released us from circumcision only by submitting to it innocently and by bestowing his right against it upon us.

23. Behold, this is putting Christ under the law, in order that he might redeem those who were under it, in Galatians 4:5. Moreover, he has subjected himself to all other laws, to none of which he was bound, being Lord and God over all. Therefore, they have all fallen into his power, have done him wrong, and must now justly be subject to him.

24. Now, all this he has also given to us. Therefore, if we believe in Christ, and the law would endeavor to punish us as sinners, and death would insist upon it, and try to drive the wretched conscience to hell, and if you then hold up to them in turn their sin and wrong, which they have done to Christ, your Lord, do you not suppose that they also shall be put to shame and be more afraid of you than you of them? Death shall feel its guilt and flee in disgrace; the law shall be compelled to give up its terror and smile friendly upon Christ. In this way, sin must be banished by sin. The sins which they have committed against Christ and now also against you on account of your faith, are greater than those which you have committed against them. In this case, God, the just judge, will not suffer that a great thief should hang a little one; on the contrary, if the great one is to be free, much more must the little one go free. Of this, Saint Paul says, in 1 Corinthians 15:55–57, "O death, where is thy sting? The sting of death is sin; but thanks be to God, who giveth us the victory through our Lord Jesus Christ; for death is swallowed up in victory." Behold, is not this a precious redemption from the law through him, who innocently subjected himself to the law?

25. Praise God, what an exceedingly rich and mighty thing faith is! It indeed makes of man a god, to whom nothing is impossible, as Christ says, in Mark 9:23, "If thou canst! All things are possible to him that believeth." Therefore, it is also said in Psalm 82:6, "Ye are gods, and all of you sons of the Most High."

26. His name is rightly called on this day Jesus, that is interpreted, Savior: for Savior we call one who saves, redeems, brings salvation, and is of help to everybody; this one, the Hebrew language calls Jesus. So the angel Gabriel spoke to Joseph in sleep, in Matthew 1:21, "She shall bring forth a son; and thou shalt call his name Jesus; for it is he that shall save his people from their sins." Here the angel himself explains why he is called Savior, Jesus, namely, because he is help and salvation to his people. We have now heard how this comes to pass through faith, to which he gives all his right and possession, that he has over sin, death, and the law. He makes it righteous, free, and blessed.

27. Now as circumcision signifies our faith, as we have heard, so the naming of children signifies that by faith we have a name and are known before God. For God knows none of those who do not believe, as is said, in Psalm 1:6, "For Jehovah knoweth the way of the righteous; but the way of the wicked shall perish." And, in Matthew 25:12, "Verily I say unto you, I know you not." What then is our name? Doubtless as Christ gives us all that is his, so he also gives his name to us; therefore, we are all called Christian from him,

all God's children from him, all Jesuses from him, all Saviors from him, and whatever is his name, that also is ours; as Saint Paul writes, in Romans 8:24, "In hope were ye saved," for you are Jesuses or Saviors. Behold, there is, therefore, no measure to the dignity and honor of a Christian! These are the superabundant riches of his goodness, which he pours out upon us, so that our heart may be free, joyous, peaceable, and unterrified, and willingly and cheerfully keep the law. Amen.

The Epiphany

‑‑‑‑‑‑

On the Visit of the Magi

[Editor's Note: Two parts of this sermon were added at a later period, and have been omitted from this collection. Paragraphs 143–216 appeared under the title: "An Exposition and Explanation of the Papacy in Its Own Colors," by Dr. Martin Luther, 1522. Paragraphs 232–249 appeared in two editions of a pamphlet under the title: "The Difference between True and False Worship, Dr. Martin Luther, 1522, and 1646." There is no paragraph 318 in the original.]

N ow when Jesus was born in Bethlehem of Judea in the days of Herod the king, behold, wise men from the east came to Jerusalem, saying, "Where is he that is born King of the Jews? for we saw his star in the east, and are come to worship him." And when Herod the king heard it, he was troubled, and all Jerusalem with him. And gathering together all the chief priests and scribes of the people, he inquired of them where the Christ should be born. And they said unto him, "In Bethlehem of Judea: for thus it is written through the prophets,

'And thou Bethlehem, land of Judah,
Art in no wise least among the princes of Judah:
For out of thee shall come forth a governor,
Who shall be shepherd of my people Israel.' "

Then Herod privily called the wise men, and learned of them exactly what time the star appeared. And he sent them to Bethlehem, and said, "Go and search out exactly concerning the young child; and when ye have found him, bring me word, that I also may come and worship him." And they, having heard the king, went their way; and lo, the star, which they saw in the east, went before them, till it came and stood over where the young child was. And when they saw the star, they rejoiced with exceeding great joy. And they came into the house and saw the young child with Mary his mother; and they fell down and worshiped him; and opening their treasurers they offered unto him gifts, gold and *frankincense and myrrh. And being warned of God in a dream that they should not return to Herod, they departed into their own country another way.* — MATTHEW 2:1–12.

1. This Gospel harmonizes with the Epistle and speaks of the temporal coming of the heathen to Christ, by which their spiritual coming to Christ, mentioned in the Epistle, is signified and commenced. It is both a terrifying and consoling Gospel: terrifying to the great and wise, the self-satisfied and the mighty, because they all reject Christ; consoling to the humble and despised, because to them alone Christ is revealed.

I. THE HISTORY OR LESSON STORY

2. The evangelist first refers to Herod the king, in order to recall the prophecy of Jacob the patriarch, who said, "The scepter shall not depart from Judah, nor the ruler's staff from between his feet, until Shiloh come; and unto him shall the obedience of the peoples be," in Genesis 4:9–10. From this prophecy is evident that Christ must come, when the kingdom or government of the Jews is taken from them, so that no other king or ruler from the house of Judah might sit on the throne. This was fulfilled now when Herod, who was not of the house of Judah, nor of Jewish descent but of Edom, hence a foreigner, was made king over the Jews by the Romans to the great dissatisfaction of the Jewish people. Hence for thirty years he warred with them before he finally silenced and subdued them.

3. Now when this foreigner had ruled over the Jews for thirty years, had taken possession of the government, and the Jews had acquiesced therein, having no hopes of getting rid of him and thus the prophecy of Jacob was fulfilled, then the time was at hand, then Christ came and was born under this first stranger and appeared according to the prophecy, as though he would say, The scepter has now departed from Judah, a stranger is ruling over my people. It is now time that I should appear and become king; the government now belongs to me.

4. These wise men are usually called the three kings. As not much depends on this, we will grant this opinion to the simple-minded people. However, it is not known whether there were two, three, or more. But they certainly came from the rich country Arabia or Sheba, which is evident from their gifts, namely, gold, frankincense, and myrrh. All three of these are very precious in that country. It can certainly not be assumed that they had bought these elsewhere, for it is customary in these Eastern countries to do homage

and make presents of the choice fruits and wealth of the country. Just like Jacob commanded his sons to carry presents of the choice fruits of the land to Joseph in Egypt, in Genesis 43:11. Had these gifts of the wise men not been of their own country, why should they then have brought frankincense, myrrh, and gold produced in the land of Judea, instead of silver and precious stones or fruits of some other country?

5. Therefore, these gifts were not presented to Christ like artists paint the scenery that one offers gold, another frankincense, and the third myrrh, but they presented the gifts in common as one man. And probably there were quite a number present, a few of them being the leaders, just as now a prince or a city sends a few brave men as messengers to the emperor with presents.

6. The evangelist calls these men wise men, which means in German *weissager*, i.e., predictors, diviners; not in the same manner as the prophets predicted, but like those whom we call wise men and wise women, who can tell people all kinds of things; who know a great deal about the secret arts and follow adventures. The art of such people is called magic, which is sometimes accomplished by the black arts and the help of the devil, but not in all things as by the witches and sorcerers. For the wise men imitate the true prophets and prophesy like the true prophets, though not by the spirit of God. For this reason, they sometimes happen to be correct as their work is not, like that of the witches, altogether the devil's work, but rather human reason aided by the devil.

7. Again, their miraculous deeds are not altogether done by the devil's cunning, like the doings of the witches, but by a combination of natural forces and the power of the devil. Hence a magician always imitates the real natural arts. For there are many hidden forces in nature, and he who knows how to apply them performs miracles in the eyes of those who know no better as, for instance, the alchemists make gold out of copper.

8. Of these secret forces of nature Solomon knew a great deal by the spirit of God, and made good use of this knowledge when he judged between the two women concerning the living and the dead child, in 1 Kings 3:25, discovering the real mother by appealing to the deepest feelings of nature. Again, Jacob also made use of this art when he used the peeled rods and the flocks brought forth speckled and spotted lambs, in Genesis 30:39.

9. This is a fine and a truly natural art by which is derived all that physicians and others know about the properties of herbs, plants, metals, stones, etc. The Scriptures also recognize this art when they make comparisons of animals, stones, trees, plants, etc. This art was especially practiced and studied among the Persians, Arabians and, in other Eastern countries, was an honorable art and made wise people.

10. But later on, swine and blockheads meddled with it, as usually happens with all arts and doctrines, and have gone far from the truth, have confounded this noble art with juggling and sorcery, and have tried to follow and master both. But when they could not do this, they relinquished the real art and became jugglers and conjurers, prophesying and doing miracles by the help of the devil, though sometimes through the forces of nature. For the devil has retained much of this art and at times uses it through the magicians. Thus the word magic has become disreputable, meaning nothing else now than foretelling and doing miraculous deeds through the evil spirit, though at times it is reliable and helps men because natural forces, which are always reliable, are coupled with it, and used by evil spirit.

11. Hence these magi, or wise men, were not kings, but men learned and experienced in this natural art though without doubt they also practiced conjury. Even to this day, men from these Eastern countries are possessed of great and various magic powers and, when this real art ceased, being despised, they brought forth sorcery and spread it throughout the world; but prior to this, they relied entirely on the course of the heavenly bodies. Thus presumptuous human reason has always mixed and disgraced that which was good by imitation and indiscretion, attempting to ape everything that it sees and hears. Hence false prophets imitate the true prophets; false, work-righteous saints the true saints; and the falsely learned the truly learned. If we look at the world, we will find, that the work of human reason is but aping to imitate the good, only perverts it, and thus deceives itself and others. For the universities also claim that they teach natural arts which they call philosophy, while in reality they are teaching not only tomfoolery, but also poisonous error and idle dreams.

12. These wise men, therefore, were nothing else than what the philosophers were in Greece and the priests in Egypt, and the learned among us in the universities. In short, they were the priests and learned in the rich country of Arabia; just as if learned men are priests from the universities, were now sent to a prince with presents. For the universities also claim that they teach natural arts which they call philosophy, while in reality they are teaching not only tomfoolery, but also poisonous error and idle dreams.

13. For the natural art, which was formerly called magic but now physiology, is to learn the forces and work of nature; as for example, that a deer with its breath through the nose will draw a snake from the crevice in the rocks, kill and eat it, and then, on account of the great heat of the poison, pants for cooling streams, as stated in Psalm 42:1. Again, that a weasel will induce a snake to come out of its hiding place by wagging its tail before the opening to anger and excite the snake; and then lies in wait so that, when the snake looks up

after its enemy, the weasel fastens its teeth in the neck of the snake below the venomous fang and thus kills its enemy in its own house.

Such arts the wise men studied, and in them is concealed a great deal of wisdom concerning Christ as well as the conduct of men in life. But this art is not taught in the universities now. Hence even the peasants know more about it than our wise men or natural masters who are not wrongfully called natural fools, because in spite of so much labor and trouble they have only retrograded and are the devil's mockingbirds. If we would, therefore, truly interpret this Gospel, we must say, The masters of nature from the East or the naturalists from Arabia have come.

14. Some are also surprised that they could come such long distance in so few days, for it is believed that they appeared the thirteenth day after Christ's birth; the geographers state that the capital city Sheba in Arabia is a sixty days' journey from the Mediterranean Sea, which is not much over three German (i.e., fifteen English) miles from Bethlehem. But questions of this kind do not trouble me very much, nor is it an article of faith to believe that they appeared the thirteenth day.

15. Neither is it necessary to hold that they came from the capital city Sheba, or from the remotest parts of the country. Perhaps they came from a place near the boundary of the country and thus they had sufficient time to come in the usual way of travel.

Mary being unclean had to remain at Bethlehem according to the law for six weeks, just like any other woman, and might thus have been found there even more than twenty or thirty days. However, I will not interpret like the common idea that they came in a miraculous manner, since no one needs to hold as an article of faith the question as to how they proceeded, and what they were accustomed to do in such matters. Whatever the Scriptures do not reveal, we do not consider an article of faith.

16. Now, the thought of the evangelist is this: When Christ was born under Herod, the first foreign king, and the time of the prophecy was fulfilled, this wonderful sign occurred. He whom his own people and fellow citizens would neither seek nor acknowledge was sought by such strangers and foreigners for many days. To him whom the learned and the priests would not acknowledge and worship, came the wise men and astrologers. It was indeed a great shame for the whole Jewish land and people that Christ was born in their midst, and they should first become aware of it through these heathen people living so far away. At least in Jerusalem, the capital city, they should have known about it. An earnest admonition to seek and to acknowledge Christ was given them. But their neck was an iron sinew and their brow brass as Isaiah says, in Isaiah 48:4.

*"Where is he that is born King of the Jews? for we saw his star in the East,
and are come to worship him."*

17. Text and circumstances demand that we speak further about the natural philosophers or masters of nature, because here the wise men knew by the star of the birth of a king as they declared. It must be observed that to every man is known a certain portion of the knowledge of nature. For instance, I know that a dog's tongue is good in healing wounds, that a cat will catch mice even when she is not hungry, that a hawk catches partridges, etc. One individual may know more also than others about nature either by his own experience, or through instruction. God did not, however, reveal to us all the facts about nature, but only a small portion of them. Yet human reason is inquisitive and always wants to know more and more, and thus originated the study and investigation of nature.

18. But it is impossible that nature could be understood by human reason after the fall of Adam, in consequence of which it was perverted, any further than experience or divine illumination allows. However, restless human reason will not submit and be satisfied with this, desiring to know and see everything. For this reason, it begins to speculate and to investigate farther than is permissible, and thus despises what experience or God has given it. And yet it never attains what it seeks after. All study and wisdom is but error and folly. This is the reason why men, despising or not being able to master this natural art, are divided into numerous sects. Some have written about the earth, others about water, some about this, and others about that, so that there is no end to investigation and the making of books. Finally, when they were tired of the study of the earth, they turned to the heavens in order to master also the nature of the heavens and the stars, with which no one could ever have any experience. Here they were entirely at liberty to dream, lie, and deceive, and to say about the innocent heavens whatever they pleased. It is a true saying that: Those who lie about distant countries lie as they please, because no one has had sufficient experience to contradict.

19. So also here, because no one can reach up into the heavens and testify from experience as to the truth or falsity of their teachings, they lie without fear. Hence they teach that whoever is born in this or that sign must become a gambler; whoever is born under this or that star will become rich or wise. Again, this one must be killed, or that one who builds, marries, or makes a journey on this or that day must fare so or so. They say, it is the nature of the stars of heaven so to affect human beings that happen to be born at such a time. The Lord help us! Human reason in all sincerity has come to this,

because these are all great and glaring lies, and captivating and unprofitable fables, in which reason in its blindness finds the greatest pleasure, as it delights not so much in the truth, as in fables and lies.

20. But finally, the real champions appeared who, disdaining to deal with child's play like this, opened their eyes widely and began to investigate the whole world, whence it came and whither it was going; whether it had a beginning or existed from eternity and will continue to all eternity; whether there is a Supreme Being who rules all things, etc. Here appeared the great light of nature, the heathen master, the supreme master of all masters of nature, who now rules in Christ's stead in all the universities, namely, the great famous Aristotle, who taught and still teaches them that a stone is heavy, that a feather is light, that water is wet, and that fire is dry; again, as a special masterpiece that the earth is above and the heavens below, which he proves by the fact that the roots of trees and all kinds of plants are in the ground, and the limbs grow heavenward. Now that part which receives nourishment must always be above, and that part to which the nourishment goes, must always be below as we observe in a human being. Therefore, man is a tree turned upside down. And thus, when a feather flies upward, it goes downward, and when a stone falls, it rises upward.

21. Furthermore, when he speaks of the Supreme Being, he concludes that the world existed from all eternity and will exist forever, and that all souls die together with the body. And the Supreme Being sits above the heavens, seeing nothing that occurs, but constantly turns as blind fortune is pictured, the heavens around once every day. In this way, all things happen just as they do. His argument is this: Should the Supreme Being see all things, he would see much evil and wrong, and that would make him unhappy. In order to remain happy, he must see nothing but himself and, consequently, rule the world blindly, just like a mother cradles her child in the night.

22. This is the wisdom of the universities. Whoever knows or learns this will have a brown cap placed upon his head and be addressed, Worthy *magister artium et philosophiae*! i.e., worthy master of the arts and of philosophy. He who does not know this art, can never become a theologian nor understand the holy Scriptures; yes, he is considered a heretic and can never become a Christian. Tell me, what shall we call these people? They are neither wise men nor sorcerers nor jugglers, but are mad, frantic, and senseless. Therefore, consider whether Christ did not rightly chastise us in that we have despised the Gospel, being unthankful, in that he permitted us to become such disgraceful and vile dupes of the devil that we not only do not apprehend the fact, but even with great expense, trouble, and labor seek after it as the greatest wisdom.

23. Saint Paul prophesied all this, saying, "Take heed lest there shall be any one that maketh spoil of you through his philosophy and vain deceit, after the tradition of men, after the rudiments of the world, and not after Christ," in Colossians 2:8. Again, "O Timothy, guard that which is committed unto thee, turning away from the profane babblings and oppositions of the knowledge which is falsely so called; which some professing have erred concerning the faith," in 1 Timothy 6:20–21. Here the apostle surely condemns in plain words the teachings of the universities so emphatically that none can contradict him, and wills that everything that is not from Christ should be avoided. Surely everyone must confess that Aristotle, the chief master of all the universities, teaches not only nothing about Christ, but even teaches such foolish things, as has been stated, that the apostle properly commands us to guard the doctrine committed unto us, calling the natural art of Aristotle unchristian, profane, meaningless babblings in opposition to Christ, knowledge falsely so-called. How could the apostle have explained it more plainly than by designating it thus? There is no greater glory than that of Aristotle in the universities, and yet it is but a false glory. For this art is nothing but an opposition that has arisen for the purpose of destroying Christ.

24. Therefore, my dear hearer, let natural art depart. If you do not know what powers the stars, stones, wood, animals, or any creatures possess, after which knowledge the natural art strives, even doing its best, then be satisfied with that which your experience and common sense teach you. Nor does it matter much whether you know all this or not; it is enough for you to know that fire is hot and water cold and wet, that in summer time different work must be done than during the winter; to know how to attend to your farm, stock, home, and children. This is enough for you as to natural art. Beyond this, think only of how you can learn to know Christ. He will teach you to know yourself, who you are and what power lies in you. In this way, you will know God and yourself, which no master of the arts of nature ever learned, as Saint Paul says in 1 Corinthians 2:8.

25. Coming back to the text, you might say, Yes, but the Gospel says that these wise men learned from the stars the birth of a king and, therefore, it proves that astrology is to be taught and known—God himself giving encouragement by causing a star to rise and thus teaching the wise men.

26. Answer: Keep to the example and learn as these wise men learned from the star, and then you will do right and not fall into error, for there is no doubt about it that the sun, moon, and stars were created to be signs and to serve the earth with their light, as Moses says, in Genesis 1:14. When the sun rises, you learn that the day begins; when it sinks, that the day has ended; and

when it stands in the meridian, that it is noonday. Furthermore, it has been fixed as a sign and measure of time and of the hours in which to do your work; so also the moon and the stars at night. Again, you also need the sun as a guide in tilling your farm and in caring for your stock, its heat determining your work. Let it be sufficient to know this much about the sun and the heavens. Whatever more you desire to know, you do not need and is but idle curiosity for the most part, unreliable and inclined to error; for instance, when fools pretend to know how large the sun is, how far it is from the earth, what particular power it has over gold, and that one born in the sign of the sun will become wise, and more such tomfoolery, for which they can give no sure reason.

27. Furthermore, you should also know that when the sun loses its brightness, it is surely a sign which forebodes disaster; and likewise when a comet appears. This is taught by experience; and Christ says, in Luke 21:25, that such signs will appear in the sun, moon, and stars, and will signify the final destruction of the world. Great storms, lightning, floods, and fire in the air and on earth are also great signs. But how these things occur or what kind of natural forces there are in all of these signs, or what effect they mysteriously produce, about which the magicians inquire and juggle, all this is of no value to you nor necessary for you to know. It is enough that you behold in all of these signs the wrath of God, and amend your life. During these years, there have also occurred many eclipses, and many signs have been seen in many countries, presaging great disturbances. Thus the eclipse at the suffering of Christ signified the calamity which rests upon the Jews to this day. These are indeed certain signs for which purpose God created them, but those of which astrologers dream are unreliable.

28. Hence these wise men had nothing else in this star than a sign and only used it as such according to the decree of God. Therefore, astrologers and fortune tellers cannot find encouragement for their false art in this Gospel. For though these wise men may also have been infatuated by this art, in this case they used this star only as a sign. They do not at all foretell what Christ would be in the future, what should happen to him, do not concern themselves about it. They are satisfied that it was a sign of a great king, and only ask where he is to be found.

29. And in order that Christ might forever stop the mouth of such babblers, he created for his birth a special new star as yet unsullied by their babbling. Knowing that they might say that he was born under the power of this star, he meets them beforehand and says, This star is not like one of those about which you are speculating. If the future fate of all men rests in the stars, as you teach, then there can be no such power in this star, which is new and of a different nature than the other stars, of which you have hitherto not heard or

known anything. Again, if none of the other stars had any power over Christ, having his own new star, it follows that they have no power over any human being, because Christ was in every respect a man like other men. Furthermore, if this new star had no power over other men, existing only for a short time, it certainly had also no power over Christ, as he is just like all other men. For this reason, astrology is mere tomfoolery.

30. But how these wise men could see in this star a sign that unmistakably signified a newborn king, I do not know. Perhaps they read in their histories and chronicles that aforetime the birth of other kings had been signified in the heavens or through a star. For we find also in the histories of the Romans and the Greeks that the coming or birth of some great princes and extraordinary men had been foretold by miracles and signs in the air and in the heavens. These wise men also knew quite well that these Jews were the chosen people of God, who were and had been above all other people, especially favored of God. Therefore, as this was such a beautiful star, they certainly thought that God had given this people a new king. But the claim of some that these wise men knew the saying of Balaam, "There shall come forth a star out of Jacob," etc., in Numbers 24:17, will avail nothing, as this passage speaks mainly of the spiritual coming of Christ, who is the star himself. But whoever is not satisfied with this may think as he pleases about it. Perhaps they knew all by divine revelation.

31. At first they did not consider this king to be God, but in the usual manner took him for a temporal king, just as the queen of Sheba considered Solomon a king, coming to him with presents from her country. For this reason, they also come to Jerusalem, the capital city, hoping to find him in the king's palace and in splendor. For the star that they saw over the Jewish country when they were yet at home in Arabia, must have disappeared so that they did not see it again on their journey until they proceeded from Jerusalem to Bethlehem, as the Gospel states.

32. But when they say, We have seen his star, they do not yet think that Christ had created it, but that it was his star because it signified his birth, just as the astrologers today call each man's sign in which he was born his sign, not as though he had created it himself. For the glory of Christ's divinity remained unseen until his ascension, though glimpses were sometimes afforded.

33. So also when they worshiped him, they did it after the manner of those Eastern countries, as the Scriptures state, not as though they considered them gods. The falling down before them and the homage given is called worship by the Scriptures and it is applied both to men and God, just as the words lord and king, yea, even the name of God are applied to man as when Jehovah said to Moses, "See, I have made thee as God to Pharaoh," in Exodus 7:1.

II. THE ATTITUDE OF HEROD TO THE ARRIVAL OF THE WISE MEN

And when Herod the king heard it, he was troubled,
and all Jerusalem with him.

34. Why are they troubled? Were not the Jews waiting for Christ who was promised them by God, as we have seen from Genesis 49:10? Were not Simeon and Anna and many more pious people at Jerusalem at that time looking for Christ's coming and rejoicing in it? That Herod was troubled, there was good reason. He feared the loss of his kingdom because he well knew that he was a foreigner and merited the ill will of the Jews. He also knew that the Jews looked for the Christ who should deliver them as Moses had done. Troubled by his conscience, he feared an insurrection against him and that he be driven from his kingdom. On the other hand, the Jews feared Herod and the Romans, believing that to have a new king would mean much bloodshed for them. They had before this, to their own great misfortune, revolted against the Romans and Herod, hence they were minded like the people of Israel in Egypt, who, when Moses was to lead them out and they were oppressed more than before, murmured against Moses. This was a sign of their weak faith, just as this fear of the Jews at Jerusalem indicates unbelief, and more trust in human than divine power.

35. However, the true believers were not frightened, but rather rejoiced. And when the evangelist says that all Jerusalem was troubled together with Herod, he does not mean all the inhabitants and citizens of the city, but speaks after the manner of the Scriptures, namely, that when it mentions a city only and not its inhabitants also, it means not all who dwell in it but the majority of them. Thus it is often said in the book of Joshua that he destroyed this and that city, killing all the inhabitants and whatever lived in it, but meaning only the largest part and number of them.

And gathering together all the chief priests and scribes of the people,
he inquired of them where the Christ should be born. And they said unto
him, "In Bethlehem of Judea, for thus it is written through the prophet,
'and thou Bethlehem, land of Judah, art in no wise least among
the princes of Judah: for out of thee shall come forth a governor,
who shall be shepherd of my people Israel.'"

36. Here we ask, why did not Christ lead these wise men to Bethlehem by the star instead of allowing his birth, which was now known, to be

learned from the Scriptures? This was done that he might teach us to adhere to the Scriptures and not depend on our own wisdom nor the teaching of any man. The Scriptures have been given for a purpose. In them, he desires to be found, and nowhere else. Whoever despises and rejects these shall and will never find him.

We have also heard, in Luke 2:12, that the angel also gave the shepherds a sign, but not to Mary nor to Joseph nor to any other men, no matter how pious they were, but gave to them only the swaddling clothes and the manger in which he was wrapped and laid; that is, the writings of the prophets and the law; in these he is wrapped, they contain him, they speak only of him and bear witness of him; they are his sure sign, as he says himself, "Ye search the Scriptures because ye think that in them ye have eternal life; and these are they which bear witness of me," in John 5:39. And Paul says, "A righteousness of God hath been manifested, being witnessed by the law and the prophets," in Romans 3:21. Furthermore, we have also heard that Simeon and Anna represent the Scriptures, which manifest Christ and bear him in their arms. And according to Luke 16:29–31, Abraham would not grant the request of Dives in hell that Lazarus be sent to his brothers, but points to the Scriptures, saying, "They have Moses and the prophets; let them hear them. If they hear not Moses and the prophets, neither will they be persuaded if one rise from the dead."

37. Against this divine doctrine our learned men have until now set up all kinds of means to learn the truth. We must speak of a few in order to guard ourselves against them. In the first place, they have set up innumerable laws, statutes, articles, and teachings invented by men, such as clerical canons, orders, regulations, etc., all of which are without doubt not the swaddling clothes and the manger of Christ, neither do they represent Simeon nor Anna. Saint Paul has earnestly warned us against such teachings and urged us to abide in the Word of God alone. For all human doctrines are dangerous and cause us to depart from the faith, just as Solomon was led astray by strange women and as Paul says, in Titus 1:14, "That fables and commandments of men turn away from the truth."

38. If anyone were to use human doctrines as he eats and drinks and wears clothing, they might be harmless. No one eats or drinks or clothes himself for the purpose of becoming holy and being saved thereby. Such an opinion or conviction would be base folly for anyone. His intention and desire to become holy rests upon this, that he strives firmly to believe in Christ and thus become holy and be saved. Such intention is correct and the desire good. Hence let him who fasts, labors, wears the garments of monks or priests, or

keeps the rules of his order, consider this just as he considers eating and drinking, not as making him holy by doing it, or as making him unholy by omitting it. Let him know that he can become holy only through faith. Doing this he will be safe, and human teachings will do him no more harm than eating and drinking or the wearing of clothing. But where are they that are doing this? Among a thousand there is scarcely one, for they usually all say, If I do not become holy and am not saved by such a life, order, regulations, and work, what a fool I am to walk in them and observe them.

39. It is, therefore, not possible for human doctrines not to lead away from the truth, as Paul says. For one of two things must take place, namely, they will either be despised and rejected when it is understood that they will not make us holy nor save us; or they will ensnare and deaden conscience and conviction if it is believed that they do make us holy and must, therefore, be kept. In this case, faith is destroyed and the soul must perish. There is no help nor rescue. For true faith cannot exist nor can it tolerate that anyone should conscientiously hold something else to be necessary to become holy and be saved than faith in Christ alone. Therefore, whoever has this faith cannot trust in human teachings, but observes them when and wherever he pleases, being lord over them. But he who follows human doctrines without having faith, can never apprehend faith, remains forever a slave of human commandments, and will never do a really good work, as Saint Paul says, in Titus 1:16. For this reason, we must hold fast to the plain teaching of Scripture which presents Christ only, and that by faith in him we become true Christians and then freely do all kinds of good works to the good of our neighbor, as has often been said.

40. In the second place, they point us to tradition and the examples of the saints to strengthen and prove their man-made teachings. And this is very effective and leads many souls to destruction. It leads away from the Scriptures and faith in such a smooth, unsuspecting manner that no one is aware of it. Thus they point to Saint Benedict, Gregory, Bernard, Augustine, Francis, Dominic, and many other saints, whom we all recognize as holy men, and say that they observed such human ordinances and regulations and, by virtue of them, became holy men. Tell me, how can the simple-minded Christian withstand such arguments and still keep the faith? It must be an apostolic or evangelical spirit that will here remain firm. Oh, how sure they are and how boldly they parade! When they produce such examples of holy men they think that they have kindled a great light.

41. Now, if I say to them, these holy men also ate, drank, slept, and wore clothing, does it, therefore, follow that we should also establish an eat-order, drink-order, sleep-order, and clothes-order? They will answer, Oh, these holy

fathers did not observe this, namely, eating and drinking, etc., to become pious and holy men, as they observed these other regulations which they believed to be good and holy institutions. Here I answer, if you say that these holy fathers become pious and holy through such human ordinances more than by eating and drinking, sleeping, and wearing clothing, then you are quite mistaken. For God has wisely desisted from ever honoring one of these saints with a miracle on account of his good works; rather were they all full of the spirit and faith. You seem to care not for their spirit and faith, but instead cling to their external deeds only. A fool would do the same if he were to sleep all his life because he heard that Saint Bernard also slept once, and were to hope thereby to become holy and be saved. Therefore, these holy men are wronged if it is claimed that they observed these ordinances to become holy and be saved, and the people are deceived by the life and in the name of these saints.

42. But you may say, Yes, but they still kept them, did not reject them, nor consider them so important as you seem to teach. Answer: It is not for you or me to judge their hearts and intentions; but we say this, It is not impossible that they considered them of too great importance. If so, they, as human beings, have erred concerning them. For everybody must confess that the saints have also erred and sinned. Therefore, God demands that we look to his Word only, and not follow the example of the saints except as these agree with the Word of God. But whenever they, as human beings, follow also their own inventions or human teachings, then we should do as the pious Shem and Japheth, who covered the wickedness of their father, and not like the impious Ham, who went around talking about it. Thus we should keep silent about the infirmities of the saints and not make them known that we may follow them only in their strength.

It is no wonder that these saints have stumbled and erred in these things. The knowledge of Christ and of faith is so above the natural man that only God's grace can work it in us. Flesh and blood cannot reveal it unto us, but only the Father in heaven, as Christ says, in Matthew 16:17. Even greater saints than Augustine, Benedict, Gregory, and others like them have erred in these things. At the time of the apostles, there were already such teachers, against whom Saint Paul wrote all his Epistles, in order to keep the faith altogether free from works and human doctrines.

43. And that you may marvel still more, the whole Christian Church in its early days, and at its best, erred in these things, only Peter, Paul, and Barnabas standing firm and holding that neither law nor good works are profitable and

necessary for salvation. Saint Luke clearly states it in Acts 15. There were great saints there, the apostles and their disciples, who insisted and would have continued to insist that the law and good works were necessary for salvation, had not Saint Paul and Peter declared against it. And even they themselves would not have known this had not God by miraculous signs from heaven confirmed them in their opinion that only faith is profitable and necessary for salvation, as we read, in Acts 10:43.

44. More than this, although Saint Peter knew all this and helped to defend it, yet at Antioch he also erred and made improper use of his Christian liberty, and only Saint Paul understood him, as he writes, in Galatians 2:11. Not as though Saint Peter believed that he must keep the law, but that he did not at once make proper use of his Christian liberty, which he well understood, thinking that he had to hesitate for the sake of others. This was wrong and was censured by Paul.

Therefore, it amounts to nothing whatever if those works of the saints are referred to which they did outside of the Scriptures. They are deceiving just as well and even more than the errors of heretics and false teachers, because real and true holiness adorns such infirmities altogether too much. God permits such things in order that he might hold us to his Word and doctrine, without which there is neither life nor light, even if all the angels were to teach such things.

45. In the third place, they hold up to us the saints' interpretations of the Scriptures, and consider them a great light. They finally adhere to them and believe that in these interpretations they possess something that no one could reject, and claim again and again in order to keep us away from the pure Word that the Scriptures are obscure and make many heretics.

46. Is not this a masterpiece of blasphemy? But who guarantees them that the fathers are not also obscure? Or who will give us the guaranty that the fathers did not err in their interpretations? Indeed it is well known that they did often err, often contradicted themselves, often contradicted each other, and very seldom were unanimous in their agreement. God permitted this to happen to make uncertain also the interpretations of the fathers and to warn us on all sides not to depart from the Scriptures. And yet we stumble here and do not permit ourselves to be guided by the Scriptures. Therefore, we should know that it is not true when they say, The fathers give light to the obscure Scriptures. They are doing injustice to the fathers, and belie them. The work of the fathers was not to give light to the Scriptures with their comments, but rather to set forth the clear Scriptures and thus interpret Scripture by Scripture only without any additions of their own.

47. However, that heretics originated from the Scriptures, is true. From where else should they have come? There is no other book that teaches the Christian faith but the Scriptures. Therefore, as no one can become a Christian except by the Scriptures, so also can no one become a heretic but by the same Scriptures. Christ is indeed a sign spoken against and set for the falling and rising of many. Should we on that account reject him or set up another Christ by his side? You do not at the same time need wine and bread, but should we on that account quit tilling the farm and the vineyards or start others besides them? Satan is the enemy of the Scriptures and, therefore, he has decried and calumniated them by this clamor and blasphemy.

48. But what does this Gospel teach? In the first place, these wise men did not inquire after the chief priests and do not ask, Where is Annas or Caiaphas, or how did this or that man live? But they ask, Where is the newborn king of the Jews? Yes, Christ permits them, as a warning to us, to go astray and to seek him in Jerusalem in the holy city among the priests, the learned, and the royalty. He is not found in the holy place nor in the holy customs. Nor did they receive as an answer any human opinions, but only what the Scriptures say about Christ, which alone are to be sought among the holy people and in holy places.

49. Sufficient examples are here given to show us that disregarding all human works, teachings, comments, and life, we should be mindful only of the clear Scriptures, and as to the life and teachings of the saints preserve the right not to rake or snatch up everything that they teach or live, but rather to sit in judgment on these things and accept with discretion only that which is compatible with the Scriptures. But what is their own, without Scripture proof, we should consider as human inventions and avoid, as Saint Paul teaches, Prove all things; hold fast that which is good, in 1 Thessalonians 5:21. Moses has also indicated this, in Leviticus 11:3 and in Deuteronomy 14:6, where he describes clean and unclean beasts; that all animals which are not cloven footed and ruminant are unclean. These are the men who are not cloven footed, who spend their lives carelessly, rake up whatever comes before them, and follow it. But the clean animals are those men who, by the spirit, act with discretion in all external things and doctrines. Whatever they see harmonizing with the Scriptures, they keep, but whatever is without scriptural foundation and mere human inventions, they dismiss, no matter how great and famous the saints who taught it may be. For no saint has been so perfect as to be free from flesh and blood, or the continued struggle with flesh and blood, so that it is scarcely possible that all their teachings and works were spiritually perfect and are to be accepted as examples. Human nature and reason often concurred in their

work, and these are not to be trusted at all. Hence Moses commands us to be cloven footed, and Paul to discern the spirits and not to accept all the works and doings of men.

50. Now, in these three things, namely, human teachings, examples of the saints, and the comments of the fathers, they think and many believe it, that they are quite right, that no one dares to doubt or contradict them, and that they rule here in perfect safety. They imagine that no one but they alone possess the holy Scriptures, which they have so beautifully summarized in these three vessels.

51. In addition, they sink still deeper into the abyss of spiritual darkness when they claim that natural light or intellect and heathen philosophy are also safe means of discovering the truth. In this direction, the universities have gone so far astray that they teach that no one can be a theologian, i.e., one of the best Christians, without Aristotle. O blindness above all blindness!

It might be tolerated if they were to refer here to truths of nature as would call this natural philosophy, namely, that fire is hot, that three and five are eight, etc., which reason at once recognizes. But they soar high and invent idle dreams and useless thoughts about things that are vain and of which they know nothing; and it is grievous to think of their senseless, absurd studying. They go to so much expense and trouble that even Satan mocks at them, whereby God deservedly punishes them because they would not abide in the pure Word. For this reason, they must devour the very pollution of hell and be lost.

52. They then meddled even with the work of the devil and followed the example of the souls or spirits appearing and praying for help, and believed everything that these spirits said without fear or hesitation. Thus the Mass, i.e., the Lord's Supper, has been so abused by saying Mass for souls in purgatory and by the selling of indulgences, that the whole world by shedding tears of blood day and night could not bewail it sufficiently.

Thus the devil has permitted himself to be conjured and constrained to reveal the truth and has turned our faith and sacrament into play and mockery to his own liking. All this is the result and reward of our overcuriousness, which has not been satisfied with the Scriptures of God, and has made our true and faithful God and Father a fool and clown, who pretends to teach us by his Word and yet does not care to teach us that which we ought and necessarily need to know. For this reason, he serves us right in permitting us to become the devil's pupils, inasmuch as we despised his school.

53. But you say, Should we then deny that wandering spirits go astray and seek for help? Answer: Let wander who will, you listen to what God commands.

If you hold all these spirits in suspicion, you are not sinning; but if you hold some of them to be genuine and honest, you are already in danger of erring. And why? Because God does not want you to seek and learn the truth from the dead. He himself wants to be your living and all-sufficient teacher. To his Word you should cling. He knows best what to tell you about the living and the dead, for he knows all things. But whatever he does not want to tell you, you should not desire to know, and give him the honor to believe that he knows what is not necessary, profitable, nor good for you to know.

54. Therefore, you should freely and unhesitatingly cast all such ghostly apparitions to the winds and not be afraid of them; they will then leave you in peace. And should it seem, that perhaps in your house you hear a hobgoblin or rumbling spirit, then make no ado about it, but be assured that it cannot be a good spirit come from God. Make the sign of the cross and firmly hold to your faith. Has he been sent by God to chastise you, like Job, then be ready to endure it willingly, but should it be the spirit's own sport, then defy him by strong faith and joyfully depend on God's Word. Depend upon it; he will not attack that.

However, I hold that none of these hobgoblins are ordained of God to molest us, but it is their own mischief to terrify the people, because they have no longer any power to harm. If they had any power to harm, they would surely not engage in much racketing, but do their evil work before you could be aware who had done it. But if a good spirit were to visit you, it would not occur with such noise and frivolity. Do this and manifest strong faith and you will find that such a spirit is not of God, and will cease its work. If you have not such faith, then he will have easy work, for then God's Word which alone he fears is not with you.

55. The words of the Scriptures upon which you should boldly rely are in Luke 16:29, where Abraham said to Dives in hell, who desired the departed Lazarus to be sent to his brothers living on earth, but Abraham, refusing to do this, said, "They have Moses and the prophets, let them hear them." From these words, it is plain that God will not have us taught by the dead, but have us abide in his Word. Therefore, no matter how and where a spirit comes to you, do not ask whether he be good or evil, but bravely, quickly, and defiantly cast into his teeth the words, "they have Moses and the prophets," and he will soon understand what you mean. Is it a good spirit, he will only love you the more for adhering so gladly and firmly to the Word of your God. Is it an evil spirit, as are all those that are noisy, he will soon bid you adieu.

Again, another word of God is spoken by Moses in Deuteronomy 18:11, "When thou art come into the land which Jehovah thy God giveth thee, thou shalt not learn to do after the abominations of those nations. There shall not be found with thee any one that maketh his son or his daughter to pass through fire, one that useth divination, one that practiceth augury, or an enchanter, or a sorcerer, or a charmer, or a consulter with a familiar spirit, or a wizard, or a necromancer."

Here you are told that it is an abomination in the sight of God to consult the dead or the spirits, and it is strictly forbidden. To this word of Moses, Abraham looked when he did not permit Lazarus to come back to the earth. You can also use this passage against these spirits, saying, "Thou shalt not consult the dead, saith the Lord."

56. God has insisted on this so firmly, that there is no example recorded in the Scriptures, where the saints have ever consulted the dead about anything. And this is the third argument that you can use against these spirits, No one ever heard or read of an example in the Scriptures as to such spirits and their work, hence the whole must be condemned and avoided as of the devil.

57. From this, we may easily learn, that the coming up of Samuel was an apparition, in 1 Samuel 28:13, inasmuch as it is altogether contrary to this commandment of God. It is, therefore, not to be assumed that the real prophet Samuel came up by the power of the witch of En-dor. But that the Scriptures are silent on this point, not telling us whether it was the real or false Samuel, is because they demand of everybody to remember well that, through Moses, God forbade to consult the dead. And he never revokes his Word, as Job says, and Balaam also, in Numbers 23:19. How can the witch have any power over the saints, who are resting in God's hands?

58. However, should it be said, In this way, purgatory will also be denied, I will answer, You are not a heretic for disbelieving in purgatory, as there is nothing said about it in the Scriptures. And it is better not to believe that which is outside of the Scriptures, than to depart from that which is in the Scriptures. Let pope and papists here rage as they please, who have made purgatory an article of faith because it has brought to them the wealth of the earth but also countless souls to hell, souls that depended and relied on good works for redemption from it. God gave no command concerning purgatory, but he did command us in no way to consult the dead nor to believe what they say. Consider God more truthful and trustworthy than all angels, to say nothing of the pope and the papists who, as all their work is but lying and deceiving, awaken but little faith in purgatory. However, if you want to pray for the dead, I will not interfere. I am of the opinion that purgatory is not so general as they say, but that only a few souls will enter it. Still as I have said, it is without any danger to your soul if you do not believe in a purgatory. You are not called upon to believe more than what the Scriptures teach.

But should they advance also the sayings and comments of Gregory, Augustine, and other saints concerning purgatory, then remember that I have already told you how far these saints are to be followed and believed. Who will assure us that they did not err and were not deceived here as in many other things.

59. Our faith must have a sure foundation, God's Word, and not the sand or bog of human custom and inventions. With this, Isaiah also agrees when he says, "And when they shall say unto you, Seek unto them that have familiar spirits and unto the wizards, that chirp and that mutter. Should not a people seek unto their God? On behalf of the living should they seek unto the dead? To the law and the testimony! If they speak not according to this Word, surely there is no morning for them, etc.," in Isaiah 8:19–20. This is certainly a clear passage that urges and compels us to seek in God's law and testimony all that we want to know. And he who will not do this, shall be deprived of the morning light which no doubt means Christ and the truth itself. Note also that after Isaiah said we should seek unto God, so that no one might stare at the heavens and expect something extraordinary from God, he shows where and whence we should seek unto God, saying, To the law and to the testimony. He will not permit any seeking unto God in himself outside of the Scriptures, much less will he permit it in others.

60. Moses mentions many ways by which men seek knowledge, in Deuteronomy 18:10–11. There are eight classes as follows:

1. The users of divination. They are those who reveal the future, like the astrologers and false prophets by inspiration of the devil.
2. Those that practice augury. They designate some days as lucky for making a journey, for building, for marrying, for wearing fine clothes, for battle, and for all kinds of transactions.
3. The enchanters or rather diviners—I know no better name to call these, who conjure the devil by means of mirrors, pictures, sticks, words, glass, crystals, fingers, nails, circles, rods, etc., and expect in this way to discover hidden treasures, history, and other things.
4. The sorcerers, or witches, the devil mongers who steal milk, make the weather, ride on goats, brooms, and sails (mantles); shoot the people, cripple and torture and wither, slay infants in the cradle, bewitch certain members of the body, etc.
5. The charmers, who bless people and animals, bewitch snakes, bespeak steel and iron, bluster and see much, and can do wonders.

6. The consulters of familiar spirits, who have the devil in their ears and tell the people what they have lost, what they are doing or what they will do in the future, just as the gypsies do.
7. The wizards, who can change things into different forms so that something may look like a cow or an ox, which in reality is a human being, that can drive people to illicit love and intercourse, and more such works of the devil.
8. The necromancers, who are walking spirits.

61. Behold, Moses did not forget anything, stopping up every avenue where men seek to learn, outside of the Word of God. Thus he has often denounced self-conceit and human reason, especially in Deuteronomy 12:8, Ye shall not do after all the things that we do here this day, every man whatsoever is right in his own eyes. And, in Proverbs 3:5, Trust in Jehovah with all thy heart and lean not upon thine own understanding. He does this that we might know that God wants us to follow neither our own reason nor that which is above reason, but only his Word, as Isaiah said above, not to seek unto the living nor the dead, but to seek unto God only in the law and testimony.

Saint Peter also says, in 2 Peter 1:19, "And we have the word of prophecy made more sure; whereunto ye do well that ye take heed, as unto a lamp shining in a dark place, until the day dawns, and the day-star arise in your hearts." Does not Saint Peter here agree nicely with Isaiah as to God's Word and the dawn of the morning? And when Saint Peter says that the Word alone is a light that shines in a dark place, does he not clearly show that there is only darkness where God's Word is absent?

62. This digression was necessary in order to reply to the false teachers and doctrines of men, and to preserve the Scriptures in their purity. We now come back to our text and learn of these wise men to ask, "Where is the newborn king of the Jews?" Let Herod consult the priests and scribes, we will only inquire after the newborn king. Let the universities ask, Where is Aristotle? Where is the pope? What does human reason teach? What says Saint Bernard, Saint Gregory, the church councils, and the learned doctors, etc.? We ask, Where is Christ? We are not satisfied until we hear what the Scriptures say about him. We are not concerned as to how great and holy Jerusalem is, nor how great and mighty Rome may be. We seek neither Jerusalem nor Rome, but Christ the King in the Scriptures. If we have the Scriptures, we cast aside Herod, the priests, and the scribes, Jerusalem and Rome, and search in them until we find Jesus.

63. However, we learn here that the Scriptures and Christ have three kinds of disciples. The first are the priests and the scribes. They know and teach the Scriptures to all, but do not come to him. Is not this great hardness of heart and contempt on the part of the learned? They hear and see that great and honest men come from a far country to seek Christ, and they are told that a star in the heavens testified to his birth; in addition, they themselves produce testimony from the Scriptures. Since they were the priests and most learned men, they should have been the first, joyfully and eagerly, to hurry to Bethlehem. Yes, if they had been told that Christ had been born in some Eastern country, they should even then by all means have hurried to him, inasmuch as all their hopes and consolation rested in Christ's coming.

64. But they feared Herod, who would surely have killed them, if they had without word confessed Christ and their willingness to accept him as their king, as he had before killed Hircanus and many others and slew innocent babes. Hence because they feared death they forsook their Lord and king, and remained with the tyrant Herod and the devil.

65. Afterward, when Christ did not appear with splendor and power, they looked with contempt and disregard upon all this, believing that the wise men had been deceived. Hence Christ grew up among them entirely unknown, and no one knew finally whence he should come as stated, in John 1:26.

There are disciples of Christ who indeed know the truth, but dare not confess it nor defend it, and are, therefore, lost, as Christ says, in Matthew 10:32–33, "Everyone therefore who shall confess me before men him will I also confess before my Father who is in heaven. But whosoever shall deny me before men, him will I also deny before my Father who is in heaven."

66. The second class of disciples are Herod and his people. Herod searched the Scriptures, believing that it was the truth, and that the coming of Christ was predicted therein, and that Christ had now been born; otherwise, he would despise all this and not have been concerned about it. Hence it is certain that he held the Scriptures to be the Word of God which must be fulfilled, and that in Christ's birth the work of God was revealed. Yet he at once determines to set himself intentionally and directly against God's Word and work, and thinks he can bring to naught that which God has spoken and done, in spite of better knowledge. Therefore, he searched the Scriptures diligently to learn about Christ, but only for the purpose of bringing to naught and destroying all. He was concerned lest that which God, who cannot lie, spoke, would come to pass. Is not this incredibly foolish arrogance? Who would have thought that such intentions could have ever entered the human heart? And yet the world is always full of such people, and they are generally the rulers and upper classes.

67. The third class of disciples are the pious wise men, who left their country, home, and possessions, forsaking all in order to find Christ. They represent the people who fearlessly confess Christ and the truth; but Herod stands for those who persecute and destroy the former, though they still claim to serve God, and enter the house of God just as other pious persons do.

The Prophecy of Micah

68. One may be interested in asking why the evangelist changed the words of the prophet and said, "And thou Bethlehem, land of Judah, art in no wise least among the princes of Judah; for out of thee shall come forth a governor, who shall be shepherd of my people Israel," while the prophet Micah says, "But thou, Bethlehem Ephrathah, which art little to be among the thousands of Judah, out of thee shall one come forth unto me that is to be ruler in Israel," in Micah 5:2.

Matthew says, Thou art in no wise the least, but Micah says, Thou art little. How do these two statements agree with each other?

69. The other difference between Matthew and Micah, the former saying, Among the princes of Judah, the latter, Among the thousands of Judah, can easily be adjusted, as the Hebrew word *aleph* means both a prince and a thousand; hence whoever chooses may interpret the prophet either way.

For instance, if I say, There comes a duke, by this one may understand either a prince or an army, as duke means a prince, and also a leader of an army, and whatsoever an army is doing we usually say the duke did it. The law of Moses also provides that men should be made rulers over thousands, in Exodus 18:21, so that we can say among the princes or rulers as well as among the thousands. For the prince stands for the army of thousands into which the people were divided. And among them the princes or thousands in Judah the city of Bethlehem is mentioned as being the least, just as though we were to say, Among the cities of Saxony, Wittenberg is the least. But it pleased the evangelist to say among the princes rather than among the thousands, as it is not necessary that there should be just a thousand men, it being sufficient that there be a regiment in which there may be a thousand men, and always having a prince who may rule over a thousand.

So also might we call the mayor of each city, or the community, Aleph, i.e., a thousand, or a community in which there may be about a thousand inhabitants who have an Aleph, i.e., a prince or a mayor. Hence we might render the words of the evangelist and the prophet thus, And thou Bethlehem art a humble and common city among the communities or cities of Judah. And in comparison to such cities as Hebron, Kariath, and Sephar, etc., it was but a small city at that time.

70. That the prophet calls the city Bethlehem Ephrathah, and the evangelist Bethlehem in Judah, is after all the same, for both of them undoubtedly intended to point out that city which aforetime was called Ephrathah, but now Bethlehem in the land of Judah. We heard in the first Gospel lesson for Christmas why this city was called Ephrathah and Bethlehem, that is, a country rich in grain, from which it perhaps has its name. For Bethlehem means a house of bread, and Ephrathah means fruitful, so that it must have been a rich country and blessed with plenty (with plenty of food in it.)

71. Nor does it present any difficulty that the prophet says, "A ruler in Israel," and the evangelist, "A governor, who shall be a shepherd of my people Israel." The latter speaks of a government without saying how blessed it is nor how it rules.

72. But how can we harmonize the fact that the prophet calls the city little, and the evangelist in no wise least. These seem diametrically opposed to each other. It would not be a sufficient answer to say that the books were falsified. There can be no doubt that the evangelist looks more at the spiritual greatness which is also indicated by the prophet, as though he would say, Thou Bethlehem art little before men, but before God thou really art in no wise the least, inasmuch as the ruler of Israel shall come out of thee. Hence what the prophet meant but did not express, the evangelist states clearly. The figure of speech by which a certain thing is not directly mentioned but only indicated is also used in common conversation. If I say, for instance, You are my friend, yet you side with my enemies, I really said, You are not of the least among my enemies. Again, The beggars are poor, yet they have much money, that is, they are not the poorest. So also when Paul says in Romans 2:22, "Thou that abhorrest idols, dost thou rob temples?", he means thou dost not infrequently abhor idols in order to rob the temples.

73. Let this suffice for it does not afford much pleasure to argue very much on this point, nor is it necessary for a true believer to do so for he gives all glory to God and never doubts that everything is truly and correctly stated in the Scriptures, though he is not able to prove everything. For the learned, it is necessary in order to defend the Scriptures against the blasphemers and perverse. Therefore, we return to the sense and meaning of the Scriptures, which do not speak here of a common master in Israel such as there had been many before, whom the prophets so highly honored and predicted must be altogether different from others. For the passage of Micah reads as if there had been no ruler in Israel before, because he says out of Bethlehem shall he come forth that shall be a ruler in Israel. That sounds as though he would say, I will give the people of Israel a ruler, so that they may also have their own prince.

So far, the kings and princes have only been servants, and the people were not their own. This one, however, shall be a ruler to whom the people belong.

74. For this reason, the fathers among them always understood such passages to mean that Christ would be not only man, but God, and that his government would be without end, and not be a temporal but a spiritual government. For no man, nor angel, has a people of his own. God alone is the Lord of his own people, as David says, "The Lord ministereth judgment to the people," in Psalm 7:8. And when Gideon was asked by the people to rule them, he replied, "I will not rule over you, neither shall my son rule over you: The Lord shall rule over you," in Judges 8:23. And when the people asked for a king of Samuel, God said, "They have not rejected thee, but they have rejected me, that I should not be king over them," in 1 Samuel 8:7. Not that it was a sin to have a king, for he gave them one; but they trusted more in human power and government than in God. And that was a great sin.

75. Now if Christ was to be a ruler over his own people, then his government could be neither temporal nor corporeal, but he must rule over the entire people past, present, and future. Therefore, he must be an eternal king. And this he can only be spiritually. But as God bestows on Christ his own government, he could not be a human being only. For it is not possible for God to bestow his glory, government, property, or people on one who is not true God, as he himself declares, "And my glory will I not give to another," in Isaiah 42:8.

76. Therefore, Micah continues, "Whose goings forth are from of old, from everlasting." As if he would say, I proclaim the ruler that shall come out of Bethlehem, but he does not there begin to be; he has been already from the beginning before the world began, in that no day or beginning can be named in which he did not already have his being. Now from all eternity and before the creation of the world there existed nothing but God alone. Hence the going forth from everlasting could not be by one person only, for going forth signifies that there was someone from whom he came forth. Hence Micah proves that this ruler must be God's own true Son, born of God the Father, and that the one true God must be with him eternally before all creation began.

77. Again, if he shall come out of Bethlehem in time, then he must be a true and natural man. And this, namely, that Christ is God and man is the cornerstone of Christian faith. Those are his own people and the true Israel, who acknowledged him as such a ruler and permit him to rule and work in their hearts.

78. From this, we can easily conclude why Christ had to die and rise again in order to rule spiritually to all eternity. For though the passage here proves

that he had to become a true natural man, it yet follows that he had to change this bodily life into a spiritual invisible life, as it was impossible for him to rule bodily as widely and as long as the prophet indicates.

79. Micah continues, and says, "Therefore, will he give them up until the time that she which travaileth hath brought forth: then the residue of his brethren shall return unto the children of Israel. And he shall stand and shall feed his flock in the strength of the Lord, in the majesty of the name of the Lord his God: and they shall abide; for now shall he be great unto the ends of the earth."

From these words, it is clear that Christ's kingdom should be extended to the ends of the earth by preaching and suffering, of which the prophet says that in the majesty of the name of Jehovah he would preach and feed his flock, showing also that he would be persecuted on account of his preaching. Therefore, the prophet also says that they should be given a respite as to their temporal existence and government until a new people had been born. The woman in travail represents the little flock of the apostles which, during the sufferings of Christ, was in the agony of the birth of a new spiritual people for this ruler of Israel, as Christ himself foretells in John 16:2.

Then Herod privily called the wise men, and learned of them exactly what time the star appeared. And he sent them to Bethlehem and said, "Go and search out exactly concerning the young child; and when ye have found him, bring me word, that I also may come and worship him."

80. From this text, we learn that the wise men were not kings nor princes, but common, honest people, like the learned and the clergy. Herod does not treat them as belonging to royalty, but sends them to Bethlehem, tells them to attend to their mission and, as if they were his subjects, commands them to bring him word again. He would not have done this if they had been kings or lords; he would have invited them to his palace, accompanied them on their journey, and treated them with great honor. For all historians agree that Herod was a pompous man, who knew how to treat people royally after the way of the world, and wished to be admired by the people. As, however, he calls the men privily and without display and parade they must have been of much lower rank than he was.

81. But why does he call them privately, since the land was his and in his full control? He did it for this reason. He knew quite well that the Jews were his sworn enemies and wished to be rid of him. He was afraid, therefore, that if he called the men publicly and the Jews became aware of it, they would go

to the wise men and enjoin them not to acquaint Herod with the true state of affairs, so that the new king may live before his eyes.

82. When he asks them about the time of the star he does it out of the same anxiety. He was already resolved in his heart to slay the innocent children. He reasoned thus, If the new king is born, the Jews will rejoice, and will secrete him for a while until he is grown up, and then will espouse his cause, put him on the throne, and banish me. I must forestall them, therefore, and carefully inquire into the time of his birth; and although he is hidden from me I shall still find him among the people when I slay all the children, and their disguise will avail them nothing. He pursues this plan diligently so that the new king might be made known to him, commands the wise men to bring him word again, and puts on a pious and devout face as if he wished to worship the child also.

83. Humanly speaking, he acted wisely enough in his purpose of slaying Christ. But it is true what Solomon says, in Proverbs 21:30, "There is no wisdom nor understanding nor counsel against Jehovah." And, in Psalm 33:10, "Jehovah bringeth the counsel of the nations to naught; he maketh the thoughts of the people to be of none effect." And in Psalm 37:32–33, "The wicked watcheth the righteous and seeketh to slay him. Jehovah will not leave him in his hand." Herod is here compelled to fulfill such passages against his will, and be an illustration of the same for our own comfort, in order that we might be free and secure and need fear none but God alone. If he is with us, neither guile nor force can harm us.

III. HOW THE WISE MEN CONTINUE THEIR JOURNEY, FIND CHRIST, AND WORSHIP HIM

And they having heard the king, went their way; and lo, the star,
which they saw in the east, went before them, till it came and stood over
where the young child was. And when they saw the star,
they rejoiced with exceeding great joy.

84. It is not said here that they promised the king to return, but that they heard his request to bring him word again. Yet it appears from the warning they received in a dream that, in the simplicity of their hearts, they were willing to return to Herod, not knowing his depravity nor his purpose and thinking him to be an artless honest man. We learn from this that the children of God may be so misled by the pleasing manners and false pretensions of unbelieving saints that they take that to be good which is not. But they do not always remain in deception, for they are directed and delivered, if need be, from heaven. Their hearing of the king, as mentioned by the evangelist, may

also be understood to mean that they listened to the words of the prophet, that in Bethlehem was to be born the new king for whom they inquired, and who was the object of their search.

85. This is an illustration of how the enemies of Christ may at times be of service and teach others rightly, as Caiaphas teaches, in John 11:50, that it was expedient that one man should die for the people, and as Balaam, in Numbers 24, utters many beautiful words concerning Christ, although they do it sometimes unintentionally and in ignorance. So Christ instructs the people, in Matthew 23:2–3, they should listen to the scribes and Pharisees, and follow them when they sit in Moses' seat; but forbids them to do after their works. These wise men were right, therefore, and give us a good example by listening to Herod, not for Herod's sake, neither as said by him, but for the sake of the Scriptures, which he taught them; and they followed this and not Herod's works. From this is derived the good rule that we should hear the evil bishops and priests, as well as the good ones, and should follow, not their lives, but their teachings, provided their teaching is Scripture and not idle talk. For, as we are to listen to the teachings of Holy Writ, even when spoken by Herod, though he also commit murder, so we are not to listen to human doctrine, even if spoken by Saint Peter, Paul, or an angel, and accompanied by many wondrous signs.

86. It was said above that the saints often err and give offense by human doctrines and works. It is God's will, therefore, that we shall not be guided by their examples, but by his Word. For this reason, he permits the saints often to deliver human doctrine and works. Again, he disposes that the impious sometimes teach the clear and plain Scriptures, in order to guard us against offenses, on the one hand, and from the wicked life of the ungodly; on the other hand from the shining deeds of the saints. For, if you do not follow the Scriptures alone, the lives of the saints are ten times more dangerous and offensive than those of the ungodly. These commit gross sins, which are easily recognized and avoided, but the saints exhibit a subtle, pleasing appearance in human doctrines, which might deceive the very elect, as Christ says, in Matthew 24:24.

87. But now such offense of the saints is directly against the articles of faith and its doctrine; gross sins, however, do not oppose faith and doctrine. If they desert it, they do not rail against it, while human doctrine is nothing but rebellion against faith and its doctrine, for it makes men rely upon themselves and upon their works. From this, Christ rescues his saints in the midst of human doctrine and work, just as he preserved the three men, Shadrach, Meshach, and Abednego, in Daniel 3, at Babylonia, in the midst of the fiery

furnace. Hence the lives of the saints are not to be followed as an example in this, but are rather to be avoided, like miracles which are only to be admired and praised. For he does not desire to do wonders to everyone in the fiery furnace, neither does he wish to make everyone a Bernhard, Francis, Gregory, Benedict, or Augustine.

88. This was the evangelist's intention when he omitted Herod's name, saying, they heard the king. He calls him by the name of his office and dignity, just as John 11:51 says that Caiaphas uttered his prophesies, not because his name was Caiaphas, but because he was high priest. The offices of king and priest are good and by divine institution, although wicked people make evil use of them, as gold and silver and all creatures are good, and yet may be put to good or evil use.

God uses Herod when he may be used to advantage as God's creature, and offers him to the wise men for their service. Hence they did not look upon or listen to Herod but to the king. It did not concern them that he was wicked within himself; they took hold of what was good in him, as the bee sucks the honey from the flower and leaves the poison to the spider. They listened to him when he told them to go to Bethlehem and search diligently for the child, as the prophet had foretold, which intelligence he had not from himself but from the priests. They could not, however, know his wicked counsel and purpose, nor his evil life. Thus we are to learn to hate the vices of men, but love the men; we are to distinguish the honey from the poison.

89. It is also indicated here that this star was not high in the heavens like the other stars, but hung above them in the air; otherwise, it would have been impossible for them to discover whether it stood over Jerusalem or over Bethlehem. For, according to astronomy and experience, it cannot be discerned on account of their height over the town the stars of heaven really are suspended, since two cities, ten or more miles apart, both think the star above them. Again, you cannot perceive their movement with the eye, although they move more swiftly than time or lightning. This star, however, they did not see move swiftly but glide slowly before them according to the speed of their journey. A star in heaven moves farther in one moment than ten journeys from Jerusalem to Bethlehem, for they move once around earth and heaven every day and night. Besides, all stars move from east to west.

90. But this star accompanying them from Jerusalem to Bethlehem, traveled from north to south. This was proof that it was of another kind, its course and place in the sky different from the other stars in the heavens. It was not a fixed star, as astronomers call them, but rather a movable star that could

rise and descend and move from one place to another. With this, those astronomers are again silenced who say that the star had no special significance in Christ's birth or life. It was probably not as large as the stars in the heavens, although it appeared larger on account of its nearness. In short, it was a servant of Christ and had no power or authority over Christ's birth.

91. It seems strange, however, that the star reappears to them now when they do not need it any more, when they know the town of Christ's birth, while it was hidden before, when they needed it and knew not the town. But this was done to strengthen their faith, as the law of Moses says, that in the mouth of two or three witnesses every word may be established. The wise men first heard the word of the prophet in Jerusalem, as a witness of Christ's birth; with this, the second witness, the star, agrees and announces the same birth, so that they may be sure of their ground. The prophet speaks only of the child at Bethlehem; in like manner the star does not go any farther than where the child is, to Bethlehem, and remains over him. And they rejoiced with exceeding great joy.

> And they came into the house and saw the young child with Mary his mother; and they fell down and worshiped him; and opening their treasures they offered unto him gifts of gold and frankincense and myrrh.

92. It was diligently prevented that the wise men should find Christ through themselves, or men. On the contrary, they found him alone through the Scriptures of the prophet and by the aid of the stars of heaven that there might be put to naught all natural ability, all human reason, all light outside of the spirit and of grace, which now boasts and pretends to teach the truth and lead people aright, as was said above is done in the universities. Here it is concluded that Christ, the knowledge of salvation, is not taught or acquired by human teaching or assistance, but the Scriptures and divine light must reveal him, as he says, in Matthew 16:17, "Blessed art thou, Simon Bar-Jonah: for flesh and blood hath not revealed it unto thee, but my Father who is in heaven." With this, Christ distinctly casts aside flesh and blood with its revelation, i.e., man and all human wisdom, which, being nothing but darkness, cannot reveal Christ.

Christ says, in John 6:44, "No man can come to me, except the Father that hath sent me draw him." By this all boasting of human reason is condemned, since it cannot guide aright and all who follow it must go astray. So strongly does God everywhere resist our natural haughtiness and will, that we may know we are blind, despair of our own light, put ourselves into his hands, and be led by him into the ways which reason cannot know nor follow.

Of the Faith of the Wise Men

93. The wise men here teach us the true faith. After they heard the sermon and the word of the prophet, they were not slow to believe, in spite of obstacles and difficulties. First, they came to Jerusalem, the capital, and did not find him, the star also disappearing. Do you not think they would have said within themselves, if they had followed human reason alone, Alas, we have traveled so far in vain, the star has misled us, it was a phantom. If a king were born, he should, of course, be found in the capital and lie in the royal chamber. But when we arrived, the star disappeared and no one knew anything about him. We strangers are the first to speak of him in his own country and royal city! Indeed, it must be all false!

94. Besides, his own people are troubled and do not care to hear of him, and direct us from the royal city to a little village. Who knows what we shall find? The people act so coldly and strangely, no one accompanies us to show us the child; they do not believe themselves that a king is born to them, and we come from afar and expect to find him. O how odd and unusual everything appears at the birth of a king! If a young pup were born, there would be a little noise. A king is born here, and there is no stir. Should not the people sing and dance, light candles and torches, and pave the streets with branches and roses? O the poor king whom we seek! Fools we are to permit ourselves to be deceived so shamefully.

95. Having been flesh and blood, doubtless they were not free from such thoughts and views, and they had to battle for their faith. Natural reason could here not have held its own; if they had not found the king as they had expected, they would have murmured and complained, and said, The devil must have led us here. A king cannot have been born since everything is so quiet and nothing is going on. There is more noise when a child is born to our shepherd, and a calving cow is more talked about than this king.

96. Reason and nature never proceed any further than they can see and feel. When they cease to feel, they at once deny God's existence and say, as Psalm 14:1 says, "There is no God," therefore, the devil must be here. This is the light of the universities which is to lead men to God, but rather leads to the abyss of hell. The light of nature and the light of grace cannot be friends. Nature wants to feel and be certain before she believes; grace believes before she perceives. For this reason, nature does not go further than her own light. Grace joyfully steps out into the darkness, follows the mere word of Scripture, no matter how it appears. Whether nature holds it true or false, she clings to the Word.

97. For the sake of this very strife and struggle, by which the wise men accepted the word of the prophet and followed it into such wild, unnatural

appearance of a royal birth, God comforted and strengthened them by this star which went before them more friendly than before. Now they see it near, it is their guide, and they have an assurance which needs no further question. Before it was far from them, and they were not certain where they would find the king.

98. So it is always with the Christian, after affliction has been endured, God becomes more dear to him and is so near and so distinctly seen that man not only forgets anxiety and affliction, but has a desire for greater affliction. He gradually becomes so strong that he does not take offense at the insignificant, unattractive life of Christ. For now he experiences and realizes that to find Christ it must appear as though he found nothing but disgrace.

99. Even so, the wise men must have been ashamed of themselves if they had doubted and had said, as perhaps they did say secretly in their hearts, We were so successful, let us travel a little farther on and seek new kings.

I call this buffoonery, as Dame Gay, i.e., nature, conducts herself in the presence of divine words and works. For from the fact that the wise men were so much rejoiced when they saw the star, we can infer that they were in such temptation and were heavy-minded when everything appeared so inconsistent. Their joy indicates that they were perhaps despondent and tempted with unbelief. There was cause enough if you look at nature alone. Hence Christ says, in Matthew 11:6, "Blessed is he whosoever shall find no occasion of stumbling in me." Blessed, indeed, but how difficult since appearances were against Christ's presence.

100. When the wise men had overcome their temptation and were born again by the great joy they were strong and took no offense at Christ, they had overcome in the trial. For although they enter a lowly hut and find a poor young wife with a poor little child, and find less of royal appearance than the homes of their own servants presented, they are not led astray. But in a great, strong, living faith, they remove from their eyes and their minds whatever might attract and influence human nature with its pretense, follow the word of the prophet and the sign of the star in all simplicity, treat the child as a king, fall down before him, worship him, and offer gifts. This was a strong faith indeed, for it casts aside many things which impress human nature. Perhaps there were some people present who thought, What great fools are these men to worship such a poor child. They must indeed be in a trance to make of him a king.

101. This is the kernel of the Gospel, in which the nature and character of faith is explained as an assurance of things not seen. It clings alone to the words of God and follows the things that are not seen, as alone conveyed in the Word of God, and looks askance at many things which urge it to disbe-

lieve the Word. What nature calls playing the fool, faith calls the true way. Nature may be wise and clever, faith remains nature's fool and idiot, and thus comes to Christ and finds him. Saint Paul's words, in 1 Corinthians 1:25, apply here, "The foolishness of God is wiser than men, and the weakness of God is stronger than men." For feeling and believing do not get together.

102. When they give three presents and worship him, it does not imply that each gave a separate gift but, as mentioned above, it was a common gift of the goods of their country, with which they honored him as a king. Nor was the worship like that due to God for, in my opinion, they did not yet recognize him as God, but after the usages of the Scriptures, kings and dignitaries were worshiped, i.e., honored and respected, by the bending of the knee as we do today.

103. What conversation they had with Mary and Joseph I leave to the imagination of idle minds. The languages in the Orient are not so foreign to the Hebrew, so that they may easily have understood each other. They had spoken with Herod and the priests and the citizens of Jerusalem, hence they no doubt spoke with Mary and Joseph. If they had a different language, the Jews still had such business connections and were so well known at the Red Sea that in both countries both languages were no doubt known as, in German lands, you find French and, in France, German. The Red Sea country is on one side exclusively Arabic, and from there the wise men came.

IV. HOW THE WISE MEN BY THE COMMAND OF GOD RETURNED TO THEIR FATHERLAND

And being warned of God in a dream that they should not return to Herod they departed into their own country another way.

104. Here it appears that those who believe in God enjoy his special protection. He has an eye upon these wise men so that he keeps watch over their return and directs them in a dream.

105. And why does he not allow them to return to Herod since he could have shielded the child from all the world even if Herod had known and found him? It is done for the purpose of teaching us not to tempt God. Whatever can be accomplished by ordinary means should be done. We should not presume upon faith and say in idleness, I trust in God everything will grow that is to grow. His creatures have no purpose if we make use of them. In Genesis 1, he created and ordained all creatures with their works, and indicated the use man shall make of them. This will he never recall and ordain something special for you.

106. Here the question arises, How can I strike the golden mean to believe and yet not tempt God, for you preach and praise faith alone and cannot extol it enough? Answer: You should not believe save where you have a word of God. It is the character and nature of faith to be built and to rely on the Word of God. Where there is no Word of God, there cannot and shall not be any faith. Is this not stated clearly and positively enough? Hence the Word of God is called in Scripture: testament, *testimonia*, *pacta*, *foedera*, testimonies, agreements, covenants, as these postulate faith; nor did God ever command us to believe any of his works without his Word.

107. Again, he has confirmed his works and wonders, as Christ says, in John 10:38, "Though ye believe not me believe the works." If you have not God's Word, you should continue to make use of your power, of your goods, of your friends, and of all that God has given you, and thus abide in the dispensation, established by God, in Genesis 1. For he did not give it to you in vain; he will not, for your sake, turn water into wine or stone into bread, but you should use according to his order whatever he has created until he forces you by word or work to use it differently.

108. But when the hour comes that the creature cannot help you anymore, and all your strength fails, behold then God's Word begins. For then, he has commanded us to acknowledge him as God, i.e., expect everything that is good from him. This word, though in force all the time, will yet be only understood and made use of in need, when nothing else avails. Of this he speaks, in Psalm 50:15, "Call upon me in the day of trouble: I will deliver thee, and thou shalt glorify me." From this, it is clear that we cannot make trial of God in need, for all his words and promises point to the time of trouble, when no one but he is able to help. Hence we read, in Matthew 4:7, that when the devil tempted Christ to cast himself down from the temple, Christ said, no, for it is written, "Thou shalt not make trial of the Lord thy God," as if to say, I can go down by the steps, it is not necessary to do signs and wonders.

Again we read in the legends of the fathers that two brothers journeyed and one of them died of hunger for God's sake; that is, he went to hell; for they came among wicked people, who offered them something to eat, and the one said he would not take bread from these people, but expect his food from heaven. The other took and ate and lived. That fool did nothing else but set aside God's order and tempted him. However sinful people may be, they are still God's creatures as well as thorns and thistles. You make use of a thorn to open a boil or for some other purpose; will you look contemptuously upon it, because it is a prickly brush? Thus we read that Abraham and Isaac gave up their own wives and had them taken from them in order not to tempt God. Therefore, God preserved them so that no harm was done to them or to their wives, while great kings were punished. From this, it is clear that to tempt God is mere wickedness and frivolity except in time of trouble.

109. There is another temptation, also in the time of trouble, which was punished severely among the people of Israel and which, alas, is common as compared to the other temptation and equally irrational. That temptation occurs before God's Word is heard; this after we hear the Word, namely, thus, when we know that God has promised help in the time of any trouble, but are not content with it, go forward, and will not abide his promise, but prescribe time, place, and manner for his help; and then, if he does not come as we expect and desire, faith vanishes. There faith is too long, here it is too short; there it is too early, here it is too late. In both cases, men fall from the Word. Those have faith without Word, these have Word without faith, both of which are of no avail. Middle ground is blessed, both Word and faith united in one, as God and man are one in Christ.

110. He who holds fast to the Word alone, trusts and abides in it, does not doubt that what the Word says will come to pass; he who does not dictate aim or time or means and ways, but resigns all freely to God's will and pleasure as to when, how, where, and by whom he will fulfill his Word; he, I say, has a true, living faith which does not nor cannot tempt God.

111. Learn then what it means to tempt God. It is easily understood; it is a deficiency of true faith. To faith belongs above all the Word of God, as the foundation and rock of faith.

Hence to tempt God is nothing else than to deal with him aside from his Word, i.e., to believe when he did not command faith and gave us no Word, or to disbelieve when he bids believe and gives us his Word. He did not give orders to believe that he would feed you when you have food before you or can find it without a miracle. But where you cannot find it, he has commanded that you firmly believe he will not forsake you. But you should not set time or measure for him, for he deserves to be free, which is becoming, and will not forsake you, which is divine; what more could you desire?

112. Such was the lot of Christ. God could have rescued him from the power of Herod. But since without apparent necessity of a miracle all could be adjusted, he used for our example ordinary means, and led the wise men into their own country by another way. It would have required an unnecessary exhibition of miracles if they had returned to Herod and made known the house wherein the child was to be found. But even this has its meaning, as we shall see later.

V. THE SPIRITUAL SIGNIFICANCE OF THIS GOSPEL

113. Christ's natural birth always signifies his spiritual birth, since he is born in us and we in him, as Saint Paul says in Galatians 4:19, "My little children, of whom I am again in travail until Christ be formed in you." Now, in order to complete this birth, God's Word and faith are necessary, because only through these can Christ's spiritual birth be wrought in us. Therefore, this Gospel signifies spiritually nothing more than the nature of the divine Word and of faith; also, how they fare who are born spiritually; what temptations and conflicts faith must encounter.

114. First, God used the circumstance that Herod, a stranger, reigned over his people to signify thereby the kind of reign existing within the soul. They had rejected God, so that he could no more govern them by faith. The Jews had become nothing but a Pharisaical, Sadducaical, hypocritical, and selfish people, who wanted to save themselves by human doctrines and outward works. They have no faith, which the entire Gospel and the life of Christ prove. As they, unbelieving in spirit, made for themselves a Herod in the place of Christ, they had to submit bodily and spiritually to a Herod instead of one who descended from the royal line of David and, therefore, in both relations there was purely a kingdom of Herod. In the Greek language, we are accustomed to call those who are noted for great clamor and deeds heroes, as were Hercules, Hector, Achilles, and the like, who in German are called giants, but in Saxon a fellow (Kerl), hence the name Carolus or Carl means among us what hero or Herod does in Greek. Herod comes from hero, because he was like a fellow, like a giant, a boaster, a Dieterich from Bern, a Hildebrand, a Roland, or by whatever other name you may call these great murderers and devourers of the people, who were also before the flood and whom Moses calls in Hebrew *Nephilim* (giants), in Genesis 6:4, which means that the people who fall upon others and with force suppress them will themselves fall. The people of Israel destroyed many of them in the land of Canaan, as the Anakims, Rephaims, and *Emims*. Anak is called a golden chain; hence the *Anakims*, in Deuteronomy 2:11, were called giants in the land and wore golden chains. The *Rephaims* were called rescuers, because they rescued the land and the people. The Emims were called terrible and frightful because the people were afraid of them.

115. Thus there always have been Herods, only in a different way and under other names; and thus there always will be Herods until the day of judgment, whom Christ at his coming will destroy. They are now called pope, cardinal, bishop, priest, monks, spiritual lords, and holy fathers, who are very unjustly called shepherds and sheep of Christ, but who are in reality ravenous wolves that flay and devour Christ's people in body, soul, and property. They

are in these last days the mighty fellows, giants, devourers of the people, and Herods, whom none but Christ from heaven can destroy.

116. Now Christ and Herod are entirely different and diametrically opposed, one to the other. Christ's merit consists not in a great clamor and in pretentious deeds. With him, there are no doings such as the giants and the fellows boast of, but only pure humanity that thinks not of self, is despised and content to let God be all in all and to do all and also to give him all the glory. Herod's ambition is to do great things, to possess every ability, to make a loud clamor, to be everything, and to lack nothing.

117. Since the Jews were inwardly veritable Herods, boasting much of themselves and of their deeds, commanding great respect on account of their ostentatious lives, Christ's humble demeanor amounted to nothing with them; therefore, God sent them a king, Herod, who dealt with them in temporal things as they dealt with souls in spiritual things. They rejected Christ and God; therefore, he rejected their royal family. Since he could not reign in their souls, he did not allow their own flesh and blood to reign over their bodies and property; and as they destroyed and suppressed the people spiritually with their government and with human doctrines, therefore, he permitted them to be destroyed, suppressed, and tormented through Herod. The physical Herod was a chastisement and a sign of their spiritual Herod.

118. As in all sin, one feels and hates the punishment, but loves the sin without being conscious of it; so it was with the Jews. They indeed felt the physical Herod and hated him, but the spiritual Herod, their unbelief, spiritual tyranny, they considered excellent, arrogantly claiming, through their Pharisaical, sectarian conduct in human doctrines and works of the law, to have earned much before God, and they could not discern that they had thereby earned the kingdom of Herod, from which they were not able to free themselves, however much they desired it, and they considered themselves worthy on account of their spiritual and holy conduct.

119. Thus we now also keenly feel our Herod, who is flaying and devouring us in body and estate; and since we are not sincere Christians and do not permit Christ to be our king in a pure and free faith, but are satisfied with the spiritual affairs now existing and with our own works, we are unable to rid ourselves of this Herod and there is no hope of relief. We must suffer ourselves to be devoured and ruined; there is no help; he must be our bodily and spiritual Herod.

120. Let this be an established truth, that in the first place Herod signifies a kingdom; not simply a kingdom such as worldly lords rule, but a spiritual kingdom. Therefore, the kingdom does not include only the temporal possessions of people but also their spiritual possessions; that is, their con-

sciences and the affairs belonging to salvation, such as good works, a pious life, the sacraments, and the Word of God.

121. Furthermore, this spiritual kingdom may be governed in a twofold manner: first, in a blessed way, when Christ alone governs in the true faith and the pure Gospel; secondly, in a pernicious way, when man governs with works and human doctrines. Just as the people of Israel were governed at one time by one of their own kindred, by their own king, and then again by Herod, a foreign king. Therefore, Herod signifies nothing else than such a spiritual kingdom, in which people are governed, not through faith and the Gospel, but through works and doctrines of men. It has the name, indeed, and the appearance of being the true way to heaven and of teaching the people right but, in reality, it is nothing else than the broad road to hell. The sum of it all is that Herod is the pope with his spiritual kingdom. There we see no faith, no Gospel, but simply human doctrines and works, and he has an enormous, Herod-like power and makes a loud clamor in the world. The consciences of men should be guided, fed, and preserved through God's Word alone, but he leads and feeds them only with his own swivel and blabber, with indulgences, orders, masses, prayers, fasts, and the like and, in this respect, is a mighty giant, a Roland and a fellow, a Kerl.

122. They say that if the Christian Church were not sustained by the state, she would founder, when the truth is that faith in Christ alone should govern her. Hence it is in this respect as the peasants say, Kuntz Hildebrand, the great whale, carries the world on his tail; that is, if it were not for what the pope did with his kingdom, God would be entirely too weak, the apple of the world would certainly fall out of his hand, and neither faith nor Gospel could avail anything. But now since the pope comes to his assistance and lays the foundation for him with his many tonsures, caps, robes, wooden shoes, bishop and cardinal hats, organ peals and smoke of incense, sounding of bells and candlesnuffing, bawling in the church and turkeys in their bellies, particularly in those who fast, eating neither milk, eggs, nor meat, and the like, in which the pope's holiness consists, everything will be sustained. And if the pope were in favor of doing away with such spiritual, orderly, holy government, where would the world be? Here we have what Herod and Christ are, two spiritual kingdoms, one unbelieving and the other believing.

123. Now, what is the "star"? It is nothing else than the new light, the oral and public preaching of the Gospel. Christ has two witnesses of his birth and kingdom; the one is the Scripture, the written Word; the other is the voice, or the word preached orally. The same word Paul calls in 2 Corinthians 4:6, and Peter in 2 Peter 1:19, a light and lamp.

124. The Scriptures are not understood until the light is risen, for through the Gospel the prophets arose; therefore, the star must first arise and shine. In the New Testament, sermons must be preached orally, with living voices publicly, and that which formerly lay concealed in the letter and secret vision must be proclaimed in language to the ear. The New Testament is nothing else than a resurrection and revelation of the Old Testament, as Revelation 5:9 testifies, where the Lamb of God opens the Book with its seven seals. We furthermore see that all the preaching of the apostles was nothing else than a presentation of the Scriptures upon which they built. Christ did not write his doctrines himself as Moses did, but he gave them orally, and commanded that they should be published abroad by preaching, and he did not command that they should be written. Likewise, the apostles wrote very little, except Peter, Paul, John, Matthew, and a few others; from the rest, we have nothing, for many do not consider the Epistles of James and Jude apostolic writings. Those who have written do nothing more than direct us to the Scriptures of the Old Testament, just as the angel directed the shepherds to the manger and the swaddling clothes, and the star led the wise men to Bethlehem.

125. Nor do we need any more New Testament books concerning Christian doctrine, but we need good, learned, spiritual, faithful preachers in every locality who, without books, can draw forth the living Word from the old Scriptures and make it plain and simple to the people, just as the apostles did; for previous to their writing, they preached and conferred with the people by word of mouth, which was strictly the apostolic and New Testament mode of evangelical work. This is also the right star, testifying of Christ's birth and the angelic message concerning the swaddling clothes and the manger.

126. That there was a necessity of writing books was in itself a great detriment and denotes an infirmity of the human spirit and does not arise out of the nature of the New Testament. For instead of pious preachers, there came heretics, false teachers, and all kinds of errorists, giving the sheep of Christ poison in the place of pasture. Hence in order to rescue at least some of the sheep from the wolves, it was necessary to write books in harmony with the Scriptures, so that, as much as possible, the lambs of Christ might be fed and the Scriptures preserved in their purity, thereby enabling the sheep to protect themselves against the wolves, and to be their own guides when their false shepherds would not lead them into the green pastures.

127. Luke says in his preface, in Luke 1:1, that he was influenced to write his Gospel by the fact that some had undertaken to write the history of Christ in whose reliableness he did not have full confidence. It was the object of all

the Epistles of Paul to guard and foster what he had taught before, doubting not that he had preached much more abundantly than he wrote. If wishing did any good, one could wish nothing better than that all books were simply destroyed and that nothing remained in the world except that which Christians formerly had, namely, the pure Scriptures alone or the Bible. It contains more than is necessary of all kinds of art and doctrine which man ought to know, but wishing is now to no purpose; would to God there were only good books besides the Bible.

128. Let it suffice for the present that this star is the visible sermon and the bright revelation of Christ as he is concealed and foreshadowed in the promises of the Scriptures. Therefore, whoever sees the star certainly recognizes the king of the Jews, the newborn Christ. For the Gospel teaches nothing else but Christ and, therefore, the Scripture contains nothing else than Christ. But he who does not recognize Christ may hear the Gospel, or indeed carry the book in his hands, but he has not yet its real meaning. To have the Gospel without its meaning, is to have no Gospel; and to have the Scripture without recognizing Christ, means to have no Scripture, and is nothing else than to let this star shine and yet not see it.

129. Therefore, the Herodites and the people of Jerusalem fare thus: the star rises over their land and over their heads, but they do not see it. Hence when the Gospel arose over the Jewish people, as Isaiah says in the Epistle, in Romans 10:21, they let it shine but did not acknowledge it. Of this, Paul writes, in 2 Corinthians 4:3, 4, "And even if our Gospel is veiled, it is veiled in them that perish: in whom the god of this world," that is, the devil, "hath blinded the minds of the unbelieving, that the light of the Gospel of the glory of Christ, who is the image of God, should not dawn upon them." From this, it is evident, that unbelief alone is the cause of blindness, on account of which they do not see the Gospel although it shines and is preached without ceasing. That it is impossible for Christ and his Gospel to be acknowledged by reason, but by faith alone, is here plainly taught. And the seeing of the star signifies this individual star.

130. The wise men signify, and are themselves, the first fruit of heathendom converted unto faith through the Gospel. For the heathen were the wise men, that is, people of nature, living according to their reason, who did not have the law and the prophets, as the Jews, but walked only according to nature, without the divine law and the Word. Now, as the natural masters, the wise men, generally deviated from the line of right, and converted the natural art into witchcraft and sorcery, as stated above, so the natural reason when left to itself, and not assisted by the doctrines of God, most certainly will

go astray, and will loose itself in error and blindness, as a veritable witch, full of all manner of unbelief.

131. Thus Paul writes, in Romans 2:14, that the heathen, although the law of God had not been given to them, nevertheless had a natural law of conscience and performed the works of the law, which they found written in their hearts. But though they were far from the truth, and were without the law of God, they were brought to faith much more easily and much sooner than the Jews, for the reason, that the Jews, having the law depended upon it, and thought they had sufficiently satisfied it by their works. Therefore, they despised the Gospel as something entirely superfluous and false, because it rejected works, concerning which they boasted so much, and lauded faith alone. The heathen had no ground for such vain boasting, because they were without the law; hence they more easily yielded to the Gospel, acknowledged its necessity, and their need of it.

132. That the wise men came to Jerusalem and inquired after the newborn king, signifies nothing else than that the heathen were enlightened through the Gospel, came into the Christian Church, and sought Christ. For Jerusalem is a figure of the Christian Church, into which God's people are gathered, which in German may be called, vision of peace, because in the Christian Church peace is seen, that is, when all have a good conscience, and peaceful confidence of heart, who, being in the Christian Church and being true Christians, have forgiveness of sins through the grace of God.

133. Now in this peaceful place, Herod the devourer of men, would reign at all times; for all the doctrines and works of men have in them this vexatious evil, that they in their very nature mislead, oppress, and destroy the true Jerusalem, ensnaring good consciences and pious hearts, teaching them to trust in themselves and in their good works, thereby causing faith to perish, peace and a good conscience to be destroyed, while the rule of Herod with its great show and clamor and faithless works, alone remains. This is what our Gospel wishes to say, that thus Christ was born and sought after at the time of Herod, in the very city of his kingdom. For evangelical truth wages its whole warfare with the false holiness of Herod and every time it renews the strife it finds Herods, who rule the people with their doctrines and human works, and these things are so for no other reason than that the truth condemns these doings of theirs and teaches the pure grace of God instead of works and pure faith instead of law, in order to rescue the people of God from the reign of Herod, and save them for the true Jerusalem.

134. When Herod heard this he was troubled and all Jerusalem with him. Why? Because Herod was afraid of another king, the true king, for he himself,

with force wanted to be the only king. It came to pass, that through the Gospel the heathen began to praise Christ and to have faith, contrary to the works and doctrines of men; thereupon the Jews became enraged, because they could easily perceive that if this matter should grow and spread, their affairs would soon be considered worthless, and their great and false doings would surely be brought to shame. This they could not endure, and, therefore, they began to rage, as is shown by the history of the apostles. For they knew very well that the progress of the Gospel, their government, honor, power, and riches, which they had in such abundance under the spiritual reign of Herod, would receive a powerful blow.

135. Human works and doctrines at all times yield much revenue and carnal gain, while the doctrines of God and the work of Christ bring the cross, poverty, ignominy, and all kinds of calamity, which the holiness of Herod cannot endure. Thus it happens always, that they who have ensnared and oppressed the poor with an erring conscience and with human doctrines, do not like to hear that poor, miserable consciences receive instruction, attain a right understanding, and seek the simple, pure Word of God and faith. Many say that they want a new king, and have seen his star; for thus the pope, bishops, holy fathers, and lords could not indulge their carnal desires.

136. Therefore, it is not at all agreeable nor serviceable to the reign of Herod that the wise men, the learned, the laity, who know nothing, should begin to speak of the light of the Gospel, and to inquire about another matter in the midst of Jerusalem, paying no attention to spiritual pomp of the rulers. This must indeed have frightened Herod and his associates because it concerned their purses and their belly. Yes, it also frightened all Jerusalem; for many pious people, though they hated the reign of Herod and wished that it were not thus, also were afraid that the truth might be brought to light at an unpropitious time, that through it a tumult and confusion might be caused in the world, that the government might be attacked, and that perhaps this tumult could not, without great detriment, be suppressed. Therefore, they thought that it might be better to withhold the truth for a time, or to bring it forth in such a manner as not to frighten Herod, and arouse him to some desperate action.

137. But the wise men do not inquire after his fright and anger, but speak openly of the star and the new king, and are not in the least concerned that the heavens might fall. For one must neither confess nor deny the Gospel on account of any particular person; it is God's Word; Herod must yield to it and follow it. Does he rage, however? Then let him rage; Christ must remain in preference to him.

138. And now, behold! Herod is foremost to learn of the new king, not with sincerity but with deceit, and so he gathers together all the learned men and diligently searches the Scripture, as though he were anxious to learn the truth, and yet we know that it was his determination to accomplish his own will and intention instead of obeying the Scripture. Here we arrive at the real character of Herod; here we see the pope and his followers truly portrayed.

139. But that no one may blame me for applying this to the pope, and comparing his holy order and its reign so contemptuously with that of Herod, I want it understood that I do it because it is my Christian duty and a debt of faithfulness which I feel in my conscience that I owe everyone. If the truth and experience do not prove all that I say, then let anyone who will, chastise me for lying; I will fulfill my fraternal office satisfactorily and be excused before God. If anyone despises my faithful warning, let him answer for it himself; I want to say to him, that Christ and his doctrine shall not suffer on account of the pope and his spiritual rule. Therefore, let everyone guard himself against them, as against his eternal destruction, and adhere alone to Christ. Whether it brings the pope and his divines any fortune or honor, does not concern me in the least; I must preach Christ and not the fortune and honor of the pope and his divines. What is said of the pope and his divines, is said of all those who oppress the people with their works and doctrines, and do not teach the true faith, the pure Scripture, and the one Christ, as the Jews also did but accomplished very little against the pope and his associates. He who will suffer himself to be misled has herewith heard my warning: I am innocent of his blood and ruin.

140. That Herod called the princes, priests, and scribes of the people together and inquired of them concerning the birth of Christ, is the same as our spiritual kingdom, and is what the unbelieving tinkers are doing; they keep the Scriptures to themselves, and what they teach is presumably contained in the Scripture, but in this sense, that their own opinion comes first, and the Scriptures must be twisted so as to agree with their opinion. For their intention is to use the Scripture only to this end, that it may suppress the truth and satisfy their own doings, just as Herod searched in the Scriptures for no other purpose than that he might slay Christ.

141. Thus our Herod is doing, with his Herodites, the people; he indeed searches the Scripture and uses it, but he explains it only in such a way that he may destroy its real sense, and read into it his own sense. With such show, even the elect are deceived; for there is no greater show, which frightens and deceives every conscience, than that which sets forth the name of God and claims only to search and follow God's Scripture and Word, while at the same time it seeks

thereby only to oppose and to quell the Scriptures with all their contents. Therefore, the wise men do not see the star of Jerusalem, and do not know where they shall go. And all who walk among such genteel and glittering folks will be deceived and will lose the real Christian sense on account of the great bustle and glittering exterior of unbelieving divines, unless they grasp firmly the pure Scripture.

142. Although both Herod and the wise men received the Scriptures here from the priest, Herod received them in a false and vicious sense. The wise men received them in a right and good sense; therefore, they see again the star shining, and are rescued from Herod's hypocrisy under which they had lost the star. As here the strife between Herod and the wise men is signified, so also is signified the strife between the true and the false divines who place themselves over the Scriptures, that the true divines are indeed a trifle in error, and for a little while lose the true light, but they do not continue in error. They finally grasp the true sense of Scripture, come again to the clear light, and let the Herods praise themselves in their false understanding of the Scripture.

⋘⋙

217. That Herod called the wise men and inquired of them secretly as to when the star appeared, indicates that the spiritual Herods do not deny the Gospel outwardly, but learn it from the true Christians, however, only, with this intention that they will use it to do mischief; just as Herod here intended to use the time the star appeared to kill Christ and confirm his own kingdom. Thus also now, when we hold up the Gospel to our clergy, they do not deny that it is the Gospel, they hear and accept it. They deny, however, that this is not the correct meaning, that it has a gloss and an interpretation which we shall get from no one but them, and that everyone must acknowledge their interpretation. Thus they do not deny the Gospel, but rob it of its power and, under the name and appearance of the Gospel, they teach their own dreams. This Saint Paul, in 2 Timothy 2:5, calls, "Holding a form of godliness, but having denied the power thereof." He does not say they have the power of the divine essence, although that is true also; but he says much more forcibly that they deny it. Thereby he gives us to understand clearly, that they are godless not only in their life and walk, but also in their doctrine and government; that they lead themselves with their lives, and others with their doctrine, away from the Gospel and salvation. This, the pope and the clergy now do in all their sermons. Though they cry loudly, Gospel! Gospel!, yet they deny, damn, and curse everything that is in the Gospel with all its contents, just as Herod learned of the star, but endeavored to destroy everything the

star signified. We will now consider a few of their doctrines, and guard against them.

218. The Gospel teaches that salvation is by faith alone. This they hear and do not deny; nevertheless, they destroy all its power by saying that faith without works is useless. Thus they secretly depart from faith to works, and publicly condemn faith and ascribe everything to works. Therefore, they retain the little word faith only in appearance, and deny, condemn, and curse everything of the nature of faith, and begin to divide it into many parts; some say there is a natural faith, others a spiritual, some a common, some others a particular, some a simple, others a complex, and they themselves, these blind leaders, know less of what they are juggling than any natural fool. The Gospel knows nothing of their manifold faith, has but the one, which is founded upon the pure grace of God, without any merit of works; of this they have not the faintest idea, yes, condemn it as the worst heresy, and yet they say that they will defend the Gospel and the Christian faith.

219. Again, the Gospel says that Christ is our Savior; this they hear, but then loosen and weaken every natural work, manner, and attribute of Christ, inasmuch as they publicly teach that man can, through natural strength and works, earn the grace of God; therefore, they condemn Christ and all his works, as Saint Peter, in 2 Peter 2:1, has prophesied of them, "There shall be false teachers among you denying even the Master that bought them." For if nature itself can attain the grace of God, as now all high schools, institutions, and cloisters hold and teach in harmony with the pope, then Christ was born and died to no purpose. Why should Christ have shed his blood to acquire grace for us, if we through our nature could have acquired ourselves? Yet they wish to be Christians, and raise aloft the name of Christ, under the appearance of which they revile and condemn as heresy the entire Christian essence.

220. Again, the Gospel teaches that the law of God is spiritual and cannot possibly be fulfilled by nature; but that the Spirit of God must fulfill it in us through faith, in Romans 8:2–3. Therefore, they deny neither the Spirit nor the law, but they nevertheless destroy all its power, and teach that man, without the help of the Spirit, can fulfill the law naturally in all its works, although he cannot thereby earn heaven. This is nothing less than denying the power of the law and of the Spirit, retaining only the name.

221. Then they proceed and tear the law of God asunder where they think it too difficult for nature, making superfluous, unnecessary things of it; as, for example, that it is neither necessary nor commanded that we should love God with the entire heart, that we give the cloak with the coat; again, that we should not go to court; again, that we should loan and give to everybody,

without profit or gain. Again, that we should suffer evil and do good unto our enemies, etc. Thus they have destroyed the true nature of Christianity, which consists alone in this that we suffer wrong and do good to everybody. And then they institute in its stead their own command, that they wear tonsures and caps, eat no meat, eggs, butter, and milk, make a great noise in the church; that nothing remains now of the law of God.

222. Again, the Gospel praises the pure grace of God as pardoning and destroying sin. Now they do not deny the little word grace, but hold it seemingly in high esteem; besides this, however, they teach a multiplicity of satisfactions for sin, payments of money, orders, divisions of repentance in order to purchase from God the forgiveness of sin, and to pay him for his grace. Therefore, the nature and work of grace are destroyed and condemned to the very foundation; for grace is pure grace or nothing at all.

223. Again, the Gospel teaches that through original sin all men are under wrath and disfavor, and that all their works are thereby rendered sinful. They do not deny the expression, original sin, but destroy its force by saying that nature is still good, and its works are not sinful, and can as yet well prepare itself, yet for grace. They say also that original sin did not injure nature so that it should be condemned, but simply weakened it toward the good, and disposed it to evil. If it does not follow its inclination, which of itself it does not need to do, it does not deserve hell, and can also acquire the grace of God. Behold, this is as much as to say, original sin is not original sin; and under this name they deny the work and nature of sin.

224. Again, the Gospel teaches that love does not seek its own, but serves others only. Now they indeed hold to the little word love, but curtail its entire nature, inasmuch as they teach, ordinary love begins with itself and loves itself first and most. Then they say, it is loving enough if one simply wishes another well; it is not necessary to add the deed of serving him. For it would be dishonest for the pope to humble himself and serve his subject, but he permits his feet to be kissed, and thinks it enough simply to say, I wish everybody well except my enemies. Behold! here lie in ruins the nature and power of love, and nothing remains but the simple empty name.

225. Again, the Gospel teaches how hope builds alone upon pure divine revelation; they confess the little word, hope, teach, however, that hope does not rest upon divine revelation, but upon its own merits.

226. Again, the Gospel teaches how God's providence is eternally sure; they, however, teach that it rests upon the free will and is uncertain.

227. In short, they confess God and his name, but root out and condemn as the worst heresy whatever God orders, wills, does, establishes, and executes,

from which we can clearly see how Christ's suffering is now spiritually fulfilled under the rule of the pope. Behold, see they have in their teaching the appearance of faith, of hope, of love, of grace, of sin, of the law, of Christ, of God, of the Gospel; yet they deny all strength and nature of the same, and even condemn it all as the worst heresy. On this account, the apostle spoke so sharply when he said, They deny the power of the whole divine worship and life, and live only the pretense of it. Oh, Lord God of heaven, where are the streams of water, yes, of blood, that rightly should flow from our eyes in this last terrible and dreadful time of the unspeakable, immeasurable wrath of God upon the world because of its sin and thanklessness.

228. Further, Herod sends the wise men to Bethlehem and commands them diligently to seek the child, pretending that he also wished to come and worship him. Here our Herodians are shown another thing, namely, that they ought to live as they preach. Teaching and living are with them empty show and denial of the truth, for the life must be as the teaching directs. However, the pope and the religious orders now do allow Christians to be pious, and command them to seek Christ and the truth, yet with this addition, that they must be his betrayers, and serve the priesthood in thus seeking Christ. For the pope now shamelessly and eagerly declares this to all the world: Anyone is allowed to seek Christ and to live righteously; but, if he does not also obey the pope's orders and command, and serve him, with all his good life, be subject to his authority, he still cannot be saved. The people are thus made to think that more, or at least just as much, depends upon obedience to the pope than upon God's commands.

229. See, this is Herod's addition, that he not only sends the wise men to Bethlehem, but also holds them subject to himself and feels bound treacherously to destroy Christ. For what do all who thus hold that obedience to the pope is necessary to salvation, and that whoever does not hold it is condemned, do, except betray and surrender Christ that Herod may find and kill him. For Christian faith cannot exist beside such obedience or such conscience, as has often been said. For faith alone must save, and such obedience be counted useful and permitted, faith must perish, and Herod reign in Christ's stead. That means then really to surrender and betray Christ and one's faith.

230. But when Herod says, I, too, will come and worship him, everyone sees that he lies, that these are mere words and a clear pretense, beneath which he is still planning something quite different, namely, to kill Christ and to destroy his kingdom. Here you have in Herod the image of all unbelieving saints well and briefly set forth. In the first place, Herod does not pretend any common thing: he does not say that he wishes to give him gold or

myrrh, neither that he wishes to help him or to be his true friend; but undertakes the very highest and best thing that there is in the service of God, namely, humility and worship. I will come, he says, as a lowly one, and show the highest honor, even worship.

231. Thus do now also the Herodians, the priests, who do not undertake any ordinary work, but the very highest, the service of God. This they appropriate to themselves, in that they exercise themselves, saying openly that the life of other men is temporal and worldly, but that they are in the service of God day and night and, while others labor, they pray and serve God for the poor people.

Do you not believe this? Well then, ask the bells about it which ring for their worship. To this they go in humble manner, let themselves be proclaimed God's servants before all men, fattening their bellies right well in so doing, gather for themselves riches out of all the world, and build houses, as if they expected to live here forever. Accordingly, we must here note the difference between true and false worship, that we may recognize and avoid the spirit of the villain Herod.

⋰⋱

The True and False Worship of God

250. According as we have now learned to know Herod's worship and perceived his artful hypocrisy, let us now see, too, his evil purpose and maliciousness, with which he plans to destroy not only the true worship, but also Christ, the king, and his whole kingdom. He attempts to do this in three ways. First, with the same hypocritical appearance of this false worship. For such an appearance of worship is so strong an enticement from true worship that it can be overcome only by especial grace, so that Saint Paul well names it *energiam erroris*, a strong working of error. The people cannot defend themselves against such seduction, where there are not true bishops and preachers who preach the only true worship, hold the people to the pure Word of God, and forbid the false worship, as the prophets did in Israel, and were all for that reason put to death.

251. In the second place, Herod destroys true worship through his teaching, of which we have already spoken. Thus he teaches works instead of faith, contrary to the first commandment to honor and serve God; in the second and third commandments, he perverts and teaches one's own works and sufficiency, and forbids to confess the faith and God's name. As has been said, he

teaches disobedience to father and mother, contrary to the fourth commandment. Contrary to the fifth, he teaches that it is not necessary to love one's enemy and to do him good. Contrary to the sixth, he tears matrimony to pieces. He robs and steals and even justifies so doing, thus breaking the seventh commandment. He teaches also that it is not necessary to lend and give. *Summa summarum*, he teaches that it is not necessary to love God and one's neighbor from the heart. That means, to be sure, that he destroys the whole Scripture and worship of God.

252. In the third place, he is not satisfied with such poisonous examples and deadly teachings, but goes ahead and exercises two kinds of force in them; he banishes and execrates the souls that do not follow him, also burns, hunts, and persecutes their bodies, property, and honor in the most shameful way. What more could he do that is evil? I mean to say that he is a Herod; nevertheless, he must leave Christ alone, and cannot carry out his will. He destroys many, but faith remains to the end of the world, although hidden, a fugitive, and unknown.

253. But here, perhaps, you ask me, What then should they do who are spiritual captives under Herod in false worship, in convents and monasteries? I answer: You cannot do otherwise than lay aside the false worship and hold to God's Word and true worship; or do as the wise men did, and drink the poison, firmly believing that it will not hurt you. You will find no other means: God's Word will remain unchanged to all eternity. But although I have already spoken of this in another gospel, I must speak of it again.

254. Well now, we place before us one who holds fast in this matter and argues against us that a priest, a monk, or a nun, or any other person who has gone into orders, is bound to keep his spoken vow and may not in any way during his whole life leave it or turn aside. Such a man may take his stand in the Scripture, which says that one should fulfill what one has vowed. But let us, however, speak of vows which God has not commanded, but which men make of their own accord. For, since in baptism we vowed to serve God and keep his commandment, such a vow is demanded by God of all men, as the Scripture says, in Psalm 22:25, "I will pay my vows before them that fear him," and, in Psalm 116:18, "I will pay my vows unto Jehovah, yea, in the presence of all his people." But the vow of the religious orders he has not commanded.

255. With this opponent we shall deal in two ways. First, let us decide definitely upon those things in which there is no doubt or argument; secondly, let us dispute with him, explore, and seek the truth. First, no one can or should doubt that all contrary to God's command, whether it be to live or to die, to

vow or to become free, to speak or to be silent, is to be condemned and by all means to be changed and to be avoided. For the will of God must soar above all and be done in heaven and on earth, as we pray, even if a man could work all miracles. This is clear and certain enough. So there is now no doubt or argument, but it is certainly determined: If anyone has been consecrated as priest, monk, or nun against God's will, such priesthood and monkery is nothing and altogether to be condemned, and he is bound to let it all go and change. Thus if anyone has become priest or monk only for the purpose of stealing a chalice or ornaments, he has certainly taken the vow against God's commandment, and has also sinned in so doing and his vow does not bind him. Such a man may and should return to secular life, or he must take the vow anew and from right motives. For his purpose has never been to enter the clergy; but if thievishness had not urged him, he would certainly not have taken the vow and considered entering the order. Accordingly, God cannot accept the vow, nor is it binding upon the man to observe it.

256. But before men it is different, for whoever has vowed anything must keep his vow, although he did not intend it in his heart. For man does not see his neighbor's heart and, accordingly, accepts his vow as honest and believes it to be from the heart. So he has the right to ask him to fulfill it, and may honestly state that he is not bound to believe that the promiser has changed his mind and rued his bargain. If, however, the other lied, the loss is his. But God cannot be deceived, and he judges only by the heart. Accordingly, such a vow counts for nothing with him, and he does not ask it, but is angry to have anyone thus tempt him.

257. If now anyone had taken vows against the first great commandment of God of the first table, he would be much more obliged to give up his vow than that thief who had vowed against the seventh commandment, as the first commandment is higher than the seventh commandment. For whoever thus steals contrary to the seventh commandment steals only worldly property, the very least of created things. But he who deals contrary to the first commandment robs and denies God himself, the highest good and the Creator of all. The priests and monks, then, who sin against the first commandment, are many times worse than that thievish cheat and breaker of the seventh commandment. What, if we could now prove that nearly all priests and monks enter orders against the first commandment, and that they become spiritual just as little, or even less than these thievish roguish knaves. Oh, this means to throw open monasteries and convents and to set free the monks and priests. Well now, consider and listen.

258. The first commandment contains the Christian faith, for he who does not believe cannot have a God or know him; all unbelief is idolatry. This is Christian faith that trusts in God's grace alone, gained for us and bestowed upon us through the blood of Christ, and that counts no work useful or good to win God's favor. For this were too hard for nature, which is conceived and born in sin, and also lives, works, and dies in it if Christ would not come to its help, gaining God's mercy for us by his works alone and not by our own. Through him, too, we fulfill the first commandment and have a God on whose mercy we can depend with all confidence, so that without our merit he forgives all our sins and saves us in Christ, as has often already been said. Therefore, it is impossible that this faith should permit besides itself a trust in works, as though anyone could obtain forgiveness of sins and grace and become holy and be saved by them, for this belongs to Christ alone, who does all this through his work. Thus we have only to believe and confidently to entrust ourselves to him

259. Therefore, there is no penance, no satisfaction for sin, no acquiring of grace, no becoming holy, for we believe only in Christ, that he has done enough for our sin, won mercy for us, and saved us. After that, we should first of all do good works of free will, to his honor and for the good of our neighbor, not that we may become holy or be saved or put away sin thereby, for that must remain entrusted to Christ alone through faith. He does not grant to angels, much less to our good works, that they should put away sin, win grace, and make holy: that belongs to him; he has done and does it alone. This he wishes to have us believe and, if we believe it, then we have it.

Of this, Saint Paul says, I do not make void the grace of God; for if righteousness is through the law, then Christ died for naught, in Galatians 2:21. That is to say, if we are able to do so much that God forgives our sins and gives grace and salvation on account of our works, then we do not need Christ. For what other reason did he die, except to atone for our sins and win grace, that we give up hope in ourselves and our works, make nothing of them, confide in Christ alone, and hold with a fixed faith that he is the one whom God regards in our place and through whose merit alone forgives us our sins, becomes reconciled, and saves us. This is a Christian faith, of which Christ says, in Mark 16:16, "He that believeth and is baptized shall be saved, but he that disbelieveth shall be condemned."

260. Now let us consider the religious orders and estimate them over against the first commandment and Christian faith. Does anyone wish to become a priest or to take a vow in the Christian spirit so that he does not run

against the first commandment and tempt God, then the intention of his heart must be that he can say, Well, I intend to become a priest, a monk, or nun, or to take some other vow, not that I consider the station of life or order a way to salvation, neither because I expect through such a life to become holy, to atone for sin, and to win God's grace. God protect me against this, for this would be against Christ and his blood, this would be destroying all his merit and honor and the worst scorn and mockery of God. For all that will I expect from him in pure faith, since I do not doubt that he has done it for me. However, since I must do something on earth, I will take up this life, exercise myself in it, chastise my body, and serve my neighbor, just as another man works in the field or garden or at his trade without regard to merit and good in his works. See, where this purpose is not, there Christ must be denied and the first commandment destroyed, and vain, unchristian, unbelieving, Jewish, and heathen life be found. This, also, says the mighty Scripture truth of Saint Paul, in Romans 14:23, "Whatsoever is not of faith is sin." And, For without faith no one will be saved, in Mark 16:16. So, too, without faith, there can be no righteousness nor truth.

261. Tell me now how many priests and monks, think you, are to be found who take vows and live under vows with so Christian a purpose? Do not nearly all of them speak thus, Well, if my order does not count more for me in atoning for sin, in becoming holy, and in getting to heaven than a farmer's plough or a tailor's needle does for him, then what am I doing in the order of priesthood? No, I will do good works, hold many masses, pray, and do penance for myself and other people. What kind of word is that of an unbelieving heart that has denied Christ and that ascribes to its order and works that which should be expected of Christ alone through faith?

262. Moreover, as has been said above, it is the meaning and teaching of all those in the religious orders that one can, through his own work, win God's grace and put away sin. They are so devoid of shame that they sell, promise, and divide to others their good works, merit, and brotherhood; they are so bold as to do for men what Christ alone is able to do, namely, to put away men's sins and to make them holy. Of this, Christ has especially prophesied and said, in Matthew 24:5, "For many shall come in my name, saying, I am the Christ." Beloved, give heed to the word. Is it not true, as has just been said, that our priests and monks make themselves Christ? Although no one of them says with the mouth, I am Christ; nevertheless, they say, I help other people, give them my merit, win grace for them, put away their sin, which is Christ's work and office only. Accordingly, they are Christ, although they do not call themselves Christ. For Matthew 24 does not say that they will say, I am called

Christ, but I am Christ. It is not the name, but the office and work of Christ that they take for themselves.

263. Therefore, we conclude here without any dispute or question or doubt that all in religious orders who are not priests, monks, or nuns from the above-named Christian purpose have certainly taken vows and live against the first commandment of God, and are ten times worse than the thievish, tricky rascal of whom we have spoken. And they are truly the lost multitude, heathen and Jews, the devil's own, as they come and go; they are truly and exactly those of whom Saint Peter says, in 2 Peter 2:1–3, "Among you also there shall be false teachers denying even the Master that bought them. And in covetousness shall they with feigned words make merchandise of you." This they do to perfection, for all possessions and tribute come to the religious orders, because of their false, unchristian life, which they hold up with false words.

264. Accordingly, all these are to be advised to leave tonsures and caps, monastery and convent, and to cease keeping their vow; or to begin anew to vow such a life in Christian faith and purpose. For the vow observed in the Christian purpose counts no more before God than this much: See here, God, I vow to you not to be a Christian as long as I live, I recall the vow of my baptism, and will now make and keep for thee a better vow, apart from Christ, in my own doings and works. Is not that a terrible, horrible vow? Now it is nothing different, as can clearly be seen from the above. But these are the ones who take vows in the best way, as they suppose.

265. For the great, mad crowd who become priests and monks for their bellies' sake, that they may be provided for in this world, and who compose the larger part of the clergy, are not worthy to be discussed and much less is their vow of any validity. These can surely become secular, if they wish, for they have never become nor been religious. And it would indeed be necessary for them to cease mocking God with their mummery, to give up their prebend, tenure, priesthood, monkery, and nuns' life. O Lord God, how totally blind is the world, how perverted it is! The world now is religious, and religious orders are now the world. How strong is the rule of Antichrist!

266. In the second place, we shall now argue and say, Although someone had honestly taken the vow with Christian intention, has he not the power, if occasion demand, to return to secular life? Here I desire that only pious, honest spirits would give heed, who are not swift to judge, but are eager to learn and reason. For nothing can be said to the mad papists and Herodians; no one can argue with them: they can only hold their ears, gnash their teeth, and scream: Heretic, heretic, fire, fire, fire! We let these alone as irrational and talk

with those who would gladly have their own and other people's conscience instructed.

267. It is undeniable that a Christian purpose to take vows consists, as has been said above, in this, that it does not take the vow because the order is useful and necessary to abolish sin, to win grace, to become pious, to especially serve God, and to be saved. These are properties of the common Christian faith only which nowhere, except in Christ, expects such blessings, but which, free and exempt from such unchristian madness, thinks only of accepting a good discipline of the body in this life. Just so undeniable it is that God accepts no vow or religious order, except it be taken with this Christian purpose, since Saint Paul stands firmly here and says, in Romans 14:23, "Whatsoever is not of faith is sin." But God cannot accept sin, as in Psalm 5:5 and in Habakkuk 1:13. Because, therefore, God does not accept such vow and order otherwise than as voluntary and unnecessary to salvation, and because true Christian purpose does not begin nor vow otherwise, I should like to hear the man who thoroughly and with honest reason could deny that one in religious orders could re-enter secular life without injury to his soul and with a good conscience before God, especially if he had cause to do so.

268. That many say, It is not customary, the holy fathers have done and written differently, settles nothing, as anyone can see. We ask here, not what custom does or what the writings of the fathers ask, but what is right and pleasing before God. Who will assure that custom is not wrong and that the fathers are not in error, since even Christ declares, in Matthew 24:24, that even the elect shall be deceived by false Christs, such as those in the religious orders. Say what you will, it cannot be made to agree that anything which is free and unnecessary to the soul's salvation as undertaken or vowed before God and the conscience, cannot be let go but, on the contrary, must, at the risk of the soul's salvation, be kept until death. The two things are exactly opposite, as you can see for yourself.

269. A Christian vow to take religious orders must before God be thus, See, dear God, I vow to thee to lead this life, which can be led free by nature and without regard to salvation. Ought not God answer here, Well, what then have you vowed to me here, and what are you keeping? Have you not enough necessary things to observe? In this you vow nothing to me, since you may observe it and again let it go. Good, this I will allow. And thus the vow before God naturally excludes that the life under the vow remains free to be observed or to be let go. It is just as if your servant made you a vow and promised, Master, I vow to you on this extra day free service, which I may do or leave undone; on the

other days, I am bound to serve you. Here, I think, whether the servant did or left undone, as it may happen, he would have done enough for his vow.

270. I cannot understand differently but that the vow of all those who are in religious orders is the same; for the reason that faith makes all things free, and it is impossible that anything should be necessary or should be made necessary to salvation, either through ourselves, through angels, or through any creatures, faith alone excepted. And this is the liberty which Christ has won for us, of which Saint Paul teaches, in Galatians 5:1, and says against all the teaching of men, "For freedom did Christ set us free: stand fast therefore." Therefore, the vow of all those who are in orders must naturally have in it liberty again to leave this life and should read thus, I vow to God and you, chastity, poverty, and obedience, according to the rule of Saint Augustine, to be freely held or given up, until death.

271. Here, probably, someone begins to laugh and to say that would be a foolish, ridiculous vow and a mere deception. I answer: Do not be surprised if men do ridiculous and foolish things when they leave God's ordering to follow their own blindness and to do, not what God's Word teaches, but what suits them. Ridiculous, foolish, and worthless such a vow is; but nevertheless by it, God's wrath is fulfilled and countless souls are led astray, so that scarcely the elect escape.

272. Men have invented such vows and such a life; therefore, it is and remains a human order. Many years ago, when young people were accepted to be taught and reared in a Christian way, as now ought to be done in the schools, they were allowed, of their own free will, to remain for a while under discipline. Now, some remained willingly in this state all their lives and became so accustomed to it that few forsook the company, but remained altogether in it until their end; thus finally, monasteries and convents arose.

Since now the masters have become lazy and the youth intractable, men invented these cords and chains of the vow, and with it took the conscious prisoners and rid themselves with care and oversight by making each one constrain himself to be and to remain disciplined and pious for the sake of the bond of his vow; just as in the higher schools also, the abominable practice prevails of guarding and carrying out everything with oaths and vows to bind the poor youth so shamefully without any necessity.

273. Thus convents and cloisters have grown out of the free Christian schools, and faith has been perverted into works, and liberty destroyed and bound through vows. Accordingly, it is not surprising that, where Christian liberty again shines forth, human vows appear ridiculous and foolish. Christian

liberty can at no time exist together with the timid vows of external works. One of the two must yield; that is unavoidable. Faith makes all external things free; the vow binds them fast; how then can both remain together? Thus faith is divine; the vow is human. Therefore, it is not possible that God should let faith go and regard our vow. Therefore, it is not possible that he should sin against God or break his vow who remains priest, monk, or nun as long as he wishes, and returns to secular life when he wishes.

274. We would further discuss this for the comfort of the wretched, imprisoned consciences, oppressed under this Herod and Antichrist. If we take for granted that vows made in a Christian way ought to be kept, what then will you say if one of these would become impossible for someone to observe? I take up the one that is the most plausible, the vow of chastity, which, as we see with our own eyes, cannot be kept by the majority, for nature is far too weak to keep it where special grace is not present.

275. Moses has written much of the natural sexual intercourse between man and woman, both while awake and asleep, of which no one dare now speak openly. So much purer have our ears become than the mouth of the Holy Ghost, that we are ashamed where there is nothing to be ashamed of, and are not ashamed where there is cause for shame. Yet it is necessary that everyone should know and be instructed in these things, and especially the youth. Where special heavenly grace is not found, there nature must be satisfied according to its constitution. If man and woman do not come together, nature takes its own course and is unrestrained, so that it would be better for man and woman to come together, as God created them and as nature prompts. Many teachings and books have been written about this; would to God they were all well written and helpful!

276. So now I ask, How will they advise one for whom it is impossible to restrain himself? You say that such should guard themselves with prohibitions. Well then, one of these three things will follow, where there is not special grace. Man and woman will come together, if they can, as now takes place among priests; or nature will relieve itself; or, where neither of these happens, there will be a continual burning and secret suffering. Here, then, you have a diabolical torture, and it comes about that the man would take the ugliest woman on earth, and the woman the most disgusting man because of the raging evil lust of the flesh.

277. Modest ears should and will pardon me; I must lay hold on the sickness of souls as a physician does of the excrement and secret places if I am to help at all. Now God can and will have no forced, unwilling chastity, which is no chastity to him; it must be voluntary, as all other services of God must be

voluntary. or he does not regard it. What are you doing, then, that you hold this poor man for his whole life in unchaste chastity, that without cessation he sins with the heart against his vow, so that it would be better for the young man to have a young woman and for the young woman to have a young man?

278. Here some teach that it is enough if one willingly begins the life of chastity and takes the vow accordingly for, by virtue of the willing beginning, it will not harm, if he afterward become unwilling. Oh, ye betrayers and blind leaders who adapt the service of God to works and not to the Spirit! All is in vain that is unwillingly done, and it would better be left undone. For it may happen that the man and the woman who live together have much less fire and lust than such solitary men and women; but the greater the lust, the greater is the sin of unchastity. So now these three kinds of men can find no counsel; the pope lets them burn and be martyred, as they may, so that I consider these to be the children who, among the people of Israel, were offered and burned before the fiery idol of Moloch.

279. Then you say, What shall I do otherwise? It is not fitting to let them marry, on account of the vow, since the Scriptures say, *Vovete et reddite*, vow and observe. That answer I would have. Now answer me again. It is not fitting to let them marry, you say; why, then, is it fitting to let them play the profligate, to have secret sexual intercourse, and to burn? Will not the vow be violated worse here than if they were married? How cleverly this helps the vow when you forbid marriage and when you see that you cannot prevent profligacy and lust. I think to do the latter would be to leave the beam in the eye and to draw out the mote.

280. Yes, say you, the man may at last leave the woman and live chastely, and this he could not do if married. My dear man, give me a few examples. It would happen sooner that married people separate and voluntarily abstain than such people. But let that go until another time. Answer me here: Saint Augustine makes a rule that his brethren are not to go alone, but two by two. This I have vowed until death; well, then, I am taken prisoner and compelled to be alone; tell me, what becomes of my vow? Shall I keep my vow here, then I must let myself be killed, rather than be alone. But what if they will not kill me, and keep me alone by force, then my vow must be broken or I must always have made for myself this condition, that I vow to keep the rule in this and this particular, as far as it is possible for me.

281. Further, I vow to pray, to wear a habit, and other things of the kind according to the rule. Well, then, I become sick, must keep my bed, and cannot observe any of them. What becomes now of the command, *Vovete et reddite*, vow and observe? It does not help me that I am sick, for God's commandment

should always be kept in death as well as in life, in sickness as well as in health. What will you say to this? It does not count to invent careless, lazy, unfounded excuses here; we are to do with serious matters, on which the salvation of the soul depends, so that one should answer honestly, uprightly, and thoroughly. Accordingly, if you should say, If I am imprisoned and forced to be alone, if I am sick that I cannot keep the other rules, it is enough that I have the will to keep them and that I act contrary to the rule against my will; God accepts the will, where the act cannot follow; then I say, My friend, that does not help; my vow rests on the deed and embraces not only the will but also the work prescribed in the rule.

282. Therefore, where the work does not follow, the vow is broken, or the vow excludes the possibility of the lack of ability. Otherwise, I, too, might take a woman and say, I do this unwillingly, and I would gladly by choice remain chaste, but it is impossible for me, my nature forces, seizes, and draws me on. Who in the world is there who would not prefer to live chaste and alone if he could do as he would? You must answer here differently.

283. Now, see, as in other points in religious vows impossibility is reserved (as no one can deny), and as no one sins, though he never in his life keeps the vow, because of impossibility, I should like to hear honest reasons why chastity alone must be observed, whether it is possible or impossible to observe it, and why not in the vow this condition should be made: I vow chastity, as far as it is possible for me. If we would speak without foolish talk, we must say that either the impossible chastity, like the other impossible things, shall never be vowed, or there never was a monk on earth. For there never has been one who has not at one time been sick or otherwise hindered that he had to leave undone certain parts of his rule which is contrary to his vow.

284. Concerning all this, it is in accord with their usual custom to leave such parts of the rule in the power of the abbot, that he may give his inferiors dispensation and excuse them from keeping what he will; not only because of impossibility, but also for convenience' sake, and as it seems good to him, all of which is contrary to the vow, where vows are to be understood without any condition. For what you vow to God to keep, no creature can take away. Now, you vow the whole rule and your prelate excuses you in whatever point he will or you have need, so that, without doubt, all monks' vows can be considered as having this meaning, I vow to keep the rule as far as is possible for me and agreeable to my superior. If that is not the contents and meaning of the vow, then all orders and cloisters are false and damnable, or there never has been a monk on earth. For no one has ever believed and regarded this point differently. Why, then, should not a superior have the

power to give a brother permission to become secular and to marry, when he sees how the fiery and restless temptations of the flesh are tormenting him? If he cannot release from the vow of chastity, how then can he release from the others? But if he can release from the others, why not also from the vow of chastity, for which there is so much more cause than for the others?

285. Therefore, it has come about that they have divided vows into *substantialia* and *accidentialia*; that is, some vows are fixed and others are removable. Of fixed vows, they have made three: poverty, chastity, and obedience. All the others, with the whole rule and order, they call removable.

286. What a rascal the devil is, and how full of a thousand tricks! If we ask them here for what reason they make such a difference, and who has given them the power to do this, they cannot say anything else than that they do it of their own power and without all reason and cause. For when they saw that it was impossible to vow the order and rule, and that it could not be kept, they thought, Well, what shall we do now; this is all vowed and will not be kept. If they should all be condemned, there is no monk in a state of holiness, and all orders and rules would be nothing else than impossible, foolish things. We will do thus with it. We will exclude three points that shall be called fixed, and whoever does not keep these shall be damned; the others shall be called removable and not damnable. And so it has also happened; so they all hold, practice, and teach. But wait, dear sirs, we have something to discuss with you about this.

287. If it is true that you have the power to make vows fixed and removable, you have also the power to condemn people and to save them. But tell me, how shall I be sure that this division of yours is right and pleasing to God? Who will quiet my conscience and assure it, when it is pressed with the commandment, *Vovete et reddite*? Do you think that it will be enough for me that you so divide, or that you point out how it is not to be observed? No, your division and non-observance will not satisfy me against this storm: *Vovete et reddite*. I have vowed not only the fixed vows, but the whole rule, with removable and fixed vows. The judge of all will not permit that I change his word and say, *Omnia vovete, aliqua reddite*; but he will say, *Quodcunque voveris, redde. Et iterum; Redde vota tua.*

288. Therefore, to exclude these three vows is surely a senseless, misleading thing, invented by mere human presumption, or all vows must be alike removable; for they are all vowed alike, demanded by the same commandment, and must alike be kept or given up. What can you say to this, dear sirs? You will say, Such a religious life is an impossible and useless thing. That is certainly true. We are fools; we vow and do not know what we vow. Afterward,

we would help ourselves and make possible, impossible, observe, let go, remove, and fix as it suits us. But the Highest will not permit us this; he will not allow his commandment to move this way and that according to our will.

289. You have learned such things from the pope; he, too, takes this commandment of God, *Vovete et reddite*, and stretches it as far as he will. He will set aside all vows, except those of chastity and pilgrimages to Rome, to Saint James, and to Jerusalem, and God's commandment is now taking this meaning, Vow chastity and a pilgrimage to Saint James, Rome, and Jerusalem; observe this; what you have vowed otherwise, you dare not observe. See, it is to be in his power which of God's commands are to be observed and what are not to be observed. Oh, thou cursed abomination, how impudent, how trifling is thy insolence toward thy God! But what reason and cause has he for this? No other but that chastity and pilgrimage are great things, and that the other vows are little.

Behold here the senseless fool and blasphemer who sets aside God's commandment if it commands a little thing and teaches to observe it if it commands a great thing. This is directly contrary to Christ, in Matthew 5:19, "Whosoever therefore shall break one of these least commandments, and shall teach men so, shall be called least in the kingdom of heaven." You should not hold, like the pope, that a thing is trifling. We listen to the command, *Vovete et reddite*, even in little things, while the religious orders do as their father, the pope, teaches them, and say, *Vovete et reddite* the three fixed vows, but *Vovete et non reddite* the removable vows. See, then, whether the religious orders are not the devil's own government and nature, founded on mere lies and blasphemy.

290. Is it not so, my dear man? Be it little or great, whatever is comprehended in God's commandments should and must be observed. One must here direct himself, not according to works, but according to the commandment. You must not consider whether the work is great or little, but only whether it is commanded. If it is commanded, there should be no neglecting it, be the case as it may. For Christ says, Not one jot or tittle shall pass from the law till all be fulfilled. But the pope and his disciples take away not only jot and tittle from this commandment, *Vovete et reddite*, but also letters, text, meaning, and everything.

291. The religious orders cannot deny that they vow removable vows which they include under the word *Vovete*; for they call them *Vota*, vows, although they change them into removable ones. So they can never deny that they are bound to observe these, and that they are also to remain under the word *Reddite*. Otherwise, you might be an enemy to your neighbor in your heart, and say

that you are not bound to love him, but that it is sufficient that you do not kill him, thus keeping the larger part of the fifth commandment and neglecting the smaller part. Henceforth, we could divide all God's commandments into great and small, or into removable and fixed parts, and say that we are not bound to observe the small or removable ones. This is contrary to God, although the pope and the universities thus hold and teach, and the religious orders follow them.

292. What shall we now do? If the religious orders hold all their vows and rules as fixed, who among them can be saved? Will you then condemn them all? I would not willingly condemn one, but would far rather that they all escaped from the cloisters or became holy in another way. In this way, they must certainly all be condemned, if they tear and twist God's Word according to their whims. I have discussed all this in order that I conclude beyond contradiction that all vows be made removable or all fixed and equal; one must be like the other. And if one among them can be given up with a good conscience for some cause, then the vow of chastity, too, and all the others can and should be given up, where need and cause demand. I hope I have now stopped the mouth of all gainsayers so that they, on this account, must be silent and have nothing to answer.

293. Since we now see plainly that the impossible vows must be given up, even by the holy people, and that God does not ask these of them, I shall have concluded that no vow will be otherwise accepted by God, or can otherwise be made, except with the restriction and meaning, If it is possible and pleases the Superior. Accordingly, we may give all young monks and nuns wives and husbands and let them re-enter secular life, where it is necessary, and where we cannot hold them with a good conscience so as to please God. By this means, we shall restore the cloisters to their original purity and nature as Christian schools, in which boys and girls learn discipline, reverence, and faith, after which they may freely remain there until death, or as long as they wish, if God has not otherwise planned and willed for them.

294. Further, we would have another encounter with them, that we may see how wholly confused and groundless a thing the "religious" life is. I grant that their dream of the three fixed vows, poverty, chastity, and obedience, is true. Poverty is of two kinds, spiritual and bodily. Concerning spiritual poverty Christ says, in Matthew 5:3, "Blessed are the poor in spirit: for theirs is the kingdom of heaven." This means that man is content and ready to deny himself all riches, and that he bears in his heart only a renounced desire for them, although he may have and control great riches, as Abraham,

Isaac, Jacob, and many pious Christians. This poverty of spirit is vowed by all Christians in common at baptism, and is not vowed by the religious orders; for their vow demands that the Christian, evangelical, common poverty first exist.

295. Bodily poverty means to possess or have no property outwardly. This is not possible. Christ neither demanded nor practiced it, for man cannot live without bodily food and clothing. Therefore, they have made it mean this that bodily purity is, not to have anything of one's own. This poverty, Luke has described in Acts 4:34, "For neither was there among them any that lacked: for as many as were possessors of lands or houses sold them and brought the prices of the things that were sold." Christ also practiced this, for his purse, which Judas carried, was common to all the apostles, so that John does not say that Judas had Christ's purse to carry, but, "Having the bag, took away what was put therein," in John 12:6. This word proves that the purse was common to all; otherwise, he had said, He had Christ's purse and carried what was given to Christ.

296. Now, see, Saint Bonaventura was a cardinal; Eugene, the pope, was Saint Bernhard's disciple, and many in religious orders have become bishops and popes. Tell me, what has become of their vow of poverty? They are always holy. And if their vow had not been removable and free before God, they would certainly have been damned, since they did not keep their vow until death. Now, popes, cardinals, and bishops always have their own property, and do with it what they will; which is directly contrary to the vow of poverty, so that being a pope, cardinal, or bishop is considered by everyone as secular, as over against the monkish orders.

297. Will you say here, They have followed obedience and have risen to a more perfect order, and do not have their own property but that of the church in their control? My dear man, observe what you say; are not these empty words? Or do you think to stop my mouth with this? Is it not so, dear brother? I would say, first, Obedience here, obedience there; to keep one's vows is God's commandment and obedience, from which we ought not follow even an angel, as Saint Paul says, in Galatians 1:8, "But though we, or an angel from heaven should preach unto you any gospel other than that which we have preached unto you, let him be anathema." Also Saint Peter, in Acts 5:29, "We must obey God rather than man." Have they now left God's obedience for the sake of the pope's obedience? Then they have left heaven for hell. No, you dare not thus throw away God's commandment and obedience. Then I, too, would say that you may depart also from the vow of chastity for the pope's sake, and set aside all God's commandments. If you can set aside one command of God, for the sake of men, then you can set them all aside.

298. Secondly, even if the orders of pope, cardinals, and bishop were a perfect order, we ought, nevertheless, not free ourselves from God's commandment. For without God's commandment there is no order, much less a perfect order, but nothing but error and seduction. Perfection is not contrary to God's commandment, but it much rather follows God's commandments and sees none but observes all. See, with what great lies and foolishness the people have to do, that it does not know what and of what it speaks, that it establishes perfection without God's commandment, and wishes thereby to abolish God's commandment. But now, because the orders of pope, bishop, and cardinal form a real aristocracy, and are the most imperfect, we shall not keep these saints, unless we confess that all vows exist before God only for a time and can be changed, as we see that this vow of poverty is here changed. For why should not the vow of chastity be changed on account of necessity and cause, since it is not vowed more strongly than poverty? But now let it be that such saints have passed out of the vow of poverty into the perfect state, then you must grant me that the state of matrimony is perfect over against the state of unchastity, or against impossible chastity, as Saint Paul says, in 1 Corinthians 7:9, "It is better to marry than to burn." It is always better to have a lawful wife than to live with a woman unlawfully or to burn. Well, then, let those pass out into this perfect state of marriage who hold an unchaste chastity or an imperfect, unwilling state of chastity; or, if you will not have that, then your excuse of the perfect state counts for nothing.

299. In the third place, how can you be so bold as to say that the vow of poverty is not broken for the reason that they care not for their own property, but for that of the church. If that now were true, in what were they better than a secular servant or official? Why then do you not consider these also as "religious," since they do not control their own property? This is empty, foolish chatter. But now is it not true that the bishops hold property of their own, and that, in respect of poverty, their life is a thousand miles removed from that of the monks? Accordingly, nothing can be claimed here; you must acknowledge that poverty is vowed no further than the prelate wishes or cause demands, if we would keep our saints.

300. And what is the need of so much round-about talk? It is clear that a man in a religious order vows only the childish, slavish poverty, which consists in this that he has no property in his hands, but is subordinate and takes what people give him. As soon, however, as he comes into power and stands before others to administer property, he is no longer under the vow of poverty, unless he is deposed and again becomes subordinate. For what difference is there between such a ruler and the secular housefather or official, as far as having,

using, ruling over, and administering property is concerned? These are only feigned words, as Saint Peter says, what men speak to the contrary: in reality, it is a purely secular office, work, and order. Therefore, we see that God does not accept vows, unless they be free and removable; otherwise, no cloister could have a prelate; so that necessity compels us to support the cloisters or schools for the training of young people.

301. In the same way, obedience may and cannot be understood otherwise than as childish and slavish obedience; for the words of the vow clearly demand obedience to the abbot or prior. If, then, one becomes a bishop or prelate, what becomes of his vow of obedience? People must now be obedient to him, and he is not obedient.

302. Will you again bring forward your foolish pretense that such a one passes into a higher obedience, or keeps his heart willing to become again obedient? All this has already been set aside; for it says, *Vovete et reddite.* Against this word, there is no gloss; God will not have his command destroyed for the sake of either higher, middle, or lower obedience. It is clear, then, that those in the religious orders vow a subjection, not of the heart, but only of the body; for the willing subjection of the heart toward everyone is common to all Christians, as Saint Paul says, in Romans 12:10, "In love of the brethren be tenderly affectioned one to another; in honor preferring one another." But now again, the cloisters dare have no prelates and supply no bishops; or the word subjection ends with the vow. See, therefore, how cleverly those two vows are called immovable and what fables and feigned words they use. God allows his saints both to vow and to live; he suffers their folly, but he does not accept the fixed vows, as you see from all this discussion, since they are contrary to Christian liberty and all good order, and exist only that Satan may have his sport with the unbelieving, and may work his deception in them, as Saint Paul teaches.

303. Now there remains only the vow of chastity; that alone must remain fixed and unchangeable which justly should be the first of all and most removable. In all the others, they say *Vovete et non reddite;* here alone, it is like iron and steel, *Vovete et reddite.* Is not this a horrible perversion? But Satan has done it for this reason, that he may the more firmly hold souls in unchastity, and he grasps just where they are the weakest and most easily held; for he saw clearly that all other vows could be more easily kept. Accordingly, he did not insist upon them; but he insists upon this impossible thing alone, that he may be sure of his tyranny. Alas, O God, what illusion and foolery does he carry on with the religious orders!

304. We find then in the whole "religious" life nothing fundamental, certain, or permanent; everything shakes and moves without Scripture or reason,

so that there is cause enough that we should run away from the whole thing. There is the special reason that it has no Scripture foundation, and that it has so many kinds of errors and lies in its leading points. Moreover, it is so condemned and cursed by Christ in Matthew 24, by Saint Paul in 2 Timothy 3, by Saint Peter, in 2 Peter 2, that, if you had taken ten vows and you saw that it was the devil's doing and against God, you would be obliged to give it up or to vow in a new, free way, as has been said above.

305. They have one thing that they advance: There have been holy fathers in the religious orders. But here they should be terrified when Christ says, that the elect may be deceived by them, as here the magi were deceived by Herod, and many other examples. The three children of Israel, Ananias [Hananiah], Azarias [Azariah] and Misael [Mishael], remained in the fiery oven of Babylon. Naaman the Syrian alone remained pious in the temple of the false god. Joseph remained pious in Egypt. What shall I say? Saint Agnes remained chaste in an ordinary brothel, and the martyrs remained pious in dungeons, and Christians still daily remain pious in the flesh, in the world, and in the midst of devils. Could God, then, not have been able to preserve Francis, Bernhard, and their like in the midst of error and, although they have sometimes erred, to rescue them from this error again?

306. He has allowed hardly any great saint to live without error. He allowed Moses and Aaron and Miriam, David, Solomon and Hezekiah, and many more to stumble, that no one should rely without Scripture upon the mere example and work of the saints. But we throw in whatever we see and hear of the saints, and so we come upon and generally find that as men they have erred in their infirmity. This error has then to be for us a fundamental truth, and thus we build on the crooked wall of which Psalm 62:3–4 speaks, "How long will ye set upon a man, that ye may slay him, all of you; like a leaning wall, like a tottering fence. They only consult to thrust him down from his dignity; they delight in lies. They bless with their mouth, but they curse inwardly."

307. But if all other things were good in the priesthood, the abuse of the Mass would be enough to cause one to flee wherever one hears of it. I think that such abuse of the holy sacrament is reserved for this order as the worst, most destructive, and horrible that has come upon earth, and which will be the greatest and last among evil things. Thus they make out of the Mass a sacrifice and a good work which they sell to people and make all kinds of money out of it. Oh, the terrible perversion! What wrath ought it not merit? Would to God that all secondary masses were done away with; then there might be hope that God would be a little more merciful to us. But now, blinded as we are, we think that we should commit a great sin if we were to drop the

masses; and we intend with such horrible abuse to propitiate and serve God. Thus there is no end to his wrath, and all our prayer becomes only sin, as Psalm 109:1–7 has declared. Only one Mass a day should be held, and this should be treated as a sacrament for all, yes, one Mass a week would be still better. But the matter cannot be improved; it is too deeply seated.

308. This utterance I wish to have made for the benefit of whom will use it; it makes no difference to me if the priests are angry at and cry over me. I prefer that they should be angry rather than Christ. I know that I am obliged to advise and help wretched consciences and souls, and to share with everyone that which God has given me. I will not leave the blame upon myself. I shall not be responsible for the man who does not accept it; he must take care of himself. He has my true service and advice so far; if I could do more for him, I would do more. Whoever will, can enter and remain in a religious order; but whoever wishes to be saved, must see to it that he becomes a Christian, and let priests and monks be priests and monks.

309. Here, probably, the chaste hearts and holy priests of God, whom nothing pleases except what they themselves speak and write, will pucker up their mouths, and say, Oh, how the cowl presses the monk, how he wishes he had a wife! But let them slander and enjoy their malice, the chaste hearts and great saints; let them be iron and steel, as they set themselves up to be; but do you not deny that you are a man of flesh and blood, and let God afterward judge between the strong, angelic heroes and you, the poor, despised sinner. I hope I have come so far that, by the grace of God, I shall remain as I am, although I am not yet over the mountain, and I do not venture to compare myself with the chaste hearts. I should be sorry to do this, and may God in his mercy keep me from it. For if you know them, who they are who pretend so great chastity and make a show of discipline, and what it is that Saint Paul says, in Ephesians 5:12, "For the things which are done by them in secret it is a shame even to speak of," you would not consider their much-praised chastity fit for a whore to wipe her shoe with. Here, too, the perversion is found, that the chaste are the unchaste, and that whatever glitters, deceives.

310. Dear youth, do not be ashamed that you desire a girl, and that the girl desires a boy; only let this result in marriage, not unchastity, and then it is no more a disgrace than eating and drinking. Celibacy ought to be a virtue which happens among God's miracles, as the instance of a man who neither eats nor drinks. It is beyond healthy nature, not to mention sinful, fallen nature. God has not let many virgins live long, but quickly hastened them out of the world, as Caccilia, Agnes, Lucia, Agatha, and their like, for he well knows how noble the treasure is, and how difficult it is to preserve long. If in every

city there were five young men and five young women, twenty years old and entirely pure who had discovered nothing of the natural flowings, then I could say that Christianity of today were better than in the times of the apostles and martyrs.

311. Alas, Lord God, I consider that in no other way has unchastity been able to spread faster or more terribly than through such a command and vow of chastity. What a Sodom and Gomorrah that the devil established through such a command and vow, and how altogether vile has he made this same chastity to indescribable wretchedness. There is neither the common house of prostitution nor any other allurement so destructive in this command and vow invented by the devil himself.

312. Here I shall say something of the boys and girls who have taken the vow before they felt what flesh and blood are, when they were only fifteen, sixteen, or twenty years old. These should be taken out at once, if they so desire; for their vow is as yet nothing at all, as if a child had engaged itself to marry. Here the Shrove Tuesday consecration is not to be regarded, whether the man be a priest, a deacon, or hold any other religions rank. Such consecration is jugglery and counts for nothing with God. But enough of this; let us come again to our subject, where we left it.

313. When the wise men came from Herod, and turned to Bethlehem, the star appeared to them again, and they became very glad. This always happens when, after the error and deception of human teaching, the heart comes again to the knowledge of the pure truth and of the Gospel. Then at once it is free from Herod and sees how altogether certain and light the way of the truth is, over against the appearances that the Herodians pretend; so the heart is made glad. For the Gospel is a comforting doctrine, which leads us out of human presumption into the confidence of the pure grace of God, as Psalm 4:7–8 says.

314. Again, all who wander in the teachings of men and in their own strength, lead a hard, anxious life, and still it does not help them. What heart should not rejoice to discover that the pope's rule is merely trouble and burden for the conscience, and that it deceives the whole world with its pretense. Heavenly light and truth has this nature, that it lifts up the conscience, comforts the heart, and creates a free spirit; just as, on the other hand, the teaching of men naturally oppresses the conscience, tortures the heart, and quenches the spirit.

315. The star thus goes before them and does not leave them until it brings them to Christ, yet it goes no farther, but remains at rest over where the child is. So, too, the light of the holy Gospel does; it is as a light in the

darkness, as Saint Peter calls it, in 2 Peter 1:19, and goes before us and leads us, if we only cherish it with a strong faith; it does not leave us until it brings us to Christ and to the truth; but it goes no further for, besides Christ, it teaches us nothing.

316. Accordingly, in this leading of a star, the manner and work of the Gospel is shown, and through the wise men all believers; so that, as the star led them bodily to Christ, and they followed it in the body, so the Gospel spiritually guides the hearts of men in this world, and believing hearts see it and follow it with joy until they come to Christ.

So, too, Saint Paul boasts, in 1 Corinthians 2:2, "For I determined not to know anything among you, save Jesus Christ and him crucified." And in Colossians 2:8, he forbids us to follow any doctrine which does not teach Christ. What else is this than that the star points to Christ alone, and nothing else, and goes no farther? In this figure, therefore, all doctrines of men are condemned, and should no longer be preached to Christians, but only the pure, simple light of the Gospel is to be preached, and we should follow this star only. Therefore, pope, bishops, priests, and monks, with all their rule and teachings, are here condemned, and are to be avoided as the tyranny of Herod.

317. Here, too, the mouth of the papists and Herodians is closed, and their lies rightly punished, since they teach with deliberate sacrilege that we can find the Christian Church and faith only with them; and whoever does not hear them, should be considered as if he did not hear the Christian Church. They wish to be the sign and the star that leads to Christ, but this is all a lie. Do you wish to know where Christ and the truth are? Learn that here from this history. Do not look to the pope nor to the bishops, nor to the universities and monasteries. Do not be led astray by their abundant preaching, praying, singing, and holding of masses. Do not mind that they sit in the place of the apostles and usurp spiritual jurisdiction that may all deceive, and does deceive continuously; they are in error and teach error. There is only one sure sign whereby you can recognize where Christ and his church are, namely, the star, the holy Gospel; all else is false. But where the Gospel is preached, there this star shines; there Christ certainly is; there you surely find the church, whether it be in Turkey, Russia, Bohemia, or anywhere else. It is not possible that God's Word should be heard, and God, Christ, and the Holy Ghost not be there. On the other hand, it is not possible that God, Christ, the Holy Ghost, the church, or anything holy should be where God's Word is not heard, even if they worked all miracles; but there can be only Herodians and the devil's rule at such a place. Now everyone can see how the pope and the clergy are occupied not with God's Word but with human teaching.

And they came into the house and saw the young child with Mary
his mother; and they fell down and worshiped him.

319. This house is the Christian Church, the assembly of all believers on earth, in which alone you can find Christ and his mother; for in the Christian Church alone are those who, being filled by the Holy Ghost, bring forth the fruits of Christianity and lead a Christian life. Everything that is outside of this house, however beautiful it may appear, however reasonable it may be, has neither Christ nor his mother; that is, there is no Christian there, for these cannot exist without faith and the Holy Ghost.

320. Therefore, if the pope, bishops, or anyone else demand of you that you should look to them, if you wish to see the church, then think of this Gospel, and look to the star. Be assured that where the star does not stand, there is not the house where Christ and his mother are to be found. In other words, where the Gospel does not give its light, there the Christian Church is certainly not found. This star will never fail you and, without it, you will never arrive at the right place. It leads to this house and remains over this house and, just so, the Gospel brings you into the church, and remains over the church, keeping its place and not letting itself be driven away by any persecution. Here it sounds and shines freely and clearly, to the vexation of all its enemies, as we see entirely fulfilled in the apostles, martyrs, and all saints, and still daily, where it is preached.

And opening their treasures they offered unto him gifts,
gold and frankincense and myrrh.

321. All bodily sacrifices in the law of Moses, wherever they occur, point to the spiritual sacrifice of which Hebrews 13:15 speaks, "Through him let us offer up a sacrifice of praise to God continually, that is, the fruit of the lips which make confession to his name." And in Hosea 14:1–2, "O Israel, return unto Jehovah thy God; for thou hast fallen by thine iniquity. Take with you words, and return unto Jehovah; say unto him, Take away all iniquity, and accept that which is good," that is, take away the evil, which thou bringest over us through thy hand, and take the good into thy hand, that thou mayest give it to us; "so will we render as bullocks the offering of our lips," that is, praise and thanksgiving. These are the true bullocks that we should offer thee, of which also Psalm 51:21 speaks, "Do good in thy good pleasure unto Zion: Build thou the walls of Jerusalem. Then wilt thou delight in the sacrifices of righteousness, then will they offer bullocks upon thine altar." Also in Psalm 50:7–15, "Hear, O Israel, I am thy God. I will not reprove thee for thy sacrifices.

What will you offer me? Will I eat the flesh of bulls, or drink the blood of goats? If I were hungry I would not tell thee: For the world is mine, and all the birds of the mountains, and the wild beasts of the field. Offer unto God the sacrifice of thanksgiving; and pay thy vows unto the highest. The sacrifice of thanksgiving honors me, and that is the way to salvation." From these verses, we can see that sacrifice, if it is to find favor before God, must be praise and thanksgiving, or at least not without praise and thanksgiving. And where a sacrifice is offered without praise and thanksgiving, he will reject it, as he says, in Isaiah 1:11, "What unto me is the multitude of your sacrifices? I have had enough of the burnt offerings."

322. Moreover, we could not give God anything else, for everything is his already, and we have everything from him; praise, thanks, and honor only we can give him. So also Psalm 116:12–13 teaches, "What shall I render unto Jehovah for all his benefits towards me? I will take the cup of salvation and call upon the name of Jehovah. Thou hast loosed my bonds, I will offer to thee the sacrifice of thanksgiving." Now, praise is nothing else than recognizing the favor received from God, and ascribing this, not to ourselves, but to him. And this praise and confession is rendered in two ways; first before God alone, and then before men, and is a true work and fruit of faith. Saint Paul teaches of this in Romans 10:9–10, "If thou shalt confess with thy mouth Jesus as Lord, and shalt believe in thy heart that God raised him from the dead, thou shalt be saved: for with the heart man believeth unto righteousness; and with the mouth confession is made unto salvation." This is as though Saint Paul were to say, That is not the true faith, if you were to believe in Christ secretly in your heart and praise him in some hidden place; you must freely confess him with your mouth before everyone, even as you believe in your heart. This perhaps may cost you your life. For devils and men do not like to hear such confession, and the cross goes with such confession, as you see that even now the pope, bishops, priests, and monks cannot bear or endure Christ's Word, so that the prophet well says, "I will take the wholesome cup, and preach the name of the Lord." This is as though he were to say, If I praise and confess God, they will afflict and persecute me with the cup of the martyrs; well, I will take it in God's name, and not cease from praising God. He will not harm me, but will be a Savior to me, and help me quickly to salvation. This, Christ, too, will do, in Mark 8:38, "For whosoever shall be ashamed of me and my words in this adulterous and sinful generation, the Son of man also shall be ashamed of him, when he cometh in the glory of his Father with the holy angels."

323. Many have commented upon these three offerings, one in this way, another in that, yet all agree that it is a threefold confession. Therefore, we shall take from all what seems true to us. The offering of gold, they say, means that they confess Christ as king; the frankincense, that he is a priest; the myrrh, that he died and was buried. All three articles apply to Christ according to his human nature; yet so that he is God, and that such things have happened to his humanity because of his divinity.

324. In the first place, the Christian faith confesses and rejoices that Christ is a king and lord over all things, according to the sayings of Psalm 8:6, "Thou makest him to have dominion over the works of thy hands; thou hast put all things under his feet."

Also in Psalm 110:1, "Jehovah saith unto my Lord, Sit thou at my right hand, until I make thine enemies thy footstool."

This confession of the true faith is a high and strong defense and boast for all who believe in Christ against all that is against them, though it be, as Saint Paul says, in Romans 8:36, sword, hunger, cold, or any other creature. Who can injure or terrify a Christian, if he offers this gold, believes and confesses that his Lord Christ is Lord also over death, hell, over the devils and over all other creatures, and that everything lies in his hands, yes, under his feet?

325. If anyone has a gracious prince, he fears nothing that is under the power of this prince; he boasts of glories and declares his master's favor and power. How much more does a Christian boast and glory against pain, death, hell, and the devil, and say confidently to him, What can you do to me? Are you not under the feet of my Lord? Attach and devour me without his will! See, such a free heart makes this offering of gold. Oh, how rare has that become! Therefore, it is truly comforting, if anything terrifies or injures you, to come out openly, confess Christ, and say, *Omnia subjecisti sub pedibus ejus,* all things are under his feet; who will then be against me?

326. In the second place, they use incense in divine services, according to the law of Moses, to burn incense in the temple, which pertains to the office of priest. Therefore, to offer incense is nothing else than to recognize Christ as a priest who is an intercessor between God and us, as Saint Paul says, in Romans 8:34, that he speaks for us, and is our intercessor before God, which is most necessary for us. For through his kingdom and rule, he protects us against evil in all things; but through his priesthood, he defends us against all sin and the wrath of God, takes his place before us, and offers himself to propitiate God, that we through him may have confidence toward God, and that our conscience may not be terrified before his wrath and judgment, as Saint

Paul says, in Romans 5:12, "Through him we have peace with God and access by faith into his grace."

327. Now, this is a much greater thing, that he makes us safe toward God and sets our consciences at peace, that God and ourselves are not at enmity, than that he should make the creatures harmless to us. For guilt is much greater than pain, and sin than death, since sin brings death, and without sin there would be no death, or it would not be injurious. As Christ is now Lord over sin and death, and has it in his power to give grace and life to all who believe on him; so to offer gold and incense is to recognize these two offices and works of his, and to thank him, as Saint Paul does, in 1 Corinthians 15:55–56, "O death, where is thy victory? O death, where is thy sting? The sting of death is sin; and the power of sin is the law; but thanks be to God, who giveth us the victory through our Lord Jesus Christ."

328. This is surely a strong defense, that a man can set this high priest against his sin, against his bad conscience, against God's terrible anger and judgment, and with unshaken faith say and confess, *Tu es saderdos in aeternum*, thou art a high priest forever. But, if thou art a high priest, thou intercedest for all sin of those who confess you as such a priest. As little as God's judgment and anger, sin, and a bad conscience may condemn or terrify you, do they condemn and terrify me, for whom thou art such a priest. See, this is to offer true incense, to be undismayed against all sin and the wrath of God through faith in Christ.

329. In the third place, they used myrrh to anoint dead bodies, that they should not corrupt in the grave. Therefore, the death and resurrection of Christ are here set forth; since it is he alone who died and was buried and is not corrupted, but arose again from the dead, as Psalm 16:10 says, "For thou wilt not leave my soul to Sheol, neither wilt thou suffer thy holy one to see corruption." And his incorruptibility is indicated through all who are preserved and kept through bodily myrrh. Accordingly, to offer myrrh is as much as to confess that Christ died and yet remained incorrupt, that is, that death has been overcome by life, and that he never died according to his divinity, and that his human nature again awoke from death.

330. This confession is the most important of all the three, although all three are necessary and must be undivided. For, since he has become a king and priest for you, and given you so great a possession, you must not think that it has been done in vain, or that it has cost little, or come to you through your own merit. Sin and death have been overcome for you in him and through him, and grace and life given you; but it was bitter for him, and cost him much, and has been bought for a high price, namely, with his own blood,

body, and life. For it was impossible to put away God's wrath and judgment, conscience, hell, death, and every evil thing; divine righteousness must be satisfied, sin atoned for, and death overcome by justice. Accordingly, it was Saint Paul's practice, when he preached God's grace in Christ, to mention his suffering and blood together, that he might show how all our good things have been given through Christ, but not without his unspeakable merit and cost, as he says in Romans 3:25, "God has set him forth, to be a propitiation through faith." Also in 1 Corinthians 2:2, "For I determined not to know anything among you, save Jesus Christ, and him crucified," etc. Therefore, to offer myrrh is to confess the great cost and pains that it meant for Christ to become our priest and king.

331. See, these are the three parts in which we should praise and confess his three works which he has shown us, and will show us daily until the day of judgment. And the order, too, is fine: but the evangelist puts gold in the first place. For it would not be possible that he should be king over all things for our good, if he had not first reconciled us to God and assured our conscience, that with calm and peace he might rule and work in us as in his own kingdom. Accordingly, he must first be priest for us. But, if he is to be priest and to reconcile us to God according to his priestly office, he must fulfill God's righteousness for us. But there was no other satisfaction; he had to give himself to death and, in his own person, overcome sin with death. So, too, through death he came to the priesthood, through his priesthood to the kingdom, thus receiving the myrrh before the incense, and the incense before the gold. But the Scripture at all times declares the kingdom to be first, then the priesthood and, finally, his death, as Psalm 110:1–7 also does, which Psalm describes for the first time his kingdom, as follows, "Jehovah saith unto my lord, Sit thou at my right hand, until I make thine enemies thy footstool." It follows, then, from his priesthood thus, "Jehovah hath sworn, and will not repent: Thou art a priest forever after the order of Melchizedek." Finally, he closes with his martyrdom thus, "He will drink of the brook in the way: Therefore will he lift up his head." Here, too, he wishes to say, He will taste the myrrh, therefore he will become a priest; he is a priest and therefore he will also be king; so that one follows from the other; one is the cause of the other, and they follow one upon another.

332. With these simple and plain interpretations, I let the matter rest, and commend the lofty considerations to people of leisure. Here it concerns us most to have care that we do not take any one of these three confessions alone, but offer them together. And although Isaiah 60:6 speaks of gold and incense only, and is silent about the myrrh, it may readily be on this account,

namely, that Christ's kingdom and priesthood have been from the beginning of the world, as Saint Paul says, in Hebrews 13:8, "Jesus Christ is the same yesterday and today, yea and for ever." For all the saints have been redeemed from death and sin through him and his faith; and yet at that time, the third part, his Passion, the myrrh, had not yet been accomplished, which properly belonged to the evangelist to announce after its fulfillment.

333. But the Herodians and papists have not only separated these three offerings, but also by an unspeakable outrage have destroyed them, retaining, however, the names and confessing with words that Christ is a king and priest, and that he has died for us. However, with other, contradictory words they deny all this with the heart and their whole life, and condemn it in the most shameful way. We, to observe such a thing, have begun with the myrrh, but they teach that man, without the grace of God, of himself and from the natural power of his reason and free will, may make himself worthy and receptive of divine favor. What else is this than to desire, without Christ's blood and suffering, to satisfy through one's own act the divine righteousness, to appease the worth and judgment of God, and to give the conscience peace? This is indeed to make nothing of Christ's blood and all his suffering, yea, his whole humanity and all his work, to regard them as useless and to tread them under foot, of which Saint Paul says, in Hebrews 6:5–6, "It is impossible to renew to repentance those who fell away; seeing they crucify to themselves the Son of God afresh, and put him to an open shame." For without Christ, there is no grace nor repentance, but wrath only. Nevertheless, the papists teach that we can seek and find grace without him. Accordingly, the offering of myrrh is entirely done away with.

334. Then the offering of incense must first cease to be. For how shall Christ be their priest and intercessor, if they are so good and pure that they do not need his blood and intercession, but intercede through themselves, and stand of themselves before God, and attain grace and eternal life through their own ability?

Thereby they confess and teach that natural ability is pure and good and, therefore, Christ need not be priest. Who would ever have believed that Christians would arrive at such a stage when someone would teach and hear such things which are dreadful to think of?

335. But now, we see that all higher schools as well as the pope and his clergy do not teach and hold differently, yes, they condemn as heresy whatever does not conform to their teaching. How clearly has Peter described them, when he says, in 2 Peter 2:1, "Among you also there shall be false teachers, denying even the Master that bought them." He does not say, They will

deny Christ, but "the Master that bought them," as if he wished to say, Christ they will confess with words; but they will not regard him as having bought them with his blood; but without his blood they will redeem themselves, through their own natural power they will attain God's grace, which Christ alone has bought for us all with his blood. This is what they mean, when they say that it costs and affords nothing to attain God's grace. Therefore, they wish to redeem themselves and cannot bear to hear of Christ's redemption.

336. Where, however, Christ is not acknowledged as priest, there he is much less acknowledged as king. For they are in no wise subject to him; they are their own masters, that is, the devil's own household. Although they do not suffer him to rule over them and to exercise his power in them, he is, nevertheless, a king, priest, and redeemer, without their consent, over all creatures. Behold, thus you see that now is the time when Saint Peter thrice denies Christ. Would to God that they would hear the cock's crow, that they would recover from their error, acknowledge their fall, cry bitterly, and go out from the house of Caiaphas, that is, out from the diabolical assembly of the pope, where the fire of worldly love has been kindled, and where the pope's household is to warm itself; for the divine love is utterly extinguished in them. Let this suffice of the spiritual offerings. We come now to,

And being warned of God in a dream that they should not return
to Herod, they departed into their own country another way.

337. This is the outcome and end, namely, that we are to shun human teaching, and are not to relapse into it, when we have once been redeemed therefrom; just as the wise men, having once been freed from Herod, do not return to him. Thus I also say that we are to shun the pope's and all papists' law and teaching, if we do not wish to incur God's displeasure and hazard our soul's salvation, since we have already experienced the true evangelical truth. For their teaching brings us away from God and makes us follow our own reason and work. Thereby God's work is hindered, who should and would give us and work in us all things, and who desires us also to expect that of him.

338. Human teaching, however, leads us so that we just begin all works, desire to be the first ones to seek God, and that we then expect God to come after a while and to look at what we have begun. Let me give you this for an example: Those that seem to be the best teachers of young people say to them that they are willing to pray and to go to church, to live chaste, and to be pious; however, they do not tell them where they are to begin and to seek all this; just as it were enough that they had instructed them to be pious. Again, when after this they are to marry or to enter orders, they think it is enough

that they themselves have begun, they do not look at God, neither do they consult him about it; but, when they have begun, then they want God to come, to see what they have made and to be satisfied with it.

339. Yes, the young people are educated so that a girl is ashamed to ask God for a young man, and a young man to ask God for a girl; they consider it foolish to ask God for a such a thing, they want to do it themselves. Ought not a girl to be taught with all earnestness to come to God and to say with all confidence, See, dear God, I have become old enough to marry, be thou my Father and let me be thy child, give me a pious young man, and graciously help me to enter the estate of matrimony or, if it pleases thee, give me a spirit to remain chaste. Thus also a young man is to ask for a girl, and is to begin nothing himself, but is to ask God that he may begin and to lay the first stone. These would be true children of God indeed, who begin nothing but consult God about it, no matter how insignificant it may be. Thus Christ would remain our king, and all our works would be his works and would be done well. But human teachings do not allow this, they act as if there is no God, and as if they would have to do whatever is to be done well. Behold, from these examples you can learn how all human teaching is seductive and against God.

340. There are, however, three ways in which human teaching can be avoided: first, that it is avoided by the conscience only and not by the deed. For instance, when I confess, pray, and fast according to the pope's canon, not as if it were necessary for us to do so, or as if it were sin, if I were not to do it; but when I do it willingly, of my own accord, not compelled by necessity, when I can leave it undone, if I wish so. Here the deed is under human teaching, but the conscience is free, it considers the doing no more nor no less than the not doing, it does not think it a sin to neglect it, nor a good work to do it; for it is not obedient but does it of its own accord. This is the best way.

341. Thus the wise men are still in Herod's land, they also travel under his rule, but they do not regard him, do not come to him, and are not obedient to him. He, therefore, who now also is under the pope, and who observes his law, not for the sake of obedience, but of his own accord, how, when, where, and as long as he pleases, he, I say, suffers no harm. This understanding, however, is above the average mind and is found with but few people, and as it was given to the wise men secretly in their sleep, so we experience it only in our heart through God's Spirit; it cannot be given to anyone with a heart from without, if the heart itself does not receive it from heaven.

342. The second way is that human teaching is avoided by the conscience as well as by deeds, as those do who trample it under foot and only do the contrary with a glad secure conscience. And this way is the most necessary and

best for weak consciences that they may be liberated and made strong, perfect, and free, as the foregoing. This cannot be very readily accomplished with words and conscience alone, if you do not show the contrary by examples; just as Christ did, who allowed his disciples, contrary to the law of the Pharisees, to neglect to wash their hands. Thus it were good, if we would neglect the prescribed confession, prayer, and fasting for a certain time and show by examples that the pope's laws are foolery and deception, and if we would at another time do all this of our own accord.

343. The third way is that it is avoided by the deed alone and not by the conscience, as those do who boldly neglect human teaching and still believe that they do wrong in not observing it. And alas, such a conscience is ever to be found among the common people. For their sake, Saint Paul calls these times grievous times, in 2 Timothy 3:1. For such consciences sin continually whether they observe or do not observe, and the pope with his law is the murderer of their souls and the cause of such danger and sin. If they observe, they do it against faith, which is to be free from all human teaching. If they do not observe, they do it against their conscience which believes that it must be observed. It is necessary that these are well instructed in the free Christian faith, and that they put aside this false conscience or, if they are not able to do this, that we bear their infirmities for a time, as Saint Paul teaches in Romans 15:1, and that we suffer them to follow and observe such a conscience together with faith, until they also have become large and strong.

344. Behold, this is the other way to depart into one's own country and not to return to Herod. For generally, when people begin to be pious, they do it through human teaching and outward holiness, but we must abandon this and come to pure faith and not suffer ourselves again to fall from faith into works. Thus we surely come into our fatherland, from which we have come, that is, to God, by whom we have been created. The end thus comes together with the beginning as in a golden ring. God grant this through Christ, our king and priest, who be blessed to all eternity.

The First Sunday in Lent

❦

The Fast and the Temptation of Christ

T hen was Jesus led up of the Spirit into the wilderness to be tempted of the devil. And when he had fasted forty days and forty nights, he afterward hungered. And the tempter came and said unto him, "If thou art the Son of God, command that these stones become bread." But he answered and said, "It is written, Man shall not live by bread alone, but by every word that proceedeth out of the mouth of God." Then the devil taketh him into the holy city; and he set him on the pinnacle of the temple, and saith unto him, "If thou art the Son of God, cast thyself down: for it is written, 'He shall give his angels charge concerning thee: 'and,' On their hands they shall bear thee up, lest haply thou dash thy foot against a stone.'"

Jesus said unto him, Again it is written, Thou shalt not make trial of the Lord thy God. Again, the devil taketh him unto an exceeding high mountain, and showeth him all the kingdoms of the world, and the glory of them; and he said unto him, All these things will I give thee, if thou wilt fall down and worship me. Then saith Jesus unto him, Get thee hence, Satan: for it is written, Thou shalt worship the Lord thy God, and him only shalt thou serve. Then the devil leaveth him; and behold, angels came and ministered unto him.
— MATTHEW 4:1–11

I. THE FASTING OF CHRIST

1. This Gospel is read today at the beginning of Lent in order to picture before Christians the example of Christ, that they may rightly observe Lent, which has become mere mockery: first, because no one can follow this example and fast forty days and nights as Christ did without eating any food. Christ rather followed the example of Moses, who fasted also forty days and nights, when he received the law of God on Mount Sinai. Thus Christ also wished to fast when he was about to bring to us, and give expression to, the new law.

In the second place, Lent has become mere mockery because our fasting is a perversion and an institution of man. For although Christ did fast forty days, yet there is no word of his that he requires us to do the same and fast as he did. Indeed, he did many other things, which he wishes us not to do; but whatever he calls us to do or leave undone, we should see to it that we have his Word to support our actions.

2. But the worst of all is that we have adopted and practiced fasting as a good work: not to bring our flesh into subjection, but, as a meritorious work before God, to atone for our sins and obtain grace. And it is this that has made our fasting a stench and so blasphemous and shameful, so that no drinking and eating, no gluttony and drunkenness, could have been as bad and foul. It would have been better had people been drunk day and night than to fast thus. Moreover, even if all had gone well and right, so that their fasting had been applied to the mortification of the flesh, but since it was not voluntary, and it was not left to each to do according to their own free will, but was compulsory by virtue of human commandment, and they did it unwillingly, it was all lost and to no purpose. I will not mention the many other evils as the consequences, as that pregnant mothers and their offspring, the sick and the weak, were thereby ruined, so that it might be called a fasting of Satan instead of a fasting unto holiness. Therefore, we will carefully consider how this Gospel teaches us by the example of Christ what true fasting is.

3. The Scriptures present to us two kinds of true fasting: one, by which we try to bring the flesh into subjection to the spirit, of which Saint Paul speaks in 2 Corinthians 6:5, "In labors, in watchings, in fastings." The other is that which we must bear patiently, and yet receive willingly, because of our need and poverty, of which Saint Paul speaks in 1 Corinthians 4:11, "Even unto this present hour we both hunger, and thirst," and Christ in Matthew 9:15, "When the bridegroom shall be taken away from them, then will they fast." This kind of fasting, Christ teaches us here while in the wilderness alone, without anything to eat, and while he suffers his penury without murmuring. The first kind of fasting, one can end whenever he wills, and can satisfy it by food; but the other kind, we must observe and bear until God himself changes it and satisfies us. Hence it is much more precious than the first, because it moves in greater faith.

4. This is also the reason that the evangelist with great care places it first: Then was Jesus led up of the Spirit into the wilderness, that he might there fast and be tempted, so that no one might imitate his example of their own choice and make of it a selfish, arbitrary, and pleasant fasting; but instead wait for the Spirit, who will send him enough fastings and temptations. For whoever,

without being led by the Spirit, wantonly resorts to the danger of hunger or to any temptation, when it is truly a blessing of God that he can eat and drink and have other comforts, tempts God. We should not seek want and temptation; they will surely come of themselves. We ought then do our best and act honestly. The text reads, Jesus was led up of the Spirit into the wilderness, and not, Jesus himself chose to go into the wilderness. "For as many as are led by the Spirit of God, these are sons of God," Romans 8:14. God gives his blessings for the purpose that we may use them with thanksgiving, and not that we may let them lie idle, and thus tempt him; for he wishes it, and forces us to fast by the Spirit or by a need which we cannot avoid.

5. This narrative, however, is written both for our instruction and admonition. First, for instruction, that we should know how Christ has served and helped us by his fasting, hunger, temptation, and victory; also, that whoever believes on Christ shall never suffer need, and that temptation shall never harm him; but we shall have enough in the midst of want and be safe in the midst of temptation; because his Lord and Head triumphed over these all in his behalf, and of this he is assured, as Christ says in John 16:33, "Be of good cheer; I have overcome the world." God, who was able to nourish Christ forty days without any food, can nourish also his Christians.

6. Secondly, this is written for our admonition, that we may in the light of this example also cheerfully suffer want and temptation for the service of God and the good of our neighbor, like Christ did for us, as often as necessity requires it, which is surely accomplished if we learn and confess God's Word. Therefore, this Gospel is sweet consolation and power against the unbelief and infamy of the stomach, to awaken and strengthen the conscience, that we may not be anxious about the nourishment of our bodies, but be assured that he can and will give us our daily bread.

II. THE TEMPTATION OF CHRIST

7. But as to how temptation takes place and how it is overcome, is all very beautifully pictured to us here in Christ. First, that he is led up into the wilderness, that is, he is left solitary and alone by God, angels, and men, by all creatures. What kind of a temptation would it be, if we were not forsaken and stood not alone? It is, however, painful when we do not feel anything that presents its back to us; as, for example, that I should support myself and have not a nickel, not a thread, not a twig, and I experience no help from others, and no advice is offered. That means to be led into the desert and to be left alone. There I am in the true school, and I learn what I am, how weak my faith is,

how great and rare true faith is, and how deeply unbelief is entrenched in the hearts of all men. But whoever has his purse, cellar, and fields full, is not yet led into the desert, neither is he left alone; therefore, he is not conscious of temptation.

8. Secondly, the tempter came forward and attacked Christ with these very same cares of food for the body and with the unbelief in the goodness of God, and said, "If thou art the Son of God, command that these stones become bread," as if he should say, Yes, trust thou in God and bake and cook nothing; only wait patiently until a roasted fowl flies into your mouth; do you now say that you have a God who cares for you; where is now your heavenly Father, who has charge of you? Yea, it seems to me he lets you in a fine condition; eat now and drink from your faith; let us see how you will satisfy your hunger; yea, when you have stones for bread. What a fine Son of God you are! How fatherly he is disposed toward you in that he fails to send you a slice of bread and permits you to be so poor and needy; do you now continue to believe that you are his son and he is your father? With like thoughts, he truly attacks all the children of God. And Christ surely felt this temptation, for he was no stock nor stone; although he was and remained pure and without sin, as we cannot do.

9. That Satan attacked Christ with the cares for daily food or with unbelief and avarice, Christ's answer proves, in that he says, "Man shall not live by bread alone"; that sounds as if he said, Thou wilt direct me to bread alone and dost treat me as though I thought of nothing but the sustenance of my body. This temptation is very common also among pious people, and they especially feel it keenly who have children and a family, and have nothing to eat. Therefore, Saint Paul says in 1 Timothy 6:10, that avarice is a root of all kind of evil; for it is a fruit of unbelief. Do you not think that unbelief, care, and avarice are the reasons people are afraid to enter married life? Why do people avoid it and live in unchastity, unless it be the fear that they must die of hunger and suffer want? But here we should consider Christ's work and example, who suffered want forty days and nights, and finally was not forsaken, but was ministered to even by angels.

10. Thirdly, behold how Christ resists this temptation of bread, and overcomes; he sees nothing but stones and what is uneatable, then he approaches and clings to the Word of God, strengthens himself by it, and strikes the devil to the ground with it. This saying all Christians should lay hold of when they see that there is lack and want and everything has become stones, so that courage trembles, and they should say, What were it if the whole world were

full of bread, still man does not live by bread alone, but more belongs to life, namely, the Word of God. The words, however, are so beautiful and powerful that we must not pass over them lightly, but carefully explain them.

11. These words Christ quotes from Deuteronomy 8:3, where Moses says, "Thy God humbled thee, and suffered thee to hunger, and fed thee with manna, which thou knewest not, neither did thy fathers know; that he might make thee know that man doth not live by bread only, but by everything that proceedeth out of the mouth of Jehovah doth man live." That is as much as to say, Since God permits you to hunger and you still continue to live, you ought indeed to grasp the thought that God nourishes you without bread through his Word; for if you should live and sustain yourself by bread alone, then you must continually be full of bread. But the Word that nourishes us is, that he promises us, and causes it to be published, that he is our God and desires to be our God.

12. Thus now, the meaning of Moses and of Christ is, Whoever has here God's Word and believes, has both blessings: the first, where he is in want and has nothing, but must suffer hunger, that Word will sustain him, so that he will not die of hunger nor perish, just as well as if he had abundance to eat; for the Word he has in his heart nourishes and sustains him without eating and drinking. But has he little to eat, then a bite or slice of bread will feed and nourish him like a kingly meal; for not only bread but the Word of God also nourishes the body naturally, as it creates and upholds all things, in Hebrews 1:3. The other blessing he will also enjoy, namely, that finally bread will surely be at hand, come whence it will, and should it rain from heaven like manna where none grows and none can grow. In these two thoughts, every person can freely trust, namely, that he must in time of hunger receive bread or something to eat or, if not, then his hunger must become so moderate and bearable that it will nourish him even as well as bread does.

13. What has been said of eating and feeding the body should be understood also of drinking, clothing, house, and all our needs, namely, that although he still permits us to become naked and suffer want for clothing, house, etc., clothing must finally be at hand, and before it fails the leaves of the trees must become coats and mantles; or, if not, then the coats and garments that we wear must never grow old; just as happened to the children of Israel in the desert, in Deuteronomy 8:2–4, whose clothing and shoes never wore out. Likewise the wild wilderness must become their houses, and there must be a way where there is no way; and water, where there is no water; stones must become water. For here stands God's Word, which says, "He cares for you"; and Saint Paul in 1 Timothy 6:17, "God giveth us richly all things to

enjoy"; and in Matthew 6:33–34, "But seek ye first the kingdom of God and his righteousness; and all these things shall be added unto you. Be not therefore anxious for the morrow." These and like words must continue true and stand forever firm.

14. All this one may indeed learn from his own daily experiences. For it is held, and I almost believe it, that there are not as many sheaves of wheat grown as there are people living on the earth; but God daily blesses and increases the wheat in the sack, the flour in the tray, the bread on the table and in the mouth, as Christ did, in John 6:12ff. It is also noticeable that as a rule poor people and their children are fatter and their food reaches farther and agrees with them better than is the case among the rich with all their provisions. However, that the godless at times suffer need, or in times of famine many die of hunger, is caused by a special plague as pestilence, war, etc. In other ways, we see that in all things it is not the food, but the Word of God that nourishes every human being.

15. Now that God sustains all mankind by bread, and not by the Word alone, without bread, is done to the end, that he conceals his work in the world in order to exercise believers; just as he commanded the children of Israel to arm themselves and to fight, and yet it was not his pleasure that victory should come through their own sword and deeds; but he himself was to slay their enemies and triumph with their swords and through their deeds. Here it might also be said, The warrior was not victorious through his sword alone, but by every Word that proceeded out of the mouth of God, as David sings, in Psalm 44:6, "For I will not trust in my bow, neither shall my sword save me." Also, in Psalm 147:10 and in Psalm 33:16–17, "He taketh no pleasure in the legs of a man. A mighty man is not delivered by great strength. A horse is a vain thing for safety." Yet he uses man and the horse, the sword and bow: but not because of the strength and power of man and of the horse, but under the veil and covering of man and the horse he fights and does all. This he proves in that he often did and daily does the same without man and the horse, where there is need and he is not tempted.

16. Thus he does also with the bread; since it is at hand, he nourishes us through it and by means of it, so that we do not see it and we think the bread does it; but where it is not at hand, there he nourishes us without the bread, only through the Word, as he does by means of the bread; so that thus bread is God's helper, as Paul says in 1 Corinthians 3:9, "We are God's fellow workers," that is, through and under our outward ministerial office, he gives inwardly his grace, which he also could give and does give indeed without our office; but since the office is at hand, one should not despise it nor tempt God. Thus

God sustains us outwardly by bread; but only inwardly he gives that growth and permanency, which the bread cannot give. And the summary is, All creatures are God's larva and mummery, which he permits to work with him and to help to do everything that he can do and does do otherwise without their cooperation, in order that we may cleave alone to his Word. Thus if bread is at hand, that we do not therefore trust the more; or if there is no bread present, that we do not therefore despair the more; but use it when it is at hand, and do without it, when there is none; being assured that we shall still live and be sustained at both times by God's Word, whether there be bread or no bread. With such faith, one overcomes avarice and temporal care for daily bread in the right way.

17. Christ's second temptation is opposed to the first and is repugnant to common sense. Its substance is that the devil teaches us to tempt God; as he here calls to Christ to cast himself down from the pinnacle of the temple, which was not at all necessary, since there were surely good steps upon which he could descend. And that this temptation was for the purpose of tempting or making trial of God, the answer of Christ also clearly proves, when he says, "Thou shalt not make trial of the Lord thy God." By this, he shows that the devil wished to lead him into temptation.

18. And this very appropriately follows the first temptation. For where the devil feels a heart trusts God in times of want and need, he soon ceases his temptation of bread and avarice and thinks, Wait, wilt thou be very spiritual and believing, I will assist you: He approaches and attacks on the other side, that we might believe where God has not commanded us to believe, nor wills that we should believe. For example, if God gave you bread in your homes, as he does yearly everywhere in the world, and you would not use it, but instead you would cause need and want yourselves, and say, Why, we are to believe God; I will not eat the bread, but will patiently wait until God sends me manna from heaven. See, that would be tempting God; for that is not believing where all is at hand that we need and should have. How can one believe that he will receive what he already has?

19. Thus you see here that Satan held before Christ want and need where there was neither want nor need, but where there was already good means by which to descend from the temple without such a newly devised and unnecessary way of descending. For this purpose, Satan led Christ to the top of the temple, in the holy city, says the evangelist, and placed him in a holy place. For he creates such precious thoughts in man that he thinks he is filled with faith and is on the true way of holiness; and yet he does not stand in the temple, but is only on the outside of the temple, that is, he is not in the true holy mind

or life of faith; and yet he is in the holy city; that is, such persons are found only in Christendom and among true Christians, who hear a great deal of preaching about faith. To these persons, he applies the sayings of Scripture. For such persons learn Scripture also by daily hearing it; but not farther than they can apply it to their erroneous opinions and their false faith. For Satan here quotes from the Psalter, in Psalm 91:11–12, that God commanded the angels that they should protect the children of God and carry them on their hands. But Satan, like a rogue and cheat, fails to quote what follows, namely, that the angels shall protect the children of God in all their ways. For the psalm reads thus, "For he will give his angels charge over thee to keep thee in all thy ways. They shall bear thee up in their hands, lest thou dash thy foot against a stone"; hence the protection of the angels does not reach farther, according to the command of God, than the ways in which God has commanded us to walk. When we walk in these ways of God, his angels take care of us. But the devil omits to quote "the ways of God" and interprets and applies the protection of the angels to all things, also to that which God has not commanded; then it fails and we tempt God.

20. Now, this temptation seldom takes place in outward material things as bread, clothing, house, etc. For we find many foolhardy people, who risk and endanger their body and life, their property and honor, without any need of doing so; as those do who willfully enter into battle or jump into the water, or gamble for money, or in other ways venture into danger, of whom the wise man says in Sirach 3:27, "Whoever takes pleasure in danger, will thereby be overcome"; for in the degree one struggles to get a thing, will he succeed in obtaining it; and good swimmers are likely to drown and good climbers likely to fall. Yet it is seldom that those of false faith in God abstain from bread, clothing, and other necessities of life, when they are at hand. As we read of two hermits who would not accept bread from the people, but thought God should send it to them directly from heaven: so the consequence was that one died and went to his father, the devil, who taught him such faith and left him fall from the pinnacle.

21. But in spiritual matters, this temptation is powerful when one has to do with the nourishment not of the body but of the soul. Here God has held before us the person and way by which the soul can be forever nourished in the richest manner possible without any want, namely, Christ, our Savior. But this way, this treasure, this provision, no one desires. Everybody seeks another way, other provisions, to help their souls. The real guilty ones are those who would be saved through their own work; these the devil sets conspicuously on the top of the temple. They follow him and go down where there is no stairway; they

believe and trust in their own work where there is no faith nor trust, no way nor bridge, and break their necks. But Satan makes use of and persuades them through the Scriptures to believe that the angels will protect them, and that their way, works, and faith are pleasing to God, and who called them through the Scriptures to do good works; but they do not care how falsely they explain the Scriptures.

22. Who these are, we have identified often enough and very fully, namely, work-righteous persons and unbelieving hypocrites under the name of being Christians and among the congregation of Christian people. For the temptation must take place in the holy city, and one temptation is seldom against another. In the first temptation, want and hunger are the reasons that we should not believe, and by which we become anxious to have a full sufficiency, so that there is no chance for us to believe. In the second temptation, however, the abundance and the full sufficiency are the reasons that we do not believe, by which we become tired of the common treasure, and everyone tries to do something through his own powers to provide for his soul. So we do; if we have nothing, then we doubt God and believe not; if we have abundance, then we become tired of it and wish to have something different and, again, we fail to believe. There we flee and turn against want and seek abundance: here we seek want and flee from the abundance we have. No, whatever God does for us, is never right. Such is the bottomless wickedness of our unbelief.

23. Christ's third temptation consists in temporal honor and power; as the words of the devil clearly teach, when Satan shows and offers Christ all the kingdoms of the world if he would worship him. To this class those belong who fall from their faith for the sake of honor and power, that they may enjoy good days, or not believe further than their honor and power extend. Such are also the heretics who start sects and factions in matters of faith among Christians, that they may make a great parade before the world and soar aloft in their own honor. Hence one may place this third temptation on the right, and the first on the left side. The first is the temptation of misfortune, by which man is stirred to anger, impatience, and unbelief; the third and last, the temptation of prosperity, by which man is enticed to lust, honor, joy, and whatever is high. The second or middle temptation is spiritual, and deals with the blind tricks and errors that mislead reason from faith.

24. For whom the devil cannot overcome with poverty, want, need, and misery, he attacks with riches, favor, honor, pleasure, power, and the like, and contends on both sides against us; yea, "he walketh about," says Saint Peter, in 1 Peter 5:8, so that if he cannot overthrow us either with suffering or love, that is, with the first temptation on the left or the third on the right, he

retires to a higher and different method and attacks us with error, blindness, and a false understanding of the Scripture. If he wins there, we fare ill on all sides and in all things; and whether one suffers poverty or has abundance, whether he fights or surrenders, all is lost. For when one is in error, neither patience in misfortune nor firmness in prosperity helps him; seeing that in both heretics are often powerful and the devil deliberately acts as if he were overcome in the first and last temptations, although he is not, if he has only won in the middle or second temptation. For he lets his own children suffer much and be patient, even at times to spurn the world, but never with a true and honest heart.

25. Now these three temptations taken together are heavy and hard; but the middle one is the greatest, for it attacks the doctrine of faith itself in the soul, and is spiritual and in spiritual matters. The other two attack faith in outward things, in fortune and misfortune, in pleasure and pain, etc., although both severely try us. For it is sad that one should lay hold of heaven and ever be in want and eat stones where there is no bread. Again, it is sad to despise favors, honor and possessions, friends and associates, and let go what one already has. But faith, rooted in God's Word, is able to do all things; is faith strong, then it is also easy for the believer to do this.

26. The order of these temptations, as they met Christ, one cannot absolutely determine; for the evangelists give them in different order. The temptation Matthew places as the middle one, Luke places last, in Luke 4:4ff.; and again, the temptation Luke places in the middle, Matthew places last, as if little depended on the order. But if one wished to preach or speak of them, the order of Luke would be the better. For it is a fine opportunity to repeat and relate that the devil began with want and misfortune; when that did not work, then he began with prosperity and honor; and last, when all fails, that he wantonly and wickedly springs forth and strikes people with terror, lies, and other spiritual tricks. And since they have no order in practice and experience, but as it happens that a Christian may be attacked at one time with the last, and another time with the first, etc., Matthew gave little attention to the order for a preacher to observe in speaking of this theme. And perhaps it was also the same with Christ through the forty days that the devil held to no order, but today attacked him with this and tomorrow with another temptation, and again in ten days with the first, and so on, just as occasion was given.

27. At last, angels approached and served him. This must have taken place in a literal sense, that they appeared in a bodily form and gave him to eat and drink, and just as at a table, they ministered to all his wants. For the service is offered outwardly to his body, just like, no doubt, the devil, his tempter, also

appeared in a bodily form, perhaps like an angel. For, seeing that he places him on the pinnacle of the temple and shows him all the kingdoms of the world in a moment, he must have been a higher being than a man, since he represents himself as a higher being, in that he offers him all the kingdoms of the world and permits himself to be worshiped. But he surely did not bear the form of the devil, for he desires to be beautiful when he lies and deceives, as Saint Paul says of him in 2 Corinthians 11:14, "For even Satan fashioneth himself into an angel of light."

28. This, however, is written for our comfort, that we may know that many angels minister also to us, where one devil attacks us; if we fight with a knightly spirit and firmly stand, God will not let us suffer want; the angels of heaven would sooner appear and be our bakers, waiters, and cooks, and minister to all our wants. This is not written for Christ's sake, for he does not need it. Did the angels serve him, then they may also serve us.

The Second Sunday in Lent

⁓✣⁓

The Faith of the Syrophenician Woman, and the Spiritual Interpretation of This Gospel

And Jesus went out thence, and withdrew into the parts of Tyre and Sidon. And behold, a Canaanitish woman came out from those borders and cried, saying, "Have mercy on me, O Lord, thou son of David; my daughter is grievously vexed with a demon." But he answered her not a word. And his disciples came and besought him, saying, "Send her away; for she crieth after us." But he answered and said, "I was not sent but unto the lost sheep of the house of Israel." But she came and worshiped him, saying, "Lord, help me." And he answered and said, "It is not meet to take the children's bread and cast it to the dogs." But she said, "Yea, Lord: for even the dogs eat of the crumbs which fall from their masters' table." Then Jesus answered and said unto her, "O woman, great is thy faith: be it done unto thee even as thou wilt." And her daughter was healed from that hour. — MATTHEW 15:21–28

I. HER FAITH

1. This Gospel presents to us a true example of firm and perfect faith. For this woman endures and overcomes in three great and hard battles, and teaches us in a beautiful manner the true way and virtue of faith, namely, that it is a hearty trust in the grace and goodness of God as experienced and revealed through his Word. For Saint Mark says, she heard some news about Jesus, in Mark 7:25. What kind of news? Without doubt, good news, and the good report that Christ was a pious man and cheerfully helped everybody. Such news about God is a true Gospel and a word of grace, out of which sprang the faith of this woman; for had she not believed, she would not have thus run after Christ, etc. In like manner, we have often heard how Saint Paul, in Romans 10:17, says that faith cometh by hearing, that the Word must go in advance and be the beginning of our salvation.

2. But how is it that many more have heard this good news concerning Christ, who have not followed him, and did not esteem it as good news? Answer: The physician is helpful and welcome to the sick; the healthy have no use for him. But this woman felt her need, hence she followed the sweet scent, as is written in the Song of Solomon 1:3. In like manner, Moses must precede and teach people to feel their sins in order that grace may be sweet and welcome to them. Therefore, all is in vain, however friendly and lovely Christ may be pictured, if man is not first humbled by a knowledge of himself and he possesses no longing for Christ, as Mary's song says, "The hungry he hath filled with good things; and the rich he hath sent empty away," in Luke 1:53. All this is spoken and written for the comfort of the distressed, the poor, the needy, the sinful, the despised, so that they may know in all times of need to whom to flee and where to seek comfort and help.

3. But see in this example how Christ like a hunter exercises and chases faith in his followers in order that it may become strong and firm. First when the woman follows him upon hearing of his fame and cries with assured confidence that he would according to his reputation deal mercifully with her, Christ certainly acts differently, as if to let her faith and good confidence be in vain and turn his good reputation into a lie, so that she could have thought, Is this the gracious, friendly man? or, Are these the good words, that I have heard spoken about him, upon which I have depended? It must not be true; he is my enemy and will not receive me; nevertheless he might speak a word and tell me that he will have nothing to do with me. Now he is as silent as a stone. Behold, this is a very hard rebuff, when God appears so earnest and angry and conceals his grace so high and deep; as those know so well, who feel and experience it in their hearts. Therefore, she imagines he will not fulfill what he has spoken, and will let his Word be false; as it happened to the children of Israel at the Red Sea and to many other saints.

4. Now, what does the poor woman do? She turns her eyes from all this unfriendly treatment of Christ; all this does not lead her astray, neither does she take it to heart, but she continues immediately and firmly to cling in her confidence to the good news she had heard and embraced concerning him, and never gives up. We must also do the same and learn firmly to cling to the Word, even though God with all his creatures appears different than his Word teaches. But, oh, how painful it is to nature and reason, that this woman should strip herself of self and forsake all that she experienced, and cling alone to God's bare Word, until she experienced the contrary. May God help us in time of need and of death to possess like courage and faith!

5. Secondly, since her cry and faith avail nothing, the disciples approach with their faith, and pray for her, and imagine they will surely be heard. But while they thought he should be more tenderhearted, he became only the more indifferent, as we see and think. For now he is silent no more nor leaves them in doubt; he declines their prayer and says, "I was not sent but unto the lost sheep of the house of Israel." This rebuff is still harder since not only our own person is rejected, but the only comfort that remains to us, namely, the comfort and prayers of pious and holy persons, are rejected. For our last resort, when we feel that God is ungracious or we are in need, is that we go to pious, spiritual persons, and there seek counsel and help, and they are willing to help as love demands; and yet, that may amount to nothing, even they may not be heard and our condition becomes only worse.

6. Here one might upbraid Christ with all the words in which he promised to hear his saints as, in Matthew 18:19, "If two of you shall agree on earth as touching anything that they shall ask, it shall be done for them." Likewise, in Mark 11:24, "All things whatsoever ye pray and ask for, believe that ye receive them, and ye shall have them"; and many more like passages. What becomes of such promises in this woman's case? Christ, however, promptly answers, and says, Yes, it is true, I hear all prayers, but I gave these promises only to the house of Israel. What do you think? Is not that a thunderbolt that dashes both heart and faith into a thousand pieces, when one feels that God's Word, upon which one trusts, was not spoken for him, but applies only to others? Here all saints and prayers must be speechless, yea, here the heart must let go of the Word, to which it would gladly hold, if it would consult its own feelings.

7. But what does the poor woman do? She does not give up, she clings to the Word although it be torn out of her heart by force, is not turned away by this stern answer, still firmly believes his goodness is yet concealed in that answer, and still she will not pass judgment that Christ is or may be ungracious. That is persevering steadfastness.

8. Thirdly, she follows Christ into the house, as Mark 7:24–25 informs us, perseveres, falls down at his feet, and says, "Lord, help me!" There she received her last mortal blow, in that Christ said, in her face, as the words tell, that she was a dog, and not worthy to partake of the children's bread. What will she say to this! Here he presents her in a bad light, she is a condemned and an outcast person, who is not to be reckoned among God's chosen ones.

9. That is an eternally unanswerable reply, to which no one can give a satisfactory answer. Yet she does not despair, but agrees with his judgment and concedes she is a dog, and desires also no more than a dog is entitled to, namely,

that she may eat the crumbs that fall from the table of the Lord. Is not that a masterly stroke as a reply? She catches Christ with his own words. He compares her to a dog, she concedes it, and asks nothing more than that he let her be a dog, as he himself judged her to be. Where will Christ now take refuge? He is caught. Truly, people let the dog have the crumbs under the table; it is entitled to that. Therefore, Christ now completely opens his heart to her and yields to her will, so that she is now no dog, but even a child of Israel.

II. THE SPIRITUAL INTERPRETATION OF THIS GOSPEL

10. All this, however, is written for our comfort and instruction, that we may know how deeply God conceals his grace before our face, and that we may not estimate him according to our feelings and thinking, but strictly according to his Word. For here you see, though Christ appears to be even hard-hearted, yet he gives no final decision by saying "no." All his answers indeed sound like no, but they are not no, they remain undecided and pending. For he does not say, I will not hear thee; but is silent and passive, and says neither yes nor no. In like manner, he does not say she is not of the house of Israel; but he is sent only to the house of Israel; he leaves it undecided and pending between yes and no. So he does not say, Thou art a dog, one should not give thee of the children's bread; but it is not meet to take the children's bread and cast it to the dogs; leaving it undecided whether she is a dog or not. Yet all those trials of her faith sounded more like no than yes; but there was more yea in them than nay; aye, there is only yes in them, but it is very deep and very concealed, while there appears to be nothing but no.

11. By this is set forth the condition of our heart in times of temptation; Christ here represents how it feels. It thinks there is nothing but no and yet that is not true. Therefore, it must turn from this feeling and lay hold of and retain the deep spiritual yes under and above the no with a firm faith in God's Word, as this poor woman does, and say God is right in his judgment which he visits upon us; then we have triumphed and caught Christ in his own words. As, for example, when we feel in our conscience that God rebukes us as sinners and judges us unworthy of the kingdom of heaven, then we experience hell, and we think we are lost forever. Now, whoever understands here the actions of this poor woman and catches God in his own judgment, and says, Lord, it is true, I am a sinner and not worthy of thy grace; but still thou hast promised sinners forgiveness, and thou art come not to call the righteous, but, as Saint Paul says in 1 Timothy 1:15, "to save sinners." Behold, then must God according to his own judgment have mercy upon us.

12. King Manasseh did likewise in his penitence as his prayer proves; he conceded that God was right in his judgment and accused himself as a great sinner, and yet he laid hold of the promised forgiveness of sins. David also does likewise in Psalm 51:4, and says, "Against thee, thee only, have I sinned, and done that which is evil in thy sight; that thou mayest be justified when thou speakest, and be clear when thou judgest." For God's disfavor in every way visits us when we cannot agree with his judgment nor say yea and amen, when he considers and judges us to be sinners. If the condemned could do this, they would that very moment be saved. We say indeed with our mouth that we are sinners; but when God himself says it in our hearts, then we are not sinners, and eagerly wish to be considered pious and free from that judgment. But it must be so; if God is to be righteous in his words that teach you are a sinner, then you may claim the rights of all sinners that God has given them, namely, the forgiveness of sins. Then you eat not only the crumbs under the table as the little dogs do, but you are also a child and have God as your portion according to the pleasure of your will.

13. This is the spiritual meaning of our Gospel and the scriptural explanation of it. For what this poor woman experienced in the bodily affliction of her daughter, whom she miraculously caused to be restored to health again by her faith, that we also experience when we wish to be healed of our sins and of our spiritual diseases, which is truly a wicked devil possessing us; here she must become a dog and we become sinners and brands of hell, and then we have already recovered from our sickness and are saved.

14. Whatever more there is in this Gospel worthy of notice, as that one can obtain grace and help through the faith of another without his own personal faith, as took place here in the daughter of this poor woman, has been sufficiently treated elsewhere. Furthermore, that Christ and his disciples along with the woman in this Gospel exhibit to us an example of love, in that no one acts, prays, and cares for himself but each for others, is also clear enough and worthy of consideration.

The Third Sunday in Lent

❧❧❦

Christ's Defense Against Those Who Slandered Him

And he was casting out a demon that was dumb. And it came to pass, when the demon was gone out, the dumb man spake; and the multitudes marveled. But some of them said, By Beelzebub the prince of the demons casteth he out demons. And others trying him, sought of him a sign from heaven. But he, knowing their thoughts, said unto them, Every kingdom divided against itself is brought to desolation; and a house divided against a house falleth. And if Satan also is divided against himself, how shall his kingdom stand? because ye say that I cast out demons by Beelzebub. And if I by Beelzebub cast out demons, by whom do your sons cast them out? therefore shall they be your judges. But if I by the finger of God cast out demons, then is the kingdom of God come upon you. When the strong man fully armed guardeth his own court, his goods are in peace: but when a stronger than he shall come upon him, and overcome him, he taketh from him his whole armor wherein he trusted, and divideth his spoils.
— Luke 11:14–23

I. CHRIST'S DEFENSE AGAINST HIS SLANDERERS

1. This is a beautiful Gospel from which we learn many different things, and in which nearly everything is set forth as to what Christ, his kingdom, and his Gospel are: what they accomplish and how they fare in the world. In the first place, like all the Gospels, this one teaches us faith and love; for it presents Christ to us as a most loving Savior and helper in every need, and tells us that he who believes this is saved. For we see here that Christ had nothing to do with people who were healthy, but with a poor man who was greatly afflicted with many ills. He was blind, as Matthew says; also dumb and possessed with a demon, as Luke tells us here. Now, all mutes are also deaf, so that in the Greek language deaf and dumb are one word. By this act, Christ draws us to himself, leads us to look to him for every blessing, and to go to him in every

time of need. He does this that we also, according to the nature of love, should do unto others as he does unto us. This is the universal and the most precious doctrine of this Gospel and of all the Gospels throughout the church year. This poor man, however, did not come to Christ without the Word; for those who brought him to Christ must have heard his love preached and were moved thereby to trust in him. We learn, therefore, that faith comes through the Word; but more of this elsewhere.

2. Secondly, it is here demonstrated how Christ and his Gospel fare in the world, namely, that there are three kinds of hearers. Some marvel at him; these are pious and true Christians, who consider this deed so great that they are amazed at it. Some blaspheme the Gospel; these are the Pharisees and scribes, who were vexed because they could not do the like, and were worried lest the people should hold Christ in higher esteem than themselves. Some tempt him, like Herod desired a sign after his own heart, that they may make sport of it. But he answers both parties; at first, the blasphemers in this Gospel, and later on the tempters, saying that no sign shall be given this wicked generation except the sign of the prophet Jonah, of which we read in the verses following. He answers the blasphemers in a friendly way and argues five points with them.

3. In the first place, with honest and reasonable arguments, he concludes from two comparisons that one devil cannot cast out another; for if that were so, the devils would be divided among themselves and Satan's kingdom would indeed not stand. For nature teaches that if a kingdom is divided against itself and its citizens drive out each other, it is not necessary to go to war against it, for it will come to ruin soon enough of itself. Likewise, a house divided against itself needs no other destruction. Even the heathen author Sallust, teaching only from the light of nature and experience, says, "Great wealth passes away through discord, but through concord small means become large." If now the devils were divided among themselves to such a degree that one should drive out the other, Satan's dominion would be at an end, and we would have rest from his attacks.

4. What, then, were these blasphemers able to say to such clear arguments? They were put to silence, but their hearts were hardened, so that they did not heed his words. A hardened heart will not be instructed, no matter how plainly and clearly the truth is presented; but the faith of the righteous is strengthened when they see that the ground of their faith is right and good. And for the sake of such we must answer those whose hearts are hardened, and put them to silence. Even though they will not be converted nor keep silence, still it serves to reveal their hardened hearts, for the longer they talk

the more foolish they become, and they are caught in their folly, and their cause is robbed of the appearance of being right and good, as Solomon also says in Proverbs 26:5, "Answer a fool according to his folly, lest he be wise in his own conceit." That is, answer him according to his folly that his folly may be put to shame for the sake of others, that they may not follow him and be deceived, thinking that he is right. Otherwise, where no such condition exists, it is better to keep silent, as Solomon also says in the same chapter, verse 4, "Answer not a fool according to his folly, lest thou also be like unto him."

5. Nor could they say here that the devils only pretended to be divided among themselves and to yield to one another in order to deceive the people, for it is publicly seen how they resist and contend, cry and rave, tear and rage, when they see that Christ means to expel them. It is then clearly seen that they are opposed to Christ and his Spirit, and they are not united with him, to whom they must yield so unwillingly. Therefore, it is only a flagrant, blasphemous lie, in which they are caught and put to shame, by which they try in venomous hate to give the devil credit for a work of God. From this, we learn not to be surprised when our doctrine and life are blasphemed, and stubborn hearts will not be convinced nor converted, although they are overwhelmed, as it were, with tangible truth and completely put to silence. It is enough that through our arguments their obstinate folly is revealed, acknowledged, and made harmless to pious people, so that the latter may not be misled by its fine pretension. They may then go whither they will; they have condemned themselves, as Saint Paul says, in Titus 3:11.

6. In the second place, he replies with a public example and a similar work, when he says, "By whom do your sons cast them out?" As if he would say, "Is this not simple idiocy? Just what you praise in your sons, you condemn in me. Because your sons do it, it is of God; but because I do it, it must be of the devil." So it is in this world. What Christ does, is of the devil; if someone else did it, it would be all right. Thus the tyrants and enemies of the Gospel do now, when they condemn in us what they themselves do, confess, and teach; but they must proceed thus in order that their judgment may be publicly approved, when they are condemned by all justice. The sons, of whom Christ here says that they drive out devils, were, I think, certain exorcists among the people, for God, from the beginning, had given this people manifold spiritual gifts and he calls them their "sons," as though to say, I am the Son of God and must be called a child of the devil, while those who are your sons, begotten by you, do the same things and are not to be considered children of the devil.

7. "Therefore shall they be your judges," that is, I appeal to them. They will be forced to decide that you wrongfully blaspheme me, and thus condemn

yourselves. For if one devil does not drive out another, then some other power must do it that is neither satanic nor human, but divine. Hence the words, "But if I by the finger of God cast out demons, then is the kingdom of God come upon you." This finger of God is called in Matthew 12:28, the Holy Ghost, for the words read thus, "But if I by the Spirit of God cast out demons," etc. In short, Christ means to say, If the kingdom of God is to come unto you, the devil must be driven out, for his kingdom is against God's kingdom, as you yourselves must confess. But demon is not driven out by demon, much less by men or the power of men, but alone by the Spirit and power of God.

8. From this follows that where the finger of God does not cast out the devil, there the devil's kingdom still exists; where Satan's kingdom still exists, there the kingdom of God cannot be. The unavoidable conclusion then is that, as long as the Holy Spirit does not enter our hearts, we are not only incapable of any good, but are of necessity in the kingdom of Satan. And if we are in his kingdom, then we can do nothing but that which pleases him, else it could not be called his kingdom. As Saint Paul says to Timothy, "The people are taken captive in the snares of the devil unto his will," in 2 Timothy 2:26. How could Satan suffer one of his people to take a notion to do something against, and not for, his kingdom? Oh, it is a striking, terrible, and powerful statement that Christ here admits such a dominion, which we cannot escape except by the power of God; and that the kingdom of God cannot come to us until that kingdom is driven out by divine, heavenly power.

9. This truth is proved in the case of this poor man, who was bodily possessed of the devil. Tell me, what could he and all mankind do to free him from the devil? Without a doubt, nothing. He had to do and suffer just as his master the devil willed, until Christ came, with the power of God. Now then, if he could not free himself from the devil as to his body, how could he, by his own power, deliver his soul from Satan's spiritual dominion? Especially is this the case since the soul, because possessed of sin, is the cause of all bodily possession as a punishment, and sins are more difficult to remove than the punishment of them, and the soul is always more firmly possessed than the body. This is proved by the fact that the devil permits the body to have its natural powers and functions; but he robs the soul of reason, judgment, sense, understanding, and all its powers, as you readily see in the case of this possessed man.

10. He answers them in the third place, by a comparison taken from life, namely, that of a strong man overcome by one stronger, and robbed of all his armor and goods, etc. By this, he testifies also that no one but God can

overcome the devil, so that again no man can boast of being able of himself to drive out either sin or the devil. Notice how he pictures the devil! He calls him a mighty giant who guards his court and home, that is, the devil not only possesses the world as his own domain, but he has garrisoned and fortified it, so that no one can take it from him. He rules it also with undisputed sway, so that it does whatever he commands. Just as little as a house or court may withstand or contend against the tyrant who is its master, can man's free will and natural powers oppose sin and Satan, that is, not at all; but they are subject to them. And as that house must be conquered by a stronger man and thus wrested from the tyrant, so must man also be ransomed through Christ and wrested from Satan. We see again, therefore, that our works and righteousness contribute absolutely nothing toward our salvation; it is effected alone by the grace of God.

11. He answers them fourthly, with pointed proverbs and teachings, as, "He that is not with me is against me," and, "He that gathereth not with me, scattereth." "The devil is not with me for I drive him out, hence he must of necessity be against me." But this saying does not apply to the devil alone, but also to the blasphemers whom he here convicts and condemns, as being against him since they are not for him. "To be with Christ" is to have the same mind and purpose as Christ, that is, to believe in Christ that his works save us and not our own, for this is what Christ holds and teaches. But "to gather with Christ" is to do good out of love to him, and to become rich in good works. He that does not believe is, by his own free will, not with Christ but against him, because he depends upon his own works. Therefore, he that does not love, does not gather with Christ, but by fruitless works becomes only more sinful and drifts farther and farther from the faith.

12. In the fifth place, he answers with a threat, namely, that the last state always is worse than the first. Therefore, we should take heed that we not only refrain from blaspheming the Gospel and Christ, who does such great things for us and drives the devil out of us; but with zeal and fear hold fast to them, in order that we may not become possessed of seven worse devils whereas one possessed us before. For thus it was with the Jews, who had never been so wicked as while the Gospel was being preached to them. So also under the papacy, we have become seven times (that is, many times) worse heathen under the name of Christ than we ever had been before; as Saint Peter says, "The last state is become worse with them than the first," in 2 Peter 2:20. And if we neglect the great light which we now have, it will come to pass in our case also, that we shall become worse than we were before, for the devil does not slumber. This should be sufficient warning.

13. Finally, when the woman cries out to Christ and praises him, saying, "Blessed is the mother that bore such a son," etc., he opposes her carnal worship and takes occasion to teach all of us the substance of this Gospel, namely, that we should not go gaping after the works or merits of the saints but rather see to it that we hear and keep the Word of God. For it does not concern or profit us in the least to know how holy and honorable the mother of this child might be, nor how noble this Son of hers may be; but rather what this Son has done for us, namely, that, by grace, without any merit or worthiness on our part, he has redeemed us from the devil. This fact is proclaimed to us through the Word of God, and this we are to hear and hold in firm faith; then shall we, too, be blessed like this mother and her child.

Although such a Word and work will be blasphemed, we should suffer it and give an answer with meekness, as Saint Peter teaches, for the improvement of others.

II. THE SPIRITUAL MEANING OF THIS GOSPEL

14. This dumb, deaf, blind, and demon-possessed man represents all the children of Adam, who through the flesh are possessed of Satan in original sin, so that they must be his slaves and do according to his will. Hence they are also blind, that is, they do not see God. They are deaf, for they do not hear God's Word, and are not obedient or submissive to it. They are also dumb, for they do not give him one word of thanks or praise, nor do they preach and proclaim Christ and the grace of God. But they are all too talkative about the teachings of the devil and the opinions of men. In these things, they see only too well and are wiser than the children of light in their undertakings, opinions, and desires. In these things, they hear with both ears and readily adopt the suggestions of flesh and blood. So then, whatever we do, in word and deed, as to both body and soul, is of the devil, whether it be externally good or bad, and must be redeemed through the work of God. We are in his kingdom and, therefore, we acknowledge him, see, hear, and follow him, and praise and proclaim his name. All this takes place through the Spirit of God in his Word, which casts out the devil and his kingdom.

15. The Jews called the chief of the devils Beelzebub. The Hebrew word "zebub" means a fly; "baal" or "beel," a man or ruler, as a householder. When the two words form a combination, they mean an archfly or chief fly or, in plain German, "Fliegenkoenig oder grosse Hummel," that is, king fly or the great drone. They gave Satan this contemptuous epithet as though they were entirely free from him, secure against him, and lords over him. That is the way all conceited, corrupt hypocrites do; they imagine they are so pure and holy,

that the devil is a helpless, feeble fly compared with them, and that they do not need the grace of Christ nor the Word of God. Still, they think he is strong enough for others, yet, that whatever God-fearing people teach and do must be the devil's own work, and they consider it such a trifling thing as though it were a dead fly. The devil can well endure such contempt, for by it he is placed above the true God in their hearts.

16. The tyrant in the court or palace is the devil, as I said before. He is in peace, however, as long as God's Word and finger do not oppose him and, just like this deaf-mute, his people do whatever he wishes, for they know no better. His weapons and armor are the carnal conceit, doctrines, and traditions of men, by which he terrifies the conscience and protects himself.

17. But when the stronger man, the Gospel, comes, peace flees, and he rages like a madman, for he resents being condemned, unmasked, punished, and publicly branded. Then he gathers up his armor, the powerful, wise, rich, and holy people, and sets them all to attacking God's Word, as we see in the persecution of the teachers of the Gospel. Such rage and persecution signify that the devil retires very unwillingly and raves in his whole body; for as he acts in the body and its members when he must depart, so he also behaves in the whole world, resisting with all his power when he is to give place to the Gospel; but it is all in vain; he must be expelled.

18. For a stronger one, that is, Christ, comes and overpowers him, and takes away his whole armor, that is, he converts some of those same persecutors and, to that extent, makes him weaker and his own kingdom stronger. He divides the spoils, too, that is, those he converts he uses for various offices, graces, and works in Christendom, of which Paul writes, in Romans 12:6. He is also in the courtyard or anteroom of the palace, for the devil's kingdom consists in outward appearances and pretenses of wisdom, holiness, and strength; but when it is captured by the Gospel, it is found to consist of pure folly, sin, and weakness.

19. The text continues, "When the unclean spirit has gone out, he wanders through dry places, seeking rest," etc. This means as much as the saying, "The devil never takes a vacation" and "The devil never sleeps," for he is seeking how he may devour man. "Dry places" are not the hearts of the ungodly, for in such he rests and dwells like a mighty tyrant, as the Gospel here says; but there are dry and waste places here and there in the country where no people live, as forests and wildernesses. To these he flees in wicked rage because he is driven out. You will remember that the devil found Christ in the wilderness. Now, in Judea, there is not much water; hence we read that it contains many arid wastes. In other countries, however, as in our own, which are

well watered, the devils stay in rivers and lakes, and there they sometimes drown those who bathe or sail upon them. Furthermore, at some places, there are water spirits, who entice the children from the shores into the water and drown them. These are all devils.

20. That he comes again and finds the house swept and garnished (Matthew adds "empty"), signifies that the man is sanctified and adorned with beautiful spiritual gifts, and that the evil spirit clearly sees that he can do nothing there with his familiar tricks, for he is too well known. Thus when the worship of idols was driven from the heathen, he never attacked the world with that device again. But what did he do then? He tried something else, went out, took with him seven spirits, more evil than himself, and entered in with them and dwelt there, and the last state of that man was worse than the first. So he has dealt with us. When Christ had become known in the world and the devil's former kingdom with its idol worship had been destroyed, he adopted another plan and attacked us with heresy and introduced and established the papacy, in which Christ was entirely forgotten, and men became worse heathen under the name of Christ than before he was preached, as we can see now with our own eyes. Such also was the lot of the Jews after the destruction of Jerusalem, and of the Greeks under the Turks [Muslims]. And so all will fare, who at first hear the Word of God and afterward become secure and weary of it. Saint Matthew says, in Matthew 12:14, that Satan finds the house empty. And, in Matthew 13:25, he sowed tares among the wheat, by night, while men slept. Therefore, it is necessary for us to watch as the apostles always admonish us, especially Saint Peter, in 1 Peter 5:3, "Brethren, be sober, be watchful: your adversary the devil, as a roaring lion, walketh about, seeking whom he may devour"; for wherever he overthrows faith, he easily restores again all former vices.

The Fourth Sunday in Lent

※

The Feeding of the Five Thousand

Afer these things Jesus went away to the other side of the sea of Galilee, which is the sea of Tiberias. And a great multitude followed him, because they beheld the signs which he did on them that were sick. And Jesus went up into the mountain, and there he sat with his disciples. Now the Passover, the feast of the Jews, was at hand. Jesus therefore lifting up his eyes, and seeing that a great multitude cometh unto him, saith unto Philip, "Whence are we to buy bread, that these may eat?" And this he said to prove him: for he himself knew what he would do. Philip answered him, "Two hundred shillings' worth of bread is not sufficient for them, that every one may take a little." One of his disciples, Andrew, Simon Peter's brother, saith unto him, "There is a lad here, who hath five barley loaves, and two fishes: but what are these among so many?" Jesus said, "Make the people sit down." Now there was much grass in the place. So the men sat down, in number about five thousand. Jesus therefore took the loaves; and having given thanks, he distributed to them that were set down; likewise also of the fishes as much as they would. And when they were filled, he saith unto his disciples, "Gather up the broken pieces which remain over, that nothing be lost." So they gathered them up, and filled twelve baskets with broken pieces from the five barley loaves, which remained over unto them that had eaten. When therefore the people saw the sign which he did, they said, This is of a truth the prophet that cometh into the world.

Jesus therefore perceiving that they were about to come and take him by force, to make him king, withdrew again into the mountain himself alone. — JOHN 6:1–15

I. THE FEEDING OF THE FIVE THOUSAND

1. In today's Gospel, Christ gives us another lesson in faith, that we should not be overanxious about our daily bread and our temporal existence, and

stirs us up by means of a miracle; as though to say by his act what he says by his words in Matthew 6:33, "Seek ye first the kingdom of God, and his righteousness, and all these things shall be added unto you." For here we see, since the people followed Christ for the sake of God's Word and the signs, and thus sought the kingdom of God, he did not forsake them but richly fed them. He hereby also shows that, rather than those who seek the kingdom of God should suffer need, the grass in the desert would become wheat, or a crumb of bread would be turned into a thousand loaves; or a morsel of bread would feed as many people and just as satisfactorily as a thousand loaves; in order that the words in Matthew 4:4 might stand firm, that "Man shall not live by bread alone, but by every word that proceedeth out of the mouth of God." And to confirm these words, Christ is the first to be concerned about the people, as to what they should eat, and asks Philip, before they complain or ask him; so that we may indeed let him care for us, remembering that he cares more and sooner for us than we do for ourselves.

2. Secondly, he gives an example of great love, and he does this in many ways. First, in that he lets not only the pious, who followed him because of the signs and the Word, enjoy the food; but also the slaves of appetite, who only eat and drink, and seek in him temporal honor; as follows later when they disputed with him at Capernaum about the food, and he said to them in John 6:26, "Ye seek me, not because ye saw signs, but because ye ate of the loaves," etc., and also because they desired to make him king; thus here also he lets his sun shine on the evil and the good, in Matthew 5:45. Secondly, in that he bears with the rudeness and weak faith of his disciples in such a friendly manner. For that he tests Philip, who thus comes with his reason, and Andrew speaks so childishly on the subject, all is done to bring to light the imperfections of the disciples, and on the contrary to set forth his love and dealings with them in a more beautiful and loving light, to encourage us to believe in him, and to give us an example to do likewise; as the members of our body and all God's creatures in their relation to one another teach us. For these are full of love, so that one bears with the other, helps, and preserves what God has created.

3. That he now takes the five loaves and gives thanks, etc., teaches that nothing is too small and insignificant for him to do for his followers, and he can indeed so bless their pittance that they have an abundance, whereas even the rich have not enough with all their riches; as Psalm 34:11 says, "They that seek Jehovah shall not want any good thing; but the rich must suffer hunger." And Mary, in her song of praise, says, "The hungry he hath filled with good things; and the rich he hath sent empty away," in Luke 1:53.

4. Again, that he tells them so faithfully to gather up the fragments, teaches us to be frugal and to preserve and use his gifts, in order that we may not tempt God. For just as it is God's will that we should believe when we have nothing and be assured that he will provide, so he does not desire to be tempted, nor to allow the blessings he has bestowed to be despised, or lie unused and spoil, while we expect other blessings from heaven by means of miracles. Whatever he gives, we should receive and use, and what he does not give, we should believe and expect he will bestow.

II. THE ALLEGORICAL INTERPRETATION

5. That Christ by the miraculous feeding of the five thousand has encouraged us to partake of a spiritual food, and taught that we should seek and expect from him nourishment for the soul, is clearly proved by the whole sixth chapter of John, in which he calls himself the bread from heaven and the true food, and says, "Verily, verily, I say unto you, ye seek me, not because ye saw signs, but because ye ate of the loaves, and were filled. Work not for the food which perisheth, but for the food which abideth unto eternal life, which the Son of man shall give unto you," in John 6:26–27. In harmony with these words, we will explain also this evangelical history in its spiritual meaning and significance.

6. First, there was much hay or grass in the place. The evangelist could not fail to mention that, although it appears to be unnecessary; however, it signifies the Jewish people, who flourished and blossomed like the grass through their outward holiness, wisdom, honor, riches, etc., as Isaiah 40:6–7 says, "All flesh is grass, and all the goodliness thereof is as the flower of the field. The grass withereth, the flower fadeth, because the breath of Jehovah bloweth upon it; surely the people is grass." From the Jewish people, the Word of God went forth and the true food was given to us; for salvation is of the Jews, in John 4:22. Now, as grass is not food for man, but for cattle, so is all the holiness of the outward Jewish righteousness nothing but food for animals, for fleshly hearts, who know and possess nothing of the Spirit.

7. The very same is taught by the people sitting on the grass; for the true saints despise outward holiness, as Paul does in Philippians 3:8, in that he counted his former righteousness to be filth and even a hindrance. Only common and hungry people receive the Word of God and are nourished by it. For here you see that neither Caiaphas nor Annas, neither the Pharisees nor the scribes, follow Christ and see Christ's signs, but they disregard them; they are grass and feed on grass. This miracle was also performed near the festive time of the Jewish Passover; for the true Easter festival, when Christ should be

offered as a sacrifice, was near, when he began to feed them with the Word of God.

8. The five loaves signify the outward, natural word formed by the voice and understood by man's senses; for the number five signifies outward things pertaining to the five senses of man by which he lives; as also the five and five virgins illustrate in Matthew 25:1. These loaves are in the basket, that is, locked up in the Scriptures. And a lad carries them, that means the servant class and the priesthood among the Jews, who possessed the sayings of God, which were placed in their charge and entrusted to them, in Romans 3:2, although they did not enjoy them. But that Christ took these into his own hands, and they were thereby blessed and increased, signifies that by Christ's works and deeds, and not by our deeds or reason, are the Scriptures explained, rightly understood, and preached. This he gives to his disciples, and the disciples to the people. For Christ takes the Word out of the Scriptures; so all teachers receive it from Christ and give it to the people, by which is confirmed what Matthew 23:10 says, "For one is your master, even the Christ," who sits in heaven, and he teaches all only through the mouth and the word of preachers by his Spirit, that is, against false teachers, who teach their own wisdom.

9. The two fishes are the example and witness of the patriarchs and prophets, who are also in the basket; for by them the apostles confirm and strengthen their doctrine, and the believers like Saint Paul does in Romans 4:2–6, where he cites Abraham and David, etc. But there are two, because the examples of the saints are full of love, which cannot be alone, as faith can, but must go out in exercise to its neighbor. Furthermore, the fishes were prepared and cooked; for such examples are indeed put to death by many sufferings and martyrdoms, so that we find nothing carnal in them, and they comfort none by a false faith in his own works, but always point to faith and put to death works and their assurance.

10. The twelve baskets of fragments are all the writings and books the apostles and evangelists bequeathed to us; therefore, they are twelve, like the apostles, and these books are nothing but that which remains from and has been developed out of the Old Testament. The fishes are also signified by the number five (Moses' books); as John 21:25 says, "Even the world itself would not contain the books that should be written" concerning Christ, all which nevertheless was written and proclaimed before in the Old Testament concerning Christ.

11. That Philip gives counsel as how to feed the people with his few shillings, and yet doubts, signifies human teachers, who would gladly aid the soul with their teachings; but their conscience feels it helps nothing. For the

discussion Christ here holds with his disciples takes place in order that we may see and understand that it is naturally impossible to feed so many people through our own counsel, and that this sign might be the more public. Thus he lets us also disgrace ourselves and labor with human doctrines, that we may see and understand how necessary and precious God's Word is and how doctrines do not help the least without God's Word.

12. That Andrew pointed out the lad and the loaves, and yet doubted still more than Philip, signifies the teachers who wish to make the people pious and to quiet them with God's laws; but their conscience has no satisfaction or peace in them, but only becomes continually worse, until Christ comes with his Word of grace. He is the one, and he alone, who makes satisfaction, delivers from sin and death, gives peace and fullness of joy, and does it all of his own free will, gratuitously, against and above all hope and presumption, that we may know that the Gospel is devised and bestowed, not through our own merit, but out of pure grace.

13. Finally, you see in this Gospel that Christ, though he held Gospel poverty in the highest esteem and was not anxious about the morrow, as he teaches in Matthew 6:34, had still some provisions, as the two hundred shillings, the five loaves, and the two fishes; in order that we may learn how such poverty and freedom from care consist not in having nothing at all, as the barefooted fanatics and monks profess, and yet they themselves do not hold to it; but it consists in a free heart and a poor spirit. For even Abraham and Isaac had great possessions, and yet they lived without worry and in poverty, like the best Christians do.

The Fifth Sunday in Lent

⚜

Christ's Defense Against His Enemies

W hich of you convicteth me of sin? If I say truth, why do ye
not believe me? He that is of God heareth the words of God:
for this cause ye hear them not, because ye are not of God." The Jews
answered and said unto him," Say we not well that thou art a
Samaritan, and hast a demon? Jesus answered, "I have not a demon;
but I honor my Father, and ye dishonor me. But I seek not mine own
glory; there is one that seeketh and judgeth. Verily, verily, I say unto
you, If a man keep my word, he shall never see death." The Jews said
unto him. "Now we know that thou hast a demon. Abraham died, and
the prophets; and thou sayest, 'If a man keep my Word, he shall never
taste of death.' Art thou greater than our Father Abraham who died?
and the prophets died: whom makest thou thyself?" Jesus answered, "If
I glorify myself, my glory is nothing: it is my Father that glorifieth me;
of whom ye say, that he is your God; and ye have not known him: but
I know him; and if I should say, 'I know him not,' I shall be like unto
you, a liar; but I know him and keep his Word. Your father Abraham
rejoiced to see my day; and he saw it, and was glad." The Jews therefore
said unto him, "Thou art not yet fifty years old, and thou hast seen
Abraham?" Jesus said unto them, "Verily, verily, I say unto you, Before
Abraham was born, I am." They took up stones therefore to cast at him:
but Jesus hid himself, and went out of the temple. — JOHN 8:46–59

I. HOW AND WHY CHRIST IN HIS DEFENSE DEMANDS A REASON WHY HIS ENEMIES DO NOT BELIEVE

1. This Gospel teaches how hardened persons become the more furious, the more one teaches them and lovingly stirs them to do their duty. For Christ asks them here in a very loving way for a reason why they still disbelieve, since they can find fault neither with his life nor with his teaching. His life is blameless, for he defies them and says, "Which of you convicteth me of sin?" His

teaching also is blameless, for he adds, "If I say truth, why do ye not believe me?" Thus Christ lives, as he teaches.

2. And every preacher should prove that he possesses both: first, a blameless life, by which he can defy his enemies and no one may have occasion to slander his teachings; secondly, that he possesses the pure doctrine, so that he may not mislead those who follow him. And thus he will be right and firm on both sides: with his good life against his enemies, who look much more at his life than at his doctrine, and despise the doctrine for the sake of the life; with his doctrine among his friends, who have much more respect for his doctrine than for the kind of life he leads, and will bear with his life for the sake of his teaching.

3. For it is indeed true that no one lives so perfect a life as to be without sin before God. Therefore, it is sufficient that he be blameless in the eyes of the people. But his doctrine must be so good and pure as to stand not only before man but also before God. Therefore, every pious pastor may well ask, Who among you can find fault with my life? Among you, I say, who are men; but before God I am a sinner. Thus Moses also boasts in Numbers 16:15, [sic] that he took nothing from the people and he did them no injustice. Samuel did likewise, in 1 Samuel 12:3; also Jeremiah and Hezekiah, who rightly boasted of their blameless life before the people, in order to stop the mouths of blasphemers. But Christ does not speak thus of his doctrine; he says not, "Who among you can find fault with my doctrine"; but, "If I tell you the truth." For one must be assured that his doctrine is right before God and that it is the truth and, accordingly, care not how it is judged by the people.

II. HOW AND WHY IN HIS DEFENSE HE PASSES SUCH A SEVERE JUDGMENT UPON HIS ENEMIES

4. Hence the Jews have no ground for their unbelief than that they are not the children of God; therefore, he passes judgment upon them, and says, "He that is of God heareth the words of God; for this cause ye hear them not, because ye are not of God," which cannot mean anything else than that you are of the devil.

5. The Jews could not stand this, for they wished to be God's children and people; therefore, they are now raging and slander both Christ's life and his doctrine; his doctrine, in that they say, "Thou hast a devil," that is, thou speakest moved by the devil and thy doctrine is his lie; and they slander his life, in that they say, "Thou art a Samaritan," which sounds among the Jews worse than any other crime. In this way, Christ teaches us here the fate that awaits us Christians and his Word; both our life and our doctrine must be condemned

and reviled, and that by the foremost, wisest, and greatest of earth. Thus one knows the corrupt tree by its fruits, as they, under the pretense of being good, are so bitter, angry, impatient, cruel, and mad as to condemn and pass sentence when one touches them at their tender spot and rejects their ideas and ways.

III. HOW AND WHY CHRIST IN HIS DEFENSE DID NOT ESTEEM HIS OWN LIFE, BUT POWERFULLY DEFENDED HIS TEACHINGS

6. What does Christ do here? His life he abandons to shame and dishonor, is silent and suffers them to call him a Samaritan while he takes pains to defend his doctrine. For the doctrine is not ours, but God's, and God dare not suffer in the least, here patience is at an end; but I should stake all that I have and suffer, all that they do, in order that the honor of God and of his Word may not be injured. For if I perish, no great harm is done; but if I let God's Word perish, and I remain silent, then I do harm to God and to the whole world. Although I cannot now close their mouth nor prevent their wickedness, I shall nevertheless not keep silent, nor act as if they are right, as I do about my good life, so that they retain their right. Although they do me injustice at the time, yet it remains right before God. Further, Christ excuses himself, and says, "I have not a demon," that is, my doctrine is not of the devil's lies; "but I honor my Father," that is, I preach in my doctrine the grace of God, through which he is to be praised, loved, and honored by believers. For the evangelical office of the ministry is nothing but glorifying God, in Psalm 19:2, "The heavens declare the glory of God," etc. "But you dishonor me," that is, you call me the devil's liar, who reviles and dishonors God.

7. Why does he not say, I honor my Father, and ye dishonor him, but says, "Ye dishonor me"? Impliedly, he proves by this, that the Father's and his honor are alike and the same, as he and the Father are one God; yet along with this, he also wishes to teach that if the office of the ministry, which God honors, is to be duly praised, then it must suffer disgrace. In like manner, we will also do to our princes and priests; when they attack our manner of life, we should suffer it and show love for hatred, good for evil; but when they attack our doctrine, God's honor is attacked. Then love and patience should cease, and we should not keep silent, but also say, I honor my Father, and you dishonor me; yet I do not inquire whether you dishonor me, for I do not seek my own honor. But, nevertheless, be on your guard; there is one who seeks it and judges, that is, the Father will require it of you, and judge you, and never let you go unpunished. He seeks not only his honor, but also mine, because I seek his honor, as he says in 1 Samuel 2:30, "Them that honor me I will

honor." And it is our consolation that we are happy; although the whole world reviles and dishonors us, we are assured that God will advance our honor and, therefore, will punish, judge, and revenge. If one could only believe it and persevere, he will surely come.

"Verily, verily, I say unto you, if a man keep my word,
he shall never see death."

IV. HOW CHRIST IN HIS DEFENSE ASCRIBES A VERY POWERFUL EFFICACY TO HIS DOCTRINE

8. By these words, he spoils it entirely, in that he does not only defend his doctrine as right and good, which they attribute to the devil, but also ascribes such virtue to his teaching that it becomes a powerful emperor over Satan, death, and sin, to give and sustain eternal life. Behold here, how divine wisdom and human reason conflict with one another. How can a human being grasp the thought, that a corporeal, an oral word should redeem forever from death? But let blindness run its course; we shall consider this beautiful saying. Christ is speaking here not of the word of the law, but of the Gospel, which is a discourse about Christ, who died for our sins, etc. For God did not wish to impart Christ to the world in any other way; he had to embody him in the Word and thus distribute him, and present him to everybody; otherwise, Christ would have existed for himself alone and remained unknown to us; he would have thus died for himself. But since the Word places before us Christ, it thus places us before him who has triumphed over death, sin, and Satan. Therefore, he who grasps and retains Christ, has thus also eternal deliverance from death. Consequently, it is a Word of Life, and it is true, that whoever keeps the Word shall never see death.

9. And from this, we may well understand what Christ meant by the word "keep"; it does not refer to such keeping as one keeps the law by good works; for this word of Christ must be kept in the heart by faith and not with the fist or by good works, as the Jews in this case understand it. They fearfully rage against Christ, that Abraham and the prophets are dead; they know nothing of what it is "to keep," "to die," or "to live." And it is not called "to keep" in vain, for there is a conflict and battle when sin bites, death presses, and hell faces us; then we are to be in earnest in holding firmly to the Word and let nothing separate us from it. Thus see now how Christ answers the Jews and praises his own teachings. You say, my Word is of the devil and wish to sink it to the bottom of perdition; on the contrary, I say to you that it has divine power in it, and I exalt it higher than the heaven of heavens, and above all creatures.

10. How does it then come to pass that man does not see nor taste death, and yet Abraham and all the prophets are dead, who notwithstanding had the Word of God as the Jews say? Here we must give attention to the words of Christ, who makes the distinction that death is a different thing than to see or taste death. We all must face death and die; but a Christian neither tastes nor sees it, that is, he does not feel it, he is not terrified before it, and he enters death calmly and quietly, as though falling asleep, and yet he does not die. But a godless person feels and experiences death, and is terrified before it forever. Thus to taste death may well be called the power and reign or the bitterness of death, yea, it is the eternal death and hell. The Word of God makes this difference. A Christian has that Word and clings firmly to it in death; therefore, he does not see death, but his eyes are filled with the life and the Christ in that Word; therefore, he never feels death. But the godless possess not that Word, therefore, they see no life, but only death; and they must also feel death; that is then the bitter and eternal death.

11. Now, Christ means here that whoever clings to his Word will in the midst of death neither feel nor see death, as he also says in John 11:25, "I am the resurrection, and the life: he that believeth in me though he die, yet shall he live," that is, he will not experience real death. Here we see now what a glorious estate it is to be a Christian, who is already released from death forever and can never die. For his death or dying seems outwardly indeed like the dying of the godless, but inwardly there is a difference as great as between heaven and earth. For the Christian sleeps in death and in that way enters into life, but the godless departs from life and experiences death forever; thus we may see how some tremble, doubt and despair, and become senseless and raging in the midst of the perils of death. Hence death is also called in the Scriptures a sleep. For just as he who falls asleep does not know how it happens, and he greets the morning when he awakes, so shall we suddenly arise on the last day, and never know how we entered and passed through death.

12. Let us take another example. When Israel marched out of Egypt and came to the Red Sea, they were free and experienced no death, but only life. However when King Pharaoh arrived behind them with all his forces, then they stood in the midst of death, then no life was in sight. For before them was the sea, through which they could not pass, behind them King Pharaoh, and on both sides of them high mountains; on all sides they were seized and enclosed by death, so that they said to Moses, "Because there were no graves in Egypt, hast thou taken us away to die in the wilderness?" in Exodus 14:11, so completely and wholly did they despair of life. Just then, Moses came and brought them God's Word that comforted them in the midst of death and preserved

them alive, when he said, in Exodus 14:13, "Fear not, stand still, and see the salvation of Jehovah, which he will work for you today: for the Egyptians whom ye have seen today, ye shall see them again no more for ever." They clung to this Word and held out until victory came; through it life appeared in the presence of death, because they believed the Word, that it would come to pass, and relying upon it they marched into the midst of the Red Sea, which stood on both sides of them like two walls. Then it came to pass that nothing but life and safety were in the sea, where before there were only death and danger. For they would have never become so bold as to go into the sea, had it divided a hundred times, if God's Word had not been present, which comforted them and promised life. Thus man triumphs over death through the Word of Life, if he cleaves to it and believes, and marches into death with it.

13. Likewise, Christ also says here in replying to the Jews, that Abraham and the prophets still live and they never died, but have life in the midst of death; they, however, only lie and sleep in death. For "Abraham," he says, "rejoiced to see my day; and he saw it, and was glad." Thus the prophets also saw it. Where and when did Abraham see it? Not with his bodily eyes, as the Jews interpret it, but with the sight of faith in the heart; that is, he recognized Christ when he was told in Genesis 22:18, "In thy seed shall all the nations of the earth be blessed." Then he saw and understood that Christ, born of his seed through a pure virgin, so as not to be cursed with Adam's children but to remain blessed, should suffer for the whole world, cause this to be preached, and thus overwhelm the whole world with blessing, etc. This is the day of Christ, the dispensation of the Gospel, that is, the light of this day, which radiates from Christ as from the sun of righteousness, and shines and enlightens the whole world. This is a spiritual day, yet it arose at the time Christ was on the earth in the flesh, a day like Abraham saw. But the Jews understood nothing about such a day because of their carnal minds, and hence they reviled Christ as a liar.

14. Therefore, Christ proceeds farther and gives the ground and reason why it is just his Word and not the word of anyone else, that gives life, and says it is because he was before Abraham or, in other words, because he was the one true God. For if the person who offered himself as a sacrifice for us were not God, it would not help or avail anything, even if he were born of the Virgin Mary and suffered a thousand deaths. But the fact that the Seed of Abraham, who gave himself for us, is also true God, secures blessing and victory for all sinners. Therefore, Christ speaks not of his human nature that they saw and experienced, for they could easily see he was not yet fifty years of age, and did not live before Abraham, but with that nature by which he

existed long before the time of Abraham, by which he existed also before all creatures and before the whole world. Just as he was man according to his spiritual nature before Abraham, that is, in his Word and in the knowledge of faith was he in the saints; for they all knew and believed that Christ, as God and man, should suffer for us, as is written, in Hebrews 13:8, "Jesus Christ is the same yesterday and today, yea and for ever"; and, in Revelation 13; 8, "The Lamb of God that hath been slain from the foundation of the world." Yet now he [John] is speaking here especially of his divine nature.

15. But here reason is terribly offended and becomes mad and furious because God should become man; this reason cannot harmonize and understand. And this is the article of faith to which the Jews still in our day cannot reconcile themselves; hence they cannot cease their throwing stones and their blasphemy. But Christ also continues on the other hand to hide himself from them and to go out of their temple so that they cannot see nor find him in the Scriptures, in which they search daily. Again, this narrative is not a little terror to all who are so foolhardy about the Scriptures and never approach them with a humble spirit. For even in our day it happens, that many read and study in the Scriptures and yet they cannot find Christ; he is hid and has gone out of the temple. And how many there are who say with their mouth that God is become man, and yet they are without the spirit in their hearts; who, whenever tested, prove that they were never in real earnest. This is sufficient on this subject.

Palm Sunday

~◦✠◦~

Christig: An Example of Love

Have this mind in you, which was also in Christ Jesus: who, existing in the form of God, counted not the being on an equality with God a thing to be grasped, but emptied himself, taking the form of a servant, being made in the likeness of men; and being found in fashion as a man, he humbled himself, becoming obedient even unto death, yea, the death of the cross. Wherefore also God highly exalted him, and gave unto him the name which is above every name; that in the name of Jesus every knee should bow, of things in heaven and things on earth and things under the earth, and that every tongue should confess that Jesus Christ is Lord, to the glory of God the Father. — PHILIPPIANS 2:5–11

1. Here Paul again presents to us as a powerful example of the celestial and eternal fire, the love of Christ, for the purpose of persuading us to exercise a loving concern for one another. The apostle employs fine words and precious admonitions, having perceived the indolence and negligence displayed by Christians in this matter of loving. For this, the flesh is responsible. The flesh continually resists the willing spirit, seeking its own interest and causing sects and factions. Although a sermon on this same text went forth in my name a few years ago, entitled "The Twofold Righteousness," the text was not exhausted; therefore, we will now examine it word by word.

Have this mind in you, which was also in Christ Jesus.

2. You are Christians; you have Christ, and in him and through him all fullness of comfort for time and eternity: therefore, nothing should appeal to your thought, your judgment, your pleasure, but that which was in the mind of Christ concerning you as the source of your welfare. For his motive throughout was not his own advantage; everything he did was done for your sake and in your interest. Let men, therefore, in accord with his example, work every good thing for one another's benefit.

Who, existing in the form of God, counted not the being on an equality
with God a thing to be grasped, but emptied himself,
taking the form of a servant.

[Who, being in the form of God, thought it not robbery to be equal with
God; but made himself of no reputation, and took upon him
the form of a servant.]

3. If Christ, who was true God by nature, has humbled himself to become servant of all, how much more should such action befit us who are of no worth, and are by nature children of sin, death, and the devil! Were we similarly to humble ourselves, and even to go beyond Christ in humility—a thing, however, impossible—we should do nothing extraordinary. Our humility would still reek of sin in comparison with his. Suppose Christ to humble himself in the least degree—but a hair's breadth, so to speak—below the most exalted angels; and suppose we were to humble ourselves to a position a thousand times more abased than that of the devils in hell; yet our humility would not compare in the least with that of Christ. For he is an infinite blessing—God himself—and we are but miserable creatures whose existence and life are not for one moment secure.

4. What terrible judgment must come upon those who fail to imitate the ineffable example of Christ; who do not humble themselves below their neighbors and serve them, but rather exalt themselves above them! Indeed, the example of Christ may well terrify the exalted, and those high in authority; and still more the self-exalted. Who would not shrink from occupying the uppermost seat and from lording it over others when he sees the Son of God humble and eliminate himself?

5. The phrase "form of God" does not receive the same interpretation from all. Some understand Paul to refer to the divine essence and nature in Christ; meaning that Christ, though true God, humbled himself. While Christ is indeed true God, Paul is not speaking here of his divine essence, which is concealed. The word he uses, *"morphe,"* or *"forma,"* he employs again where he tells of Christ taking upon himself the form of a servant. "Form of a servant" certainly cannot signify "essence of a real servant"—possessing by nature the qualities of a servant. For Christ is not our servant by nature; he has become our servant from good will and favor toward us. For the same reason, "divine form" cannot properly mean "divine essence"; for divine essence is not visible, while the divine form was truly seen. Very well; then let us use the vernacular, and thus make the apostle's meaning clear.

6. "Form of God," then, means the assumption of a divine attitude and bearing, or the manifestation of divinity in port and presence; and this not privately, but before others, who witness such form and bearing. To speak in the clearest possible manner: Divine bearing and attitude are in evidence when one manifests in word and deed that which pertains peculiarly to God and suggests divinity. Accordingly, "the form of a servant" implies the assumption of the attitude and bearing of a servant in relation to others. It might be better to render *"Morphe tu dulu,"* by "the bearing of a servant," that means, manners of such character that whoever sees the person must take him for a servant. This should make it clear that the passage in question does not refer to the manifestation of divinity or servility as such, but to the characteristics and the expression of the same. For, as previously stated, the essence is concealed, but its manifestation is public. The essence implies a condition, while its expression implies action.

7. As regards these forms, or manifestations, a threefold aspect is suggested by the words of Paul. The essence may exist without the manifestation; there may be a manifestation without the corresponding essence; and finally, we may find the essence together with its proper manifestation. For instance, when God conceals himself and gives no indication of his presence, there is divinity, albeit not manifest. This is the case when he is grieved and withdraws his grace. On the other hand, when he discloses his grace, there is both the essence and its manifestation. But the third aspect is inconceivable for God, namely, a manifestation of divinity without the essence. This is rather a trick of the devil and his servants, who usurp the place of God and act as God, though they are anything but divine. An illustration of this we find in Ezekiel 28:2, where the king of Tyre is recorded as representing his heart, which was certainly decidedly human, as that of a god.

8. Similarly, the form, or bearing, of a servant may be considered from a threefold aspect. One may be a servant and not deport himself as such, but as a lord, or as God; as in the instance just mentioned. Of such a one Solomon speaks, in Proverbs 29:21, saying, "He that delicately bringeth up his servant from a child shall have him become a son at the last." Such are all the children of Adam. We who are rightly God's servants would be God himself. This is what the devil taught Eve when he said, "Ye shall be as God," in Genesis 3:5. Again, one may be a servant and conduct himself as one, as all just and faithful servants behave before the world; and as all true Christians conduct themselves in God's sight, being subject to him and serving all men. Thirdly, one may be not a servant and yet behave as one. For instance, a king might minister to his servants before the world. Before God, however, all men

being servants, this situation is impossible with men; no one has so done but Christ. He says at the Supper, in John 13:13–14, "Ye call me, Teacher, and, Lord: and ye say well; for so I am," and yet I am among you as a servant. And in another place, Matthew 20:28, "The Son of man came not to be ministered unto, but to minister."

9. From these explanations, Paul's meaning must have become clear. His thought is, Christ was in the form of God; that is, both the essence and the bearing of deity were his. He did not assume the divine form as he did that of a servant. He was, I repeat it; he was in the form of God. The little word "was" expresses that divinity was his both in essence and form. The meaning is, Many assume and display an appearance of divinity, but are not themselves actually divine; the devil, for instance, and Antichrist and Adam's children. This is sacrilege—the assumption of divinity by an act of robbery. See Romans 2:22. Though the offender does not look upon such conduct as robbery, it is none the less robbing divine honor, and is so regarded by God and angels and saints, and even by his own conscience. But Christ, who had not come by divinity through arrogating it to himself, but was divine by nature according to his very essence, did not deem his divinity a thing he had grasped, nor could he, knowing divinity to be his very birthright, and holding it as his own natural possession from eternity.

10. So Paul's words commend Christ's essential divinity and his love toward us and, at the same time, correct all who falsely assume a divine form. Such are we all so long as we are the devil's members. The thought is, The devil's members all would be God, would rob the divinity they do not possess; and they must admit their action to be robbery, for conscience testifies, indeed must testify, that they are not God. Though they may despise the testimony of conscience and fail to heed it, yet the testimony stands, steadfastly maintaining the act as not right—as a malicious robbery.

But the one man, Christ, who did not assume the divine form but was in it by right and had a claim upon it from eternity, who did not and could not hold it robbery to be equal with God, this man humbled himself, taking upon him the form of a servant—not his rightful form—that he by the power of his winning example, might induce them to assume the bearing of servants who possessed the form and character of servants, but who, refusing to own them, appropriated the appearance of divinity upon which they had no claim, since the essence of divinity was forever beyond them.

11. That some fail to understand readily this great text, is due to the fact that they do not accept Paul's words as spoken, but substitute their own ideas of what he should have said, namely, Christ was born true God and did not

rob divinity, etc. The expression "who, existing in the form of God" sounds, in the Greek and Latin, almost as if Christ had merely borne himself as God, unless particular regard be given to the words "existing in," which Paul contrasts with the phrase "took upon him." Christ took upon himself the form of a servant, it is true, but in that form was no real servant. Just so, while dispensing with a divine appearance, behind the appearance chosen was God. And we, likewise, take upon ourselves the divine form, but in the form we are not divine; and we spurn the form of servants, though that is what we are, irrespective of appearance. Christ disrobes himself of the divine form wherein he existed, to assume that of a servant, which did not express his essential character; but we lay aside the servant form of our real being and take upon ourselves, or arrogate to ourselves, the form of God to which we are not fitted by what we are in reality.

12. They are startled by this expression also, "Christ thought it not robbery to be equal with God." Now, at first sight, these words do not seem to refer solely to Christ, since even the devil and his own, who continually aspire to equality with God, do not think their action robbery in spite of the testimony of their conscience to the contrary. But with Paul, the little word "think," or "regard," possesses a powerful significance, having the force of "perfect assurance." Similarly, he says, in Romans 3:28, "We reckon therefore that a man is justified by faith apart from the works of the law"; and, in 1 Corinthians 7:40, "I think [deem] that I also have the spirit of God." But the wicked cannot boast it no robbery when they dare take upon themselves the form of God; for they know, they are satisfied in themselves, that they are not God. Christ, however, did not, nor could he, think himself not equal to God; in other words, he was confident of his equality with God, and knew he had not stolen the honor.

Paul's words are chosen, not as an apology for Christ, but as a severe rebuke for those who arrogate to themselves the form of God against the protest of conscience that it is not their own but stolen. The apostle would show how infinitely Christ differs from them, and that the divine form they would take by theft is Christ's by right.

13. Paul does not use this expression, however, when he refers to Christ's assumption of the servant form which is his, not by nature, but by assumption. The words produce the impression that Christ took by force something not his own. Paul should be expected to say, "He held it not robbery to assume the form of a servant." Why should he rather have chosen that form of expression in the first instance, since Christ did not assume the divine form,

but possessed it as his very own—yes, laid it aside and assumed a form foreign to his nature? The substance of the matter is that he who becomes a servant does not and cannot assume anything, but only gives, giving even himself. Hence there is no warrant here to speak of robbery or of a disposition to look upon the matter in this light.

On the other hand, assumption of the divine form necessarily involves taking, and altogether precludes giving. Hence there is warrant to speak of robbery in this connection, and of men who so view it. But this charge cannot be brought against Christ. He does not render himself guilty of robbery, nor does he so view his relation, as all others must do. Divinity is his by right, and so is its appropriate form a birthright.

14. Thus it seems to me, this text very clearly teaches that to have divine form is simply to assume in regard to others, in word and deed, the bearing of God and Lord; and that Christ meets this test in the miraculous signs and life-giving words, as the Gospels contend. He does not rank with the saints who lack the divine essence; he has, in addition to divine form, the divine essence and nature. On the other hand, the servant, or servile, form implies acting toward others, in word and deed, like a servant. Thus Christ did when he served the disciples and gave himself for us. But he served not as the saints, who are servants by nature. Service was, with him, something assumed for our benefit and as an example for us to follow, teaching us to act in like manner toward others, to disrobe ourselves of the appearance of divinity as he did, as we shall see.

15. Unquestionably, then, Paul proclaims Christ true God. Had he been mere man, what would have been the occasion for saying that he became like a man and was found in the fashion of other men? and that he assumed the form of a servant though he was in form divine? Where would be the sense in my saying to you, "You are like a man, are made in the fashion of a man, and take upon yourself the form of a servant"? You would think I was mocking you, and might appropriately reply, "I am glad you regard me as a man; I was wondering if I were an ox or a wolf. Are you mad or foolish?" Would not that be the natural rejoinder to such a foolish statement? Now, Paul not being foolish, nor being guilty of foolish speech, there truly must have been something exalted and divine about Christ. For when the apostle declares that he was made like unto other men, though the fact of his being human is undisputed, he simply means that the man Christ was God, and could, even in his humanity, have borne himself as divine. But this is precisely what he did not do; he refrained: he disrobed himself of his divinity and bore himself as a mere man like others.

16. What follows concerning Christ, now that we understand the meaning of "form of God" and "form of a servant," is surely plain. In fact, Paul himself tells us what he means by "form of a servant." First: He makes the explanation that Christ disrobed, or divested himself; that is, appeared to lay aside his divinity in that he divested himself of its benefit and glory. Not that he did, or could, divest himself of his divine nature; but that he laid aside the form of divine Majesty—did not act as the God he truly was. Nor did he divest himself of the divine form to the extent of making it unfelt and invisible; in that case, there would have been no divine form left. He simply did not affect a divine appearance and dazzle us by its splendor; rather he served us with that divinity. He performed miracles. And during his suffering on the cross he, with divine power, gave to the murderer the promise of paradise, in Luke 23:43. And in the garden, similarly, he repelled the multitude by a word, in John 18:6.

Hence Paul does not say that Christ was divested by some outside power; he says Christ "made himself" of no repute. Just so the wise man does not in a literal way lay aside wisdom and the appearance of wisdom, but discards them for the purpose of serving the simple-minded who might fittingly serve him. Such man makes himself of no reputation when he divests himself of his wisdom and the appearance of wisdom.

17. Secondly: Christ assumed the form of a servant, even while remaining God and having the form of God; he was God, and his divine words and works were spoken and wrought for our benefit. As a servant, he served us with these. He did not require us to serve him in compensation for them, as in the capacity of a Lord he had a just right to do. He sought not honor or profit thereby, but our benefit and salvation. It was a willing service and gratuitously performed, for the good of men. It was a service unspeakably great, because of the ineffable greatness of the minister and servant—God eternal, whom all angels and creatures serve. He who is not by this example heartily constrained to serve his fellows, is justly condemned. He is harder than stone, darker than hell, and utterly without excuse.

18. Thirdly: "Being made in the likeness of men." Born of Mary, Christ's nature became human. But even in that humanity he might have exalted himself above all men and served none. But he forbore and became as other men. And by "likeness of men," we must understand just ordinary humanity without special privilege whatever. Now, without special privilege, there is no disparity among men. Understand, then, Paul says, in effect, Christ was made as any other man who has neither riches, honor, power, nor advantage above his fellows; for many inherit power, honor, and property by birth. So lowly did Christ become, and with such humility did he conduct himself, that no mortal

is too lowly to be his equal, even servants and the poor. At the same time, Christ was sound, without bodily infirmities, as man in his natural condition might be expected to be.

19. Fourthly: "And being found in fashion as a man." That is, he followed the customs and habits of men, eating and drinking, sleeping and waking, walking and standing, hungering and thirsting, enduring cold and heat, knowing labor and weariness, needing clothing and shelter, feeling the necessity of prayer, and having the same experience as any other man in his relation to God and the world. He had power to avoid these conditions; as God, he might have demeaned and borne himself quite differently. But in becoming man, as above stated, he fared as a human being, and he accepted the necessities of ordinary mortals while all the time he manifested the divine form which expressed his true self.

20. Fifthly: "He humbled himself," or debased himself. In addition to manifesting his servant form in becoming man and faring as an ordinary human being, he went farther and made himself lower than any man. He abased himself to serve all men with the supreme service—the gift of his life in our behalf.

21. Sixthly: He not only made himself subject to men, but also to sin, death, and the devil, and bore it all for us. He accepted the most ignominious death, the death on the cross, dying not as a man but as a worm, in Psalm 22:6; yes, as an archknave, a knave above all knaves, in that he lost even what favor, recognition, and honor were due to the assumed servant form in which he had revealed himself, and perished altogether.

22. Seventhly: All this Christ surely did not do because we were worthy of it. Who could be worthy of such service from such a one? Obedience to the Father moved him. Here Paul with one word unlocks heaven and permits us to look into the unfathomable abyss of divine Majesty and to behold the ineffable love of the fatherly heart toward us—his gracious will for us. He shows us how from eternity it has been God's pleasure that Christ, the glorious one who has wrought all this, should do it for us. What human heart would not melt at the joy-inspiring thought? Who would not love, praise, and thank God and, in return for his goodness, not only be ready to serve the world, but gladly to embrace the extremity of humility? Who would not so do when he is aware that God himself has such precious regard for him, and points to the obedience of his Son as the pouring out and evidence of his fatherly will? Oh, the significance of the words Paul here uses! such words as he uses in no other place! He must certainly have burned with joy and cheer. To gain such a glimpse of God—surely this must be coming to the Father through Christ.

Here is truly illustrated the truth that no one comes to Christ except the Father draw him; and with what power, what delicious sweetness, the Father allures! How many are the preachers of the faith who imagine they know it all, when they have received not even an odor or taste of these things! How soon are they become masters who have never been disciples! Not having tasted God's love, they cannot impart it; hence they remain unprofitable babblers.

Wherefore also God highly exalted him.

23. As Christ was cast to the lowest depths and subjected to all devils, in obeying God and serving us, so has God exalted him Lord over all angels and creatures, and over death and hell. Christ now has completely divested himself of the servant form—laid it aside. Henceforth, he exists in the divine form, glorified, proclaimed, confessed, honored, and recognized as God.

While it is not wholly apparent to us that "all things are put in subjection" to Christ, as Paul says, in 1 Corinthians 15:27, the trouble is merely with our perception of the fact. It is true that Christ is thus exalted in person and seated on high in the fullness of power and might, executing everywhere his will; though few believe the order of events is for the sake of Christ. Freely the events order themselves, and the Lord sits enthroned free from all restrictions. But our eyes are as yet blinded. We do not perceive him there nor recognize that all things obey his will. The last day, however, will reveal it. Then we shall comprehend present mysteries; how Christ laid aside his divine form, was made man, and so on; how he also laid aside the form of a servant and resumed the divine likeness; how as God he appeared in glory; and how he is now Lord of life and death, and the King of Glory.

This must suffice on the text. For how we, too, should come down from our eminence and serve others has been sufficiently treated of in other postils. Remember, God desires us to serve one another with body, property, honor, spirit, and soul, even as his Son served us.

Maundy Thursday

Confession and the Lord's Supper

I. OF CONFESSION AND THE LORD'S SUPPER IN GENERAL

1. Although I have often preached and written on the Lord's Supper and Confession, yet annually the time appointed for the consideration of these subjects, for the sake of those who desire to commune, returns, and so we must review them in a summary and speak of them once more.

2. In the first place, I have often enough said that Christians are not obliged to commune on this particular festive day, but that they have the right and authority to come whenever they desire; for God established the office of the ministers for the purpose that they might at all times serve the people and provide them with God's Word and the sacraments. It is, therefore, unchristian to force people under pain of committing mortal sin to commune just at this time, as has been done heretofore, and is still done in many places. For it is not and cannot be in keeping with the Lord's Supper to force or compel anyone to partake of it; on the contrary, it is intended only for a hungry soul that compels itself and rejoices in being permitted to come; those who must be driven are not desired.

3. Therefore, until the present the devil has ruled with unrestrained power and authority through the pope, compelling him to drive and force the whole world to commune; and in fact, everybody did come running, like swine, because of the pope's command. In this way, so much dishonor and shame have been brought upon the Lord's Supper, and the world has been so filled with sin that one is moved with compassion to think of it. But since we know these things, we ought to let no command bind us, but to hold fast the liberty wherewith Christ has made us free. I say this for the sake of those who will not commune except at this time of the year, and who come only because of the custom and the common practice. There is, to be sure, no harm in coming at this Easter festival, if only the conscience be free and not bound to the time, and is properly prepared to receive the Lord's Supper.

II. OF CONFESSION

4. In the second place, we must say the same thing concerning Confession. First of all, we know that the Scriptures speak of three kinds of confession. The first is that which is made to God, of which the prophet David speaks in Psalm 32:5, "I acknowledged my sin unto thee, and my iniquity did I not hide: I said, I will confess my transgressions unto Jehovah; and thou forgavest the iniquity of my sin." Likewise, in the preceding third verse, David says, "When I kept silence, my bones wasted away as with the drought of summer"; that is, before God no one is able to stand unless he come with this confession, as Psalm 130:4 declares, "But there is forgiveness with thee, that thou mayest be feared"; that is, whoever would deal with thee must deal so that this confession proceeds from his heart, which says, Lord, if thou be not merciful, all is lost, no matter how pious I may be. Every saint must make this confession, as again we read, in the Psalm mentioned, verse 6, "For this let everyone that is godly pray unto thee."

This kind of confession, therefore, teaches us that we are all alike, wicked and sinners, as the saying is, If one of us is good, all of us are good. If anyone have special grace, let him thank God and refrain from boasting. Has anyone fallen into sin, it is because of his flesh and blood; nor has any fallen so low but that another who now stands may fall even lower. Therefore, as far as we are concerned, there is no difference among us, the grace of God alone is dividing us.

5. This kind of confession is so highly necessary that it dare not cease for a moment, but must constitute the entire life of a Christian, so that without ceasing he praise the grace of God and reproach his own life in the eyes of God. Otherwise, if he dare to plead some good work or a good life before God, his judgment, which can tolerate nothing of the kind, would follow; and no one is able to stand before it. Therefore, this kind of confession must be made, that you may condemn yourself as worthy of death and the fire of hell; thus you will anticipate God so that he will not be able to judge and condemn you, but must show you mercy. Concerning this kind of confession, however, we will not speak at this time.

6. The second kind of confession is that made to our neighbor, and is called the confession springing from love, as the other is called the confession springing from faith. Concerning this kind of confession we read in James 5:16, "Confess therefore your sins one to another." In this confession, whenever we have wronged our neighbor, we are to acknowledge our fault to him, as Christ declares in Matthew 5:23–25, "If therefore thou art offering thy gift at the altar, and there rememberest that thy brother hath aught against thee,

leave there thy gift before the altar, and go thy way, first be reconciled to thy brother, and then come and offer thy gift. Agree with thine adversary quickly, while thou art with him in the way, etc." God here requires of both parties that he who hath offended the other ask forgiveness, and that he who is asked, grant it. This kind of confession, like the former, is necessary and commanded; for God will be merciful to no one, nor forgive his sins, unless he also forgive his neighbor. In like manner, faith cannot be true unless it produce this fruit, that you forgive your neighbor, and that you ask for forgiveness; otherwise, a man dare not appear before God. If this fruit is absent, faith and the first kind of confession are not honest.

7. The third kind of confession is that ordered by the pope, which is privately spoken into the ears of the priest when sins are enumerated. This confession is not commanded by God; the pope, however, has forced the people to it and, in addition, has invented so many kinds and varieties of sin that no one is able to keep them in mind; thus consciences have been troubled and tortured in a manner that is pitiful and distressing. Concerning this, however, we will say that God does not force you to confess by faith to him, or by love to your neighbor, when you have no desire to be saved and to receive his grace. Neither does he want you to make confession against your will and desire; on the contrary, he wants you to confess of your own accord, heartily, with love and pleasure. In like manner, he does not compel you to make a private confession to the priest when you have no desire of your own to do so, and do not long for absolution.

This the pope disregarded, and proceeded as though it were a part of the civil government requiring that force be employed; he did not inquire whether a person felt willing or not, but he simply issued the order, that whosoever does not confess at this time shall not have burial in the cemetery. But God cares not whether a thing is done or not, as long as it is not done with pleasure. It is better, therefore, to postpone a duty than to perform it unwillingly. For no one can come to God unless he come gladly and of his own free will; hence no one can compel you to come. If you come because of the command and in order to show obedience to the pope, you do wrong. Yet it is the custom in the whole world that everybody runs to the Lord's Supper solely because it is commanded; hence this is very properly called the week of torture, since in it the consciences of the people are tortured and tormented so that they are really to be pitied, besides the injury and destruction of souls. Moreover, Christ himself is also tortured far more shamefully than when he hung upon the cross. Therefore, we may well lift up our hands and thank God for giving us such light. For although we do not bear much fruit and amend, still we have the right knowledge. Hence it is much better to stay away from confession and communion than to go unwillingly; then at least our consciences remain untortured.

8. Hence we say of private confession, that no one is compelled to observe it. Still it is for this reason a commendable and good thing. Wherever and whenever you are able to hear God's Word, you ought not to despise it, but receive it with heartfelt desire. Now, God has caused his Word to go forth through all the world, so that it fills every nook and corner, and wherever you go you find God's Word. If I preach the forgiveness of sins, I preach the true Gospel. For the sum of the Gospel is, Whosoever believeth in Christ shall receive the forgiveness of his sins. Thus a Christian preacher cannot open his mouth unless he pronounces an absolution. Christ also does the same in the Gospel lesson when he says, *"Pax vobiscum,"* Peace be unto you. That is, I proclaim unto you, as of God, that you have peace and forgiveness of sins; this is even the Gospel itself, and absolution. So also the words of the Lord's Supper, "This is my body which is given for you; this is my blood which is shed for you for the remission of sins, etc." If I were to say, I will not go to confession because I have the Word in the Lord's Supper, I will be like him who declares, Neither am I going to hear the preaching. The Gospel must ring and echo without ceasing in every Christian's mouth. We are, therefore, to accept it with joy wherever and whenever we can hear it, lift up our hands, and thank God that we can hear it everywhere.

9. Therefore, when you go to private confession, give more heed to the priest's word than to your own confessing; and make this distinction, What you say is one thing, and what he says who hears you is another. Do not place much value on what you do, but give heed to what he says, to wit, that in God's stead he proclaims to you the forgiveness of sins. It makes no difference whatever whether he be a priest, called to preach, or merely a Christian. The word which he speaks is not his, but God's Word; and God will keep it as surely as if he had spoken it. This is the way he has placed his holy Word into every corner of the world. Since, therefore, we find it everywhere, we ought to receive it with great thankfulness, and not cast it to the winds.

10. For in Confession as in the Lord's Supper, you have the additional advantage, that the Word is applied to your person alone. For in preaching it flies out into the whole congregation, and although it strikes you also, yet you are not so sure of it; but here it does not apply to anyone except to you. Ought it not to fill your heart with joy to know a place where God is ready to speak to you personally? Yea, if we had a chance to hear an angel speak we would surely run to the ends of the earth. Are we not then foolish, wretched,

and ungrateful people not to listen to what is told us? Here the Scriptures stand, and testify that God speaks through us, and that this is as valid as though he were to speak it with his own mouth; even as Christ declares in Matthew 18:20, "Where two or three are gathered together in my name, there am I in the midst of them"; again in John 20:23, "Whose soever sins ye forgive, they are forgiven unto them; whose soever sins ye retain, they are retained." Here God himself pronounces the absolution, just as he himself baptizes the child; and do you say we don't need Confession? For although you hear the same thing in the Lord's Supper, you ought not on that account to reject it, especially since it applies to you, as already stated, personally.

11. Besides this, you have another advantage: in Confession, you are enabled to disclose all your failings and to obtain counsel regarding them. And if there were no other reason, and God did not himself speak in Confession, I would not willingly give it up for this one reason, that here I am permitted to open my heart to my brother and tell him what troubles me. For it is a deplorable thing to have the conscience burdened and prostrate with fear, and to know neither counsel nor consolation.

This is why it is such an excellent and comforting thing for two to come together, and the one to offer advice, help, and consolation to the other, proceeding in a fine brotherly and affectionate manner. The one reveals his ailment, whereupon the other heals his wounds. I would, therefore, not give Confession up for all the treasure of the world. Still it dare not be made a command, lest it be turned into a matter of conscience, as though a person would not dare to commune without first making confession; nevertheless, we ought never to despise Confession; you cannot hear God's Word too frequently, nor impress it so deeply upon your heart that it could not be done still better.

12. Therefore, I said that confession and absolution must be carefully distinguished from each other, that you give attention chiefly to the absolution, and that you attend Confession not because of the command, or in order to do a good work by your confessing, thinking that because of this good work your sins are forgiven; on the contrary, we are to go only because we there hear God's Word and by it receive consolation. To this incline your ears, and be persuaded that God speaks through men and forgives you your sins; this, of course, requires faith.

Hitherto, the manner of our Confession was as follows: when people were absolved, so many works were required of them as to render satisfaction for their sins. This was called absolving, whereas in truth it meant binding worse than ever. Sins ought to be completely removed by the absolution;

but they first imposed the task of rendering satisfaction for them, and thus force people away from faith and absolution, and induce them to rely upon their own works.

They should be taught thus, Behold, this word which I speak to you in God's stead you must embrace in true faith. If you have not this faith, postpone your confession; yet this does not mean that when your faith is too weak you are not to come and demand consolation and strength. If you cannot believe, tell the brother to whom you would confess of it, and say to him, I do indeed feel that I have need of confession and absolution, but I find I am too cold and too weak in faith. For to whom are you going to confide your weakness if not to God? And where can you find him except in your brother? He can strengthen and help you by his words. This is confessing in the right way; and would to God the whole world were brought far enough at least for everyone to confess that he cannot believe.

13. Let it be said now concerning Confession that everything ought to be free, so that each person attends without constraint, of his own accord. But what ought one to confess? Here is where our preachers in the past have pounded a great deal into us by means of the five senses, the seven deadly sins, the Ten Commandments, etc., thereby perplexing our consciences. But it should be, that you first of all feel that which weighs you down, and the sins that pain you most and burden your conscience you ought to declare and confess to your brother. Then you need not search long nor seek all kinds of sins; just take the ones that come to your mind, and say, This is how frail I am and how I have fallen; this is where I crave consolation and counsel. For confession ought to be brief. If you recall something that you have forgotten, it is not to trouble you; for you confessed not in order to do a good work, or because you were compelled, but in order to be comforted by the word of absolution. Moreover, you can easily confess to God in secret what was forgotten, or you can hear the absolution for it during the communion service.

We are, therefore, not to worry even if sins have been forgotten; though forgotten they are still forgiven; for God looks not to the excellence or completeness of your confession, but to his Word and how you believe it. So also the absolution does not state that some sins are forgiven and others not; on the contrary, it is a free proclamation declaring that God is merciful to you. But if God is merciful to you, all your sins must be blotted out. Hold fast, therefore, to the absolution alone and not to your confession; whether you have forgotten anything makes no difference; as much as you believe, so much are you forgiven. This is the way we must ever trust in God's Word in spite of sin and an evil conscience.

III. OF THE LORD'S SUPPER

14. In the third place, we must speak of the Lord's Supper. We said above that no one should be compelled to commune at any special time, but that this should be left free. It remains for us to speak of the two elements in the Lord's Supper. I have already said that among us one element alone is not to be offered to the communicant; he who wants the Lord's Supper should receive the whole of it. For we have preached and practiced this long enough and cannot assume that there should be anyone unable to understand it; yet if there be one so dense, or claiming to be so weak that he cannot grasp the true meaning of it, we will excuse him; it is just as well that he remains away. For anyone to hear God's Word so long, to have himself coddled like a child, and after all to continue saying, I do not understand, is no good sign. For it is impossible for you to hear so long and still be unenlightened; since then you remain blind, it is better for you not to receive the Lord's Supper. If you cannot grasp the Word that is bright, clear, and certain, you need not grasp the sacrament; for the sacrament would be nothing if there were no Word.

Moreover, this Word has now resounded again and again throughout the whole world, so that even they who oppose it, know it. These, however, are not weak but obdurate and hardened; they set their heads against the doctrine they hear us prove from the Scriptures with such clearness that they are unable to reply or establish the contrary; yet they simply remain in the Romish Church and try to force us to follow them. It is, therefore, out of the question for us any longer to yield or to endure them, since they defy us and maintain as their right what they teach and practice. Hence we wish to receive both elements in the Lord's Supper, just because they wish to prevent us from having them. The thought of causing offense no longer applies to those people.

But if there were a locality where the Gospel had not been heard, it would be proper and Christian to adapt one's self for a time to those who are weak, as also we did in the beginning when our cause was entirely new. Now, however, since so much opposition is offered, and so many efforts at violent suppression are made, forbearance is out of the question.

15. It is, moreover, a fine example of God's providential ruling and guidance that the Lord's Supper is not devoid of persecution, for in instituting it he intended it to be a token and mark whereby we might be identified as Christians. For if we were without it, it would be impossible to tell where to find Christians, and who are Christians, and where the Gospel has borne fruit. But when we go to the Lord's Supper, people can see who they are that have heard the Gospel; moreover, they can observe whether we lead Christian lives. So this is a distinctive mark whereby we are recognized, whereby

we also confess the name of God and show that we are not ashamed of his Word.

When now the pope sees me going to the Lord's Supper and receiving both elements, the bread and the wine, according to the Gospel, it is a testimony that I am determined to cling to the Gospel. If then he grows angry and endeavors to slay me, it is just as it was in the early days of Christianity when the Christians confessed God in the same way by this token of the Lord's Supper. Our bishops have forbidden both elements as contrary to God's ordinance and command. If now we mean to confess Christ, we must receive both elements, so that people may know that we are Christians and abide by the Word of God. If for this cause they slay us, we ought to bear it, knowing that God will abundantly restore life to us again. Hence it is proper for us to suffer persecution on this account; otherwise, if everything were to go smoothly, there would be no real confession. In this way, we remain in the right state, always expecting shame and disgrace, yea, even death, for the Lord's sake, as it was in the ancient church.

16. Furthermore, I said it is not enough to go to the Lord's Supper, unless you are assured and know a defense to which you can refer as the foundation and reason that you do right in going; in order that you may be armed when attacked, and able to defend yourself with the Word of God against the devil and the world. On this account, you dare not commune on the strength of another's faith; for you must believe for yourself, even as I must, just as you must defend yourself, as well as I must defend myself. Therefore, above all, you must know the words Christ used in instituting the Lord's Supper. They are these:

> Our Lord Jesus Christ, the same night in which he was betrayed, took
> bread; and when he had given thanks, he broke it and gave it to his
> disciples and said, "Take, eat; this is my body which is given for you:
> this do in remembrance of me."

> After the same manner also he took the cup, when he had supped, gave
> thanks and gave it to them, saying, "Take, drink ye all of it; this cup is the
> New Testament in my blood, which is shed for you for the remission of
> sins: this do ye, as oft as ye drink it, in remembrance of me."

17. These are the words which neither our opponents nor Satan are able to deny; on them we must stand. Let them make whatever comments they please; we have the clear Word of God, saying the bread is Christ's body given for us; and the cup, his blood shed for us. This he bids us do in remembrance of him; but the pope commands that it be not done.

Well, they say, we are only erring laymen, we do not understand, nor are we able to explain the words. But we reply, It is for us to explain just as much as it is for them; for we are commanded to believe in Christ, to confess our faith, and to keep all the commandments of God, just as well as they are. For we have the same God they claim to have. How, then, are we to believe without knowing and understanding his Word? Since I am commanded to believe, I must know the words I am to believe; for how can I believe without the words? Moreover, it is my duty to stand firm, and I must know how to defend myself and how to refute the arguments to the contrary. This is how you can stop their mouths and bring them to silence. My faith must be as good as yours; therefore, I must have and must know the Word as well as you. For example, the evangelist here says Jesus took the cup and gave it to his disciples, saying, "Take, drink ye all of it; this cup is the New Testament in my blood, which is shed for you," etc. These words are certainly clear enough; and there is no one so stupid that he cannot understand what is meant by, "Take, drink ye all of it; this cup is the New Testament in my blood," etc. Therefore we reply, Unless they prove to us that drinking here signifies something different from what all the world understands by the term, we shall stick to the interpretation, that we are all to drink of the cup. Let them bring forward what they please, custom or councils, we reply, God is older and greater than all things.

18. Likewise, the words are clear, "This do in remembrance of me." Tell me, who is to remember the Lord? Is this said to the priests alone, and not to all Christians? And to remember the Lord, what is that but to preach him and to confess him? Now if we are all to remember the Lord in his Supper, we must certainly be permitted to receive both elements, to eat the bread and to drink the cup; this surely no one can deny. There is, therefore, no use for you to cover up these words and tell us that we are not to know them. If we are not to know them, what are you here for? You claim to be a shepherd and, therefore, you ought to be here to teach these words and preach them to me and now, by your own rotten defense, you are forced to confess your own shame and bite your own tongue, having so shamefully spoken in contradiction of the truth.

19. Thus you see how we are to understand the words of the institution of the Lord's Supper and firmly hold to them, for in them all the virtue is centered; we all must know them, understand them, and cling to them in faith, so as to be able to defend ourselves and to repulse the foe. When you wish to go to the Lord's Supper, listen to the words spoken, and be assured that they contain the whole treasure on which you are to stand and rely, for they are

really spoken to you. My body is given, my blood is shed, Christ declares. Why? Just for you to eat and drink? No; but for the remission of sins. This is what strikes you; and everything else that is done and said has no other purpose than that your sins may be forgiven. But if it is to serve for the forgiveness of sins, it must be able also to overcome death. For where sin is gone, there death is gone, and hell besides; where these are gone, all sorrow is gone and all blessedness has come.

20. Here, here the great treasure lies; on this keep your eyes and dismiss the follies which occupy and trouble the great schools when they inquire how the body of Christ can be present and concealed in so small a space. Be not puzzled about the marvel, but cleave to the Word, and endeavor to obtain the benefit and fruit of the Lord's Supper, namely, that your sins be forgiven.

You must, therefore, act so that the words mean you. This will be when you feel the sting and terror of your sin, the assault of the flesh, the world, and the devil. At one time you are angry and impatient; at another you are assailed by the love of money and the cares of life, etc.; so that you are constantly attacked, and at times even gross sins arise, and you fall and injure your soul. Thus you are a poor and wretched creature, afraid of death, despondent, and unable to be happy. Then it is time, and you have reason enough to go, make confession, and confide your distress to God, saying, Lord, thou hast instituted and left us the sacrament of thy body and blood that in it we may find the forgiveness of sin. I now feel that I need it. I have fallen into sin. I am full of fear and despair. I am not bold to confess thy Word. I have all these failings, and these. Therefore, I come now that thou mayest heal, comfort, and strengthen me, etc.

21. For this reason, I made the statement that the Lord's Supper is to be given only to him who is able to say that this is his condition; that is, he must state what troubles him, and must long to obtain strength and consolation by means of the Word and the symbol. Let him who is unable to use the Lord's Supper in this way remain away, nor let him do like those who wretchedly torture themselves at this time, when they come to the sacrament, and have no idea what they are doing.

Now, when you have received the Lord's Supper, go forth and exercise your faith. The sacrament serves to the end that you may be able to say, I have the public declaration that my sins are forgiven; besides, my mouth has received the public symbol, this I can testify, as also I have testified before the devil and all the world. When death now and an evil conscience assail you, you can rely on this and defy the devil and sin, and thus strengthen your faith and gladden your conscience toward God, and amend your life day by day, where otherwise you would be slothful and cold, and the longer you remained away the more unfit you would be. But if you feel that you are unfit, weak, and lacking in faith, where will you obtain strength but here? Do you mean to wait until you have grown pure and strong, then indeed you will never come and you will never obtain any benefit from the Holy Communion.

22. This is the right use of the Lord's Supper, serving not to torture, but to comfort and gladden the conscience. For by instituting it for us, God did not intend it to be poison and torture to frighten us; this is what we made of it by our false doctrine, when we imagined we were to bring the offering of our piety to God, and hid the words that were to give comfort and salvation, strengthen our consciences, refresh, gladden, and free them from every distress. This is the meaning of the Lord's Supper, and we are to look upon it only as containing sweet grace, consolation, and life. It is poison and death to those who approach it with insolence, who feel no weakness, frailty, or distress to impel them, who act as if they were pure and pious from the start. The Lord's Supper welcomes those who perceive their frailties and feel that they are not pious, yet would like to be. Thus it all depends on this feeling, for we are all frail and sinful, only we do not all confess it.

23. Let this suffice on how we ought to prepare ourselves to receive the communion and conduct ourselves toward it, namely, that we are to exercise and strengthen our faith by the words of the institution of the Supper which say that Christ's body and blood are given and shed for the remission of sins. These words sufficiently show the benefit, fruit, and use of the Lord's Supper as far as partaking of it for ourselves is concerned.

But the second thought springing from the first is Christian love, and this also deserves attention. It is our duty to let the benefit and fruit of the Lord's Supper become manifest, and we ought to show that we have received it with profit. We at present see it received throughout all the world in so many celebrations of the Mass, but where do you see the least fruit following from it?

24. Now, this is the fruit, that even as we have eaten and drunk the body and blood of Christ the Lord, we in turn permit ourselves to be eaten and drunk, and say the same words to our neighbor, Take, eat and drink; and this by no means in jest, but in all seriousness, meaning to offer yourself with all your life, even as Christ did with all that he had, in the sacramental words. As if to say, Here am I myself, given for you, and this treasure do I give to you; what I have you shall have; when you are in want, then will I also be in want; here, take my righteousness, life, and salvation, that neither sin, nor death, nor hell, nor any sorrow may overcome you; as long as I am righteous and alive, so long shall you also be righteous and alive.

These are the words he speaks to us; these we must take, and repeat them to our neighbor, not by the mouth alone, but by our actions, saying, Behold, my dear brother, I have received my Lord; he is mine, and I have more than enough and great abundance. Now you take what I have, it shall be yours, and I place it at your disposal. Is it necessary for me to die for you, I will even do that. The goal placed before us in the Lord's Supper is that the attainment of such conduct toward our neighbor may appear in us.

25. Of course, it is true, we will not become so perfect that one places his soul and body, goods, and honor at the disposal of the other. We still live in the flesh, and this is so deeply rooted in us that we are unable to furnish this symbol and evidence as perfectly as we should. On account of these our short-comings, Christ has instituted the Lord's Supper for our training, that here we may obtain what we lack. For what will you do when you miss in yourself what we have described? You must even come and tell him, Behold, this is what I need. Thou dost give thyself to me so richly and abundantly, but I am unable to do likewise toward my neighbor; this I lament before thee, and I pray thee, let me grow rich and strong enough to accomplish it. Though it is impossible for us to reach such perfection, we are nevertheless to sigh for it, and not to despair when we fall short, only so the desire to obtain it continue in our hearts.

26. Yet the least part of love and devotion is not the sacrifice of my pride. I can indeed give my neighbor temporal goods and bodily service by my efforts and labor; I can also render him service by offering instruction and intercession; likewise, I can visit and comfort him when he is sick and in sor-row, feed him when hungry, loose him when bound, etc. But to bear my neighbor's weakness is far greater than all these. Yet with us the trouble will always be that we will not be able to do it as perfectly as Christ did. He is the bright, radiant sun without a single shadow, whereas our light, compared with this sun, is only a gleaming bit of lighted straw. Yonder a glowing oven full of fire and perfect love; and he is satisfied if we light only a little taper and endeavor somewhat to let love shine forth and burn.

This is the shortcoming we all see and feel in each other. But never let any-one conclude and say, This is not Christ. On the contrary, see what he did in the Gospel story when so often he suffered his disciples to stray and stumble, making his wisdom yield and serve their folly. He condemns them not, but endures their weakness, and tells them in John 13:7–33, "Whither I go, ye can-not come." Likewise, to Peter, "What I do, thou knowest not now." By such love, he abandons his righteousness, judgment, power, vengeance, and pun-ishment, and his authority over us and our sins. He could indeed condemn us for our folly, but all he does is to say, You do wrong, you do not know; yet casts us not away, but comforts us. Therefore I said, it is no small evidence of love to be able to bear with one's neighbor when he is weak in faith or in love.

27. On the other hand, Christ's dealing so kindly with his disciples is no permission for us to approve of human weaknesses or of sin. For later he tells Peter, "What I do thou shalt understand hereafter." Here he merely gives his weakness time and bears with it. It is as though he said, I will bear with your ignorance and weak faith for your sake and will spare you as long as you understand that you must do better, and intend to later on; not that you may grow idle and secure.

28. Therefore, when we have received the Lord's Supper, we must not allow ourselves to become indolent, but must be diligent and attentive to increase in love, aid our neighbor in distress, and lend him a helping hand when he suffers affliction and requires assistance. When you fail to do this, you are not a Christian, or only a weak Christian, though you boast of having received the Lord and all that he is, in the Lord's Supper.

29. If, however, you would be sure of partaking profitably of the Lord's Supper, there is no better way than to observe your conduct toward your neighbor. You need not reflect on the great devoutness you experienced, or on the sweetness of the words in your heart. These indeed are good thoughts, but they will not give you assurance; they may deceive you. However, you will be sure as to whether the sacrament is efficacious in your heart if you watch your conduct toward your neighbor. If you discover that the words and the symbol soften and move you to be friendly to your enemy, to take an interest in your neighbor's welfare, and to help him bear his suffering and affliction, then it is well.

On the other hand, if you do not find it so, you continue uncertain even if you were to commune a hundred times a day with devotions so great as to move you to tears for very joy; for wonderful devotions like this, very sweet to experience, yet as dangerous as sweet, amount to nothing before God. Therefore, we must above all be certain for ourselves, as Peter writes in 2 Peter 1:10, "Give the more diligence to make your calling and election sure." The Word and the sacrament are indeed certain in themselves; for God himself, together with all the angels and saints, testify to this; the question is in regard to yourself, whether you furnish the same testimony. Therefore, even if all the angels and the whole world were to testify that you had received the Lord's Supper profitably, it would be weaker testimony than that furnished by yourself. This you cannot reach unless you consider your conduct, whether it shines forth, works in you, and bears fruit.

30. Now, when fruit fails to appear, when you feel that constantly you remain just as you were, and when you care nothing for your neighbor, then you have reason to take a different attitude in these things; for this is no good sign. Even Peter had to hear the same who was godly and ready to die and to do wonderful deeds for Christ. What then will you do? If you still experience evil desires, anger, impatience, etc., you are again in trouble, and that should urge and impel you to go to Christ and lay it before him, saying, I partake of the Lord's Supper, still I remain as I was, without fruit. I have received the great treasure, yet it remains inactive and dormant within me: This I lament before thee. As thou hast bestowed this treasure upon me, grant now that it may also produce fruit and a new life within me, manifesting themselves toward my neighbor. Now when you begin a little to prove this, you will continually grow stronger and break forth in good deeds to your neighbor more from day to day.

31. For this life is nothing more than a life of faith, of love, and of sanctified affliction. But these three will never be perfect in us while we live here on earth, and no one possesses them in perfection except Christ. He is the sun and is set for our example, which we must imitate. For this reason, there will always be found among us some that are weak, others that are strong, and again some that are stronger; these are able to suffer less, those more; and so they must all continue in the imitation of Christ. For this life is a constant progress from faith to faith, from love to love, from patience to patience, and from affliction to affliction. It is not righteousness, but justification; not purity, but purification; we have not yet arrived at our destination, but we are all on the road, and some are farther advanced than others. God is satisfied to find us busy at work and full of determination. When he is ready he will come quickly, strengthen faith and love, and in an instant take us from this life to heaven. But while we live on earth we must bear with one another, as Christ also bore with us, seeing that none of us is perfect.

32. Christ has shown this to us not only by his own example and by his Word, but he has also pictured it to us in the form of the Sacrament of the Altar, namely, by means of the bread and the wine. We believe that the true body and blood of Christ is under the bread and wine, even as it is. Here we see one thing and believe another, which describes faith. For when we hear the Word and receive the Lord's Supper, we have merely a word and an act, yet by it we embrace life and every treasure, even God himself. Likewise, love is pictured in these signs and elements—first of all, in the bread. For as long as the grains of wheat are in a pile before they are ground, each is a body separate for itself, and is not mingled with the others; but when they are ground, they

all become one body. The same thing takes place with the wine. As long as the berries are not crushed, each retains its own form; but when they are crushed, they all flow together and become one drink. You cannot say, this is the flour from this grain, or this is a drop from that berry; for each has entered the form of the other, and thus was formed one bread and one drink.

This is the interpretation of Saint Paul in 1 Corinthians 10:17, "Seeing that we, who are many, are one bread, one body: for we all partake of the one bread." We eat the Lord by the faith of the Word which the soul consumes and enjoys. In this way, my neighbor also eats me: I give him my goods, body, and life and all that I have, and let him consume and use it in his want. Likewise, I also need my neighbor; I, too, am poor and afflicted, and suffer him to help and serve me in turn. Thus we are woven one into the other, helping one another even as Christ helped us. This is what it means spiritually to eat and drink one another.

33. Let me say now in conclusion in regard to the Lord's Supper that when we have received it, we ought to give heed to love and, in this way, assure ourselves that we have received the sacrament profitably and, at the same time, furnish evidence to others; so that we may not always come and still continue unchanged. Therefore, as I said, we must turn from our devotions and thoughts to our conduct toward our neighbor, and examine ourselves in this mirror with all seriousness. The sacrament is to act upon us so that we may be transformed and become different people. For God's Word and work do not intend to be idle, but are bound to produce great things, to wit, set us free from sin, death, and the devil, and every kind of fear, and make us servants even of the least among men on earth, and this without the slightest complaint on our part, rejoicing rather to find someone in need of our help, and fearing only lest after receiving so much we may not apply it all.

34. Whenever the Lord's Supper fails to produce this result, there is reason to fear it has wrought injury. Nevertheless, even if the result is not great, we are not to reject those that are imperfect and weak, but those that are indolent and insolent, who imagine they have done enough when they have partaken of the sacrament. A change must take place in you, and there must be evidence of it, then you will be able to perceive through the symbol that God is with you, and your faith will grow sure and strong. For you can easily feel whether you have grown more joyous and bold than you were before. Formerly, the world seemed too narrow for us when we heard of death and thought of sin. If now we feel different, it is not because of our own strength, for in the past we could not get so far, although we put forth greater exertions and endeavored to help ourselves by means of works. Likewise, you can feel

whether you are kind to him who injured you, and whether you are merciful to him who is sick. Thus you can discover, whether the Lord's Supper is producing any fruit through your own life. If you experience nothing, go to God and tell him of your shortcomings and troubles; we all must do the same thing as long as we live, for, as we have said, not one of us is perfect. For the present, let this suffice on this subject.

Good Friday

—⊸⟋⟍⊷—

How to Contemplate Christ's Holy Sufferings

THE TRUE AND THE FALSE VIEWS OF CHRIST'S SUFFERINGS

I. THE FALSE VIEWS OF CHRIST'S SUFFERINGS

1. In the first place, some reflect upon the sufferings of Christ in a way that they become angry at the Jews, sing and lament about poor Judas, and are then satisfied; just like by habit they complain of other persons, and condemn and spend their time with their enemies. Such an exercise may truly be called a meditation not on the sufferings of Christ but on the wickedness of Judas and the Jews.

2. In the second place, others have pointed out the different benefits and fruits springing from a consideration of Christ's Passion. Here the saying ascribed to Albertus is misleading, that to think once superficially on the sufferings of Christ is better than to fast a whole year or to pray the Psalter every day, etc. The people thus blindly follow him and act contrary to the true fruits of Christ's Passion; for they seek therein their own selfish interests. Therefore, they decorate themselves with pictures and booklets, with letters and crucifixes, and some go so far as to imagine that they thus protect themselves against the perils of water, of fire, and of the sword, and all other dangers. In this way, the suffering of Christ is to work in them an absence of suffering, which is contrary to its nature and character.

3. A third class so sympathize with Christ as to weep and lament for him because he was so innocent, like the women who followed Christ from Jerusalem, whom he rebuked, in that they should better weep for themselves and for their children. Such are they who run far away in the midst of the Passion season, and are greatly benefited by the departure of Christ from Bethany and by the pains and sorrows of the Virgin Mary, but they never get further. Hence they postpone the Passion many hours, and God only knows whether it is devised more for sleeping than for watching. And among these fanatics are those who taught what great blessings come from the holy Mass

and, in their simple way, they think it is enough if they attend Mass. To this we are led through the sayings of certain teachers, that the Mass *opere operati, non opere operantis*, is acceptable of itself, even without our merit and worthiness, just as if that were enough. Nevertheless, the Mass was not instituted for the sake of its own worthiness, but to prove us, especially for the purpose of meditating upon the sufferings of Christ. For where this is not done, we make a temporal, unfruitful work out of the Mass, however good it may be in itself. For what help is it to you, that God is God, if he is not God to you? What benefit is it that eating and drinking are in themselves healthful and good, if they are not healthful for you, and there is fear that we never grow better by reason of our many masses, if we fail to seek the true fruit in them?

II. THE TRUE VIEWS OF CHRIST'S SUFFERINGS

4. Fourthly, they meditate on the Passion of Christ aright, who so view Christ that they become terror-stricken in heart at the sight, and their conscience at once sinks in despair. This terror-stricken feeling should spring forth, so that you see the severe wrath and the unchangeable earnestness of God in regard to sin and sinners, in that he was unwilling that his only and dearly beloved Son should set sinners free unless he paid the costly ransom for them as is mentioned in Isaiah 53:8 "For the transgression of my people was he stricken." What happens to the sinner, when the dear child is thus stricken? An earnestness must be present that is inexpressible and unbearable, which a person so immeasurably great goes to meet, and suffers and dies for it; and if you reflect upon it really deeply, that God's Son, the eternal wisdom of the Father, himself suffers, you will indeed be terror-stricken; and the more you reflect, the deeper will be the impression.

5. Fifthly, that you deeply believe and never doubt the least, that you are the one who thus martyred Christ. For your sins most surely did it. Thus Saint Peter struck and terrified the Jews as with a thunderbolt in Acts 2:36–37, when he spoke to them all in common, "Him have ye crucified," so that three thousand were terror-stricken the same day and tremblingly cried to the apostles, "O beloved brethren what shall we do?" Therefore, when you view the nails piercing through his hands, firmly believe it is your work. Do you behold his crown of thorns, believe the thorns are your wicked thoughts, etc.

6. Sixthly, now see, where one thorn pierces Christ, there more than a thousand thorns should pierce thee, yea, eternally should they thus and even more painfully pierce thee. Where one nail is driven through his hands and feet, thou shouldest eternally suffer such and even more painful nails; as will be also visited upon those who let Christ's sufferings be lost and fruitless as far

as they are concerned. For this earnest mirror, Christ, will neither lie nor mock; whatever he says must be fully realized.

7. Seventhly, Saint Bernard was so terror-stricken by Christ's sufferings that he said, I imagined I was secure and I knew nothing of the eternal judgment passed upon me in heaven, until I saw the eternal Son of God took mercy upon me, stepped forward, and offered himself on my behalf in the same judgment. Ah, it does not become me still to play and remain secure when such earnestness is behind those sufferings. Hence he commanded the women, "Weep not for me, but weep for yourselves, and for your children," in Luke 23:28; and gives, in verse 31, the reason, "For if they do these things in the green tree, what shall be done in the dry?", as if to say, Learn from my martyrdom what you have merited and how you should be rewarded. For here it is true that a little dog was slain in order to terrorize a big one. Likewise, the prophet also said, "All generations shall lament and bewail themselves more than him"; it is not said they shall lament him, but themselves rather than him. Likewise, were also the apostles terror-stricken in Acts 2:27, as mentioned before, so that they said to the apostles, "O, brethren, what shall we do?" So the church also sings, I will diligently meditate thereon, and thus my soul in me will exhaust itself.

8. Eighthly, one must skilfully exercise himself in this point, for the benefit of Christ's sufferings depends almost entirely upon man's coming to a true knowledge of himself, and becoming terror-stricken and slain before himself. And where man does not come to this point, the sufferings of Christ have become of no true benefit to him. For the characteristic, natural work of Christ's sufferings is that they make all men equal and alike, so that as Christ was horribly martyred as to body and soul in our sins, we must also like him be martyred in our consciences by our sins. This does not take place by means of many words, but by means of deep thoughts and a profound realization of our sins. Take an illustration: If an evildoer were judged because he had slain the child of a prince or king, and you were in safety, and sang and played as if you were entirely innocent until one seized you in a horrible manner and convinced you that you had enabled the wicked person to do the act behold, then, you would be in the greatest straits, especially if your conscience also revolted against you. Thus much more anxious you should be, when you consider Christ's sufferings. For the evildoers, the Jews, although they have now judged and banished God, they have still been the servants of your sins, and you are truly the one who strangled and crucified the Son of God through your sins, as has been said.

9. Ninthly, whoever perceives himself to be so hard and sterile that he is not terror-stricken by Christ's sufferings and led to a knowledge of him, he should fear and tremble. For it cannot be otherwise; you must become like the

picture and sufferings of Christ, be it realized in life or in hell; you must at the time of death, if not sooner, fall into terror, tremble, quake, and experience all Christ suffered on the cross. It is truly terrible to attend to this on your deathbed; therefore, you should pray God to soften your heart and permit you fruitfully to meditate upon Christ's Passion. For it is impossible for us profoundly to meditate upon the sufferings of Christ of ourselves, unless God sink them into our hearts. Further, neither this meditation nor any other doctrine is given to you to the end that you should fall fresh upon it of yourself, to accomplish the same; but you are first to seek and long for the grace of God, that you may accomplish it through God's grace and not through your own power. For in this way it happens, that those referred to above never treat the sufferings of Christ aright; for they never call upon God to that end, but devise out of their own ability their own way, and treat those sufferings entirely in a human and an unfruitful manner.

10. Tenthly, whoever meditates thus upon God's sufferings for a day, an hour, yea, for a quarter of an hour, we wish to say freely and publicly, that it is better than if he fasts a whole year, prays the Psalter every day, yea, than if he hears a hundred masses. For such a meditation changes a man's character and, almost as in baptism, he is born again, anew. Then Christ's suffering accomplishes its true, natural, and noble work; it slays the old Adam, banishes all lust, pleasure, and security that one may obtain from God's creatures, just like Christ was forsaken by all, even by God.

11. Eleventhly, since, then, such a work is not in our hands, it happens that sometimes we pray and do not receive it at the time; in spite of this, one should not despair nor cease to pray. At times it comes when we are not praying for it, as God knows and wills; for it will be free and unbound: then man is distressed in conscience and is wickedly displeased with his own life, and it may easily happen that he does not know that Christ's Passion is working this very thing in him, of which perhaps he was not aware, just like the others so exclusively meditated on Christ's Passion that in their knowledge of self they could not extricate themselves out of that state of meditation. Among the first, the sufferings of Christ are quite and true; among the others, a show and false, and according to its nature God often turns the leaf, so that those who do not meditate on the Passion, really do meditate on it; and those who hear the Mass, do not hear it; and those who hear it not, do hear it.

III. THE COMFORT OF CHRIST'S SUFFERINGS

12. Twelfthly, until the present we have been in the Passion week and have celebrated Good Friday in the right way: now we come to Easter and Christ's

resurrection. When man perceives his sins in this light and is completely terror-stricken in his conscience, he must be on his guard that his sins do not thus remain in his conscience, and nothing but pure doubt certainly come out of it; but just as the sins flowed out of Christ and we became conscious of them, so should we pour them again upon him and set our conscience free. Therefore, see well to it that you act not like perverted people, who bite and devour themselves with their sins in their heart, and run here and there with their good works or their own satisfaction, or even work themselves out of this condition by means of indulgences and become rid of their sins; which is impossible, and, alas, such a false refuge of satisfaction and pilgrimages has spread far and wide.

13. Thirteenthly, then, cast your sins from yourself upon Christ, believe with a festive spirit that your sins are his wounds and sufferings, that he carries them and makes satisfaction for them, as Isaiah 53:6 says, "Jehovah hath laid on him the iniquity of us all"; and Saint Peter, in his 1 Peter 2:24, says, "Who his own self bare our sins in his body upon the tree" of the cross; and Saint Paul in 2 Corinthians 5:21, "Him who knew no sin was made to be sin on our behalf; that we might become the righteousness of God in him." Upon these and like passages you must rely with all your weight, and so much the more the harder your conscience martyrs you. For if you do not take this course, but miss the opportunity of stilling your heart, then you will never secure peace, and must yet finally despair in doubt. For if we deal with our sins in our conscience and let them continue within us and be cherished in our hearts, they become much too strong for us to manage, and they will live forever. But when we see that they are laid on Christ and he has triumphed over them by his resurrection and we fearlessly believe it, then they are dead and have become as nothing. For upon Christ they cannot rest; there they are swallowed up by his resurrection, and you see now no wound, no pain in him, that is, no sign of sin. Thus Saint Paul speaks in Romans 4:25, that he was delivered up for our trespasses and was raised for our justification; that is, in his sufferings he made known our sins and also crucified them; but by his resurrection, he makes us righteous and free from all sin, even if we believe the same differently.

14. Fourteenthly, now, if you are not able to believe, then, as I said before, you should pray to God for faith. For this is a matter in the hands of God that is entirely free, and is also bestowed alike at times knowingly, at times secretly, as was just said on the subject of suffering.

15. Fifteenthly, but now bestir yourself to the end: first, not to behold Christ's sufferings any longer; for they have already done their work and terrified you; but press through all difficulties and behold his friendly heart, how

full of love it is toward you, which love constrained him to bear the heavy load of your conscience and your sin. Thus will your heart be loving and sweet toward him, and the assurance of your faith be strengthened. Then ascend higher through the heart of Christ to the heart of God, and see that Christ would not have been able to love you if God had not willed it in eternal love, to which Christ is obedient in his love toward you; there you will find the divine, good Father heart and, as Christ says, be thus drawn to the Father through Christ. Then will you understand the saying of Christ in John 3:16, "God so loved the world that he gave his only begotten Son," etc. That means to know God aright, if we apprehend him not by his power and wisdom, which terrify us, but by his goodness and love; there our faith and confidence can then stand unmovable and man is truly thus born anew in God.

16. Sixteenthly, when your heart is thus established in Christ, and you are an enemy of sin, out of love and not out of fear of punishment, Christ's sufferings should also be an example for your whole life, and you should meditate on the same in a different way. For hitherto we have considered Christ's Passion as a sacrament that works in us and we suffer; now we consider it, that we also work, namely, thus: if a day of sorrow or sickness weighs you down, think how trifling that is compared with the thorns and nails of Christ. If you must do or leave undone what is distasteful to you, think how Christ was led hither and thither, bound and a captive. Does pride attack you, behold, how your Lord was mocked and disgraced with murderers. Do unchastity and lust thrust themselves against you, think how bitter it was for Christ to have his tender flesh torn, pierced, and beaten again and again. Do hatred and envy war against you, or do you seek vengeance, remember how Christ with many tears and cries prayed for you and all his enemies, who indeed had more reason to seek revenge. If trouble or whatever adversity of body or soul afflict you, strengthen your heart, and say, Ah, why then should I not also suffer a little since my Lord sweat blood in the garden because of anxiety and grief? That would be a lazy, disgraceful servant who would wish to lie in his bed while his lord was compelled to battle with the pangs of death.

17. Behold, one can thus find in Christ strength and comfort against all vice and bad habits. That is the right observance of Christ's Passion, and that is the fruit of his suffering, and he who exercises himself thus in the same does better than by hearing the whole Passion or reading all masses. And they are called true Christians who incorporate the life and name of Christ into their own life, as Saint Paul says in Galatians 5:24, "And they that are of Christ Jesus have crucified the flesh with the passions and the lusts thereof." For Christ's Passion must be dealt with not in words and a show, but in our lives

and in truth. Thus Saint Paul admonishes us in Hebrews 12:3, "For consider him that hath endured such gainsaying of sinners against himself, that ye wax not weary, fainting in your souls"; and Saint Peter, in 1 Peter 4:1, "As Christ suffered in the flesh, arm ye yourselves also with the same mind." But this kind of meditation is now out of use and very rare, although the Epistles of Saint Paul and Saint Peter are full of it. We have changed the essence into a mere show, and painted the meditation of Christ's sufferings only in letters and on walls.

Easter Sunday

—∾⊂∾—

Of Christ's Resurrection

A nd when the Sabbath was past, Mary Magdalene, and Mary the mother of James, and Salome, bought spices, that they might come and anoint him. And very early on the first day of the week, they came to the tomb when the sun was risen. And they were saying among themselves, "Who shall roll us away the stone from the door of the tomb?" and looking up, they saw that the stone is rolled back: for it was exceeding great. And entering into the tomb, they saw a young man sitting on the right side, arrayed in a white robe; and they were amazed. And he saith unto them, "Be not amazed: ye seek Jesus, the Nazarene, who hath been crucified: he is risen: he is not here: behold, the place where they laid him! But go tell his disciples and Peter, 'He goeth before you into Galilee: there shall ye see him, as he said unto you.'" And they went out, and fled from the tomb; for trembling and astonishment had come upon them: and they said nothing to any one; for they were afraid. —MARK 16:1–8

I. THE STORY OF CHRIST'S RESURRECTION

1. In the first place, we shall briefly examine the text of this narrative, and afterward speak of the benefits of the resurrection of Christ, and how we should build upon it. The text reads, "And when the Sabbath was past." Here we must remember Mark writes of the Sabbath according to the custom of the Hebrews, for according to the Jewish reckoning, the day began in the evening and lasted until the evening of the next day, as the first chapter of Genesis says, "And there was evening and there was morning, one day," "a second day," "a third day," and so forth. Thus the first and greatest Sabbath began on the evening of the day when Christ was crucified, that is to say, at the time of sunset on the evening of Friday. Our reckoning conveys the wrong sense. Yesterday was the great Sabbath, when Christ lay in the grave; in addition to this, the Jews had seven full days which they celebrated, and all of which they

called Sabbaths, counting them from the first holiday after the great Sabbath and calling it prima *sabbathorum* (first of the Sabbaths), and the third holiday *secundam sabbathorum* (second of the Sabbaths), and so forth. On these days, they ate only wafers and unleavened bread, for which reason they are also called by the evangelist the days of unleavened bread. From this, we must conclude that Christ rose before sunrise and before the angel descended in the earthquake. Afterward, the angel only came to open the empty grave, etc., as has been clearly described by the evangelists.

2. The question now arises, How can we say that he rose on the third day, since he lay in the grave only one day and two nights? According to the Jewish calculation, it was only a day and a half; how shall we then persist in believing there were three days? To this we reply that he was in the state of death for at least a part of all three days. For he died at about two o'clock on Friday and, consequently, was dead for about two hours on the first day. After that night, he lay in the grave all day, which is the true Sabbath. On the third day, which we commemorate now, he rose from the dead and so remained in the state of death a part of this day, just as if we say that something occurred on Easter Day, although it happens in the evening, only a portion of the day. In this sense, Paul and the evangelists say that he rose on the third day.

3. For this period and no longer, Christ was to lie in the grave, so that we might suppose that his body remained naturally uncorrupted and that decomposition had not yet set in. He came forth from the grave so soon that we might presume that corruption had not yet taken place according to the course of nature; for a corpse can lie no longer than three days before it begins to decompose. Therefore, Christ was to rise on the third day, before he saw corruption.

4. The great longing and love of the women for the Lord must also be particularly noted here, so that unadvised and alone they go early to the grave, not thinking of the great stone which was rolled before the tomb. They might have thought of this and taken a man with them. But they act like timid and sorrowing persons and, therefore, they go on their way without even thinking of the most necessary things. They do not even think of the watchers who were clad in armor, nor of the wrath of Pilate and the Jews, but boldly they freely risk it and alone they venture on their way. What urged these good women to hazard life and body? It was nothing but the great love they bore to the Lord, which had sunk so deeply into their hearts that for his sake they would have risked a thousand lives. Such courage they had not of themselves, but here the power of the resurrection of Christ was revealed, whose Spirit makes these women, who by nature are timid, so bold and courageous that they venture to do things which might have daunted a man.

5. These women also show us a beautiful example of a spiritual heart that undertakes an impossible task, of which the whole world would despair. Yet a heart like this stands firm and accomplishes it, not thinking the task impossible. So much we say for the present on this narrative, and now let us see what are the fruits and benefits of the resurrection of Christ.

II. THE FRUITS AND BENEFITS OF THE RESURRECTION OF CHRIST

6. Saint Paul writes in Romans 4:25, as follows, "Christ was delivered up for our trespasses, and was raised for our justification." Paul is indeed the man who extols Christ in a masterly manner, telling us exactly why and for what purpose he suffered and how we should conform ourselves to his sufferings, namely, that he died for our sins. This is a correct interpretation of the sufferings of Christ, by which we may profit. And as it is not sufficient to know and believe that Christ has died, so it will not suffice to know and believe that he rose with a transfigured body and is now in a state of joy and blessedness, no longer subject to mortality, for all this would profit me nothing or very little. But when I come to understand the fact that all the works God does in Christ are done for me, nay, they are bestowed upon and given to me, the effect of his resurrection being that I also will arise and live with him, that will cause me to rejoice. This must be brought home to our hearts, and we must not merely hear it with the ears of our body nor merely confess it with our mouth.

7. You have heard in the story of the Passion how Christ is portrayed as our exemplar and helper, and that he who follows him and clings to him receives the Spirit, who will enable him also to suffer. But the words of Paul are more Christian and should come closer home to our hearts and comfort us more, when he says: "Christ was raised for our justification." Here the Lamb is truly revealed, of whom John the Baptist testifies, when he says in John 1:29, "Behold, the Lamb of God, that taketh away the sin of the world." Here is fulfilled that which was spoken to the serpent, "I will put enmity between thee and the woman, and between thy seed and her seed: he shall bruise thy head," which means that for all those who believe in him, hell, death, and the devil and sin have been destroyed. In the same manner, the promise is fulfilled today which God gave to Abraham, when he said in Genesis 22:18, "In thy seed shall all the nations of the earth be blessed." Here Christ is meant, who takes away our curse and the power of sin, death, and the devil.

8. All this is done, I say, by faith. For if you believe that by this seed the serpent has been slain, then it is slain for you; and if you believe that in this seed all nations are to be blessed, then you are also blessed. For each one individually

should have crushed the serpent under foot and redeemed himself from the curse, which would have been too difficult, nay, impossible for us. But now it has been done easily, namely, by Christ, who has crushed the serpent once, who alone is given as a blessing and benediction, and who has caused this Gospel to be published throughout the world, so that he who believes, accepts it, and clings to it, is also in possession of it, and is assured that it is as he believes. For in the heart of such a man, the Word becomes so powerful that he will conquer death, the devil, sin, and all adversity, like Christ himself did. So mighty is the Word that God himself would sooner be vanquished than that his Word should be conquered.

9. This is the meaning of the words by Saint Paul, "Christ was raised for our justification." Here Paul turns my eyes away from my sins and directs them to Christ, for if I look at my sins, they will destroy me. I must, therefore, look unto Christ, who has taken my sins upon himself, crushed the head of the serpent, and become the blessing. Now, they no longer burden my conscience, but rest upon Christ, whom they desire to destroy. Let us see how they treat him. They hurl him to the ground and kill him. O God; where is now my Christ and my Savior? But then God appears, delivers Christ, and makes him alive; and not only does he make him alive, but he translates him into heaven and lets him rule over all. What has now become of sin? There it lies under his feet. If I then cling to this, I have a cheerful conscience like Christ, because I am without sin. Now I can defy death, the devil, sin, and hell to do me any harm. As I am a child of Adam, they can indeed accomplish it that I must die. But since Christ has taken my sins upon himself, has died for them, has suffered himself to be slain on account of my sins, they can no longer harm me, for Christ is too strong for them; they cannot keep him; he breaks forth and overpowers them, ascends into heaven (takes sin and sorrow captive, Ed. 1531), and rules there over all throughout eternity. Now I have a clear conscience, am joyful and happy, and am no longer afraid of this tyrant, for Christ has taken my sins away from me and made them his own. But they cannot remain upon him; what then becomes of them? They must disappear and be destroyed. This then is the effect of faith. He who believes that Christ has taken away our sin, is without sin, like Christ himself, and death, the devil, and hell are vanquished as far as he is concerned, and they can no longer harm him.

10. Here we also refer to the passage in Hosea 13:14, which Paul quotes in reference to the victory that Christ has won by his resurrection, and by which he has conquered sin, death, hell, and all our enemies. Paul says that death is swallowed up in this victory, and he defies death with these words, "O

death, where is thy victory? O death, where is thy sting?" Just as if Paul would say, O death, where are thy teeth? Come, bite off one of my fingers. Thou formerly hadst a spear, what has become of it now? Christ has taken it from thee. Death, where is now thy spear, etc.? Sin, where is now the edge of thy sword and thy power? Paul says that the power of sin is the law. The more clearly we understand the law, the more sin oppresses and stings us. For this reason, Paul says that Christ has completely destroyed and annihilated the spear and whetstone of death. Now, this Gospel he has not taken with him into heaven, but he caused it to be preached throughout the world, so that for him who believes in Christ, spear and whetstone, nay, sin and death, should be destroyed. This is the true Gospel, which bestows life, strength, power, and marrow, and of which all the passages of Scripture speak.

11. Therefore, seek and learn to know Christ aright, for the whole Scriptures confer upon us the righteousness of the true knowledge of Christ. But this must be brought about by the Holy Spirit. Let us, therefore, pray God that his Gospel may prosper, that we all may truly learn to know Christ and thus rise with him and be honored by God as he was honored.

12. The question now arises, If Christ has taken away death and our sins by his resurrection and has justified us, why do we then still feel death and sin within us? For our sins torment us still, we are stung by our conscience, and this evil conscience creates the fear of hell.

13. To this I reply, I have often said before that feeling and faith are two different things. It is the nature of faith not to feel, to lay aside reason and close the eyes, to submit absolutely to the Word, and follow it in life and death. Feeling, however, does not extend beyond that which may be apprehended by reason and the senses, which may be heard, seen, felt, and known by the outward senses. For this cause, feeling is opposed to faith, and faith is opposed to feeling. Therefore, the author of the Epistle to the Hebrews writes of faith, "Now faith is assurance of things hoped for, a conviction of things not seen." For if we would see Christ visibly in heaven, like the visible sun, we would not need to believe it. But since Christ died for our sins and was raised for our justification, we cannot see it nor feel it, neither can we comprehend it with our reason. Therefore, we must disregard our feeling and accept only the Word, write it into our heart, and cling to it, even though it seems as if my sins were not taken from me, and even though I still feel them within me. Our feelings must not be considered, but we must constantly insist that death, sin, and hell have been conquered, although I feel that I am still under the power of death, sin, and hell. For although we feel that sin is still in us, it is only permitted that our faith may

be developed and strengthened, that in spite of all our feelings, we accept the Word, and that we unite our hearts and consciences more and more to Christ. Thus faith leads us quietly, contrary to all feeling and comprehension of reason, through sin, through death, and through hell. Then we shall see salvation before our eyes, and then we shall know perfectly what we have believed, namely, that death and all sorrow have been conquered.

14. Take as an illustration the fish in the water. When they are caught in the net, you lead it quietly along, so that they imagine they are still in the water; but when you draw them to the shore, they are exposed and begin to struggle, and then they first feel they are caught. Thus it also happens with souls that are caught with the Gospel, which Christ compares with a net, in Matthew 13:47. When the heart has been conquered, the Word unites this poor heart to Christ and leads it gently and quietly from hell and from sin, although the soul still feels sin and imagines to be still under its power. Then a conflict begins, the feelings struggling against the Spirit and faith, and the Spirit and faith against our feelings; and the more faith increases, the more our feelings diminish, and vice versa. We have still sins within us, as for instance pride, avarice, anger, and so forth, but only in order to lead us to faith, so that faith may increase from day to day, and the man become finally a thorough Christian and keep the true Sabbath, consecrating himself to Christ entirely. Then the conscience must become calm and satisfied, and all the surging waves of sin subside. For as upon the sea one billow follows and buffets the other, as though they would destroy the shore, yet they must disappear and destroy themselves, so also our sins strive against us and would fain bring us to despair, but finally they must desist, grow weary, and disappear.

15. In the second place, death is still at our elbow. It also is to exercise the faith of him who believes that death has been killed and all his power taken away. Now, reason feels that death is still at our elbow and is continually troubling us. He who follows his feelings will perish, but he who clings to the Word with his heart will be delivered. Now, if the heart clings to the Word, reason will also follow; but if reason follows, everything will follow, desire and love and all that is in man. Yea, we desire that all may come to the point when they may consider death to be dead and powerless. But this cannot come to pass until the old man, that is, the old Adam, be entirely destroyed and, meanwhile, that process has been going on of which Christ speaks in Matthew 13:33, where he compares the kingdom of God to leaven, which a woman took and hid in three measures of meal. For even if the kneading has begun, the meal is not yet thoroughly leavened. So it is here. Although the heart

clings to the belief that death and hell are destroyed, yet the leaven has not yet worked through it entirely. For it must penetrate and impregnate all the members of the body, until everything becomes leavened and pure, and there remains nothing but a pure faith. This will not be brought about before the old man is entirely destroyed; then all that is in man is Christlike from center to circumference.

16. These two things, sin and death, therefore, remain with us to the end, that we might cultivate and exercise our faith, in order that it may become more perfect in our heart from day to day and finally break forth, and all that we are, body and soul, become more Christlike. For when the heart clings to the Word, feelings and reasoning must fail. Then in the course of time, the will also clings to the Word, and with the will everything else, our desire and love, until we surrender ourselves entirely to the Gospel, are renewed, and leave the old sin behind. Then there comes a different light, different feelings, different seeing, different hearing, acting, and speaking, and also a different outflow of good works. Now, our Scholastics and papists have taught an external piety; they would command the eyes not to see, and the ears not to hear, and would put piety into our hearts from the outside. Ah, how far this is from the truth! But it comes in this way: When the heart and conscience cling to the Word in faith, they overflow in works, so that, when the heart is holy, all the members become holy, and good works follow naturally.

17. This is signified by the Sabbath that was to be hallowed, and on which the Lord lay quietly in the grave. It signifies that we should rest from all our works, should not stir, nay, should not allow any sin to stir within us, but we should firmly believe that death, hell, sin, and the devil are destroyed by the death of Christ, and we are righteous, pious, holy, and, therefore, contented, experiencing no longer any sin. Then all the members are calm and quiet, being convinced that sin and death are vanquished and prostrated. But this cannot be brought about, as I have said, until this impotent, wretched body and the old Adam are destroyed. Therefore, it is indeed necessary that we are required to keep this Sabbath. For as Christ lies in the grave on the Sabbath, never feels nor moves, so it must be with us, as we have heard: Our feelings and actions must cease. And I say again that this cannot be accomplished before the old Adam is annihilated. Nevertheless, we still experience sin and death within us, wrestle with them and fight against them. You may tie a hog ever so well, but you cannot prevent it from grunting (until it is strangled and killed, Ed. 1531). Thus it is with the sins in our flesh. As they are not yet entirely conquered and killed, they are still active, but when death comes, they

must also die, and then we are perfect Christians and pure, but not before. This is the reason why we must die, namely, that we may be entirely freed from sin and death. These words on the fruits of the resurrection of Christ may suffice for the present, and with them we will close. Let us pray God for grace that we may understand them and learn to know Christ aright.

Easter Sunday

❧❧❧

The Manifestation of Christ After His Resurrection, and the Sermon He Preached to His Disciples

A nd as they spake these things, he himself stood in the midst of them, and saith unto them, "Peace be unto you." But they were terrified and affrighted, and supposed that they beheld a spirit. And he said unto them, "Why are ye troubled? and wherefore do questionings arise in your heart? See my hands and my feet, that it is I myself: handle me, and see, for a spirit hath not flesh and bones, as ye behold me having". And when he had said this, he showed them his hands and his feet. And while they still disbelieved for joy, and wondered, he said unto them, "Have ye here anything to eat?" And they gave him a piece of a broiled fish. And he took it, and ate before them.

And he said unto them, "These are my words which I spake unto you, while I was yet with you, that all things must needs be fulfilled, which are written in the law of Moses, and the prophets, and the psalms, concerning me." Then opened he their mind, that they might understand the Scriptures; and he said unto them, "Thus it is written, that the Christ should suffer, and rise again from the dead the third day; and that repentance and remission of sins should be preached in his name unto all the nations, beginning from Jerusalem." — LUKE 24:36–47

I. CHRIST'S MANIFESTATION AFTER HIS RESURRECTION

1. I think, beloved, you have heard enough in these days on the resurrection of Christ, what it works, why it came to pass, and what fruit it bears. But since the Lord has commanded those who preach the Gospel to be steadfast and diligent in this proclamation, we must dwell upon it ever more and more. Our Gospel shows, first, who hear of the Lord's resurrection profitably and fruitfully, namely, they that are here assembled in fear and dread behind closed doors. To them it ought also to be preached most of all, although it must be

preached to all nations, as the Lord says at the end of the Gospel of Matthew. Therefore, let us learn first of all what kind of persons hear the Gospel aright.

2. The disciples are gathered there together in seclusion. They are afraid of the Jews and are, indeed, in danger of their lives; they are fearful and fainthearted, and afraid of sin and death. Had they been strong and courageous, they would not thus have crept into a corner; even as afterward they were made so courageous, when the Holy Spirit came and strengthened and comforted them, that they stepped forth and preached publicly without fear. This is written for us, that we might learn that the Gospel of Christ's resurrection comforts only the fainthearted. And who are these? They are the poor, conscience-stricken ones, whose sins lie heavily upon them, who feel their faint heart, are loath to die, and are well-nigh startled by the sound of a rustling leaf. To these contrite, poor, and needy souls, the Gospel offers comfort; to them it is a sweet savor.

3. This is also learned from the nature of the Gospel, for the Gospel is a message and a testimony, which declares how the Lord Jesus Christ rose from the dead, that he might remove sin, death, and all evil from all who believe on him. If I recognize him as such a Savior, I have heard the Gospel aright, and he has in truth revealed himself to me. If now the Gospel teaches naught but that Christ has overcome sin and death by his resurrection, then we must indeed confess that it can be of service to none save those who feel sin and death. For they who do not feel their sin, and are not dismayed, nor see their infirmities, profit not a whit by it, nor do they delight in it. And though they hear the Gospel, it has no effect upon them, except that they learn the words, and speak of what they heard. They do not treasure them in their hearts, and receive neither comfort nor joy from them.

4. Hence it were well, if the Gospel could be preached only where such fainthearted and conscience-stricken ones are found. But this cannot be and, for this reason, it bears so little fruit. For this they reproach us, and say that we wish to preach many new things, and yet no one is better because of our doctrine. The fault is not in the Gospel, but in the hearers. They hear it, indeed, but they do not feel their own affliction and misery, nor have they ever tried to feel it; they simply go on, secure and reprobate, like dumb brutes. Hence none need marvel if the Gospel does not everywhere bring forth fruit. For besides the good hearers, of whom we have spoken, there are many others that have no regard for it at all, have neither a conscience nor a heart for it, and think neither of death nor of the salvation of souls. These must be driven by force, like asses and dumb brutes and, for this purpose, the civil sword is established.

Again, there are some who do not despise the Gospel, but fully understand it, yet do not amend their lives, nor strive to walk in it. They carry away only the words and prate much about them, but neither deeds nor fruit follow. The third class, however, are they that taste it and use it aright, so that it bears fruit in them.

5. This is then the conclusion of the matter: the Gospel is a testimony of the resurrection of Christ, which serves to comfort and refresh the poor, sorrowing, and terrified consciences. There is need that we have clearly apprehended this truth when we come to die, and also that we may provide for it in every other need. If you think, Behold, now death is approaching and staring me in the face; would that I had someone to comfort me that I might not despair; then know that for this purpose the Gospel is good; here it belongs, here its use is blessed and salutary. As soon as a man knows and understands this, and believes the Gospel, his heart finds peace, and says, If Christ, my Lord, has overcome my sin, and trodden it under foot by his resurrection, wherefore should I fear, and of what should I be afraid? Why should not my heart rejoice and be of good cheer? But such comfort, peace, and joy of heart are felt by none save by the small company which was before greatly dismayed and full of sorrow, and felt its infirmities. Hence also the rude and impenitent understand neither this nor any other Gospel, for he that has not tasted the bitter cannot relish the sweet, and he that has not seen adversity does not understand happiness. For as in the world, that man who neither cares nor attempts to do anything and endures naught, is good for nothing, so, in a more eminent degree in spiritual things, it is not possible that anyone should understand the Gospel except he who has such a dismayed and terrified heart.

6. From this, you should learn that it is no marvel, that many who hear the Gospel do not receive it nor live according to it. Everywhere there are many who reject and persecute it, but we must let them go and grow accustomed to their work. Where the Gospel is preached, such people will surely be found and, if it were otherwise, it would not be right, for there must be many kinds of hearers. Again, many will be found who do not persecute it and yet do not receive it, for they bear no fruit and continue to live as before. Be not worried because of this! for even though a man preach and continue in the Gospel for many years, he must still lament, and say, Aye, no one will come, and all continue in their former state. Therefore, you must not let that grieve nor terrify you.

7. For note what took place at Jerusalem, where the Gospel was first heard, and where there were so many people that it is said, there were in the city at the feast of the Passover eleven hundred thousand men. How many of

these were converted? When Saint Peter stood up and preached, they made a mockery of it and considered the apostles drunken fools. When they had urged the Gospel a long time, they gathered together three thousand men and women. But what were they among so many? Yea, no one could discern that the Gospel had accomplished anything, for all things continued in the same state as before. No change was seen, and scarcely anyone knew that there were Christians there. And so it will be at all times.

8. Hence the Gospel must not be measured by the multitude that hear, but by the small company that receive it. They, indeed, appear as nothing; they are despised and persecuted, and yet God secretly works in them.

9. Besides this, there is another thing that hinders the free movement of the Gospel, namely, the infirmities of the believers. This we see in many examples. Thus although Peter was filled with faith and the Holy Spirit, yet he fell and stumbled, he and all that were with him, when he walked not according to the Gospel nor according as he had taught, so that Paul had to reprove him openly, in Galatians 2:14. There clung to him many great and holy men, and all stumbled with him. Again, we read that Mark journeyed with Paul, but afterward fell away and withdrew from him; and in Acts 15:37, we read again that Paul and Barnabas strove together, and there arose a sharp contention between them. And, before this, we read in the Gospels how often the apostles erred in weighty matters, though they were the best of Christians.

10. These infirmities of Christians and believers darken the Gospel most of all, so that men who deem themselves wise and learned stumble and are offended in them. Few there are who can well reconcile these things so as to take no offense and hence say, Yes, these desire to be good Christians, and are still so wayward, envious, filled with hate and wrath, that one thinks the Gospel has been preached in vain. This really signifies to be offended in the weak and sick Christ.

11. It was also thus with the disciples. At first, when Christ wrought great and excellent works, and gained great honors, and began the work only to fulfill it, they remained steadfast, though many great and noble saints and learned men were offended, because he would not join them. The common man on the contrary was instructed, and the people clung to him, because they saw that with great power he wrought such excellent works; and also walked so that none could reproach him, but all must needs say, Truly this is a great and holy prophet! But when his suffering began, they all turned back and forsook him, and not one of his disciples continued with him. Why was this? Because they considered him not the strong, but the weak Christ. He now was in the hands of the Jews, did no more works and miracles just as if

he had lost all his power and was forsaken of God. Then perished completely his power and his great name. Before, they counted him a prophet, the like of whom had never appeared; now, he is rated as a murderer and a condemned man. Who could now see that this was Christ, the Son of God? Here all reason must fall, yea, all the great and holy saints; for they thought, If he were the Christ, there would needs appear the fruits whereby we might know that it is he, but now we see in him only weakness and sin and death.

12. Therefore, it is the highest wisdom on earth, though it is known by very few men, how to bear with the weak Christ. For if I see a pious, holy man leading a beautiful godly life, who will thank me for praising him, and saying, There is Christ, and there is righteousness? For although bishops and great dunces be offended in such a one, the common people will be instructed. But if he be feeble and falter, straightway everyone will be offended and say, Alas! I had imagined him to be a good Christian, but I see that he falls short of it. However, if they look about them, they will find none without like infirmities, yea, they will perceive it in themselves. Still they think that the Gospel has come to naught. Thus might they think, if God were not able, in his wisdom, to hide it, even as he put a covering over Christ when he drew over him death and weakness, and Christ was under it, though no man could see it. Hence he told his disciples in advance, in Matthew 26:31, "All, all ye, shall be offended in me, and shall no more think nor believe that I am the Christ." Hence if we judge the Gospel, as I have said, according to the infirmity and weakness of Christians, as they stumble at times, a very great obstacle is presented at which offense is taken, and the Gospel is thought to be without power.

13. Therefore, he that would know Christ aright must not give heed to the covering. And though you see another stumble, do not despair, nor think all hope is lost; but rather think, God, perchance, will have this one bear the weak Christ, even as another bears the strong; for both must be and abide on earth, though the greater part appear weak and are such especially in our day. But if you pierce through such weakness, you will find that Christ lies hidden in that weak person; he will come forth and show himself.

14. That is what Paul means when he says to the Corinthians, in 1 Corinthians 2:2, "I determined not to know anything among you, save Jesus Christ, and him crucified." What kind of glory is this that impels him to write that he knows nothing, save Christ crucified? It is a thing that neither reason nor human wisdom can understand, nor yet they who have studied and learned the Gospel; for this wisdom is mighty, hidden, and mysterious, and seems of no value, because he was crucified and emptied himself of all power and divine strength, and hung upon the cross like a wretched, forsaken man, and it

seemed as if God would not help him. Of him alone I speak and preach, says Saint Paul. For the Christ, that sits on high, does wonders, comes and breaks through with power, that all may see who he is, and may quickly come to know him. But to know the weak Christ, that is hanging upon the cross and lying in death, one needs great wisdom; for they who know him not, must needs stumble and be offended.

15. Yea, some are also found who really know the Gospel, but are offended at their own manner of life. They have a desire to walk in godliness, but they feel they make no progress. They begin to despair and think that with them all is lost because they do not feel the strength which they ought to have, also earnestly desire Christ to become strong in them and manifest himself in mighty deeds. But Jehovah, our God, hereby designs to humble us, that we may see what feeble creatures we are, what wretched, lost, and condemned men, if Christ had not come and helped us. Behold, that is the great wisdom we have, and at which all the world is offended.

16. But thereby we have no furlough, to continue for all time in weakness, for we do not preach that any should be weak, but that we should know the weakness of Christians and bear with it. Christ did not hang upon the cross, that he might appear as a murderer and evildoer, but that we might learn thereby how deeply strength lies hidden under weakness, and might learn to know God's strength in weakness. Thus our weakness is not to be praised, as though we should abide in it, but rather must we learn not to think that those who are weak are not Christians, nor yet to despair when we feel our own weakness. Therefore, it behooves us to know our own weaknesses and ever to seek to wax stronger, for Christ must not suffer always, nor remain in the grave, but must come forth again and live.

17. Hence let none say that this is the true course and condition. It is only a beginning, in which we must grow day by day, giving heed only that we turn not away and despair when we are so weak, as though all were lost. Rather must we continue to exercise ourselves until we wax stronger and stronger, and endure and bear the weakness, until God helps and takes it away. Hence even though you see your neighbor so weak that he stumbles, think not that he is beyond hope. God will not have one judge another and be pleased with himself, inasmuch as we are all sinners, but that one bear the infirmity of the other, Romans 14 and Galatians 5. And if you will not do that, he will let you fall and cast you down, and raise the other up. He desires to have us help one another and bear each other's weaknesses.

18. I have thus spoken of our infirmity in order that you may have a good understanding of it, for such knowledge is very necessary, especially at this

time. Oh, if our bishops, pastors, and prelates had had this wisdom, for they needed it the most, how much better would conditions be in Christendom! They would then be able to bear with the weak consciences, and would know how to minister to them. But now it has come to this, that they look only to the strong Christians, and can never bear with the weak; but deal only harshly with them and proceed with force. In times past, when conditions were yet good, the bishops were sorely wanting in this, for, though they were great and holy men, they yet constrained and oppressed the consciences too much. Such things do not take place among Christians, for it is Christ's will to be weak and sickly yet a while, and to have both flesh and bones together, as he says here in the Gospel, "Handle me and see, for a spirit hath not flesh and bones, as ye behold me having." He would have both, not bones only, nor flesh only. Thus we read, in Genesis 2:23, that when God created Eve, Adam said, "This is now bone of my bones, and flesh of my flesh." He says not flesh only nor bones only; he speaks of having both himself, for he, too, must needs have both. So it is also with Christ and with us, and hence he says here, I have both flesh and bones; you will find in me not only bones, nor yet only flesh; you will find that I am both strong and sick.

19. Thus also my Christians must be so mingled together, that some are strong and some weak. They that are strong walk uprightly, are hale and hearty, and must bear the others; they are the bones. The others are the weak that cleave unto the strong. They are also the greater number, as in a body there will always be found more flesh than bones. Hence Jesus was crucified and died, and likewise was quickened again and glorified, that he might not be a spirit, as the disciples here deem him to be and were filled with fear of him, thinking that because he is not only bone and the strong Christ, it is not he, but a ghost.

20. This wisdom was diligently urged by the apostles and by Christ himself and, besides this, I know of no book in which it is urged. It is, indeed, sometimes touched upon, but nowhere urged. Only this one book, the New Testament, urges it constantly, and everywhere strives to set before the people the weak and strong Christ. Thus says Saint Paul, in Romans 15:1–3, "Now we that are strong ought to bear the infirmities of the weak and not to please ourselves. Let each one of us please his neighbor for that which is good, unto edifying. For Christ also pleased not himself." Hence we must do the same, and this is the wisdom we are to learn here.

21. To this school belong all that are pictured here in this Gospel, whom Christ finds terrified and affrighted. The others, who do not belong here, are easily identified, for they reject and despise the Gospel. In like manner, everyone can know himself, whether he truly takes pleasure in the Gospel. And if

you see in another's behavior evidence of an earnest desire to be made holy, you should not despise him.

22. This Gospel, therefore, shows the following: first, that the Lord stands among the disciples and is now strong, having overcome sin, death, and the devil; but they do not stand as yet, but sit there, and he comes and stands in the midst of them. Where does he stand at the present time? In the midst of the weak and fainthearted company, that sit in fear and weakness, while he is strong and mighty, though it is not yet apparent to the world. But even though the world does not see it, God sees it. Secondly, he shows them his hands and his feet, and comforts them, saying, "Why are ye troubled? and wherefore do questionings arise in your hearts? See my hands and my feet, that it is I myself: handle me and see; for a spirit has not flesh and bones," etc.

23. This is nothing but a sermon that teaches us not to be offended in the weak Christ. He does not rebuke the disciples harshly, does not say, Away with you; I do not want you. You should be strong and courageous, but here you sit and are dismayed and terrified! He does not do these things, but lovingly comforts them, that he might make them strong and fearless. Hence they were also made strong and fearless, and not only this, but also cheerful and of good courage. Therefore, we ought not to cast away the weak, but so deal with them that, from day to day, we may bring them to a condition that they may become strong and of good cheer. This does not signify that it is well, if they are weak, and that they should continue weak; for Christ does not stand among them for that purpose, but that they might grow in faith and be made fearless.

24. Here we may also speak, as the text gives occasion, of ghosts or walking spirits, for we see here that the Jews and the apostles themselves held that spirits roam about and are seen by night and at other times. Thus, in Matthew 14:25ff., when the disciples sailed in a ship by night and saw Jesus walking on the sea, they were affrighted, as before a ghost, and cried out in fear. And here we learn that Jesus does not deny it but confirms it by his answer that spirits do appear, for he says, "A spirit has not flesh and bones," etc.

25. But the Scriptures do not say, nor give any example, that such are the souls of dead persons walking among the people and seeking help, as we, in our blindness and deluded by the devil, have heretofore believed. Hence the pope has, also, invented purgatory and established his shameful annual market of masses. We may well see in this false doctrine and abomination as a fruit, that the foundation on which it is built, namely, the doctrine of the migration of souls, comes from the father of lies, the devil, who has deluded the people in the name of the dead.

26. We have good reason not to believe such apparitions of roaming erring spirits that profess to be souls. First, because the Scriptures nowhere say that the souls of the deceased, that have not yet risen, should wander about among the people; whereas everything else we need to know, is clearly revealed in the Scriptures. Not one word concerning this is given for our instruction, nor is it possible that we should grasp and understand the state of the spirits that have departed from the body, before the resurrection and the day of judgment; for they are sundered and separated altogether from the world and from this generation. Moreover, it is clearly forbidden in the Scriptures to consult the dead or to believe them who do, in Deuteronomy 18:11 and in Isaiah 28:19. And, Luke 16:31 proves that God will neither let one rise from the dead nor preach, because we have Moses and the Scriptures.

27. Know, therefore, that all ghosts and visions, which cause themselves to be seen and heard, especially with din and noise, are not men's souls, but evidently devils that amuse themselves thus either to deceive the people with false claims and lies, or unnecessarily frighten and trouble them. Hence with a specter that makes a pretense in the name of a soul, a Christian should not deal otherwise than as with the very devil himself. He should be well girded with God's Word and faith, that he may not be deceived nor affrighted, but abide in the doctrine that he has learned and confessed from the Gospel of Christ, and cheerfully despise the devil with his noise. Nor does he tarry long where he feels a soul trusts in Christ and despise him. This I say that we may be wise and not suffer ourselves to be misled by such deception and lies, as in the past he deceived and mocked even excellent men, like Saint Gregory, under the name of being a soul.

28. Now what does it signify that he shows the disciples his hands and his feet? He would thereby say, Come, and learn to know me. Now I am strong, but you are weak, as I also was. Therefore, see to it now that you become strong also.

II. THE SERMON CHRIST PREACHED TO HIS DISCIPLES

29. The above is one chief part of this Gospel; the other follows at the end of the Gospel, where the Lord concludes by saying,

> *"Thus it is written, that the Christ should suffer, and rise again from the dead the third day; and that repentance and remission of sins should be preached in his name unto all the nations."*

30. Here you see that the Gospel is the preaching of repentance and remission of sins. And it should not be preached in a corner, but before all men,

whether it be received or not, for it is to spread even farther that it may be heard and bear fruit. Hence we are not to be offended though but few receive it, nor say it has been given in vain. We should, rather, be content with it, that Christ has given command to preach it in all the world, that he who will may receive it. But we must note here in particular, that he says,

31. First, let us consider two thoughts. By repentance he means a change for the better; not as we have called it repentance, when one scourges and castigates himself and does penance to atone for his sin, or when the priest imposes this or that upon anyone for penance. Scripture does not speak of it in this sense. Repentance rather signifies here a change and reformation of the whole life; so that when one knows that he is a sinner, and feels the iniquity of his life, he desists from it and enters upon a better course of life, in word and deed, and that he does it from his heart.

32. What then is repentance in his name? Hereby he singles out the repentance that is not made in his name, and hence the text compels us to consider two kinds of repentance. First, a repentance not in his name is, when I come with my own works and undertake to blot out sin with them, as we all have hitherto been taught and have tried to do. This is not repentance in God's name, but in the devil's name. For this is striving to propitiate God by our own works and by our own strength, a thing God cannot allow.

33. But on the other hand, to repent in his name is done thus: in those who believe in Christ, God, through the same faith, works a change for the better, not for a moment, nor for an hour, but for their whole life. For a Christian is not instantaneously or suddenly cleansed perfectly, but the reformation and change continue as long as he lives. Though we use the utmost diligence, we will always find something to sweep or clean. For even though all wickedness be overcome, we have not yet overcome the fear of death, for few have come so far as to desire death with a spirit of rejoicing; hence we must grow better day by day. This is what Paul means when he says in 2 Corinthians 4:16, "Though our outward man is decaying, yet our inward man is renewed day by day." For we hear the Gospel every day, and Christ shows us his hands and his feet every day that our minds may be still more enlightened, and we be made more and more godly.

34. For this reason, Christ would say, let no one strive to amend his life by his own works and in his own name; for of themselves no one is an enemy of sin, no one will come to repentance and think of amending his life. Nothing will be accomplished except in my name. That name alone has power to do it, and brings with it willingness and desire to be changed. But if the works and doctrines of men be taught, I will go and say to myself, O, that I might not

need to pray, nor make confession, nor go to the Lord's Supper! What will your repentance profit you, if you fail to do it gladly or willingly, but are constrained by the commandment or by fear of shame, otherwise you would rather not do it? But what is the reason? Because it is a repentance in the devil's name, in your own name, or in the pope's name. Hence you go on and do worse things, and wish there were no confession and sacrament, so that you might not be constrained to attend them. This is repentance in our own name, and proceeds from our own strength.

35. But when I begin to believe in Christ, lay hold of the Gospel, and doubt not that he has taken away my sin and blotted it out, and comforts me with his resurrection, my heart is filled with such gladness that I myself take hold willingly, not through persuasion, nor of necessity; I gladly do what I ought, and say, Because my Lord has done this for me, I will also do his will in this, that I may amend my ways and repent out of love to him and to his glory. In this way, a true reformation begins that proceeds from the innermost heart, and that is brought forth by the joy that flows from faith, when I apprehend the greatness of the love Christ has bestowed upon me.

36. Secondly, we should preach also forgiveness of sins in his name. This signifies nothing else than that the Gospel should be preached, which declares unto all the world that in Christ the sins of all the world are swallowed up, and that he suffered death to put away sin from us, and arose to devour it and blot it out. All did he do, that whoever believes, should have the comfort and assurance, that it is reckoned unto him even as if he himself had done it; that his work is mine and thine and all men's; yea, that he gives himself to us with all his gifts to be our own personal property. Hence as he is without sin and never dies by virtue of his resurrection, even so I also am, if I believe in him; and I will, therefore, strive to become more and more godly, until there be no more sin in me. This continues as long as we live, until the day of judgment. As he is without sin, he sets before us an example, that we might be fashioned like unto him, though while we live here, we shall be fully like the image.

37. Saint Paul speaks of this in writing to the Corinthians, "We all, with unveiled face beholding as in a mirror the glory of the Lord, are transformed into the same image from glory to glory," in 2 Corinthians 3:18. Christ, even as he is risen, is the image, and is set before us that we might know that he rose from the dead to overcome our sin. This image stands before us and is set before our eyes by the Gospel, and is so mirrored in our hearts that we may grasp it by faith, if we hold it to be true and daily exercise ourselves in it. Thus the glory is imparted by him to us, and it comes to pass that we become ever more glorious, and grow into the same image that he is. Hence he also says

that we are not at once made perfect and strong, but must grow from day to day until we become like him. Many similar passages are here and there in the Scriptures.

38. This then is preaching the forgiveness of sins in his name, that we do not point only to confession, or to a certain hour; for we must act in view of the fact that it deals not with our works but with the whole person. Even when we begin to believe, our sin and infirmity are always present so that there is nothing pure in us, and we are indeed worthy of condemnation. But now forgiveness is so great and powerful, that God not only forgives the former sins you have committed but looks through his fingers and forgives the sins you will yet commit. He will not condemn us for our daily infirmities, but forgives all, in view of our faith in him, if we only strive to press onward and get rid of sin.

39. Here you may see what a difference there is between this and that which has heretofore been preached, of buying letters of indulgence, and of confessions, by which it was thought sin could be blotted out. So far as this pressed and such confidence was there put in it, that men were persuaded if anyone should die upon it, he would straightway mount to heaven. They did not know that we have still more sin and will not be rid of it, as long as we live. They supposed that all is well if only we have been to confession. Hence this is a forgiveness in the name of the devil. But see that you understand it correctly: By absolution you are absolved and declared free from sin, that is, you are put into that state, where there is forgiveness of sin that never ends. And not only is there forgiveness of past sins, but of those also you now have, if you believe that God overlooks and forgives your sins; and although you stumble still, yet he will neither reject nor condemn you, if you continue in faith. This teaching is heard indeed in all the world, but few there be that understand it.

40. Thus you have heard what the Gospel is, and what repentance and forgiveness of sins are, whereby we enter into another, a new state, out of the old. But take heed, lest you trust in this and become sluggish, thinking that when you sin there is no danger, and thus boldly persist in sin. This would be sinning in spite of God's mercy and would tempt God. But if you desire to be delivered from sin, it is well with you, and all is forgiven. So much then on the second part of this Gospel, and with it we shall, for the present, content ourselves.

The Sunday After Easter

❦

Of True Piety, the Law and Faith, and of Love to Our Neighbor

When therefore it was evening, on that day, the first day of the week, and when the doors were shut where the disciples were, for fear of the Jews, Jesus came and stood in the midst, and saith unto them, "Peace be unto you." And when he had said this, he showed unto them his hands and his side. The disciples therefore were glad, when they saw the Lord. Jesus therefore said to them again, "Peace be unto you: as the Father hath sent me, even so send I you." And when he had said this, he breathed on them, and saith unto them, "Receive ye the Holy Spirit: whose soever sins ye forgive, they are forgiven unto them; whose soever sins ye retain, they are retained."

But Thomas, one of the twelve, called Didymus, was not with them when Jesus came. The other disciples therefore said unto him, "We have seen the Lord." But he said unto them, "Except I shall see in his hands the print of the nails, and put my finger into the print of the nails, and put my hand into his side, I will not believe."

And after eight days again his disciples were within, and Thomas with them. Jesus cometh, the doors being shut, and stood in the midst, and said, "Peace be unto you." Then said he to Thomas, "Reach hither thy finger, and see my hands; and reach hither thy hand, and put it into my side: and be not faithless, but believing". Thomas answered and said unto him, "My Lord and my God." Jesus saith unto him, "Because thou hast seen me, thou hast believed: blessed are they that have not seen, and yet have believed."

Many other signs therefore did Jesus in the presence of the disciples, which are not written in this book: but these are written, that ye may believe that Jesus is the Christ, the Son of God; and that believing ye may have life in his name. — JOHN 20:19–31

I. OF TRUE GODLINESS; OF THE LAW AND FAITH

1. In today's Gospel is presented to us, what the life of a Christian is to be and that it consists of two parts: first, that the Lord shows Thomas his hands and feet; secondly, that he is sent as Christ is sent. This is nothing else than faith and love, the two thoughts that are preached to us in all the Gospel texts.

2. Formerly you heard, and alas! it is preached in all the world, that if anyone desires to become righteous, he must begin with human laws. This was done under the reign of the pope, and nearly all the very best preachers preached nothing else than how one is to be outwardly pious, and about good works which glitter before the world. But this is still far from the true righteousness that avails before God.

3. There is another way to begin to become righteous, which commences by teaching us the laws of God, from which we learn to know ourselves, what we are, and how impossible it is for us to fulfill the divine commandments. The law speaks thus, Thou shalt have one God, worship him alone, trust in him alone, seek help and comfort from him alone, in Exodus 20. The heart hears this and yet it cannot do it. Why then does the law command such an impossible thing? In order, as I have said, to show us our inability, and that we may learn to know ourselves and to see ourselves as we are, even as one sees himself in a mirror. When now the conscience, thus smitten by God's law, begins to quake and finds that it does not keep God's commandment, then the law does its proper work; for the true mission of the law is only to terrify the conscience.

4. But there are two classes of men who fulfill the law, or who imagine they fulfill it. The first are those who, when they have heard it, begin with outward works; they desire to perform and fulfill it by works. How do they proceed? They say, God has commanded thou shalt have one God; I surely will worship no other God; I will serve him and no idol, and will have no heathen idolatrous image in my house or in my church; why should I do this? Such persons make a show with their glittering, fabricated service of God, like the clergy in our day, and they think they keep this law, when they bend their knees and are able to sing and prate much about God. By this show, the poor laity also are deceived; they follow after and also desire to obey the law by their works. But the blind guides the blind and both fall into a pit, in Luke 6:39. This is the first class, who take hold and imagine they will keep the law, and yet they do not.

5. The other class are those who know themselves by the law and study what it seeks and requires. For instance, when the law speaks, "Thou shalt have one God, and worship and honor him alone," this same heart meditates,

What does this mean? Shalt thou bend the knees? Or what is it to have one God? It surely is something else than a bodily, outward reverence; and finally it perceives that is a very different thing than is generally supposed; that it is nothing but having trust and hope in God, that he will help and assist in all anxiety and distress, in every temptation and adversity, that he will save him from sin, from death, from hell, and from the devil, without whose help and salvation he alone can do nothing. And this is the meaning of having one God. A heart, so thoroughly humble, desires to have God, namely, a heart that has become quite terrified and shaken by this commandment, and in its anxiety and trouble flees to God alone.

6. This now the hypocrites and work saints, who lead a fine life before the world, are not able to do; for their confidence is based alone upon their own righteousness and outward piety. Therefore, when God attacks them with the law and causes the poor people to see that they have not kept the law, aye, not the least of it, and when overwhelmed by anxiety and distress, and an evil conscience, and they perceive that external works will not suffice and that keeping the commandments of God is a very different thing from what they thought, then they rush ahead and seek ever more and more, and other and still other works, and fancy that they will thereby quiet their conscience, but they greatly miss the right way. Hence it comes to pass that one wishes to do it by rosaries, another by fasting; this one by prayer and that one by torturing his body; one runs to Saint James, another to Rome, this man to Jerusalem, that to Aix; here one becomes a monk, another a nun, and they seek their end in so many ways that they can scarcely be enumerated.

7. Why do they do all this? Because they wish to save themselves, to rescue and help themselves. The consequence of this is great blasphemy of God, for they also boast mightily of these works, and vaunt, and say, I have been in an order so long, I have prayed so many rosaries, have fasted so much, have done this and that; God will give me heaven as a reward. This then means to have an idol. This also is the meaning of Isaiah, when he says, "They worship the work of their own hands," in Isaiah 2:8. He is not speaking of stone and wood, but of the external works, which have a show of goodness and beauty before men. These hypocrites are ingenious enough to give the chaff to God and to keep the wheat for themselves. This then is true idolatry, as Saint Paul writes to the Romans, "Thou that abhorrest idols, dost thou rob temples?" in Romans 2:22. This is spiritual robbery.

8. Therefore, you will find that there is nothing good in any man of himself. But you have this distinction, that the upright, in whom the law has exercised

its work, when they feel their sickness and weakness, say, God will help me; I trust in him; I build upon him; he is my rock and hope. But the others, as hypocrites and work saints, when trial, distress, and anxiety are at hand, lament, and say, Oh, whither shall I go? They must at last despair of God, of themselves, and of their works, even if they have ever so many of them.

9. Such in the first place are these false and unrighteous pupils of the law, who presume to fulfill it by their works. For they have an appearance and glitter outwardly, but in their hearts they have nothing but filth and uncleanness. Therefore, they also merit nothing before God, who regards not external works that are done without any heart in them.

10. In the second place, they are the true and real pupils, who keep the law, who know and are conscious that they do evil, and make naught of themselves, surrender themselves, count all their works unclean in the eyes of God, and despair of themselves and all their own works. They who do this, shall have no trouble, except that they must not deceive themselves with vain fruitless thoughts and defer this matter until death; for if anyone persistently postpones this until death, he will have a sad future.

11. But we must give heed that we do not despair, even if we still feel sinful inclinations and are not as pure as we would like to be. You will not entirely sweep out of your heart all this rubbish, because we are still flesh and blood. This much can surely be done: outward wicked deeds can be prevented and carnal, shameful words and works avoided, although it is attained with difficulty. But it will never come to pass here that you are free from lust and evil inclination. Saint Jerome undertook to root such inclinations out of his heart by prayer, fasting, work, and torture of the body, but he found out what he accomplished. It was of no avail; the concupiscence remained. Works and words can be restrained, but lust and inclinations no one can root out of himself.

12. In short, if you desire to attain the true righteousness that avails before God, you must despair altogether of yourself and trust in God alone; you must surrender yourself entirely to Christ and accept him, so that all that he has is yours, and all that is yours, becomes his. For in this way you begin to burn with divine love and become quite another man, completely born anew, and all that is in you is converted. Then you will have as much delight in chastity as before you had pleasure in unchastity, and so forth with all lusts and inclinations.

13. This now is the first work of God, that we know ourselves, how condemned, miserable, weak, and sickly we are. It is then good and God's will, that

a man desponds and despairs of himself, when he hears, This shalt thou do and that shalt thou do. For everybody must feel and experience in himself, that he does not and cannot do it. The law is neither able nor is it designed to give you this power of obeying it; but it effects what Saint Paul says, "The law worketh wrath," in Romans 4:15, that is, nature rages against the law, and wishes the law did not exist.

14. Therefore, they who presume to satisfy the law by outward deeds, become hypocrites; but in the others it works wrath only, and causes sins to increase, as Saint Paul says in another place, "The power of sin is the law," in 1 Corinthians 15:56. For the law does not take sin away, aye, it multiplies sin, and causes me to feel my sin. So he says again to the Corinthians, "The letter killeth," in 2 Corinthians 3:6, that is, the law works death in you; in other words, it reduces you to nothing; "but the Spirit giveth life." For when he comes through the Gospel, the law is already fulfilled, as we shall hear.

15. Therefore, the world errs when it tries to make men righteous through laws; only pretenders and hypocrites result from such efforts. But reverse this and say, as Saint Paul says, The law produces sin. For the law does not help me the least, except that it teaches me to know myself; there I find nothing but sin; how then should it take sin away? We will now see how this thought is set forth in this Gospel. The text says,

When therefore it was evening, on that day, the first day of the week, and the doors were shut where disciples were for fear of the Jews.

16. What do the disciples fear? They fear death; aye, they were in the very midst of death. Whence came their fear of death? From sin; for if they had not sinned, they would not have feared. Nor could death have injured them; for the sting of death, by means of which it kills, is sin, in 1 Corinthians 15:56. But they, like us all, had not yet a true knowledge of God. For if they had esteemed God as God, they would have been without fear and in security; as David says, "Whither shall I go from thy Spirit? Or whither shall I flee from thy presence? If I ascend up into heaven, thou art there: if I make my bed in Sheol, behold, thou art there. If I take the wings of the morning, and dwell in the uttermost parts of the sea; even there shall thy hand lead me, and thy right hand shall hold me," in Psalm 139:7–10. And, as he says in another place, "In peace will I both lay me down and sleep; for thou, Jehovah, alone makest me dwell in safety," in Psalm 4:8. It is easy to die, if I believe in God; for then I fear no death. But whoever does not believe in God, must fear death, and can never have a joyful and secure conscience.

17. Now God drives us to this by holding the law before us, in order that through the law we may come to a knowledge of ourselves. For where there is not this knowledge, one can never be saved. He that is well needs no physician; but if a man is sick and desires to become well, he must know that he is weak and sick; otherwise, he cannot be helped. But if one is a fool and refuses to take the remedy that will restore him to health, he must certainly die and perish. But our papists have closed our eyes, so that we were not compelled, and not able, to know ourselves, and they failed to preach the true power of the law. For where the law is not properly preached, there can be no self-knowledge.

18. David had such knowledge, when he said, "Have mercy upon me, O God, according to thy lovingkindness; according to the multitude of thy mercies blot out my transgressions. Wash me thoroughly from mine iniquity, and cleanse me from my sin. For I know my transgressions; and my sin is ever before me. Against thee, thee only, have I sinned, and done that which is evil in thy sight, that thou mayest be justified when thou speakest, and be clear when thou judgest. Behold, I was brought forth in iniquity; and in sin did my mother conceive me," in Psalm 51:1ff. Just as if David wished to say, Behold, I am so formed of flesh and blood, which of itself is sin, that I cannot but sin. For although you restrain your hands and feet or tongue that they sin not; the inclinations and lusts always remain, because flesh and blood are present, you may go whither you please, to Rome or to Saint James.

19. If now an upright heart that comes to the point of knowing itself is met by the law, it verily will not begin and seek to help itself by works; but it confesses its sin and helplessness, its infirmity and sickness, and says, Lord God, I am a sinner, a transgressor of thy divine commandments: help thou, for I am lost. Now when a man is in such fear and cries out thus to God, God cannot refrain from helping him; as in this case, Christ was not long absent from the disciples tormented by fear; but he is soon present, comforts them, and says, "Peace be unto you!" Be of good courage; it is I; fear not. The same happens now. When we come to a knowledge of ourselves through the law and are now in deep fear, God arouses us and has the Gospel preached to us, by which he gives us a joyful and secure conscience.

20. But what is the Gospel? It is this, that God has sent his Son into the world to save sinners, in John 3:16, and to crush hell, overcome death, take away sin, and satisfy the law. But what must you do? Nothing but accept this and look up to your Redeemer and firmly believe that he has done all this for your good and freely gives you all as your own, so that in the terrors of death,

sin, and hell you can confidently say and boldly depend upon it, and say, Although I do not fulfill the law, although sin is still present and I fear death and hell, nevertheless, from the Gospel I know that Christ has bestowed upon me all his works. I am sure he will not lie, his promise he will surely fulfill. And as a sign of this, I have received baptism. For he says to his apostles and disciples, "Go ye into all the world, and preach the Gospel to the whole creation. He that believeth and is baptized shall be saved; but he that disbelieveth shall be condemned," in Mark 16:15–16. Upon this I anchor my confidence. For I know that my Lord Christ has overcome death, sin, hell, and the devil all for my good. For he was innocent, as Peter says, "Who did no sin, neither was guile found in his mouth," in 1 Peter 2:22. Therefore, sin and death were not able to slay him, hell could not hold him, and he has become their Lord, and has granted this to all who accept and believe it. All this is effected not by my works or merits; but by pure grace, goodness, and mercy.

21. Now, whoever does not appropriate this faith to himself, must perish; and whoever possesses this faith, shall be saved. For where Christ is, the Father will come and also the Holy Spirit. There will then be pure grace, no law; pure mercy, no sin; pure life, no death; pure heaven, no hell. There I will comfort myself with the works of Christ, as if I myself had done them. There I will no longer concern myself about cowls or tonsures, Saint James or Rome, rosaries or scapulars, praying or fasting, priests or monks.

22. Behold, how beautiful the confidence toward God that arises in us through Christ! You may be rich or poor, sick or well, yet you will always say, God is mine, I am willing to die; for this is acceptable to my Father, and death cannot harm me; it is swallowed up in victory, as Saint Paul says in 1 Corinthians 15:57, yet not through us, but "Thanks be to God," says he, "who giveth us the victory through our Lord Jesus Christ." Therefore, although we must die, we have no fear of death, for its power and might are broken by Christ, our Savior.

23. So then you understand that the Gospel is nothing but preaching and glad tidings, how Christ entered into the throes of death for us, took upon himself all our sins and abolished them; not that it was needful for him to do it, but it was pleasing to the Father; and that he has bestowed all this upon us, in order that we might boldly stand upon it against sin, death, Satan, and hell. Hence arises great, unspeakable joy, such as the disciples here experience. The text says, "The disciples therefore were glad, when they saw the Lord"—not a Lord, who inspired them with terror or burdened them with labor and toil, but who provided for them and watched over them like a father is the lord of his estate and cares for his own. Aye, then first they rejoiced most on his

account, when he spoke to them, "Peace be unto you! It is I," and when he had showed them his hands and feet, that is, his works, all which were to be theirs.

24. In the same manner, he still comes to us through the Gospel, offers us peace, and bestows his works upon us: if we believe, we have them; if we believe not, we have them not. For the Lord's hands and feet really signify nothing but his works, which he has done here upon earth for men. And the showing of his side is nothing but the showing of his heart, in order that we may see how kind, loving, and fatherly his mind is toward us. All this is set forth for us in the Gospel as certainly and clearly as it was revealed and shown to the disciples bodily in our text. And it is much better that it is done through the Gospel than if he now entered here by the door; for you would not know him, even if you saw him standing before you, even much less than the Jews recognized him.

25. This is the true way to become righteous, not by human commandments, but by keeping the commandments of God. Now nobody can do this except by faith in Christ alone. From this flows love that is the fulfillment of the law, as Saint Paul says in Romans 13:10. And this results not from the exercise of virtues and good works, as was taught hitherto, which produced only true martyrs of Satan and hypocrites; but faith makes righteous, holy, chaste, humble, and so forth. For as Paul says to the Romans, "The Gospel is the power of God unto salvation to every one that believeth; to the Jew first and also to the Greek. For therein is revealed a righteousness of God from faith unto faith: as is written, But the righteous shall live by faith," in Romans 1:16–17. As if Saint Paul should say, Your works will not save you but the Gospel will, if you believe; your righteousness is nothing, but Christ's righteousness avails before God; the Gospel speaks of this and no other writing does. Whoever now wishes to overcome death and blot out sins by his works, says that Christ has not died; as Saint Paul says to the Galatians, "If righteousness is through the law, then Christ died for naught," in Galatians 2:21. And they who preach otherwise are wolves and seducers.

26. This has been said of the first part of our Gospel, to show what is to be our attitude toward God, namely, we are to cling to him in faith; and it shows what true righteousness is that is availing before God and how it is attained, namely, by faith in Christ, who has redeemed us from the law, from death, sin, hell, and the devil; and who has freely given us all this in order that we may rely upon it in defiance of the law, death, sin, hell, and the devil. Now follows how we are to conduct ourselves toward our neighbor; this is also shown to us in the text, where the Lord speaks thus:

II. OF LOVE TO YOUR NEIGHBOR

"As the Father hath sent me, even so send I you."

27. Why did God the Father send Christ? For no other purpose than to do the Father's will, namely, to redeem the world. He was not sent to merit heaven by good works or to become righteous thereby. He did many good works, aye, his whole life was nothing else than a continual doing good. But for whom did he do it? For the people who stood in need of it, as we read here and there in the evangelists; for all he did, he did for the purpose of serving us. "As the Father hath sent me," he says here, "even so send I you." My Father hath sent me to fulfill the law, take the sin of the world upon myself, slay death, and overcome hell and the devil; not for my own sake, for I am not in need of it; but all for your sakes and in your behalf, in order that I may serve you. So shall you also do.

28. By faith you will accomplish all this. It will make you righteous before God and save you, and likewise also overcome death, sin, hell, and the devil. But this faith you are to show in love, so that all your works may be directed to this end; not that you are to seek to merit anything by them; for all in heaven and earth is yours beforehand; but that you serve your neighbor thereby. For if you do not give forth such proofs of faith, it is certain that your faith is not right. Not that good works are commanded us by this Word; for where faith in the heart is right, there is no need of much commanding good works to be done; they follow of themselves. But the works of love are only an evidence of the existence of faith.

29. This also is the intent of Saint Peter, when he admonishes us in 2 Peter 1:5, to give diligence to make our faith sure and to prove it by our good works. But good works are those we do to our neighbor in serving him, and the only one thing demanded of a Christian is to love. For by faith he is already righteous and saved; as Saint Paul says in Romans 13:8, "Owe no man anything, save to love one another: for he that loveth his neighbor hath fulfilled the law." Therefore Christ says to his disciples in John 13:34–35: "A new commandment I give unto you, that ye love one another; even as I have loved you, that ye also love one another. By this shall all men know that ye are my disciples, if ye have love one to another."

30. In this way, we must give proof of ourselves before the world, that everyone may see that we keep God's commandment; and yet not that we would be saved or become righteous thereby. So then I obey the civil government for I know that Christ was obedient to the government, and yet he had

no need to be; he did it only for our sakes. Therefore, I will also do it for Christ's sake and in behalf of my neighbor, and for the reason alone that I may prove my faith by my love; and so on through all commandments. In this manner, the apostles exhort us to good works in their writings; not that we become righteous and are saved by them, but only to prove our faith both to ourselves and others, and to make it sure. The Gospel continues,

"Receive ye the Holy Spirit: Whose soever sins ye forgive, they are forgiven unto them; whose soever sins ye retain, they are retained."

31. This power is here given to all Christians, although some have appropriated it to themselves alone, like the pope, bishops, priests, and monks have done: they declare publicly and arrogantly that this power was given to them alone and not to the laity. But Christ here speaks neither of priests nor of monks, but says, "Receive ye the Holy Spirit." Whoever has the Holy Spirit, power is given to him, that is, to everyone that is a Christian. But who is a Christian? He that believes. Whoever believes has the Holy Spirit. Therefore, every Christian has the power, which the pope, bishops, priests, and monks have in this case, to forgive sins or to retain them.

32. Do I hear then, that I can institute confession, baptize, preach, and administer the Lord's Supper? No. Saint Paul says in 1 Corinthians 14:40, "Let all things be done decently and in order." If everybody wished to hear confession, baptize, and administer the Lord's Supper, what order would there be? Likewise, if everybody wished to preach, who would hear? If we all preached at the same time, what a confused babble it would be, like the noise of frogs! Therefore, the following order is to be observed: the congregation shall elect one, who is qualified, and he shall administer the Lord's Supper, preach, hear confession, and baptize. True we all have this power; but no one shall presume to exercise it publicly, except the one who has been elected by the congregation to do so. But in private, I may freely exercise it. For instance, if my neighbor comes and says, Friend, I am burdened in my conscience; speak the absolution to me; then I am free to do so, but I say it must be done privately. If I were to take my seat in the church, and another and all would hear confession, what order and harmony would there be? Take an illustration: If there are many heirs among the nobility, with the consent of all the others they elect one, who alone administers the estate in behalf of the others; for if everyone wished to rule the country and people, how would it be? Still they all alike have the power that he has who rules. So also is it with this power to forgive sins and to retain them.

33. But this word, to forgive sins or to retain sins, concerns those who confess and receive more than those who are to impart the absolution. And

thereby we serve our neighbor. For in all services the greatest is to release from sin, to deliver from the devil and hell. But how is this done? Through the Gospel, when I preach it to a person and tell him to appropriate the words of Christ, and to believe firmly that Christ's righteousness is his own and his sins are Christ's. This I say, is the greatest service I can render to my neighbor.

34. Accursed be the life, where one lives only for himself and not for his neighbor; and on the contrary, blessed be the life, in which one lives not for himself but for his neighbor and serves him by teaching, by rebuke, by help, and by whatever manner and means. If my neighbor errs, I am to correct him; if he cannot immediately follow me, then I am to bear patiently with him; as Christ did with Judas, who had the purse with the money and went wrong and stole from it. Christ knew this very well; yet he had patience with him, admonished him diligently, although it did no good, until he disgraced himself.

35. So we are to give heed to do everything in behalf of our neighbor, and ever to be mindful, that Christ has done this and that for me; why should I not also for his sake freely do all for my neighbor? And see to it that all the works you do are directed not to God, but to your neighbor. Whoever is a ruler, a prince, a mayor, a judge, let him not think that he is a ruler to gain heaven thereby or to seek his own advantage; but to serve the public. And so with other works, I assume to do for the good of my neighbor. For example, if I take a wife, I make myself a captive; why do I do this? In order that I may not do harm to my neighbor's wife and daughters, and thus may bring my body into subjection; and so forth with all other works.

36. Thus then you have finely portrayed in this Gospel, as in almost all the Gospel lessons, these two thoughts, faith and love. Through faith we belong above to God, through love below to our neighbor. That we may thus lay hold of this truth, may God give us his help! Amen.

The Second Sunday After Easter

⮜⦿⮞

Christ's Office and Kingdom: A Sermon on the Good Shepherd

I am the good shepherd: the good shepherd layeth down his life for the sheep. He that is a hireling, and not a shepherd, whose own the sheep are not, beholdeth the wolf coming, and leaveth the sheep, and fleeth, and the wolf snatcheth them, and scattereth them: he fleeth because he is a hireling, and careth not for the sheep. I am the good shepherd; and I know mine own, and mine own know me, even as the Father knoweth me, and I know the Father; and I lay down my life for the sheep. And other sheep I have, which are not of this fold: them also I must bring, and they shall hear my voice; and they shall become one flock, one shepherd." — JOHN 10:11–16

1. This is a comforting Gospel, which so beautifully portrays the Lord Jesus and teaches us what manner of person he is, what kind of works he does, and how he is disposed toward men. And there is no better way to understand it than to contrast light and darkness, and day and night; that is, the good shepherd with the wicked one, as the Lord himself does.

2. Now, you have often heard that God has given the world two different proclamations. One is that which is declared in the Word of God when it says, Thou shalt not kill, not commit adultery, not steal, in Exodus 20:13–15, and when it adds the threat that all who do not keep these commandments shall die. But this declaration will make no one godly at heart. For though it may compel a man outwardly to appear godly before men, inwardly it leaves the heart at enmity with the law, and wishing that there were no such law.

3. The other proclamation is that of the Gospel. It tells where one may obtain that which will meet the demands of the law. It does not drive or threaten, but tenderly invites us. It does not say, Do this and do that, but rather, Come, I will show you where you may find and obtain what you need to make you godly. See, here is the Lord Jesus; he will give it to you. Therefore, the two are as contrary to each other as taking and giving, demanding

and presenting; and this distinction must be well observed. Thus God ever has ruled and still rules the world today. To coarse and rude persons, who are not influenced by the Gospel, the law must be declared, and they must be driven until they are humbled and acknowledge their imperfections. When this has been accomplished, the Gospel is to be applied.

4. These are the two divine proclamations, which come from heaven. Besides these, there are others that are not from heaven, but are human prattle, which the pope and our bishops have invented that they might terrify our consciences. Such men are not worthy of being called shepherds or hirelings, but they are here designated by the Lord Jesus as thieves, murderers, and wolves. For if men are to be savingly governed, it must be done with the Word of God; and if it is not done by the Word of God, they are not properly governed.

I. THE NATURE OF THE OFFICE AND KINGDOM OF CHRIST EXPLAINED

5. Now, here Jesus has in mind the second proclamation. He explains it and sets himself forth as the chief shepherd, yea, as the only shepherd; for that which he does not tend is not kept. This comforting and sweet proclamation we will now consider.

6. You have heard that after his sufferings and death, Christ our Lord arose from the dead and entered upon, and was enthroned in, an immortal existence. Not that he might sit up there in heaven idly and find pleasure in himself, but that he might take charge of the kingdom of which the prophets and all the Scriptures have so fully spoken, and might rule as a king. Therefore, we should think of him as being present and reigning among us continually, and never think of him as sitting up there doing nothing, but rather that he from above fills and rules all things, as Paul says to the Ephesians, in Ephesians 4:10, and especially that he is taking care of his kingdom, which is the Christian faith, and that, therefore, his kingdom among us here on earth must prosper. This kingdom, as we have said, is so constituted that we all must daily increase and grow in holiness, and it is not governed by any other power save the oral proclamation of the Gospel.

7. This proclamation is not of men, but Christ himself sent it forth, and then put it into the hearts of the apostles and their successors so that they understood it, and into their mouths so that they spoke and declared it. This is his kingdom, and so does he rule that all of his power is comprehended in and connected with the Word of God. They who hear and believe it belong to this kingdom, and the Word then becomes so mighty that it provides all that man may need and bestows all the blessings that we may desire. For it is the

power of God, and it can and will save all who believe it, as Saint Paul declared to the Romans, in Romans 1:16. If you believe that Christ died to save you from all evil, and will hold fast to that Word, you will find it so certain and sure that no creature can overthrow it; and as no one can overthrow the Word, neither can anyone harm you who believe it. Accordingly, with the Word you will overcome sin, death, the devil, and hell, and you will find a refuge in the Word and attain that which is found where the Word is, namely, everlasting peace, joy, and life. In short, you will be participants in all the power that is in the Word. Therefore, it is a peculiar kingdom. The Word is present and is orally proclaimed to all the world, but its power is deeply hidden, so that none but they who believe realize that it is so effective and that it accomplishes such great things. It must be experienced and realized by the heart.

8. Hence all that we preachers can do is to become the mouthpieces and instruments of Christ our Lord, through whom he proclaims the Word bodily. He sends forth the Word publicly so that all may hear it, but that the heart inwardly experiences it, that is effected through faith and is wrought by Christ in secret where he perceives that it can be done according to his divine knowledge and pleasure. That is why he says, "I am the good shepherd." And what is a good shepherd? "The good shepherd," says Christ, "layeth down his life for the sheep; and I lay down my life for the sheep." In this one virtue, the Lord comprehends and exemplifies all others in the beautiful parable of the sheep. Sheep, you know, are most foolish and stupid animals. When we want to speak of anybody's stupidity we say, "He is a sheep." Nevertheless, it has this trait above all other animals, that it soon learns to heed its shepherd's voice and will follow no one but its shepherd and, though it cannot help and keep and heal itself, nor guard itself against the wolf, but is dependent upon others, yet it always knows enough to keep close to its shepherd and look to him for help.

9. Now, Christ uses this trait or nature of the animal as an illustration in explaining that he is the good shepherd. In this manner, he plainly shows what his kingdom is, and wherein it consists, and would say, My kingdom is only to rule the sheep; that is, poor, needy, wretched men, who well see and realize that there is no other help or counsel for them.

10. But that we may make it the plainer, and may understand it the better, we will cite a passage from the prophet Ezekiel, where he speaks of the wicked shepherds that are against Christ, when he says, in Ezekiel 34:2ff., "Should not the shepherds feed the sheep? Ye eat the fat, and ye clothe you with the wool, ye kill the fatlings; but ye feed not the sheep. The diseased have ye not strengthened, neither have ye healed that which was sick, neither have ye bound up that which was broken, neither have ye brought back that which

was driven away, neither have ye sought that which was lost; but with force and with rigor have ye ruled over them. And they were scattered, because there was no shepherd; and they become food to all the beasts of the field and were scattered. My sheep wandered through all the mountains, and upon every high hill: yea, my sheep were scattered upon all the face of the earth; and there was none that did search or seek after them," and so forth. Accordingly, God reproves the shepherds who do not keep the sheep. And now mark well what he has written. His earnest intent in this paragraph is that the weak, sick, broken, those who are driven away, and the lost, are to be strengthened, bound up, healed, and sought again, and that they are not to be torn to pieces and scattered. This you should have done, says he to the shepherds, but you have not done it; therefore, I will do it myself. As he says further on, in verse 16, "I will seek that which was lost, I will bring back that which was driven away, and will bind up that which was broken, and will strengthen that which was sick."

11. Here you see that Christ's kingdom is to be concerned about the weak, the sick, the broken, that he may help them. That is, indeed, a comforting declaration. The only trouble is that we do not realize our needs and infirmities. If we realized them, we would soon flee to him. But how did those shepherds act? They ruled with rigor, and applied God's law with great severity; and, moreover, they added their own commandments, as they still do, and when these were not fulfilled, they raved and condemned, so that they were driving and driving and exhorting and exacting, continually. That is no proper way to tend and keep souls, says Christ. He is no such shepherd as that; for no one is benefited, but is rather wholly undone, by such a course, as we shall presently hear. Now let us consider this citation from the prophet in its order.

12. First, he says, The sheep that are weak are to be strengthened; that is, consciences weak in faith and troubled in spirit and of tender disposition are not to be driven and told, You must do this. You must be strong. If you are weak, you are lost. That is not strengthening the weak. Saint Paul, speaking to the Romans, in Romans 14:1, says, "But him that is weak in faith receive ye, yet not for decision of scruples." And shortly afterward, in Romans 15:1, he says, "Now we that are strong ought to bear the infirmities of the weak." Accordingly, they should not be driven with rigor, but should be comforted, even though they are weak, lest they be driven to despair; and in time they will grow stronger.

13. Isaiah, the prophet, speaks of Christ likewise, in Isaiah 42:3, "A bruised reed will he not break, and a dimly burning wick will he not quench." The bruised reeds are poor, tender consciences, which are easily distracted so that they tremble and despair of God. He does not fly at them then, and trample

them under foot; that is not his way. But he deals with them gently, lest he break them to pieces. Again, the dimly burning wick, which still burns at least, though there be more smoke than fire there, he does not wholly quench, but lights, and again and again trims it. That is a great consolation, indeed, to such as experience it; and, therefore, he who does not deal gently with tender consciences is no good shepherd.

14. Secondly, the prophet says, "Neither have ye healed the sick." Who are the sick? They are those who are manifestly deficient in certain of their works. The first clause has reference to tender consciences; the second, to outward conduct. As, for instance, when one growls and sulks, and now and then lapses and, in anger and other foolish ways, oversteps the bounds; even as the apostles, at times, grievously stumbled. But even those who in their outward works before men manifest their shortcomings, so that people are offended at them and say that they are rude and peculiar, he will not cast away; for his kingdom here below is not so constituted as to embrace only the strong and the whole, as it will be in the life to come. Christ is sent here that he might receive and help just such people.

15. Therefore, even though we are weak and sick, we must not despair and say we are not in the kingdom of Christ. But the more we realize our sickness, all the more should we turn to him; for that is what he is here for, to heal and make us whole. Accordingly, if you are sick and a sinner, and realize your condition, you have all the more reason to go to him, and say, Dear Lord, I come just because I am a sinner; that thou mayest help me, and make me good. Thus necessity drives you to him; for the greater your ailment, the more imperative it is that you seek relief. And that is what he wants; therefore, he tenderly bids us to be of good cheer, and to come unto him. They who are not good shepherds, however, expect to make people good by hatefully scolding and driving them, whereas they are thereby only making matters worse. And this may be seen when we look upon present conditions, brought about by this wrong method, when everything is so piteously scattered, even as the prophet has here said.

16. Thirdly, "Neither have ye bound up that which was broken." To be broken is as though one had a bone fractured or were otherwise wounded. As when a Christian is not only weak and infirm, so that he makes a misstep at times, but when he falls into such great temptation that he breaks his leg; for instance, if he should fall and deny the Gospel, as Saint Peter did, when he denied Christ. Well, even though one should make such a misstep as to be impeded or overthrown—even then you should not cast him away, as though he no more belonged to this kingdom. For you must not rob Christ of his

characteristic, that in his kingdom abounding grace and mercy alone prevail, so that he helps those who realize their misery and wretchedness, and desire to be helped, and that his kingdom is wholly one of consolation, and that he is a comforting, friendly shepherd, who tenderly invites, and would induce, all men to come unto him.

17. Now, all this is effected through the Gospel alone, by means of which we are to strengthen all the weak and heal all the sick; for this Word will satisfy every want of those whose consciences are troubled, and will give full consolation to all, so that no one, no matter how great a sinner he has been, need despair. Hence Christ alone is the good shepherd, who heals all our infirmities and raises up again those who have fallen. He who does not do that is no shepherd.

18. Fourthly, the prophet says, "Neither have ye brought back that which was driven away." What is meant by "that which was driven away"? It is that despised soul that is fallen so low that all efforts to reclaim it seem to be in vain. Nevertheless, Christ would not have even such dealt with rigorously. He would not have his kingdom narrowed down so as to include only such as are strong and healthy and perfect. That will be the case in the future kingdom that follows this life, as has been said, Now, because he reigns, pure grace and bliss only shall prevail. Even as God promised the children of Israel, in Exodus 3:8, that the Promised Land would be a land flowing with milk and honey, likewise Saint Paul says that our uncomely parts shall have more abundant comeliness, in 1 Corinthians 12:23.

19. Fifthly, he concludes, "Neither have ye sought that which was lost." That which was lost is that which is given up as already condemned, so that there is no expectation that it ever will return; as the publicans and harlots mentioned in the Gospel, and as the dissolute and intractable in our day, were and are. And yet, even these he would not have us pass by, but would have everything possible done to reclaim them. This was done by Saint Paul, on different occasions; as, for example, when he delivered two men unto Satan, as he said to Timothy, in 1 Timothy 1:20, "Whom I delivered unto Satan that they might be taught not to blaspheme." And, again, to the Corinthians he said, in 1 Corinthians 5:5, "I have concluded to deliver such a one unto Satan for the destruction of the flesh, that the spirit may be saved in the day of the Lord Jesus." He had cast these away as condemned, and yet he goes after them again.

20. Therefore, we should so preach Christ as one who will reject nobody, however weak he may be, but will gladly receive and comfort and strengthen everybody; that we may always picture him to ourselves as a good shepherd.

Then hearts will turn to him of their own accord, and need not be forced and driven. The Gospel graciously invites and makes men willing, so that they desire to go, and do go, to him with all confidence. And it begets a love for Christ in their hearts, so that they willingly do what they should, whereas formerly they had to be driven and forced. When we are driven, we do a thing with displeasure and against our will. That is not what God desires; therefore, it is done in vain. But when I see that God deals with me graciously, he wins my heart, so that I am constrained to fly to him; consequently, my heart is filled with happiness and joy.

21. Now see what an evil it is when one person judges another. Christ's kingdom, as we have heard, is calculated to heal and sanctify only such souls as are sick and needy; therefore, all must err who look only upon those who are strong and holy. Consequently, the knowledge that rightly apprehends Christ is great and mighty. By our nature, we are knaves to the very hide, and yet we expect everyone to be pious. With open mouth, we do not want to look at anybody but strong Christians. We ignore the sick and weak, and think that if they are not strong then they are not Christians at all. And others who are not perfectly holy, we reckon among the wicked, and yet we, ourselves, are more wicked than they. That is what our evil nature does, and our blind reason, that wants to measure God's kingdom by its own imagination, and thinks that whatever does not appear pure in its eyes is not pure in the sight of God.

22. Therefore, we must get that idea out of our minds; for if we keep it before us too much, we will finally get into such a state of mind as to think, Oh, what will become of me if only they are Christians who are strong and healthy and holy? When will I ever reach that state? And thus we, ourselves, will make it impossible. Therefore, we must eventually be driven to say, Dear Lord, I realize that I am very weak, very sick, and despondent. Nevertheless, I will not allow that to confound me, but I will come to thee, that thou mayest help me; for thou art ever the good and pious shepherd, which I also confess thee to be and, therefore, will I despair of my own works.

23. Let us, therefore, ever be wise and learn to know Christ well, and to know that in his kingdom there are only weak and sickly people, and that it is nothing but a hospital, where the sick and infirm, who need care, are gathered. And yet there are so few who understand that! And this fact seems so obscured that even they who have the Gospel and the Spirit are lacking in the knowledge of it; for it is the most profound wisdom that man can attain. For even though they see that the Scriptures praise this kingdom and speak of its preciousness, yet they do not realize what the words mean, and do not

understand that they contain that true wisdom which is far above the wisdom of men. For it is not our wisdom that we deal with, and that we speak of and preach to sensible, prudent, and wise people; but it is this, that we go among fools and simpletons, and care for them, not because we find pleasure in so doing, but in order that we may help them to get rid of their sins and foolishness, and to find righteousness and true knowledge.

24. So you see that Christian wisdom does not consist in raising our eyes to that which is lofty and wise, to see ourselves reflected there, but in lowering our eyes to that which is lowly and foolish. Let him who knows this, thank God; for such knowledge will fit him to accommodate himself to, and guide him under, all circumstances in this life. Therefore, you will yet find many even among those who preach the Gospel, who have not yet attained it. They never taught us thus before, and we were accustomed to think we did not dare to come to Christ until we had first become perfectly pure. Now, you must get out of that way of thinking and come to a proper understanding of Jesus, and learn to know him as a true shepherd. But we have heard enough on this point for the present.

II. CHRIST ILLUSTRATES HIS OFFICE AND KINGDOM BY COMPARING THE GOOD SHEPHERD WITH THE HIRELING

25. Now, he contrasts the good shepherd with a wicked one, or a hireling, and says,

> *"The good shepherd layeth down his life for the sheep.*
> *He that is a hireling, and not a shepherd, whose own the sheep are not,*
> *beholdeth the wolf coming, and leaveth the sheep, and fleeth, and the wolf*
> *snatcheth them and scattereth them: he fleeth because he is a hireling,*
> *and careth not for the sheep."*

26. In the strictest sense, he alone is the shepherd; and yet, as he alone is Christ but nevertheless calls us by the same name, Christians, even so, though he alone is the shepherd, he designates all those who exercise the office of the ministry among Christians by that name also. In like manner in Matthew 23:9, he forbids us to call any man on earth father, for one is our father, even he who is in heaven, yet Paul calls himself a father of the Corinthians when he says, "I begat you through the Gospel," in 1 Corinthians 4:15. Thus God acts as though he alone would be our father, and yet he attributes the name to men also, so that they are called fathers. But they have no right to this name in themselves; only in Christ is it theirs: even as we are called Christians though

we have nothing of our own, but all we have has been given to us, in him. Now, "the hireling," says he, "whose own the sheep are not, beholdeth the wolf coming, and leaveth the sheep, and fleeth," etc. That is a hard saying, indeed, that some who truly preach and administer the Gospel and strengthen and heal the sheep, finally allow themselves to be carried away and leave the sheep when they are most in need of help. As long as no wolf is in sight, they are active and tend the sheep; but when they see the wolf breaking in, they forsake the sheep. If the sheep have been well kept, until they are strong and healthy and fat, they will then be all the more acceptable to the wolf, for whom they have been kept.

27. How does that happen? Well, says Christ, in my kingdom, whose whole object is to strengthen the weak, heal the sick, comfort the sorrowing, and so forth, the holy cross will not be wanting. For, if we preach that Christ alone must receive, strengthen, heal, and help us poor sheep, and that we cannot, by our own strength and works, help ourselves, and that, therefore, all works and whatever else the world pretends to offer in its many religious services are of no avail, the world cannot abide such preaching. Hence it is but natural that the Gospel should bring with it the holy cross, and that they who confess it before the world should risk their necks in so doing.

28. Because this is so, the good shepherds are thus distinguished from the hirelings. Whoever is a hireling will preach the Gospel only so long as they say of him that he is a learned, pious, and good man; but when he is attacked, and men begin to denounce him as a heretic and a knave, and challenge him to a dispute, he recants or runs away, and abandons the poor sheep in their distress, and things are in a worse state than they were before. For what advantage has it been to the poor sheep that they had once been well kept? Had the shepherds been faithful, they would have sacrificed their bodies and lives for the sake of the sheep, and would have given their necks to the executioner for the Gospel's sake. Accordingly, they are never true shepherds who, in preaching, have their own popularity, profit, and advantage in view. They are surely hirelings; for they seek their own advantage, even when they dispense the true doctrine and Word of God. Therefore, they continue only as long as they are honored and praised. Hence they retract and deny the Word when the wolf comes, or flee and leave the sheep in the lurch. The sheep bleat for pasture and for the shepherd to protect them from the wolves, but there is no one to succor them; thus they are deserted when they most need someone to help them.

29. Such will be the result when men once begin to lay hands on and persecute us in earnest. There will be preachers who will hold their tongues and flee, and the sheep will be pitiably scattered, the one running here and the

other there. God grant that there may be at least some who will stand firm and risk their lives to rescue the sheep. Thus Christ has here portrayed the hireling. He then proceeds,

"I am the good shepherd; and I know mine own."

30. There is a great deal contained in these words, far too much to be exhaustively treated here. He speaks here of his own peculiar calling. "I know mine own," he says, "and mine own know me." How is this to be understood? That he explains further when he says,

"Even as the Father knoweth me, and I know the Father."

III. THE SPECIAL OFFICE CHRIST ADMINISTERS EXPLAINED

31. How is he known of the Father? Not with an earthly, but with a heavenly, knowledge. Of that we have spoken more fully before, and the substance of it is this: Christ recognizes us as his sheep, and we recognize him as our shepherd. Now, we have heard what a good shepherd is, and also who the weak sheep are. He knows us to be such sheep as are weak, sick, and broken. That is, It does not make any difference in his regard for them that they are weak and sickly, and he does not despise and reject them on that account; but he pities and heals them, even though they be so diseased that the whole world concludes they are not his sheep. Such is the world's knowledge, but that is not the way that Christ distinguishes them. He does not look upon their condition, but looks to see whether they are sheep, whether they may be designated sheep. He looks at the sheep, not at the wool.

32. Now, they are good shepherds who imitate Christ and know the sheep in the same way; who look at the person, not at the faults, and know how to distinguish between the sheep and the disease.

33. Even so the Father knows me also, says Christ, but the world does not know me. When the time comes for me to die a shameful death upon the cross, all the world will say, Well, is that the Son of God? That must be a malefactor, owned, body and soul, by the devil. And thus the world will look upon and know me; but my Father will say, This is my beloved Son, my King, my Savior. For he will not look upon my sorrows, nor upon my wounds, nor upon my cross and my death, but he will see the person that I am. Therefore, though I were in the midst of hell and in the jaws of the devil, I must again come forth, for the Father will not desert me. And thus I know my sheep and am known of them. They know that I am the good shepherd and know me;

and, therefore, they come to me and abide with me, and they are not afraid because they are weak and sick, for they know that I will receive such sheep. He now concludes, and says,

> *"And other sheep I have, which are not of this fold;*
> *them also must I bring, and they shall hear my voice;*
> *and they shall become one flock, one shepherd."*

34. Some have explained this passage in such a way as to make it appear that it will be fulfilled shortly before the last day, when the Antichrist appears, and Elias and Enoch. That is not true, and it is the devil himself who is responsible for this belief of some, that the whole world will become Christian. The devil did this that the true doctrine might be so obscured so that it might not be understood. Therefore, be on your guard; for this passage was verified and fulfilled shortly after Christ ascended into heaven, and is still in process of fulfillment. When the Gospel was first proclaimed, it was preached to the Jews; that nation was the sheepfold. And now he says here, "And other sheep I have, which are not of this fold: them also must I bring." Here he declares that the Gospel is to be preached to the gentiles also, so that they also might believe in Christ, that there might be one Christian communion, composed of Jews and gentiles. This was afterward brought about through the apostles, who preached to the gentiles and converted them to the faith. Accordingly, there is now but one church or communion, one faith, one hope, one love, one baptism, etc. And this continues to be so at the present day, and will continue until the day of judgment. Hence you must not understand this to mean that the whole world, and all men, will believe in Christ; for this holy cross will always be with us. They are in the majority who persecute Christ and, therefore, the Gospel must ever be preached, that some may be won for Christ. The kingdom of Christ is in process of growing and is not something that is completed. This is, in brief, the explanation of this Gospel.

The Third Sunday After Easter

≈≈≈

A Sermon of Comfort That Christ Preached to His Disciples

A little while, and ye behold me no more; and again a little while, and ye shall see me." Some of his disciples therefore said one to another, "What is this that he saith unto us, 'A little while, and ye behold me not; and again a little while, and ye shall see me:' and, 'Because I go to the Father?'" They said therefore, "What is this that he saith, 'A little while?' We know not what he saith." Jesus perceived that they were desirous to ask him, and he said unto them, "Do ye inquire among yourselves concerning this, that I said, 'A little while, and ye shall behold me not, and again a little while, and ye shall see me?' Verily, verily, I say unto you, that ye shall weep and lament, but the world shall rejoice: ye shall be sorrowful, but your sorrow shall be turned into joy. A woman when she is in travail hath sorrow, because her hour is come: but when she is delivered of the child, she remembereth no more the anguish, for the joy that a man is born into the world. And ye therefore now have sorrow: but I will see you again, and your heart shall rejoice, and your joy no one taketh away from you. And in that day ye shall ask me no question. Verily, verily, I say unto you, If ye shall ask anything of the Father, he will give it you in my name."
— JOHN 16:16–23

I. WHAT MOVED CHRIST TO DELIVER THIS SERMON OF COMFORT

1. Here in this Gospel we see how the Lord comforts and imparts courage to his children whom he is about to leave behind him, when they would come in fear and distress on account of his death or of their backsliding. We also notice what induced the evangelist John to use so many words that he indeed repeats one expression four times, which according to our thinking he might have expressed in fewer words. There is first of all presented to us here the nature of the true Christian in the example of the dear apostles. In the second place, how the suffering and the resurrection of Christ are to become effective in us.

2. We also see that Christ announces to his disciples, how sorrowful they should be because he would leave them, but they are still so simple-minded and ignorant, and also so sorrowful on account of his recent conversation at the Last Supper, that they did not understand at all what he said unto them; yea, the nature of that which Christ presents to them is too great and incomprehensible for them. And it was also necessary that they should first become sorrowful before they could rejoice, even as Christ himself was an example to us that without the cross we could not enter into glory. Hence he says, in Luke 24:26, to the two, with whom he journeyed to Emmaus, "Behooved it not the Christ to suffer these things and to enter into his glory?" If, therefore, the dear disciples were to have joy, they must first of all pass through great sorrow. But this joy came to them through the Lord Jesus; for it is decreed in the Gospel, that without Christ there is no joy; and on the other hand, where Christ is, there is no sorrow, as is plainly stated in the text. Hence when Christ was taken from them, they were in great sorrow.

3. And these words here in this Gospel Christ the Lord spoke unto his disciples after the Last Supper, before he was apprehended. Let us look at them:

"A little while and ye behold me no more, and again a little while and ye shall see me, for I go to the Father."

II. THE SERMON OF COMFORT ITSELF

A. Contents of This Sermon

4. "A little while," he says, "and ye behold me no more," for I shall be taken prisoner and they shall deliver me to death. But it will not last long and, during this short time, ye shall be sorrowful, but only remain steadfast in me and follow me. It will soon have an end. Three days I will be in the grave; then the world will rejoice as though it had gained a victory, but ye shall be sorrowful and shall weep and lament. "And again a little while, and ye shall see me; and, Because I go to the Father." That is, on the third day I will rise again; then ye shall rejoice and your joy no man shall take from you; and this will not be a joy of only three days, like the joy of the world, but an eternal joy. Thus the evangelist John most beautifully expresses the death and resurrection of Christ in these words, when Christ says, "A little while, and ye behold me not; and again a little while, and ye shall see me; and, Because I go to the Father."

5. An example is here given us, which we should diligently lay hold of and take to heart; if it went with us as it did in the time of the apostles, that we should be in suffering, anxiety, and distress, we should also remember to be

strong and to rejoice because Christ will arise again. We know that this has come to pass; but the disciples did not know how he should be raised, or what he meant by the resurrection, hence they were so sorrowful and so sad. They heard indeed that they should see him, but they did not understand what it was or how it should come to pass. Therefore, they said among themselves, "What is this that he saith to us, A little while? We know not what he saith." To such an extent had sadness and sorrow overcome them, that they quite despaired, and knew not what these words meant and how they would see him again.

6. Therefore, we must also feel within us this "a little while" as the dear disciples felt it, for this is written for our example and instruction, so that we may thereby be comforted and be made better. And we should use this as a familiar adage among ourselves; yea, we should feel and experience it, so that we might at all times say, God is at times near and at times he has vanished out of sight. At times I remember how the Word seems neither to move me nor to apply to me. It passes by; I give no heed to it. But to this "a little while" we must give heed and pay attention, so that we may remain strong and steadfast. We will experience the same as the disciples. We cannot do otherwise than is written here; even as the disciples were not able to do otherwise.

7. The first "a little while" in that he says, "A little while, and ye shall behold me no more," they could soon afterward understand, when they saw that he was taken prisoner and put to death, but the second "a little while" in that he says, "And again a little while, and ye shall see me," that they could not understand, and we also cannot understand it. Yea, and when he says, "Because I go to the Father," that they understand still less. Thus it also goes with us: although we know and hear that trials, misfortune, and sorrow endure but a little while, yet we see that it constantly appears different than we believe. Then we despair and waver, and cannot be reconciled to it. We hear and we know very well that it shall not last very long, but how that result shall be accomplished we can never understand, as the disciples here cannot understand it.

8. But since they are unable to understand it, why does Christ relate it to them or why is it written? In order that we should not despair but hold fast to the Word, assured that it is indeed thus and not otherwise, even though it seems to be different. And although we do at times depart from the Word, we should not, therefore, remain altogether away from it, but return again, for he makes good his Word. Even though man cannot believe it, God will nevertheless help him to believe it, and this he does without man's reason or free will and without man's adding anything thereto. Yea, the evangelist tells us that the disciples could not understand the words the Lord spoke to them; how much less could they understand his works that followed afterward. So

very little does the free will and understanding of man know of the things pertaining to the salvation of the soul. These temporal things the free will can perceive and know, such as the cock crowing, which he can hear and his reason can also understand it; but when it is a question of understanding the work and Word of God, then human reason must give it up; it cannot make head or tail of it, although it pretends to understand a great deal about it. The glory thereof is too bright, the longer he beholds it, the blinder he becomes.

9. This is presented very plainly to our minds in the disciples who, though they had been so long with the Lord, yet they did not understand what he said to them. Well, neither will we be able to learn nor to understand this until we experience it; as when we say, Such and such a thing happened to me; this I felt and thus it went with me, then I was in anxiety; but it did not last long. Then I was encompassed by this temptation and by that adversity, but God delivered me soon out of them, etc.

10. We should take to heart and firmly hold fast to these words and keep them in mind when in sorrow and distress, that it will not last long, then we would also have more constant joy, for as Christ and his elect had their "a little while," so you and I and everyone will have his "a little while." Pilate and Herod will not crucify you but, in the same manner as the devil used them, so he will also use your persecutors. Therefore, when your trials come, you must not immediately think how you are to be delivered out of them. God will help you in due time. Only wait. It is only for a little while; he will not delay long.

11. But you must not lay the cross and sorrow upon yourself as some have indeed done, who chose for themselves death and imprisonment, and said, Christ willingly entered into death; he willingly permitted himself to be apprehended and delivered. I will also do the same. No, you dare not do this. Your cross and suffering will not long delay coming. These good people did not understand it. The dear disciples also said in Matthew 26:35, that they would remain with Christ and die with him. Peter said in John 13:37, he would not deny Christ, or would give his life for him; but how was it in the end? Christ went into the garden, trembled and quaked, was apprehended, put to death; Peter, however, forsook him. Where was now this great confidence, this boldness and courage of Peter? He thought Christ would die with joyful courage, and he would also follow him, but alas he was badly mistaken.

12. Here you easily see that the sorrow and sufferings, in which we expected to remain permanently, were of our own choosing, but when the hour finally comes, of which you never thought before, you will hardly be able to stand, unless you become a new man. The old Adam despairs; he does not abide; he cannot abide, for it goes against his nature, against his purpose,

and against his designs. Hence you must have your own time, then you must suffer a little. For Christ withdraws himself from you and permits you to remain in the power of sin, of death, and of hell. There the heart cannot accomplish very much to calm the conscience, do whatever it will, for Christ departs and dies. Then you will have the refrain, "A little while, and ye shall not behold me." Where will you go? There is no comfort. There is no help. You are in the midst of sin; in the midst of death; in the midst of hell. If Christ would not come now independent of any merit of your own, then you would be compelled to remain in this tribulation and terror eternally, for thus it would have happened also to the disciples, if Christ had not risen from the dead and become alive. It was, therefore, necessary for him again to arise from the dead.

13. Now, this everyone must experience and suffer, either now or upon his deathbed when he dies, but how much better it is to experience it now, for when at some future time we shall be cast into the fire for the sake of the Gospel and be counted as heretics, then we shall see of what profit this is; for if the heart is not strong at such a time, what shall become of us, for there our eyes shall see the torture and the terror of death. Whither shall we go? Therefore, if Christ is not present, and if he should then withdraw his hand, we are already lost; but if he is with us to help, the flesh may indeed die, but all is well with the soul, for Christ has taken it to himself. There it is safe; no one shall pluck it out of his hand, in John 10:28.

14. But this we cannot accomplish with words; an experience is here needed for that. Well it is for him who experiences this now; then surely it will not be hard for him to die. It is very perilous indeed if we must learn this upon our deathbed, namely, how to wrestle with and conquer death. Therefore, it was indeed a great favor and mercy of God, which he showed to the holy martyrs and apostles in whom he had first conquered death, then afterward they were prepared without fear to suffer everything that could be laid upon them.

B. This Sermon of Comfort Explained

15. All this is presented to us in our Gospel, but since the disciples could not understand what he meant in that he said "A little while" and he noticed that they were desirous to ask him, he continues and explains it to them in these simple words, and says,

> *"Verily, verily, I say unto you, ye shall weep and lament,*
> *but the world shall rejoice; ye shall be sorrowful,*
> *but your sorrow shall be turned into joy."*

16. This is spoken to all Christians, for every Christian must have temptations, trials, anxieties, adversities, sorrows, come what may. Therefore, he mentions here no sorrow nor trial, he simply says they shall weep, lament, and be sorrowful, for the Christian has many persecutions. Some are suffering loss of goods; others there are whose character is suffering ignominy and scorn; some are drowned, others are burned; some are beheaded; one perishes in this manner, and another in that; it is, therefore, the lot of the Christian constantly to suffer misfortune, persecution, trials, and adversity. This is the rod or foxtail with which they are punished. They dare not look for anything better as long as they are here. This is the court color by which the Christian is recognized and, if anyone wants to be a Christian, he dare not be ashamed of his court color or livery.

17. Why does God do this and permit his own to be persecuted and hounded? In order to suppress and subdue the free will, so that it may not seek an expedient in their works, but rather become a fool in God's works and learn thereby to trust and depend upon God alone.

18. Therefore, when this now comes to pass, we shall not be able to accommodate ourselves to it, and shall not understand it, unless Christ himself awakens us and makes us cheerful, so that his resurrection becomes effective in us, and all our works fall to pieces and be as nothing. Therefore, the text here concludes powerfully, that man is absolutely nothing in his own strength. Here everything is condemned and thrust down that has been and may still be preached about good works; for this is the conclusion: where Christ is not, there is nothing. Ask Saint Peter how he was disposed when Christ was not with him. What good works did he do? He denied Christ. He renounced him with an oath. Like good works we do, when we have not Christ with us.

19. Thus all serves to the end that we should accustom ourselves to build alone upon Christ, and to depend upon no other work, upon no other creature, whether in heaven or upon earth. In this name alone are we preserved and blessed, and in none other, in Acts 4:12 and in Acts 10:43. But on this account, we must suffer much. The worst of all is, that we must not only suffer shame, persecution, and death, but that the world rejoices because of our great loss and misfortunes. This is indeed very hard and bitter. Surely it shall thus come to pass, for the world will rejoice when it goes ill with us. But this comfort we have, that their joy shall not last long, and our sorrow shall be turned into eternal joy. Of this the Lord gives us a beautiful parable of the woman in travail, when he says,

"A woman when she is in travail hath sorrow, because her hour is come,
but when she is delivered of the child, she remembereth no more
the anguish for joy that a man is born into the world."

C. This Sermon of Comfort Is Illustrated by a Parable

20. With this parable he also shows that our own works are nothing, for here we see that if all women came to the help of this woman in travail, they would accomplish nothing. Here free will is at its end and is unable to accomplish anything, or to give any advice. It is not in the power of the woman to be delivered of the child, but she feels that it is wholly in the hand and power of God. When he helps and works, then something is accomplished, but where he does not help, all is lost, even if the whole world were present. In this, God shows to the woman her power, her ability, and her strength. Before this, she could dance and leap; she rejoiced and was happy, but now she sees how God must do all. Hereby we perceive that God is our Father, who also must deliver us from the womb and bring us forth to life.

21. Christ says here to his disciples, So it will also go with you. The woman is here in such a state of mind that she is fearful of great danger, and yet she knows that the whole work lies in the hands of God; in him she trusts; upon him it is she depends; he also helps her and accomplishes the work, which the whole world could not do, and she thinks of nothing but the time that shall follow, when she shall again rejoice; and her heart feels and says, A dangerous hour is at hand, but afterward it will be well. Courage and the heart press through all obstacles. Thus it will also be with you, when you are in sorrow and adversity, and when you become new creatures. Only quietly wait and permit God to work. He will accomplish everything without your assistance.

22. This parable of the woman is a strong and stubborn argument against free will, that it is entirely powerless and without strength in the things pertaining to the salvation of our souls. The Gospel shows very plainly that divine strength and grace are needed. Man's free will is entirely too weak and insignificant to accomplish anything here. But we have established our own orders and regulations instead of the Gospel and through these we want to free ourselves from sin, from death, from hell, and from all misfortune, and finally be saved thereby. A great mistake.

23. Here you see in this example, that if a man is to be born the mother must become first as though she were dead; that is, she must be in a condition as though she were already dead; she thinks it is now all over with her. Thus

it shall be also with us. If we want to become godly, we must be as dead, and despair of all our works, yea, never think that we shall be able to accomplish anything. Here no monastic life, no priest craft, and no works will be able to help; but wait patiently and permit God to do with you according to his will. He shall accomplish it; permit him to work. We shall accomplish nothing ourselves, but at times we shall feel death and hell. This the ungodly shall also feel, but they do not believe that God is present in it and wants to help them. Just as the woman here accomplishes nothing; she feels only pain, distress, and misery, but she cannot help herself out of this state.

24. But when delivered of the child, she remembers no more her sorrow and pain, but is as though she had become alive again. She could not before even think that her sorrow and pain should have an end so soon. Thus it is also with us in the trials of sin, of death, and of hell; then we are as though we were dead; yea, we are in the midst of death, and Christ has forsaken us. He has gone a little while from us. Then we are in great pain and cannot help ourselves; but when Christ returns, and makes himself known to us, our hearts are full of joy, even though the whole world be to the contrary.

25. This no one can realize unless he has once been encompassed by death. He who has once been delivered from death must then rejoice; not that such a person cannot again fall and be sorrowful at times, but since this joy is at hand he worries about nothing. He also fears nothing, no matter by what dangers he may be surrounded. This joy can indeed be interrupted, for when I fall again into sin, then I fear even a driven leaf, in Leviticus 26:36. Why? Because Christ has departed a little while from me and has forsaken me; but I will not despair, for this joy will return again. I must not then continue and cling to the pope, nor endeavor to help myself by works; but I must quietly wait until Christ comes again. He remains but a little while without. When he then looks again upon the heart and appears and shines into it, the joy returns. Then shall I be able to meet every misfortune and terror.

26. All this is said and written that we may be conscious of our weakness and inability, and that as far as our works are concerned all is nothing, all is utterly lost. But this joy is almighty and eternal when we are dead; but now in this life, it is mixed. Now I fall and then I rise again, and it cannot be eternal, because flesh and blood are still with me. Therefore, Christ says to his disciples,

"And ye now have sorrow, but I will see you again,
and your heart shall rejoice, and your joy no man taketh from you."

27. All this David has described in a psalm in a most masterly and beautiful manner, when he says in Psalm 30:1–8, "I will extol thee, O Jehovah, for

thou hast raised me up, and hast not made my foes to rejoice over me. O Jeho-vah, my God: I cried unto thee and thou hast healed me. O Jehovah, thou hast brought up my soul from Sheol, thou hast kept me alive, that I should not go down to the pit. Sing praise unto Jehovah, O ye saints of his, and give thanks to his holy memorial name for his anger is but for a moment; his favor is for a lifetime; weeping may tarry for the night, but joy cometh in the morning. As for me, I said in my prosperity, I shall never be moved. Thou, Jehovah, of thy favor hadst made my mountain to stand strong: thou didst hide thy face; I was troubled. I cried to Thee, O Jehovah; and unto Jehovah I made supplication." Where is now the man who just said, "I shall never be moved"? Well, he replies, when thou, Jehovah, of thy favor didst make my mountains to stand strong, then I spoke thus. "But when thou didst hide thy face, I was troubled," I fell. If Christ were continually with us, I really believe we would never be afraid; but since he occasionally departs from us, we must, therefore, at times be afraid.

28. In this psalm is beautifully portrayed to us how to recognize and expe-rience a good conscience, for here David considers the whole world as a drop, and is not the least afraid of it, even though it should storm and rage against him, for he has the Lord with him. He has made his mountain to stand strong, but when he fell and the Lord hid his face from him, then he was afraid. Then were heart, courage, and mountain gone. Then was he afraid of a driven leaf, who before was not afraid of the whole world, as he also says in another psalm unto the Lord, "Yea, though I walk through the valley of the shadow of death, I will fear no evil, for thou art with me; thy rod and thy staff they comfort me," in Psalm 23:4. Likewise in Psalm 3:6, he says, "I will not be afraid of ten thousands of the people that have set themselves against me round about." Passages like these can be multiplied in the psalms, all of which show how an upright, good conscience stands, namely, when God is with it, it is courageous and brave, but when God has departed, it is fearful and terrified.

29. Here we rightly understand now what the words of Christ signify, "I go to the Father." Before this, no one understood them, not even the disciples. But this is the road, I must die, he saith, and ye must also die. Peter vowed boastfully, for according to the old Adam he wanted to die with the Lord, and we all think we want to die with Christ, as all the other disciples said that they would enter into death with Christ, in Matthew 26:35. But all this must perish in us. You must come to the moment of trial, when Christ does not stand by you and does not die with you, when you cannot help yourself, just like the woman in travail. When this takes place, then you come to the Father. That

is, you are filled with his power, and he makes a new man of you, who thereafter is not afraid, whose character is already here a heavenly character, as Saint Paul calls it, in Philippians 3:20; and this has its beginning here, by faith. Then you become courageous and brave, and can say as the prophet in the psalm, "I will not be afraid of ten thousands of people," and "Though I walk through the valley of the shadow of death, I will fear no evil." Why all this? Because you have come to the Father. Who can now overthrow God's omnipotence? No one. Aye, then no one can do anything to you or cause you any harm.

30. This no one will understand until it has come to pass. Have you been encompassed by death and been delivered from it, then you will say, I was in death, and if the Lord had not delivered me, I would have remained in death's grasp forever. The entire thirtieth Psalm refers to this, which you will do well to examine thoroughly and consider faithfully.

31. Here you have now the fruit and the example of the death and the resurrection of Christ, and how free will is nothing, and everything reason concludes regarding these things, which pertain to our salvation. May God give grace that we may lay hold of it and regulate our lives accordingly. Amen.

APPENDIX TO THE FOREGOING SERMON

CHRIST

"Verily, verily, I say unto you, that ye shall weep and lament,
but the world shall rejoice," etc. –JOHN 16:20

1. No one should lay his cross upon himself, as some foolish persons have done and are still doing. They even court the prison and death, and say, Since Christ of his own free will entered death, I will follow him in his example as he commanded us to do. There is no need whatever to do this, for your martyrdom and cross will not be wanting. Such people, however, do not understand divine things; they think they will suddenly enter death with Christ, whom they have never learned to know except in words. Thus was Peter also disposed, but he stood before Christ like a rabbit before one beating a drum. Notice, how the old Adam lacks courage when under the cross! The new man, however, can indeed persevere through grace. In suffering, pious persons have no aim of their own; but if it be God's will, they bear good fruit like the tree planted by the streams of water; and that is pleasing to God and, besides, all presumption is condemned, all show and every excuse, however good they

may be. But he who battles heroically will receive for his suffering here joy, the eternal in place of the temporal. Of this Christ says, "Your joy shall be turned into sorrow."

2. This saying of Christ is addressed to all Christians in general. For things may go well or ill, still a Christian must contend with persecution, need, distress, and opposition. Moreover, Christ does not specify here any special punishment, cross or martyrdom; hence he says simply, You will weep, lament, and be sorrowful; for Christians suffer many kinds of persecutions. Some have their property damaged, others have their name dishonored, some are drowned, others burned or beheaded. Thus Christians die, being put to death by many different hands, each with greater contempt than the other, so that misfortune, persecution, and adversity are constantly weighing upon the neck of Christians, by which they are stricken, and there is nothing more certain for them to hope for as long as they crawl here upon the earth. And this is the court dress by which Christians are identified. Now, whoever wishes to be a Christian dare not be ashamed of his colors.

3. But why has God appointed his own children to be driven here and there by persecution? On account of free will, that it may be humbled to the ground and become a perfect fool in the works of God, and learn to trust in God alone; as a result give to God good works, things, and at last give ourselves and thus rightly trust in God and cling to Christ. It may, however, well grieve one that the world rejoices over our misfortunes. It is a common thing, the jaybird can never stop jumping. But the comfort of the Christian is, that the world's joy will not last long, and that his own distress shall be changed into joy eternal. Amen.

The Fourth Sunday After Easter

～ာ၅๛～

Of Sin, of Righteousness, and of the Cross

B ut now I go unto him that sent me; and none of you asketh me,
Whither goest thou? But because I have spoken these things unto
you, sorrow hath filled your heart. Nevertheless I tell you the truth: It
is expedient for you that I go away; for if I go not away, the Comforter
will not come unto you; but if I go, I will send him unto you. And he,
when he is come, will convict the world in respect of sin, and of
righteousness, and of judgment: of sin, because they believe not on me;
of righteousness, because I go to the Father, and ye behold me no more;
of judgment, because the prince of this world hath been judged. I have
yet many things to say unto you, but ye cannot bear them now. Howbeit
when he, the Spirit of truth, shall come, he shall guide you into all the
truth; for he shall not speak from himself; but what things soever he
shall hear, these shall he speak; and he shall declare unto you the
things that are to come. He shall glorify me: for he shall take of mine,
and shall declare it unto you. All things whatsoever the Father hath
are mine; therefore said I, that he taketh of mine, and shall declare it
unto you." — JOHN 16:5–15

I. THE HOLY SPIRIT CONVICTS THE WORLD OF SIN

1. Christ pictures to us in this Gospel what his kingdom is and what takes
place in it, how it is governed, and what it accomplishes. Here you learn that
there is a kingdom upon the earth and that it is invisible, and that it cleaves to
and rests upon the Word of God alone. Christ does not say that he wishes his
disciples to follow him up into heaven at once; but that he will send them the
Holy Spirit and that he departs from them for the very purpose of sending
them the Holy Spirit, in order that thereby his kingdom may be further developed. Therefore, he says, "I have yet many things to say unto you, but ye cannot bear them now." They could not understand that kingdom, how it should
exist and be administered. Their reason and senses were still too carnal; they

had never seen a spiritual kingdom, nor heard of one; therefore, they continually thought of a temporal, outward kingdom. And here as in other Gospels, faith and trust in Christ are preached. We wish now to consider the leading thoughts in this Gospel and to explain them as far as God gives us his grace to do so. The Lord addresses his disciples thus:

> *"When the Comforter is come, he will convict the world in respect of sin,*
> *and of righteousness, and of judgment; of sin,*
> *because they believe not on me."*

2. Here we must let that be "sin" which is ascribed to, and included in, sin by the high Majesty of heaven. In the text, only unbelief is mentioned as sin, "because," says the Lord, "they believe not on me."

3. But what is it to believe on Christ? It is not simply to believe that he is God, or that he reigns in heaven in equal power with God the Father; many others believe that: But I believe on Christ when I believe that he is a gracious God to me and has taken my sins upon himself and reconciled me with God the Father, that my sins are his and his righteousness mine, that there is an intermingling and an exchange, that Christ is a mediator between me and the Father. For the sins of the whole world were laid upon Christ, and the righteousness of the Father, that is in Christ, will swallow up all our sins.

No sins dare and can remain upon Christ. Such faith makes me pure and acceptable to the Father. Of this faith, the pope and our highly educated leaders know nothing to speak, much less to believe. They teach that man should do many good works if he is to be acceptable to God and be free from sin, and that then God imparts to him his grace.

4. However, here the Lord speaks quite differently, and says, "The Holy Spirit will convict the world in respect of sin, because they believe not on me." Unbelief only is mentioned here as sin, and faith is praised as suppressing and extinguishing the other sins, even the sins in the saints. Faith is so strong and overpowering that no sin dare put it under any obligation. Although sins are present in pious and believing persons, they are not imputed to them, nor shall their sins condemn them. This is Paul's meaning when he says in Romans 8:1, "There is therefore now no condemnation to them that are in Christ Jesus, who walk not after the flesh, but after the Spirit." Their hearts are cleansed by faith, as Peter says in Acts 15:9. Therefore, whatever they do in this faith, in this assurance is all good, pure, and pleasing to God. On the contrary, without this faith, all their doings are sin and destruction, though their good works may shine and glitter as beautifully as they will, and even though they raise the dead. For Paul says, "Whatsoever is not of faith is sin," in Romans 14:23.

5. What will now become of all the priests, nuns, and monks who, wishing to escape sin, run into cloisters and undertake to do many good works without this faith? Unbelief is called sin, as I said, but to believe on Christ—that he takes my sins upon himself, reconciles me to the Father and at the same time makes me his heir of all that is in heaven and earth—this is good works. In John 6:28–29, the Jews asked Christ, "What must we do, that we may work the works of God?" Jesus answered, "This is the work of God, that ye believe on him whom he hath sent." Yea, and should we preach thus, who will then enter the cloisters or contribute anything for them? The purses of the monks would then surely become flat, their kitchens scanty, their cellars empty and neglected. For this reason, they will not allow faith to be preached; nay, they condemn this doctrine and banish its preachers. Indeed they have already set about it in good earnest. Christ further says,

"Of righteousness, because I go to the Father."

II. THE HOLY SPIRIT CONVICTS THE WORLD OF RIGHTEOUSNESS

6. Here all the learned come armed, yea, the whole world besides, and tell us what kind of righteousness this is. Yes, and they shall err. For the world has never known this righteousness; it does not yet know it, and it does not wish to know it. Hence the Lord says here that the Holy Spirit will convict the world of this righteousness.

7. But what are we to understand here by "the world"? We dare not understand by it the coarse, outward sins, as adultery, murder, stealing, and theft. There are instituted for such characters the wheels and gallows, with which the worldly powers, the kings, emperors, and princes, have to do. But we will interpret "the world" as the subtle and secret sins, of which the Holy Spirit convicts, which the world does not know as sin. Yea, it pronounces them divine works; it applauds them and will not permit them to be called sins. How else can unbelief and other secret sins live in the heart while the heart itself is not conscious of them and knows not that they are sins? But those who convict the world must, on that account, be reviled as heretics and be banished from the country, as we see at present. Therefore, the Holy Spirit must convict the world.

8. The rod, however, by which the world is convicted and punished, is the divine Word and the holy Gospel, proclaimed by the apostles and preachers, as God the Father says to his Son in Psalm 2:9, "Thou shalt break them with a rod of iron; thou shalt dash them in pieces like a potter's vessel." That is, you

shall humble them with the holy Gospel. But the world resents such conviction and punishment; yet it punishes severely, and even more severely than the Holy Spirit does. The Holy Spirit takes rods, but the world uses swords and fire. Isaiah also speaks in like terms of Christ our Lord in Isaiah 11:4, "He shall smite the earth with the rod of his mouth; and with the breath of his lips shall he slay the wicked."

9. What is now the righteousness the Lord means here? Some say righteousness is a virtue that gives to every person his own. Although this is a fine definition, yet it is misleading, in that we do not know how we are indebted to everyone, to God and to man. This God desires and demands of us. Therefore, his righteousness is nothing more than the faith and grace of God, by which God makes us pious and righteous. Such righteousness we must have and thus be righteous, if we are to be found righteous and unblamable before God, and not only before man. For the smallest letter or tittle of the law shall not fail, but all will be fulfilled.

10. Noah was found to be such a righteous man. It is written of him in Genesis 6:8–9, "Noah was a righteous man, and blameless in his generation; he walked with God. Therefore he found favor in the eyes of Jehovah." It is also written of Job, in Job 1:1, that he was a perfect and upright man, one that feared God and turned away from evil. But that is done only by faith, when one believes that God has strangled and swallowed up one's sins in his righteousness. For this righteousness is nothing but to believe that Christ is seated at the right hand of the Father; that he is equal with God, possessing equal power; that he has become Lord by virtue of his Passion, by which he has ascended to the Father, reconciled us with God, and is there as our Mediator. This is what the prophet means in Psalm 110:1, "Jehovah saith unto my Lord, sit thou at my right hand, until I make thine enemies thy footstool." Therefore, Saint Paul calls Christ now a Mediator, in 1 Timothy 2:5 and in Hebrews 8:6; then a throne of grace, in Romans 3:25; a propitiation, in 1 John 2:2; and other like names. God requires this honor from us, and faith demands it that we possess him as our Lord and Savior; and this glory he will not concede to anyone else, as he says through the prophet, "My glory will I not give to another," in Isaiah 42:8.

11. His way to the Father is his glory. For "to go" means to die, and to pass through death to the Father and enter upon another existence. He glories in his future course when he says, "I go unto the Father." Therefore, here righteousness is nothing more than traveling by faith the road through death unto the Father. This faith makes us righteous before God, this faith by which we believe that he delivered us from sin, death, Satan, and hell, through his

Passion, and that thereby God, the Father, is reconciled, and our sins are blotted out by his blood. This is also the reason that he mentions his going, when he says, in respect of righteousness, not that he is with the Father, but that he goes to the Father. In this going, sin is swallowed up in righteousness and Christ passes cheerfully through death, so that no one is even aware of it. Therefore, it follows,

"And ye behold me no more."

12. The nature and art of faith are here set forth: faith neither feels nor gropes, nor do the things connected with it require a science; but it bestirs itself cheerfully to believe the things it neither feels nor can measure with all its powers inwardly or outwardly. Paul says in Romans 8:24, "Who hopeth for that which he seeth?" Therefore, the Lord aptly says, "And ye behold me no more." As if he would say that this way of good works which he is traveling, will not be seen nor grasped by the senses, but it must be believed. Now follows the third and last part of our Gospel.

III. THE HOLY SPIRIT CONVICTS THE WORLD OF JUDGMENT, OR THE CROSS

"Of judgment, because the prince of this world is judged."

13. The prince of this world is Satan, and his members include all unbelieving and godless persons; all flesh with all its powers is condemned by these words; and what the world praises is condemned by God, including both the godly and the ungodly, believers and unbelievers, friends and enemies, as Saint Peter cites, in 1 Peter 4:17, when he says, "For the time is come for judgment to begin at the house of God," that is, with the elect, in whom God dwells. The righteous, while they live here, have flesh and blood, in which sin is rooted. To suppress this sin, God will lead them into great misery and anxiety, poverty, persecution, and all kinds of danger, as Paul writes to the Romans, in Romans 7:18ff. and in Romans 8:4, and to the Corinthians, until the flesh becomes completely subject to the Spirit.

14. That, however, does not take place until death, when the flesh is completely turned to ashes. We must be in all points like Christ. Since he was here despised, mocked, and tried, so that, as the prophet Isaiah says, in Isaiah 53:3, he was esteemed and held as one stricken and smitten of God, the most despised and unworthy, full of grief and sorrow, his disciples must also go through the same experiences. Everyone should carefully consider this. It is so decreed, as Christ himself before declared to his disciples, saying, "Remember

the word that I said unto you, A servant is not greater than his lord. If they persecuted me they will also persecute you," in John 15:20. Hence Paul says in very plain words in 2 Timothy 3:12, "All that would live godly in Christ Jesus shall suffer persecution."

15. Therefore, Saint Peter carefully discriminates, and says, "If judgment begin first at us, what shall be the end of them that obey not the Gospel of God? And if the righteous is scarcely saved, where shall the ungodly and sinner appear?" in 1 Peter 4:17–18. This discrimination is between the sufferings of the godly and of the wicked. Godly and believing persons know their sins; they bear all their punishment patiently, and are resigned to God's judgment without the least murmur; therefore, they are punished only bodily, and here in time, and their pain and suffering have an end. Unbelievers, however, since they are not conscious of their sins and transgressions, cannot bear God's punishment patiently, but they resent it, and wish their life and works to go unpunished, yea, uncensured. Hence their punishment and suffering are in body and soul, here in time, and last forever beyond this life. The Lord says here, "The prince of this world is already judged." As if he were to say, All that the world and humanity in the world discover, praise, and condemn, amounts to nothing; and whatever God judges, the world cannot suffer nor bear, but rejects, repudiates, and condemns.

16. Thus three thoughts have been presented to us in this Gospel: Sin, righteousness, and, finally, the cross and persecution. We shall be freed from sin through faith. If we believe that Christ made satisfaction for our sins and that his satisfaction is ours, that is then the righteousness. When we are free from sin, and are just and pious, then the world, Satan, and the flesh will arise and contend and battle against us. Then come persecution and the cross. This we wish to have set forth in brief at present from this Gospel. May God grant his grace that we learn it thus, and know how to govern ourselves by it when we need it.

The Fifth Sunday After Easter
or Prayer Sunday

❧❧❧

A Sermon by Christ on Prayer

A nd in that day ye shall ask me no question. Verily, verily, I say
unto you, If ye shall ask anything of the Father, he will give it
you in my name. Hitherto have ye asked for nothing in my name: ask,
and ye shall receive, that your joy may be made full.

These things have I spoken unto you in dark sayings: the hour cometh,
when I shall no more speak unto you in dark sayings, but shall tell you
plainly of the Father. In that day ye shall ask in my name: and I say not
unto you, that I will pray the Father for you; for the Father himself
loveth you, because ye have loved me, and have believed that I came
forth from the Father. I came out from the Father, and am come into the
world: again, I leave the world, and go unto the Father. His disciples
say, Lo, now speakest thou plainly, and speakest no dark saying. Now
know we that thou knowest all things, and needest not that any man
should ask thee; by this we believe that thou camest forth from God."
— JOHN 16:23–30

1. We are accustomed to read today's Gospel on this Sunday because it
treats of prayer, and this week is called Rogation (Supplication) week, in which
we give ourselves to prayer and to processions with crosses. Those who first
instituted it, no doubt, meant it well, but it has proved to work harm. For, in
the processions heretofore, many unchristian things have been practiced, and
there has been no praying at all or very little; so that the processions were
rightly abolished and discontinued. Often have I admonished that we should
persevere in prayer, for there is great need of it. Since the outward prating and
muttering of prayer is done away with, we no longer pray in any way. This is
a good indication that we heretofore, notwithstanding our many prayers,
never prayed.

2. The Lord points out here five things necessary to constitute true prayer. The first is God's promise, which is the chief thing and is the foundation and power of all prayers. For he promises here that it shall be given us if we ask; and besides he swears: "Verily, verily, I say unto you, If ye shall ask anything of the Father, he will give it you in my name." He promises that we might be sure of being heard in prayer; yea, he censures the disciples for the reason that they are lazy and have not therefore been praying. As if he would say, God is ready to give more quickly, and to give more than you ask; yea, he offers his treasures if we only take them. It is truly a great shame and a severe chastisement for us Christians that God should still upbraid us for our slothfulness in prayer, and that we fail to let such a rich and excellent promise incite us to pray. We let this precious treasure lie there, and seek it not, nor exercise ourselves to receive the power in such a promise.

3. So God himself now founds our prayer upon his promise and thereby encourages us to pray. If it were not for this promise, who would have the courage to pray? We have hitherto resorted to many ways of preparing ourselves to pray—ways with which the books are filled; but if you wish to be well prepared, take the promise and lay hold of God with it. Then your courage and desire to pray will soon grow, which courage you will never otherwise get. For those who pray without God's promise, imagine in themselves how angry God is, whom they wish to propitiate by means of their prayers. Without faith in the promise, there is then, neither courage nor desire to pray, but mere uncertain delusion and a melancholy spirit; there is, therefore, no hearing of prayers, and both prayer and labor are lost.

4. By these words, Christ now chastises the unbelief of those who, by reason of their foolish worship, consider themselves unworthy to pray, and gauge the worthiness of their prayer according to themselves and their own ability, and not according to the promise of God. There is then, to be sure, nothing but unworthiness. However, you should, by all means, be conscious of your own unworthiness, taking confidence not from your own doings, but from the promise of God, and be so completely conscious, that if you were all alone, and no one else in the world prayed, you would nevertheless pray, because of this promise. For you can point me to no true saint who prayed, depending upon his own worthiness, and who did not rely only upon God's promises, be he Peter, Paul, Mary, Elijah, or anyone else. All of them have been unworthy. I would not give a nickel for all the prayers of a saint if he prayed because of his own worthiness.

5. The second requisite of true prayer, following that of God's promise, is faith—that we believe the promise is true, and do not doubt that God will give

what he promises. For the words of the promise require faith. But faith is a firm, undoubting confidence in God's promise that it is true; as James says, "But if any of you lacketh wisdom, let him ask of God, who giveth to all liberally and upbraideth not; and it shall be given him. But let him ask in faith, nothing doubting: for he that doubteth is like the surge of the sea driven by the wind and tossed. For let not that man think that he shall receive anything of the Lord," in James 1:5–7. Moreover, he who doubts and yet prays, tempts God; for he doubts in respect to God's will and grace. Therefore, his prayer is nothing, and he gropes after God like the blind for the wall. John also speaks of this assurance of faith in 1 John 5:14–15, "And this is the boldness which we have toward him, that, if we ask anything according to his will, he heareth: and if we know that he heareth us whatsoever we ask, we know that we have the petitions which we have asked of him." John describes with these words how a truly believing heart is disposed in prayer, namely, that it is concerned about nothing else than that its prayer be heard, knowing that it has even then obtained its petition. That is also true. Such faith and definite assurance, however, the Holy Spirit must impart; therefore, without the Holy Spirit, surely no prayer will be offered.

6. Try it, now, and pray thus. Then you will taste the sweetness of God's promise. What courage and consolation of heart it awakens to pray for all things! It matters not how great and high the petitions may be. Elijah was a man of like passions with ourselves; yet when he prayed, it did not rain for three years and six months, and when he again prayed, it rained, in 1 Kings 17:1 and in 1 Kings 18:45. Notice, here you see a single man prays and by his prayer he is lord of the clouds, of heaven and earth. So God lets us see what power and influence a true prayer has, namely, that nothing is impossible for it to do.

7. Let everyone now ask his heart how often he has prayed during his whole life. Singing psalms and saying the Lord's Prayer is not called praying. These are instituted for children and untutored people, as exercises, to make them athletes in the Scriptures. Your prayer, however, no one but yourself sees and feels in your heart, and you will truly know it when it hits the mark.

8. The third requisite of true prayer is, that one must name definitely something that he brings to God or for which he prays, as for strong faith, for love, for peace, and for the comfort of his neighbor. One must actually set forth the petitions, just as the Lord's Prayer presents seven petitions. This is what Christ means by the words, "If ye shall ask anything of the Father." "Anything," that is, whatever you are in need of. Besides, he himself interprets this "anything," and says, "That your joy may be made full." That is, pray for all

things you need, until you have acquired even all and your joy is made full; and his prayer will first be fully answered on the day of judgment.

9. The fourth element in true prayer is that we must desire, or wish, that the petition be granted, which is nothing but asking; as Christ says, "Ask." Others have called this *"Ascensum mentis in Deum,"* when the soul ascends to God and desires something from him, and sighs from its depths, saying, Oh, that I had this or that! Such sighing Saint Paul praises in Romans 8:26. It is an intercession of the Spirit that cannot be uttered. That is, the mouth wants to, but cannot speak as rapidly and strongly as the heart desires; the yearning is greater that any words and thoughts. Hence it is, also, that man himself does not feel how deep his sighing or desire is. When Zacchæus sought to see the Lord, he himself did not feel how strongly his heart wished that Christ might speak with him and come into his house. However, when his desire was fulfilled, he was very happy, for he had succeeded according to all his wishes and prayers; he had received more than he had dared to ask by word of mouth, or desire, in Luke 19:2ff. Moses, likewise, cried so that God spoke to him, "Wherefore criest thou unto me?" in Exodus 14:15, and yet his mouth kept silence; but his heart, in its extremity, sighed deeply, and that was called crying unto God. In like manner, Saint Paul writes to the Ephesians, "God is able to do exceeding abundantly above all that we ask or think," in Ephesians 3:20. Now, temptation, anxiety, and trouble induce this sighing; they teach us what true sighing is.

10. The fifth requisite of true prayer is, that we ask in the name of Christ. This is nothing more than that we come before God in the faith of Christ and comfort ourselves with the sure confidence that he is our Mediator, through whom all things are given to us, without whom we merit nothing but wrath and disgrace. As Paul says to the Romans, "Through whom also we have had our access by faith into this grace wherein we stand; and we rejoice in hope of the glory of God," in Romans 5:2. It is praying aright in Christ's name, when we thus trust in him that we will be received and heard for his sake, and not for our own sake. Those, however, who pray in their own name, who presume that God will hear or regard them, because they say so many, such long, such devout, such godly prayers, will merit and obtain nothing but wrath and disgrace; for they wish to be people whom God should regard without a mediator. To them, Christ here is of no consideration, nor is he of any service.

11. We observe that all five requisites of prayer may be complied within the heart, without any utterance of the mouth. The oral part of prayer is really not to be despised, but it is necessary to kindle and encourage prayer inwardly, in the heart. The additional conditions, however, of which I have written enough

elsewhere, should and must be omitted that we specify to God the time, person, place, and measure. We must leave all that to his own free will, and cling only to asking; we must not doubt that the prayer is heard, and that what we petitioned is already ordered—that it will be given—as certainly as if we already had it. This is pleasing to God, and he will do as he here promises, "Ask, and ye shall receive." Those, however, who set the time, place, and measure, tempt God, and believe not that they are heard or that they have obtained what they asked; therefore, they also receive nothing. The Gospel lesson continues,

"Hitherto have ye asked nothing in my name."

12. It may be that they knew as yet nothing of such prayer, and of this name; besides, they felt no need that urged them to pray in this name. They imagined that so long as Christ was with them, they needed nothing and had enough of everything. But now that he is to separate from them and leave them, trouble immediately comes, and they will have reason enough to move them to pray.

"These things have I spoken unto you in parables (dark sayings)."

13. When he says "these things," he means that which he had just before spoken: "A little while, and ye behold me not; and again a little while, and ye shall see me"; and, "Because I go to the Father"; also, the parable of the woman in travail. For these were nothing but parables, that is, dark, obscure sayings that they did not understand. John calls these dark, hidden sayings "parables," although the German language does not designate them so, but calls them enigmas or veiled sayings. We are accustomed to say of one who has uttered an enigmatical saying, "That is a covered dish or a covered meal," when the words have a meaning not on the surface. In parables, the meaning to be conveyed is expressed in a way that not everyone understands. Of this nature were all the sayings of Christ, which he spoke to his disciples on the night of his farewell and his going to the Father; they could understand nothing of them. They thought his going would not be dying and coming into another existence; they thought of it as a pleasure walk and that Christ should return in the body, as one journeys to another country and returns. Therefore, although he spoke plainly and clearly, yet going and parting were a "covered meal" to them. Hence he adds,

"The hour cometh when I shall no more speak unto you in dark sayings (parables), but shall tell you plainly of the Father."

14. That is, what I now speak to you, while in the body, and my parables ye understand not, that I will thoroughly explain to you through the Holy Spirit. I will plainly speak of my Father, that you may then understand who the Father is and what my going to the Father means. You will clearly see how I ascend through suffering into the Father's life and into his kingdom; that I sit at his right hand and represent you and am your Mediator; that all this is done for your sake, that you may likewise come to the Father. "I shall tell you plainly of the Father" is not to be understood to mean that he will tell us much about God's divine nature, as the sophists fancy; for that is unnecessary, and the divine nature of God is incomprehensible. But Christ will tell us how he goes to the Father, how he takes upon himself the kingdom and government of the Father; as a king's son returns to his father and assumes the government of the kingdom. Christ says further,

"In that day ye shall ask in my name."

15. For then, in your many tribulations, you will have not only reason to pray, but will also know and perceive what my name is and how you should esteem me. Then will you be taught by praying itself what you now do not at all understand, and that hitherto you have never prayed. Therefore, he adds,

"And I say not unto you, that I will pray the Father for you:
for the Father himself loveth you, because ye have loved me,
and have believed that I came forth from the Father."

16. How, then? Will Christ not be our Mediator? Shall we not pray in his name? How lovingly and sweetly the Lord can speak, and woo us to himself and, through himself, to the Father! Here he himself explains how it will be when we pray in his name: "Ye," he says, "have loved me, and have believed that I came forth from the Father." That is, ye love me and know me; have me and my name, and are in me as I in you. For Christ dwells in us, not because we can think, speak, sing, or write so much about him, but because we love him and believe in him. We know that he is come from the Father and returns to the Father; that is, how he emptied himself, in his Passion, of all his divine glory and returned again to the Father in his kingdom, for our sake. This faith brings us to the Father, and thus all then is done in his name.

17. So we are sure that Christ needs not to pray for us, for he has already prayed for us. We ourselves may now approach through Christ and pray. We no longer need a Christ who prays for us. This one Christ is enough, he who has prayed for us and accomplished this work. Therefore, he says, "The

Father himself loveth you." It is not your merit, but his love. He loves you, but for my sake, because you believe on me and love me; that is, he has regard for my name in you. Hence thereby have I fulfilled my office, and you are now brought, through me, to where you may yourselves, in my place, appear in his presence and pray. It is not necessary that I still pray for you. These are marvelous words, that we, through Christ, become like Christ and are his brethren, and may glory in being children of his Father, who loves us for Christ's sake. He says, in John 1:16, "Grace for Grace," that is, God is gracious unto us, because he is gracious to Christ, who is in us and we in him.

18. And here we also see that to "believe in Christ" does not mean to believe that Christ is a person who is both God and man; that does not help anyone. But that this same person is the Christ; that is, that he went forth from the Father and came into the world, and again leaves the world and goes to the Father. The words mean no less than that this is Christ, that he became man and died for us, rose again, and ascended to heaven. Because of this office of his, he is called Jesus Christ, and to believe this concerning him, that it is true, means to be and to abide in his name. There follows further in this Gospel,

> "His disciples say, Lo, now speakest thou plainly,
> and speakest no dark sayings."

19. Here you see that to speak "plainly" ("*frei heraus*"), or to speak in clear terms, means to speak without parables or without dark and covered words. And the good disciples think they understand very well what he tells them, that Christ comes from the Father and goes to the Father; but they do this as good, pious children of Christ. They are easily able to understand it, and in love they tell him so. In ordinary conversation, people sometimes say to one another Yes or No, or give assent, saying, It is so and, in a sense, one understands, even though he is still far from the meaning of another's words. In such case, the conversation is without hypocrisy and in true simplicity. The evangelist hereby shows what a beautiful, plain, friendly, and loving life Christ led with his disciples, since they were so very able to understand him. Then the disciples say further,

> "Now know we that thou knowest all things,
> and needest not that any man should ask thee."

20. That is, you anticipate and explain yourself and speak no more in parables, concerning which we must question you; for you know in advance where we are lacking in understanding. All this reverts to the fact that they

wished to ask what the "little while" meant, and he noticed it and explains by saying that he must go to the Father; which they still did not understand, and yet it was clearer than his words, "A little while and ye will not see me." Now, because he saw their thoughts—that they wished to question him—they confessed that he comes from God and knows all things, so that we need not to ask him, for he himself sees very well where the trouble is.

The Day of Christ's Ascension into Heaven

⚜

Christ Upbraids and Commissions His Disciples

And afterward he was manifested unto the eleven themselves as they sat at meat; and he upbraided them with their unbelief and hardness of heart, because they believed not them that had seen him after he was risen. And he said unto them, "Go ye into all the world, and preach the Gospel to the whole creation. He that believeth and is baptized shall be saved; but he that disbelieveth shall be condemned. And these signs shall accompany them that believe; in my name shall they cast out demons; they shall speak with new tongues; they shall take up serpents, and if they drink any deadly thing, it shall in no wise hurt them; they shall lay hands on the sick, and they shall recover."

So then the Lord Jesus, after he had spoken unto them, was received up into heaven, and sat down at the right hand of God. And they went forth, and preached everywhere, the Lord working with them, and confirming the word by the signs that followed. Amen.
— MARK 16:14–20

1. In today's Gospel, there is again presented to us the essence of a Christian life, namely, faith and love; just what you constantly hear in all the Gospel lessons. Since the Gospel ever holds up before you this theme, we must continually preach and discuss it; for Jesus says to his disciples, "Go ye into all the world, and preach the Gospel to the whole creation. He that believeth and is baptized shall be saved." We will consider the thoughts of this Gospel text in order.

I. CHRIST UPBRAIDS HIS DISCIPLES WITH THEIR UNBELIEF

2. First, Christ upbraids his disciples with their unbelief and hardness of heart, and reproves them for it, and shows them their faults. He does not

reject them, nor deal too severely with them, but reproves them; just as we would say to a person, Are you not ashamed that you dared to do such a thing? meaning thereby to bring him to a knowledge of himself and make him blush with shame, that he may desist from his wicked intent or deed, though we do not reject him nor turn our love from him.

3. However, it is not an insignificant matter here that the Lord rebuked the disciples; for unbelief is the greatest sin that can be named. Christ tells them the cause of their unbelief when he says that their hearts are hardened, yet he deals mildly and gently with them.

4. This is given to us all for our comfort, lest we despair when, lacking in faith, we doubt, stumble, and fall; it is to help us to rise again, to strengthen our faith and lift up our hearts to God, that we may grasp and hold fast the confidence of God, who does not deal with us severely, but can indeed bear with us and overlook much. And whoever believes him to be thus, shall find him so; if we hold him to be a merciful God, he allows himself to be found merciful, and shows himself thus to us; but a bad conscience and an unbelieving heart have no such trust in God, but flee from him, and deem him a harsh judge, which he, therefore, is found to be.

5. So should we also deal with our neighbor. If we see him fall from the faith, or err and sin, we should not strengthen him in his wickedness, nor justify his cause, but admonish him, and in meekness reprove his faults, yet neither hold enmity nor turn our love from him. Thus Saint Paul speaks to the Galatians, "Brethren, even if a man be overtaken in any trespass, ye who are spiritual, restore such a one in a spirit of gentleness," in Galatians 6:1. But our lord pope, the bishops, priests, monks, and nuns allow no one to reprove them when they do evil; they are never willing to acknowledge that any fault is theirs, but always that of their subjects, and their policy toward subjects is one of strictness and severity.

6. To sum up all, We should expose and reprove what is wrong, and exercise truth and love toward everybody; we should be plainspoken, not letting ourselves be silenced, for none of us, since we are flesh and blood, will so live as to be found without blame in all things—I in this, you in that. We all see that even the apostles were lacking in the chief things, yet they were cornerstones, the foundations and the very best part of Christendom.

7. But let no one think that the apostles were altogether unbelieving; they believed what was written in the law and the prophets, although their faith was not yet perfect. There was a faith there and yet no faith; they did not yet believe all things, although they believed that God created heaven and earth, and was the Maker of every creature. So the apostles were not

altogether without faith, for they had faith in part. Faith is a thing that always grows. It is with faith as with a man who is ill and begins to get well—is increasing in strength. Therefore, the Lord shows where they did not believe, and what they lacked; it was that they did not believe the resurrection of Christ from the dead. Although they believed the other things, they were still lacking in this. I hold that they believed that they had a gracious God. Yet this was not enough; they must believe also the resurrection of Christ. The Lord upbraided them with their unbelief, reproved them, and said that in spite of all they had seen, they were not believing; they still lacked in a certain article of faith, namely, the article on the resurrection, hence Christ's words to them at the Last Supper, "Ye believe in God, believe also in me," in John 14:1.

8. What does it mean, then, to believe the resurrection of Christ, this thing which is so important, and concerning which the disciples were called unbelieving and faithless, and without which nothing else that they believed would help them? To believe the resurrection of Christ, is nothing else than to believe that we have a mediator before God. Who is Christ, who makes us holy and acceptable to God the Father? For man's possessions, by birth and nature, are but sin and corruption, by which he brings down upon himself the wrath of God. But God is eternal righteousness and purity and, therefore, from his very nature, hates sin. Hence there is always enmity between God and the natural man, and they cannot be friends and in harmony with one another.

9. For this cause, Christ became man and took upon himself our sins and also the wrath of the Father, and drowned them both in himself, thus reconciling us to God the Father. Without this faith, we are children of wrath, able to do no good work that is pleasing to God, nor can our prayers be acceptable before him. For thus it is written in Psalm 18:41, "They cried, but there was none to save; even unto Jehovah, but he answered them not." Yea, even our noblest deeds, by which we had thought to obtain from God mercy, help, and comfort, are counted to us for sin; as the prophet says, in Psalm 109:7, "Let his prayer be turned into sin," seeing God could not be reconciled by all our strength, for there is truly no strength in us.

10. Christ, therefore, must come, that he might go before the Father's face, reconcile us to him, and obtain for us everything we lacked. Through this same Christ, we must ask of God all we need. You have heard in last Sunday's Gospel that the Lord says, "If ye shall ask anything of the Father, he will give it to you in my name." Whatever we obtain from God, we must receive through this Christ, who has gained for us a merciful Father. For Christ is our

support and refuge, where we may hide ourselves, like the young chickens hide under the wings of the mother hen. Through him alone is our prayer acceptable before God, and through him is it answered, and we obtain the favor and mercy of the Father; for Christ has made atonement for our sins, and an angry judge he has changed into a gracious and merciful God. To believe in the resurrection of Christ means, then, to believe, as I said, that Christ has taken upon his head our sins, and the sins of the whole world, also the wrath of the Father, and thus drowned them both in himself, whereby we are become reconciled with God and altogether righteous.

11. Now, observe for yourselves how few Christians there are who have this faith, by which alone man is freed from his sins and becomes entirely holy; for they believe not in the resurrection of Christ, that their sins are taken away through Christ, since they attempt to become holy through their own works. This one runs to a cloister, that one becomes a nun, one does this, another that, in order to be free from sin; and yet they always say they believe in the resurrection of Christ from the dead, notwithstanding that their works prove the contrary.

12. The apostles have insisted upon and preached this article more than any other; thus Saint Paul speaks to the Corinthians, "If Christ hath not been raised, then is our preaching vain, your faith also is vain," in 1 Corinthians 15:14. And shortly after, in verse 17, he says, "If Christ hath not been raised, your faith is vain; ye are yet in your sins." What sort of a conclusion is this? What is its logical analysis? This—If Christ be not risen from the dead, then sin and death have devoured and slain him, and we cannot get rid of our sins ourselves. Jesus Christ took them upon himself, so that he might tread under foot sin, death, and hell, and become their Master. But if he be not risen, then he has not overcome sin, but has been overcome by sin. Also, if he has been overcome by sin, then he is not risen; if he be not risen, then he has not redeemed you; then you are yet in your sins. Likewise, Paul speaks to the Romans, "If thou shalt confess with thy mouth Jesus as Lord, and shalt believe in thy heart that God raised him from the dead, thou shalt be saved," in Romans 10:9. Thereto all the Scriptures of the Old and the New Testaments agree.

13. Now, it is not enough that we believe the historic fact of the resurrection of Christ; for this all the wicked believe, yea, even the devil believes that Christ has suffered and is risen. But we must believe also the meaning—the spiritual significance of Christ's resurrection, realizing its fruit and benefits, that which we have received through it, namely, forgiveness and redemption from all sins; we must believe that Christ has suffered death, and thereby has overcome and trodden under foot sin and death, yea, everything that can

harm us, and is seated at the right hand of the Father in heaven as Almighty Lord over sin and devil, death and hell, and all that harms us, and that all this took place for our good. This, the wicked do not believe.

14. You see how much depends upon this article of faith on the resurrection. We can better dispense with all the other articles than with this one. What would it avail if we believed all the other articles, as that Christ was born of the Virgin Mary, died, and was buried, if we did not believe that he arose again? It is to this subject that God has reference, in Habakkuk 1:5, when he says, "I am working a work in your days, which ye will not believe though it be told you."

15. The importance of this subject is also the reason that Paul has urged and preached it, and in all his Epistles has treated of no work or miracle of Christ so frequently as of his resurrection. He is silent concerning the many works and wonders of Christ, and preaches and teaches emphatically the benefit and the import of the resurrection of Christ—what we have received from it. No other apostle has portrayed Christ to us in the light that Paul has. Christ did not without meaning say of him to Ananias, "He is a chosen vessel unto me to bear my name before the gentiles and kings, and the children of Israel; for I will show him how many things he must suffer for my name's sake," in Acts 9:15–16.

16. Now, no good work will help those who do not have this faith in the resurrection, let them play the hypocrite as they will. To virgins, their virginity or purity is no help; nor to monks, their long prayers. Here it avails nothing to preach of works, they are not even named; but everything must be obtained of God through Christ, as you have heard. So David prayed in Psalm 84:9, "Behold, O God, our shield, and look upon the face of thine anointed." This is enough on the first part of this Gospel. Now follows in the text the words,

"Go ye into all the world, and preach the Gospel to the whole creation."

II. THE MISSIONARY COMMISSION CHRIST GIVES TO HIS DISCIPLES

A. The Contents of This Commission

17. What shall they preach? Nothing else, he says, than just that I am risen from the dead and have overcome and taken away sin and all misery. He that believes this, shall be saved; faith alone is sufficient for his salvation. Therefore, the Gospel is nothing else than preaching the resurrection of Christ, "He that believeth shall be saved; but he that disbelieveth shall be condemned." Here all works are abolished. Here you see, also, the nature and character of faith.

Faith will compel no one to accept the Gospel, but leaves its acceptance free to everyone and makes it a personal matter. He that believes, believes; he that comes, comes; he that stays out, stays out.

18. Thus you see that the pope errs and does the people injustice in that he ventures to drive them to faith by force; for the Lord commanded the disciples to do nothing more than to preach the Gospel. So the disciples also did; they preached the Gospel and left its acceptance to those who would take it, and they did not say, Believe, or I will put you to death.

19. A question arises about this passage, "Go ye into all the world," as to how it is to be understood, since the apostles certainly did not visit all the world. No apostle came hither to us; and many a heathen island has since been discovered, where the Gospel has never been preached. Yet the Scriptures say, "Their sound went out into all the earth," in Romans 10:18. Answer: Their preaching went out into all the world, although it has not yet come into all the world. This going out has been begun and continues, although it is not yet completed; the Gospel, however, will be preached ever farther and wider, until the judgment day. When this preaching shall have reached all parts of the world, and shall have been everywhere heard, then will the message be complete and its mission accomplished; then will the last day also be at hand.

20. The preaching of this message may be likened to a stone thrown into the water, producing ripples which circle outward from it, the waves rolling always on and on, one driving the other, until they come to the shore. Although the center becomes quiet, the waves do not rest, but move forward. So it is with the preaching of the Word. It was begun by the apostles, and it constantly goes forward, is pushed on farther and farther by the preachers, driven hither and thither into the world, yet always is being made known to those who never heard it before, although it be arrested in the midst of its course and is condemned as heresy. As we say, when one sends a message, the message has gone forth, although it has not yet arrived at its destination, but is still on its way; or as we say, the emperor's message is sent to Nurenburg, or to the Turk [Muslim], although it has not yet arrived, so we are to understand the preaching of the apostles.

B. The Promise Attached to This Commission

21. But there arises here another question from this passage of today's Gospel, "He that believeth, shall be saved," whether faith is sufficient for salvation, and alone saves; or whether we must also do good works in order to be saved. Here our highly learned doctors have desired to control the Holy Spirit,

to sharpen his tongue, and to place a little stick under his tongue, as if he could not speak plainly, and have forced and strained this passage, and so worn it out and rent it that no marrow nor vitality remains in it. They have said that good works are necessary to faith, and that faith is not sufficient for salvation. This is not true. Faith alone, of itself, without any works, as the Word of God here clearly says, brings us salvation, and works help nothing at all toward righteousness or salvation. We must let this passage stand pure and unadulterated, and without any addition. If the Holy Spirit had so desired, he could easily have said different words thus, "He that believeth and doeth works, shall be saved." But he did not do this; therefore, we should and will leave it as it is.

22. This I say to the end, that you may fortify yourselves with such passages, holding to the true meaning of the words. Though there are many passages in Scripture teaching that faith alone saves, yet they have been so covered over and obscured, so shaken to pieces and stretched, by the sophists and scholars, that their right meaning has suffered. Saint Paul says to the Galatians, "If righteousness is through the law, then Christ died for naught," in Galatians 2:21. That is to say, If we can be saved in any other way or work out our salvation, then Christ has died in vain; for to presume to be justified by the law means to think that man can become righteous through his works.

23. Therefore, to conclude, The chief righteousness is faith; the chief wickedness is unbelief. There is also no sin so great that it is able to condemn man; unbelief alone condemns all who are condemned. And again, only faith saves everyone; for faith alone deals with God; no works can appear before him. For works have to do only with man, and man lets his works be made use of as he has made use of Christ's. They make no one holy; they are only the distinguishing marks of a man that has already become righteous through faith, which alone makes the heart pure.

24. I can easily assent to the saying, Works do not make you pious, but show that you are pious; or when I hear it said, He that believes, serves his neighbor, I admit that it is so. But that the explanation of this text should be, Faith is not sufficient for salvation, we must also do good—this is a liberty which the text can stand just as little as this church could stand that I should pull down its pillars. There follows further in the text,

"He that believeth and is baptized shall be saved."

25. God has always accompanied his Word with an outward sign to make it the more effective to us, that we might be strengthened in heart and never doubt his Word, nor waver. Thus he gave Noah the rainbow in the heavens as a sure sign that he would keep his promise and not destroy the world by

another flood. The rainbow is, so to speak, a seal or sign to Noah and to us all, just as a seal upon a letter certifies the document. And just as a nobleman has his own coat of arms of a particular device or color, by which he is known, so has God evidenced his words for us with signs, as with a seal, that we should never doubt. To Abraham, he gave the rite of circumcision, to show that Christ should come and bless the world. Thus has he done here, adding to this promise of his, "He that believeth and is baptized shall be saved," an outward sign, namely, baptism, and also the sacrament of the bread and the wine, which was especially instituted for use in times of temptation, and when death draws near, that by it we might strengthen our faith, and remind God of his promise, and hold him to it.

26. A man can believe even though he be not baptized; for baptism is nothing more than an outward sign that is to remind us of the divine promise. If we can have it, it is well; let us receive it, for no one should despise it. If, however, we cannot receive it, or it is denied us, we will not be condemned if we only believe the Gospel. For where the Gospel is, there is also baptism and all that a Christian needs. Condemnation follows no sin except the sin of unbelief. Therefore, the Lord says, "He that disbelieveth shall be condemned"; he says not, He that is not baptized. He is silent concerning baptism, for baptism is worth nothing without faith, but is like seals affixed to a letter in which nothing is written. He that has the signs that we call sacraments, and has no faith, has only seals upon a letter of blank paper.

27. Here you see also what is the office of the apostles, to which all the bishops, and those that call themselves ministers, should conform, inasmuch as they boast that they are the successors of the apostles in preaching the Gospel. For the Lord says here, "Go ye into all the world, and preach the Gospel." Therefore, we should not listen to those who do not preach the Gospel. Now our papists come along and quote the passage in Luke 10:16, "He that heareth you, heareth me." This verse has hitherto been the pope's sword, by which he has swayed the whole world, and none has rightly understood this passage, which means that teachers are to be obeyed only when they preach the Gospel. So the Lord here inspires the apostles to speak the Gospel, which is his Word. Christ alone is to be heard, and the apostles are but messengers and instruments for this Word of Christ. Therefore, here again are condemned pope, bishops, monks, and priests, and all who preach something else than the Gospel.

28. But what is meant when the Lord says, "Preach the Gospel to the whole creation"? Shall I preach also to trees and stones, mountains and waters? What would that profit? Saint Gregory preached on this text and said that "all creation" means man; that man is one with all creatures—with the

angels in understanding, with the animals in sensibilities, and with the trees in growth. We must, therefore, not misuse the text nor make its meaning too literal, for so we shall misconstrue it. The meaning is that the Gospel should be publicly and universally preached, given to all; it should hide in no corner, but be preached freely in all places, as is written in Psalm 19:3–4, "There is no speech nor language where their voice is not heard. Their line is gone out through all the earth, and their words to the end of the world." The beginning and going forth has been fulfilled by the apostles, but the work is not yet finished; the Gospel has not yet reached its limit, for I know not whether Germany has ever heard the Word of God. The pope's word we have surely heard.

29. The Lord here says to the apostles, "Go ye into all the world, and preach the Gospel to the whole creation," for the reason that this Gospel may be published to everyone, so that even trees and stones might hear if they had ears, and might bear witness that we have heard the Gospel; and that pillar there might say, I have heard the Gospel preached to you. Thus generally and publicly shall it be proclaimed, and preached in all the world, being withheld from no one, until it reaches the ends of the world, as the psalm records. So it has now come to us, who are dwelling at the end of the world, for we live close to the sea. This, Paul has in mind when he says to the Ephesians, "And he gave some to be apostles, and some prophets; and some evangelists; and some pastors and teachers; for the perfecting of the saints, unto the work of ministering, unto the building up of the body of Christ: till we all attain unto the unity of the faith, and of the knowledge of the Son of God," in Ephesians 44:11–13. Next, the text speaks of the signs that shall follow faith, and names five signs, one after the other, thus,

> "And these signs shall accompany them that believe: in my name shall they cast out demons; they shall speak with new tongues; they shall take up serpents, and if they drink any deadly thing, it shall in no wise hurt them; they shall lay hands on the sick and they shall recover."

30. How shall we proceed here that we may preserve the truth of the passage: he that believeth shall have power also, and be able to show these signs? For the Lord says all these signs shall accompany them. Now we know that the apostles did not present all the signs, for we read of no other that drank poison than John the Evangelist, and there are no other individual instances. If the passage shall stand literally, then few believers will be cleared and few saints be entitled to heaven; for these signs, one and all, have not accompanied them, though they have had power to work signs, and have exhibited some of them.

31. Some rush on here and explain these signs as spiritual, so as to preserve the honor of the saints; but it will not do to strain the words. They do not carry such meaning; therefore, they will not bear such an explanation. It puts upon the Scriptures uncertain construction for us.

32. Others, with equal heedlessness, say that though not every individual has the power and does the wonders mentioned, yet the church as a whole, the multitude of Christendom, has; one may drive out devils, another heal the sick, and so on. Therefore, they say, such signs are a manifestation of the Spirit; where the signs are, there is also the Christian Church, and so on.

33. But these words do not refer to the church as a whole, but to each person separately. The meaning is, If there is a Christian who has faith, he shall have power to do these accompanying miracles, and they shall follow him, as Christ says, in John 14:12, "Verily, verily, I say unto you, he that believeth on me, the works that I do, shall he do also; and greater works than these shall he do," for a Christian has equal power with Christ, is a congregation, and sits with him in joint tenure. The Lord has given Christians power, as is written, in Matthew 10:8, also against the unclean spirits, that they might cast them out and heal every disease. Thus it is written in Psalm 91:13, "Thou shalt tread upon the lion and the adder; the young lion and the serpent shalt thou trample under foot."

34. We read also that this has been fulfilled. There was once a patriarch in the wilderness, who, when he met a serpent, took it in both hands and tore it in two, and thought no more about it, but said: O what a fine thing it is to have a clear and guiltless conscience! So, where there is a Christian, there is still the power to work these signs if it is necessary. But no one should attempt to exercise this power if it is not necessary or if need does not compel. The apostles did not always exercise it, but only made use of it to prove the Word of God, to confirm it by the miracles, as is written here in the text, "And they went forth, and preached everywhere, the Lord working with them, and confirming the Word by the signs that followed."

35. But since the Gospel has now been spread abroad, and made known to all the world, there is no need of working miracles as in the apostles' times. If need should arise, and men were to denounce and antagonize the Gospel, then we verily should have to employ wonder-working rather than permit the Gospel to be derided and suppressed. But I hope such a course will not be necessary, and that such a contingency will never arise. For another example, That I should here speak in new languages, is not at all necessary, since you all can well hear and understand me; but if God should send me

where the people could not understand me, he could easily grant me their speech or language, that I might be understood.

36. Then let no one, without pressing need, undertake to work wonders. For we read of the patriarchs' children that they once brought a large number of serpents in their cloaks, and shook them out at their parents' feet; whereupon their parents reproved them for tempting God unnecessarily. In like manner, we read of many signs that believers have done. It happened once upon a time that one of the fathers by chance got hold of a basilisk. He looked at it, and thereupon exclaimed, O Lord, I must die, or this reptile must! for the basilisk kills by its looks. At once, it bursted and flew into pieces.

37. I know not what I shall say about those who venture to do signs where they are not necessary. For example, some drive out demons. But I know that it is a dangerous undertaking. The devil, indeed, lets himself be driven out, but he does not intend to suffer for it; he allows it only that he may strengthen the sign-worker in such error. I would not like to trust him. We have many such instances in our times. I know also of many that happened not long ago.

38. There was a sexton who wished to learn alchemy from the devil, that is, the art of separating gold from sand, and of making gold from other metals. The devil agreed to come to him at the hour of eleven, but the sexton should have on a gown and chasuble. See with what fool's work the devil goes about! As though he cared much about the chasuble. The sexton went and reversed the hourglass and noted the hour. At eleven, he put on the chasuble. The devil came and knocked. The sexton was afraid and asked who was there. The devil said that the sexton should come at once to the parson and attend the sacrament. The sexton threw off the chasuble and ran out in haste, but found no one. Then the devil the second time demanded of the sexton to come out. The third time the devil came and said that the parson was awaiting him impatiently; he should come without delay. The sexton then went out, but by this time the hour was past, and the sexton had not on the chasuble. Then the sexton saw for the first time that it was the devil, and wished to hurry back to the house and get the chasuble. The devil, however, would not allow this, but said, No, my dear fellow, the time is past. He seized the sexton, broke his neck, and threw him to the ground. Such occasions the devil seeks, and acts. So much for this Gospel.

The Sunday After Christ's Ascension

A Sermon of Comfort and of Admonition

But when the Comforter is come, whom I will send unto you from the Father, even the Spirit of truth, who proceedeth from the Father, he shall bear witness of me: and ye shall bear witness, because ye have been with me from the beginning. These things have I spoken unto you, that ye should not be caused to stumble. They shall put you out of the synagogues: yea, the hour cometh, that whosoever killeth you shall think that he offereth service unto God. And these things will they do, because they have not known the Father, nor me. But these things have I spoken unto you, that when their hour is come, ye may remember them, how that I told you. And these things I said not unto you from the beginning, because I was with you." — JOHN 15:26–16:4

1. Beloved, you have heretofore heard much about faith. Today you hear also of the witness of faith and of the cross that follows. Paul says to the Romans, "With the heart man believeth unto righteousness," in Romans 10:10. If one be pious, he must begin in his heart and believe. That serves only unto godliness; it is not enough for salvation. Therefore, one must also do what the Christian life requires, and continually abide in that life. Hence Paul adds, "If thou shalt confess with thy mouth Jesus as Lord, thou shalt be saved." It is these two things that constitute our salvation, faith, and the confession of faith. Faith rescues from sin, hell, Satan, death, and all misfortunes. Now, when we have this, we have enough. We then let God live here that we may reach a hand to our neighbor and help him. Besides, God desires to have his name praised and his kingdom developed and extended. Therefore, we must praise his name, confess our faith, and win others to do the same, so that God's kingdom may be extended and his name praised.

2. Thus faith must be exercised, worked, and polished; be purified by fire, like gold. Faith, the great gift and treasure from God, must express itself and triumph in the certainty that it is right before God and man, and before angels, devils, and the whole world. Just as a jewel is not to be concealed, but to be worn in sight, so also will and must faith be worn and exhibited, as it is written in 1 Peter 1:7, "That the proof of your faith, being more precious than gold that perisheth though it is proved by fire," etc.

3. Now, by confession, I must take upon myself the load of Satan, hell, death, and the whole world—kings and princes, pope and bishops, priests and monks. By faith, everything falls that reason can or ever has devised for the salvation of the soul. It must chastise the apish tricks of the whole world, and its jewel alone must be praised. The world cannot endure this, therefore it rushes in, destroys, kills, and says, "It is expedient for you that one man should die for the people, and that the whole nation perish not," as Caiaphas says in John 11:50. Thus the confession must break forth, that God alone is the Savior; and the same confession brings us into danger of losing our lives. As the Lord says later to the disciples, "They shall put you out of the synagogues."

4. One cannot paint the cross differently than it is here painted; that is its true color. But the cross of illness—to lie in bed at home ill—is nothing compared with the cross of persecution. The first is indeed suffering, but the suffering is golden when we are persecuted and put to death with ignominy; when our persecutors have the praise; when right and honor apparently are on their side, while shame, disgrace, and injustice are on our side, compared with the world that wishes them thereby to have God's honor defended, so that all the world says we are served right and that God, the Scriptures, and all the angels witness against us. There can be no right in our cause and, without trial, we must be banished and isolated in shame and disgrace. So it also was the lot of Christ—they put him to death in the most scornful and disgraceful way, and crucified him between two thieves or murderers; he was regarded as chief of sinners, and they said, with blasphemous words, Aye, he called himself God's Son; let God help him now, if he wills it differently. Since he does not, God and all the angels must be against him. So Christ says in our Gospel, "They will kill you," and not in an ordinary way, but in an infamous manner, and all the world will say that they thereby offer God a service. It is, indeed, hard to hold and confess that God is gracious to us and that we have a Savior who opposes all the world, all its glitter and shine. But let the struggle be as hard and sharp as it will, faith must express itself, even though we would like to have it otherwise.

5. Faith must expect all this, and nothing follows its confession more surely than the cross. For it is certain to come to us, either in life or at death, that all our doings will appear to be opposed to God and the Scriptures. It is better that it be learned during life, from the people, than from the devil at death; for the people cannot force it further than into the ears, but Satan has a pointed tongue that pierces the heart and makes the heart tremble. Satan torments you until you conclude that you are lost and ruined, that heaven and earth, God and all the angels, are your enemies. This is what the prophet means, in Psalm 6:7–8, when he says, "I am weary with my groaning; every night make I my bed to swim; I water my couch with my tears. Mine eye wasteth away because of grief; it waxeth old because of all mine adversaries." It is hard to endure this. Now you see how weak you are who are permitted to bear witness of this faith. One fears his wife, another his children and riches, and a third fears himself.

6. Faith is in vain where it does not continue steadfast to the end. Christ says in Matthew 10:22 and in Matthew 24:13, "But he that endureth to the end, the same shall be saved." Hence it is better to experience persecution here than punishment at the end. If one flees persecution, there is no faith in his heart—only a dead knowledge or erroneous belief, without sap and strength, marrow and bone; but where there is a true, living faith, it presses forward through sword and fire. Let us now notice how the Lord comforts his disciples. He says,

"But when the Comforter is come."

I. CHRIST'S SERMON OF COMFORT

7. That we may, under no circumstances, despair, Christ says, I will send you a Comforter, even one who is almighty. And he calls the Holy Spirit here a Comforter; for although both my sins and the fear of death make me weak and timid, he comes and stirs up the courage in my heart, and says, Ho, cheer up! Thus he trumpets courage into us; he encourages us in a friendly and comforting manner not to despair before death, but to cheerfully go forward, even though we had ten necks for the executioner, and says, Aye, although I have sinned, yet I am rid of my sins; and if I had still more, so that they overwhelmed me, I would hope that they should do me no harm. Not that one should not feel his sins, for the flesh must experience them; but the Spirit overcomes and suppresses diffidence and timidity, and conducts us through them. He is powerful enough to do that. Therefore, Christ says further,

"Whom I will send unto you from the Father."

8. For he, the Father, is the person that takes the initiative: I am the Son; and from us the Holy Spirit proceeds. And the three persons are one, and one essence, with equal power and authority, as he better expresses it when he says,

"The Spirit of truth, who proceedeth from the Father."

9. That is as much as to say, He who will comfort you is almighty and Lord over all things. How can the creatures now harm us, if the Creator stands by us? Notice how great the comfort of the Holy Spirit is. Now let all the Turks [Muslims] attack us. As long as he is our guard and rear guard, there is no danger. John also says, in 1 John 3:19–20, "Hereby shall we know that we are of the truth, and shall assure our heart before him; because if our heart condemn us, God is greater than our heart, and knoweth all things." Likewise, in the following chapter, verse 4, he says, "Ye are of God, my little children, and have overcome them: because greater is he that is in you than he that is in the world." So the Lord now says, Him will I send unto you, so that nothing can harm you. Is not that liberal comfort? Who would not be fearless and cheerful in view of this? And Christ calls him "The Spirit of truth"; that is, where he is and comes, there is a rock foundation through and through, the real truth. Neither falsehood nor hypocrisy is there, for the Spirit is not hypocritical. But wherever he is not, there is nothing but hypocrisy and falsehood. Therefore, we fall when the test comes because the Spirit of truth is not present. Christ now further says,

"He shall bear witness of me."

10. That is, if he is in the heart, he speaks through you, and assures and confirms you in the belief that the Gospel is true. Then, as a result, the confession of the Gospel springs forth. What, then, is the Gospel? It is a witness concerning Christ, that he is God's Son, the Savior, and besides him there is none other. This is what Peter means when he says, "Ye are a royal priesthood, that we are elected thereto, that we preach and show forth the excellencies of Christ," in 1 Peter 2:9. Hence there must always be witnessing. Witnessing loads upon itself the wrath of the whole world. Then the cross follows, then rebellions rise, then the lords and princes and all who are great become angry; for the world cannot hear, nor will it tolerate, this kind of preaching. Therefore, the Gospel is hated and spoken against.

11. Reason thinks, Aye, one can, nevertheless, easily preach the Gospel in a beautifully simple and plain way, without a revolution in the world, and then it will be heartily welcomed. This is the utterance of Satan; for if I believe and say that faith in Christ alone does and accomplishes all, I overthrow the monkey

play of the whole world; and that they cannot allow. Therefore, Christ's teachings and man's teachings cannot stand together; one must fall. Priests and monks, as they are at present, are dependent in name, character, and works upon human institutions, which the Gospel thrusts to the ground. Hence they dare not accept the Gospel, and they continue as they are.

12. Thus I say that the Christian faith is founded upon Christ alone, without anything additional. The priests will not permit their affairs and institutions to fall; in consequence, seditions and rebellions follow. Therefore, there must be dissension where the Gospel and the confession of Christ are; for the Gospel opposes everything that is not of its own spirit. If the teachings of Christ and the priests were not antagonistic, they could easily stand together. They are now pitted against one another. As impossible as it is for Christ not to be Christ, so impossible is it for a monk or priest to be a Christian. Therefore, a fire must be kindled. The Lord himself, in Matthew 10:34 and in Luke 12:51, says, "I came not to send peace, but a sword." Then follows in our text,

"And ye also bear witness,
because ye have been with me from the beginning."

13. Yes; then, first, when you become certain of your faith through the Holy Spirit, who is your witness, you must also bear witness of me, for to that end I chose you to be apostles. You have heard my words and teachings, and have seen my works and life and all things that you are to preach. But the Holy Spirit must first be present; otherwise, you can do nothing, for the conscience is too weak. Yes, there is no sin so small that the conscience could vanquish it, even if it were so trifling a one as laughing in church. Again, in the presence of death, the conscience is far too weak to offer resistance. Therefore, another must come and give to the timid, despairing conscience, courage to go through everything, although all sins be upon it. And it must, at the same time, be an almighty courage, like he alone can give, who ministers strength in such a way that the courage, which before a rustling leaf could cause to fear, is now not afraid of all the devils, and the conscience that before could not restrain laughing, now restrains all sins.

14. The benefit and fruit of the Holy Spirit is, that sin will be changed to the highest and best use. Thus Paul boasts to Timothy, when he was converted, that whereas he had lived such a wicked life before, he now held his sin to be so contemptible that he composed a hymn and sang about it thus, in 1 Timothy 1:12–17, "I thank him that enabled me, even Christ Jesus our Lord, for that he counted me faithful, appointing me to his service; though I was before a

blasphemer, and a persecutor, and injurious: howbeit I obtained mercy, because I did it ignorantly in unbelief; and the grace of our Lord abounded exceedingly with faith and love which is in Christ Jesus. Faithful is the saying, and worthy of all acceptation, that Christ Jesus came into the world to save sinners; of whom I am chief: howbeit for this cause I obtained mercy, that in me as chief might Jesus Christ show forth all his long-suffering, for an example of them that should thereafter believe on him unto eternal life. Now unto the King eternal, immortal, invisible, the only God, be honor and glory for ever and ever. Amen."

II. CHRIST'S SERMON OF WARNING

> *"These things have I spoken unto you*
> *that ye should not be caused to stumble."*

15. Now that Christ had comforted and strengthened his disciples, he warns them of their future sufferings, in order that they might be able to bear them valiantly. He is an especially good friend who warns one; and the evil visitation is much easier borne when one is prepared beforehand for it. Christ says,

> *"They shall put you out of the synagogues; yea, the hour cometh that*
> *whosoever killeth you shall think that he offereth service unto God."*

16. You will certainly experience this; therefore, arm yourself and be prepared. The most of all will be that, when they have treated you in the most shameless manner, they will think they did a good work in doing so, and it will appear to them as if your God had taken stand against you, and they will sing over it a Te Deum laudamus (Lord God, we praise thee), as if they had done God's will and offered unto him a service. Hence he arms them here, that they may be of good courage when it comes to pass; and he concludes with the thought that they shall have God's favor, although at the time there shall be no signs of it; for God does stand on the side of his disciples. He adds,

> *"And these things will they do,*
> *because they have not known the Father, nor me."*

17. Therefore, be patient, be prepared, be firm. See to it that ye, by no means, take offense at me. Remember that I told you before that they have known neither the Father nor me; and therefore they will heap upon you dishonor, shame, and persecution. You should never forget this, for it will give you great comfort and make you bold, cheerful, and undismayed. Therefore, Christ concludes the admonition by saying,

*"But these things have I spoken unto you, that when their hour is come,
ye may remember them, how that I told you. And these things I said not
unto you from the beginning, because I was with you."*

18. Who, now, has been considered to be worse than he who told the pope
that he knew not the Father? The pope would, of course, declare the contrary
and say, Aye, Satan has commissioned you to speak that. Now, they all say that
they know the Father. The Turk [Muslim] also says that he does. In like manner, they declare they believe God and the Scriptures. But there are two kinds
of knowledge. The first, for example, such knowledge as one might have of
the Turk [Muslim] from his noise and reputation; the other the knowledge
one would have of the Turk [Muslim] through his deeds were he to capture
and occupy Rome. In this latter sense, we do not know the Turk [Muslim].

19. It is this first kind of knowledge that some people have of God. They
know very well how to say of him, I believe in God the Father, and in his only
begotten Son. But it is only upon the tongue, like the foam on the water; it
does not enter the heart. Figuratively, a big tumor still remains there in the
heart; that is, they cling somewhat to their own deeds and think they must do
works in order to be saved—that Christ's person and merit are not sufficient.
Thy work is nothing, thy wisdom is foolishness, thy counsel is nothing, thy
truth also amounts to nothing, neither does the Mass avail anything before
God. Then they reply, Aye, the devil has prompted you to speak thus. They
say, Christ has truly died for us, but in a way that we, also, must accomplish
something by our deeds. Notice how deeply wickedness and unbelief are
rooted in the heart. The puffed-up pride of the heart is the reason why man
can know neither Christ nor the Father.

20. But to know Christ in the other and true sense is to know that he died
for me and transferred the load of my sin upon himself; to so know this that I
realize that all my doings amount to nothing. To let go all that is mine, and
value only this, that Christ is given to me as a present; his sufferings, his righteousness, and all his virtues are at once mine. When I become conscious of
this, I must in return love him; my affections must go out to such a being.
After this, I climb upon the Son higher, to the Father, and see that Christ is
God, and that he placed himself in my death, in my sin, in my misery, and
bestows upon me his grace. Then I know also his gracious will and the highest love of the Father, which no heart of itself can discover or experience.
Thus I lay hold of God at the point where he is the tenderest, and think, Aye,
that is God; that is God's will and pleasure, that Christ did this for me. And
with this experience I perceive the high, inexpressible mercy and the love in

him because of which he offered his beloved child for me in ignominy, shame, and death. That friendly look and lovely sight then sustain me. Thus must God become known, only in Christ. Therefore, Christ himself says to his disciples, "No one knoweth the Son, save the Father; neither doth any know the Father, save the Son, and he to whomsoever the Son willeth to reveal him," in Matthew 11:27.

21. On the other hand, those who parade their own works, do not know Christ. Neither do they know what the Father has done through Christ. Nor do they know that God is not interested in their good works, but in his Son alone. Thus they do not know the Father, neither do they know what they have received from the Father, through Christ. Therefore, they must fall and perish, and behold God in his severest aspect—as a judge. They try to silence the judgment with their good works, but they find no good work that is sufficient to do this, and then they must finally despair. When people see that they, themselves, are nothing, and establish the foundation of their hearts upon Christ, esteem him as the highest good, and know God as a Father in death and life—this is to "know God." Enough has been said on this Gospel. We will pray to God, to give us grace to know him and his Christ aright. Amen.

Pentecost

❦

Or, the Festival of the Outpouring of the Holy Spirit

J esus answered and said unto him, "If a man love me, he will keep
my Word: and my Father will love him, and we will come unto him,
and make our abode with him. He that loveth me not keepeth not my
words: and the word which ye hear is not mine, but the Father's who
sent me.

These things have I spoken unto you, while yet abiding with you. But
the Comforter, even the Holy Spirit, whom the Father will send in my
name, he shall teach you all things, and bring to your remembrance all
that I said unto you. Peace I leave with you: my peace I give unto you:
not as the world giveth, give I unto you. Let not your heart be troubled,
neither let it be fearful. Ye heard how I said to you, I go away, and I
come unto you. If ye loved me, ye would have rejoiced, because I go unto
the Father: for the Father is greater than I. And now I have told you
before it come to pass, that, when it is come to pass, ye may believe. I
will no more speak much with you, for the prince of the world cometh:
and he hath nothing in me; but that the world may know that I love the
Father, and as the Father gave me commandment, even so I do. Arise, let
us go hence." — JOHN 14:23–31

I. THE INTRODUCTION TO THIS SERMON OF COMFORT, TREATING OF CHRIST'S LOVE

1. In today's Gospel, Christ says plainly and bluntly, "If a man love me, he will keep my Word; he that loveth me not, keepeth not my words." The text stands there clear; whoever loves God, keeps his commandments and, on the contrary, whoever does not love God, does not keep his commandments. Christ here simply casts out of his kingdom all who do not keep his commandments with pleasure and love. Let us thoroughly understand this. It is briefly pictured to us here who are and who are not Christians. No one is a Christian unless he keeps Christ's Word, as he here says. And no one can keep

it, unless he first loves God. God had tested the plan of making people godly by means of force. For, in olden times, God dealt severely with his people, so that they were forced to keep his Word, and not to blaspheme God; to observe the Sabbath and to obey all the other commandments. To this end, he threatened to afflict and punish them, severely, as is written, in Leviticus 26:14ff. Thus God from without coerced the people to be pious by means of the fear of punishment; but their hearts were not obedient. The result is the same in the present day. Therefore, to keep God's Word is a thing that can be accomplished only by divine love.

2. Accordingly, in the New Testament, God ceased to punish and only administered the Word; for the means must yet come to the point that the divine love be present. Neither the stake nor bulls nor bans help in the least. Where this love is not, all amounts to nothing, do as we will. If one were to take all the swords in the world in his hands, he would not bring a single heretic to the faith. The people may, indeed, appear to accept the Word, but in their inward hearts there is no faith. Hence God has abolished the sword in this matter, and his plan of salvation aims to possess the heart. The bishops are commanded first to take the heart captive, so that it may find love and pleasure in the Word, and the work is then accomplished. Hence he who wishes to be a true bishop, arranges all his administration to the end that he may win souls and develop a love for and a delight in God's Word, and be able to oppose the false babblers with sound teaching, and to stop their mouths, in Titus 1:11. This will never be accomplished by means of commandments, bans, and bulls.

3. Thus the true spiritual leaders fight. They strike Satan dead and rescue souls from him; for to pierce Satan to death is nothing else than to rescue from him a human being whom he has taken captive by deceitful teaching. And that is the right kind of spiritual tactics. But in case people will not outwardly obey the Word, their parents should educate their children, and the civil government its subjects, to obedience. However, by this method, none are yet brought to believe. For it is affirmed in our text, "He that loveth me not keepeth not my words." Thus you hear what a Christian life is, namely, to love God; it is not to storm about, eat flesh, destroy pictures in churches, become monks or nuns—neither a married nor a single life avails here. It means to love, and they do this who keep his Word.

4. Now, what is God's Word? It is that we love one another as Christ loved us, and that we believe on him. If one truly possesses the Word, it must break forth out of the heart from pure love. One may possess the words and commands of man, even if he does not love; he may receive the command of a superior and execute it. But the only thing that will keep

God's commandments and Word is love. Therefore, observe how foolishly our princes and bishops act, in that they coerce and constrain the people to believe by means of force.

5. How does one now acquire this love? The human heart is so false that it cannot love unless it first sees the benefit of loving. When, in the Old Testament, God struck blows among the people as if among dogs, and he dealt severely and fearfully with them, they naturally had no love for him. Then God thought, I must show my love to you and be so affectionate that you cannot help but love me. Then he took his Son and sent him into our filth, sin, and misery, pouring out his mercy so freely and fully that we had to boast of all his treasures as if they were our own. He thus became a loving Father, and he declared his mercy and caused it to go forth into all the world that whosoever believes this and lays hold of it with his heart, shall have a gracious and merciful God, who never becomes angry nor deals blows, but who, instead, is kind and affectionate. Now, where a heart believes and experiences this, and gets glimpses of so much, then it must place all its confidence and affection in God, and deal with its neighbor as God has dealt with itself. As a result, the Word of God goes forth out of the heart, and his commandments will be kept with pleasure. Thus, first, there is no other God; secondly, man calls upon the name of the Lord; and thirdly, he lets God reign—God can do as he will, and he possesses his soul in quiet and observes the Sabbath. In this way, the commandments of the first table are fulfilled. Henceforth, he is kindly and humbly disposed toward all persons, he honors his father and mother, and serves his neighbor as his highest pleasure and with all the love of his heart. His thought is ever this, I will do to my neighbor as God has done to me. Thus love alone is the fulfillment of the law, as Paul says to the Romans, in Romans 13:10.

6. Now, no man can bring this love into the heart. Therefore, God struck in among the people with the law that man might experience and feel that no human being could love the divine, righteous, just, and holy law. In view of this, he gave us his Son, thus graciously poured out his greatest treasures, and sunk and drowned all our sins and filth in the great ocean of his love, so that this great love and blessing must draw man to love, and cheerfully be ready to fulfill, the divine commandments with willing heart. In no other way can the heart love or have any love; it must be assured that it was first loved. Now, man cannot do this; therefore, Christ comes and takes the heart captive, and says, Learn to know me. Then the heart replies, Aye, who art thou? I am Christ, who placed myself in your misery to drown your sins in my righteousness. This knowledge softens your heart, so that you must turn to him. Thus love is awakened when one learns who Christ is.

7. And a Christian should glory in this knowledge, as God says in Jeremiah 9:23–24, "Thus saith Jehovah, Let not the wise man glory in his wisdom, neither let the mighty man glory in his might, let not the rich man glory in his riches; but let him that glorieth in this, that he hath understanding, and knoweth me, that I am Jehovah who exerciseth lovingkindness, justice, and righteousness, in the earth: for in these things I delight, saith Jehovah." So also Peter, in 2 Peter 3:18, says, "But grow in the knowledge of our Lord and Savior Jesus Christ." In all the prophets, and especially in the psalms, and in many places in the Bible, there is much written about this knowledge. It is this knowledge of Christ that must convert or it will never be accomplished. No one is so hardened that he will not be converted and made tender if once his heart knows Christ. And the same knowledge causes one to steadfastly live a godly life. Isaiah says, The time will come when this knowledge shall flow forth like a deluge. This came to pass in the time of the apostles. Therefore, whoever loves God will keep his commandments, and that love brings a knowledge of God. Now Christ says, further, in our Gospel,

"And my Father will love him."

8. It comes to pass in this way: I know first, that Christ has served me by his whole life, and that Christ is God; thus I see that it is God's will that Christ should give himself for me and that the Father commissioned him to that end. Thus I climb to the Father through Christ. Then my confidence in him begins to grow, so that I esteem him as a loving Father. Christ here means to say, Man must begin with my love and then he will come to the Father; Christ is a mediator. Therefore, I must first be loved—must first feel the great treasure and blessing in Christ. Hence God takes the very first step and allows his dear child to die for me, before I ask him to do so, yea, before I ever know him. Then a confidence in and love to God grow in me; this I must feel. Christ also says here, "And my Father will love him"; that is, the convert will feel that he is placed with me in the same kingdom and co-inheritance, and will, through me and with me and with my voice, say to the Father in comforting confidence, Dearly beloved Father. Then the text continues,

"And we will come unto him, and make our abode with him."

9. When I come to the point of knowing that God is my Father, then I let him rule in my heart according to his pleasure, and allow him to be all in all. Therewith, my heart becomes a quiet, humble abode of God. Thus God is a co-laborer with me and assists me, as he says in Isaiah 66:1–2 and in Acts 7:49–50, "Thus saith Jehovah, Heaven is my throne, and the earth is my footstool: what

manner of house will ye build unto me? and what place shall be my rest? For all these things hath my hand made, and so all these things came to be, saith Jehovah: but to this man will I look, even to him that is poor and of a contrite spirit, and that trembleth at my Word." The heart must come to the point where it knows God's glory, God's power, and God's wisdom, and lets God rule in everything. It knows that all is God's work; therefore, it cannot fear anything: cold, hunger, hell, death, Satan, poverty, or any like thing. Then the heart says, My God, who has made his abode in me, is greater than Satan, death, and all the powers of hell.

10. Thus there develops in man a confident defiance of everything upon earth, for he has God and all that is God's. He does all that he is now required to do, and fears not. On the contrary, where there is no love of God, that heart does not keep God's Word; and if the heart does not keep God's Word, the hand never will. There God will never enter and make his abode. There the devil dwells, until the weak and despairing soul will even fear the sound of a driven leaf, as Moses says in Leviticus 26:36. Man cannot endure the gnawing of conscience. The conscience can never know any peace when oppressed by sin, nor can it experience a joyful confidence in God; yea, it will sink lower than hell, while confidence is higher than the heavens. There is then nothing but despair and fear for that heart. All creatures are above it. Such is a picture of the kingdom of Satan. Christ continues by saying,

"And the word which ye hear is not mine, but the Father's who sent me."

11. These words Christ speaks only in order to bring us to the Father, either in a gracious or ungracious way, either with pleasure and love or with fear, for all must lean and depend upon him. Hence whoever will not understand these words scorns God. Then no teaching, no words, nor anything else will help in his case. Now Christ comes, and says,

"These things have I spoken unto you, while yet abiding with you.
But the Comforter, even the Holy Spirit, whom the Father
will send in my name, he shall teach you all things,
and bring to your remembrance all that I said unto you."

II. THE SERMON OF COMFORT

12. Here Christ says, The Father will send you the Holy Spirit, who will bring to your remembrance what I told you, and the same Spirit will explain it to you. In other words, Your hearts are as yet rough and untutored and you cannot understand what I have spoken to you; but when the Holy Spirit

comes, he will make all so plain to you that you will experience the assurance that it is as I told you before. Thus the Holy Spirit, and he alone, has explained the Scriptures and Christ, and made them clear. This knowledge, then, is sufficient for me and enables me to fulfill God's commandments. Beyond this, however, I have no obligations. Christ comforts his disciples further, and says,

> "Peace I leave with you; my peace I give unto you; not as the world giveth, give I unto you."

13. As if he had said, I shall now leave you. Farewell! It was a common greeting among the Jews, in the Hebrew language, when they met or parted, to say, Peace be with you! That is as much as to say, Take good care of yourself, be of good spirits, hope you may prosper; as we in German say, God greet you (*Gott grüsze euch*) or God bless you!

14. And the Lord adds the kind of peace he wishes them to have, and says, My peace I give unto you; not as the world is in the habit of giving peace. In plain words, he distinguishes between his peace and the peace of the world. The disciples, however, did not understand it, just as they did not understand what it was to love and to keep God's commandments. Now, it is the nature of the world's peace that it consists only in outward things, in eating and drinking and dancing; its pleasure is in the flesh. Christian peace, however, is in the heart, although at the same time the heart may suffer great persecution, fear, want, and opposition. The Lord had told them of all these things in the words, "Ye shall weep and lament." The world will persecute you, will reject your teaching, will scourge, banish, and finally put you to death; but in the midst of all, ye shall have peace and rejoice. Cling only to me and my Word!

15. And his words were soon fulfilled. When they had received the Holy Spirit, Luke writes in Acts 5:41, Peter, John, and the other disciples, though scourged and forbidden to preach, departed from the presence of the council, rejoicing that they were counted worthy to suffer dishonor for the Name. But the disciples did not at this time understand, and they were troubled because of the Lord's discourse. Therefore, he gives them further comfort, and says,

> "Let not your heart be troubled, neither let it be fearful."

16. These are consoling words, but for the time they are not effectual. Be not afraid, he says, for you have my peace. No one will harm you; only cling to me. The words they indeed hear, as do we, but without seeing their significance. Therefore, he says in clearer language,

> "Ye heard how I said to you, I go away, and I come unto you."

17. As if he said, Be not fearful because I said to you I go away from you: I will come again to you; yea, it is especially for your sake that I go away, that afterward when I return to you, you may be the happier and be of good spirits. But neither did they understand this until the Holy Spirit later interpreted it to them. Just so it is with us in the time of temptation: we do not then understand what God intends to teach us; but later, when grace and comfort return, we understand it very well. The Lord says to the disciples,

"If ye loved me, ye would have rejoiced, because I go unto the Father."

18. His words mean, The only failing you have is that you do not love me, or do not understand what it is to love. If ye loved me, ye would gladly let me go; yea, ye would laugh for joy, because I depart from you. And the more you are visited with ill fortune and adversity, the happier you should be. But human reason does not understand this. It is certainly true that the more a Christian suffers persecution from without, the happier he is in heart, and the more peace he possesses. The reason is that he loves Christ. This Saint Paul well understood from his own experience when he wrote to the Corinthians, in 2 Corinthians 4:4–10, We are pressed on every side, yet not straitened; perplexed, yet not unto despair; pursued, yet not forsaken; smitten down, yet not destroyed; always bearing about in the body the dying of Jesus, that the life also of Jesus may be manifested in our body."

And again, he says, in verses 16 to 18, "Wherefore we faint not; but though our outward man is decaying, yet our inward man is renewed day by day. For our light affliction, which is for the moment, worketh for us more and more exceedingly an eternal weight of glory; while we look not at the things which are seen, but at the things which are not seen; for the things which are seen are temporal; but the things which are not seen are eternal."

19. This is the experience of the Christian heart when the Holy Spirit has entered it. Saint Paul writes more about this later, in 2 Corinthians 6. It made an impression upon the heathen when they saw the Christians thus hastening to death; they thought the Christians were foolish and intervened to spare their lives. The gentiles did not understand what it meant; but the Christians very well knew whence it came. Therefore the Lord adds,

"For the Father is greater than I."

20. Even if I should tell you many things, ye would not understand them; they reach no farther than the ears and never enter the heart. However, when I return to the Father, then I will take upon myself the power to send into your

hearts the Holy Spirit, through whose help ye may understand all that I said to you. For the present, I am in the service of my ministry upon earth; I only speak and preach the Word as it has been commanded me by my Father. The Arians paid no attention here to the words, "I go to the Father," which means nothing more than, I go and receive the honor the Father has. It is as if the Lord had said to his disciples, I have two offices. At present, I am upon the earth, where I am performing my office of preaching, for which I was sent by the Father. When I come to the Father, I will fulfill the other office, namely, this: I will send the Holy Spirit into your hearts. The disciples could not understand this, and neither do we understand how he administers the gift. He concludes by saying,

> *"And now I have told you before it come to pass,*
> *that when it is come to pass, ye may believe."*

21. The meaning is, I know very well that you do not understand this now; but I tell you it now so that, when it comes to pass as I have told you, you may remember that I declared it to you before, and you can then say, It is true. In what follows now in this Gospel, the Lord speaks of the hour of his suffering, that it is at hand, and says,

> *"I will no more speak much with you, for the prince of the world cometh;*
> *and he hath nothing in me; but that the world may know that I love the*
> *Father, and as the Father gave me commandment, even so I do.*
> *Arise, let us go hence."*

III. THE CONCLUSION OF THIS SERMON OF CONSOLATION

22. In other words, The time of my suffering and death is at hand. The prince of this world, the devil, is present in his adherents, and will seize me. But he will accomplish nothing, for he will unjustly lay hold of me, desiring to crush me. His tactics will fail; I will triumph over him, and I will do it justly.

23. One may reply, Did not Satan conquer Christ? Did he not put him to death? Christ himself answers this, and says that he dies for the very purpose of satisfying the will of the Father. It is not due to the power of Satan that Christ dies, but to the will of the Father, who would blot out sin through the death of his only begotten Son. Hence it does not rest in the power of the world nor of Satan to put to death either Christ or any of his followers. But it does rest in the will of the Father, who reveals his power through our weakness, before all his creatures; as Saint Paul says in 1 Corinthians 15:27. In view

of this, Christ here says to his disciples, I will indeed die, but I will rise again. I die to the end, that the world may know that I love the Father, and that I do what my Father hath commanded me. I seek the Father's glory in this, who wills that I should so do. And all this for the sake of your salvation and blessedness. Therefore, be of good cheer and let not your heart be troubled; for you will have great joy because of my death and my leaving you.

Trinity Sunday

⟨⟩

The Doctrine of the Trinity

O the depth of the riches both of the wisdom and the knowledge of God! How unsearchable are his judgments, and his ways past tracing out! For who hath known the mind of the Lord? or who hath been his counsellor? or who hath first given to him, and it shall be recompensed unto him again? For of him and through him, and unto him, are all things. To him be the glory for ever. Amen.
— ROMANS 11:33–36

1. This festival requires us to instruct the people in the dogma of the Holy Trinity, and to strengthen both memory and faith concerning it. This is the reason why we take up the subject once more. Without proper instruction and a sound foundation in this regard, other dogmas cannot be rightly and successfully treated. The other festivals of the year present the Lord God clothed in his works and miracles. For instance, on Christmas we celebrate his incarnation; on Easter his resurrection from the dead; on Whitsunday the gift of the Holy Spirit and the establishment of the Christian Church. Thus all the other festivals present the Lord in the guise of a worker of one thing or another. But this Trinity Festival discloses him to us as he is in himself. Here we see him apart from whatever guise assumed, from whatever work done, solely in his divine essence. We must go beyond and above all reason, leaving behind the evidence of created things, and hear only God's own testimony concerning himself and his inner essence; otherwise, we shall remain unenlightened.

2. Upon this subject the foolishness of God and the wisdom of the world conflict. God's declaration that he is one God in three distinct persons, the world looks upon as wholly unreasonable and foolish; and the followers of mere reason, when they hear it, regard everyone that teaches or believes it as no more than a fool. Therefore, this article has been assailed continually, from the times of the apostles and the fathers down to the present day, as history testifies. Especially the Gospel of Saint John has been subjected to attack, which was written for the special purpose of fortifying this dogma against the

attacks of Cerinthus the heretic, who in the apostolic age already attempted to prove from Moses the existence of but one God, which he assigned as reason that our Lord Jesus cannot be true God on account of the impossibility of God and man being united in one being. Thus he gave us the prattle of his reason, which he made the sole standard for heaven to conform to.

3. O shameless reason! How can we poor, miserable mortals grasp this mystery of the Trinity? we who do not understand the operation of our own physical powers—speech, laughter, sleep, things whereof we have daily experience? Yet we would, untaught by the Word of God, guided merely by our fallible head, pronounce upon the very nature of God. Is it not supreme blindness for man, when he is unable to explain the most insignificant physical operation daily witnessed in his own body, to presume to understand something above and beyond the power of reason to comprehend, something whereof only God can speak, and to rashly affirm that Christ is not God?

4. Indeed, if reason were the standard of judgment in such matters, I also might make a successful venture; but when the conclusions of even long and mature reflections upon the subject are compared with Scripture, they will not stand. Therefore, we must repeat, even though a mere stammering should be the result, what the Scriptures say to us, namely, that Jesus Christ is true God and that the Holy Spirit is likewise true God, yet there are not three Gods, not three divine natures, as we may speak of three brothers, three angels, three suns, three windows. There is one indivisible divine essence, while we recognize a distinction as to the persons.

SCRIPTURE PROOF THAT CHRIST IS GOD

Paul, speaking of Christ in Hebrews 1:3, refers to him as the express image of God's substance. Again, in Colossians 1:15, he says of Christ, "Who is the image of the invisible God, the firstborn of all creation." We must take these words for what they say—that all creatures, even angels and men, are ranked below Christ. This classification leaves room for God only: taking away the creature, only God remains. It is one and the same thing, then, to say that Christ is the firstborn of all creatures, and that Christ is true and essential God.

5. To make the matter as clear as possible, Paul uses the expression "image of the invisible God." If Christ be the image of God, he must be a person distinct from him whose image he is, but at the same time in one divine essence with the Father. He and the Father are not one person, but two, and yet Christ could not be the express image of the Father's person, or essence, if he were not equally divine. No creature can be an image of the divine essence, for it does not possess that essence. To repeat, Christ could not be called the express

image of God if he and the Father were not distinct persons; there must be one imaged and one who is the image. Expressed more clearly and according to Scripture, one person is the Father, who in eternity begets the other; the other is the Son, begotten in eternity, yet both are equally eternal, mighty, wise, and just.

6. Though the Jews and Turks [Muslims] ridicule our doctrine, as if we taught the existence of three brothers in heaven, it does not signify. Might I also cavil were it to serve any purpose here. But they do us wrong and falsify our teaching; for we do not conceive of the Trinity as in the nature of three men or of three angels. We regard it as one divine essence, an intimacy surpassing any earthly unity. The human body and soul are not so completely one as the Triune God. Further, we claim the holy Scriptures teach that in the one divine essence, God the Father begot a Son. Before any creature was made, before the world was created, as Paul says, "before the foundation of the world," in eternity, the Father begot a Son who is equal with him and in all respects God like himself. Not otherwise could Paul call Christ the express image of the invisible God. Thus it is proved that the Father and the Son are distinct persons, and that nevertheless but one God exists, a conclusion we cannot escape unless we would contradict Paul, and would become Jews and Turks [Muslims].

PAUL AND MOSES AGREE IN TESTIMONY

7. Again, Paul makes mention of Christ in different phrase, saying, "Neither let us tempt Christ, as some of them also tempted, and were destroyed of serpents," in 1 Corinthians 10:9. Now, keeping this verse in mind, note how Paul and Moses kiss each other, how clearly the one responds to the other. For Moses says, in Numbers 14:22, "All those men...have tempted me these ten times, and have not hearkened to my voice," and, in this connection, the speaker is represented by the term "Lord," everywhere in the Bible printed by us in capitals to indicate a name belonging only to the Eternal, applicable to none but the one true God. Other terms used to designate God are sometimes applied also to men, but this word "Lord" refers only to God.

Now, Moses says, "And the Lord [Adonai, the true God] said...All these men ...have tempted me these ten times." Then comes Paul, explaining who this God is—saying they tempted "Christ." Crawl through this statement if you may; the fact remains that Paul declares it was Christ who was tempted, and Moses makes him the one eternal and true God. Moreover, Christ was not at that time born; no, nor were Mary and David. Nevertheless, the apostle plainly says, They tempted Christ, let us not also tempt him.

8. Certainly enough, then, Christ is the man to whom Moses refers as God. Thus the testimony of Moses long before is identical with that of Paul. Though employing different terms, they both confess Christ as the Son of God, born in eternity of the Father, in the same divine essence and yet distinct from him. You may call this difference what you will; we indicate it by the term "person." True, we do not make a wholly clear explanation of the mystery; we but stammer when speaking of a "Trinity." But what are we to do? we cannot better the attempt. So, then, the Father is not the Son, but the Son is born of the Father in eternity; and the Holy Spirit proceeds from God the Father and God the Son. Thus there are three persons, and yet but one God. For what Moses declares concerning God, Paul says is spoken of Christ.

9. The same argument substantially Paul employs in Acts 20:28, when, blessing the church of Miletus and exhorting the assembled ministers concerning their office, he says, "Take heed unto yourselves, and to all the flock, in which the Holy Spirit hath made you bishops, to feed the church of the Lord which he purchased with his own blood." This, too, is a significant text, proving beyond all controversy that Christ our Lord, who purchased the church with his blood, is truly God, and to him the church belongs. For the apostle plainly asserts it was God who bought the church with his blood, and that the church is his own.

Now, in view of the fact already established that the persons are distinct, and of the further statement that God has purchased the church through his own blood, we inevitably conclude that Christ our Savior is true God, born of the Father in eternity, and that he also became man and was born of the Virgin Mary in time.

10. If such blood—the material, tangible, crimson blood, shed by a real man—is truly to be called the blood of God, then he who shed it must be actually God, an eternal, almighty person in the one divine essence. In that case, we truly can say the blood flowing from the side of the crucified One and spilled upon the ground is not merely the blood of an ordinary man, but God's own. Paul does not indulge in frivolous talk. He speaks of a most momentous matter; and he is in dead earnest when he, in his exhortation, reminds us that it is an exalted office to rule the church and to feed it with the Word of God. Lest we toy in the performance of such an office, we are reminded that the flock is as dear to him as the blood of his dear Son, so precious that all creatures combined can furnish no equivalent. And if we are indolent or unfaithful, we sin against the blood of God and become guilty of it, inasmuch as through our fault it has been shed in vain for the souls which we should oversee.

11. There are many passages of similar import, particularly in the Gospel of John. So we cannot evade the truth but must say God the Father, God the Son, and God the Holy Spirit are three individual persons, yet of one divine essence. We do not, as the Jews and Turks [Muslims] derisively allege, worship three Gods; we worship only one God, represented to us in the Scriptures as three persons.

Christ said to Philip in John 14:9, "He that hath seen me hath seen the Father." There Christ claims unity and equality with the Father in the one divine essence. So does Paul, in Colossians 1:15, where he calls Christ "the image of the invisible God," at the same time indicating two distinct persons: the Father is not the Son, and the Son is not the Father, yet they are one God. Such passages, I say, are frequent. By means of them, the sainted fathers valiantly maintained this dogma of the Trinity against the devil and the world, thus making it our heritage.

12. Now, what care we that reason should regard it as foolishness? It requires no skill to cavil over these things; I could do that as well as others. But, praise God, I have the grace to desire no controversy on this point. When I know it is the Word of God that declares the Trinity, that God has said so, I do not inquire how it can be true; I am content with the simple Word of God, let it harmonize with reason as it may. And every Christian should adopt the same course with respect to all the articles of our faith. Let there be no caviling and contention on the score of possibility; be satisfied with the inquiry, Is it the Word of God? If a thing be his Word, if he has spoken it, you may confidently rely upon it; he will not lie nor deceive you, though you may not understand the how and the when.

Since, then, this article of the Holy Trinity is certified by the Word of God, and the sainted fathers have from the inception of the church chivalrously defended and maintained the article against every sect, we are not to dispute as to how God the Father, the Son, and the Holy Spirit are one God. This is an incomprehensible mystery. It is enough that God in his Word gives such testimony of himself. Both his nature and its revelation to us are far beyond our understanding.

PHYSICAL LIFE INEXPLICABLE TO REASON

13. And why should you presume to comprehend, to exactly understand, the sublime, inconceivable divine essence when you are wholly ignorant of your own body and life? You cannot explain the action of your laughter, nor how your eyes give you knowledge of a castle or mountain ten miles away. You cannot tell how in sleep one, dead to the external world, is yet alive. If we

are unable to understand the least detail of our physical selves, anything so insignificant as the growth of a mere hair, for instance, can we, unaided by the revelation of God's Word, climb by reason—that reason so blind to things within its natural realm—into the realm of heavenly mysteries and comprehend and define God in his majesty?

If you employ reason from mere love of disputation, why not devote it to questions concerning the daily workings of your physical nature? for instance, where are the five senses during sleep? just how is the sound of your own laughter produced? We might without sin occupy ourselves with such questions. But as to the absolute truth in a matter such as this, let us abide patiently by the authority of the Word. The Word says that Christ is the express image of the invisible God, the firstborn of all creatures; in other words, he is God equally with the Father.

14. Again, John 5:23 testifies that all should honor the Son as they honor the Father. And in John 12:44, we read, "He that believeth on me, believeth not on me, but on him that sent me." Also, in John 14:1, "Believe in God, believe also in me." And again, in John 16:15, "All things whatsoever the Father hath are mine." These and similar passages are armor that cannot be pierced; for they are uttered by God, who does not lie and who alone is qualified to speak the truth concerning himself. Thus the dogma of the Trinity is thoroughly founded upon the holy Scriptures.

THE THIRD PERSON OF THE TRINITY

15. Now, having established the existence of Christ in the Trinity, we must next consider the third person, the Holy Spirit, in Scripture sometimes termed the "Spirit" of God and sometimes his "Soul." This person is not spoken of as "born"; he is not born like the Son, but proceeds from the Father and the Son. To express it differently, he is a person possessing in eternity the divine essence, which he derives from the Father and Son in unity in the same way the Son derives it from the Father alone. There are, then, three distinct persons in one divine essence, one divine Majesty. According to the Scripture explanation of the mystery, Christ the Lord is the Son of God from eternity, the express image of the Father, and equally great, mighty, wise, and just. All deity, wisdom, power, and might inherent in the Father is also in Christ and, likewise, in the Holy Spirit, who proceeds from Father and Son. Now, when you are asked to explain the Trinity, reply that it is an incomprehensible mystery, beyond the understanding of angels and creatures, the knowledge of which is confined to the revelations of Scripture.

16. Rightly did the fathers compose the creed, or symbol, in the simple form repeated by Christian children, "I believe in God the Father Almighty, Maker of heaven and earth, and in Jesus Christ his only Son...I believe in the Holy Ghost." This confession we did not devise, nor did the fathers of former times. As the bee collects honey from many fair and gay flowers, so is this creed collected, in appropriate brevity, from the books of the beloved prophets and apostles—from the entire holy Scriptures—for children and for unlearned Christians. It is fittingly called the "Apostle's Symbol," or "Apostle's Creed." For brevity and clearness, it could not have been better arranged, and it has remained in the church from ancient time. It must either have been composed by the apostles themselves, or it was collected from their writings and sermons by their ablest disciples.

17. It begins, "I believe." In whom? "In God the Father." This is the first person in the Godhead. For the sake of clear distinction, the peculiar attribute and office in which each person manifests himself is briefly expressed. With the first, it is the work of creation. True, creation is not the work of one individual person, but of the one divine, eternal essence as such. We must say, God the Father, God the Son, and God the Holy Spirit created heaven and earth. Yet that work is more especially predicated of the person of the Father, the first person, for the reason that creation is the only work of the Father in which he has stepped forth out of concealment into observation; it is the first work wrought by the divine Majesty upon the creature. By the word "Father," he is particularly and rightly distinguished from the other persons of the Trinity. It indicates him as the first person, derived from no other, the Son and the Holy Spirit having existence from him.

18. Continuing, the creed says, I believe in another who is also God. For to believe is something we owe to no being but God alone. Who is this second person? Jesus Christ. God's only begotten Son. Christians have so confessed for more than fifteen hundred years; indeed, such has been the confession of believers from the beginning of the world. Though not employing precisely these words, yet this has been their faith and profession.

19. The first designation of God the Son makes him the only Son of God. Although angels are called sons of the Lord our God, and even Christians are termed his children, yet no one of these is said to be the "only" or "only begotten" Son. Such is the effect of Christ's birth from the Father, that he is unequaled by any creature, not excepting even the angels. For he is in truth and by nature the Son of God the Father; that is, he is of the same divine, eternal, uncreated essence.

20. Next comes the enumeration of the acts peculiar to him: "Who was conceived by the Holy Spirit, born of the Virgin Mary, suffered under Pontius Pilate, was crucified, dead and buried. He descended into hell; on the third day he rose again from the dead; he ascended into heaven, and sits at the right hand of God the Father Almighty; from thence he shall come to judge the quick and the dead." The distinct personality of the Son is thus demonstrated by acts peculiar to himself. Not the Father and not the Holy Spirit, but the Son alone, assumed human nature of flesh and blood, like unto ours, to suffer, die, rise again, and ascend into heaven.

21. In the third place we confess, "I believe in the Holy Ghost." Here again, a distinct person is named, yet one in divine essence with the Father and the Son; for we must believe in no one but the true God, in obedience to the first commandment, "I am Jehovah thy God...Thou shalt have no other gods before me."

Thus briefly this confession comprehends the unity of the divine essence—we accept and worship only one God—and the revealed truth that in the Trinity are three distinct persons. The same distinction is indicated in holy baptism; we are baptized into the faith of one God, yet Christ commands us to baptize "into the name of the Father and of the Son and of the Holy Spirit."

22. The peculiarity of this third person is the fact that he proceeds from both the Father and the Son. He is therefore called also the Spirit of the Father and the Son; he is poured into the human heart and reveals himself in the gathering of the church of Christ in all tongues. Through the Word of the Gospel, he enlightens and kindles the hearts of men unto one faith, sanctifying, quickening, and saving them.

23. So the creed confesses three persons as comprehended in one divine essence, each one, however, retaining his distinct personality; and in order that the simple Christian may recognize that there is but one divine essence and one God, who is tri-personal, a special work, peculiar to himself, is ascribed to each person. And such acts, peculiar to each person, are mentioned for the reason that thus a confusion of persons is avoided. To the Father we ascribe the work of creation; to the Son the work of redemption; to the Holy Spirit the power to forgive sins, to gladden, to strengthen, to transport from death to life eternal.

The thought is not that the Father alone is the Creator, the Son alone Redeemer, and the Holy Spirit alone Sanctifier. The creation and preservation of the universe, atonement for sin and its forgiveness, resurrection from the dead and the gift of eternal life—all these are operations of the one divine Majesty as such. Yet the Father is especially emphasized in the work of creation, which proceeds originally from him as the first person; the Son is emphasized in the redemption he has accomplished in his own person; and the Holy Spirit in the peculiar work of sanctification, which is both his mission and revelation. Such distinction is made for the purpose of affording Christians the unqualified assurance that there is but one God and yet three persons in the one divine essence—truths the sainted fathers have faithfully gathered from the writings of Moses, the prophets, and the apostles, and which they have maintained against all heretics.

24. This faith has descended to us by inheritance and, by his power, God has maintained it in his church, against sects and adversaries, unto the present time. So we must abide by it in its simplicity and not be wise. Christians are under the necessity of believing things apparently foolish to reason. As Paul says, in 1 Corinthians 1:21, "It was God's good pleasure through the foolishness of the preaching to save them that believe." How can reason adapt itself to comprehend that three are one, and one is three; that God became man; that he who is washed with water in obedience to Christ's command, is washed with the blood of our Lord Jesus Christ and cleansed from all sins? Such articles of faith appear utterly foolish to reason. Paul aptly calls the Gospel foolish preaching wherewith God saves such as do not depend on their own wisdom but simply believe the Word. They who will follow reason in the things dealt with in these articles, and will reject the Word, shall be defeated and destroyed in their wisdom.

25. Now, we have in the holy Scriptures and in the creed sufficient information concerning the Holy Trinity, and all that is necessary for the instruction of ordinary Christians. Besides, the divinity of our Lord Jesus Christ and that of the Holy Spirit is also attested by miracles not to be lightly esteemed nor disregarded. The Lord our God brings to pass miraculous things for the Christian's sake—for the strengthening of his faith—and not merely as a rebuke to false teachers. Were he to consider the false teachers alone, he might easily defer their retribution to the future life, since he permits many other transgressors to go unpunished for ten, twenty, or thirty years. But the fact is, God openly in this life lays hold upon leaders of sects who blaspheme and slander him with their false doctrines. He inflicts upon them unusual punishments for the sake of warning others. Besides being openly convicted of blasphemy and having the condemnation of their own conscience, the misguided ones receive testimony to the fact that these false leaders are instigators of

blasphemy against God's name and his Word. All men are compelled to admit God can have no pleasure in their doctrine, since he visits them with special marks of his displeasure, destroying them with severer punishments than ordinarily befall offenders.

26. History records that John the Evangelist had as contemporary a heretic, by the name of Cerinthus, who was the first to arise in opposition to the apostolic doctrine and in blasphemy against the Lord Jesus with the claim that Jesus is not God. This blasphemy spread to such an extent that John saw himself compelled to supplement the work of the other evangelists with his Gospel, whose distinct purpose it is to defend and maintain the deity of Christ against Cerinthus and his rabble.

A feature of John's Gospel patent to all is the sublime beginning of his Gospel, which renders it distinct from the others. He does not lay stress upon the miraculous doings of Christ, but upon his preaching, wherein he reveals himself powerfully as true God, born of the Father from eternity, and his equal in power, honor, wisdom, righteousness, and every other divine work.

With respect to John and Cerinthus, it is reported that the former, having gone to a public bath with some of his disciples, became aware that Cerinthus and his rabble were there also. Without hesitation, he told his disciples to be up and away, and not to abide among blasphemers. The disciples followed his advice and departed. Immediately after their departure, the room collapsed, and Cerinthus with his followers perished, not one escaping.

27. We also read concerning the heretic Arius, the chief foe of his time toward the dogma of the deity of Christ. The injury done by this man to the cause of Christ was such as to occupy the church for four centuries after his death; and still today, his heresy has not been altogether rooted out. But the Lord took the matter in hand by the performance of a miracle which could not but be understood.

History records that Arius had ingratiated himself into the favor of Constantine, the emperor, and his counselors. With an oath, he had succeeded in impressing them with the righteousness of his doctrine, so that the emperor gave command that Alexander, bishop of Constantinople, should recognize him as a member of the Christian Church and restore him to the priestly office. When the godly bishop refused to accede to this demand, knowing full well the purpose pursued by Arius and his followers, Eusebius and the other bishops who supported Arius threatened him with the imperial edict and expressed the determination to drive him out by force and to have Arius restored by the congregation as such. However, they gave him a day to think the matter over.

28. The godly bishop was fearful. The following of Arius was large and powerful, being supported by the imperial edict and the whole court. The bishop, therefore, resolved to seek help from God, where alone it is found in all things relating to God's honor. He fell down upon his face in the church and prayed all night long that God should preserve his name and honor by methods calculated to stem the tide of evil purpose, and to preserve Christendom against the heretics. When it was morning, and the hour had come when Alexander the bishop should either restore Arius to office or be cast out of his own, Arius convened punctually with his followers. As the procession was wending its way to the church, Arius suddenly felt ill and was compelled to seek privacy. The pompous procession halted, waiting his return, when the message came that his lungs and liver had passed from him, causing his death. The narrative comments: *Mortem dignam blasphema et foetida mente*—a death worthy such a blasphemous and turpid mind.

29. We see, then, that this dogma has been preserved by God first through the writings and the conflicts of the apostles, and then by miracles, against the devil and his blasphemers. And it shall be preserved in the future likewise, so that, without a trace of doubt, we may believe in God the Father, God the Son, God the Holy Spirit. This is the faith which we confess with our children daily. To guard against a mixing of persons or the abandonment of the tri-personality, three distinct acts are predicated. This should enable the common Christian to avoid confusing the persons, while maintaining the divine unity as to essence.

We proclaim these things on this Sunday in order to call attention to the fact that we have not come upon this doctrine in a dream, but by the grace of God through his Word and the holy apostles and fathers. God help us to be found constant and without blemish in this doctrine and faith to our end. Amen.

Index by Source

The sermons included in this volume may be found in *the Sermons of Martin Luther: the Church Postils*, collected in volumes 1–4 of *the Complete Sermons of Martin Luther*, Edited by John Nicholas Lenker. Translated by John Nicholas Lenker and others. Published by Baker Books, a division of Baker Book House Company, Grand Rapids, Michigan 49516.

The First Sunday in Advent: Faith, Good Works, and the Spiritual Interpretation of This Gospel
Volume 1.1: *Sermons on Gospel Texts for Advent, Christmas, and Epiphany*, 17

The Second Sunday in Advent: The Comfort Christians Have from the Signs of the Day of Judgment; and the Spiritual Interpretation of These Signs
Volume 1.1: *Sermons on Gospel Texts for Advent, Christmas, and Epiphany*, 59

The Third Sunday in Advent: Christ's Answer to the Question John Asked Him, His Praise of John, and the Application of This Gospel
Volume 1.1: *Sermons on Gospel Texts for Advent, Christmas, and Epiphany*, 87

The Fourth Sunday in Advent: The Witness and Confession of John the Baptist
Volume 1.1: *Sermons on Gospel Texts for Advent, Christmas, and Epiphany*, 114

Christmas Day: Of the Birth of Jesus, and of the Angels' Song of Praise at His Birth
Volume 1.1: *Sermons on Gospel Texts for Advent, Christmas, and Epiphany*, 134

Christmas Day: Christ's Titles of Honor and Attributes; Christ's Coming; His Becoming Man; and the Revelation of His Glory
Volume 1.1: *Sermons on Gospel Texts for Advent, Christmas, and Epiphany*, 171

The Sunday After Christmas: Of Simeon; of Anna; of the Return of the Parents of Jesus to Nazareth, and the Childhood of Christ
Volume 1.1: *Sermons on Gospel Texts for Advent, Christmas, and Epiphany*, 255

New Year's Day: The Circumcision, and Choosing the Name, as Was the Custom at Circumcision

Volume 1.1: *Sermons on Gospel Texts for Advent, Christmas, and Epiphany*, 208

Epiphany: On the Visit of the Magi

Volume 1.1: *Sermons on Gospel Texts for Advent, Christmas, and Epiphany*, 319

The First Sunday in Lent: The Fast and the Temptation of Christ

Volume 1.2: *Sermons on Gospel Texts for Epiphany, Lent, and Easter*, 133

The Second Sunday in Lent: The Faith of the Syrophenician Woman, and the Spiritual Interpretation of This Gospel

Volume 1.2: *Sermons on Gospel Texts for Epiphany, Lent, and Easter*, 148

The Third Sunday in Lent: Christ's Defense Against Those Who Slandered Him

Volume 1.2: *Sermons on Gospel Texts for Epiphany, Lent, and Easter*, 155

The Fourth Sunday in Lent: The Feeding of the Five Thousand

Volume 1.2: *Sermons on Gospel Texts for Epiphany, Lent, and Easter*, 166

The Fifth Sunday in Lent: Christ's Defense Against His Enemies

Volume 1.2: *Sermons on Gospel Texts for Epiphany, Lent, and Easter*, 173

Palm Sunday: Christ: An Example of Love

Volume 4.1: *Sermons on Epistle Texts for Epiphany, Easter, and Pentecost*, 169

Maundy Thursday: Of Confession and the Lord's Supper

Volume 1.2: *Sermons on Gospel Texts for Epiphany, Lent, and Easter*, 193

Good Friday: How to Contemplate Christ's Holy Sufferings

Volume 1.2: *Sermons on Gospel Texts for Epiphany, Lent, and Easter*, 183

Easter Sunday: Of Christ's Resurrection

Volume 1.2: *Sermons on Gospel Texts for Epiphany, Lent, and Easter*, 238

Easter Sunday: The Manifestation of Christ After His Resurrection, and the Sermon He Preached to His Disciples

Volume 1.2: *Sermons on Gospel Texts for Epiphany, Lent, and Easter*, 301

The Sunday After Easter: Of True Piety, the Law and Faith, and of Love to Our Neighbor

Volume 1.2: *Sermons on Gospel Texts for Epiphany, Lent, and Easter*, 364

The Second Sunday After Easter: Christ's Office and Kingdom: A Sermon on the Good Shepherd — Volume 2.1: *Sermons on Gospel Texts for Pentecost*, 17

The Third Sunday After Easter: A Sermon of Comfort That Christ Preached to His Disciples — Volume 2.1: *Sermons on Gospel Texts for Pentecost*, 72

The Fourth Sunday After Easter: Of Sin, of Righteousness, and of the Cross — Volume 2.1: *Sermons on Gospel Texts for Pentecost*, 125

The Fifth Sunday After Easter or Prayer Sunday: A Sermon by Christ on Prayer — Volume 2.1: *Sermons on Gospel Texts for Pentecost*, 166

The Day of Christ's Ascension into Heaven: Christ Upbraids and Commissions His Disciples — Volume 2.1: *Sermons on Gospel Texts for Pentecost*, 195

The Sunday After Christ's Ascension: A Sermon of Comfort and of Admonition — Volume 2.1: *Sermons on Gospel Texts for Pentecost*, 244

Pentecost: Or, the Festival of the Outpouring of the Holy Spirit — Volume 2.1: *Sermons on Gospel Texts for Pentecost*, 287

Trinity Sunday: The Doctrine of the Trinity — Volume 4.2: *Sermons on Epistle Texts for Trinity Sunday to Advent*, 26

Index by Key Scripture Passage

Matthew 2:1–12   Epiphany: On the Visit of the Magi

Matthew 4:1–11   The First Sunday in Lent: The Fast and the Temptation of Christ

Matthew 11:2–10   The Third Sunday in Advent: Christ's Answer to the Question John Asked Him, His Praise of John, and the Application of This Gospel

Matthew 15:21–28   The Second Sunday in Lent: The Faith of the Syrophenician Woman, and the Spiritual Interpretation of This Gospel

Matthew 21:1–9   The First Sunday in Advent: Faith, Good Works, and the Spiritual Interpretation of This Gospel

Mark 16:1–8   Easter Sunday: Of Christ's Resurrection

Mark 16:14–20   The Day of Christ's Ascension into Heaven: Christ Upbraids and Commissions His Disciples

Luke 2:1–14   Christmas Day: Of the Birth of Jesus, and of the Angels' Song of Praise at His Birth

Luke 2:21   New Year's Day: The Circumcision, and Choosing the Name, as Was the Custom at Circumcision

Luke 2:33–40   The Sunday After Christmas: Of Simeon; of Anna; of the Return of the Parents of Jesus to Nazareth, and the Childhood of Christ

Luke 11:14–23   The Third Sunday in Lent: Christ's Defense Against Those Who Slandered Him

Luke 21:25–36   The Second Sunday in Advent: The Comfort Christians Have from the Signs of the Day of Judgment; and the Spiritual Interpretation of These Signs

Luke 24:36–47   Easter Sunday: The Manifestation of Christ After His
                       Resurrection, and the Sermon He Preached to His
                       Disciples

John 1:1–14   Christmas Day: Christ's Titles of Honor and Attributes;
                       Christ's Coming; His Becoming Man; and the Revelation
                       of His Glory

John 1:19–28   The Fourth Sunday in Advent: The Witness and
                       Confession of John the Baptist

John 6:1–15   The Fourth Sunday in Lent: The Feeding of the 5000

John 8:46–59   The Fifth Sunday in Lent: Christ's Defense Against His
                       Enemies

John 10:11–16   The Second Sunday After Easter: Christ's Office and
                       Kingdom: A Sermon on the Good Shepherd

John 14:23–31   Pentecost: Or, the Festival of the Outpouring of the
                       Holy Spirit

John 15:26–16:4   The Sunday After Christ's Ascension: A Sermon of
                       Comfort and of Admonition

John 16:5–15   The Fourth Sunday After Easter: Of Sin, of
                       Righteousness, and of the Cross

John 16:16–23   The Third Sunday After Easter: A Sermon of Comfort
                       That Christ Preached to His Disciples

John 16:23–30   The Fifth Sunday After Easter or Prayer Sunday:
                       A Sermon by Christ on Prayer

John 20:19–31   The Sunday After Easter: Of True Piety, the Law and
                       Faith, and of Love to Our Neighbor

Romans 11:33–36   Trinity Sunday: The Doctrine of the Trinity

Philippians 2:5–11   Palm Sunday: Christ: An Example of Love

Through the Year with Martin Luther

A Selection of Sermons Celebrating the Feasts and Seasons of the Church Year

The text of this book is set in DanteMT 11/14 and Delphin IA, with Plantagenet Ornaments.

Typeset in QuarkXPress.

Foreword by Evelyn Bence.

Editorial services by Suzanne Tilton.

Interior design and typesetting by
Rose Yancik
Y Design
15455 Copperfield Drive
Colorado Springs, CO 80921
www.ydesign.us